15063

Stock, Noel
    The life of Ezra Pound.   New York,
Pantheon Books [1970]
    xvii, 472 p.   illus., facsims., ports.
25cm.

    1. Pound, Ezra Loomis, 1885-
I. Title.

THE LIFE OF EZRA POUND

THE LIFE OF
EZRA
POUND

NOEL STOCK

PANTHEON BOOKS
A Division of Random House, New York

FIRST AMERICAN EDITION
Manufactured in the United States of America by
Jenkins-Universal Corporation, Richmond, Virginia

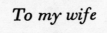
To my wife

Contents

List of Illustrations

Acknowledgments

The author has obtained permission to quote from the works of Ezra Pound, but the granting of that permission must not be taken as conveying Ezra Pound's approval of the quotations selected nor of the context in which they appear.

Excerpts from the following published works of Ezra Pound are reprinted by permission of New Directions Publishing Corporation, New York:

The Cantos: Copyright 1934, 1937, 1940, 1948, © 1956 by Ezra Pound
Personae: Copyright 1926 by Ezra Pound
A Lume Spento and Other Early Poems: Copyright © 1965 by Ezra Pound and New Directions Publishing Corporation
Redondillas: Copyright © 1967 by Ezra Pound
The Confucian Odes: Copyright 1954 by the President and Fellows of Harvard University
Translations: Copyright 1926, 1954, © 1957, 1958, 1960, 1962, 1963 by Ezra Pound
Women of Trachis: Copyright © 1957 by Ezra Pound
Literary Essays   : Copyright 1918, 1920, 1935 by Ezra Pound
Guide to Kulchur: All Rights Reserved
Pavannes and Divagations: Copyright © 1958 by Ezra Pound
Spirit of Romance: All Rights Reserved

Excerpts from *Patria Mia* are reprinted by permission of Mrs. Dorothy Pound, Committee for Ezra Pound. Copyright 1950 by Ralph Fletcher Seymour. Passages from unpublished and uncollected material are reprinted by permission of Mrs. Dorothy Pound.

Excerpts from *The Letters of Ezra Pound 1907–1941*, edited by D. D. Paige, are reprinted by permission of Harcourt, Brace & World, Inc. Copyright 1950 by Harcourt, Brace & World, Inc.

Preface

When I first began to read Ezra Pound's poetry in Melbourne in 1946 he was a figure as remote as Keats or Rimbaud. In those days I had read only a few of his books: the *Selected Poems* with an introduction by T. S. Eliot, *The Pisan Cantos*, one or two prose books, and in 1951 *The Letters of Ezra Pound*. I knew vaguely that he had been connected with the beginnings of the 'modern movement' in English poetry, that he held strong views on economics and politics, and that he had got into trouble because of some broadcasts he had made over Rome Radio during the war; but if these things made him seem different and exciting, they were also remote, for they had occurred in Europe and America. The turning-point was in 1953 when I wrote to Hugh Kenner, Professor of English at the Santa Barbara College of the University of California, about his recently published book, *The Poetry of Ezra Pound*. In a postscript to his reply of 8 August he suggested that I get in touch with Pound and gave me his address: St Elizabeths Hospital, Washington, D.C., the insane asylum to which he had been committed by an American court. I wrote, not knowing what to expect, and received a reply immediately, the substance of which was that if I was as well read as I seemed to be, then it was time for me to go into action. And from that moment he instructed me how to, writing more than a hundred letters (between forty-five and fifty thousand words) in the next five years.

I well remember Kenner's warning in 1954 to be careful of Pound's politics; I paid little heed and was soon involved in Social Credit and similar activities. I joined a Social Credit newspaper, *The New Times*, and to Pound's great satisfaction began to publish unsigned or pseudonymous items which he sent from Washington. I posted him copies of each issue which he distributed to those whom he considered active or in other respects worthy. In 1956 I also started a literary magazine called *Edge* in which he played a considerable part. It was typical of his drive and energy that shortly afterwards *Edge* was noticed in the Rome weekly *Il Caffé*; the notice was not signed by Pound but part of it had been composed by him in the exaggerated terms which he reserved for such occasions. 'In October 1956', it said, 'the centre of intellectual life of the English-speaking nations was transferred to Melbourne, Australia. After *The Little Review* (1917–29) no English or American review has approached the vigour of the Australian review *Edge.* . . .' He also praised *Edge* to a correspondent in Tokyo with the result that young Japan was informed of its importance in a periodical called *The Rising Generation.*

In 1956 I reviewed Pound's *Rock-Drill* (cantos 85 to 95) in the Australian magazine *Meanjin*, a copy of which I sent to Washington. He liked it and within a short time was distributing photo-copies of it. For the next few years I was embroiled in Poundian ferment: I received copies of dozens of periodicals and leaflets in which he had a hand or of which he approved and wanted circulated; at his behest I wrote letters to publishers urging them to publish books he thought important and to writers informing them of matters which for one reason or another Pound did not wish to mention directly; and in looking back through old material I see that I even signed a declaration which he published in the United States: 'Every man has the right to be born free of debt.'

I left Australia in 1958 to live in England and was on the high seas when in April he was released from St Elizabeths Hospital. I had met his daughter, Mary de Rachewiltz, during a visit to Rome in 1955, and now, on my way through Italy again I stayed at her home, Brunnenburg Castle, at Tirolo di Merano in the Italian Tirol, shortly before Pound himself arrived from America. The following year, with my wife and our two daughters, I moved to a flat at Brunnenburg. Pound was away at the time but told me to examine his collection of books and papers. I first met him at Rapallo in the summer of 1959 and in the autumn when he returned to Brunnenburg I edited a collection of his essays published in 1960 under the title *Impact*. I saw him often at this time and met him occasionally later when he went to live in Venice and Rapallo. His wife, Dorothy Pound, continued to spend part of each year at the castle and I had many opportunities to talk to her about Pound's life in London before and during the First World War and in Paris and Rapallo between the wars. And so, in 1966, when Routledge & Kegan Paul asked me if I would undertake a detailed biography of Pound, I reflected that the time was probably ripe to attempt a balanced account of his extraordinary life.

It remains that I should make some acknowledgments. First, I owe much to other books, particularly Charles Norman's *Ezra Pound* (The Macmillan Company, New York, 1960) and *The Case of Ezra Pound* (Funk & Wagnalls, New York, 1968); others which proved helpful were B. L. Reid's *The Man from New York, John Quinn and His*

Friends (Oxford University Press, New York, 1968); *Pound/Joyce*, The Letters of Ezra Pound to James Joyce, edited with commentary by Forrest Read (New Directions, New York, 1967); Julien Cornell's *The Trial of Ezra Pound* (John Day, New York, 1966); Patricia Hutchins's *Ezra Pound's Kensington* (Faber & Faber, London, 1965); and Michael Reck's *Ezra Pound A Close-Up* (McGraw-Hill, New York, 1967). Of great assistance in disentangling the steps leading to Pound's release from St Elizabeths Hospital was Harry Meacham's *The Caged Panther, Ezra Pound at St Elizabeths* (Twayne Publishers, New York, 1967), which was sometimes useful for other periods as well. For much information on A. R. Orage and *The New Age* I am indebted to *The New Age under Orage* (Manchester University Press, 1967) whose author Wallace Martin also kindly answered numerous questions about T. E. Hulme, Imagism, and Pound's London years. Other books consulted included *A Casebook on Ezra Pound*, edited by William Van O'Connor and Edward Stone (Thomas V. Crowell, New York, 1959); *The Annotated Index to the Cantos of Ezra Pound*, by John Edwards and William Vasse (University of California Press, 1959); and Eustace Mullins's *This Difficult Individual Ezra Pound* (Fleet, New York, 1961).

For unfailing kindness and patience in correspondence and also when I visited the United States I wish to thank Warren Roberts and his staff at the Humanities Research Centre of the University of Texas and Mrs Mary Hirth and her staff at the Academic Centre Library at the University of Texas. I owe similar thanks to Donald Gallup of Yale, not only for answering questions by post and assisting me in every way when I visited the Yale Library, but also for his *Bibliography of Ezra Pound* (Rupert Hart-Davis, London, 1963). Thanks are also due to the following: The United States Department of Justice, for answering questions about Pound's legal position at various times; A. N. L. Munby of King's College, Cambridge, for several T. S. Eliot items and other assistance; William Fleming, for information about his correspondence with Pound and for tracing material kindly made available by the Latrobe Library, Melbourne; Mrs R. McNair Wilson and Michael McNair Wilson, for making available very useful material among the papers of the late R. McNair Wilson; Mrs Mary Hemingway for placing the Pound–Hemingway correspondence at my disposal and Dr Carlos Baker for his generosity in going through it for me; Professor James McAuley and Dr Laurie Hergenhan of the University of Tasmania, for assistance concerning Frederic Manning's correspondence with Dorothy Shakespear (Mrs Dorothy Pound); Rabindra-Sadana, Visva-Bharati, Santiniketan, West Bengal, for sending me copies of Pound's letters to Tagore; and the Essay Society at St John's College, Oxford, and the college Librarian H. M. Colvin, for information regarding Pound's visit to Oxford in February 1913. Others who kindly answered questions or provided material included: Murray Schafer, author of 'Ezra Pound and Music', published in the Summer 1961 issue of the *Canadian Music Journal*; Ian Angus, Deputy Librarian, University College, London; Edmund Wilson; Allen Tate; the Public Relations office, Lloyds Bank, London; William Clowes & Sons, printers, Beccles, Suffolk; Miss Marcella Spann, Austin, Texas; and the American Academy of Political and Social Science, Philadelphia.

Special thanks are due to James Laughlin of New Directions, New York, for his assistance and kindness; Stephan Chodorov of CBS Television, New York, for numerous acts of kindness; Daniel Cory, for his help with material relating to George Santayana and for permission to quote from Santayana's letters to Pound; Mrs J. Biala of Paris for information relating to Ford Madox Ford; P. Spiro, Librarian at the Institute of Bankers, London, for information on exchange rates early this century; Mrs William Carlos Williams for permissions and assistance relating to her late husband; E. A. Harwood, librarian of the *Daily Telegraph*, London, for tracing a book review which appeared in that paper in 1909; Sanehide Kodama, for making available copies of articles published by Pound in the *Japan Times*; Miss Elizabeth Meyer, Secretary, Dept. of Paintings, the Metropolitan Museum of Art, New York, for information on Goya's 'Don Sebastian Martinez y Perez'; and Dr Gerald Fleischmann, for information on the Salzburg Festival and other assistance. I must not forget to thank the trustees of the Leverhulme Research Awards, London, for a grant to enable me to travel in connection with the book, and for their unusual thoughtfulness in the administration of it; my thanks also to their Secretary, Miss M. Branney. To others who have helped, whose names I cannot mention, either from forgetfulness on my part, or for other reason, I offer my thanks.

I should like to express my heartfelt appreciation of the assistance I received from Carl Gatter of Wyncote, Pennsylvania, who told me all he knew of Pound's early life and traced for me persons and events long passed into obscurity; he was also an enthusiastic guide when in 1967 I visited Wyncote, graciously inviting me to stay at his home, 166 Fernbrook Avenue, the house in which Ezra Pound had been brought up. He also helped me to collect photographs.

And finally I should like to thank Ezra Pound, Olga Rudge and Mary de Rachewiltz for their assistance and kindness over a period of many years; and Mrs Dorothy Pound not only for assistance in many forms but for her patience in the face of numerous questions and requests. During the course of the book I have quoted from unpublished work by Pound, unpublished letters, and also from a number of uncollected pieces, the copyright of which belongs to Ezra Pound: for permission to use this material and to quote from the poet's books I must thank Mrs Dorothy Pound in her capacity as committee for Ezra Pound.

Brunnenburg   Noel Stock

I Childhood
1885/1901

Hailey, Idaho, was a frontier town of about two thousand people when Ezra Pound was born there on 30 October 1885. His father, Homer Pound, ran the United States Land Office, a position which doubtless carried a certain prestige, but not (if we judge by the local newspaper) very much weight. When the poet's grandfather, Thaddeus Coleman Pound, arrived five months earlier on a tour of his mining properties, the *Hailey Times* of 20 May reported: 'Thad. C. Pound, former Governor of Wisconsin, and father of Homer L. Pound, register of the U.S. Land Office here, found his mining interests in a bad way when he arrived in Hailey a few days ago. His claim, the Alturas, on Warm Springs Creek was jumped, ore and all, the morning he arrived, and on his claim, the Acme, in Smoky, there was a cross location saddled. He is disgusted.' The same issue announced, much as if it were the date of the next council meeting, that horse-thieves were busy on Wood River. The general attitude of the population to the finer things of life, and the rollicking, back-slapping humour, are seen in an anecdote which Pound recalled for Ernest Hemingway in a letter of August 1955. After Homer Pound had built a house for his bride, they were joined by her mother, Mrs Mary Weston from New York. Finding no curtain in her attic window she hung up a fancy petticoat, which caused Homer to be inundated next day with inquiries about his female guest. It was some time before he lived it down.

Ezra Pound arrived into this frontier atmosphere by way of a 'disorderly trek of four or five generations across the whole teeming continent', as he wrote many years later. There were in the family the usual stories about money – all families, it seems, have seen better days – and the usual hints about ancestry. There was talk of their having arrived on the American shore aboard the *Lion*, at a suitably short interval after the *Mayflower*; of a plantation in early New England bearing the name Weston; and of Quakers and whalers by the name of Pound who landed originally in New Jersey and later settled in Pennsylvania. Pound was related on his mother's side to the poet Henry Wadsworth Longfellow and to Captain Joseph Wadsworth who in 1687 stole the Connecticut charter and hid it in Charter Oak, to protect it, apparently, from the designs of the Governor-General. He saw in childhood an engraving, possibly of the eighteenth century, of Wadsworth entering the room to steal the charter, and he heard how the captain swept out the candles on the table with a swish of his long cloak. He was taken when he was eight or nine to Hartford to look at a large stump with a young tree growing out of it, which was said to be *the* oak. Closer to his own day we may observe, among much that was thoroughly correct and dull, such curiosities as a relative who rode behind the first locomotive, a sixteenth cousin named Loomis who was said to have sent an 'electric signal' between ships, without wires, in the 1860s and was thought crazy, a grandfather who corresponded with the local bank manager in verse, and a great-uncle Albert who inclined towards the Episcopal Church because it interfered 'neither with a man's politics nor his religion'.

The most important figure in the poet's immediate background was grandfather Thaddeus (son of Elijah), who was born in a log cabin in Elk, Warren County, Pennsylvania, in or about 1832. He married Sarah Angevine Loomis from a family of horse-thieves: charming people, an old lady from Upper New York State once told Pound, in fact the nicest people in the county, but horse-thieves. It was never hinted, as far as I know, that Thaddeus contracted this weakness of his wife's family·and no breath of suspicion, that I know of, ever attached to him in regard to the thieves active at the time of his visit to Idaho. We may safely assume that his marriage into the Loomis family and the activity on Wood River in 1885 were in no way connected.

Thaddeus and Sarah travelled west to Wisconsin and settled at Chippewa Falls, where he learnt the lumber business, starting as a bookkeeper, set up the Union Lumbering Company on his own account, and for a time prospered, doing, it was said, more than a million dollars' worth of business annually. Sarah supervised the preparation of meals for about forty lumbermen and Thaddeus, to maintain his prestige, used to wrestle with them. He also 'used to watch his gang saws in person', Pound wrote, 'to be sure the planks were one and a quarter inch thick before planing'. This was to ensure that 'a foot of lumber after planing was one foot square and an inch thick', no scamped planks being delivered. Thaddeus served in the State Assembly, as member and Speaker, became Lieutenant-Governor of Wisconsin, and was three times elected to Congress. He and Sarah separated and he 'took to himself a second feminine adjunct, without sanction of clergy'. He also built three railways, and boosted Morse's telegraph.

The highest point he reached nationally, according to family tradition, was when he was promised a seat in President Garfield's cabinet;

but J. G. Blaine, a brighter luminary, refused to sit in the same cabinet with a man who was not living with his wife. Thaddeus retaliated successfully some years later when Blaine was running for President by turning Wisconsin and other western states against him.

His son Homer was thought to be the first white male child born in the northern part of Wisconsin, where he had an Indian for nurse. After military school in Minnesota he was accepted for West Point but descended from the train before it arrived, returned home, and went to work in a Chippewa Falls butcher's shop. He had himself photographed with the young Ella Wheeler, afterwards famous as Ella Wheeler Wilcox. Thence to Washington, D.C., where he received an invitation to visit New York (where he took a fancy to Isabel Weston) and, in 1883, at the instigation of Thaddeus and the invitation of President Arthur, far west to Hailey to establish a government Land Office. Miners came to the office to file their claims and have their ore assayed.

Homer's bride, Isabel, was born in New York City, although she later told a friend in Wyncote, Pennsylvania, that she came from the 'apple region' of New York State. Whereas Homer was easygoing and seems to have been universally liked, Isabel, with her 'high society' voice, was often regarded as uppish. There is a story which true or not illustrates perfectly Homer's lack of guile. It was in Rapallo in the 1930s and Homer and his son were in attendance on Max Beerbohm at his home on the road to Zoagli. Most of the time Ezra Pound talked, a barrage of historical detail and proposals for monetary reform. During a lull in which he was absent from the room, Homer leant across, and, shaking his head in wonderment, said 'You know Mr Beerbohm, there isn't a darn thing that boy of mine don't know.' Isabel, on the other hand was formal. We see her in her son's *Pisan Cantos*, stiff-backed as she listens to the orators in Congress:

> and in my mother's time it was respectable,
> it was social, apparently,
>   to sit in the Senate gallery
> or even in that of the House
>   to hear the fire-works of the senators
> (and possibly representatives)

Homer built for her the first plastered house in Hailey, a town which consisted of a single street lined with saloons, one hotel, and a newspaper. The news consisted largely of such items as 'George Choate, the carpenter, has begun work on his new residence on the bench south of the H. L. Pound home.' Homer was never more surprised in his life, he told the *Hailey Times-News-Miner* (21 May 1925), than when, in the spring of 1885 he received from Washington a wire saying that President Arthur had appointed him 'register' of the Hailey Land Office. He was unable to find Hailey on the map. 'I was given transportation over the U.P. and Oregon Short Line, Wood River branch, that passed me over the line to the "end of the road". If I remember aright I arrived on the "first train in". It was some weeks later before we were able to open the office – in July. Then the long line of applicants for lands that seemed worthless to me began to file in. Then months of contests and trials – it took about two years to get matters adjusted. . . .' It was a time, in places like Hailey, when fortunes were made overnight. The handyman you paid to saw your kindling wood might tell you (as Homer's did) when you asked him a few days later to saw some more, that he had ten thousand dollars in the bank and a mine to sell. And legal arguments were sometimes settled with revolvers. 'I assure you,' Homer said, 'that the first four years of the Land Office were somewhat interesting. There were times when it seemed as if one might be mutilated by some angry seeker after lands.' In 1919 he gave to the *Philadelphia Ledger* a story how the recently appointed American ambassador to France, Hugh C. Wallace of Tacoma, Washington, had 'once grabbed a 42-calibre six-shooter revolver from the wall of his office to avenge an insult to a friend'. Fortunately, said Homer, 'we prevailed upon him not to carry out his threat'. The incident is recorded by Ezra Pound in a number of places, notably 'Retrospect: Interlude' in *Polite Essays* (1937). He met Wallace in Paris after the Armistice of 1919, a very tired, mild, white-haired man in whom it was difficult to recognize the young man of thirty-six years earlier who had announced his intention of dealing once and for all with the 'son of a bitch' who had insulted his friend.

When Isabel's mother arrived in Hailey to see her grandson she stayed for a time at the hotel. She was horrified to discover that there was no lock on the door. A man wouldn't lock his door out there, Homer later told his son, otherwise 'they'd suspicion you'. What disturbed Isabel about the hotel was that conversations filtered through the flimsy walls.

Hailey was five thousand feet above sea-level and the air did not agree with her. When the baby was about eighteen months they moved to New York. Pound tells us in his autobiographical reverie, *Indiscretions*, published as a series of articles in 1920 and as a small book three years later, that they travelled east during the Great Blizzard of 1887, behind the first rotary snow-plough. When baby Ezra's cough disturbed the others in the sleeper, the inventor of the snow-plough cured him with a dose of sugar saturated with kerosene. The family stayed first with Frances A. Weston at her boarding-house at 24 East 47th Street. In the spring of 1888, when the baby was two and a half, he was taken to Newport for the season. His first toy, he says in a footnote to his essay on Henry James (1918), was a rather slow and well-behaved lift, in New York apparently, while he was either living there or on holiday. When he was three the family, including also Mrs Mary Weston, went to stay with Thaddeus on his farm in Wisconsin, which numbered among its other inhabitants great-grandfather Elijah and Elijah's elder brother. In June 1889, Homer, Isabel, and child moved to Philadelphia where Homer took up an appointment as assistant assayer at the United States Mint. It was here that the young Ezra grew up and went to school and began his literary career with letters to Santa Claus.

For two years the Pounds lived in a brick row-house with tiny lawn, porch and polished walnut door at 208 South 43rd Street, West Philadelphia, which was then at the city's edge. The house still stands, with a white door in place of the polished walnut. They then moved to 417 Walnut Street, Jenkintown, ten miles north of Philadelphia, but connected to the city by the Reading railroad. An old resident of Jenkintown, Miss Grace Ridpath, recalled many years later that when Ezra was about five the maid would call him so that his mother could read him 'the classics' before his afternoon nap. When he was six they bought a spacious house in nearby Wyncote, five minutes' walk from the Jenkintown station. This was 166 Fernbrook Avenue which was his home for the next sixteen years. It is still there, much as it was in Pound's day, and still bears the same street number.

The ground floor consisted of a large hall and dining-room, front and back parlours, a kitchen and a pantry. Upstairs there were four bedrooms, two bathrooms and a sitting-room, on the first floor, and three bedrooms, a bathroom, and a store-room, on the second. There was a closet in the 'Tower Room' upstairs in which his mother once placed him after some particularly odious offence. The house was furnished in Victorian style, plus a few heirlooms. There were three family portraits: 'Uncle Ezra' after whom Pound was named, a great-grandmother, Hannah How, and a William Page portrait of Mary Wadsworth Parker, who married Harding Weston and had Isabel for daughter. Homer planted a row of trees – pear, peach and cherry, and possibly others – down the right side of the yard, and in the rear garden corn and sweetpeas. There was also at the back a large apple-tree with a swing.

It seems that Pound's first school was run by a Miss Elliot, after which, at the age of six or seven, he attended for a year or more the Chelten Hills school at Wyncote run by a well-known family, the Heacocks. One of his boyhood friends was Edward (Ned) Heacock who was drowned young while canoeing on a wild river out Oregon way. His next school was a temporary establishment run by Miss Florence Ridpath in a house which is still standing at the south-west corner of Greenwood Avenue (then Station Road) and Fernbrook Avenue, only a minute or two from the Pound home. An official school, presided over by a severe mistress in marked contrast to the pleasant Miss Ridpath, was opened a quarter of a mile further up Greenwood Avenue. Out of school Ezra and his pals roamed the nearby hills, in those days still uncleared, and there was a cave in which they played by the local creek. He and another boy were almost drowned rescuing a dog caught in a flash flood. The boys built various huts and other constructions out of packing boxes in the Pound apple-tree.

Rising Philadelphia families like Widener, Stetson and Wanamaker, began to build their medieval castles, renaissance palaces and Elizabethan manor-houses in the countryside surrounding the city. Some of the grandest of these edifices were within a mile or two of the Pound house. But even in Fernbrook Avenue itself there were neighbours on the way up. The Sheip boy, next door, kept telling Ezra that his father was an important man who made cigar-boxes. The Kunkles erected a Victorian house immediately opposite and further up Fernbrook Avenue Cyrus Curtis worked on his *Ladies Home Journal*. Ezra peering over the banister when Curtis came to dinner was struck by the square-cut beard. George Horace Lorimer of the *Saturday Evening Post*, who lived only two doors away, took short-cuts through the Pound backyard. There is something in the tone of Pound's later references to Lorimer, as in *Guide to Kulchur* (1938) when he says that the 'vulgar' Lorimer 'honestly didn't know that there ever had been a civilization', which provokes the suspicion that there may have been some sort of clash, physical or intellectual, between the successful journalist and the young poet quite early in his career.

While the neighbourhood generally became richer and more pretentious, the Pounds continued to make do on Homer's salary as assistant assayer. They lived and ate well, better than the same family could ever hope to do today, and Isabel always kept a maid; but there was no money to spare and Ezra was sometimes conscious of the fact that some of his friends and acquaintances were better off than he was.

Visiting the Mint, with its Greek columns, at the corner of Juniper and Chestnut Streets in those days, he was fascinated by the inner workings, not least his father's skill with a gold balance which enabled him to weigh a man's signature scrawled for the occasion on a visiting-card. He mixed with the assayers and drank in stories about 'gold bricks', which he still remembered in 1944 when he wrote his pamphlet on the 'Economic Nature of the United States'. 'Gold bricks' were false ingots made of lead covered with a layer of gold; some even were solid gold in parts to enable the swindler to bore in and demonstrate their genuineness. It was a period in America when anybody had the right to have his own gold coined at the official mint, and many who had been duped brought their bricks to Homer to have them converted into coin, only to be told that they were mostly lead. When Grover Cleveland was elected for a second time in 1893 – he had been President 1885–89, was succeeded by Benjamin Harrison, but came back again in '93 – the Administration called for a recount of the silver coinage. The boy watched in the light of gas flares as workmen stripped to the waist in the mint vaults shovelled the coins into the counting machines. The scene remained in his memory and there was still a touch of wonder forty-two years later when he wrote to Sir Montagu Webb, a British businessman interested in monetary reform, that 'Silver I saw, as no Aladdin, for when Cleveland was elected there was the recount of four million in the Mint vaults, the bags had rotted, and the men half-naked with open gas flares, shovelled it into the counting-machines, with a gleam on tarnished discs'. And in canto 97, in the book *Thrones* (1959), he speaks of silver dollars, $371\frac{1}{4}$ grains silver, 'as I have seen them by shovels full lit by gas flares'.

He visited New York regularly to stay with Mary Weston at 596 Lexington Avenue or at the boarding-house on East 47th Street. With his great-uncle, Mr Weston, and later his great-aunt, he walked through the fruit and vegetable markets in search of provisions; on one such occasion he was struck by the fact that he alone of all the bystanders seemed curious about a huge jack-knife thrown in pursuit of a fleeing male figure. To the boy from Wyncote the incident was unique; to the others, including apparently his Aunt Frank, as she was known, it was in no way remarkable. Here in New York, as at home, politics was in the air. He listened to his elders discuss the 'Free Silver' campaign of 1896 when William Jennings Bryan and the reforming party sought (according to the oratory of the time) to prevent the banking class from its attempt to crucify mankind upon a cross of gold. He must have paid great attention to these discussions and absorbed the significance of the nodding heads and weighty pauses. How otherwise to explain the story, which we have on his own authority, in *Indiscretions*, that even at the age of six he was so seized with indignation at the result of a national election that he hurled his rocking-chair across the room.

The Pounds attended the Wyncote Presbyterian Church, called Calvary, where Homer taught Sunday school. It was a wooden building located on the north-east corner of Fernbrook Avenue and Station Road, opposite Miss Ridpath's unofficial school. It was later rolled to a new

7

site in Fernbrook Avenue, accompanied by a host of small boys including Pound. The Presbyterian minister was the Rev. Carlos Tracy Chester; his son, Hawley, with whom Pound played as a boy, called on him during a honeymoon visit to Paris about 1920. One of their childhood pranks together was to invent a djinn to scare and perplex another boy who bored them with his company. Hawley's sister, Anna, made an impression on him, mainly, it seems, because of her fanatical adherence on the metronome during piano lessons. It is not clear when exactly Pound first began to have his doubts about Presbyterianism, or Christianity in general, but the seeds of his later rejection of Christianity were sown at Sunday-school or during bible class; or, perhaps, at the Christian Endeavour Convention in Boston which he reports as having attended at 'a precocious age'. He said of the Hebrew Scriptures in his 1938 essay on 'Mang Tsze: The Ethics of Mencius' that it was only with the greatest and most tortuous difficulty that the Sunday-school had got a moral teaching 'out of these sordid accounts of lechery, trickery and isolated acts of courage'. In 1940 he complained in a letter to an American Jesuit, Fr Francis Talbot, of the 'modern habit of trying to get everything down to the level of the young men's bible class'. And in a letter in 1958 to the historian R. McNair Wilson, he said that he had been brought up a Presbyterian, 'but it began to seem phoney' under a minister by the name of Lower. This was the Rev. William Barnes Lower who in 1901 took over Calvary Church from Carlos Chester. He was a great organizer and in the words of a local historian, 'Young peoples' groups were started and the whole church was alive with activity'. Pound was still attending church sometimes, even if mainly for the music, when he was nineteen, and still thinking in what we may call Christian terms. If doubts formed early about organized religion and the meaning and import of the Bible, if he began to formulate religious thoughts independently of Christianity, there is still no single overwhelming turn to be traced and recorded because the process was a slow one, intermittent, and by no means consistent.

At the age of ten he seems to have been a happy boy: a well-behaved, slightly spoilt, only child, of above-average intelligence. He was now known by the family and among his friends as '*Ra*', pronounced *ray*. He went with his mother to New York in the spring of 1896. His father, who remained at Wyncote, was requested by Isabel, through her son, in a letter written to 'Dear Pa' on 28 April, to 'douse the palm if you haven't watered it'. 'Ma' was busy 'scribbling thread on the scurt of the dress she made the waist of the other day'. They hoped to come home the first of next week, but didn't know the day. 'Ma Weston' had been invited to return with them but had refused.

Signed 'E.L.P.' When his mother and Homer went to New York later in the year he wrote on 15 November to tell her that he had been in to Philadelphia to see a minstrel show. He declined to send her a full description which, he said, would fill ten sheets of paper, but contented himself with a list of the 'chief topics': 'McKinley Bombarded' (William McKinley, President of the United States 1897–1901), 'Bicycle Crazy' and 'Our Public Safety'. At Wanamaker's Store he had some cream, 'more than we could eat'. He asked her to buy him some stamps, a list of which she would find in the upper outside pocket of Homer's overcoat. If his handwriting was poor it was because he had sprained his little finger at football. And the letter was signed 'X Ra', which in letters a year later became 'X ray'. It was typical of Isabel's sense of duty that she went each evening to the Jenkintown station to meet her husband on his way home from work; and later when the walk back, up Fernbrook hill, became too much for her, she waited beautifully dressed at the door.

In the summer of 1897 he was in New York again with his mother. He was pleased when he wrote to Homer on 7 June because Aunt Frank had promised to have his wheels cleaned. He began to be active in tennis and fencing: repairs still visible in the stained glass on the hall-landing at Fernbrook Avenue testify to the tennis balls which hit the glass while he was practising against the side of the house. He also played chess and in winter skated on Wanamaker's pond nearby.

At the age of twelve he entered the Cheltenham Military Academy only a mile or so up the road from his home at Wyncote. There he studied English, arithmetic, history, Latin and Greek and wore a uniform. He said years later that he could stand everything about the Academy except the drill. Latin and Greek were taught by a Wyncote man, Frederick Doolittle, who was known among the cadets as 'Cassius' or 'Lean and Hungry Look'. For part of the time Pound boarded at the Academy and decked the walls of his room with photographs and posters advertising reigning beauties of stage and music-hall. Midway through January 1898 he and a boy named Reed went to Philadelphia to perform a fencing act as 'picked' representatives of the Academy. 'We did ourselves proud,' he told his mother, 'and have been excused from all drill since and will be for some time to come.'

In February Wyncote was under snow and on the 6th Ezra and a friend called Tom went sledging. They started in the Pound driveway, went down Fernbrook Avenue which falls away steeply to Station Road and then up the road to Chelten Hills. He also took a sleigh ride with Levi Bean, one of the founders of Calvary Presbyterian Church, who had the livery stable on Station Road opposite the foot of Fernbrook Avenue. Ezra helped Mr Bean to hook on the horses and they went up past Glenside – a village adjoining Wyncote – and back. Sometimes he hired a ride with Mr bean in a horse and buggy at one dollar for the afternoon. Bean had a lift whereby a carriage could enter the stable at the lower or Station Road level and be driven out of the attic door onto the top level of the hill behind. It is not clear whether this device served any important purpose but it pleased greatly Ezra and his companions.

In June 1898 as the school year came to a close he had ice-cream, cake, eight lemonades and crackers after 'Skinny' Dayton, whose name was Dayton Larzelere, beat him in the high jump at the Academy sports. He looked forward to the coming 'declamation contest' which he hoped to win. I do not know the outcome for certain but I seem to remember Pound telling me, or perhaps I read it somewhere, that he did in fact win. On 10 June he celebrated in verse the approaching end of term:

> Four more days until vacation
> Then we leave this ——— plantation,
> No more Latin, no more Greek
> No more smoking on the sneak. . . .

The summer of 1898 he spent abroad on a three months' tour with his Aunt Frank who believed in travelling prepared. She carried in her luggage ninety-seven (according to Pound) little tissue-paper parcels of green tea prepared in advance for the pot. They were distributed throughout her luggage, ever since the occasion when they had all been discovered on top of a single case, to the amazement of a customs official. Towards the end of June and early in July they saw the sights in London: the two which he liked best were the Tower and St Paul's. The 'chief warden' of the Tower he noticed had five medals and was a 'Scotchman'. They went to Kenilworth Castle and to Warwick which he was impressed to discover was 'still' the home of the Earl of Warwick who only the week before had played host to the Prince of Wales. At Stratford he saw 'Shakers birth-place, tomb and memorials', and at Cowes had large strawberries with Devonshire cream. They left London on 4 July and travelled to the Continent, Ezra celebrating American Independence Day, he told his father, by depositing his breakfast and his lunch in the depths of the English Channel. At Brussels they stayed at the Grand Hotel de Saxe where on 5 July he sat down to write an account of his travels to Homer. On receiving news of the fall of Santiago in the Spanish-American war the young patriot dashed off a postscript 'Vive l'Amerique. Hurrah, Santiago has fallen'. After Brussels the route seems to have included Cologne, a journey

down the Rhine to Bingen, Mainz and Heidelberg, a stay in the Alps
(Lucerne and Como), and then Florence, Naples, Rome and Venice. It
would appear that they also visited North Africa; for there was a
photograph in Pound's possession for many years which perpetuated
the marvellous vision of Aunt Frank's wide figure in white bodice and
hat sitting upright on a narrow mule in Tangiers. They returned to the
United States in September.

It must have been about this time or the following year that a man
by the name of H. Spencer excited his interest in Greek poetry by
reciting a long passage from Homer, after a game of tennis. The incident hung in his mind. In *Guide to Kulchur* he said that hearing the
Greek poetry read aloud was worth more to him at the age of thirteen
than grammar; and he referred to it again in canto 80 in the *Pisan
Cantos*:

> and it was old Spencer (,H.) who first declaimed me
>   the Odyssey
> with a head built like Bill Shepard's
> on the quais of what Siracusa?
>   or what tennis court
> near what pine trees?

Of his early reading and taste I know little: only that grandmother
Weston read him a great deal of Sir Walter Scott and that his awakening years were 'adorned with the bustuous noises of Kipling'. Beyond
that there is a passing reference in the essay 'The Teacher's Mission'
(1934) to the fact that Ibsen's name was known to him when he was
at preparatory school, and a letter of the same year in which he says
that as a child he heard people talking about Edward Bellamy's *Looking
Backward*. James Whitcomb Riley was a household name with his
poems of rural and semi-rural America and we know that Pound read
him: I assume it was when he was a boy but I have no proof.

From Military Academy he went to the Cheltenham Township
High School, one stop along the Reading railroad at Elkins Park, to
prepare for university. He was fifteen when he left there in 1901. The
original building of 1884 is no longer used as a school. There was no
sign of Ezra Pound either there or at the present school when I visited
them a year or two ago, nor had the school official to whom I spoke
even heard of him; the only scrap I could find was a plaque on the wall
with the name Homer L. Pound among the Board of Directors responsible for the new building of 1905.

II University
1901/1907

Pound was about fifteen when he decided to be a poet and began to learn the necessary skills. He believed (he wrote twelve years later, in an article, 'How I Began') that the 'Impulse', as he called it, was from the gods, but that technique was a man's own responsibility; and so he resolved that at thirty he would know more about poetry than any man living: would know the 'dynamic content' from the 'shell', what was accounted poetry everywhere, what part of it was indestructible and could not be lost in translation, and what effects were obtainable in one language only and were incapable of being translated at all. 'In this search I learned more or less of nine foreign languages, I read Oriental stuff in translations, I fought every university regulation and every professor who tried to make me learn anything except this, or who bothered me with "requirements for degrees".' Probably his attitude at fifteen was not as hard as he would have us believe, nor his understanding of what he would have to do, to become the poet of his dreams, quite so clear as it was here represented: a hardening had occurred in the meantime, which by 1913 when he wrote the article, was at the heart of his literary programme, and in the heat of battle it no doubt coloured his memory of 1901; but we may accept the article as a guide to his ambition and as an indication of his inkling about the importance of the craft of poetry, even at the age of fifteen.

In the autumn of 1901, within a few months perhaps of this crystallization of interest, he was admitted to the University of Pennsylvania, Philadelphia, under the name Ezra Loomis Pound, to study 'Arts and Science'. He was not quite sixteen and gained admission largely on account of his showing with Latin. His courses for the year 1901–2 were: English composition, English language and analysis, public speaking, algebra, solid geometry, plane trigonometry, German grammar and reading, Livy, Horace, American colonial history, and principles of Government in the United States. He studied English under Dr Felix E. Schelling, who was the John Welsh Centennial Professor, Dr Clarence G. Child (Assistant Professor), and Dr Cornelius Weygandt (Instructor), and he spent hours on Layamon's *Brut* for which he was grateful later. For history he had Herman Vandenburg Ames, whose classes contributed little, in a direct way, to his later study of history, but seem to have kept alive his interest in the subject when it might well have died. These classes were at times informal, owing to the fact that Ames, according to Pound later, did not make mountains out of molehills and refused to be disturbed, or even distracted, by the movement of ping pong balls to and fro on the long narrow tables of the history room. Student horseplay he neither condemned nor encouraged. And if a student by the name of James Kirkbride, who was six feet two, was sent sprawling in his path as he walked from his office into the classroom, Ezra Pound's shinbone having been the material cause, he waited until order was restored and continued on his way.

Pound's friendship with the painter, William Brooke Smith ('my first friend', he called him), began when he was fifteen or sixteen. Between 1902 and 1905 Smith was a student at the Philadelphia College of Art, also known as the School of Industrial Art, at the corner of Broad and Pine Streets, Philadelphia. Pound sometimes accompanied him to the college and was enthralled by his talk about art. When Smith moved into a studio Pound was a frequent visitor. While a student Smith appears to have lived at 1612 Diamond Street, Philadelphia, then a fashionable brownstone row-house. Later he lived in a large semi-detached townhouse at 839 Franklin Street, from which address in 1907 he wrote Pound a number of letters reflecting the rather precious world of 'arts and crafts' in which he moved. Years later Pound said that Smith died of consumption in 1908, to the 'intimate grief of his friends'. How Smith came to be in Philadelphia in those days or to be so knowledgeable, between the ages of seventeen and twenty-five, remained for him a complete mystery.

Pound went abroad again in the summer of 1902. In London he visited with his father the Royal Mint which he found more formal and less interesting than the Philadelphia Mint where he was free to walk among the stamping-presses and talk with the staff. A standard game among the workmen at Philadelphia was to tell you that you were welcome to keep one of the bags of gold if you could carry it away. It looked small enough and naturally you tried but it always proved impossible to lift. There was none of this banter and laughter when the two Americans visited the Royal Mint, and despite Homer's official letter of introduction they were not invited to view the workings below. They also visited Venice, which to the young poet was beginning to seem more attractive than Wyncote or Philadelphia.

In his second year at Pennsylvania (1902–3) he enrolled as Ezra Weston Loomis Pound and began to live in a dormitory, travelling home at the week-ends. He studied English composition, nineteenth-century English novelists, ethics, logic, constitutional history of the United States, comparative Governments, foreign relations of the United States, the Civil War and reconstruction, and the following in Latin: Catullus and Tibullus, Horace, Propertius and Ovid, and Vergil and Lucretius.

He was beginning to read Browning, Fiona McLeod, Arthur Symons, Ernest Dowson, and the Canadian poet Bliss Carman whose *Songs of Vagabondia* written in collaboration with Richard Hovey was published in the United States in 1894, to be followed by more than a dozen books of verse, under his own name, during the next ten years. Pound's own publishing career began, as far as I can determine, on 8 November 1902. On that day an unsigned poem called 'Ezra on the Strike' appeared in a local newspaper, the *Jenkintown Times-Chronicle*. It contains eight quatrains in imitation of James Whitcomb Riley; the voice is that of an old farmer on his way to town with hay who comments on the approach of Thanksgiving Day and the effects of a strike:

> Wal, Thanksgivin' do be comin' round.
> With the price of turkeys on the bound,
> And Coal, by gum! Thet were just found,
>   Is surely gettin' cheaper.
>
> The winds will soon begin to howl,
> And winter, in its yearly growl,
> Across the medders begin to prowl,
>   And Jack Frost gettin' deeper.

My reason for thinking it may be Pound's work is a statement he made when on 27 June 1958 he revisited the house at 166 Fernbrook Avenue. He told Mr Carl Gatter, whose home it now is, that his 'first publisher' was a Jenkintown newspaper; and in a letter the following year wrote: 'Believe the *Times-Chronicle* had but one poem, the earliest and political.' No other poems have been found which have a better claim than 'Ezra on the Strike', but what makes me hesitate to say definitely that Pound was the author, is that the Rev. William Barnes Lower also was a poet, a regular contributor to the *Times-Chronicle* of similar 'dialect' poems. His work, signed and unsigned, appeared both before and after 'Ezra on the Strike' and some of it was later collected into a book, *Falling Petals*.

Pound continued while at Pennsylvania to play tennis and took fencing lessons under the university coach, Signor Leonardo Terrone. He did not play football but he was interested enough to serve as a voluntary usher for the games played on Franklin Field.

It was during the Academic year 1902–3 that he met William Carlos Williams. A dormitory acquaintance when he heard that Williams wrote verse arranged a meeting with Pound. Williams was two years older, a freshman in the Department of Dentistry who changed the following year to Medicine and became a doctor; but although older he found the other more advanced in literature, 'the livest, most intelligent and unexplainable thing' he had ever met. In April 1903 Pound played one of the women of the chorus in Euripides' *Iphigenia among the Taurians*, given in Greek at the Academy of Music, with his parents in the audience. According to Williams later, he wore 'a great blonde wig at which he tore as he waved his arms about and heaved his massive breasts in ecstasies of extreme emotion'.

A survey of the thirty-three courses which he took during his freshman and sophomore years shows that he received a *pass* in four courses each semester and *good* for most of the others. There is one *distinguished* for a mathematics course, three *not passed* for two mathematics courses and one history course, and one *postponed* (or *incomplete*), for another history course. This suggests that his work was only fair and certainly nothing out of the ordinary.

In 1903 he transferred to Hamilton College at Clinton near Utica in New York State. Two reasons have been suggested for this change – that his parents were disappointed with his progress at Pennsylvania and were unhappy about the company he was keeping. Pound himself has suggested a third reason – that he wanted to know the difference between a big university and a small college. Whatever the reasons may have been he went to Hamilton in June 1903 to enrol for the coming academic year. He travelled north from New York aboard the Empire State Express at an average speed of 54 miles an hour and on the afternoon of 11 June he saw the President of the College, Dr Melancthon Woolsey Stryker, and arranged a two-year course as a third year 'special student' which would enable him to qualify for his degree in 1905. In a letter to his father on 22 July, from New York where he stayed for part of the summer, we find three of the characteristics which to a greater extent and more forcefully mark the correspondence of his mature years: the use of foreign language, dialect, and strong English. Thus the letter begins in German ('Lieber Vater'), and includes both a foreigner's broken English ('oderwise dings vas az dey vas') and straightforward speech, as when he apologizes that the letter has been written 'by bum gas light'. Queer spellings and a great variety of dialect voices gradually began to creep into his letters: sometimes, it seems, for emphasis, but often as not for the sheer fun of it. In later years he also developed oddities of typing, with strange spacing, phrasing and line-breaks, often reinforced by an array of underlinings and marginal interpolations in ink. Another peculiarity was his method of spacing out the name and address of his correspondent to cover almost the entire face of the envelope. As a result his letters were recognizable immediately and even those that were unsigned bore his unmistakable mark.

At Hamilton he was listed as Ezra Weston Pound and lived at 17 Hungerford. He may have got rid of the 'Loomis' from his name because it was cumbersome, but the deletion may also have been rendered advisable by the proximity of the college to that part of New York State in which the Loomis family achieved its fame.

Although, as I said earlier, the Pounds lived well and were by no means poor, money was always a problem, and while settling in at college Pound was forced to apply to his father for extra funds to pay for such necessary items as blankets, pitcher and washbowl. He was close on eighteen and began looking ahead to the future. His problem was how to earn a living when he had finished his education. He considered taking up Law and toyed with the idea of a career on Wall Street but his travels abroad had made him restless and he decided that the Consular Service would be more enjoyable than either. The ivy and quadrangle atmosphere at Hamilton appealed to him for a time at least and he enjoyed Dr Stryker's vigorous sermons inspired by a no-nonsense Christianity. The hearty clergyman did not express disapproval of religious 'rapture' when he preached on the Transfiguration on the Mount but he warned against the temptation to stay enraptured when you ought to be 'getting busy'. There was a side to Pound which responded to this kind of message, then and throughout his life. Dr Stryker compiled several hymnals and translated some of Luther's hymns into English. One beginning 'A Tower of Refuge is our God' was included in Pound's anthology *Confucius to Cummings*, published in 1964.

Three men, more than others, at Hamilton, played a decisive part in shaping him for poetry by opening his eyes to some of the glories of the European past: Herman Carl George Brandt, who was Munson Professor of the German Language and Literature; the Rev. Joseph Darling Ibbotson (known as 'Bib'), who was Professor of English Literature, Anglo-Saxon and Hebrew; and, the most important, William Pierce Shepard, Professor of Romance Languages and Literatures, who not only introduced him to French, Italian and Spanish but when he saw that the young man's enthusiasm was backed by ability gave him free private tuition in Provençal. Through Ibbotson Pound was steered towards those sonorities in English having their root in Anglo-Saxon, which he exploited later in 'The Seafarer' and other poems; and by Shepard he was introduced to the Europe of the Middle Ages which thereafter remained a point of reference to which continually he returned and from which he drew intellectual energy and the sustenance for many of his dreams. Both men he mentioned when later he acknowledged early influences which he believed were more important to his poetry than anything received from contemporaries. His first year (1903–4) included courses in German, French, Italian, English and mathematics; one of the highlights of the year was a lecture at the college by, he told his family, 'a personal friend of Browning's'. He was very much struck by a remark made one day by the Dean of the college, Professor A. P. Saunders, about 'that fine old word "an independence",' perhaps because it reminded him of his own position. An 'independence' was 'sufficient income to live on, so that a man could do what he liked'. Among Pound's published poems there is only one which appears to belong to 1903 or early 1904. It was called 'Motif' when published in his first book, *A Lume Spento* (1908), and re-titled 'Search' in *Personae* the following year:

> Through woodlands dim
> > Have I taken my way,
> And o'er silent waters, night and day
> Have I sought the wee wind.

Beneath his junior year photograph in *The Hamiltonian* of 1905 is this description:

> Ezra Weston Pound, Philadelphia, Pa.
> 'Bib's' pride. Leader of the anvil chorus at the Commons.
> Oh, how he throws those legs! Peroxide blonde.

For part of the time that he was away from home his parents moved to 502 South Front Street, Philadelphia, and worked among underprivileged children during the winter. Homer was also superintendent of the Italian Mission in Philadelphia and Isabel his organist.

During the spring holidays in 1904 William Carlos Williams spent a week-end with Pound at Wyncote. 'His parents are very nice people,' Williams wrote to his mother on 30 March, 'and have always been exceptionally kind to me. Mrs Pound had prepared a fine meal.' After supper he and Pound had a long talk on literature, drama, the classics and philosophy, 'subjects that I love yet have not time to study and which he is making a life work of'. He described Pound as a 'fine fellow':

If he ever does get blue nobody knows it, so he is just the man for me. But not one person in a thousand likes him, and a great many people detest him and why? Because he is so darned full of conceits and affectation. He is really a brilliant talker and thinker but delights in making himself just exactly what he is not: a laughing boor. His friends must be all patience in order to find him out and even then you must not let him know it, for he will immediately put on some artificial mood and be really unbearable. It is too bad, for he loves to be liked, but there is some quality in him which makes him too proud to try to please people.

In his second year at Hamilton beginning in the autumn of 1904 he was much more active than before; his literary tastes began to clarify and he began to follow with determination wherever they would lead, without losing sight of his immediate scholastic purpose and final examinations; and he showed signs of some of his later critical attitudes. His courses included Old English, German, French, Provençal, Spanish (the Spanish, he said, was 'not particularly exciting'), physics and analytical geometry. Under Dr Stryker he studied the 'Christian Evidences' and listened to 'hot air' about parliamentary law. Soon he was able to report home that he was being transferred to more advanced work in German. He began to read Beddoes and was particularly pleased with *Death's Jest Book*. He was flattered to discover in Edmund Gosse's introduction that Beddoes was not everybody's meat but 'a dish for a few literary epicures' only and to hear that those who enjoyed him would be able to 'pick out his excellencies' without being told. It was about this time that he met Katherine Ruth Heyman, the concert pianist, who although fifteen years older than Pound charmed him for some years to come. In volume two of his two-volume edition of Beddoes her name is inscribed in his early hand and dated 1904. Passages which he marked, then or later, in *Death's Jest Book*, such as:

> an I utter
> Shadows of words, like to an ancient ghost,
> Arisen out of hoary centuries,
> Where none can speak his language. . . .

appear thirteen years later in an article on Beddoes published in a magazine called *The Future* (September 1917), and again thirty years later in canto 80.

As the horizon broadened he took notice: he read Caedmon and began to find Anglo-Saxon 'very fascinating'; in French he sampled Descartes and Pascal and read Corneille's *Cid*; in English he explored comedy before Shakespeare; and at last he began to find something worthy of his talents in mathematics. Analytical geometry, he wrote to his mother, 'is the first respectable mathematics I have interviewed for some time'. He took part in the proceedings of a literary club which met at Ibbotson's; they read *A Midsummer Night's Dream* together and ate, talked and smoked. It was in a talk with Ibbotson, he said in a letter in 1936, that his long poem *The Cantos* originated, his first idea for a *magnum opus* having been, apparently, to write a trilogy on Marozia (d. 945), wife of Alberic I, Prince of Rome. He was also a member of the college's four-man chess team. For exercise he walked and continued to play tennis and for relaxation did odd jobs with knife and tools, which is not in itself remarkable but is interesting here because if we keep it in mind it will help us to understand later a very important aspect of Pound's make-up: his belief, almost to the point of its being part of his temperament, in the virtues of the handyman, the man who can turn his hand to anything, which though often at odds with his professionalism and belief in craft in the highest sense, in a way directed the whole bias of his thought in the 1930s and later.

It was probably in 1904 that he wrote the two short poems, 'Song' and 'To the Dawn: Defiance', which were first published in *A Lume Spento*. They provide evidence of an early stage in the formation of the dream element which is important later. 'Song', which begins, 'Love thou thy dream', and ends:

> dreams alone can truly be,
> For 'tis in dreams I come to thee.

is like a pale forerunner of 'To Καλὸν' (1914):

> Even in my dreams you have denied yourself to me
> And sent me only your handmaids.

The other, 'To the Dawn: Defiance', similarly tells of a 'dream' for which he could not yet find the right words and had therefore to be content to describe in the worn-out word-patterns of the time:

> Ye blood-red spears-men of the dawn's array
> . . .
> My moated soul shall dream in your despite
> A refuge for the vanquished hosts of night. . . .

In January 1905 we find him enjoying Taine, reading Goethe's *Egmont* and Molière's *Femmes Savantes*, looking into the subject of bibliography, via G. H. Putnam's *Books and Their Makers during the Middle Ages*, making a literary and dramatic study of the Book of Job, learning how to debate, and on the side, reading tragedy. His mother's emphasis upon proper behaviour he found rather tiresome and he could not always resist the urge to reply. An opportunity presented itself in January while he was reading Galdos's *Dona Perfecta*. 'You may tell Miss Whitechurch and Mrs Lovell,' he wrote, 'I'm reading about "a perfect lady" even if the name sounds like a cheap cigar.' Miss Whitechurch and Mrs Lovell were two ladies who boarded at the Pound home; Isabel Pound always referred to them as her 'paying guests'. When he passed his January examination in analytical geometry he was pleased to be able to report that the faculty of mathematics in consultation could not fathom the method by which he discovered the equation demanded by the key problem: 'I wrote it despite the formulae, etc., supposed to be necessary thereto, and which I didn't know.'

By February 1905 he had reached a position on Dante only a short step from the views expressed in his book *The Spirit of Romance* (1910) and throughout the rest of his life. Any developments after *The Spirit of Romance* were only in particulars or certain areas, new depth as the result of detailed readings; but his overall view was based upon his discovery in 1905 that the moderns were not so modern after all and that the Middle Ages knew a few things too. 'Find me', he wrote to his mother, 'a phenomenon of any importance in the lives of men and nations that you cannot measure with the rod of Dante's allegory . . . I shall continue to study Dante and the Hebrew prophets.' And he added that Dante (poet, scholar, lover, soldier and upholder of 'clean politics') had put a pope in hell centuries before Luther. He wrote again within a few days to defend Catholicism against what he believed to be Protestant detraction and to give credit where credit was due in the past.

With the end of the college year in sight and all going well he had himself measured for his gown. In April he was reading the Old Spanish *Cid*, the *Chansons de Geste*, the troubadours, Chaucer and Jean Paul Richter's German. He acknowledged the receipt of coffee from home (presumably in response to his earlier request for a quarter pound of Acker's best pulverized Java), and was able to report that he was attending church in Utica where the music was 'excellent'. His 'Belangal Alba', translated from the Provençal during 1904–5 was published in the May 1905 issue of the *Hamilton Literary Magazine*:

> Dawn light, o'er sea and height, riseth bright,
> Passeth vigil, clear shineth on the night.
>
> They be careless of the gates, delaying,
>   Whom the ambush glides to hinder
> Whom I warn and cry to, praying,
>   'Arise!'

He sent his father a copy on 3 May and reported having heard from William Carlos Williams. Also in May he was engrossed in a technical problem in versification: how to translate Giraut de Bornelh's Tenzon, 'S-ie-us quier', using only five rhyme-sounds over sixty-eight lines.

The money problem, which had continued to dog him throughout the college year, became serious in mid-May. Writing to his mother on 19 May he apologized for being 'too vicious' in a letter to his father. The reason was that he had had to borrow the price of his dinner for three days because his father's cheque had not arrived until the morning of the nineteenth. His letters home at this stage were signed 'Son'. On 2 June he attended a dance in Utica and had more fun, he said, than since he left home. He found that 'these desolate regions', as he described Upper New York State, were made more bearable by the company of a local girl, Viola Baxter, with whom he went driving. She obviously took his fancy and a year or two later he wrote her a number of letters full of news and poems. By 22 June he had passed all his exams except physics, which was in a day or two, and on 29 June he received his degree of Ph.B. and second prize in French.

Of the five poems in *A Lume Spento* which appear to belong to 1905, two of them, 'Plotinus' and 'Ballad for Gloom', move well enough, but the gap between his words and what he is trying to express – if at this stage he had a clear grasp of what it was – is uncomfortably wide; he has had the experience but as yet lacks means to turn it into genuine poetry. Two others of the five were successful and are rightly collected among the author's shorter poems: 'On His Own Face in a Glass' and 'For E.McG', the latter a memorial to a University of Pennsylvania student, Eugene McCartney, 'That was', says the subtitle, 'my counter-blade under Leonardo Terrone, Master of Fence'. The fifth poem, 'In Tempore Senectutis' is of little interest now except to the student who wants to examine the young poet's attempts to digest Dowson, which he never really succeeded in doing. There is a note in Dowson, a perfection in a frail narrow sphere, which he could hear, as witness his footnote on the villanelle in his preface to the *Poetical Works of Lionel Johnson* (1915), but was never able to reproduce.

Returning to the University of Pennsylvania for the year 1905–6, to work for his Master's degree, he studied Spanish drama (Tirso de Molina, Lope de Vega and Moreto), Spanish literature, Old French (*Erec und Enid*), Provençal and Italian and made a 'special study' of Martial, Catullus and Tacitus. Pound told me in conversation in 1959 that he thought his search for clarity and hardness in verse had its roots in his early reading of Martial and Catullus, so it may have been in the period after his return to Pennsylvania that these qualities first struck him as desirable. There is no saying that 'The Cry of the Eyes', which he probably began in 1905 and finished the following year, reflects this awakening, and we must admit that it is couched in a rather artificial language; but there is a delightful turn, here and there, in the movement:

> would feel the fingers of the wind
> Upon these lids that lie over us
> Sodden and lead-heavy.

and there is a certain simplicity of style, and possibly – it is hard to tell, the margin is so fine – a gain in straightforwardness of presentation:

> The yellow flame paleth
> And the wax runs low.

and

> this ever-flowing monotony
> Of ugly print marks, black
> Upon white parchment.

It first appeared in *A Lume Spento* and is preserved by Pound in later collections as 'The Eyes'.

Of the three teachers who left a mark on him at this stage it is impossible to say for certain who was the most important but we may guess that it was Walton Brooks McDaniel, assistant Professor of Latin, from whom he received a schooling which enabled him to read Latin easily and with pleasure for the rest of his life. He was to say later that he considered the hours spent copying out McDaniel's prose translation of Catullus, like his instruction under Ibbotson and Shepard, more important to his poetry than any contemporary influences. As with any intelligent young man who is beginning to use his mind beyond the requirements of the classroom it was often the small things with universal meaning, rather than general ideas of no particular significance to his present mood, which caught his mind's eye. Thus Ovid came alive because of a chance remark about Daedalus (probably by McDaniel), in which he suddenly saw the human curiosity which causes the small boy to watch his father at work and copy his every move. 'I am much more grateful', he wrote in his 'Notes on Elizabethan Classicists' in 1918, 'for the five minutes during which a certain lecturer emphasized young Icarus begorming himself with Daedalus' wax than for all the dead hours he spent trying to make me a scholar.' When he became interested in the Latinists of the Renaissance it was apparently McDaniel who warned him that 'after all if one confined oneself to the accepted authors one was sure of reading good stuff, whereas there was a risk in hunting about among the unknown'. Pound was considering the possibility of doing a thesis on material outside the list of classic authors included in the curriculum, which caused irritation, especially when he pointed out that a thesis was supposed to contain original research. He quotes McDaniel as saying, 'And besides, Mr Pound, we should have to do so much work ourselves to verify your results'.

His other teachers for the years 1905–7 were Dr Hugo A. Rennert, Professor of Romance Languages and Literatures, and author of a life of Lope de Vega, and Felix Schelling. Rennert was handsome and something of a dandy. There are three glimpses of him in Pound's later writings. In canto 28 he sighs heavily and looks despairingly over the top of his glasses when a chronic late-comer arrives puffing at the foot of the stair below the classroom. There is another in a note written about 1930 for a revised edition of *The Spirit of Romance*; the subject is the 'irregular' metre of the *Poema del Cid*: 'I can still see Dr Rennert manicuring his finger nails in seminar, pausing in that operation, looking over his spectacles and in his plaintive falsetto, apropos someone who had attempted to reprint the *Cid* with ten syllables in *every* line: "Naow effa man had sense enough to write a beautiful poem like this is, wudn't yeow think he wudda had sense enough to be able to keount ep to ten on his fingers *ef he'da wanted tew?*"' The third glimpse is in an article on economics in the paper *New Democracy* (15 October 1935): 'I remember Hugo Rennert remarking on some ballyhoo about "the plant", the U. of Penn. "plant" was, according to the ballyhoo, not to lie idle. Rennert observed on the part of himself and faculty: "But damn it *we* are the plant".'

One of Pound's friends was Hilda Doolittle, later the poet H.D., whose father, Charles Doolittle, was Professor of Astronomy at Pennsylvania and director of the Flower Astronomical Observatory in nearby Upper Darby which was then in the country. Pound, Williams, Hilda Doolittle and a few others made up a group from about 1905 when she began her freshman year at Bryn Mawr. They took woodland walks together near the observatory, went to parties and dances and sometimes met at the Pound home at Wyncote where they sang in the front parlour while Mrs Pound accompanied on the upright piano. Pound gave Hilda a ring to wear and they were unofficially engaged; soon, however, as the result of Professor Doolittle's opposition or some other cause it petered out. But not before Pound had celebrated their friendship by presenting her with a bound collection of twenty-five poems written between 1905 and 1907. Called simply *Hilda's Book*, it is now in the Harvard Library. It is about four inches by three-and-a-half and consists of fifty-four rather badly typed pages, with numerous

autograph corrections and notes, sewn and bound in vellum – all by
Pound himself. Four of the poems were published in *A Lume Spento*:
'La Donzella Beata', 'Li Bel Chasteus', 'Era Venuta' and 'The Tree'.
The first two are readable but nothing more. 'Era Venuta' when it
appeared in print was considerably altered and bore a new title,
'Comraderie'. In the latter form it has a good ending:

> Or on still evenings when the rain falls close
> There comes a tremor in the drops, and fast
> My pulses run, knowing thy thought hath passed
> That beareth thee as doth the wind the rose.

which seems to look ahead to later poems like 'Ballatetta' and 'Ione,
Dead the Long Year'. 'The Tree' is a genuine poem with a finely-
timed conclusion which appeals through the absence of rhyme in the
final line:

> Nathless I have been a tree amid the wood
> And many new things understood
> That were rank folly to my head before.

Slightly altered:

> And many a new thing understood
> That was rank folly to my head before.

it now heads the poet's own selection of his collected poems. The only
other point of interest in *Hilda's Book* is this ingenious experiment in
sound and versification:

> Tho the elfin horn shall
>   call to you
> 'true   be true
> By the violets in thy
>   leaf brown hair
> 'ware   be ware
> . . .
> Tho night shall dwell in thy
>   child eyes
> 'wise   be wise
> That thy child heart to mine
>   emprise
> 'plies   replies

For night shall flee
    from the fore-suns flame
'shame   in shame
Tho my heart to thee embeggared
               came
'same   'tis the same. . . .

He uses an echo effect in some of his mature verse but nothing quite like this. We cannot but feel disappointed that he did not at some later stage, when he was in the full possession of his skills, see fit to pursue the possibilities these lines of youth suggest. Another young writer with whom he was friendly was Phyllis Bottome, the novelist, who credits Pound with giving her sound literary advice while they were at Pennsylvania together. They met again in London and years later in Italy.

Three or four minor points in the story which I have not been able to date, even to within a year or two, probably belong to this period after his return to the University of Pennsylvania when he took up again old threads, renewed friendships and created new ones and sought to build for himself an artistic and intellectual life in Wyncote and Philadelphia. He began to play chess with the Rev. James Biddle Halsey who from 1901 to 1908 was Vicar at All Hallows Episcopal Church at the corner of Greenwood Avenue and Bent Road, Wyncote. In the social scale at Wyncote the Episcopal Church came first and the Presbyterian second. He became friends with the landscape painter, Frank Reed Whiteside, who lived a few minutes away in Washington Lane. Born in Philadelphia in 1866 Whiteside studied first at the Pennsylvania Academy of Fine Arts and later in Paris under Laurens and Constant. Pound used to visit his home, whether at Wyncote or when Whiteside moved to Philadelphia I do not know; but the artist, who was nineteen years older than Pound, told Wyncote residents that he benefited from the younger man's comments on his paintings. In the long poem 'Redondillas, or Something of that Sort', which Pound wrote in 1910, he praised God 'for a few royal fellows . . . like Whiteside'. The painter was shot outside his Philadelphia home in 1929; no one was caught and no motive discovered.

As Pound sought to find an artistic milieu close to home he began to live more consciously the life of 'the artist' and to introduce a little mild eccentricity into his behaviour. Miss Adele Polk who lived in Washington Lane, close to Whiteside, told me in Jenkintown in 1967 that she remembered one day at the Pound home when Ezra, using a sideboard or buffet for chair, methodically pulled out the tail of his shirt as he talked, carefully tore off a square of material, with gravity placed the square on his knee, and tapped it during the rest of the conversation. She could not fathom his purpose but she was impressed. Her father however, who was an Englishman, was not one to tolerate anything that smacked of nonsense. One day when he found Ezra on his front lawn, explaining to Adele the art of fencing by bearing down dramatically on an imaginary opponent with his rapier, Mr Polk intervened: 'Young man, I'm afraid you will end up in gaol.' On another occasion while learning to drive, Pound broke the steering on a Pullman horseless carriage.

It may have been as early as the spring of 1906 that he composed the nineteen lines which appear in *A Lume Spento* under the title 'Vana', and as the opening section of 'Praise of Ysolt' in *Personae* and later collections. They are still fresh in their contrasts of rhythm (for example 'In vain have I striven' against 'In vain have I said to him') and still worth reading for the way in which emphasis is brought to bear on a key word – on 'greater', for instance, in the line 'There be many singers greater than thou'. With two other poems which appear to belong to this period he was not so lucky. 'From Syria' is a translation of a song by Peire Bremon, 'made for his Lady in Provença', says Pound in a prefatory note, 'he being in Syria a crusader'. It has all the vices of the young poet struck with admiration for a distant time and place, without any compensating virtues. It begins in April when 'new flowers' blow in 'mead and garden', progresses by way of 'my Love's land' to 'Syrian strand' ('God keep me there for a fool, alway!'), and ends with the news that he is 'desirous' and 'grief-filled', his days 'full long', etc. A note at the end, signed E.P., says it is the 'only bit of Peire Bremon's work that has come down to us, and through its being printed with the songs of Giraut of Bornelh he is like to lose credit for even this', which suggests that Bremon having been forced upon him in his Provençal studies he tried to make the best of it. The other poem similarly defunct is 'From the Saddle', with subtitle 'D'Aubigne to Diane'. It opens well: 'Wearied by wind and wave', but is immediately unseated:

> death goes
> With gin and snare right near alway
> Unto my sight. . . .

and does not recover, despite a brave attempt at the end:

> since mid war I bear love's pain
> 'Tis meet my verse, as I, show sign
> Of powder, gun-match and sulphur stain.

Pound used them only once, to fill out *Exultations* (1909), and then allowed them to rest.

On 13 June he received his Master of Arts degree, which would seem to have been the occasion of his composing for his parents' amusement a fifty-five line poem called 'The Mourn of Life'. The well-written *Envoi* suggests what I believe to be the truth of the matter, that he was hoping to be a full-time writer but didn't know how he was going to manage, his family naturally enough having no inclination at this stage to support him in such an unusual enterprise, which from their point of view would amount to him doing nothing.

THE MOURN OF LIFE

There comes a time in the lives of men
   That makes their blood turn cold
And their fathers say
   In a gentle way
   'Thou canst not stay
Any more in the dear home fold.'

'Twill come some time to you,
   When your noble Dad,
   Your loving Dad
Your dear Dad, kind and true,
   Will no more pay
   In that generous way
Your bills as he used to do.

But will gently say
   In his old sweet way
Though the tone may ring some cool
   'I paid the stake
   The damned high stake
While you loafed "round school".

While you rushed the can
   And played the man
A smokin' your fine cheroots
   I had to pay
   In a hefty way
For a coon to black your boots.

Now you're a Master of Arts
   And a man of parts;

Go forth, get on the job.'
There comes a time in the lives of men
That makes their blood turn cold.

For the world is a place
They've glanced upon
From ethereal heights afar
Where each has fussed his chorus girl
And each has dined his star;
And each has spent
What Dad has sent
In ways a bit bizarre.

L'Envoi
Go little verse
Go forth and be damned
Throughout your limited sphere
But prithee tell
To the bards in hell
Who live on nothing a year
That a Master of Arts
And a man of parts
Is trying the same thing here.

Tell thou the ancient story
To the singers of long ago
Who left their ills
And unpaid bills
And their mortgages on glory
For good warm rooms below,
Unto such, when hell gets slow
Go, little verse, by gumbo, go.

Also in June he received from the university a notice informing him
that the trustees meeting on 5 June had appointed him Harrison Fellow
in Romanics for one year from 1 September 1906, at a salary of $500
payable in eight instalments from 30 September 1906 to 31 May 1907.
For a student to be eligible he had to possess (among other things) a
good reading knowledge of French and German. This 'pittance from
Sugar Trust money' (as he described it in a letter to me in 1955) was
very important to him at the age of twenty; it made him for the first
time independent financially, even if only for a short while, and
enabled him in the summer of 1906 to make his first independent trip

to Europe. He was admitted to the British Museum Reading Room on 2 July, for one week, to study the role of the Gracioso in the plays of Lope de Vega which was to be the subject of his thesis for a doctorate at Pennsylvania. In London he stayed at Miss Ann Withey's boarding-house at 8 Duchess Street, Portland Place. It was in July that he wrote the poem 'Scriptor Ignotus', which appeared in *A Lume Spento* with a dedication to 'K.R.H.' (Katherine Ruth Heyman). He draws a parallel between himself and Miss Heyman, on the one hand, and the eighteenth-century poet Bertold Lomax and his lady, an organist of Ferrara, on the other. A note at the end of the poem says: 'Bertold Lomax, English Dante scholar and mystic, died in Ferrara in 1723, with his "great epic" still a mere shadow, a nebula crossed with some few gleams of wonder light. The lady of the poem was an organist of Ferrara, whose memory has come down to us only in Lomax's notes.' 'Scriptor Ignotus' contains Pound's first promise of a long poem to come: a vision in which he sees his 'greater soul-self bending Sybilwise with that great forty-year epic' as yet 'unwrit'; which is rephrased at the end, after the manner of the concluding lines of Dante's *Vita Nuova*, to say that if it be God's will, he will make for her and the beauty of her music a new thing 'As hath not heretofore been writ'. The Temple Classics edition of the *Vita Nuova*, which was published by J. M. Dent in 1906, has: 'So that if it be the pleasure of him, by whom all things live, that my life persever for some few years, I hope to write of her what hath never been written of any woman.' In his 1934 essay on Laurence Binyon's translation of the *Inferno* Pound says: 'One was thankful in 1906 to Dent for the Temple bilingual edition' (he is referring to both the *Divine Comedy* and the *Vita Nuova*) but whether he consulted the Dent *Vita Nuova* before writing 'Scriptor Ignotus' I do not know.

He also went to Paris and to Spain and with the assistance of the American Consul in Madrid he received permission to work on Lope de Vega in the royal library. He was helped in his studies by a young priest, Father José Maria de Elizondo, with whom he struck up a friendship; they met again in London in 1917. He also met the play-wright José Echegaray, winner of the Nobel Prize in 1904, who told him that the reason Lope's plays were not then being staged in Spain was that there weren't any actors who were capable: the last actress who could do them was in South America. In the Prado Museum where he encountered one after the other the paintings of Velasquez, he experienced some of the richest moments in a life devoted to the appreciation of art. So strong was the enchantment, that thirty-one years later he could still call to mind – whether accurately or not does not matter – the order of the paintings as he strolled through the long galleries, great halls and smaller rooms of the museum, minute details in the brushwork clear in his mind: *Las Meniñas*, with a glimpse of Velasquez 'by the far door painting the picture'; the *Coronation of the Virgin*, differing greatly in workmanship from the others, 'designed . . . for church lighting and not for a palace'; the *Surrender of Breda*, with the upraised spears; portraits of Philip IV of Spain, on foot with a hunting gun, on horseback, 'the horse's foot having been done first in a different position'; a portrait of Don John of Austria, in which the fire in the background 'is there with two strokes or perhaps *one* of the brush'; *Los Boracchos*, and so on.

Pound was in a crowd outside the palace which witnessed an assassination attempt against King Alfonso and his bride. There was an immediate drive against anarchists and Pound thought it wise to leave Madrid because 'anarchist suspects and uncatalogued foreigners began to be confused in the eyes of the law'.

While in Spain he also explored Burgos and the surrounding countryside where eight hundred years before roamed Rodrigo Diaz de Bivar, hero of the *Poema del Cid*. Looking from the castle of Burgos, out over Old Castile, he 'was tempted to forget there were such prosaic things as doctors' theses to be writ'.

He returned to the University of Pennsylvania for the year 1906–7, to pursue post-graduate studies in Provençal and the *Chanson de Roland*, the Sicilian poets, the *Vita Nuova* and Boccaccio's *Decamerone*, the Old Spanish *Poema de Fernán González*, the plays of Miguel Sánchez, and Lope's *Estrella de Sevilla*. He also did 'an odd sort of post-graduate course' under Professor Cornelius Weygandt which may have been where he first heard of Lionel Johnson. Under the terms of his Harrison Fellowship he was expected to give his undivided attention to his studies and was exempt from the payment of tuition fees. The September 1906 issue of the *Book News Monthly*, a publication of the John Wanamaker store in Philadelphia, contained what appears to be his first published article, called 'Raphaelite Latin', and a review by him of two books on the troubadours by the Frenchman, M. Péladan, which he had come across in Paris. The editors of the *Book News Monthly* prefaced 'Raphaelite Latin' with these remarks:

Mr Pound, who is Fellow in Romance Languages for the University of Pennsylvania, and is especially interested in late Latin, has spent the past summer travelling in Europe, gathering material by the way. He is ready to defend the Latin of this period – which has the lifetime of Raphael as its centre – from the superficial charges of literary barrenness and inferiority of production that have been made against it. Some idea of the mere bulk of this production may be gained from the fact that the Ghero collection alone, if complete, would contain nearly three thousand pages of Latin verse.

The article itself contained, in its references to 'the Germanic ideal of scholarship' and 'the beauty of the classics', the seed of the theory upon which he based most of his later critical writings:

Perhaps the most neglected field in all literature is that containing the Latin works of the elegant poets and scholars contemporary with Raphael, and owning for the most part Pietro Bembo as their chief.

There are causes for this neglect. The scholars of classic Latin, bound to the Germanic ideal of scholarship, are no longer able as of old to fill themselves with the beauty of the classics, and by the very force of that beauty inspire their students to read Latin widely and for pleasure; nor are they able to make students see clearly whereof classic beauty consists. The scholar is compelled to spend most of his time learning what his author wore and ate, and in endless pondering over some utterly unanswerable question of textual criticism. . . .

This 'Germanic ideal' prevents the student from building 'a comfortable house for his brain to live in', and causes him to revile as a 'dilettante' anyone who tries to do so: 'No one knows the contempt and hatred that can be gathered into these few syllables until they have been hissed at him by one truly Germanised.' His review of the two French books in the same issue was headed 'Interesting French Publications', and in it we find reference to the Mysteries of Eleusis and the Albigenses, which would exercise his thought and ingenuity for many years and provide him with a basis for his religious philosophy:

Of all this year's publications of that nervy little bookshop of E. Sansot, which lucky wanderers in Paris will fall upon in the Rue St Andre des Arts 'on the other side of the river', perhaps the book most filled with the snap of brilliant conclusions, arrived at by the sort of argument that most persuadeth, is Péladan's *Le Secret de Troubadours*. The theme is the descent of the idealist from Parsifal to Don Quixote.

. . . Péladan's *Origine et Esthétique de la Tragédie* (1905) is, however, a contradiction of this, being apparently sound, and brim full of clear views of the drama from its Greek beginnings in the Mysteries of Eleusis to the point in literature where Sancho Panza takes unto himself the functions of the chorus of Euripides.

In *Le Secret* . . . Péladan invades the realm of uncertainty when he fills in the gap between these two with four centuries of troubadours singing allegories in praise of a mystic extra-church philosophy or religion, practiced by the Albigenses, and the cause of the Church's crusade against them.

In the October issue of the *Book News Monthly* Pound published 'Burgos, a Dream City of Old Castile', which tells of his trip to Spain. Although of the Cid's house there remained, he said, nothing but a

'Solar', with a few emblazoned pillars to mark the place where it lay, there were still many doorways in Burgos to which he might have come, as in the old 'Poema', battering with his lance butt at the door closed against him for fear of King Alfonso who had threatened that anyone opening to Ruy Diaz would lose all his possessions 'and the eyes of his head to boot'. The only one in Burgos who 'dared to tell these tidings to the Cid was a little maid of nine; and there are yet in Burgos window and balcony from which she might have leaned . . .'. On a tour of the hill above, which was covered with fallen fortifications, he was guided by a boy of eleven who referred to Pound as a Frenchman. When Pound explained that he was an American the boy replied: 'It is all one. Here we know no other name for strangers save "frances".' And then he came upon a pair of very big black eyes and a very small girl tugging at the gate latch, and he 'knew of a surety' that this was the little girl who had delivered the king's command to the Cid.

Pound was twenty-one, a post-graduate student with ideas germinating that would eventually draw him into the world of the pagan mystery religions; but he was still, apparently, in some sense a Christian. There is still in existence his copy of George Meredith's *Poems*, published by Scribner's Sons, New York, in 1906, with his early signature on the fly-leaf. There is an ink mark against the lines:

> Ah, what a dusty answer gets the soul
> When hot for certainties in this our life!

and in Pound's hand, the comment: 'yes, if it have not Christ'. And there is a Christian note of sorts in his first commercial success with poetry, 'A Dawn Song', published in the December 1906 issue of *Munsey's Magazine* (New York):

> God hath put me here
> In earth's goodly sphere
>   To sing the song of the day,
> A strong, glad song,
> If the road be long,
>   To my fellows in the way.

Two among his collected poems seem to date from late 1906 or early 1907: 'Mesmerism', with its remarkable embodiment of Browning's writing and personality:

> One must of needs be a hang'd early riser
> To catch you at worm turning, Holy Odd's bodykins!

and 'La Fraisne', which although it is mannered and stretches his technical equipment of 1907 to its limits, has a freshness, of conception rather than of language, and vitality of rhythm, which win it a place among his best work:

> She hath called me from mine old ways,
> She hath hushed my rancour of council,
> Bidding me praise
>
> Naught but the wind that flutters in the leaves.
>
> She hath drawn me from mine old ways,
> Till men say that I am mad;
> But I have seen the sorrow of men, and am glad,
> For I know that the wailing and bitterness are a folly.

Writing from home on 16 January 1907, he gave Felix Schelling a brief account of his current studies: he had already begun work on Giordano Bruno's *Il Candelaio* ('in which I have considerable interest'); but Roman private life, on the other hand, so disgusted him (ever since his study of Martial) that he was not inclined to travel in that direction unless Schelling so directed him; in which case, he would endeavour to make his 'hate do as good work' as his interest.

In 1907 while riding home to Wyncote aboard the last and after midnight train from Philadelphia he had an encounter with a working-man which shook him at the time. He was dead tired and had with him a pile of books appertaining to graduate study; a working-man sat nearby. Suddenly, two minutes before the train pulled into Jenkintown station, he launched a verbal attack against the young man with the books, which showed that he was envious to the point of dislike. 'He thought it just as unlikely that fellows that had "that learning" would unbuckle and hand it out to someone that hadn't, as that J. Wanamaker, whose country place lay alongside the railway, would hand out a slice of money.'

On the evening of 8 February the Wanamaker 'country place', called 'Lindenhurst', was badly damaged by fire. It lay in huge grounds beside the Reading railroad, about three-quarters of a mile from the Pound home. When the alarm was given neighbours rushed to help – Homer Pound, Ezra and some of his friends among them. Homer and a man called J. W. Hunsberger were mentioned in the newspaper next day for having rushed into the blaze and carried out paintings, in some cases cutting canvases from the frames with a penknife. One picture so rescued by Homer, a 'Crucifixion', is still on display at the Wanamaker store in Philadelphia. To Ezra it was a like a scene from the French Revolution: 'the muffler'd lads of the village tearing down gold frames in the light of the conflagration, the onyx-topped tables against the blackness'. He helped to carry out a number of Rembrandts, Van Dykes and Velasquezes, which in his opinion were all fakes. He and a friend tried to ease a grand piano down a flight of stairs, but it gathered momentum in the process and there was little of it left when it reached the bottom. On 30 March John Wanamaker sent out signed copyplate letters to Homer and other neighbours thanking them for the help given in the face of 'great peril'.

Pound's formal education ceased at the end of the academic year 1906–7; he did not continue to study for his doctorate, nor did he produce his thesis on Lope de Vega, although his work towards it went into the Lope de Vega chapter in *The Spirit of Romance*. The exact nature of his quarrel with the University of Pennsylvania is difficult to determine, but it was certainly to do with his studies or the manner in which he chose to pursue them. In an unpublished note in 1930 – written for publication but the project fell through – he said: 'In 1907 I achieved the distinction of being the only student flunked in J.P.'s course in the history of literary criticism. So far as I know I was the only student who was making any attempt to understand the subject of literary criticism and the only student with any interest in the subject. . . .' He wanted to continue his post-graduate work in a certain way, or in a certain direction, the university authorities had other ideas; there were clashes and he withdrew from further studies there when his fellowship was not renewed for a further year. There is a letter he wrote in the summer of 1907 in reply to a suggestion by L. Burtron Hessler (a classmate and later a professor at the University of Michigan), that he continue to work for his doctorate. He had decided not to; an M.A. and a fellowship were enough, anything more would smack of professionalism; and besides 'I have spatted with nearly everybody'. It is clear from what he says in this letter, and from the way he says it, that he rather prided himself on his self-assumed role as gadfly among the professoriate. He had no plans for the immediate future: 'I may go to Carolina before you get here but don't expect to. . . . Am preparing a little booklet of satire that may amuse you slightly. It is a teeny weeny bit caustic in places but you won't mind, and the world is so very ridiculous that one can scarcely help smiling now and then. We will converse at leisure when you arrive. Bed and grub for yours in Wyncote.' In July he ventured into art criticism with an essay on Rembrandt and Fra Angelico but neither the essay nor the 'booklet of satire' seems to have found its way into print.

It was during this period that Pound met Mary S. Moore of 136

West State Street, Trenton, New Jersey. Her father, Henry C. Moore, was vice-president of the Trenton Street Railway. Their first meeting took place at Scudders Falls, just north of Trenton, at the country home of a young man, John Scudder, whom the poet was tutoring in preparation for college. Pound was lying in a hammock on the porch when Scudder and Miss Moore drove up in a buggy. 'Who is that curly mop?' she asked, and later that evening they met at dinner. They were immediately attracted to one another and their romance continued throughout the summer and autumn of 1907, with invitations to lunch at Wanamaker's Tea Rooms, dozens of letters to and fro, and with Pound visiting the Moore home and Miss Moore a guest at 166 Fernbrook Avenue.

III From Crawfordsville to Venice 1907/1908

Pound spent much of the summer of 1907 searching for an academic job that would allow him a certain amount of time in which to write and travel; and in August he succeeded in 'nailing' (as he put it) a post at Wabash College, a Presbyterian institution at Crawfordsville, Indiana, where he would be free to run as he saw fit an entire department – French, Spanish and Italian – with the chance in two years of a full professorship. When he wrote to tell his mother of his success he could not resist a gibe: he had got the job, he said, despite the fact that his shoes were not shined. But he was still restless, and even as he planned his trip west to Indiana he talked of retiring to Venice to live and loaf as he pleased; and the trip itself through the tidy but characterless farmlands of Ohio and Indiana only made matters worse: 'Gawsh, I won't be near so caustic about European decadence the next time I see it.'

His first impression of Crawfordsville when he arrived early in September was that it was not so bad after all; everyone he met at the college seemed 'kindly disposed', and the surroundings, which he described as 'southish', could have been worse. Crawfordsville was a town of 8,500 inhabitants, in central Indiana, which boasted of Wabash College, then in its seventy-fifth year, and little else. The President of the college was a Presbyterian minister, the Rev. George Lewes Mackintosh, a stern Scot and a widower. Romance Languages was a department newly established by the trustees in a reshuffle of the college and Pound was the sole instructor, with fifty-seven students for French, thirty for Spanish and fifteen for another class in French. He took a comfortable room in Milligan Terrace, in 'the most delightful place in town', not only with gas and bath but gothic windows, trees and a private door. And soon he had as large a circle of acquaintances as he had time for. The Dean of the college, a man named Thomas, and his wife, were 'quite charming' when he got to know them and there was an assistant in English by the name of Stephens who was a 'sane and joyous companion', and two others, Milford (English literature) and Cragwell (mathematics), who seemed 'agreeable and intelligent'.

What seemed early to be the foundations of a good life soon proved to be a deception and he grew quickly to dislike his job, the college, and Crawfordsville; but having nothing else in view he tried to make the best of it, telling himself that the full professorship which he would 'slide into' more or less automatically, if he persisted, was worth waiting for. But he was hoping for release from some other quarter. As early as 2 October he wrote that things were much better than could have been expected but that he would be likely to abandon his high calling in Indiana if a similar job was offered in the 'effete east'. There is no doubt that he felt a complete outsider; it was not his world and he wanted to leave. If he was miserable in these circumstances the poet in him was nourished by them and he wrote 'In Durance':

> And I am homesick
> After mine own kind that know, and feel
> And have some breath for beauty and the arts.

But 'In Durance' is a poem not autobiography and his 'own kind' were not simply his friends back in the east, such as William Brooke Smith, nor even those who peopled his thoughts of Europe, but beings at once more substantial yet harder to grasp, who inhabit a realm which is certainly not in, but can only be reached through, the imagination:

> My fellows, aye I know the glory
> Of th'unbounded ones, but ye, that hide
> As I hide most the while
> And burst forth to the windows only whiles or whiles
> For love, or hope, or beauty or for power,
> Then smoulder, with the lids half closed
> And are untouched by echoes of the world.

Shut in, as he felt, he was glad to visit Indianapolis for a football match between Wabash and Michigan. The match was worth while – only one touchdown against Wabash in the first half and in the second half they managed to put up a good resistance against the superior team; but he was glad also of the opportunity to enjoy what he described as 'a touch of civilization'.

When his mother suggested editorial work on a magazine as a possible means of exit from Indiana he replied that he would consider it if the salary were right but 'hack writing' did not appeal to him unless he chanced on something which would enable him to show off his 'goldarsted brilliancy'. He devoted much of his spare time to writing and at least two poems which have stood the test of time –

'Cino' and 'Na Audiart', both in *A Lume Spento* – appear to have been written in October with Crawfordsville and the college weighing down on him. They suggest that his mind was elsewhere. The subtitle to 'Cino' is '*Italian Campagna* 1309, *the open road*', and the verse itself opens out into other worlds:

> Eyes, dreams, lips, and the night goes.
> . . .
> I will sing of the white birds
> In the blue waters of heaven,
> The clouds that are spray to its sea.

'Na Audiart' is set in twelfth-century Provence and the plying of strands of sound by the young poet was a remarkable achievement in its time and remains so today:

> Broken of ancient pride
> Thou shalt then soften
> Knowing I know not how
> Thou wert once she
>   Audiart, Audiart
> For whose fairness one forgave
>   Audiart, Audiart
> Que be-m vols mal.

He wrote constantly to Mary Moore, sometimes enclosing a poem, and they both thought of marriage as a distinct possibility in the near future. They discussed the question of acquiring rooms or a house in preparation for her arrival and in one of his first letters he reported that he had just inspected the surroundings and was not at all afraid that 'you will be disappointed when I bring you here'. He addressed her variously as 'Miss Mary Moore', 'Grey Eyes', 'Your Ladyship', 'Maridhu', 'Beloved Your Grace', etc., and his letters ranged widely from a request for some 'real cigarettes' (unprocurable in Crawfordsville) to the news that he had been 'joying in translations from the Hindoo'. The only 'jangle' in his room, he told her, was the red cloth on his table, which he was determined to eliminate; and shortly afterwards he informed her that he had just spent half an hour doing what in all conscience she should be there doing for him – namely fixing the hem of his new green table cover.

It is difficult to say how serious he was, but when the question of engagement was discussed he sent her a ring he had received from Katherine Heyman (which had belonged to her mother and which

Kitty told him to keep 'till we are both very old'), explaining that this would do until they could buy one together. In another letter about this time he insisted that they would be going abroad together the following summer and that it would be futile to dispute the matter.

Pound's room was in a lodging-house frequented by passing actors and entertainers and he began to show greater interest in the theatre. He read Shaw's *Cashel Byron's Profession* and lent his copy of Beddoes's *Death's Jest Book* to an actor, Kirk Brown, who was 'repertoiring in the provinces'. He continued his Dante studies – in the local Carnegie rooms when the college library proved 'utterly useless'. In remarking in 1928 how he had come across an intelligent essay on Dante's 'metre' buried away in a century-old Italian school-book found by chance in a Sicilian hotel, he said the author did not lay down rules, he merely observed that Dante's hendecasyllables were composed of combinations of rhythm units of various shapes and sizes, and that these pieces were put together in lines to make, roughly, eleven syllables in all – 'roughly', because of the liberties allowed in elision. He went on to say that he had discovered this fact for himself in Indiana twenty years before and in his own work and made use of the knowledge continually.

'Famam Librosque Cano', one of the best among his early poems, belongs to the Wabash period, possibly November, and was published in its present form in *A Lume Spento*. Whatever it contains of Browning or others has been absorbed in the making and the old scholar, scrawny, be-spectacled and out at heels, who emerges as a 'sort of curse' against the world's guzzling and greed, is a true creation of Pound's:

> Such an one picking a ragged
> Backless copy from the stall,
> Too cheap for cataloguing,
> Loquitur,
>
>   'Ah-eh! the strange rare name . . .
> Ah-eh! He must be rare if even *I* have not . . .'
> And lost mid-page
> Such age
> As his pardons the habit,
> He analyzes form and thought to see
> How I 'scaped immortality.

There is a rare feeling for the grain of the language in the lines:

> And lost mid-page
> Such age
> As his pardons the habit

which (part II of *The Waste Land* intervening) look ahead to canto 27:

> Nothing I build
> And I reap
> Nothing; with the thirtieth autumn
> I sleep, I sleep not, I rot
> And I build no wall.

By November 1907 he was moving about among the townsfolk: he met the editor of the local paper and searched for signs of intellectual life. A student by the name of Emanuel took him to the studio of Fred Nelson Vance, an artist whose work he had seen and liked. Born in Crawfordsville in 1880, Vance studied painting first in Chicago and later at various academies in Paris and as a pupil of E. Vedder in Rome. He lived at the corner of Plumb and Jefferson Streets, Crawfordsville, and also had or was connected with an art shop. He painted mainly murals. Having lived in Paris he was regarded, apparently, as rather 'advanced' company. 'Have just met the town artist returned from 72 Notre Dame Des Champs,' Pound wrote to a friend, 'so I guess I am fer hell and gone.' He told his family: 'Vance proves human and paints pretty well, especially mural stuff.' He was one of the 'few royal fellows' celebrated in the poem 'Redondillas', among the notes to which appeared the following: '*Vance*, an American painter, chief works: "Christ appearing on the Waters" (Salon, Paris, '03) and the new bar-room in San-Diego.' When the magazine *Blast*, with its calliope pink cover, appeared in 1914–15, with contributions from Pound, Eliot, Wyndham Lewis, etc., Vance displayed copies in the art shop window.

But the painter and his friends were not enough to reconcile Pound to Crawfordsville or its countryside. 'I assure you', he wrote to Hessler in November or December, 'that Indiana is the last or at least sixth circle of desolation'. He had a 'crying need,' he said, for civilization – 'mere degenerate decadent civilization, as represented by cocktails, chartreuse and kissable girls' – which might call him from his middle-class prosperity and paths of peace 'into some inferior and less respectable walk or amble of life'. He mentions having corrected the proofs of an article on the Renaissance Latinist, M. Antonius Flaminius, which duly appeared in the *Book News Monthly* of February 1908. And he wondered whether he had sent Hessler his 'words on Beddoes', possibly the short poem 'Beddoesque':

> new-old runes and magic of past time
> Caught from the sea deep of the whole man-soul . . .

which he entered in his Venetian notebook of 1908 and published later the same year in the pamphlet *A Quinzaine for This Yule*. He also reminded Hessler that 'since Longinus you have in the field of literary criticism: Dante, De Quincey and Coleridge, and "your humble servant" – the rest are mere revisers, mere re-sayers of truism????' The letter contains an addition, written 'Next day':

Two stewdents found me sharing my meagre repast with the lady-gent impersonator in my privut apartments.

keep it dark and find me a soft immoral place to light in when the she-faculty-wives git hold of that jewcy morsel. Don't write home to me folks. I can prove an alibi from 8 to 12 p.m. and am at present looking for rooms with a minister or some well established member of the facultate. For to this house come all the travelling show folk and I must hie me to a nunnery ere I disrupt the college. Already one delegation of about-to-flunks have awaited on the president to complain erbout me orful langwidge and the number of cigarillos I consume.

And in ink he added a further explanation about the 'lady-gent impersonator': 'the lady being stranded hungry and it not being convenient to carry a dinner across the hall as I had done coffee and toast'.

That is the account closest to the event that I can find. It differs from all the others that I have seen in respect to important details and also the date, which is usually given as February. But if the letter to Hessler was written in November or December (and internal evidence suggests that it cannot have been later than December) then the encounter which is usually cited as the cause of his leaving Wabash occurred a month or more earlier than has hitherto been thought. The gist of all other accounts is contained in J. A. Robbins's summary, which I take the liberty of using here:

During a wintry night in February 1908, Pound came upon a homeless thespian, and with a generosity more native to Paris than Crawfordsville, offered her shelter for the night. It is said that she slept in Pound's bed and he on the floor of his study, although perhaps he was out of the house altogether. Next morning when Pound was in classroom, one of the maiden women [the Misses Hall] who had let him the rooms, found the girl and hastily telephoned the school authorities, and Pound's brief professorial career was ended.[1]

Unless there were two such events, and not one, which seems unlikely, we must allow that the story was added to and embroidered over the years; and in fact it is easy enough to see how one story might have

41

become the other by a simple process of modification by repetition. There is evidence to show that Pound with his 'Continental' ways was held in awe by some and by as many disliked – just the sort of person about whom myths are sure to accrue in a strait-laced little town dying for gossip. James E. Rader who was at Wabash at the time says in his account simply that Pound became involved with a chorus girl; Fred H. Rhodes who was a member of one of Pound's French classes described him as 'exhibitionist, egotistic, self-centered, and self-indulgent'; but to Mrs Viola Wildman who was an eighteen-year-old high school student, Viola Baylis, at the time of these happenings, Pound was like a breath of fresh air. Writing fifty years later she described how another young professor brought him to the home on East Wabash Avenue where she lived with her married sister. Instead of the regulation frock-coat and stiff white shirt, Pound wore a black velvet jacket, soft-collared shirt, flowing bow-tie, patent leather pumps, a floppy wide-brimmed hat and carried a malacca cane. She was intrigued with his sophistication, if a little embarrassed by his hand-kissing. He often came to the house after that and when the coloured cook served hot sweet rolls, which were a favourite of his, he buttered them lavishly and dipped them into his tea, to which he had already added a tot of rum. This was 'ambrosial nectar' and 'food fit for the gods', and if a student or faculty wife appeared, he would hastily conceal his flask of rum, explaining that the Indiana natives would never condone his Continental appetites.

His conversation in those days, if Mrs Wildman's memory is correct, was largely taken up with graphology, palmistry, spiritualism and rhythmics. In discussing the latter he would call for 'rounded voice tones' and the spacing of words 'to a mental metronome', and he would propagate such slogans as 'Strive for graceful gestures and smooth gliding stride' and 'Full circle living for mind and body'. He was stunned, she said, when he came to tell them his side of the 'chorus girl' story, which was, that out of a snowstorm he brought a stranded chorus girl to his room, heated water for tea over his gas-light flame ('to bring warmth to her frozen body'), and gave her his bed where she slept 'safe as in her mother's arms' while he lay fully clothed on the floor, wrapped in his topcoat. Thus his landlady found them and he was branded a 'libertine'.

There is a poem in *A Lume Spento* called 'Fifine Answers', which was written in 1907 and may contain echoes of the event. The motto is from Browning's 'Fifine at the Fair': '*Why is it that, disgraced, they seem to relish life the more*', and the poem is Fifine's explanation of the freedom felt, despite their fears, by those who are down-and-out and know shame:

we wastrels that the grey road's call
Doth master and make slaves, and yet make free,
Drink all of life and quaffing lustily
Take bitter with the sweet without complain
And sharers in his drink defy the pain
That makes you fearful to unfurl your souls.

In December 1907 he wrote the two poems from Villon, 'Villonaud for This Yule' and 'Ballad of the Gibbet', both of which are a delight still, and of a piece throughout, with lines of charming simplicity ('the stark winds reek with fear' and 'Drink of the winds their chill small-beer'), which remind us of what Eliot said in introducing Pound's *Literary Essays*, that he performed a great service for the English-speaking reader in emphasizing the importance of Villon. Both Villonauds appeared in *A Lume Spento* and are preserved in the collected poems.

Of his remaining few weeks at Wabash I know next to nothing. It is clear that he disliked Crawfordsville and wanted to leave, and equally clear that the college disliked him and wanted him to go – not, I think, for any one incident, but because of an accumulation of irritations, among which the 'lady-gent impersonator' was possibly the last straw, or more likely an event too public for the Rev. George Mackintosh to feel that he could deal with it in private. And so, in the words of the official historians, James Insley Osborne and Theodore Gregory Gronert, in their *Wabash College, The First Hundred Years*, published in Crawfordsville in 1932, the trustees 'were content to use the occasion to make an arrangement about their contract that encouraged Mr Pound to shake the dust of a small middle-western Presbyterian college forever from his feet, and content to rejoice in his subsequent triumphs in poetry'.

Only one minor point remains to be dealt with before we leave Wabash. In 1930 when Pound typed out a brief autobiography for Louis Untermeyer he stated that he was fired at the end of four months – that would mean about mid-January 1908 – all accusations save that of his being 'the Latin Quarter type' having been ultimately refuted. He then says, 'But the widow never married the president of the College after all.' Mackintosh, it appears, was interested in a young widow of the town who was also known to Pound. There is even a possibility that he visited her on the night of the 'lady-gent' affair and that she was his 'alibi' from eight o'clock until midnight which he mentioned in his letter to Hessler. It is said that she wrote to Mackintosh about Pound's dismissal; but whatever happened, she did not marry him.

Pound's own romance with Mary Moore was seriously shaken when she informed him that she was engaged to a man by the name of Oscar MacPherson. How many people, he asked her, 'are you intermittently betrothed to?' He blamed himself for having trusted in what he took to be another person's dream – the result, he said, of having learnt to trust his own dreams. He conceded however that MacPherson, paralysed and in a wheel-chair, needed her more than he did. A little later on he told her that he did not love her at all except as he loved all beautiful things that run around in the sunlight and are happy. Miss Moore, it seems, was frequently in love in those days; she did not marry Mac-Pherson but years later a man named Frederick Cross. Her affair with Pound seems to have ended shortly before his return home from Crawfordsville in January 1908.

A short poem, 'To the Raphaelite Latinists', appeared in the *Book News Monthly* of January 1908, under the name Weston Llewmys, a pseudonym of course for Ezra Weston Loomis Pound who may have been ashamed of the competent banality of its lilt:

Ye fellowship that sing the woods and spring,
Poets of joy that sing the day's delight, etc.

The fact that the *Book News Monthly* was willing to publish it, while rejecting good poems like 'La Fraisne' and 'Famam Librosque Cano', does seem to bear out Pound's claim some years later that in his day in America there was a seemingly automatic preference for the dull and diluted over any art of 'maximum intensity'. His Article 'M.Antonius Flaminius and John Keats, a Kinship in Genius', was published in the February issue, in which his title was given as Professor of Romance Languages in Wabash College. It is an interesting article, for it shows clearly the direction in which his thoughts were moving. What is beauty, he asks, and where shall one lay hold upon it? 'If tradition tell us truth there were days of less scholastic enlightenment, when men were permitted to find fragments thereof in the long dead poets, and when degrees in "arts" were less a sarcasm. But we advance; the universities train scientific specialists for utility, and the fugitive fragrance of old song-wine is left to the chance misfit or the much-scorned *dilettante*. This may not be applicable everywhere. I have not the slightest doubt that one might find (here and there) a professor or two who endanger their scholarly standing by being more interested in the genius of their author than in such artifice as intervenes between that genius and its expression: such as syntax, metric, errors in typography, etc.'

He put together about forty of his poems into a collection and tried to have them published by at least one American publisher, Thomas Bird Mosher, of Portland, Maine, but without success. Little wonder then, considering his restlessness and his difficulties, that about 8 February, with nothing definite in view for the future, he sailed from New York for Europe, taking his poems with him. When he landed at Gibraltar he was lucky to fall into the hands of a Jewish guide, of whom he later wrote, 'Life saved by Yusuf Benamore'. It is not clear how exactly Yusuf saved him, whether figuratively or actually, but since the same account says '1908 landed in Gibraltar with 80 dollars and lived on the interest for some time', we may guess that it was figuratively and had something to do with lending at interest.

Yusuf took him one day to a synagogue for a ceremony in which first the ritual was sung in high spirits by a levite and choir boys and the rabbi then drew out a snuff-box and had a small boy offer it in turn to the various elders. When he saw there was a stranger present the rabbi whispered to the boy to offer the box to Pound who grinned broadly like all the rest and sniffed up a thumb-full. After the snuff-taking they grew more solemn and had a procession for the scrolls of the Law. He also attended a Jewish court-house, 'behind the big patio full of wistaria', and took the opportunity while so close to visit Granada and Morocco. With the idea of making money out of literature he sent off poems to *Harpers* and other magazines and began to write what he hoped was saleable fiction. At least one poem, 'The Rune', was written in Gibraltar in March:

> O heart o' me
> Heart o' all that is true in me
> Beat again.

From Gibraltar he went to Venice where he stayed for three months. His first room was over a bakery at 861 Ponte San Vio, close to the Grand Canal, on the way from the Accademia bridge to Santa Maria della Salute. From there began an exploration of the city which raised his spirits even if it did not provide any solution to the problem of his dwindling purse. For the time being he was dependent on the money he had brought with him plus what little his father could send. He could not afford gondolas and did all his exploring on foot. For lunch sometimes he would eat baked sweet potatoes at a corner cook-stall and for supper he would have a plate of barley soup. There were times when he was hungry. Probably he was remembering this when seven years later in the essay 'The Renaissance' he wrote: 'Hunger – some experience of it – is doubtless good for a man; it puts an edge on his style, and so does hard common sense. In the end I believe in hunger, because it is an experience, and no artist can have too many experiences.' On one occasion he went in desperation to where the gondoliers were hired and asked for work. He was given a pole and allowed to take his place on the stern of a gondola for a trial run; but as he eased it out into the canal he realized that simple as it looked it would require both strength and skill even to propel these thirty-six foot craft, let alone negotiate the often crowded canals with precision; so he swung it to shore and decided he would have to look for something else. He visited an employment agency hoping for part-time work that would leave him a few hours each day free in which to write poetry; but when the man behind the desk finally understood it was because of poetry that Pound rejected a number of possible full-time jobs, he said fiercely: 'Vous êtes jeune; vous avez des illusions.'

But no matter how bad things were, Venice was all that he had hoped. For much of the time he sat and watched the changing colours. One of his spots was the steps of the customs house from which he could see across the Grand Canal to the Doge's palace, looking one way, and to the island of San Giorgio and the Giudecca, looking the other. He mixed in local literary circles and at the Lido met the composer Mascagni who as a conductor he thought did not get as much out of an orchestra as Walter Damrosch. At the Presbyterian Church in Venice he heard the Rev. Alex Robertson, D.D. (Cavaliere of the Order of St Maurice and St Lazarus) warning his congregation against contamination by Rome which he was convinced was the Scarlet Woman of the Apocalypse; even the bandits were in the pay of the pope. With sombre gusto the Doctor seemed to be saying that Italy was a land of Protestants suffering under papal tyranny – his argument being that only Protestants could have built all those beautiful buildings which were in process of destruction by the 'vandalism of the Roman Catholic Church'.

Poems written while Pound was still at San Vio speak of his 'old powers' returning and there is one in particular, called 'Alma Sol Veneziae', which indicates that Venice was indeed a turning-point:

> Thou that hast given me back
> Strength for the journey,
> Thou that hast given me
> Heart for the tourney,
>
> O sun venezian,
> Thou that through all my veins
> Hast bid the life-blood run. . . .

He reasoned that a poet with a book of poems to his credit would be more likely to attract attention than one without, so he decided to pay out of his own pocket to have a book printed. He added a few poems to the collection he had put together in America and took the manuscript to A. Antonini, printer and publisher, at Cannaregio 923. In a letter to William Carlos Williams four months later he confessed that even while he was making his final selection he thought it 'a rather gloomy and disagreeable book'. And in fact he had kept out of it a 'tremendously gloomy series of ten sonnets – à la Thompson of the *City of Dreadful Night*' which were poetically 'rather fine in spots'.

As for the money-making side of literature he was failing to make any headway. When *Harpers* informed him that the material he had sent was not suitable he decided to try some ghost stories for the *Ladies Home Journal*. In fact, he had a whole list of stories and articles, he told his mother in June 1908, which he could do before morning if he had a stenographer. As soon as the book of poems was ready he would try his luck in London and see if he could stir up some interest in America: 'Expect I'll have to dynamite Antonini if I am to get that book done in time to see Wilson in Brussels, or get to London. Want to have a month up the Thames somewhere and meet Bill Yeats' and one or two others. 'The American reprint has got to be worked by kicking up such a hell of a row with genuine and faked reviews that Scribner or somebody can be brought to see the sense of making a reprint. I shall write a few myself and get some one to sign 'em.' Ella Wheeler Wilcox, Austin O'Malley, Ibbotson, Emanuel, Milford and the Chippewa Falls newspaper would have to be persuaded to write reviews if possible. These notices plus any 'London rumblings' would then have to be collected together and sent to American publishers as an index of his fame. The letter was signed 'Modest Violet'.

The book of poems was the occasion of some heart-searching and one day while sitting correcting the proofs near where San Vio meets the Grand Canal he actually considered throwing the lot into the water. Luckily he thought better of it and delivered the proofs to the printer. This period of doubt was caused more by the seeming hopelessness of earning money through poetry in future than by the apparent inadequacies of the poems themselves. Another factor was the presence in Venice of Miss Heyman who was on a tour of Europe. In order to be near her and because managing a concert pianist promised a brighter future than verse he suddenly about the middle of June gave up poetry for music and with typical abandon had writing-paper printed and rushed to arrange a world-tour for his performer. In a letter to Hessler dated 14 June he said that with his 'usual bull-headed luck' he had desisted from lyric poetry and a staid professorship and was managing the 'greatest livin' she pyanist', the only specimen in captivity, who had played with the New York Symphony and at the White House. Such a course was not without its risks, he said, when one considered that Steinway & Sons had lost eighty thousand dollars on Paderewski's first trip to the United States. He begged Hessler not to tell his family or they would think he had 'gone clean crazy instead of part way'. He would prefer to spring the news of his new appointment on them after he had five or ten thousand dollars worth of engagements actually arranged. He promised to send Hessler the advertisements for Miss Heyman's Berlin and Wiesbaden appearances, together with cuttings from the European press, because *en route* from New York to San Francisco and Buenos Aires, he wanted to stop off for a concert at Ann Arbor and he was willing to give Hessler ('if you have the brains') ten per cent commission for any concerts he managed to secure in that part of the world. The letter ends: 'In the meantime also keep your shirt on'.

The next day he wrote to the Paris edition of the *New York Herald* a letter which appeared on 21 June: 'Katherine Ruth Heyman, whose American tournée is predicted as the event of the coming piano season there, may give certain concerts in Paris on her way West. Her playing in London before sailing is also to be announced.' Signed 'E.P.' It is recorded also that he borrowed the Benedetto Marcello hall in Venice for a press conference; and then, just as suddenly as it erupted, his career as an impresario seems to sink down again into oblivion. He continued to associate with Miss Heyman but I have not been able to find any further direct evidence of his management of her career. The closest thing that I have come across is the poem 'For Katherine Ruth Heyman (After One of her Venetian Concerts)':

> as upon a dulcimer
> 'Her' dreaming fingers lay between the tunes . . .

It was first published in an Italian paraphrase by Marco Londonio, editor of *La Bauta*, Venice, who used it as a tailpiece to his article 'Celebrità contemporanee: Miss Katherine Heyman', in the issue of 9 August. The English original was first published in the *Evening Standard & St James's Gazette*, London, of 8 December; its first appearance in book form was in *A Quinzaine for This Yule* under the title 'Nel Biancheggiar'. Williams told Pound soon afterwards that he considered it his best work. He spoke of it as a thing 'done right'.

We should observe that when Pound said to Hessler that he had given up 'lyric poetry', he may still have had in mind to write a long poem of some kind and perhaps touring the world as manager appeared at the time to be a means of gaining 'experience of life'. Certainly he did not give up poetry altogether, for on the same day that he wrote advertising Miss Heyman to the *New York Herald* and its readers, he composed in the Piazza San Marco a poem on Shakespeare:

> Master Will, so cussed human,
> Careless-clouted god o' speech,
> Is there twist o' man or woman
> Too well-hidden for thy reach?

In a postcard to his father on 26 June he said he was managing to eat despite the fact that he was still awaiting money arising out of his arrangement with Wabash College.

A Lume Spento issued from Antonini's press some time in June: a seventy-two page book in green paper wrappers. Only one hundred copies were printed (on paper left over, it is said, from a history of the Church) and it is today a rare book in the strictest sense. The dedication, which takes up all the second leaf, reads:

> This book was
> > LA FRAISNE
> > (THE ASH TREE)
>
> dedicated
> > *to such as love this same*
> > *beauty that I love, somewhat*
> > *after mine own fashion.*
>
> But sith one of them has gone out very quickly from amongst us it [is] given
> > A LUME SPENTO
> > (WITH TAPERS QUENCHED)
>
> in memoriam eius mihi caritate primus
> > WILLIAM BROOKE SMITH
> > *Painter, Dreamer of dreams.*

The word 'is', omitted from the dedication, was inserted by the author in ink and on page 24 he corrected 'immortalily' to 'immortality'. The title is from line 132 of canto III of the *Purgatorio*: 'dov'ei le trasmutò a lume spento', which refers to the burial of Manfred; the English translation, 'With Tapers Quenched', is from the Temple Classics edition. William Brooke Smith was his 'first friend', the painter who died young. In 1922 Pound wrote, 'thirteen years are gone; I haven't replaced him and shan't and no longer hope to'.

The first twenty copies of the book were trimmed by the binder in

49

error. These he sent to his father for use as review copies, together with a further twenty or so of the untrimmed. Among those who received inscribed copies from the author were Williams, Hessler, Adele Polk, Mary Moore and an Italian painter, Italico Brass. Antonini may have sold a few copies (at 5 lire) as the author's agent. The rest, or as many as he could carry, Pound took with him to London.

Much of *A Lume Spento* is merely quaint and some of it is plain bad. But fourteen of its forty-five poems have rightly survived into his collected works. One aspect of the fourteen which strikes us now is the grace and style with which a well-ordered run of words is suddenly caught up, held, and turned in a new direction. And there are signs also of one of the hallmarks of the genuine poet – the ability to make a word live beyond its normal range and strength, without distorting it. A good example is in 'Threnos'. The first five lines are easy and pleasant:

> No more for us the little sighing,
> No more the winds at twilight trouble us.
> Lo the fair dead!
>
> No more do I burn.
> No more for us the fluttering of wings

but it is in the sixth line, which suddenly changes the character of the poem, that his hand shows:

> That whirred the air above us.

He had been turning the idea over in his head as we see from the line, 'Its wings whirring above me as it passed', which occurs in 'The Wings' in 'Hilda's Book'. But only in 'Threnos' did he discover the right setting and the right way to say it. As for simplicity of the kind that comes from art, and is not to be confused with simple-mindedness, I do not think it is over-reading the words to see it in 'Aegupton':

> Manus animam pinxit –
> My pen is in my hand.

During the latter part of his stay in Venice Pound took a room in the Calle dei Frati, in the San Trovaso quarter, only a few hundred yards from San Vio. Nearby lived Italico Brass. One of Pound's windows looked into a walled garden, the other looked out over the corner where San Trovaso canal meets Ognissanti. The sonnet, 'Over the Ognissanti',

which was published in *A Quinzaine for This Yule*, describes the poet
in his room:

> I see much life below me,
>   In the garden, on the waters,
> And hither float the shades of songs they sing
> To sound of wrinkled mandolin, and plash of waters. . . .

Immediately opposite his room, on the other side of San Trovaso canal,
was the little workshop where day and night the gondolas are repaired
and repainted still: memories of which, mingled with scenes from later
visits, haunt the precious moments devoted to Venice in *The Cantos*:

> And the waters richer than glass,
> Bronze gold, the blaze over the silver,
> Dye-pots in the torch-light,
> The flash of wave under prows,
> And the silver beaks rising and crossing.
>   Stone trees, white and rose-white in the darkness,
> Cypress there by the towers,
>   Drift under hulls in the night.

In a notebook of 1908, a school exercise book with the words 'At San
Trovaso' written on the outside label, there is a poem called 'Sonnet of
the August Calm' which at the foot is marked 'San Trovaso'. It is a
reworking of a poem in 'Hilda's Book' called 'Pax', the first eight lines
of which he left almost intact: he pictured himself lying apart allowing
the world to go its way; as he watched the clouds he was visited by
dreams

>   as faint blown wind across the strings
> Of this old lute of mine imaginings. . . .

But he then deleted a reference to 'Thou maiden of the sun' and changed
what was apparently personal into something more general:

> In such a mood have I such strange sooth seen
> And shapes of wonder and of beauty's realm
> Such habitants, that times uncertainty
> Upwells within me and doth nigh o'erwhelm
> My body's life, until Truth dawns to me
> That where the treasure is the heart hath been.

It was during his 1908 visit that Pound first explored the cities of northern Italy, among which he found Pavia and Verona with their Romanesque architecture particularly appealing. He felt attracted to Verona also because it was the city that gave refuge to Dante after his expulsion from Florence. The inscription in the Piazza dei Signori, which commemorates Dante's arrival, he translated thus: 'It is here Can Grande delle Scala gave welcome to Dante Alighieri, the same which glorified him, dedicating to him that third his song eternal.' In a poem written the following year he mentioned a church service he had attended in Verona:

> San Pietro by Adige,
> Where altar candles blazed out as dim stars,
> And all the gloom was soft, and shadowy forms
> Made and sang God, within the far-off choir.

Writing to his mother in January 1910 he said the only religion he could remember seeing was in a 'little synagogue in Gibraltar and in San Pietro at Verona'[2]

I do not know when he left Venice on his way to France and England but when next we catch sight of him it is late September and he has been in London for some days at least.

NOTES

1 J. A. Robbins (ed.), *EP to LU, Nine Letters Written to Louis Untermeyer by Ezra Pound.* Indiana University Press, 1963.
2 Judging by a letter he wrote in April 1910, after a second visit to Verona, the church here called San Pietro may have been San Fermo.

IV   London
1908/1909

Pound arrived in London with only £3 in his pocket and some copies
of *A Lume Spento* tucked among his belongings. He had no idea how
far the £3 would stretch nor how he would make ends meet when it
was gone. He went to Miss Withey's boarding-house in Duchess
Street where he had stayed in 1906. It was 'the acme of comfort while
it lasted', but as his money began to run out and nothing came in to
replace it he moved to something cheaper and less comfortable at
Islington in north London. I think it was this he had in mind when he
wrote in *The New Age* a few years later of boarding-houses with
billiard-table but no cushions, of bathrooms advertised to contain h.
and c., in which only the cold tap worked, of 'pink, frilly paper
decorations', odours and unthinkable foods – complete board and
lodging for 12s. 6d. a week. When nothing happened to replenish his
purse he was forced to visit a local pawnbroker to raise ten shillings and
he may also have made a few pence by selling some of his books – for
the poet F. S. Flint came across a copy of *A Lume Spento* in an Islington
bookshop many years later. About the only person in England to whom
he had any kind of introduction was the contralto Elizabeth Granger
Kerr ('the Scotch champion of young British song-writers', Pound called
her) who lived at 38a Clanricarde Gardens, West London. To her he
confessed his plight and was able to borrow a further ten shillings.
When finally money arrived from home on 27 September he wrote to
his father, 'Thank Gawd it has come'. He pronounced himself much
wiser in the ways of the world and expected he would in future be
easier to live with as a result of his experience.

With his grasp of languages he was hoping for work as a translator
and he also applied to the Polytechnic at 309 Regent Street to fill a
vacancy left by the death of Churton Collins, the distinguished scholar
and editor. His application was placed before the Governors on 28
September and as a result he was appointed to deliver during the
following January and February a 'short course' of lectures on 'The
Development of Literature in Southern Europe', designed as introduction to a larger series to begin, if all went well, in October 1909. Thus

was he spared what he dreaded most – having to return home to America, which in his impecunious state would have meant travelling with a 'one horse line' for migrants, operating out of Liverpool.

At the end of September or early in October 1908 he took a room at 48 Langham Street, next door to a pub called the *Yorkshire Grey*; this was not far from Miss Withey's, close to the Polytechnic, and only a penny bus-ride from the British Museum. On 8 October he was admitted to the Museum Reading Room on a permanent basis, supported by the recommendations of Misses Withey and Elizabeth Granger Kerr. His subject was 'Latin Lyrists of the Renaissance'. He began to put together a new collection of verse from his 'San Trovaso' notebook and in a letter dated 21 October he answered jauntily William Carlos Williams's criticisms of *A Lume Spento*. Williams's taste was mild, it seems, and he objected to what he thought was bitterness and outspokenness; he also detected a note of vagabondism. Although Pound made a point of welcoming his friend's letter, which he said was worth 'a dozen notes of polite appreciation', he questioned his competence at several points and rejected most of his criticisms. He reminded him that some of the poems were intended as dramatic and were in the character of the person named in the title: in that sense he could no more be blamed for his characters' views than Shakespeare for Falstaff's dissipation. In justifying his achievement so far, along the road he had chosen, he said: 'To me the short so-called dramatic lyric – at any rate the sort of thing I do – is the poetic part of a drama the rest of which (to me the prose part) is left to the reader's imagination or implied or set in a short note.' His ultimate aim was:

1 To paint the thing as I see it.
2 Beauty.
3 Freedom from didacticism.
4 It is only good manners if you repeat a few other men to at least do it better or more briefly.

As he moved about and began to pierce the surface of London he took his work to Fleet Street and succeeded in breaking into print. 'Histrion' from the 'San Trovaso' notebook was published in the *Evening Standard & St James's Gazette* of 26 October. It depicts Tradition as a series of great individuals living again by taking over for a moment the very personality of an individual in the present:

Thus am I Dante for a space and am
One Francois Villon, ballad-lord and thief,
Or am such holy ones I may not write

Lest blasphemy be writ against my name;
This for an instant and the flame is gone.

He deposited copies of *A Lume Spento* at Elkin Mathews's bookshop in
Vigo Street and at the John Lane establishment nearby. For Pound in
1908 these were the 'two peaks of Parnassus'. He once spoke of his
'first little job in London' as convincing Mathews to print W. M.
Rossetti's translation of Dante's *Convito*, which came out the following
year. An *Evening Standard* reviewer, reading *A Lume Spento*, saw that
here was no ordinary talent and set Pound apart from the general run
of poets then writing in England. The book contained 'wild haunting
stuff, absolutely poetic, original, imaginative, passionate and spiritual.
Those who do not consider it crazy may well consider it inspired.
Coming after the trite and decorous verse of most of our decorous
poets, this poet seems like a minstrel of Provence at a suburban
musical evening. . . . The unseizable magic of poetry is in this queer
paper volume, and words are no good in describing it.'

During his first three or four months in England he wrote at least
six of the poems that appeared the following year in *Personae*, including 'Marvoil', 'And Thus in Nineveh' and 'The White Stag', which
have lasted into the collected works. Another was 'Piccadilly' which
came to him during his 1906 visit but remained beyond the reach of
words for more than two years and even then was not caught but only
described:

The gross, the coarse, the brazen,
God knows I cannot pity them, perhaps, as I should do,
But, oh, ye delicate, wistful faces,
            Who hath forgotten you?

In his attempt while in Venice to stir up interest in *A Lume Spento*
he had sent a copy to Ella Wheeler Wilcox asking her to review it. She
did so in the *New York American-Journal-Examiner* of 14 December
1908, a favourable but rudderless review ending 'Success to you, young
singer in Venice! Success to "With Tapers Quenched".' Pound complained to his mother in January that Ella had upset the order of a
poem she had quoted but as he had been 'fool enough to ask her' and
she kind enough to do it, he would have to put up with it. From the
practical side it was publicity, 'for which I should be glad if I made
patent medicine instead of poetry'. In Philadelphia the *Book News
Monthly* in its review said: 'Mr Pound is talented, but he is very young.
The academician bristles all over his work. . . . He affects obscurity and
loves the abstruse; he has apparently been influenced by Whitman . . .

a certain underlying force gives promise of simplicity to come – when Mr Pound has learned that simplicity and greatness are synonymous.'

About the middle of December the printers Pollock & Co., who were housed at 81 Mortimer Street, not far from his room, published his first book in England, the twenty-eight page pamphlet *A Quinzaine for This Yule*. It was dedicated to 'The Aube of the West Dawn', meaning probably Katherine Heyman. Priced at 1s. 6d. it contained seventeen poems and two pieces of prose – the latter attributed to Weston St Llewmys. Only one hundred copies were printed and as Christmas was near, it soon sold out; but before the end of December he was able to tell his parents and Hessler that Elkin Mathews was having 'a second edition' printed. This new 'edition' of one hundred copies appeared towards the end of December, identical with the earlier except for the correction of some misprints and the addition of a note, 'Printed for Elkin Mathews'. The opening prose piece is soft and dreamy and inconclusive but it shows that he was even then thinking of art as a matter of swift perceptions – an idea we find among his later theories – and convinced of the importance of curiosity in the pursuit of beauty – another of his lifelong ideas: 'Beauty should never be presented explained. It is Marvel and Wonder, and in art we should find first these doors – Marvel and Wonder – and, coming through them, a slow understanding (slow even though it be a succession of lightning understandings and perceptions) . . .' And, still speaking of beauty: 'Without holy curiosity and awe none find her.' It was Pound's opinion at the time of publication that although *A Quinzaine* lacked the more obvious vigour of *A Lume Spento* it displayed finer workmanship. And he thought that 'Sandalphon' was in many ways the 'biggest thing' he had done. No doubt it was the 'theme' of 'Sandalphon', rather than its merits as a poem, which caused him to draw this conclusion. In it he sees the great poets of past and present burning themselves away in the effort of singing; their wings like fallen leaves nourish the soil; it is Pound who survives and grows strong on their efforts and lives to speak a new language:

> even as I,
> Giving to prayer new language
> And causing the words to speak
> Of the earth-horde's age-lasting longing,
> Even as I marvel and wonder, and know not,
> Yet keep my watch in the ash wood.

His enthusiasm for 'Sandalphon' soon languished and he reprinted it once only, in *Exultations* (October 1909).

Deservedly, the best known poem in *A Quinzaine for This Yule*, and the only one that has been consistently reprinted, is 'Night Litany':

> O God of silence,
>> Purifiez nos coeurs,
>> Purifiez nos coeurs,
> O God of waters,
>> make clean our hearts within us
> And our lips to show forth thy praise.
>> For I have seen the
> Shadow of this thy Venice
> Floating upon the waters,
>> And thy stars
>
> Have seen this thing out of their far courses
> Have they seen this thing,
>> O God of waters.

Four years after publication, recalling the period of its composition, he said: 'I know that for days the "Night Litany" seemed a thing so little my own that I could not bring myself to sign it'.

By the end of December the Polytechnic was distributing leaflets giving details of its coming lectures. In a letter to Hessler written before the end of the year Pound described himself as 'undiscovered author' of two books of 'unintelligible worse' and the 'loudly advertised lecturer on "the Devil upment of Literachoor in Southern Yourup".' By 3 January 1909 his courses were being advertised in the London papers. On that day he wrote to his father (on stationer's samples, to save money) reporting that the second 'edition' of *A Quinzaine for This Yule* was out and also asking for two copies of *A Lume Spento* and telling his father to be sure to save any that were left. In addition to his work at the Museum, in preparation for his lectures, he was composing his 'next opus' called 'The Portal'.

Things were beginning to move in the right direction but he was still uncertain about the future. How would he keep himself during the seven months between his spring term lectures and the larger series to begin in October? He thought perhaps that summer work in the United States might be the answer and in case his parents heard of anything he urged them (on 8 January) to remember that for business purposes he already had a good job. But his mother and father wanted him in America.

The six spring term lectures which were delivered at five o'clock on

57

Thursday afternoons between 21 January and 25 February 1909 were outlined in the syllabus issued by the Polytechnic:

Afternoon Course
A Short Introductory Course of Lectures
on
The Development of Literature
in Southern Europe

will be given by
EZRA POUND, M.A.,
(Sometime Fellow in the University of Pennsylvania).

Author of 'A Lume Spento',
'A Quinzaine for this Yule', etc.

———————————

On THURSDAY AFTERNOONS at 5 o'clock.

———————————

Commencing January 21st, 1909,
in the Marlborough Room.

———————————————————————————————

Fee for the Course — — — — —7/6
Fee for Single Lecture — — — — — 1/6

———————————

Introductory Lecture FREE.

There followed a synopsis:

The six lectures of the course are designed as an introduction to a longer series to commence in October. At the Introductory Lecture (which is free) the Lecturer will explain fully the whole scheme.

SYNOPSIS OF THE COURSE

Jan. 18th, I. – Introductory Lecture.
The search for the essential qualities of literature.
Dicta of the great critics: – Plato, Aristotle, Longinus, Dante, Coleridge, De Quincey, Pater and Yeats.

„ 25th, II. – The Rise of Song in Provence.
The Troubadours.
The Belangal Alba, Bernard of Ventadorn, Bertrand of Born, Giraut of Borneilh, Jaufre Rudel, Arnaut Daniel, Pere Bremon Lo Tort, Peire Cardinal, Sordello and King Richard Coeur de Leon.

Feb. 1st, III – Mediaeval Religious Feeling.
The Childrens Crusade.
The Fioretti of St Francis of Assisi.

., 8th, IV. – Trade with the East.
Portuguese and Dutch Literature.
Camoens 'Os Lusiadas'.
Vondel, 'Lucifer'.

,, 15th, V. – Latin Lyrists of the Renaissance.
Period of Bembo, Sanazzaro, and Politian; Castiglione, Flamininus, Amalthei, Navgeri and the Capillupi.

,, 22nd, VI. – Books and their makers during the Middle Ages.
Papyrus, Parchment, Illumination, The Copyists, Books in the Monasteries, in the Universities. The Trade, The Early Printers: Aldus, Caxton and Elzevir.

As the dates given in the synopsis were incorrect, a slip was inserted into the syllabus booklet stating: 'The dates for Mr Ezra Pound's Lectures are: 21st and 28th January, 4th, 11th, 18th and 25th February.'

He did not write the first two lectures beforehand; all he had were some notes around which he wove improvisations and readings from books. During the first week in February he sent an article on the Renaissance Latinists to the *Book News Monthly* but it was rejected. This was probably the text prepared for his lecture of 18 February. On the day of his fourth lecture, 11 February, he told his father that the series had been ruined by fog.

Elkin Mathews, whose bookshop was a meeting-place for poets, took Pound under his wing and helped him to find his way into London literary circles. In January Mathews accepted Pound's latest collection of poems, *Personae*, giving him the same terms that he gave Maurice Hewlett who was an established author. The business side of the affair, as Pound remembered it four years later, was brief and to the point:

Mr E.M.: 'Ah, eh, do you care to contribute to the costs of publishing?'
Mr E.P.: 'I've got a shilling in my clothes, if that's any use to you.'
Mr E.M.: 'Oh well, I rather want to publish 'em anyhow.'

About the second week in January Pound met an Australian poet James Griffyth Fairfax and through him another Australian writer, Frederic Manning. Soon afterwards Pound sent a review of Manning's *Brunhild* to the *Book News Monthly* (where it appeared in April) and towards the end of January Fairfax, Manning and Pound attended a salon for young musicians and poets conducted by an American woman, Mrs Alfred Fowler, in Knightsbridge. Mrs Fowler, who was known to her friends as 'Aunt Eva', was married to an Englishman, the engineer Taffy Fowler who transacts business with King Menelik in canto 18. Also present, as a friend of the two Australians, was Olivia Shakespear, who asked Pound to tea at her house in Brunswick Gardens, Kensington. 'Tea with Manning and a certain Mrs Shakespear who is undoubtedly the most charming woman in London', he told his mother on 31 January. Olivia's daughter, Dorothy, whom Pound later married, told me in 1967 that her memory of Pound's first visit was very hazy; all she could remember was that it was winter and she sat on a low stool near the fire and listened.

The Shakespears were comfortably off: Mr H. H. Shakespear was a solicitor, a partner in the firm of Shakespear & Parkyn, of 8 John Street, Bedford Row, W.C.1., and Olivia was a novelist who moved a good deal in the literary world and was a friend of Yeats. They had lived in Porchester Square but had to move to something simpler when a partner in an earlier firm absconded. Dorothy Shakespear returned from boarding-school to find that they were living at 12 Brunswick Gardens. At sixteen she spent a year at school in Geneva learning what she described as 'eighteenth-century French'. A year later in Paris for ten days with her mother she was picked immediately as having learnt her French in Switzerland. Lionel Johnson was Olivia's first cousin and when Dorothy was a child used to come sometimes to lunch. One of Olivia's novels was dedicated to him. No wonder that on 3 February Pound wrote to Williams: 'Am by way of falling into the crowd that does things here. London, deah old Lundon, is the place for poesy.' He rejoiced that Williams's brother was planning a trip to Europe and urged Williams himself to 'come across' and broaden his mind.

Perhaps because London was proving to be much more exciting than anything he had experienced at home, he felt it his duty as an American to reaffirm his belief in the American side of his heritage. On 1 February he wrote out six pages of thoughts about Whitman, America, and himself, under the title 'What I Feel about Walt Whitman': 'From this side of the Atlantic I am for the first time able to read Whitman, and from the vantage of my education and – if it be permitted a man of my scant years – my world-citizenship: I see him America's poet. The only poet before the artists of the Carman-Hovey period, or better, the only one of the conventionally recognized "American Poets" who is worth reading.' But Whitman was only a beginning, not a classically finished work: 'I honour him for he prophesied me while I can only recognize him as a forbear of whom I ought to be proud.' And he concluded: 'It is a great thing, reading a man to know, not "His tricks are not as yet my tricks, but I can easily make them mine" but "His message is my message. We will see that men hear".'[1]

By the second week in February he had met Laurence Binyon, had spent an afternoon with friends of Yeats, had been commended by Maurice Hewlett for *A Quinzaine for This Yule* and was reading one of Hewlett's own books in proof. But he was also very short of money, apparently, and on 11 February he told his father that he was thinking of returning home in March. Two days later he wrote asking for the fare or part thereof. He had it in mind to try for a job at the Princeton Summer School and then at Temple University, Philadelphia, for the winter. Possibly his lectures were going so badly there was some doubt whether the Polytechnic would want him again in October.

But gloomy thoughts were swept aside for a while by a new wave of activity. On 18 February he had lunch at the Shakespears' and afterwards read to the company a prose and verse sequence called *The Dawn*; another day he met the great actress Ellen Terry who on this or another occasion told him she wasn't clever enough to have made a success in the music-halls; Selwyn Image, a well-known figure in literary London at the time, who knew Paris, talked to him about stained glass and 'old Verlaine'; he went to the Shakespears' again, this time for tea ('They are quite the nicest people in London'), and he also met the poet and publisher, Ernest Rhys and the feminist and novelist, May Sinclair. In a letter to his family on 21 February he summed up a busy week: 'I think the Shakespears and Selwyn Image are about the most worth while out of the lot I have come across.'

On 23 February Elkin Mathews introduced him to the Poets' Club which met once a month in the United Arts Club in St James's Street. He was not very enthusiastic about it in his letter home: George Bernard Shaw was entertaining, Hilaire Belloc sang, but in general it was 'a bore'. After his final lecture at the Polytechnic on 25 February he described the series as 'moderately successful' – as good as could be expected for a 'start'. Early in March, Laurence Binyon gave him a ticket for a lecture he was giving on 'Oriental and European Art'; he found it 'intensely interesting'. On 15 March he wrote to his family: 'I seem to fit better here in London than anywhere else, if I can only guess what's the answer to the problem of sustinence.' He added that perhaps a year teaching at Temple might help him to think of something. Two days later he had met Sturge Moore but had given up the idea of trying to see Swinburne who was reported to be stone-deaf and bad tempered. Swinburne died on 10 April. Pound's plan of action with other writers was to read their books, and if he liked the book, to meet the author. This was the plan in theory; but in practice he seems to have been more lenient, meeting as many as possible and thoroughly enjoying himself.

In April we find him working on a libretto for an opera, with two acts almost ready to be given to the composer or conductor, for I am not clear whether he was writing a new work or translating an already existing libretto into English. What became of it I do not know. One afternoon he had tea with May Sinclair and went on to dinner with her at Pagani's restaurant. Her intelligence was 'a comfort' after 'aesthetics unchastened by mental training at Sturge Moore's'.

When *Personae* reached the proof-stage Pound and Mathews went over it carefully to make sure that when the pages were made up, there would be no awkward or unsightly breaks. The book was published in mid-April, probably Friday the sixteenth, price 2*s*. 6*d*. It was dedicated to 'Mary Moore of Trenton, if she wants it.' In addition to sixteen poems from *A Lume Spento* it contains a number of more recent pieces: they are smoother than the earlier poems but as poetry they are not as good, belonging to a curious current of artificiality and false rhetoric which for a year or two ran parallel to the more lasting verse. This was not waste; it was a step in the development of technique and helped him to work out of his system misapprehensions about form and content and the handling of his themes; but there are few poems in this current which are completely satisfactory in their own right. 'Idyl for Glaucus', for example, is nicely worked, and we see a gain in knowledge – knowledge of the sentence in verse – but as poetry it has not the necessary inevitability:

> His eyes
> Were strange today. They always were,
> After their fashion, kindred of the sea.
> Today I found him.

The poem 'Revolt against the Crepuscular Spirit in Modern Poetry' surges forward but it is the surge of rhetoric alone:

> Great God, if these thy sons are grown such thin ephemera,
> I bid thee grapple chaos and beget
> Some new titanic spawn to pile the hills and stir
> This earth again.

In the longish poem 'Guillaume de Lorris Belated' there is a gain in confidence, which is reflected in the style, and signs that he has grown in knowledge; but it lacks the finality of genuine poetry:

> Wisdom set apart from all desire,
> A hoary Nestor with youth's own glad eyes,
> Him met I at the style, and all benign
> He greeted me an equal and I knew,
> By this his lack of pomp, he was himself.

Later in the poem he writes:

> I saw
> How all things are but symbols of all things,

to which is attached a footnote showing that he was acquainted with the definitions of *cogitation*, *meditation* and *contemplation*, in the work of the twelfth-century theologian Richard of St Victor (d. 1173), whom he owed originally to Dante:

In cogitation the thought or attention flits aimlessly about the subject.

In meditation it circles round it, that is, it views it systematically, from all sides, gaining perspective.

In contemplation it radiates from a centre, that is, as light from the sun it reaches out in an infinite number of ways to things that are related to or dependent on it.

The words are my own, as I have not the *Benjamin Minor* by me.

Following St Victor's figure of radiation: Poetry in its acme is expression from contemplation.

The *Benjamin Minor*, which Pound consulted in Migne's *Patrologia Latina*, some volumes of which he had managed to buy, was an influential work of mystical theology during the Middle Ages; the author Richard was a Scot who spent most of his life at the famous abbey of St Victor in Paris. Although neither then nor later did Pound understand the definitions of cogitation, meditation and contemplation within Richard's system of thought, they were useful to him in his own thought, in which they were simplified and stripped of their religious and theological significance. He used them in condensed form in *Guide to Kulchur* in 1938 but did not begin looking again at Richard's work until about 1954 when he incorporated a quotation and an idea or two into canto 90 published in the book *Rock-Drill* (1955). A year later he published a small book of twenty-one brief excerpts in Latin, under the title *Riccardo Da S. Vittore, Pensieri Sull'Amore*, and English translations of a few of them in S. V. Yankowski's *Richard of Saint Victor, Benjamin Minor*, privately published in Ansbach in 1960.

On 22 April 1909 Pound was introduced to a newly-formed group of poets led by T. E. Hulme who was two years older than Pound. Hulme had belonged to the Poets' Club but an attack on the club and its Christmas anthology by another young poet, F. S. Flint, in *The New Age*, caused him to re-examine his position and led to the formation in March of a new and livelier group consisting of Hulme, Flint, Edward Storer, Florence Farr, Joseph Campbell, Francis Tancred and sometimes Padraic Colum, Ernest Rhys and one or two others. They sought to renew English poetry and to this end they read and corrected each other's poems, discussed imagery, 'free verse' and the possibility of introducing Japanese, Hebrew and other verse-forms into English, and searched for means by which poetry might be made to take count of the modern world. Several of them, including Hulme and Flint, were aware of the relevance of modern French poetry to such an enterprise. As far back as 11 July 1908 Flint had written in *The New Age* of a similarity between Mallarmé and Japanese poetry and of the possibility of a poetry composed of suggestions rather than complete pictures; and he had declared: 'To the poet who can catch and render, like these Japanese, the brief fragments of his soul's music, the future lies open.' By November 1908 some copies of Edward Storer's *Mirrors of Illusion* had been distributed, containing short poems like 'Street Magic':

> One night I saw a theatre,
>   Faint with foamy sweet,
> And crinkled loveliness
> Warm in the street's cold side.

At the end of the book was an essay in which he spoke of good poetry as 'made up of scattered lines, which are pictures, descriptions, or suggestions of something at present incapable of accurate identification'. And on the question of form he wrote: 'Form should take its shape from the vital, inherent necessities of the matter, not by, as it were, a kind of rigid mould into which the poetry is to be poured, to accommodate itself as best it can. There is no absolute virtue in iambic pentameters as such, for instance, however well done they may be. There is no immediate virtue in rhythm or rhyme even. These things are merely means to an end.'[2] Another member of the Hulme group, Joseph Campbell, published in Dublin, in 1909, *The Mountainy Singer*, which contains several such short poems as 'The Dawn Whiteness':

> The dawn whiteness.
> A bank of slate-grey cloud lying heavily over it.
> The moon, like a hunted thing, dropped into a cloud.

But it was Hulme and Hulme alone who possessed the intellectual power necessary to draw together these hints and suggestions and weld them to his already acquired knowledge of Bergson and modern French poetry. Only Hulme, with his gift for taking from others, and clarifying and polishing, ideas which they had left undeveloped or barely knew they possessed, was able to hold the necessary ideas together and see them steadily, as in his 'Lecture on Modern Poetry' given at the Poets' Club towards the end of 1908 or early in 1909: 'verse forms, like manners, and like individuals, develop and die. They evolve from their initial freedom to decay and finally to virtuosity. They disappear before the new man, burdened with the thought more complex and more difficult to express by the old name. After being too much used, their primitive effect is lost.' In *The New Age* of 19 August 1909, only four months after Pound had joined the group, Hulme wrote:

In prose as in algebra concrete things are embodied in signs or counters, which are moved about according to rules, without being visualized at all in the process. There are in prose certain type situations and arrangements of words, which move as automatically into certain other arrangements as do functions in algebra. One only changes the x's and y's back into physical things at the end of the process. Poetry, in one aspect at any rate, may be considered as an effort to avoid this characteristic of prose. It is not a counter language, but a visual concrete one. It is a compromise for a language of intuition which would hand over sensations bodily. It always endeavours to arrest you, and to make you continuously see a physical thing, to prevent you gliding through an abstract process. . . . Prose is in fact the museum where the dead images of verse are preserved. Images in verse are not mere decoration, but the very essence of an intuitive language.

And finally, only Hulme had the creative ability at this early stage to write the first distinctively modern poems in English. His 'Autumn' appeared in the Poets' Club anthology, *For Christmas MDCCCCVIII*, which came out in January 1909:

> I walked abroad,
> And saw the ruddy moon lean over a hedge
> Like a red-faced farmer.
> I did not stop to speak, but nodded,
> And round about were the wistful stars
> With white faces like town children.

But whatever Hulme said or wrote, it does not seem to have made a great impression on Pound who was occupied for the moment with the troubadours and other past literatures. Some of it he did take in but it was several years before he was able to bring the lessons of 1909 fully into line with his own technical and theoretical interests.

One of the first reviews of *Personae* was by W. L. Courtney, editor of the influential *Fortnightly Review*; it appeared in the *Daily Telegraph* of 23 April – the day after his introduction to Hulme's new group – and he sent a cutting immediately to his father asking him to take it to the *Philadelphia Inquirer* and the *Book News Monthly* for reprinting. In the same letter he announced the composition of perhaps his most popular poem, 'Ballad of the Goodly Fere', in which Simon Zelotes speaks of Christ after the Crucifixion: 'I have this morning written a Ballad of Simon Zelotes, which is probably the strongest thing in English since "Reading Gaol" and a thing that anyone can understand.' Four years later he gave this account of it in the article 'How I Began':

In the case of the 'Goodly Fere' I was not excited until some hours after I had written it. I had been the evening before in the 'Turkish Coffee' café in Soho. I had been made very angry by a certain sort of cheap irreverence which was new to me. I had lain awake most of the night. I got up rather late in the morning and started for the Museum with the first four lines in my head. I wrote the rest of the poem at a sitting, on the left side of the reading-room, with scarcely any erasures. I lunched at the Vienna Café [24–8 New Oxford Street], and later in the afternoon, being unable to study, I peddled the poem about Fleet Street, for I began to realize that for the first time in my life I had written something that 'everyone could understand', and I wanted it to go to the people.

The poem was not accepted. I think the *Evening Standard* was the only office where it was even considered.

It was eventually published by Ford Madox Hueffer in the October issue of his magazine *The English Review*:

> Ha' we lost the goodliest fere o' all
> For the priests and the gallows tree?
> Aye lover he was of brawny men,
> O' ships and the open sea.
>
> . . .
>
> A master of men was the Goodly Fere,
> A mate of the wind and sea,
> If they think they ha' slain our Goodly Fere
> They are fools eternally.

When the time came for the ballad to be included in Pound's next book, *Exultations*, Mathews, fearing objections on religious grounds, inserted a note by which he hoped to convey to readers that inclusion of the poem in its present form was not his doing but the poet's: 'The Publisher desires to state that the *Ballad of the Goodly Fere* – by wish of the Author – is reproduced exactly as it appeared in *The English Review*.'

The poet he most wanted to talk to was Yeats, already an important figure in English poetry. From Venice, or during his first few weeks in

England, he had sent him a copy of *A Lume Spento* which the recipient described as 'charming'. But for six months or more they did not meet, owing to Yeats's absence from London and immersion in the affairs of the Abbey Theatre. Eventually, the Shakespears, Olivia and Dorothy, were able to take Pound to Woburn Buildings, near Euston station, where Yeats held court in a dimly-lighted first-floor room hung with pre-Raphaelite pictures. By the middle of 1909 he was attending Yeats's regular 'Monday evenings'. His Sundays he devoted to Victor Plarr, librarian of the Royal College of Surgeons, who, like Yeats, had been a member of the Rhymers' Club of the 1890s and was able to give him first-hand accounts of Ernest Dowson and Lionel Johnson.

On 21 May Pound thanked Williams for a copy of his first book, *Poems*, which had been privately printed at Rutherford, New Jersey, several weeks before. An earlier printing had so many errors that all copies save two or three were destroyed and the pamphlet reprinted. Its only value, Pound told Williams, was in proving 'that W.C.W. has poetic instincts'. To catch up on theory he urged him to read Aristotle's *Poetics*, Longinus *On the Sublime*, and the essays of De Quincey and Yeats; and to learn 'something about the progress of English poetry in the last century' he recommended the poetry of Yeats, Browning, Francis Thompson, Swinburne and Rossetti. He advised him not to be discouraged: 'a man's real work is what *he is going to do*, not what is behind him.' Referring to his own work he admitted that he had printed too much but he also let fall that he had been praised by Yeats and 'after eight years' hammering against impenetrable adamant' had suddenly become 'somewhat of a success'.

And in the months to come his reputation continued to grow as more and more critics reviewing *Personae* agreed with the *Evening Standard* reviewer of the previous year that here was something different for which current labels were somehow inadequate. Even *Punch* felt compelled to intervene: 'Mr Welkin Mark . . . begs to announce that he has secured for the English market the palpitating works of the new Montana (U.S.A.) poet, Mr Ezekiel Ton, who is the most remarkable thing in poetry since Robert Browning.' At twenty-three Pound was a minor celebrity.

NOTES

1 'What I Feel about Walt Whitman' was first published in March 1955 when the text of the original manuscript in the Yale Library was incorporated into an article by Herbert Bergman in the periodical *American Literature*.
2 *Mirrors of Illusion* bears the date 1909 but it was reviewed by Flint in *The New Age* of 26 November 1908.

V   The Spirit of Romance
1909/1910

Pound's first contribution to Ford Madox Hueffer's *The English Review* was 'Sestina: Altaforte' which appeared in the issue of June 1909 in the company of work by Galsworthy, Conrad, Belloc, Eden Philpotts and Wyndham Lewis. It was his first appearance in a British magazine. Possibly it was May Sinclair who introduced Pound to Hueffer and so into one of London's most distinguished literary circles.

Hueffer ran his review from an office in his flat above a fishmonger's shop at 84 Holland Park Avenue. A small gilt plaque outside announced 'English Review, Ltd.' Its first six issues beginning December 1908 contained work by Thomas Hardy, Henry James, Yeats, Walter de la Mare, Galsworthy, W. H. Hudson, Norman Douglas and chapters from Wells's *Tono-Bungay*. In his rooms above the office Hueffer entertained his contributors and gave dinner-parties for such writers as Henry James and Arnold Bennett. For Pound it was highly gratifying to be drawn into such a world and to be published as an equal among established authors. It is perhaps an indication of Hueffer's flair as an editor that the first poem by Pound that he published was one that had Pound stamped all over it: not only vigorous, which by itself would not be a virtue, but remarkably worked in sound and images which create a many-coloured impression of the troubadour Bertran de Born and his times. 'Sestina: Altaforte' was written in the British Museum Reading Room, as he explains in 'How I Began':

I had had De Born on my mind. I had found him untranslatable. Then it occurred to me that I might present him in this manner. I wanted the curious involution and recurrence of the Sestina. I knew more or less of the arrangement. I wrote the first strophe and then went to the Museum to make sure of the right order of permutations, for I was then living in Langham Street, next to the 'pub', and had hardly any books with me. I did the rest of the poem at a sitting. Technically it is one of my best, though a poem on such a theme [the stirring up of war] could never be very important.

From the opening fanfare, 'Damn it all! all this our South stinks peace' through the involutions of the remaining thirty-eight lines, 'Altaforte' holds our attention by its well-chosen line-endings (*music, peace, clash, opposing, crimson, rejoicing*) and by a display of flashing lines and images that is in keeping with the subject:

> I have no life save when the swords clash.
> But ah! when I see the standards gold, vair, purple, opposing
> And the broad fields beneath them turn crimson,
> Then howl I my heart nigh mad with rejoicing.
> . . .
> Better one hour's stour than a year's peace
> With fat boards, bawds, wine and frail music!
> Bah! there's no wine like the blood's crimson!

Pound is said to have read it so forcefully at a poets' dinner arranged by Hulme at the Tour Eiffel restaurant in Percy Street in 1909 that the management placed a screen round their table.

Three other poems of lasting interest – 'Planh for the Young English King', 'Piere Vidal Old' and 'Francesca' – were also written during the first seven months of 1909 and published in *Exultations*. Like 'Altaforte' the first two were fruit of his Provencal studies. 'Planh' is a translation of Bertran de Born's 'Si tuit li dol elh plor elh marrimen' which was a lament for 'Prince Henry Plantagenet, elder brother to Richard Coeur de Lion'. 'Piere Vidal Old' is an exciting account of Vidal's love for a noblewoman of Provence. Even in Pound's explanatory note we sense his absorption in everything to do with the troubadours and their landscape: 'It is of Piere Vidal, the fool *par excellence* of all Provence, of whom the tale tells how he ran mad, as a wolf, because of his love for Loba of Penautier, and how men hunted him with dogs through the mountains of Cabaret and brought him for dead to the dwelling of this Loba (she-wolf) of Penautier, and how she and her Lord had him healed and made welcome, and he stayed some time at that court.' But perhaps the most interesting of the three poems is 'Francesca'. Here, unperceived amid the rhetoric of so many other poems of his development, is the first clear instance of the cool flute tone, issuing in matter-of-fact yet formal language, which I believe will be acknowledged eventually as the distinctive feature of Pound's main achievement as a poet:

> You came in out of the night
> And there were flowers in your hands
> . . .
> I who have seen you amid the primal things
> Was angry when they spoke your name

In ordinary places.
. . .
So that I might find you again,
Alone.

Towards the end of July, at the height of his success with *Personae*, Pound was able to make definite arrangements with the Polytechnic to deliver a course of twenty-one lectures beginning in October and extending into 1910. He also discussed with Ernest Rhys, who ran the Everyman Library for J. M. Dent, the possibility of getting a commission from Dent to work the lectures up into a book. This was the origin of his first full-length prose work, *The Spirit of Romance*. With the lectures secure and a book possibly to follow, he again postponed his trip home until the next spring, at the earliest. A few days later he began preparing his lectures with *The Spirit of Romance* in view. He called it his 'history of the world'. Back home in Philadelphia the August *Book News Monthly* responded to his London success by reprinting 'Piccadilly' from *Personae*. About 4 August Pound delivered the typescript of *Exultations* for Mathews's consideration. As work on the lectures progressed he found that he needed some of his own books beside him and on 28 August he asked his father to send him his Moore's edition of Dante (*Tutte le Opere di Dante Alighieri*, Oxford, 1897), Gaston Paris's *Chrestomathie du moyen âge* and Karl Appel's *Provenzalische Chrestomathie*, the three of which he had had at Crawfordsville. He also asked for his tennis-racquet. By 9 September Mathews had accepted *Exultations* and the typescript had been sent to the printer. Pound was busy at the British Museum working on the Troubadours chapter of *The Spirit of Romance*. To his father he wrote on 9 September: 'I think *The Spirit of Romance* is really going to be good.'

In September Pound left Langham Street and as a stop-gap lived for a short time at 10 Rowan Road, Hammersmith, and then moved to 10 Church Walk, Kensington. But before we follow, there are two small points: at some time during his year of considerable activity at Langham Street he burnt the manuscript of a 'damn bad novel' and also noted an incident familiar to readers of *The Pisan Cantos*, for it was at Langham Street that:

Old Kait'
had puffed in, stewing with rage
concerning the landlady's *doings*
        with a lodger unnamed
az waz near Gt Tichfield St next door to the pub
'married wumman, you couldn't fool *her*'

Church Walk was well situated within easy distance of underground railways, buses, shops and restaurants. It is a narrow passage running off Kensington High Street between the Town Hall and the Library and through a graveyard belonging to St Mary Abbots nearby. The passage continues through to Holland Street; but about half way along, near a small cluster of shops, is a cul-de-sac or courtyard of small three-storied houses containing number 10. There he found a first-floor room with two windows looking out onto the courtyard; it was inexpensive at eight shillings a week and Mr and Mrs Langley from whom he rented it were (he said many years afterwards) 'positively the best England can produce at *any* level'. 'Sam' Langley, as Pound knew him, was manager of the Barham & Marriage grocery in nearby Kensington Church Street, until the central management discovered his homely ways, such as keeping his cash in a tea-tin so that burglars wouldn't find it if they tried the safe. On at least one occasion when 'Sam' was caught without an errand boy, Pound obliged by delivering groceries for him.

His new room was simply furnished even after he had added a few pieces of his own. There was an iron bed, a mahogany wash-stand that folded down to look like a desk, a 'sort of iron armchair convertible to cot', cane chairs, and a small bath-tub that he pushed under the bed. For a long time the room displayed three or more water-colours by William Henry Hunt (1790–1864) which Pound had on loan from Hueffer's mistress Violet Hunt who lived on nearby Campden Hill in a house called South Lodge. Later there were pieces of sculpture by Henri Gaudier-Brzeska and a woodcut by the young English artist Edward Wadsworth. Mrs Langley prepared lunch for him when he was home, otherwise he ate out. The one drawback was the noise made by the bells of St Mary Abbots.

In mid-September he visited the home of the artist Sir Lawrence Alma-Tadema, famous as a show-place. 'The Tadema house', he told his mother, 'is full of splendour and bad taste.' Another event was his first meeting with Arthur Symons, poet, critic, and relic of the Rhymers' Club. This may have been the meeting remembered by Dorothy Pound in 1966 when she described to me Symons arriving for tea at the Shakespear home accompanied by his American friend Alice Tobin and holding a single red rose which he presented to Olivia. Alice Tobin gave Pound a turquoise ear-ring which for a short time he wore in public as a joke.

At last, in September, he gained a contract with Dent for *The Spirit of Romance*: he was to receive a royalty of 10 per cent for the first thousand copies, 12½ per cent for the second thousand, 15 per cent for the third thousand, and 20 per cent for the fourth thousand. As he gathered material on the troubadours and Tuscan poets and prepared his lectures he began to display an antipathy to prose as compared with poetry. The effort of thinking out the connections between his insights and of planning the steps of an argument did not bore him, I think, but got on his nerves. And even while working on *The Spirit of Romance* he declared that prose was to be regarded mainly as a means of procuring food and that a thing was hardly worth while if not sufficiently interesting 'to be put into poetry'. During the third week in September he met R. A. Scott-James and Edward Thomas at a monthly dinner of the Square Club – one of London's literary clubs attended by men like Edgar Jepson, G. K. Chesterton, John Masefield and H. W. Nevinson of the *Daily News*. Pound was still short of money but fame brought its compensations: a sculptor (unknown) began to sculpt his head and he was given lunch at Claridges. There was also some talk of his being engaged to review books for the *Daily News* and the *Daily Express* but nothing seems to have come of it. At the end of September he corrected the 'first proofs' of *Exultations* and found Galsworthy's *Island Pharisees* a 'rattling good novel'. By 7 October he had finished a specimen chapter of *The Spirit of Romance* – probably the one on Tuscan poetry – for Dent to take and use in his attempt to find a publisher for the book in the United States. Dent was in the U.S. by early November and he did find a publisher – E. P. Dutton & Company of New York – who in 1910, a few weeks after publication in England, issued about three hundred copies of the English printing with a new title-page. Pound hoped that his prose-and-verse sequence *The Dawn*, which he had read at the Shakespears' in February, would be brought out by Dent in the early spring of 1910 but apparently Dent was not happy about it. Elkin Mathews considered it the following April or May and there was some talk of it coming out, with some of his *canzoni*, in the autumn of 1910, but nothing happened and it was never published.

He was seeing more of Yeats and one day early in October they talked for five hours. Two months later Yeats wrote to Lady Gregory: 'this queer creature Ezra Pound, who has become really a great authority on the troubadours has, I think, got closer to the right sort of music for poetry than Mrs Emery [Florence Farr] – it is more definitely music with strongly marked time and yet it is effective speech. However, he cannot sing, as he has no voice. It is like something on a very bad phonograph.' In 1909, the year in which Mathews published Florence Farr's *The Music of Speech*, she was a central figure in discussions of poetry and music, not only for her theories but also her poetry readings, some of which were given in Yeats's rooms in Woburn Buildings, and also at Ernest Rhys's home in Hermitage Lane, Hampstead, and at 10 Church Walk. She sometimes accompanied herself on an instrument designed for her by the reviver of old music, Arnold Dolmetsch, and called a psaltery. As he got to know Yeats better Pound became interested in the occult and by October 1909 was comparing Yeats's 'mystical studies' with Father Benson's ideas in *Light Invisible*.

He began his new course of lectures at the Polytechnic on Monday evening, 11 October. It was advertised as 'A Course of Lectures on Mediaeval Literature' to be given by Ezra Pound, M.A., author of *Personae*, on Monday evenings at half past eight. The fee for the full course of twenty-one lectures, which would continue until 28 March 1910, was twenty-five shillings, and for a single lecture, two shillings. The final talk was in fact cancelled because it fell on a bank holiday. In addition to his introductory remarks the subjects covered by the course included the Latin of Apuleius and the Pervigilium Veneris, Provence and the troubadours, the Albigenses, the *Chançon de Roland*, the *Poema del Cid*, Marie de France, Chretien de Troyes, *Tristram and Ysolt*, *Aucassin and Nicolette*, the Tuscan poets including Guido Guinicelli and St Francis, Dante, Villon, Lope de Vega, the Renaissance Latinists and finally a survey put together from Putnam's *Books and Their Makers during the Middle Ages*. On the night of the first lecture it was raining and only twenty people attended, about half the number he wanted. Among those who enrolled for the full course were Olivia and Dorothy Shakespear. For Dorothy Pound, looking back in 1965, the only word she could think of to describe her impression was 'dismal'. Ezra did not manage to get through to his very small audience because (she said) of his habit of over-estimating their intelligence.

Writing home on 18 October Pound enclosed part of the proof of *Exultations* with a suggestion that the translation from Lope de Vega, 'A Song of the Virgin Mother', might be suitable for reprinting on the family Christmas cards:

> O Bethlehem palm-trees
> That move to the anger
> Of winds in their fury,
> Tempestuous voices,
> Make ye no clamour,
> Run ye less swiftly,
> Sith sleepeth the child here
> Still ye your branches.

Homer had it printed in black on cream card as part of a calendar for 1910 which he circulated with a printed note: 'Christmas Greetings Yours Sincerely Homer L. Pound.'

Exultations was published on 25 October and sold for half a crown. Fourteen of the twenty-seven poems were written or finished in 1909, the rest were from *A Lume Spento* and *A Quinzaine for This Yule*. The book was dedicated to the former Wyncote clergyman, Carlos Tracy Chester. Eight of the poems are now in the collected works and are still of interest poetically; the rest are representative of an intermediary stage. Often they contain flashes of beauty or moments of percipience but are mostly rhetorical and essentially formless. They are fitful and uncoordinated explorations, but explorations which revealed to him the nature of the poetic terrain through which he was travelling rather than a way out of it: poems in which vision and intention are signified in the 'meaning' but not embodied in a poetic substance. The beauty and the formlessness are present in 'Laudantes Decem Pulchritudinis Johannae Templi':

> I am torn, torn with thy beauty,
> O rose of the sharpest thorn!
> . . .
> The unappeasable loveliness
>   is calling to me out of the wind,
> And because your name
>   is written upon the ivory doors,
> The wave in my heart is as a green wave
> . . .
> In the garden of the peach-trees,
> In the day of the blossoming.
> . . .
> I have rested with the voices
>   in the gardens of Ahthor,
> I have lain beneath the peach-trees
>   in the hour of the purple.

In the end it falls away completely to:

> So have the thoughts of my heart
> Gone out slowly in the twilight
> Toward my beloved,
> Toward the crimson rose, the fairest.

This looseness was overcome two years later by hard thinking and technical skill and banished from most of his work between 1912 and 1920 but reappeared in *The Cantos*. *Exultations* contained one of his earliest translations from the provençal, 'Alba Innominata':

In a garden where the whitethorn spreads her leaves
My lady hath her love lain close beside her,
Till the warder cries the dawn – Ah dawn that grieves!
Ah God! Ah God! That dawn should come so soon!

Nine years later the language of English poetry had undergone, thanks largely to Pound, a transformation which enabled him to render the same provençal with a certainty necessarily absent from the earlier version:

In orchard under the hawthorne
She has her lover till morn,
Till the traist man cry out to warn
Them. God how swift the night,
              And day comes on.

Reviews of *Exultations* generally during the next six months were favourable and in some cases interspersed with high praise; but there were possibly more mixed feelings this time than in the case of *Personae* and one or two reviews that were hostile. In the Birmingham *Daily Post* a critic wrote:

Mr Ezra Pound is a poet who, we fear, is in danger of being misled by the unwise. His technique in *Exultations* finds a parallel in the work of Mr Flint recently reviewed in these columns. Again we have the spectacle of a really sincere and vigorous artist driven by his revolt against the abuse of law and convention into mere chaos. The true poet is able to bend law to his own purpose without breaking it. Mr Pound proves this himself in his long poem on page 27,[1] when, conforming in general to a metrical scheme which has been built up on many generations of experience, he produces a really vital and notable poem. The whole thing is so finely knit together that it is impossible to detach any passage for quotation, but this, together with one or two of the quite short pieces, make the book one to be kept; for the rest we can find nothing but evidence of a highly interesting personality unable to express itself.

Mr Laurence Binyon, on the other hand, affords an excellent illustration of the poet who is able to adhere rigidly to the law and yet impress it with his own individuality. In *England and Other Poems* (Mathews) he is working with all his accustomed finish and apparent facility.

In the December issue of *The English Review*, F. S. Flint wrote of Pound as 'hammering, as it were, word into word' and said 'we can have no doubt as to his vitality and as to his determination to burst his way into Parnassus'. *Exultations* and Flint's first book, *In the Net of the Stars*, were reviewed together in the *Spectator* of 11 December:

Mr Ezra Pound is that rare thing among modern poets, a scholar. He is not only cultivated, but learned . . . We feel that this writer has in him the capacity for remarkable poetic achievement, but we also feel that at present he is somewhat weighted by his learning. His virility and passion are immense, but somehow we seem to know their origins. He strikes us as a little too bookish and literary, even when he is most untrammelled by metrical conventions . . . Mr Flint's *In the Net of the Stars* has something of the same manner, but the writer has not Mr Pound's richness or strength of thought.

A reviewer in *The Observer* of 24 December wrote: 'One is glad to welcome another tiny volume of most delicate verse from Mr Ezra Pound, whose *Personae* had a charm of fancy and of finish that has carried it to a high degree of success. It is quite safe to say that few new poets have so quickly become known to literary London.'

Pound sent a copy of *Exultations* to his father with the inscription:

> *al padre mio*
> *from that scurrilous scion*
> *of his house.*
> > *Ezra Pound.*

Beneath the inscription the father wrote 'Received Nov 17th 1909' and later he lovingly pasted into the book two photographs of his son, full-face from the *Philadelphia Bulletin* and half-face from the New York *Literary Digest*. His mother was more demanding and there was an exchange of letters about the conditions necessary for an epic and his own duties as an American poet. The conditions necessary for an epic, he told her, were (1) a beautiful tradition, (2) a unity in the outline of that tradition, as was to be found in the *Odyssey*, (3) a Hero, mythical or historical, and (4) a 'damn long time for the story to lose its garish detail and get encrusted with a bunch of beautiful lies'. Dante, he thought, escaped these necessities by dipping into a multitude of traditions and unifying them 'by their connection with himself'. A suggestion from his mother that he devote his talents to writing an epic of the American West drew a scornful reply in which he defended his unwillingness to become a spokesman for America. An epic in the real sense, he said, was the speech of a nation through the mouth of one man. Whitman had let America speak through him and the result was 'interesting as ethnology'. He remained in England because 'Praise from Yeats or appreciation from a circle that have listened to Swinburne reading his own verse are if you come to consider it rather preferable to competing with Munyon and Beecham Pills for American celebrity.'

At this time Pound was on friendly terms with D. H. Lawrence who between 1909 and 1912 was a teacher at the Davidson Road school at Croydon. Hueffer discovered Lawrence about October 1909 when Jessie Chambers sent a sheaf of his poems to *The English Review*. Hueffer recognized him immediately as a writer of more than ordinary merit: he published the sequence 'Dreams Old and Nascent' in November 1909 and 'Yesternight' in February 1910. One day when Ford took Lawrence and Miss Chambers to lunch at South Lodge, Pound was there also and according to Miss Chambers inclined to show off. She claimed that he speared an apple with his knife, cut it into quarters and gobbled it ostentatiously, as an example (he said) of how an American eats an apple; and turning to Hueffer he asked: 'How would *you* speak to a working-man?' to which Hueffer, after a moment's hesitation, replied: 'I should speak to a working-man in exactly the same way that I should speak to any other man, because I don't think there is any difference.'

In mid-November Pound and Lawrence attended an 'at home' held by Violet Hunt at the Reform Club in Adelphi Terrace. Afterwards Pound took Lawrence to supper at Pagani's and then back to his room. In a letter of 20 November Lawrence reported to his friend Louisa Burrows that Pound was not only 'jolly nice' and 'a good bit of a genius' but also 'rather remarkable' and a good poet. One of his main accomplishments in Lawrence's eyes was that he knew W. B. Yeats 'and all the Swells'. Summing up the difference between them he said that whereas Pound's god was beauty his own was 'life'. Lawrence told Miss Burrows that the following afternoon he was going to tea with Pound, after which they would go on to some friends' who would not require evening dress.

It was about this time Pound invited Lawrence to visit Mrs Derwent Wood who kept Saturday evenings free for her friends and any they chose to invite. On this or another occasion Lawrence missed his train to Croydon and spent the night at 10 Church Walk.

In November 1909 Pound went to stay with Arthur Galton and Frederic Manning at Edenham in Lincolnshire where he had a four-teenth-century church outside his window. Galton was a Church of England minister who read Voltaire; he left his set of Voltaire to Olivia Shakespear on condition that eventually it went to Dorothy who became as ardent an admirer of the great sceptic as the donor could have wished. Earlier Galton had been secretary to a Governor or Governor-General in Australia and it had been due to his influence that Manning had chosen to live in England. In November Pound sent a copy of a poem by Manning entitled 'Korè' for publication in *The English Review*. It was, he told Hueffer, 'quite beautiful' and he could praise it without reservation. Hueffer used it immediately and Pound's own 'Canzon: The Yearly Slain', which was a reply to 'Korè', was published in *The English Review* of January 1910. Even the stodgy *Fortnightly Review* accepted one of Pound's poems in November 1909 and paid for it immediately, which was a welcome relief, however slight, for he was still not able to support himself – he received £4 from Homer in October – and fog was not helping attendance at his lectures. In such a world, where men like Ford seemed to care about literature and treated it with some sense of urgency, he felt at home. Not only was he beginning to find a place in it, but his name was being mentioned in high company, as when R. B. Cunninghame Graham, in a letter to the *Saturday Review* of 27 November wrote: 'I observe with pleasure that our best writers – as Conrad, Hudson, Galsworthy, George Moore, Henry James, and Ezra Pound – are devoting themselves more and more to short pieces, and in them doing some of their finest work.'

The feeling that his real future lay in London was strengthened by the fact that much of the growing interest in his work in America was quite plainly due to his success in England. Thus when the *Literary Digest* of 27 November published an article on 'An American Poet Discovered in England', it was based in part on *Punch's* 'Mr Ezekiel Ton': 'To have *Punch* pun on your name and then make amends by saying that your verse is "the most remarkable thing in poetry since Robert Browning", ought to be something of a guaranty of fame.' In the same issue was a reprint of 'And Thus in Nineveh' from *Personae*. The *Philadelphia Bulletin* of 2 December ran a story which began, 'Few Philadelphians – even those of the innermost literary circle – are aware that they can claim citizenship with Ezra Pound, the young American poet, who has been "discovered" in England.' The story was picked up by the *Boston Herald* and published on 8 December:

This mood of hope and expectancy makes interesting the sudden fame of a young man who hails from Philadelphia, bearing the somewhat prosaic name of Ezra Pound, the son of an assistant assayer of the Mint and grandson of a former governor of Wisconsin. He is a graduate of Hamilton College, with a graduate course in the Romance languages in the University of Pennsylvania. Since the age of thirteen he has been writing verse. He is now twenty-four, and for several years has been delving in the libraries of Spain, England and Italy. But he has also been rarely productive for one of his years, and it is in England that he has put forth his most ambitious efforts, and there that appreciation and almost fame have overtaken him.

He is certainly getting a hearing, as he is now delivering a course of lectures on 'Medieval Literature' at the London Polytechnic, which is no mean honour for a mere youth. He has published four small books of verse, but he has written much more that has not seen the light for he is said to be his own most unsparing critic, having destroyed the manuscripts of two novels and three hundred sonnets.

This was followed on 12 December by an article in a 'Weekly Review' in one of the Philadelphia newspapers: 'Mr Pound is now delivering a course of lectures at the London Polytechnic on Mediaeval Literature and we are jealous of the fact that England should have discovered and honoured his genius rather than his own native America, but we are duly proud of him as a son of Pennsylvania.' Curtis Page in the *Book News Monthly* wrote: 'The most original note struck in English verse, since the publication of Ernest Dowson's poems some years ago, rings through the songs and dramatic lyrics of Ezra Pound . . . poetry that is original and sincere, expressing the varied moods of our own time. This poet is a true singer, genuinely carrying on the tradition of Henley, Symons, Hovey, Dowson – and Browning; a strange combination, but truly representing the literary spirit of today.'

On 4 December 1909 he saw Wilde's *The Importance of Being Earnest*; it was 'delightfully done'. Yeats had been away but was back in town again and was glad to talk about poetry and music and listen to Pound on the troubadours. Although Pound had no definite contract yet for an American edition of his poems, he wrote home on 5 December asking Homer and Isabel to make a list of twenty-five poems each to help him with a selection. As he was still searching for a way to make money he asked his father to post back to him the stories he had sent from Italy the previous year so that he might try to knock them 'into sellable shape'. Arrangements were made early in December for him to be a guest of the Poets' Club on the twentieth and to give an address on Arnaut Daniel. In view of this the club elected him an honorary member beforehand. About 11 December he began work on the lecture and the chapter of *The Spirit of Romance* dealing with Lope de Vega and Spanish dramatic poetry. Two days later he wrote to his mother to say that his poems had been praised in the *Mercure de France* but that there had been 'several more or less violent attacks' in daily papers in Britain.

As the Poets' Club dinner drew near he was excited to hear that S. H. Beerbohm Tree and the American Ambassador would be present. In the end the Ambassador did not show up, but the evening was a success, with more than sixty members attending. Joseph Campbell attired in bardic robes delivered 'Ballad of the Goodly Fere' and Pound lectured on 'Arnaut Daniel finest of the troubadours' (which became chapter two of *The Spirit of Romance*) and afterwards answered questions. Four of his poems were published in the club's anthology for Christmas 1909, including 'Paracelsus in Excelsis':

> We seem as statues round whose high-riven base
> Some overflowing river is run mad,
> In us alone the element of calm.

The anthology also included two poems by Hulme, 'Conversion' and 'The Embankment'.

A few hours after Yeats left London for Dublin on New Year's Day 1910 Pound wrote to his mother: 'He is the only living man whose work has anything more than most temporary interest – possible exceptions on the Continent.' He gave her his other news (a visit to May Sinclair, tea with Ernest Rhys) and also attacked the American Academy of Art and Letters, conceding only that the establishment of it was an attempt at 'intelligence' and admitting that when asked he would probably 'join the damn thing'. Continuing their previous discussion on the epic he jokingly described what the world's last epic would be like – before the advent of the literary Dark Age which would begin before the year 2000 and continue until about 2700. It would be a 'rhetorical epic' through which 'would move Marconi, Pierpont Morgan, Bleriot, Levavasour, Lathan, Peary, Dr Cook, etc.'

Under the influence of his recent study of Dante and the troubadours he wrote a number of *canzoni* which were published in his two books, *Provenca* (1910) and *Canzoni* (1911). None of them has survived into the collected poems but they were important to him at the time, both as an exercise in converting essentially foreign forms into English and as part of a hard lesson he still had to learn: that such forms were not really successful when transferred baldly, for the intellectual driving force which had brought them into being was gone and all that was left to the modern English poet was the empty shell. Three of these *canzoni* appeared in *The English Review* of January 1910. 'Canzon: The Yearly Slain' – the one written in reply to Manning's 'Korè':

> Barren the heart and dead the fires there,
> Blow! O ye ashes, where the winds shall please,
> But cry, 'Love also is the Yearly Slain'.

'Canzon: The Spear':

> 'Tis the clear light of love I praise
> That steadfast gloweth o'er deep waters,
> A clarity that gleams always.

And 'Canzon (To be Sung Beneath a Window)':

> Heart mine, art mine, whose embraces
> Clasp but the wind that past thee bloweth?

Towards the end of January he lectured on the *Divina Commedia*; and on those occasions when he had dined out beforehand he wore evening clothes to his lectures. Also in January he went dancing, read Kipling's *Actions and Reactions*, prepared his lecture on Villon and on the twentieth delivered to J. M. Dent & Sons the typescript of the first half of *The Spirit of Romance*.

Although his mother and father were proud of his achievements abroad they wanted him settled at home and he began to consider the possibility of getting back to the University of Pennsylvania on a fellowship, at the same time declaring to Isabel (20 January) that 'Continued residence in America is of course most revolting to think of. But I might survive one winter and it would be useful perhaps.' When he heard from his mother on the following day about the discouragement at Wyncote of a local child with artistic talent, he replied that the 'typical American attitude' was to admire art only when told to do so by 'some third-rate journalist'. By the end of the month he had submitted his application for a fellowship and was expecting to 'drift home' during the summer if it was successful. He had just heard from Small, Maynard & Company, publishers, of Boston that they were prepared to give 'extended consideration' to any of his work submitted. If this was the occasion of some delight it did nothing to alter his opinion of the American literary scene in general and a day or two later he claimed that Bliss Carman was about the only living American poet who 'would not improve by drowning'.

By the first week in February it was clear that his lectures were not going nearly as well as he had hoped, either financially or as publicity. But he was also taking a private class and this was proving lucrative. He finished his chapter on Lope de Vega and read some of his verse at Mrs Fowler's. Good news was received in mid-February from William Carlos Williams who was doing post-graduate work in medicine at Leipzig: he would be arriving in London during the first week in March. By 19 February Pound had finished the final chapter of *The Spirit of Romance* and had begun translating a group of French and Italian songs for Mrs Derwent Wood, a singer, who under her maiden name Florence Schmidt was giving a recital at the Bechstein Hall in Wigmore Street in March and wanted to include the English texts in the printed programme. Mrs Wood's husband, the sculptor Derwent Wood, R.A., took Pound to the Chelsea Arts Club where *Hedda Gabler* was performed after dinner.

Pound began to show an interest, probably under Yeats's influence, in astrology, and he wrote to his mother on 19 February asking for the exact hour of his birth and drawing her attention to 'planetary influences'. He believed that when astrology was taken in hand

systematically by 'modern science' there would be some definite discoveries. 'In the meantime there is no reason why one should not
indulge in private experiment and investigation.'

During the last week in February he read the final chapters of *The
Spirit of Romance* at the Shakespears' and afterwards made a few
changes and additions. The last of the book was delivered to the printer
on 26 February and he planned to take the proofs with him to Verona
at Easter where he hoped to have 'sunlight and quiet' for the final
revision. While working on the Lope de Vega chapter he had noticed
similarities between the Spanish playwright's *El Desprecio Agradecido*
and modern plays like Shaw's *Arms and the Man* and Wilde's *The
Importance of Being Earnest*; he had also noticed that F. W. Cosens's
translation of Lope's plays, published in London in 1869, was too
Shakespearian in diction; so in February he began translating *El
Desprecio Agradecido*, possibly in the hope of having it performed on
the London stage. Towards the end of the month he applied for a job
teaching at Hobart College, Geneva, New York, where the pay for a
professor, he had heard, was $1300 a year. He told his parents that
apparently there was little hope of a fellowship at Pennsylvania.

March opened with an urgent appeal to his father to send £4 care of
Poste Restante, Verona, as his income in the immediate future appeared
precarious. That night (1 March) at a quarter-past eight he attended
the Bechstein Hall recital: songs by Mrs Wood (accompanied by Miss
Daisy Bucktrout on the piano) and 'Pianoforte Soli' performed by Miss
Elsie Hall. Only two of the translations in the seven-page programme
were attributed to Pound but it seems likely that he was responsible for
all of the following:

Cantata Spirituale	Leonardo Leo
'Tre giorni son che Nina'	Pergolesi
Non so più cosa son'	Mozart
Clair de Lune [text by Verlaine]	Gabriel Fauré
Lied Maritime [text by the composer]	Vincent d'Indy
'Ariettes Oubliées' (No. 3) [text by Verlaine]	Debussy
'Aquarelles' (Green) [text by Verlaine]	Debussy
'Fêtes Galantes' – Fantoches [text by Verlaine]	Debussy
'Lisette' (Bergerette) [Old French text]	XVIII Century
Chanson Provençal	
'Manon'	Massenet

Next day he sent a copy of the printed programme to his father with
the comment: 'The concert was agreeable'. His own translations, however, were not particularly valuable, he said, 'having been scribbled

off, the lot of them, in one day' – all except the first Verlaine which he had done earlier.

Williams arrived in London about 3 March and Pound began immediately the attempt 'to broaden his mind by showing him the wonders of our dusky and marvellous city'. He introduced him to other writers, took him to see as many examples as possible of Turner's art, took him to dinner at the Shakespears', after which they all went to one of Yeats's evenings at Woburn Buildings, and on 11 March before Williams's departure for Paris they attended a 'delightful dinner' at the Fowlers'.

During his stay Williams witnessed Pound's coffee-making ritual at 10 Church Walk. A teaspoonful of finely-ground Dutch coffee, extracted carefully from an air-tight jar, was placed on a piece of cloth which had been stretched over the cup. Boiling water was then poured over the powder a drop at a time. Williams remembered many years later that the result was coffee both 'strong and good'. The day after his departure Pound expressed satisfaction to his mother: 'I feel that Bill's mind has been duly benefited by his brief sojourn'.

Many years later Williams mentioned that on the dresser in Pound's room was the photograph of a woman with a lighted candle always burning before it. Williams did not know her and Pound did not explain. Possibly it was a photograph of Bride Scratton, a married woman a few years older than Pound whom he had met at Yeats's. She was bored by drawing-room life, preferring the company of poets and artists to upper middle class conversation and gossip. Something of what she thought about her life is contained in a small prose work called *England* which Pound was instrumental in having published in Paris in 1923, under her maiden name, B.M.G.-Adams. Soon after they first met Pound wrote several letters to her in his own hand, one of which was accompanied by a separate sheet dated 'Saturday' containing a single line: 'To build a dream over the world.' In one of the letters he spoke of a lamp burning before a shrine.

About the middle of March 1910 *The English Review* paid him at the rate of about £5 a poem for the three poems published in January, which meant that his fare to Italy later in the month was more than covered. In the week or so that remained he lectured on Leopardi and Metastasio, received proofs of the poem accepted by the *Fortnightly Review* the previous November, and was busy socially. On 12 March he dined at the Woods', a few days later Hueffer took him to Lady Low's, and on the day of his departure, the twenty-third, he had lunch with Violet Hunt and tea with the Shakespears. He left London at a quarter to nine that night for Paris, with a promise from Olivia and Dorothy Shakespear that they would join him if possible, in Italy, in April or May.

After a 'charming time' in Paris for two days with the American pianist Walter Morse Rummel, who lived there, he went on to Verona where he tried to rent an apartment in a 'pink marble palace'. When this failed, he went almost by accident to Lake Garda a few miles away. He left the train at Desenzano and walked across to Sirmione, the Sirmio of Catullus, which juts out a narrow peninsula at the southern end of the lake. There, facing immediately onto the water, he found a 'real hotel', clean and full of sunlight, where he could have three good meals and a room for about 5s. 6d. a day, which was a price he could afford. It was called Hotel Eden and is still there under the same name. During his first meal before he had made arrangements for full-board he trembled at the thought of how much it was going to cost, but when the bill was brought it was only about 2s.

From his window he looked out over the lake towards the dome and towers of Brescia in the hills to the west and when he leant out he could see the snow-capped mountains to the north. Just behind the hotel, guarding the one approach into Sirmione by land, was the castle of the Scaligeri. Next morning he fetched his luggage by boat from Desenzano (which crouched 'in proper Whistlerian fashion on the opposite ledge of the lake'), sunbathed for two hours, shaved, and then wrote to his mother that save for electric light and a few details it was 'the same old Sirmio that Catullus raved over a few years back, or M. A. Flaminius more recently'. Within a day or two he heard from Small, Maynard & Company that they had read his poems and would like to bring out an American edition. The money which in March he had asked his father to send urgently to Verona arrived in April but there was some difficulty in cashing it at first as Homer had made out the order to *Postmaster, Italy*.

Neither Homer nor Isabel could understand his enthusiasm for Verona and Italy and said so. In reply he explained that Verona was where Dante had written 'a good deal' of his *Commedia* and was 'perhaps the most beautiful city in North Italy'. The church of San Zeno was 'the ultimate perfection'. If not bound by necessity he would 'live in Italy most of the time' and now and then visit Spain. As for Lake Garda, he knew paradise when he saw it and urged them if they could find $500 a year to buy a plot of land beside the lake and 'save me the pain of crossing the Atlantic'. His love of the lake was celebrated in two poems published the following year in *Canzoni* – 'Blandula, Tenulla, Vagula' and 'The Flame', but especially in the former:

If at Sirmio,
My soul, I meet thee, when this life's outrun,
Will we not find some headland consecrated

By aery apostles of terrene delight,
Will not our cult be founded on the waves,
Clear sapphire, cobalt, cyanine,
On triune azures, the impalpable
Mirrors unstill of the eternal change?

Through April he lazed and worked as he saw fit. In correcting the proofs of *The Spirit of Romance* he may have added (or strengthened) the remarks on San Zeno at the beginning of chapter two; he may also have added the notes on Quevedo and Herrera near the end of chapter eight, for in Paris a Miss Scarborough had given him a book of Spanish poets and he had been intending to add something when he corrected the chapter on Lope de Vega. To the *Fortnightly Review* he returned the proofs he had received before leaving London, but what happened to the poem after this is hard to say: the only poem by Pound which seems to fit the situation is 'Canzone: Of Angels' but this did not appear in the *Fortnightly* until February 1912. He sent three poems to *The English Review* and received payment for two others which had just appeared in the April issue: 'Canzon: Of Incense' and 'Thersites; on the Surviving Zeus'. At Sirmione in April he decided that Dante's contemporary, Guido Cavalcanti, was worth more than the few paragraphs in *The Spirit of Romance*, a decision which blossomed into a translation of the complete poems and a lifetime's advocacy of Cavalcanti's importance. In the midst of these not too strenuous labours he was able to spare, in a letter to his father, a moment's thought for Theodore Roosevelt and American politics.

Meanwhile his fame continued to grow and beside the lake he was able to contemplate with satisfaction the fact that his reputation had spread even to farthest Australia, where the newspapers, he was told, had published his photograph with comments. What is interesting is that the critics continued to see his work as something apart from the general run; it seemed to them that in some way a corner had been turned even if the results were not always pleasing. We see it in Flint's article in *The New Age* of 6 January, 1910:

Mr Pound is an American, and a hotchpotch of picturesqueness, made of divers elements – in literature, words from divers tongues – is the American idea of beauty. Thank heaven that Mr Pound is a poet also, and that his picturesqueness is only the sauce in the dish. . . One thing is proved by these two little books of his, *Personae* and *Exultations*, and that is that the old devices of regular metrical beat and regular rhyming are worn out; the sonnet and the three-quatrain poem will probably always live; but for the larger music verse must be free from all the restraints of a regular return and a squared-up frame; the poet must forge his rhythm according to the impulse of the creative emotion working through him.

In New York the *Literary Digest* of 26 February published two poems from *A Lume Spento* and these remarks on *Personae* and *Exultations*:

At first the books seem to be an imbroglio of egotistical nonsense, but gradually we are able to discern the arcs of out-running laws – laws of their own – which we are finally able to bring to a full circle. Of course, in common with all reformers and revolutionaries, Mr Pound's work revolves to a large extent around 'mein liebes ich'. His style, moreover, is often involved, obscure, and pedantic, and there is a certain disagreeable insistence upon the value of the poetic rind itself. But on the other hand the lines are almost oppressive with their unexpanded power, with their intensity and passion, and they are full to the fingertips with an extremely interesting personality. Mr Pound has given the vessel of poetry a rather violent shaking, but we are thankful to him for it, even though many dregs should be brought to the surface.

In the Melbourne *Book Lover* of 6 April Griffyth Fairfax reviewed *Personae* and *Exultations* under the heading 'A New Experience':

Mr Pound's two little books . . . might almost be used as touch-stones for the finding of what is genuine in the poetry of our time . . . Mr Pound is obedient to some instinctive harmony, which, if one will lay aside prejudice and dance to his piping, creates for us a new world of transfigured sound and colour. . . In his interpretation of Provençal literature, a subject on which he lectured at the Polytechnic in London, he occupies a unique position. . . It is disgracefully easy to lose critical sobriety in the presence of Mr Pound. When he reads his own work, he creates an atmosphere which delight and enthusiasm can alone inhabit. . . If anyone be disposed to question the vitality and promise of poetry in the Twentieth Century, this experience, if his perceptions be not beyond hope blunted and dulled, will oblige him to recant; will besides make him glad of the occasion.

Olivia and Dorothy Shakespear arrived at Sirmione bearing agreeable news from London: Yeats had been saying 'nice things' about him in private. In particular he had described Pound as 'a solitary volcano', a remark which Pound took care to pass on to his family. For Dorothy Shakespear, who sketched and painted, Sirmione presented a delightful opportunity to practise her skill and the result was a series of water-colours of the lake which happily have survived. Something of her original pleasure in the Garda landscape and water may be felt in a remark she made to me a few years ago. 'Sirmione', she said, 'that was the first time I ever saw colour'.

From Desenzano the Shakespears took the train to Venice with Pound as escort. On the way they were amused to hear some Italians sitting opposite speculating whether Dorothy and Pound were brother and sister or an engaged couple. In Venice he dined with people called

Snively, from Philadelphia, whose son he had known at the University of Pennsylvania. Back at Garda by 8 May he told his father that Venice was 'like a machine-shop after Sirmione'. In May he wrote to Hilda Doolittle who was thinking of visiting Europe. If she was free to choose he advised her to let London go and come to Garda: 'I've been about a bit and I know paradise when I see it.' The church of San Zeno at Verona, he told her, 'is the ultimate perfection' and 'has in it the abiding spirit as no other church in Europe'. He hoped she would arrive by 15 June because he was due then to sail from England for the United States. He stayed at Sirmione until about the middle of May, spent a few days at Verona and Vicenza, went to Venice for a week and then left for Paris and London. Shortly before he sailed from England he filled in a form sent by the Alumni Catalogue Committee of the University of Pennsylvania requesting biographical information. He listed himself as Lecturer to the Regent Street Polytechnic, London, and author of *Personae*, *Exultations* and *The Spirit of Romance* ('about to appear'). In case they did not grasp the significance of these items he pasted into the four-page form one of Elkin Mathews's advertising leaflets for *Exultations* giving extracts from favourable reviews of *Personae*. He sailed for home in June and it may have been at the start of this voyage that he was struck by the 'nickel-plate warning which is hurled at one in the saloon of any great transatlantic boat; the awfulness that engulfs one when one comes, for the first time unexpectedly on a pile of all the *Murkhn* magazines laid, shingle-wise, on a brass-studded, screwed-into-place, baize-covered steamer table. The first glitter of the national weapons for driving off quiet and all closer signs of intelligence.' He may have been on the water still when *The Spirit of Romance* was published by Dent on 20 June: two hundred and fifty-one pages, price six shillings.

Whatever faults and errors it may contain it is a work of considerable charm and understanding which more than half a century later can still be read with pleasure. The preface, which is quite remarkable for a man of twenty-five, is authentically Pound:

This book is not a philological work. Only by courtesy can it be said to be a study in comparative literature.

I am interested in poetry. I have attempted to examine certain forces, elements or qualities which were potent in the mediaeval literature of the Latin tongues, and are, as I believe, still potent in our own.

The history of an art is the history of masterwork, not of failures, or of mediocrity.

There are a number of sciences connected with the study of literature. There is in literature itself the Art, which is not, and never will be, a science.

What we need is a literary scholarship, which will weigh Theocritus and Mr Yeats with one balance, and which will judge dull dead men as inexorably as dull writers of today, and will, with equity, give praise to beauty before referring to an almanack.[2]

A number of ideas prominent in Pound's later campaigning are to be found already formed in *The Spirit of Romance*. His later call for 'objectivity' and precision is already there in chapter six: 'Dante's precision both in the *Vita Nuova* and in the *Commedia* comes from the attempt to reproduce exactly the thing which has been clearly seen.' His later insistence on the prose element in verse is there in chapter two: 'Daniel is also to be praised because, through his most complex and difficult forms the words run often with an unperturbed order, almost that of prose.' His fondness for describing poetry or art in terms of science or mathematics is indulged in chapter one: 'Poetry is a sort of inspired mathematics, which gives us equations, not for abstract figures, triangles, spheres, and the like, but equations for human emotions.' In chapter three there is a brief glimpse of a discussion with Yeats: 'Mr Yeats gives me to understand that there comes in the career of a great poet, a certain time when he ceases to take pleasure in riming "mountain" with "fountain" and "beauty" with "duty".' In illustrating in chapter six the difference between works of art which are beautiful in themselves and those which provide a key to a deeper knowledge or a finer perception of beauty, he gives Burne-Jones as an example of the former and Whistler of the latter. An earlier version of this comparison occurred in a letter to his mother in January 1909. The examples he gave there were Waterhouse, whose pictures, he said, contained their own 'answer', and those of Whistler and Turner which caused him to find beauty outside in mists and shadows where before he had never dreamed of looking.

NOTES

1 'Laudantes Decem Pulchritudinis Johannae Templi'.
2 From the first, not a revised, edition.

VI　Return to America
1910/1911

After a 'pleasant trip' from England aboard R.M.S. *Slavonia* and a short stay in New York, Pound sent a telegram on 24 June 1910 to his father at the U.S. Mint in Philadelphia announcing that he would be 'home tomorrow night'. As far as I have been able to discover he did not go to the house at Wyncote, which had been let, but either to 2103 Spring Garden Street, Philadelphia, a brick mansion not far from the Mint which Homer had rented in 1909, or to Swarthmore where for at least part of the second half of 1910 his parents lived in a house belonging to a man named Ellis. For his father he brought from London a copy of *The Spirit of Romance* which Homer signed and dated 27 June 1910. Pound seems to have spent most of the summer and part of the autumn at Swarthmore translating Cavalcanti. Isabel told a friend at Wyncote later that at Swarthmore one night Ezra and a companion arrived at the Ellis house singing to the accompaniment of a stringed instrument.

In July Dutton & Co. issued *The Spirit of Romance* at $2.50 which Pound claimed was much too dear and bore no relation to the price charged by Dent for the sheets shipped to New York. The book was well enough received in both England and America but there were signs of impatience, as in a review signed 'E.J.O.' in the Boston *Evening Transcript*: 'A noble ambition is revealed by Mr Pound in this volume . . . Mr Pound is a man of clear insight and happy enthusiasm, who is potentially a great critic. But within him there is a hunger for publicity which weakens the fibre of his work. We need him, for his insight and his idealism. As a genuine poet, he should prove a sympathetic critic. But to find himself he must first get lost.' In England a review in the *Manchester Guardian* of 10 August was signed 'G.H.M.': 'there is a solid foundation of good sense and penetrating criticism and a quite remarkable forethought in the planning of the book . . . Mr Pound, for all his excess of emphasis, never aims at forcing his judgement on the reader; there is always material enough for you to form one of your own.'

From Swarthmore Pound went to New York and stayed at 164

Waverly Place in Greenwich Village. He called on Yeats's father, the painter John Butler Yeats, who lived at 317 West 29th Street, and in August they went with John Quinn, the New York lawyer and patron of the arts, to Coney Island 'amusement park' in Brooklyn – 'marvellous against the night as one approaches or leaves it'. Five years later Pound wrote to Quinn from London: 'I have still a very clear recollection of Yeats père on an elephant (at Coney Island), smiling like Elijah in the beatific vision, and of you plugging away in the shooting gallery.' On a visit to the former Weston boarding-house at 24 East 47th Street he met a jobber by the name of Francis Bacon who made a living on the fringes of the business world – distributing orders for commercial writing-paper to printers and selling 'odd sorts of insurance'. Bacon outlined a business proposition, a certainty, for which only the money was lacking. Pound was enthusiastic and wrote immediately to his father asking him to invest but Homer replied that he had no money to spare. Pound wrote also to 'Aunt Frank' who apparently was no longer living in New York, but what happened I do not know.

In October the New York *Forum* published his poem, 'The Vision':

When first I saw thee 'neath the silver mist
Ruling thy bark of painted sandal-wood,
Did any know thee? By the golden sails
That clasped the ribbands of that azure sea,
Did any know thee, save my heart alone?

Under the title 'Canzon: The Vision' it was included in his next book, *Provença*, and also in *Canzoni*. During the first week in October he sent a review of Hudson Maxim's *The Science of Poetry and the Philosophy of Language* to the *Book News Monthly* where it appeared in December.

Throughout October he continued to work on his translations of Cavalcanti and explored New York:

Here in the flurry of Fifth Avenue,
Here where they pass between their teas and teas . . .

which is from 'Und Drang', a series of poems published in *Canzoni*. He was delighted to discover at the Metropolitan gallery one of the finest Goya's he had ever seen. (Twenty-eight years later in *Guide to Kulchur* it was no longer one of the best he knew, but 'the best'. This was probably Goya's oil portrait of Don Sebastian Martinez y Perez (1747–1800), lawyer and patron of art, who was general treasurer of the financial council in Cadiz. In the portrait, which was purchased by the Metropolitan Museum in 1906, Don Sebastian is seated and wears a light blue coat. Towards the end of October he met Witter Bynner, poet and editor, who earlier seems to have played a part in putting him in touch with Small, Maynard & Company. He dined and spent the night with William Wadsworth who was probably his grandmother's cousin, on his mother's side – the Longfellow connection. Hilda Doolittle arrived in New York and together they visited Williams in New Jersey.

Early in November he received a welcome payment of $50 from the *Sunday School Times* in Philadelphia for a poem called 'Christmas Prologue' which they published on 3 December. It is inhabited by one of the Magi, a shepherd, and various spirits and angels, including 'Christ, the eternal Spirit in Heaven', who comment in their various ways on the miraculous birth of 'the child of Mary':

> What might is this more potent than the spring?
> Lo, how the night
> Which wrapped us round with its most heavy cloths
> Opens and breathes with some strange-fashioned brightness!

When he included it in *Canzoni* he added four lines giving the final say to Diana in Ephesus:

> Behold the deed! Behold the act supreme!
> With mine own hands have I prepared my doom,
> Truth shall grow great eclipsing other truth,
> And men forget me in the aging years.

About 4 November he began work on the introduction to his translations of Cavalcanti and apparently had it in reasonable shape by the fifteenth which is the date it bears in the *Sonnets and Ballate of Guido Cavalcanti* published in 1912. During the first half of the month he read Disraeli's *Endymion* and began to take an interest in Propertius, part of whose twenty-sixth Elegy, Book III, he published in translation in *Canzoni*:

> Here let thy clemency, Persephone, hold firm,
> Do thou, Pluto, bring here no greater harshness.
> So many thousand beauties are gone down to Avernus
> Ye might let one remain above with us.

About 11 November he met John Butler Yeats on the Avenue of the Americas and reported the meeting in a letter to his mother who was always eager for cultural news. Towards the middle of November he visited Wyncote to see friends including the painter Frank Reed Whiteside. When he called at 166 Fernbrook Avenue it was let to a large family named Wallis and he carried away the impression of babies stacked in packing-cases and drawers. He also dined with grandmother Sarah Angevine and 'Aunt Frank', but whether this was at 2020 Estaugh Street, Philadelphia, where his grandmother lived from 1902 until 1925, or elsewhere, I do not know. About the same time he met another Wadsworth – Charles – probably William's brother who 'stood by' members of the family, even unto remote cousins: 'He even', Pound said later, 'did me a turn once, who, being the grandson of a cousin, couldn't decently have been supposed to be in the running.' As Pound changed their names to Henry and Edward when he wrote about them in *Indiscretions* I am not certain which one 'stood by' members of the family in times of difficulty, but I think it was Charles.

Back in New York during the third week in November he was taken by the drama editor of the *New York Herald*, named Walsh, to the first night of a play called *Nobody's Widow* and was looking forward to the 'Russian Symphony'. About 21 November he posted the completed typescript of his Cavalcanti book to Small, Maynard & Company and began to plan his next book of poems in London.

Provença, his first book of poetry in America, was published by Small, Maynard & Co. in Boston on 22 November, price $1. The jacket said: 'Mr Pound is the American poet who has so significantly won his spurs in London. *Provença* is the first American edition of his work and contains the best of the two volumes, *Personae* and *Exultations*, already brought out in England, with new poems which are to be issued in England separately under the title *Canzoniere* [*Canzoni*]. It is not too much to say that no other poet in recent years has made so marked an impression on the critics.' But 'W.S.B.' writing in the *Boston Evening Transcript* of 9 December was not impressed:

We began the examination of this book of poems with great expectations and we lay it down with considerable contempt for the bulk of English criticism that has pretended to discover in these erratic utterances the voice of a poet . . . The great faults in Mr Pound are the hopes by which he may yet achieve and justify what has been prematurely awarded him by his English sponsors . . . Mr Pound may, as he declares, have no deep regard for Longfellow, who, it seems, is related to him on his mother's side, but he can learn a great deal from the Cambridge poet that would be profitable to his art when he attempts to embody his ideas and feelings into poetry.

In the 'Friday Literary Review' of the *Chicago Evening Post* of 6 January 1911 Floyd Dell linked *Provença* with the Post-Impressionist Exhibition which had opened at the Grafton Galleries in London in November and was the subject of violent argument:

Mr Pound is a very new kind of poet. Thinking of the art exhibition just held in London, one might, for want of a better figure, call him a Neo-Impressionist poet. Like the Neo-Impressionist painters, like the Impressionists in their day, Mr Pound is open to misunderstanding, and even to ridicule. . . But though these poems have often an unconventional form, bizarre phraseology, catalectic or involved sentence structure and recondite meanings, yet it is always apparent that the poet knows what he is doing. . . Ezra Pound is a true poet; his singing has distinctive spiritual and stylistic qualities which command the most respectful attention; and to those who approach his work in some humility of spirit it is capable of giving a deep aesthetic satisfaction.

The final section of *Provença*, called 'Canzoniere: Studies in Form', was dedicated to Olivia and Dorothy Shakespear and when he gave Dorothy a copy he inscribed it 'Mistress Dorothy Shakespear' and on the tan cover wrote: 'Publisher responsible for the colour of this cover. The peculiar taste of Boston or his own obliquity? Heaven knows, I consign him to suitable justice.'

Immediately after the publication of *Provença* Pound spent the Thanksgiving Day holiday with Williams at Rutherford. It was possibly on this visit that Williams's father objected to a misleading expression in Pound's 'The House of Splendour' (in those days part of the sequence 'Und Drang') and forcefully suggested that the young man stick closely to what he meant and not try to express the thing he intended by means of something else. Another incident was recalled forty years later by Williams in his *Autobiography*:

It was at this time that Ezra made the proposal, which, when I asked my father about it, caused him only to shake his head. It was as follows: That we get a big supply of '606', the new anti-syphilitic arsenical which Ehrlich had just announced to the world, and go at once with it to the north coast of Africa and there set up shop. Between us, I with my medical certificate and experience, he with his social proclivities, we might, he thought, clean up a million treating all the wealthy old nabobs there – presumably rotten with the disease – and retire to our literary enjoyments within, at most, a year. Maybe there was something in it, I don't know.

Pound left behind at Rutherford a copy of Metastasio's *Varie Poesie* (Venice 1795) which ten years later gave Williams the idea used in his prose work *Kora in Hell* of drawing a straight line across the page to separate each item. In Olivia Shakespear's copy of *The Spirit of Romance*, Metastasio's beautiful lyric, 'L'età d'oro', was inserted by Pound in his own hand.

At some stage during his long stay in New York Pound went to live at 270 Fourth Avenue (now Park Avenue South), about half a block from Gramercy Park. Not far away on 29th Street, near Fifth Avenue, was a bookshop run by an Englishman, Laurence J. Gomme, and Pound would sit and talk there sometimes with other poets, Orrick Johns, Joyce Kilmer, Harry Kemp, etc., who used the shop as a meeting-place. From his room on Fourth Avenue he looked across Gramercy Park at a new building which made 'delightful use' of the campanile motif. 'But the ass who built it has set a round water-tank just where it spoils the sky-line.' West of the park he found a block of flats on which the architect had imposed the façade of a Gothic cathedral. The result was bad, but such a spirit, he thought, was bound to win through to something better. The new public library in New York he considered a botch and he went to the architect's office and explained this to a younger member of the firm, but 'found it impossible' to make him understand. The two buildings he admired most in New York as architectural achievements were the Pennsylvania station (now demolished) and the 'Metropolitan Life' tower. As he imbibed the city he was both attracted and repelled: attracted by the urban nights as he looked from high windows and saw the 'great buildings lose reality and take on their magical powers', only the lighted windows visible; and repelled even while fascinated by the 'surging crowd on Seventh Avenue' whose gods were not his gods, whose interests were far removed from and possibly even hostile to his own.

During the winter of 1910–11 he wrote down his thoughts about New York and American civilization. He may have tried to get them published in America – this I do not know; but eighteen months later in London he worked them into a series of articles for *The New Age* and then into a small book, *Patria Mia*.

About 10 January 1911 he received from the treasurer of the Barnard Club, Carnegie Building, a letter informing him that he had been elected a member by the Committee of Admission at a meeting on 6 January. Apparently he attended for a while: he remembered a young woman by the name of Mabelle sitting behind a large silver tea-urn and a discussion about motorcars to which he contributed the suggestion that the automobile would ultimately divorce the American leisured class from all reading-matter fit for consumption. He also attended one of the first meetings of the Poetry Society of America and moved about among painters such as Carlton Glidden and Warren Dahler. But there were things he found intolerable – not least the attitude to poetry of magazines like *The Atlantic* and *Harpers* and the lax standards which he described in *Patria Mia*:

I met a man in New York.[1] He is over thirty, he has never had time to get 'educated'. I liked some of his lyrics. I said, 'Give me some more and I'll take 'em to London and have 'em published'.

94

I found the rest of his work, poem after poem, spoiled. I said: 'Why do you do this and this?'

He said: 'They told me to.' I said: 'Why have you utterly ruined this cadence, and used this stultifying inversion to maintain a worn-out metre that everyone is tired of?'

Same answer. I said: 'Why do you say what you don't mean to get more rhymes than you need?' He said: 'They told me it was paucity of rhyme if I didn't.'

Then he read me the chorus of a play – in splendid movement. The form was within it and of it. And I said: 'Mother of God! Why don't you do that sort of thing all the time?' And he said: 'Oh! I didn't know that was poetry. I just did it as I wanted to – just as I felt it.'

And, of course, the way to 'succeed', as they call it, is to comply. To comply to formulae, and to formulae not based on any knowledge of the art or any care for it.

As he surveyed the American scene his passion for achievement and getting things done was stirred by what he saw and heard and felt. But in another sense the people everywhere around him with whom the future lay were not his people and he decided to leave. There is a glimpse of him in New York in a letter which J. B. Yeats wrote to his son on 11 February:

Have you met Ezra Pound? Carlton Glidden, an artist of talent who has a lot to learn, but who is a very nice fellow indeed, told me today that Ezra Pound was at his studio a few days ago and talked a lot about you, quoting quantities of your verse, which he had by heart, placing you very high, and as the best poet for the last century and more. I tell you this as he is going in a few days to Europe to stay in Paris, etc. Quinn met him and liked him very much. The Americans, young literary men, whom I know found him surly, supercilious and grumpy. I liked him myself very much, that is, I liked his look and air, and the few things he said, for though I was a good while in his company he said very little.

On 13 February Pound paid a visit to Williams in Rutherford and on the evening of the 21st in New York he attended a performance of *Carmen*. Next day, 22 February, he sailed aboard the R.M.S. *Mauretania* for England and Europe. To his father he wrote that it was not easy for him to go and as far as his physical comfort was concerned he was leaving more than awaited him abroad. It was twenty-eight years before he set foot again in America.

NOTES

1 Probably Orrick Johns

VII   Paris, Italy, Germany
1911

By 27 February 1911 he was in London again; it was 'splendid' to be back. He stayed in England only a day or two and then went on to Paris where by 3 March he was installed in a *pension* 'by the Odeon'. In mid-March he dined with Arnold Bennett and saw him again later but Bennett did not interest him. Quick to use or develop a point once he had seen it Pound was often slow to catch it in the first place. Bennett knew much more of what was going on in Paris than Pound did and in his reports on French literature in *The New Age* he was drawing attention not only to men like Romain Rolland and Claudel whom Pound never liked but to others, Remy de Gourmont and Tristan Corbière, for instance, whom Pound had not yet discovered but was later to consider very important. A few weeks before they dined together Bennett had written: 'Who among you has ever heard of Paul Valéry? Yet Paul Valéry is one of the very finest intelligences in France today.' And in an article published on 23 March he praised *The Brothers Karamazov* and Stendhal's *Chartreuse de Parme* 'as the most heroical novels in European literature . . . fiction raised to the highest power'. When we think of Pound's later praise of Stendhal and *Chartreuse de Parme* it is difficult not to believe that here was an opportunity missed; but Pound was not able to take in things quickly if unprepared: he could learn only when ready, only when he had developed at his own pace to the required point. Yeats came to Paris about the third week in March and together they visited Notre Dame and Versailles.

By 21 March Pound was staying with Walter Morse Rummel, attending concerts and working with Rummel on Arnaut Daniel and the problem of how to interpret the music of the troubadours. I do not know how or where they first met but as Rummel set to music words by Katherine Heyman in 1906 it seems likely that it was through her or her circle. Many years later Miss Granger Kerr told Peter Russell that it was Rummel who gave Pound her name in 1908. This suggests that if they did not already know one another from New York or Philadelphia, their first meeting took place in Paris in 1908 when Pound was

on his way from Venice to London. In 1911 they had much in common
including admiration for Debussy who highly praised Rummel's
interpretation of his piano works. 'Maestro di Tocar' in *Canzoni* is
dedicated to Rummel's playing:

> You, who are touched not by our mortal ways . . .
> Have but to loose the magic from your hands
> And all men's hearts that glimmer for a day,
> And all our loves that are so swift to flame
> Rise in that space of sound and melt away.

During March and April Pound had his portrait painted by an artist
named Ullman who finished it about 17 April. After floods and a hard
winter which persisted into the last week of April, Paris in May was
bright with sun and blossom. With Yeats he called on Davray and
Legouis at the Sorbonne and met a few poets. His verdict in a letter
home was that the poets in Paris were 'a gutless lot'. Matisse was a
subject of much discussion but Pound found only one canvas he was
prepared to consider 'well painted'. By 16 May he had seen a group by
Cézanne in a private gallery and had met Rummel's brother who
painted and played the 'cello. He apparently made some adjustments to
the introduction to his Cavalcanti book, judging by an unpublished
note of twenty years later – it was intended for publication – in which
he supposed that the introduction must have been finished 'in Margaret
Craven's apartment in Paris in the Spring of 1911'. Margaret Craven
was, I think, a friend of Rummel's brother. Pound attended a performance of Debussy's 'St Sebastien': the music was 'wonderful' but
D'Annunzio's libretto was the worst thing he had ever done. Once
again Pound had approached the University of Pennsylvania about the
possibility of a fellowship or appointment but in May he was told there
was nothing available.

About the middle of May he received from Elkin Mathews the page-
proofs of *Canzoni* which he corrected and returned by the end of the
month. He altered his early poem 'The Tree' so that the second line
read 'And knew the truth of many hidden things', which was not as
good as the original 'Knowing the truth of things unseen before'.
Fortunately he repented and returned to the original before publishing
his 'Collected Shorter Poems'. From 'De Aegypto' he deleted four lines,
this time to advantage. And in 'Abelard', first published in *Canzoni* and
not reprinted, a soul which in the original version *keened* an answer was
restrained in proof to *giving* an answer. Much of *Canzoni* was affected
and 'literary' to a hopeless degree but it contained in one of the poems
in 'Und Drang' an attempt at 'modernism':

97

> How our modernity
> Nerve-wracked and broken, turns
> Against time's way . . .

And also a new note in 'Au Salon':

> Have tea, damn the Caesars,
> Talk of the latest success, give wing to some scandal,
> Garble a name we detest, and for prejudice?
> Set loose the whole consummate pack
> to bay like Sir Roger de Coverley's. . . .

In his adaptations of Heine he played with tones of voice and speech accents within a fairly tight form:

> O ye lips that are ungrateful,
> Hath it never once distressed you,
> That you can say such *awful* things
> Of *any* one who ever kissed you?

And there is a new certainty in some of the rhetoric in 'Her Monument, the Image Cut Thereon' (from the Italian of Leopardi):

> With all the admirable concepts that moved from it
> Swept from the mind with it in its departure.

Included in the collection as it first went to the printer was a poem of one hundred and fourteen lines entitled 'Redondillas, or Something of that Sort', which he deleted entirely from the published book. It was an attempt to create poetry out of history, his friendships with Victor Plarr, Fred Vance, and Frank Whiteside, his own tastes in food and art, and his opinions about goings-on in the world around him. Like much whimsical verse it was serious, too serious for the author's comfort when he saw the proofs. First he tried correcting and re-writing it and even gave it a new title ('Locksley Hall forty years further on') in the hope of saving some of it for publication. When this failed he withdrew it completely by drawing two heavy ink lines from top to bottom of each page. Broadly it was an attempt to contrast natural beauty and the 'best' of past and present with 'squalor' ancient and modern. He mentioned Theodore Roosevelt, Russian dancers, Spinoza and Verlaine, hinted that he was reaching towards perceptions 'scarce heeded', and threw in two lines which might almost belong to his *Homage to Sextus Propertius* of seven years later:

    O Virgil, from your green elysium
      see how that dactyl stubs his weary toes.

He claimed in passing that he was 'that terrible thing, the product of American culture', but in his case improved by considerable care and attention. He was, he said, a modern, despite his 'affecting the ancients'. Medical science, Bergson, modern painting and Nietzsche, Ibsen, Mozart, Strauss and Debussy, and even himself as 'London's last foible in poets' all came in for mention. In its crude way it summarized his development and aspirations. He told of the places he had been:

    I would sing of exquisite sights,
            of the murmur of Garda;
    I would sing of the amber lights,
            or of how Desenzano
    Lies like a topaz chain
            upon the throat of the waters.

Of Ehrlich and his anti-syphilis drug – of which Williams has already informed us:

    I've just heard of a German named Ehrlich.
    Medical science is jolted. . . .

Of his dreams:

    At times I am wrapped in my dream
            of my mistress 'Tomorrow'. . . .

Of his feelings about America and Europe:

    I would sing the American people,
            God send them some civilization;
    I would sing of the nations of Europe,
            God grant them some method of cleansing
    The fetid extent of their evils.

And running through the poem was the suggestion that Pound was the one to catch this 'cosmopolite civilization' and hold it in a work of art:

    They tell me to 'Mirror my age',
      God pity the age if I do do it.

As well as 'Redondillas' he crossed out three worthless sonnets and an amusing parody which he wrote for Hulme and the Irish poet Desmond Fitzgerald who sometimes attended Hulme's gatherings in 1909:

> Although my linen still is clean,
> My socks fine silk and aa that,
> Although I dine and drink good wine –
> Say, twice a week, and aa that;
> For aa that and aa that,
> My tinsel show and aa that,
> These breeks 'll no last many weeks
> 'Gainst wear and tear and aa that.

This latter poem was published in the anthology *Des Imagistes* in 1914. In a letter to Mathews in 1916 Pound wondered whether deleting these rougher poems had not been a mistake, for it left the book unbalanced: 'I don't know that I regret it . . . for the poems weren't good enough, but even so the book would have been better if they had been left in, or if something like them had been put in their place.' Also struck out were the notes at the back of the book which included an interesting defence of his *canzoni*:

The canzoni have already been assailed and on this account I feel that I may be permitted to venture toward that dangerous thing, an explanation; or rather, I ask you to consider whether it be not more difficult to serve that love of Beauty (or, even of some particular sort of Beauty) which belongs to the permanent part of oneself, than to express some sudden emotion or perception which being unusual, being keener than normal, is by its very way of being, clearly defined or at least set apart from those things of the mind among which it appears.

After correcting the proofs he left Paris for Sirmione and was in Italy when the *Philadelphia Evening Bulletin* of 29 June published a detailed story of his exploits under the heading 'Philadelphian Wins Renown with Verse'. The paper described him as formerly 'an obscure graduate of the University of Pennsylvania' who had been 'caught up on the wings of recognition and hurried to a place of eminence'. The story obviously came from Homer who had been drilled by his son what to say to the newspapers:

When the echoes of acclaim sounded here Philadelphians were startled to realize that they had the claim of citizenship upon Ezra Pound whose *Exultations, Personae, A Lume Spento* and *A Quinzaine for This Yule* brought forth unqualified praise from the English critics.

Now another volume, the *Canzori of Ezra Pound* is on the verge of publication in London and will shortly be issued. Early proofs of these songs have been sent by Mr Pound to his father, Homer Loomis Pound, who lives at 1834 Mount Vernon Street, and is assistant assayer in the United States Mint, 17th and Spring Garden Streets.[1]

At present Ezra Pound is in Sirmione, Lago di Garda, in Italy, where he is writing almost constantly. Last spring he spent four months with his parents and then went to Paris where he was joined by Walter Rummel, the American composer, who is the grandson of Samuel W. Morse. The composer is setting one of Pound's poems, 'The Song of the Virgin Mother', to a full orchestra score and a number of his other lyrics have been adapted to music by English and French composers.

At present Pound has two other books in preparation, one of which is a translation of the poems of Arnaut Daniel. His own prose work, *The Spirit of Romance*, which is a study in the pre-renaissance literature of Latin Europe, was published a year ago, and is a collection of the lectures which he delivered on 'Mediaeval Literature' at the London Polytechnic College.

On his mother's side he is distantly related to the poet Longfellow, 'whose poetry he does not admire'.

He has lived with Arnold Bennett in Paris, visited Maurice Hewlett in Italy, and made a warm friend of William Butler Yeats, the Irish poet, who speaks of Pound as 'the solitary volcano' in modern poetry.

The smallness of the writer's output need not be reckoned as barrenness or indolence for he has a faculty of self-criticism; he has written and burned two novels and three hundred sonnets.

The recognition which has come so unreservedly to the American poet abroad is now being gradually yielded to him by his own countrymen. Pound however, cares nothing for that, he declares. He is only twenty-five years old now, and in his own estimation 'has not yet begun to write'. He prefers to live abroad and make only intermittent visits to his parents.

In a letter from Sirmione in July Pound told his parents that he wanted to write a book on 'philosophy' from Richard of St Victor to Pico della Mirandola. Later in the month he met William Carlos Williams's brother, Edward, who was an architect, and together they inspected architecture in and around Mantua, Goito and Verona. At San Zeno when they came upon columns that are signed by their maker at the base, Williams commented that such hand-made stone-work was impossible under modern conditions when columns were ordered by the gross. In Verona Pound wrote the sonnet 'Silet' which in May the following year appeared in the *Smart Set* in New York and afterwards in the book *Ripostes*. It is perhaps his most successful handling of a regular form, nicely balanced between the demands of natural language and the forward steps of the metre:

> It is enough that we once came together;
> What is the use of setting it to rime?

When it is autumn do we get spring weather,
Or gather may of harsh northwindish time?

It is enough that we once came together;
What if the wind have turned against the rain?
It is enough that we once came together;
Time has seen this, and will not turn again. . . .

From the Hotel Chiave d'Oro in Verona Pound returned to the Eden
at Sirmione and spent the next few days reading the poetry of Lorenzo
di Medici and Sismondi's *Italian Republics*. He later held that Lorenzo's

Quant'è bella giovinezza,
Che si fugge tuttavia.
Chi vuol esser lieto sia;
Di doman' non c'è certezza.

was the source of Shakespeare's

What is love? 'tis not hereafter;
Present mirth hath present laughter;
    What's to come is still unsure:
In delay there lies no plenty:
Then come kiss me, sweet-and-twenty,
    Youth's a stuff will not endure.

While on the continent Pound had been negotiating with Macmillan
in London for the publication of some of his work, possibly the
Cavalcanti book, and about the third week in July he received an
encouraging letter; but if the matter was taken further I have not
found any trace of it and it came to nothing in the end. The following
week he left Sirmione on the first stage of his return to London and by
27 July he was staying at the Hotel Belle Venise in Milan, working on
new poems of his own and exploring Milan and finding it delightful.
At the Ambrosian Library he discovered among some manuscript of
songs by Arnaut Daniel two of what appeared to be the original
melodies. The musical notation, he told his parents, 'accords exactly
with my theories of how his music should be written'. Excited by his
discovery he copied out both melodies and set out for Giessen, a small
university town north of Frankfurt, where Hueffer, no longer editor of
The English Review, was expecting him. On the way he stopped at
Freiburg-im-Breisgau, in the south-west corner of Germany, there to
meet Emil Levy, author of a Provençal dictionary in the course of

publication. Hugo Rennert had recommended him to Pound as the most knowledgeable student of the Provençal language. Levy was so interested in Pound's discovery that he walked 'half way across Freiburg' to see the two strips of copy.

In London Hueffer had been living with Violet Hunt at South Lodge. When his wife refused to divorce him he went to Germany and on the strength of his German descent he apparently sought a divorce there. He was at Giessen in vain awaiting proceedings when Pound arrived from Italy bearing a copy of *Canzoni*, which had come out in July with dedication to Olivia and Dorothy Shakespear. Hueffer when he read the book was so horrified by the artificial language that he rolled on the floor. The only account of this event is by Pound almost thirty years later in his obituary on Hueffer in the August 1939 issue of *The Nineteenth Century and After*. Hueffer, he says,

felt the errors of contemporary style to the point of rolling (physically, and if you look at it as mere superficial snob, ridiculously) on the floor of his temporary quarters in Giessen when my third volume displayed me trapped, fly-papered, gummed and strapped down in a jejune provincial effort to learn, *mehercule*, the stilted language that then passed for 'good English' in the arthritic milieu that held control of the respected British critical circles . . . that roll saved me at least two years, perhaps more. It sent me back to my own proper effort, namely, toward using the living tongue. . . .

We may doubt whether it happened quite so inevitably or suddenly as this but in the next six months Pound did in fact consider the place of the living tongue in English poetry and in his own verse gave evidence of new ability.

NOTES

1 1834 Mount Vernon Street was a large, fashionable townhouse which the Pounds rented during 1911. The following year they went to a similar house at 1640 Green Street, before returning to Wyncote where they remained apparently until 1928.

VIII　Hulme and Orage
1911/1912

Pound returned to London in August 1911 and went to stay at the
home or boarding-house of a Mrs Worthington – his room at Church
Walk having been let in his absence. During the next few months he
gathered up the threads he had let fall in June 1910 and began to look
in earnest for means of support. It was with work in mind that in
September he sought a meeting with G. R. S. Mead of the Quest Society
who was also editor of *The Quest*, a quarterly review devoted to gnosti-
cism, Theosophy and the pagan mystery religions. Something of an
expert in such matters Mead had edited and translated texts of the
Naassenes and other sects active during the early years of Christianity.
They met about 16 September when it was agreed that at a date to be
fixed Pound would lecture for the society on pagan elements in the
troubadours. In a letter to his father on 17 September he mentioned
the possibility of a job at Hamilton College but the idea seems to have
died immediately. As Homer was still helping to support him it was
possibly little more than a gesture on Pound's part to satisfy his father
that he was not idle and was always on the lookout for new opportunities. Two days later Augener Ltd of London published separately at
two shillings each the sheet music of three songs by Pound with
instrumental accompaniment by Walter Morse Rummel: 'Madrigale',
'Au bal masqué', and 'Aria'. At half-a-crown each they were still being
sold by Augener as late as 1957.

By 6 October Hilda Doolittle was in London and no doubt at Pound's
recommendation was installed at 8 Duchess Street. About 21 October
Pound and Rummel took a house at 39 Addison Street North, London,
W., but in November when his old room became vacant he returned to
Church Walk.

He began to see T. E. Hulme again and it was probably at one of
Hulme's Tuesday evenings in Mrs Ethel Kibblewhite's home at 67
Frith Street, Soho, that he first met A. R. Orage, editor of *The New
Age*. Orage was quick to see Pound's worth and in November agreed to
publish a series of his translations from Anglo-Saxon, Provençal and
Tuscan poetry accompanied by prose comments. Not only would his

contributions appear weekly but he would have a fairly free hand as well. Pound was extremely happy at this turn of events which he saw as a firm start in the world of periodicals. Looking ahead in November to future issues he asked his father to send him the unpublished articles he had written in America during the previous winter.

His first series, entitled 'I Gather the Limbs of Osiris', was published in twelve parts between 30 November 1911 and 22 February 1912. The first instalment was a translation of the Anglo-Saxon poem, 'The Seafarer', which in Pound's career was the first clear sign of major ability:

> There I heard naught save the harsh sea
> And ice-cold wave, at whiles the swan cries,
> Did for my games the gannet's clamour,
> Sea-fowls' loudness was for me laughter,
> The mews' singing all my mead-drink.
> Storms, on the stone-cliffs beaten, fell on the stern
> In icy feathers; full oft the eagle screamed
> With spray on his pinion.

As a contributor to *The New Age* Pound began to frequent Orage's small office in Rolls Passage which intersects Chancery Lane just below Cursitor Street and on Monday afternoons began to take a tuppeny tea and cake at the informal editorial conferences which Orage held in the basement of the ABC restaurant in Chancery Lane. Surrounded by contributors the editor went through the proofs of Thursday's issue and by incisive comment provoked articles for future issues. Afterwards they might all go to an Italian restaurant near the corner of Gray's Inn Road or to the Café Royal. Orage also presided over weekly discussions at the Kardomah Café in Fleet Street and occasionally held lunches at the Sceptre, off Regent Street. Through Orage, Pound was introduced into worlds hitherto unsuspected, for contributors during the next few years included not only men like Hulme, Sturge Moore, Wyndham Lewis and Rupert Brooke, but others who might have remained completely outside his ken, such as Allen Upward, Middleton Murry, Llewelyn Powys, Katherine Mansfield and the drama critic A. E. Randall of whom Shaw said: '*The New Age* has had the rare fortune to secure the services of a critic of the theatre who understands what is happening on the stage technically.'

Orage did not interfere with his contributors' freedom of expression; he controlled the paper through his 'Notes of the Week' and a literary column entitled 'Readers and Writers' which he signed 'R.H.C.' For the rest his contributors were free to express their own thoughts so long as they did so in reasonably straightforward English. And he was quick as well to admit new ideas into the field to be tested by this free discussion, as witness the fact that Freud's name was first mentioned in *The New Age* in 1912 and that soon afterwards Orage opened the paper to M. D. Eder who was one of the pioneers of psychoanalysis in England. But it was not only the contact with new and dissimilar views which for Pound was important, there was also the matter of money: during the next ten years Orage published nearly three hundred of his articles and this regular payment was the biggest single factor in keeping the wolf from the door.

Another influence on Pound at this time was T. E. Hulme who was aggressive and brilliant where Orage was quiet and incisive but similarly able to charm writers, painters and intellectuals of widely differing views. He was interested in art and philosophy as well as poetry and in April 1911 had attended a philosophical congress at Bologna, at which Henri Bergson discussed 'the image': 'But what we shall manage to recapture and to hold is a certain intermediary image between the simplicity of the concrete intuition and the complexity of the abstractions which translate it, a receding and vanishing image, which haunts, unperceived perhaps, the mind of the philosopher, which follows him like his shadow through the ins and outs of his thought and which, if it is not the intuition itself, approaches it more closely than the conceptual expression.' Hulme gave an account of the congress in *The New Age* of 27 April. Some years earlier he had read Bergson's *Essai sur les données immédiates de la conscience* in which the philosopher linked these images with poetry: 'Whence indeed comes the charm of poetry? The poet is he with whom feelings develop into images, and the images themselves into words which translate them while obeying the laws of rhythm. In seeing these images pass before our eyes we in our turn experience the feeling which was, so to speak, their emotional equivalent.' Hulme spent three months in Italy, returning to England about the time Pound left Garda for Giessen. In *The New Age* of 24 August he published a review of Tancrède de Visan's *L'Attitude du lyrisme contemporain* in which he mentioned having read Andre Beaunier's *La Poesie nouvelle* in 1905 or 1906. Both books contain detailed discussion of symbols and images.

The two young men met again after their return to London and Pound attended the series of lectures on Bergson which Hulme gave at the home of Mrs Franz Liebich between 23 November and 14 December. The two essays, 'Bergson's Theory of Art' and 'The Philosophy of Intensive Manifolds', which Hulme's editor, Herbert Read, published in *Speculations*, were probably delivered as lectures during this series. In 'Bergson's Theory of Art' Hulme speaks of the process of artistic creation as a process of discovery and disentanglement. The great artist or innovator dives down into the inner flux of life and comes back with 'a new shape' which he endeavours to fix. He cannot be said to have created it, but to have discovered it, because when he has definitely expressed it by means of fresh metaphors and epithets we are overcome by a vivid conviction that it is true. The great artist is able to see emotions and other things more clearly than his fellows and this vision breeds in him a dissatisfaction with the conventional means of expression which allow all the individualities of the things perceived to escape. By a certain tension of mind he is able to force the mechanism of expression out of the common rut in which it normally runs and into the way he wants. Pound was impressed and early in December wrote to his mother that Hulme was giving rather good lectures on Bergson. Fresh from his own work on Guido Cavalcanti, he drew Hulme's attention to a related aspect of the search for the exact means of expression. Here is his account of the conversation written sixteen years later in an essay on Cavalcanti:

When the late T. E. Hulme was trying to be a philosopher in that [British] milieu, and fussing about Sorel and Bergson and getting them translated into English, I spoke to him one day of the difference between Guido's precise interpretive metaphor, and the Petrarchan fustian and ornament, pointing out that Guido thought in accurate terms; that the phrases correspond to definite sensations undergone; in fact very much what I had said in my early preface to the Sonnets and Ballate.[1]

Hulme took some time over it in silence, and then finally said: 'That is very interesting'; and after a pause: 'That is more interesting than anything I ever read in a book.'

On 4 December Hilda Doolittle wrote to Isabel Pound to say that Ezra had been most kind to her since her arrival in London. Her cordial reception had been 'due to the efforts of his friends, spurred on by himself'. According to Dorothy Pound's memory it was Miss Doolittle and not Pound who introduced Rummel to her mother; on at least one occasion about this time Miss Doolittle was present when Rummel played Debussy on the Shakespears' baby-grand. Rummel returned to Paris about the beginning of December but was expected back the following spring. Early in December Pound received £21 for his translations of a selection of French songs published by Augener in April 1912 under the title Selection from Collection Yvette Guilbert. The songs ranged from Villon to the eighteenth century and were given in French and English with piano accompaniment arranged by Gustave Ferrari. It may have been purely coincidental but soon after receiving this money from Augener he took Dorothy Shakespear to lunch and from the tone in which he informed his mother of the event in advance we may suppose that he was seldom able to afford such outings. To this period of affluence may belong a story told by Pound to William McNaughton some forty years later and by McNaughton recounted to me in 1967. Pound, it seems, approached Mr Shakespear and asked for his daughter's hand in marriage. Having heard something of poets in general and knowing something of Pound in particular Mr Shakespear asked: 'How will you keep her?' Flustered by this direct approach Pound drew a handful of recently acquired banknotes from his pocket and exclaimed defensively, 'But look! I have money here!' Dorothy Pound remembered another occasion when he strode into her parents' house in Brunswick Gardens and announced, with only an hour to spare, that he had tickets to take Dorothy and her mother to see Nijinsky and Pavlova at the Russian Ballet. It was, he told them, 'worth seeing'.

In part two of 'I Gather the Limbs of Osiris' which appeared in *The New Age* of 7 December he boldly outlined his 'New Method of Scholarship':

When I bring into play what my late pastors and masters would term, in classic sweetness, my 'unmitigated gall', and by virtue of it venture to speak of a 'New Method of Scholarship', I do not imagine that I am speaking of a method by me discovered. I mean merely a method not of common practice, a method not yet clearly or consciously formulated, a method which has been intermittently used by all good scholars since the beginning of scholarship, the method of Luminous Detail, a method most vigorously hostile to the prevailing mode of today – that is, the method of multitudinous detail, and to the method of yesterday, the method of sentiment and generalization. The latter is too inexact and the former too cumbersome to be of much use to the normal man wishing to live mentally active.

This 'Luminous Detail' consists of certain facts which 'give one a sudden insight into circumjacent conditions, into their causes, their effects, into sequence, and law', and the artist is one who seeks out this detail and presents it without comment. In part four of the series (21 December) he says he will apply the method to Arnaut Daniel and this leads to a description of Daniel's achievement in the twelfth century as the rediscovery of literary style – a manner of writing which treats the poem as an organism in which each word should make its special contribution to the effect of the whole.

Pound spent Christmas 1911 with Maurice Hewlett at the Old Rectory, Broad Chalke, Salisbury. This was a former nunnery built in 1487 which still retained many of its original features inside and a mill-race outside. Occasionally they motored over to Henry Newbolt who lived not far away at Netherhampton House, Salisbury. In December, possibly while he was with Hewlett, he wrote for Harold Monro the essay 'Prolegomena' containing his poetic 'Credo'. After a year or two abroad, mainly in Italy, Monro had returned to London in September 1911 to assist the cause of poetry and by December was preparing to launch, from a dingy top-floor room at 93 Chancery Lane, the sixpenny *Poetry Review*. Pound's contribution to Monro's campaign was first of all to prefer poetry and leisure to theory and explanations: 'I would much rather lie on what is left of Catullus' parlour floor and speculate the azure beneath it and the hills off to Salò and Riva with their forgotten gods moving unhindered amongst them, than discuss any processes and theories of art whatsoever.' But if he had to talk about it then he would insist upon the highest standards: 'I believe in an "absolute rhythm", a rhythm, that is, in poetry which corresponds exactly to the emotion or shade of emotion to be expressed.' He also believed that the 'proper and perfect symbol' was the natural object and that if a poet used symbols he should so use them that their symbolic function did not obtrude; so that a sense, and the poetic quality of the passage, was not lost to those who did not understand the symbol as such, to whom, for instance, a hawk was simply a hawk. Technique, he said, was the test of a man's sincerity and this meant the trampling down of every convention that impeded or obscured the determination of the law or the precise rendering of the impulse. There were two kinds of content in poetry, one 'fluid' and the other 'solid'; or in other words a poem might have form as a tree has form or as water poured into a vase. Although most symmetrical forms had certain uses, he said, there were many subjects that could not be precisely, and therefore not properly rendered in such forms. Towards the end he praised Bridges, Hewlett and Manning for seriously attempting to overhaul metric and Hueffer for his 'experiments in modernity', and he then forecast the future:

As to twentieth-century poetry, and the poetry I expect to see written during the next decade or so, it will, I think, move against poppy-cock, it will be harder and saner, it will be what Mr Hewlett calls 'nearer the bone'. It will be as much like granite as it can be, its force will lie in its truth, its interpretative power (or course, poetic force does always rest there); I mean it will not try to seem forcible by rhetorical din, and luxurious riot. We will have fewer painted adjectives impeding the shock and stroke of it. At least for myself, I want it so, austere, direct, free from emotional slither.

At the beginning of 1912 Pound was at last launched upon the literary career he had for years looked forward to. He was twenty-six: a tall figure with a shock of yellow-gold hair and small red beard, his green eyes slightly apprehensive. Attached to *The New Age* and with new literary projects beginning to blossom on every side he grew rapidly in ability and from his base at 10 Church Walk he ventured forth to explore and digest as much of London as fell within the range of his interests and sensibilities. Much of his activity in the next few years took place in Kensington which he came to know 'stone by stone' as he knew Venice and later Perugia. In Church Street, opposite St Mary Abbots, was De Mario's restaurant which he used occasionally in an emergency because it was close. But more often he went to a small tea-shop in Holland Street that was run by Miss Ella Abbott, described by Pound fifty years later as an American in 'flight from U.S.A. toward civilization'. She preferred to serve only customers connected with Art or Letters, 'at 1*s*. 3*d*, per scrambled eggs on one slice of toast'. Near Miss Abbott's was a bookshop and on the corner of Holland Place a coffee-shop conveniently housing a telephone. Other shops handy to his room included a butcher's (run by a Scot), a game and fish shop with telephone, a tobacco shop, a barber's and a chemist's. And within walking distance were numerous friends and writers such as May Sinclair who lived in Edwards Square before moving to Hampstead, the Shakespears at 12 Brunswick Gardens, Violet Hunt at South Lodge, Florence Farr and G. R. S. Mead, over towards Earls Court, and the novelist Gilbert Cannan, a friend of Hueffer's, who for a time lived just around the corner from Church Walk. To reach friends in Soho or Mayfair he went by foot through Kensington Gardens and Hyde Park, sometimes accompanied by Hueffer, and occasionally they were joined by Cannan with James Barrie's large dog; but for longer journeys, when he wanted to visit Ernest Rhys in Hampstead, for example, he took a bus; and from about 1912 onwards the top of a bus was his main means of exploring the areas he could not reach on foot.

In a London studio one day in 1911 Pound had been approached by an American woman on behalf of the *North American Review* and asked to contribute something. He sent two poems including a neat imitation from the Greek Anthology called 'Two Cloaks', later re-titled 'The Cloak':

> Thou keep'st thy rose-leaf
> Till the rose-time will be over,
> Think'st thou that Death will kiss thee?

The review not only paid him well for the poems, which appeared in January 1912, but the editor wrote to congratulate him and to say that a revered member of the American Academy, Dean Howells, was also very pleased with his work. In response to this enthusiasm Pound sent them one of his best poems, 'Portrait d'une Femme', which deals with a 'modern' subject in 'modern' terms:

> Your mind and you are our Sargasso Sea,
> London has swept about you this score years
> And bright ships left you this or that in fee:
> Ideas, old gossip, oddments of all things,
> Strange spars of knowledge and dimmed wares of price.
> Great minds have sought you – lacking someone else.
> You have been second always. Tragical?
> No. You preferred it to the usual thing:
> One dull man, dulling and uxurious,
> One average mind – with one thought less, each year. . . .

This was too much for the *North American Review* which rejected it on the ground that the opening line contained too many 'r's' – a flagrant disregard on Pound's part apparently of Tennyson's condemnation of a certain line containing four 's's'. Both 'The Cloak' and 'Portrait d'une Femme' were included in his next collection, *Ripostes*.

Towards the end of January 1912 Pound attended a lecture by Yeats at the Shakespears' and in his attempt to educate Monro in the secrets of the craft took him to one of Yeats's Monday evenings. The first number of *The Poetry Review* came out in January and the second number, containing Pound's 'Prolegomena' and six of his poems, in February. Two of the poems are of lasting interest – 'Sub Mare' mainly for its conclusion:

> Pale slow green surgings of the underwave,
> 'Mid these things older than the names they have,
> These things that are familiars of the god.

and '*Δώρια*', as the first poem in which he consciously captured some of the 'hardness' called for in 'Prolegomena':

> Be in me as the eternal moods
>   of the bleak wind, and not
> As transient things are –
>   gaiety of flowers.
> Have me in the strong loneliness
>   of sunless cliffs
> And of grey waters. . . .

'*Δώρια*' was reprinted in *Ripostes* and also in the anthology *Des Imagistes*.

About the first week in February Pound met Henry James in a London drawing-room. They do not seem to have engaged in much conversation but 'glared at one another', he told his family, 'across the same carpet'. In *The New Age* of 15 February he published in part eleven of 'I Gather the Limbs of Osiris' a statement of his immediate aims: 'As far as the "living art" goes, I should like to break up *cliché*, to disintegrate these magnetized groups that stand between the reader of poetry and the drive of it, to escape from lines composed of two very nearly equal sections, each containing a noun and each noun decorously attended by a carefully selected epithet gleaned, apparently, from Shakespeare, Pope, or Horace.' Not until poetry lived again 'close to the thing' would it be a vital part of contemporary life. As long as the poet said not what he, 'at the very crux of a clarified conception', meant, but was content to say something ornate and approximate, just so long would serious people, intently alive, consider poetry as balderdash – a sort of embroidery for dilettantes and women. 'We must have a simplicity and directness of utterance', he said, 'which is different from the simplicity and directness of daily speech, which is more "curial", more dignified. This difference, this dignity, cannot be conferred by florid adjectives or elaborate hyperbole; it must be conveyed by art, and by the art of the verse structure, by something which exalts the reader, making him feel that he is in contact with something arranged more finely than the commonplace.'

About the third week in February he met and liked W. H. Hudson, found that Mead was interesting to talk to, and to his family on 21 February declared that Hulme was 'a very good sort'. In the same letter he said that Flint, in return for being 'resurrected', had put him onto some very good French authors, and he mentioned Remy de Gourmont, Henri de Regnier, 'etcetera'. Earlier Pound had fallen in with a new publisher, the poet Charles Granville of Stephen Swift & Co., 16 King Street, Covent Garden. He agreed to give them his future books in return for £100 a year advance royalties for a period of ten years. The first book they received under this scheme was his Cavalcanti and towards the end of February he delivered the typescript of *Ripostes*.

Early in March he again met Henry James and liked him 'still more on further acquaintance'. And there was a further meeting about 13 March when a mutual friend, Mrs Dilke, included them both in a party of four for lunch. James was always friendly and on one occasion discussed America: 'It is strange', he said, 'how all taint of art or letters seems to shun that continent.' But the differences were too great for intimacy and Pound never visited James at his home at Rye. In a memorial essay published six years later he described James's 'wonderful conversation':

The massive head, the slow uplift of the hand, *gli occhi onesti e tardi*, the long sentences piling themselves up in elaborate phrase after phrase, the lightning incision, the pauses, the slightly shaking admonitory gesture with its 'wu-a-wait a little, wait a little, something will come'; blague and benignity and the weight of so many years' careful, incessant labour of minute observation always there to enrich the talk. I had heard it but seldom, yet it is all unforgettable.

In a letter to his mother in March he reported having attended a very good lecture by Mead and advised her to read Aquinas and Aristotle. This lecture was one of a series held by the Quest Society at the Kensington Town Hall in 1912 and attended by Pound and Dorothy Shakespear. Included in the series was his own lecture on the troubadours, which was later published in the October 1912 issue of *The Quest*. It is a strange mixture of random fact and interesting speculation on the origins of the troubadour love-cult. As a survey it is useless because he did not know his subject beyond its literary surface; but it shows that he was trying to fit his knowledge of the pagan mysteries and the cults of Provence into the general scheme of Theosophy, or at any rate to prove that they did not run counter to it; and it shows also that he was hoping to preserve the truths available in this field by linking them to 'Science': trying to save the 'spiritual', in other words, by showing it to be natural rather than supernatural. From 1932 onwards the lecture appeared as chapter five ('Psychology and Troubadours') of *The Spirit of Romance*.

Rummel was back in London and about the middle of March gave a successful recital. About the same time Pound received approximately £20 for the first of several lectures in Lord Glenconner's 'private gallery'. Mrs Pound recalled in 1967 that at one of these lectures he gave a very good reading of 'The Seafarer'. He had by now met the English poet Richard Aldington, aged twenty, and both Aldington and Hilda Doolittle took rooms across the courtyard from Pound in Church Walk. Among the visitors to Pound's room to whom he introduced Aldington was a University of Pennsylvania classmate, Henry Slominsky, a student of the presocratic philosophers whose *Heraklit und Parmenides* came out that same year, 1912.

The *Forum* for April published an article by Pound, 'The Wisdom of Poetry', which shows him translating Hulme's material into his own terms. The function of an art, he said, was to free the intellect and the perceptive faculties from encumbrance, 'such encumbrances, for instance, as set moods, set ideas, conventions. . . .' Language, which was the 'medium of thought's preservation', was constantly wearing out and it was the poet's job to 'new-mint' it. Thus poets might be kept on as 'conservators of the public speech' and because they were also 'the advance guard of the psychologist on the watch for new emotions, new vibrations', on the alert for 'colour perceptions of a subtler sort, neither affirming them to be "astral" or "spiritual" nor denying the formulae of theosophy'.

NOTES

1 'Than Guido Cavalcanti no psychologist of the emotions is more keen in his understanding, more precise in his expression; we have in him no rhetoric, but always a true description . . .' (Introduction to *Sonnets and Ballate of Guido Cavalcanti*).

IX   Imagism
1912/1914

The first Futurist Exhibition in London opened at the Sackville Gallery on 1 March 1912 and the movement's leader, Marinetti, lectured on the nineteenth. Although Pound was never a Futurist and either indifferent or opposed to most of their principles, he shared with them a common pugnacity in aesthetic matters and a common feeling that the artist had to 'break up the surface of convention' and art be made to speak with the voice of the present. That such a feeling was 'in the air' we may deduce from the fact that even Henry Newbolt in the January–March *English Review* wrote: 'We are witnessing the natural recovery from a period of decadence . . . Poets are bent on getting nearer to the inward melody, on moving faithfully to the inward rhythm.' When we consider Pound's desire to 'break up cliché', to 'escape from lines containing two very nearly equal sections', and his search for 'hardness', 'directness' and 'simplicity'; when we observe the desire for change that was already abroad at the time, as well as economic and political currents working parallel; and, not least, when we remember that the five poems comprising 'The Complete Poetical Works of T. E. Hulme' appeared in *The New Age* of 25 January 1912, we shall see immediately that for one of Pound's temperament the way was open to the formation of a new 'movement' in poetry. And so it was that one day probably in April, Pound, Aldington and Hilda Doolittle decided they were agreed upon three principles of good writing: (1) direct treatment of the subject, (2) to allow no word that was not essential to the presentation, and (3) in their rhythms to follow the musical phrase rather than strict regularity. Then, or within a month or so, Pound gave to the members of this new movement the title *Les Imagistes*. The first use of this title in print was in Pound's *Ripostes*, in a note he placed at the back to accompany the publication in book-form of Hulme's 'Complete Poetical Works':

In publishing his *Complete Poetical Works* at thirty, Mr Hulme has set an enviable example to many of his contemporaries who have had less to say.
    They are reprinted here for good fellowship; for good custom, a custom

out of Tuscany and of Provence; and thirdly, for convenience, seeing their smallness of bulk; and for good memory, seeing that they recall certain evenings and meetings of two years gone, dull enough at the time, but rather pleasant to look back upon.

As for the 'School of Images', which may or may not have existed, its principles were not so interesting as those of the 'inherent dynamists' or of *Les Unanimistes*, yet they were probably sounder than those of a certain French school which attempted to dispense with verbs altogether; or of the Impressionists who brought forth:

'Pink pigs blossoming upon the hillside';

or of the Post-Impressionists who beseech their ladies to let down slate-blue hair over their raspberry-coloured flanks.

Ardoise rimed richly – ah, richly and rarely rimed! – with *framboise*.

As for the future, *Les Imagistes*, the descendants of the forgotten school of 1909, have that in their keeping.

Even if this note or the reference to *Les Imagistes* was inserted at one of the proof-stages it can hardly have been done later than August as the book was published in October. But whatever difficulty there may be in discovering when Pound invented the term *Les Imagistes*, the first stirrings of the movement itself, named or unnamed, almost certainly occurred in April.

Towards the end of April Mary Moore of Trenton, New Jersey, to whom *Personae* had been dedicated, arrived in London on holiday and Pound was pleased to take her round and show her the sights before he left for Paris on 1 May.

He spent the next three months in France – first at 92 rue Raynouard in Paris and later in the south exploring the land of the troubadours. Fossicking among the book-stalls on the *quais* of Paris one day in May he turned up some old books which he decided to buy: 'several ancient tomes', he told his family, 'that I may be able to use in my work'. He did not name them but most likely they were a Latin version of the *Odyssey* by Andreas Divus Justinopolitanus (Paris, 1538), an *Iliad* by Hugues Salel in French (1545) and another *Iliad* by M. de Rochefort (1772). The Andreas Divus contained also the *Batrachomyomachia* by Aldus Manutius, and the *Hymni Deorum* rendered by Georgius Dartona Cretensis. The Divus he mentioned in an article published the following year and a passage from it later served as the basis of the first canto of his long poem *The Cantos*. All three books he used in preparing his series of articles on translations from the classics which appeared in *The Egoist* between 1917 and 1919.

Also in Paris in May were Aldington and Hilda Doolittle and the three of them spent much of their time seeing the city together. One of the main attractions, for Aldington and Hilda, if not for Pound, was

Slominsky who on a bench in the 'Jardins du Luxembourg' filled their nights with talk of Hellas and Hellenism.

In May, Swift & Company published Pound's *Sonnets and Ballate of Giudo Cavalcanti* – identical with the American edition published by Small, Maynard on 27 April, except for a few minor revisions in the introduction and some of the poems. The dedication read: 'As much of this book as is mine I send to my friends Violet and Ford Madox Hueffer.' The introduction contains a formulation of an ideal arising out of his ambitions and the dreams aroused by his study of past literatures: 'I believe in an ultimate and absolute rhythm', he says, 'as I believe in an absolute symbol or metaphor. The perception of the intellect is given in the word, that of the emotions in the cadence. It is only, then, in the perfect rhythm joined to the perfect word that the twofold vision can be recorded.' He made much of this later and also of the related idea that music is composed of 'rhythm and nothing else' since variations in pitch are variations in the rhythms of the individual notes. 'When we know more of overtones,' he predicted, 'we will see that the tempo of every masterpiece is absolute, and is exactly set by some further law of rhythmic accord. Whence it should be possible to show that any given rhythm implies about it a complete musical form.' The rhythm of a line of poetry, therefore, 'connotes its symphony, which, had we a little more skill, we could score for orchestra'.

While in Paris he corrected the proofs of *Ripostes* and in the Bibliothèque Nationale studied the troubadours, taking notes in the manuscript-room from a medieval 'lives of the troubadours' written by Miquel de la Tour at Nîmes. He worked on translations for a small book devoted to Arnaut Daniel and also gave thought to the possibility of writing plays for a living when he returned to London; and he did in fact write later a short skit which he submitted to Yeats for the Abbey Theatre, but it was rejected by the manager, Pound said, on the grounds that its indecencies would cause a riot in Dublin. In June, two of his poems, 'The Return' and 'Apparuit', were published in *The English Review* and included later in *Ripostes*. 'The Return' is one of his most perfect pieces, in which simple direct speech is tethered to rhythms which seem to fall naturally into a formality scarcely yet undeniably present:

> See, they return; ah, see the tentative
> Movements, and the slow feet,
> The trouble in the pace and the uncertain
> Wavering!
>
> See, they return, one, and by one,
> With fear, as half-awakened;

As if the snow should hesitate
And murmur in the wind,
            and half turn back. . . .

The other poem, 'Apparuit', was an attempt to find an equivalent in
English of the ancient Sapphic measure:

Half the graven shoulder, the throat aflash with
strands of light inwoven about it, loveli-
est of all things, frail alabaster, ah me!
            swift in departing.

The line, 'when love dies down in the heart', from 'Planh' in *Exultations*, is given new life in:

Life died down in the lamp and flickered,
            caught at the wonder.

    Travelling south-east from Paris Pound explored Poitiers and Chalais;
from Limoges and Charente he walked the hills and followed the
rivers; he moved through the Dordogne, on one occasion losing the
road between Perigord and Excideuil and entering a cottage in search
of an omelet. Inside mending his children's shoes was a huge peasant
with a beard red like his own who welcomed him with 'gentleness
and dignity'. On 2 July he was in Rhodez, having passed through
Cahors; on the 6th he was in Toulouse, travelling south to Foix and
Carcassonne, and going as far as Narbonne. On a wet road near Cler-
mont he met a stray gipsy, 'a brown upstanding fellow' who asked him
whether he had seen a party of gipsies with apes or bears:

The wind came, and the rain,
And mist clotted about the trees in the valley,
And I'd the long ways behind me,
            gray Arles and Biaucaire,
And he said, 'Have you seen any of our lot?'
I'd seen a lot of his lot . . .
            ever since Rhodez,
Coming down from the fair
            of St John,
With caravans, but never an ape or a bear.

Pound carried with him an unstamped membership card and tin
button of the Touring Club de France which helped him to get into a
small inn at Chalus 'when covered with twenty miles of mud'. He

mentioned his explorations in the article 'Troubadours – Their Sorts and Conditions' in the October 1913 issue of the *Quarterly Review*: 'a man may walk the hill roads and river roads from Limoges and Charente to Dordogne and Narbonne and learn a little, or more than a little, of what the country meant to the wandering singers, he may learn, or think he learns, why so many canzos open with speech of the weather; or why such a man made war on such and such castles.'

He was back at Church Walk in August 1912, excited at having just discovered Flaubert whose novels were a completely new experience unlike anything he had encountered before. Another experience of some importance was Flint's fifty-nine page expository article on 'Contemporary French Poetry' in the August *Poetry Review* – an enthusiastic survey of the field which showed that Flint knew much more about the subject than any of his London contemporaries when it came to the actual texts of the poets concerned and their aims and theories. His general remarks on symbolism were not perhaps as important as his descriptions of the work of individual poets, but these too had an effect upon the general atmosphere among the poets in London. Symbolism, he said, was an attempt to 'evoke the subconscious element of life, to set vibrating the infinite within us, by the exquisite juxtaposition of images'. The music of symbolist language he likened to 'the revelation of the chromatic scale to a nation that had only known the diatonic,' so that for poets of the day 'the conception of their art had been enlarged until it was as wide and deep as life itself'. This kind of talk, backed by news of *vers libre* and new schools in France, was heady wine and played a part in provoking the poetic warfare which broke out over 'Imagisme' during the next few years.

Pound decided that his own group of three had as much right to call itself a 'school' as some of the French groups and so he began an advertising campaign on behalf of *Les Imagistes*. One of the first opportunities which presented itself was in August when Harriet Monroe in Chicago wrote asking him to contribute to a serious magazine she was about to publish under the title *Poetry*. She was a spinster twenty-five years older than Pound who had been introduced to his work by Elkin Mathews in London during the summer of 1910 while Pound was in America. She bought *Personae* and *Exultations* and read and re-read them on her way home to Chicago via Siberia. On 18 August 1912 Pound agreed to collaborate, at the same time warning her that for him poetry was an art of some complexity which ought not to be confused with the faded 'sociological dogma' in regular metre which passed for poetry among the magazine public. He sent two poems, 'Middle-Aged' and 'To Whistler, American', letting her know that the former was an 'Imagiste' piece. Harriet Monroe had no way of knowing what this meant since the new movement existed hardly at all outside Pound's own mind, but it was a beginning and no doubt served to arouse her curiosity.

Full of zeal now and hungry for activity in favour of the arts he began to hold 'Tuesday evenings' at his room; anybody wanting to see him on business, to discuss new projects, or to introduce other poets or artists could always find him at home on that evening. Florence Farr came, though not perhaps on a Tuesday, and read from the works of Rabindranath Tagore and it was through her, towards the end of August or at the beginning of September, that Pound first met the Bengali poet – a 'very great person' indeed. Influenced in part at least by Yeats's admiration for Tagore, he was seized with enthusiasm for the 'very beautiful English prose, with mastery of cadence' which Tagore used in translating his own Bengali poems. Pound was at this time reading 'more' of Henry James and early in September attended a performance of *Rebecca of Sunnybrook Farm*. He also made a discovery which he invited Aldington, Hilda and his friend Brigit Patmore to share. Brigit Patmore whom he had met through Violet Hunt was married to a successful insurance broker but spent much of her time in literary circles and moved a good deal with the *Imagistes*. When Pound's three friends arrived at his room on the evening of 3 September he introduced them to Marjorie Kennedy Fraser. According to Brigit Patmore's account half a century later Pound did not dwell upon trivialities but asked Mrs Fraser if she felt like singing right away. She placed a book of music on her knee and immediately began to sing some of the Gaelic folk songs which later became known to a wider public.

Using the unpublished articles he had written in America during the winter of 1910–11 Pound worked up a series on America called 'Patria Mia' which ran weekly in *The New Age* from 5 September until 14 November. In it he attempts to explain America to England and states his belief in the possibility of an American renaissance, with numerous asides and fleeting illustrations which while they presumably were clear to the writer of the articles are not always so to the reader. It is a mass of uncategorized impressions to which Pound has not properly addressed himself: there are delightful observations and flashes of intelligence but the greater part of the material remains outside the author's reach. The articles were revised the following year in the light of a second series called 'America: Chances and Remedies' which ran from 1 May until 5 June 1913. The typescript was sent to Chicago in 1913 for publication as a small book by Seymour, Daughaday & Company but disappeared in 1915 owing to the dissolution of the publishers' partnership. It came to light again in 1950 when it was published by Ralph Fletcher Seymour, one of the partners of the original firm. In 'America: Chances and Remedies' he discusses what are the necessary elements for a renaissance and decides they are two: 'an indiscriminate enthusiasm' and 'a propaganda'. Whilst his own activities stop short of 'indiscriminate enthusiasm' it was no doubt with a renaissance in mind that he threw himself so wholeheartedly into propaganda on behalf of Imagism and later of the arts generally.

Upon receiving Pound's agreement to collaborate with *Poetry* Harriet Monroe sent off immediately asking him to become the magazine's foreign correspondent. 'All right', he replied on 21 September, 'you can put me down as "foreign correspondent" or foreign editor if you like, and pay me whatever or whenever is convenient.' And before Miss Monroe had time to know what was happening Pound had stepped into his new post which he saw as twofold: to gather contributions worth publishing and to educate or if necessary to bully the editor into publishing them. In September he sent poems by Aldington and went after work by Tagore and Yeats. Tagore's poems, he assured her, were going to be '*the* sensation of the winter'. One day in the Museum Street tea-shop with Aldington and Hilda Doolittle he read through and corrected a poem by Hilda called 'Hermes of the Ways' and when he had finished he signed it 'H.D., Imagiste'. This he sent with a group of her poems in October, with a covering letter: 'I've had luck again, and am sending you some *modern* stuff by an American, I say modern, for it is in the laconic speech of the Imagistes, even if the subject is classic.' It was, he told Miss Monroe, the sort of American poetry he could show in London and Paris without its being ridiculed: 'no excessive use of adjectives, no metaphors that won't permit examination. It's straight talk, straight as the Greek!' A few days later he sent her a group of 'ultra-modern, ultra-effete' poems of his own under the general title 'Contemporania', but asked her not to use them until she had used the 'H.D.' and Aldington.

He was hoping to round-up for *Poetry* the best poets writing in English, no matter where they lived, and even discovered the 'faint beginnings of salvation' in the work of a New Zealand poet, Alice Kenny (1875–1960), whose poems sometimes appeared in *The Triad* published in Wellington, New Zealand. On 25 October he sent her an invitation to submit some poems for consideration but warned her that his standards were 'the stiffest' in Europe. It is possible that she submitted work but none ever appeared in *Poetry*.

Zealously applying the second Imagist principle, which was to use no word that was not essential to the presentation, Pound began to attack with a pencil any manuscript that was offered to him for his advice or comment. In Flint's first book, *In the Net of the Stars*, the poem 'A Swan' began thus:

> Among the lily leaves the swan,
> The pale, cold lily leaves, the swan,
> With mirrored neck, a silver streak,
> Tipped with a tarnished copper beak,
> Toward the dark arch floats slowly on;
> The water is deep and black beneath the arches.
>
> The fishes quiver in the pool
> Under the lily shadow cool,
> And ripples gilded by the whin,
> Painted, too, with a gloom of green,
> Mingled with lilac blue and mauve. . . .

After listening to Pound's comments Flint rewrote it:

> Under the lily shadow
> and the gold
> and the blue and mauve
> that the whin and the lilac
> pour down on the water
> the fishes quiver.
>
> Over the green cold leaves
> and the rippled silver
> and the tarnished copper
> of its neck and beak,
> toward the deep black water
> beneath the arches,
> the swan floats slowly.

Several years later however Flint wondered whether the first was not really a better Imagist poem than the second. Pound also suggested changes in the first sixteen lines of Harold Monro's 'The Strange Companion', some of which Monro incorporated into the final version published in his book *Children of Love* (1914).

The first issue of *Poetry* came out in October. It contained the announcement by Miss Monroe that 'Mr Ezra Pound, the young Philadelphian poet whose recent distinguished success in London led to wide recognition in his own country, authorizes the statement that at present such of his poetic work as receives magazine publication in America will appear exclusively in *Poetry*.' Among the poems in the first issue were the two sent by Pound in August:

And so the space
Of my still consciousness
Is full of gilded snow. . . .
   ('Middle-Aged')

You had your searches, your uncertainties,
And this is good to know – for us, I mean,
Who bear the brunt of our America
And try to wrench her impulse into art. . . .
            ('To Whistler, American', written following the
            1912 loan exhibition at the Tate.)

Yeats responded to Pound's appeal on behalf of *Poetry* by sending five poems, with a request to Pound to check the punctuation. Once he began to go through them Pound was unable apparently to resist the temptation to make three small changes in the wording. When he showed Yeats what he had done the older man was astounded at his cheek. Pound did what he could to placate him and Yeats when he looked more closely at the changes agreed that his wording was not perfect. In the end he accepted one change, refused another but altered the punctuation in an attempt to overcome the weakness Pound had pointed to, and in the third case refused to accept the change but later re-wrote the passage entirely.

In 1912, probably in the autumn, Pound was invited to read a paper at Cambridge. Among those who attended were T. E. Hulme and Edward Marsh. Hulme had been 'sent down' in 1904 but supported by a warm recommendation from Bergson he returned to St John's College in 1912. From 5 St Andrew Hill, Cambridge, Hulme sent a postcard to Marsh in London: 'Pound's paper is to be on Saturday instead of Sunday, at a man called J. Alford's rooms in King's at 8:30. If you come up in the afternoon will you come along to my place to tea. Pound will be here, or to dinner at 7 if you are up later.' As John Alford of King's College was one of the founders of an arts club called 'The Gods' it appears likely that Pound read his paper to the club.

In September 1912 Rupert Brooke and Edward Marsh had decided to publish a selection of the best recent verse, to be called *Georgian Poetry* after the new era ushered in by the coronation of George V. Marsh was secretary to the First Lord of the Admiralty, Winston Churchill, and an influential figure linking the world of poets with the world of power. He wrote asking Pound for two of his poems but they could not agree on which two, even after Marsh called at Church Walk one Tuesday evening to talk over the matter. *Georgian Poetry* was published in December by Harold Monro under the imprint of his

Poetry Bookshop then in process of opening at 35 Devonshire Street, Theobalds Road, not far from the British Museum. It was an immediate success, far beyond expectations and was followed by four similar volumes in 1915, 1917, 1919 and 1922. Although their paths crossed again later Pound and Marsh did not take to one another from the beginning and antipathy soon turned into hostility.

In mid-October another anthologist, Arthur Quiller-Couch, sought two other poems. 'Quiller-Couch wrote me', Pound told Harriet Monroe on 22 October, 'a delightful old-world letter a week ago. He hoped I did not despise the great name Victorian, and he wanted to put me in the *Oxford Book of Victorian Verse*. This is no small honour – at least I should count it a recognition.' The poems included at Quiller-Couch's suggestion were 'Ballad for Gloom' (*A Lume Spento*) and 'Portrait' (*Exultations*) which Pound had marked to be omitted from future editions of his work.

His *Ripostes*, dedicated to William Carlos Williams, was published by Swift & Co. in October, a big step forward from *Canzoni*. In twenty-two out of twenty-six poems he displays a new certainty of phrasing and movement, having cast off a number of stilted mannerisms and got closer to the directness he was seeking. His diction is clearer and he applies more art with less visible effort. Feelings or ideas which previously would have carried him automatically – in his *Canzoni* period, if not always earlier – towards an elevated discourse are dealt with now in a fashion formal yet relaxed. But most noticeable is the gain in simplicity:

> This thing, that hath a code and not a core,
> Hath set acquaintance where might be affections. . . .
> > ('An Object')

> for the day
> Hath lacked a something since this lady passed;
> Hath lacked a something. 'Twas but marginal.
> > ('Quies')

There is also a new effort to find just the right word:

> Come Beauty barefoot from the Cyclades,
> She'd find a model for St Anthony
> In this thing's sure *decorum* and behaviour.
> > ('Phasellus Ille')

and the right word turns out often to be the everyday word given new life:

These comforts heaped upon me, smother me!
I burn, I scald so for the new,
New friends, new faces,
Places!
Oh to be out of this,
This that is all I wanted
   – save the new.

('The Plunge')

In only two of the poems, 'Salve Pontifex' and 'Effects of Music upon a Company of People', both of them long, does the matter remain outside the control of the poet and of his versification and outside therefore of the poem.

A few weeks after the publication of *Ripostes* the firm of Swift & Co. collapsed. Pound wrote to his parents on 5 November: ' "Swift" is busted. They caught the *manager* in Tangier with *some* of the goods.' Three weeks later he was able to report that he was 'getting satisfactory terms out of Swift's liquidator'. He was more or less under contract to them to produce a book on Provençal poetry and was now glad that he did not have to finish it; he even destroyed some of his notes which was most annoying when four or five years later he took up again where he had left off. Elkin Mathews who took over the remaining copies and sheets of *Ripostes* issued in May 1913 a composite volume of *Canzoni & Ripostes of Ezra Pound* and in April 1915 *Ripostes* by itself, clad in heavy wrappers with a cubist design by Dorothy Shakespear Pound. Acting as agent for Pound he also sold copies of the Swift edition of *Sonnets and Ballate of Guido Cavalcanti*; but the bulk of the edition, still unbound, was destroyed by fire sometime between November 1915 and April 1917.

The second number of *Poetry*, issued in November, contained three poems by Richard Aldington who in the magazine's 'Notes and Announcements' was described as 'a young English poet, one of the "imagistes", a group of ardent Hellenists who are pursuing interesting experiments in *vers libre*; trying to attain in English certain subtleties of cadence of the kind which Mallarmé and his followers have studied in French. Mr Aldington has published little as yet, and nothing in America.' The poems included 'Choricos':

And of all the ancient songs
Passing to the swallow-blue halls
By the dark stream of Persephone,
This only remains:
That we turn to thee,

> Death,
> That we turn to thee, singing
> One last song.

and 'To a Greek Marble':

> I have told thee of the hills
> And the lisp of reeds
> And the sun upon thy breasts
> . . .
> Thou hearest me not.

Among the Aldington poems sent by Pound was one which Miss Monroe declined to print; it was called 'To Atthis (*After the Manuscript of Sappho now in Berlin*)' and was considered by University of Chicago scholars to whom Miss Monroe referred it to be too far from the Greek original. Writing to Pound on 9 November she said that the scholars 'wouldn't stand for it' and she thought it advisable not to antagonize them. In his reply Pound said that the original text was too mutilated for scholars to be able to talk about it in absolutes. Although at the time he said he did not altogether agree with Aldington's version he used it in his anthology *Des Imagistes*, mentioned it in 1918 as one of the few beautiful poems of the period that still rang in his head, and in canto 5 drew upon it in writing the passage about Sappho, beginning:

> and from 'Hesperus . . .'
> Hush of the older song: 'Fades light from sea-crest,
> 'And in Lydia walks with pair'd women
> 'Peerless among the pairs, that once in Sardis
> 'In satieties . . .'

and ending:

> So many things are set abroad and brought to mind
> Of thee, Atthis, unfruitful.

Pound introduced Aldington to Orage who used a number of his poems in *The New Age* between November 1912 and January 1913.

The December issue of *Poetry* contained five poems by Yeats, including the disputed three, and six by Tagore in his own prose translations. Pound contributed a two-page note on 'Tagore's Poems': 'The Bengali brings to us the pledge of a calm which we need over-much in an age of steel and mechanics. It brings a quiet proclamation of the fellowship between man and the gods; between man and nature.' It was all very well to object that this was not the first time such fellowship had been proclaimed, but in the arts alone could be found the inner heart of a people. There was, he said, a deeper calm and a deeper conviction 'in this eastern expression' than had yet been attained in the West. 'I speak with all gravity when I say that world-fellowship is nearer for the visit of Rabindranath Tagore to London.'

During the second week in December he sat down and wrote for *Poetry* a report on the state of things in London; it was published in January:

London, December 10, 1912. The state of things here in London is, as I see it, as follows:

I find Mr Yeats the only poet worthy of serious study. Mr Yeats's work is already a recognized classic and is part of the required reading in the Sorbonne. There is no need of proclaiming him to the American public.

As to his English contemporaries, they are food, sometimes very good food, for anthologies. There are a number of men who have written a poem, or several poems, worth knowing and remembering, but they do not much concern the young artist studying the art of poetry. . . .

I would rather talk poetry with Ford Madox Hueffer than with any man in London. Mr Hueffer's beliefs about the art may be best explained by saying that they are in diametric opposition to those of Mr Yeats.

Mr Yeats has been subjective; believes in the glamour and associations which hang near words. 'Works of art beget works of art.' He has much in common with the French symbolists. Mr Hueffer believes in an exact rendering of things. He would strip words of all 'associations' for the sake of getting a precise meaning. He professes to prefer prose to verse. You will find his origins in Gautier or in Flaubert. He is objective. This school tends to lapse into description. The other tends to lapse into sentiment.
. . .

The youngest school here that has the nerve to call itself a school is that of the *Imagistes*. To belong to a school does not in the least mean that one writes poetry to a theory. One writes poetry when, where, because, and as one feels like writing it. A school exists when two or three young men agree, more or less, to call certain things good; when they prefer such of their verses as have certain qualities to such of their verses as do not have them.

Space forbids me to set forth the programme of the *Imagistes* at length but one of their watchwords is Precision, and they are in opposition to the numerous and unassembled writers who busy themselves with dull and interminable effusions, and who seem to think that a man can write a good long poem before he learns to write a good short one, or even before he learns to produce a good single line.

Among the very young men, there seems to be a gleam of hope in the work of Richard Aldington, but it is too early to make predictions.

There are a number of men whose names are too well known for it to seem necessary to tell them over. America has already found their work in volumes or anthologies. Hardy, Kipling, Maurice Hewlett, Binyon, Robert Bridges, Sturge Moore, Henry Newbolt, McKail, Masefield, who has had the latest cry; Abercrombie, with passionate defenders, and Rupert Brooke, recently come down from Cambridge.

There are men also, who are little known to the general public, but who contribute liberally to the 'charm' of the 'atmosphere', of London; Wilfred Scawen Blunt, the grandest of old men, the last of the great Victorians; great by reason of his double sonnet, beginning –

> He who has once been happy is for aye
> Out of destruction's reach;

Ernest Rhys, weary with much editing and hack work, to whom we owe gold digged in Wales, translations, transcripts, and poems of his own, among them the fine one to Dagonet; Victor Plarr, one of the 'old' Rhymers' Club, a friend of Dowson and of Lionel Johnson. His volume, *In the Dorian Mood*, has been half forgotten, but not his verses *Epitaphium Citharistriae*. One would also name the Provost of Oriel, not for original work, but for his very beautiful translations from Dante.

In fact one might name nearly a hundred writers who have given pleasure, with this or that matter in rhyme. But it is one thing to take pleasure in a man's work and another to respect him as a great artist.

On 13 December he jotted down his earnings over the past three months and sent the list to his father. For October he showed a total of £16 15s 0d from *The New Age*, *The English Review*, *Poetry* and Small, Maynard & Company; for November a total of £4 13s 6d from *The New Age*, Dent and *Poetry*; and in December a total of £20 from *The New Age*, Small, Maynard & Company (who had undertaken to publish an American edition of *Ripostes*) and Anglo-German Amity. This last was, I take it, for a lecture, but I have not found any trace of it.

Tagore had left England for America; Pound wrote to him there towards the end of December:

> The little notice in *Poetry* was nothing. As you can see, the space in that magazine permits but the briefest sort of review.
>
> I have received proofs of my real article from the *Fortnightly Review*. I do not know how long it will be before they print it, their editor is prone to delay.
>
> I am sending you a brief volume of my own [*Ripostes*] as New Year's greeting. *Poetry* sent your draft with mine to London, but you will find it simpler if I send you the American cheque (as enclosed). I am sorry they send you prose rates but I have nothing to do with the finances of the magazine.
>
> Would you, even so, be willing to let us have some of the new translations. I will ask the editor to write you direct.

My father sends his appreciation of your poems.

I hope you will have the pleasantest of New Years in my country, and I shall await you here in the spring. I enjoy meeting your pupil Mr Ghose from whom I hear more of Bengal.

By correcting and polishing a literal translation supplied by Tagore's pupil, Kali Mohan Ghose, Pound prepared English versions of the great Hindi poet, Kabir (1440–1518). They were published in the *Modern Review*, Calcutta, in June 1913; they are of little importance poetically but may perhaps serve to give the English reader a rough idea of Kabir's work:

> The love between thee and me is from beginning to ending,
> How can it end in time?
> Saith Kabir: As the river is immersed in the ocean,
> My mind is immersed in thee.

The reader of Pound's *Pisan Cantos* will recognize in the oft-repeated 'Saith Kabir' of these poems the source of the 'Saith Kabir' in canto 77.

On 5 January 1913 Tagore wrote to Pound from 508 W. High Street, Urbana, Illinois, sending some more translations for *Poetry*:

I send you the recent translations that I made here. I am not at all strong in my English grammar – please do not hesitate to make corrections when necessary. Then again I do not know the exact value of your English words. Some of them may have their souls worn out by constant use and some others may not have acquired their souls yet. So in my use of words there must be lack of proportion and appropriateness perhaps, that also could be amended by friendly hands.

On 25 January Pound sent Tagore a copy of *Personae* for the sake, he said, of one poem in it, 'La Fraisne', which Ghose had found sympathetic. 'Your poems which I read at my lecture on Thursday were very well received and Mr Courtney promises to use my article in the February number of the *Fortnightly Review*, if possible, which is sooner than I expected he would.' But the article did not appear until the issue of 1 March. Writing from Felton Hall, Cambridge, Massachusetts, in February, Tagore thanked Pound for *Personae*: 'Your muse (pardon me for using this phrase) has come out, clothed in her own youthful body, full of life, vigour, and suggestive of incalculable possibilities of growth.'

In addition to Pound's report on the state of things in London the January 1913 issue of *Poetry* included a group of poems signed 'H.D., Imagiste' who was described as 'an American lady resident abroad, whose identity is unknown to the editor. Her sketches from the Greek are not offered as exact translations, or as in any sense finalities, but as experiments in delicate and elusive cadences, which attain sometimes a haunting beauty.' One of the poems was 'Hermes of the Ways':

> The hard sand breaks,
> And the grains of it
> Are clear as wine.

> Far off over the leagues of it,
> The wind,
> Playing on the wide shore,
> Piles little ridges,
> And the great waves
> Break over it.

Pound was beginning to be more and more important to Yeats who at the younger man's insistence was trying to overcome his tendency to rhetoric and to write more plainly and naturally. 'My digestion has got rather queer again', he wrote to Lady Gregory on 3 January, 'a result I think of sitting up late with Ezra and Sturge Moore and some light wine while the talk ran. However, the criticism I got from them has given me new life and I have made that Tara poem a new thing and am writing with new confidence having got Milton off my back. Ezra is the best critic of the two. He is full of the middle ages and helps me to get back to the definite and concrete away from modern abstractions. To talk over a poem with him is like getting you to put a sentence into dialect. All becomes clear and natural. Yet in his own work he is very uncertain, often very bad though very interesting sometimes. He spoils himself by too many experiments and has more sound principles than taste.'

John Cournos, a Russian-born journalist and poet who had given up his job as art critic on the *Philadelphia Record* to go abroad, interviewed Pound in December 1912 and sent back a story which appeared in the *Record* of 5 January 1913 under the heading 'Native Poet Stirs London'. After a standard opening, 'In years to come Philadelphia may brag of having furnished the world a great poet', and a rather ragged and approximate account of Pound's career, with quotations from *Canzoni*, *Ripostes* and 'Patria Mia', the article ends: 'In his own particular domain of poetry, however – to judge from the discontented progressive nature of the poet – no one need be astonished if, after having passed through the various stages of his wide-ranged development and manifold experiment, he shall achieve something altogether new and distinctly his own, just as in the art of painting a certain distinguished countryman of Pound's succeeded in being Whistler, despite Velasquez and the Japanese.' Pound introduced Cournos to Yeats and Hueffer, took him to a poets' dinner attended by Edward Marsh, Henry Newbolt and others, encouraged him in the writing of a book on American painting, and managed to sell some of his work for him when he needed the money. Cournos described him years later as 'one of the kindest men that ever lived'.

While there is every indication that Pound was not well liked in literary and artistic circles, except by a few, he was by many respected and seen to hold a special position in the literary affairs of the day; he was a writer you could not altogether ignore even though you were puzzled by some of his behaviour and enthusiasms – which attitude perhaps accounts for the couplet in *Punch* of 22 January 1913:

> The bays that formerly old Dante crowned
> Are worn today by Ezra Loomis Pound.

And so naturally there were young men at Oxford who wanted to hear more of him at first hand, which led to an invitation to address the St John's College Essay Society in Hilary Term. The evening was arranged by the society's Vice-President, W. G. Lawrence, brother of T. E. Lawrence. And in fact some of the stimulus may have come from T.E. who on 12 September 1912 had written to his mother from Carchemish: 'The great risk of Pound's poetry is the symbolic for its own sake. He has educated himself on old books and never correlated them. A good poet though.'

The address was fixed for nine o'clock Sunday evening, 2 February, but at W. G. Lawrence's request Pound was invited by Ernest Barker to dine in Hall beforehand; it was almost certainly this dinner at which he encountered 'a very ancient Oxford "head"' who gave evidence, according to Pound, of the benefit of a classic education. In the middle of dinner discovering that Pound was a poet the old reverend gentleman turned and said that someone had the other day shown him 'a new poem', *The Hound of Heaven*. When Pound asked, 'Well, what did you think of it?' he answered, 'Couldn't be bothered to stop for every adjective.' Inserting an account of this incident a few months later into the book *Patria Mia* Pound said he could scarcely have heard such independent criticism from anybody in America who like the Oxonian was speaking outside his own field. 'Nothing under the American heaven would have evoked that swift and profound censure, that scrap of criticism which touches the root and seed of Thompson's every defect.' Of Pound's address later in the evening I have been able to find only a brief note in the Essay Society's minute book for 1913: 'A public meeting was held in Mr George's rooms on Feb. 2nd when Mr Ezra Pound, poet, gave a study of "Guido Cavalcanti". The V.P. thanked the reader in the name of the Society, and the President [S. M. Ball, M.A.] opened a discussion in which Mr Barker and Mr Snow were prominent. The Society adjourned about 11.0 p.m. There was an innumerable company present. [Signed] W. G. Lawrence, V.P.' When he heard of the address, T. E. Lawrence wrote to his mother on 6 March: 'I am glad Will got Ezra Pound: and that he was a success: sounds a very curious person.' Will Lawrence visited Pound in London on 2 June, and was introduced to Tagore. He went out to India later in the year and on 24 December wrote to his mother from Bolphur, Bengal: 'It's very pleasant meeting Tagore in his own home. You'll remember Ezra Pound introduced me to him.'

Early in 1913 Pound called on F. S. Flint and asked if he would care to conduct an interview with Pound on behalf of *Poetry*. Flint said yes, what questions would be appropriate. No need of questions, Pound replied, and drew from his pocket the typescript of an already completed interview if Flint would just sign on the last page. But when the other pointed to certain stylistic idiosyncrasies it was agreed he should re-write it closer to his own style. The second version with certain revisions by Pound appeared in the March 1913 issue of *Poetry* under the title 'Imagisme'. It was prefaced by an editorial note saying that 'In response to many requests for information regarding *Imagism* and *Imagistes*, we publish this note by Mr Flint, supplementing it with further exemplification by Mr Pound. It will be seen from these that *Imagism* is not necessarily associated with Hellenic subjects, or with *vers libre* as a prescribed form.' Unable, says Flint, to find anything about *Imagism* in print, he sought out an *Imagiste* to discover whether the group itself knew anything about a 'movement':

The *imagistes* admitted that they were contemporaries of the Post Impressionists and the Futurists; but they had nothing in common with these schools. They had not published a manifesto. They were not a revolutionary school; their only endeavour was to write in accordance with the best tradition, as they found it in the best writers of all time, – in Sappho, Catullus, Villon. They seemed to be absolutely intolerant of all poetry that was not written in such endeavour, ignorance of the best tradition forming no excuse. They had few rules, drawn up for their own satisfaction only, and they had not published them. They were:

1. Direct treatment of the 'thing' whether subjective or objective.

2. To use absolutely no word that does not contribute to the presentation.

3. As regarding rhythm: to compose in the sequence of the musical phrase, not in sequence of a metronome.

By these standards they judged all poetry, and found most of it wanting.

The Imagistes also held, he said, a certain '"Doctrine of the Image",' which they had not committed to writing; it did not, they said, concern the public and would only provoke useless discussion. If another poet submitted his work to them they showed him his own thought already splendidly expressed in some classic ('and the school musters altogether a most formidable erudition'); they also rewrote his verses before his eyes, using about ten words to his fifty. He found among them, he said, an earnestness that was amazing to one accustomed to the usual London air of poetic dilettantism; they considered that Art was 'all science, all religion, philosophy and metaphysic'. It was true that *snobisme* might be urged against them but it was *snobisme* in its most dynamic form with a great deal of sound sense and energy behind it: 'and they are stricter with themselves than with any outsider.'

This 'interview' was followed by Pound's 'A Few Don'ts by an Imagiste' in which he defined an image as that which presents an intellectual and emotional 'complex' in an instant of time. In this he was following the English psychologist Hart, who was indebted to Freud. This complex, Pound said, gives rise to a sense of sudden liberation from the limits of time and space – an idea which may have owed something to Bergson's theory of intuition, but like most of Pound's criticism was probably born of Pater. The actual 'Don'ts' dealt with technique:

Use no superfluous word, no adjective which does not reveal something.

Don't use such an expression as 'dim lands *of peace*'. It dulls the image. It mixes an abstraction with the concrete. It comes from the writer's not realizing that the natural object is always the *adequate* symbol.

Go in fear of abstractions. Do not retell in mediocre verse what has already been done in good prose.

. . .

Don't chop up your stuff into separate *iambs*. Don't make each line stop dead at the end, and then begin again every next line with a heave. Let the beginning of the next line catch the rise of the rhythm wave, unless you want a definite longish pause.

Not long after Robert Frost came to live in England he attended by accident the official opening on 8 January 1913 of Monro's Poetry Bookshop and there met Flint. 'I was only too childishly happy', he wrote to Flint on 21 January, 'in a company in which I hadn't to be ashamed of having written verse. Perhaps it will help you to understand my state of mind if I tell you that I have lived for the most part in villages where it were better that a millstone were hanged about your neck than that you should own yourself a minor poet.' Flint later introduced him to Pound who when he heard that Frost's first book, *A*

Boy's Will, was in the process of publication, went with him to the office of the publisher, David Nutt, and obtained an advance copy. As soon as he saw that Frost in his verse had the gift of speaking naturally in his own voice, and of describing things simply, Pound sat down and wrote a review. 'Have just discovered another Amur'kn', he wrote to Alice Corbin Henderson of *Poetry* in March. 'Vurry Amur'kn, with, I think, the seeds of grace. Have reviewed an advance copy of his book, but have run it out too long. Will send it as soon as I've tried to condense it – also some of his stuff if it isn't all in the book.' Frost's story was that only one advance copy was available at the publisher's and that Pound commandeered it for his review. Sent to *Poetry* later in March and published in the May number this was the first review of Frost's work to appear in the United States. But things did not always run smoothly even in promoting work as straightforward as Frost's. Harriet Monroe was not very keen on the first examples of his work that reached her and it was some months before she could allow herself to publish him. The promotion of William Carlos Williams's work in London and America at this time was also in large measure due to Pound. The previous October he had written an introduction to a selection of his poems published in *The Poetry Review* and in March 1913 Williams's *The Tempers* was brought out by Elkin Mathews. During the following twelve months Pound reviewed *The Tempers*, put Williams in touch with Harriet Monroe who published his 'Postlude' in June, included 'Postlude' in his Imagist anthology and saw to the publication of Williams's long poem-sequence 'The Wanderer: A Rococo Study' in *The Egoist*.

Pound's own poetry meanwhile had reached a new stage with the composition in 1912 and publication in *Poetry* in April 1913 of his 'Contemporania' – a collection of short poems in which he sought to render things directly and clearly in verse that was closely related to the spoken language. He had sent them to Harriet Monroe in two lots in October and December 1912 but for a time at least she considered them too outspoken. In a letter to his mother in January 1914 Pound claimed that 'it was Tagore who poked my "Contemporania" down the Chicago gullet. Or at least read it aloud to that board of imbeciles on *Poetry* and told 'em how good the stuff was.' Sometimes the poems are conversational:

> You were praised, my books,
>> because I had just come from the country;
> I was twenty years behind the times
>> so you found an audience ready.
>
> ('Salutation the Second')

At other times they are firmer and more 'chiselled':

> I mate with my free kind upon the crags;
>   the hidden recesses
> Have heard the echo of my heels,
>   in the cool light,
>   in the darkness.
>
>   ('Tenzone')

There are traces of this firmness in his earlier poetry but in 'Contemporania' he is able to maintain it throughout the length of most of the poems. Whether this is the 'Latin tone' which he strove for, or the 'hardness' of Catullus and Martial, as he thought, I must leave to experts to decide; but without doubt he achieves a coolness in presentation which leaves the poem free to speak for itself. The ideas are the poet's but in these poems preserved as it were in glass:

> Dawn enters with little feet
>   like a gilded Pavlova,
> And I am near my desire.
>
>   ('The Garrett')

> Like a skein of loose silk blown against a wall
> She walks by the railing of a path in Kensington
>   Gardens,
> And she is dying piece-meal
>   of a sort of emotional anaemia.
>   ('The Garden')

He has so well pared back his thought and so patiently listened to get the bare force of it into appropriate words that this same impression of ideas preserved in glass applies even to a poem like 'A Pact' which is made of statements rather than images:

> I make a pact with you, Walt Whitman –
> I have detested you long enough.
> I come to you as a grown child
> Who has had a pig-headed father;
> I am old enough now to make friends.

One of the poems in the group was 'In a Station of the Metro' which first came to him in Paris in the spring of 1911. He gave a brief account of it in the article 'How I Began' which was written about eighteen months after the experience of which it tells and published in *T.P.'s Weekly* of 6 June 1913:

For well over a year I have been trying to make a poem of a very beautiful thing that befell me in the Paris Underground. I got out of a train at, I think, La Concorde, and in the jostle I saw a beautiful face, and then, turning suddenly, another and another, and then a beautiful child's face, and then another beautiful face. All that day I tried to find words for what this made me feel. That night as I went home along the rue Raynouard I was still trying. I could get nothing but spots of colour. I remember thinking that if I had been a painter I might have started a wholly new school of painting. I tried to write the poem weeks afterwards in Italy, but found it useless. Then only the other night, wondering how I should tell the adventure, it struck me that in Japan, where a work of art is not estimated by its acreage and where sixteen syllables are counted enough for a poem if you arrange and punctuate them properly, one might make a very little poem which would be translated about as follows:

> The apparition of these faces in the crowd;
> Petals on a wet, black bough.

And there, or in some other very old, very quiet civilization, some one else might understand the significance.

In April 1913 Pound went to Paris where he met the poets Jules Romains and Charles Vildrac and was present at a meeting of their 'group' attended by about twenty writers including Georges Duhamel and Jean Pierre Jouve. He had read some Romains a year or two before and in February 1913 had published in *Poetry* a short review of Jouve's *Présences*: 'I take pleasure in welcoming, in Monsieur Jouve, a contemporary. He writes the new jargon and I have not the slightest doubt that he is a poet. Whatever may be said against automobiles and aeroplanes and the modernist way of speaking of them . . . still it is indisputable that the vitality of the time exists in such work.' At the group's meeting he was impressed by the fact that the one older man he heard them mention with sympathy, the one to whom, it seemed, they could look for comprehension, was Remy de Gourmont. He could even be relied on, they said, to send a telegram to be read at a public meeting they were planning. This contact with an active French group was a step in the development of his interest in modern French poetry. Flint had stimulated his curiosity about living French poets; now he was meeting some of them for himself. One immediate result was a review of Romains' *Odes et prières* in the August *Poetry*. In Paris he also met for the first time two American poets, John Gould Fletcher, from Little Rock, Arkansas, and Skipwith Cannell, from Philadelphia, both like himself living abroad. In London a month or two later he borrowed Fletcher's collection of books by modern French poets and wrote a series called 'The Approach to Paris' which appeared in *The New Age* in seven instalments from 4 September to 16 October. Among those dealt with were Remy de Gourmont, Henri de Regnier, Jules Romains, Charles Vildrac, Laurent Tailhade, Tristan Corbière, Francis Jammes, Arthur Rimbaud, Paul Fort, Henri-Martin Barzun and André Spire. In the October issue of *Poetry* he summarized his conclusions: one could form 'a not inaccurate idea' of what the term 'Modern French poetry' meant, he said, by reading Corbière, De Regnier, Tailhade, De Gourmont and Jammes. There was no mention of Jules Laforgue but Rimbaud and Apollinaire were tacked on at the end: 'M. Rimbaud is also very important, if you do not know him already . . . Also *Alcools*, by Guillaume Apollinaire (Mercure) is clever.' He did not meet Apollinaire but the latter apparently heard that Pound was writing about recent French poetry and sent him a copy of *Alcools* for review. 'Clever' appears to have been Pound's only word on the subject.

From Paris he went to Sirmione (where he 'Rec'd £28, with thanks, salaams etc' from *Poetry*) and then on to Venice. Among the friends he met there were Professor and Mrs Doolittle and also Hilda Doolittle and Richard Aldington. 'All Venice went to a rather interesting concert at "La Fenice" on Wednesday,' he wrote to his mother in May, 'and I also, thanks to Signora Brass, for the entrance is mostly by invitation.' He wondered whether she remembered 'La Fenice', a very beautiful eighteenth-century theatre 'where you might meet anyone from Goethe to Rossini'. He sent her postcards of what he believed to be a Donatello madonna and an interior which he thought she had missed during her visit there. From Venice he went to Munich and before the end of May he was back in London scouting for new material for *Poetry*.

His first success was to obtain a long article by Hueffer, 'Impressionism: Some Speculations', which he described to Harriet Monroe as 'the best prose we've had or are likely to get'. Published in the August and September issues it impressed him first of all because he was greatly under the other's influence but also because buried amongst the meandering prose were ideas which recommended themselves to him – which helped him in the way he was already going. The business of poetry, Hueffer said, was 'not sentimentalism so much as the putting of certain realities in certain aspects', or the putting of 'one thing in juxtaposition with the other' because 'such juxtapositions suggest emotions'. For Pound, who was already thinking of poems composed of images, here was an invitation to 'suggest emotions' by the placing of a number of images one after the other. Hueffer gave as an example 'the ashbucket at dawn' which was a symbol of poor humanity, of its aspirations, its romance, its ageing and its death. 'The ashes represent the sociable fires . . . the orange peels with their bright colours represent all that is left of a little party of the night before . . . The empty tin of infant's food stands for birth; the torn-up scrap of a doctor's prescription for death.' Another aspect of the article which no doubt pleased Pound was Hueffer's declaration in favour of the language of his own day, a language clear enough for certain matters, he said, employing slang where slang was felicitous and vulgarity where it seemed that vulgarity was the only weapon against dullness. 'I am for ever on the look-out for some poet who shall render modern life with all its values. I do not think that there was ever, as the saying is, such a chance for the poet; I am breathless, I am agitated at the thought of having it to begin upon.' The article was published again later as the preface to Hueffer's *Collected Poems* (1914).

Pound was now playing tennis regularly with Hueffer on the court available to the tenants of South Lodge; he would listen to what Hueffer had to say about style in the afternoon and that evening he would use it as a lure to draw out Yeats. In this way he encouraged Yeats towards a new gauntness in his poetry and between the two older men managed also to clarify some of his own ideas about style. By all accounts Pound's tennis was a strange sight to behold, with much extraneous leaping and many oddities but often effective against more conventional opponents.

On 31 May he and Dorothy went to 'a terribly literary dinner' attended by Tagore and his son, Maurice Hewlett, May Sinclair, Evelyn Underhill and George Prothero, editor of the *Quarterly Review*. Evelyn Underhill collaborated with Tagore in bringing out a book of *One Hundred Poems of Kabir* in 1914. Pound was very pleased with a new poem by Frost called 'Death of the Farm Hand'; it was better, he thought, than anything in his recent book. Without asking permission he sent it to the *Smart Set* in New York; Frost was angry and demanded that it be recalled. It was not printed but their brief partnership was dissolved. Tagore lectured 'very finely' on 2 June and although Pound was still interested in the Bengali's work and reviewed his second book, *The Gardener*, towards the end of the year, he was beginning to grow tired of his cadenced prose and also of his philosophy which was too passive and too consistently and vaguely optimistic for Pound who thrived on activity and liked occasionally a dash of realistic pessimism.

Skipwith Cannell and his wife Kathleen visited him at Church Walk where later he found a room for them below his. He sent some of Cannell's poetry to Harriet Monroe and took the couple to South Lodge and to one of Yeats's evenings. Fletcher also visited him and although they never hit it off together Pound sent some of his work to *Poetry* and reviewed favourably two of his books in the December issue. Other visitors to Church Walk included Henri-Martin Barzun, over from Paris, John Helston, a turner and fitter who in 1913 published a book called *Aphrodite and Other Poems*, and Paul Selver who contributed articles and translations of Slav poetry to *The New Age* and other journals. When Pound wrote to his father on 3 June, he was finishing the typescript of the book *Patria Mia* for Ralph Fletcher Seymour and 'doing a tale of Bertrans de Born'. It is not clear whether this was a story or a first attempt perhaps at the long poem, 'Near Perigord', published in *Poetry* in December 1915. Rummel was in London again and on Friday 6 June he played for some of his friends and their guests at Mrs Fowler's. The following week Pound attended a concert at 3 p.m. Thursday 12 June at the Aeolian Hall in New Bond Street when Rummel gave 'the first entire performance in England' of Debussy's twelve preludes (book II) of 1912–13. On 26 March Augener had published Rummel's *Hesternae Rosae*, nine troubadour songs with piano accompaniment and a translation of each song into English by Pound and into modern French by M. D. Calvocoressi. In his preface dated 1912 Rummel wrote: 'The two Daniel melodies are here published for the first time to the writer's knowledge, and he is indebted to Mr Ezra Pound, M.A., for communicating them from the Milan Library. . . The writer with the help of Mr Ezra Pound, an ardent proclaimer of the artistic side of mediaeval poetry, has given these melodies the rhythm and the ligature, the character which, from an artistic point of view, seems the most descriptive of the mediaeval spirit.'

Imagism was now beginning to attract attention. The June issue of Harold Monro's magazine, now called *Poetry and Drama*, mentioned 'a new school of English poetry still at present very small and under the formidable dictatorship of Ezra Pound'. Word also got about that Pound was contemplating an anthology of the new school. On 22 June when *Georgian Poetry* after only six months was in its sixth edition, Marsh wrote to Rupert Brooke: 'Wilfred [Gibson] tells me there's a movement for a "Post-Georgian" Anthology, of the Pound-Flint-Hulme school, who don't like being out of *GP*, but I don't think it will come off.' At Brookline, Massachusetts, a rich American poet, Amy Lowell, after reading about Imagism in *Poetry*, secured from Harriet Monroe a letter of introduction to Pound and headed for London to make further enquiries.

Taking his cue from Hueffer, Pound began to promote the work of D. H. Lawrence despite his lack of sympathy for the man himself and much of what he wrote. 'Detestable person', he said to Harriet Monroe in March 1913, 'but needs watching. I think he learned the proper treatment of modern subjects before I did.' He later sent some of Lawrence's work to *Poetry* and also to the *Smart Set*, whose editor, Willard Huntington Wright, had recently called on Pound in London. In his review of Lawrence's *Love Poems and Others* in the July *Poetry* Pound said: 'When Mr Lawrence ceases to discuss his own disagreeable sensations, when he writes low-life narrative, as he does in "Whether or Not" and in "Violets", there is no English poet under forty who can get within shot of him.' As a result of Lawrence's prose training his characters were real, Pound said, not just stock figures done from the outside and provided with cliché emotions. 'Mr Lawrence has attempted realism and attained it. He has brought contemporary verse up to the level of contemporary prose, and that is no mean achievement.' Writing to Harriet Monroe on 13 August about the inclusion of some of Lawrence's poems in *Poetry*, he said that although Lawrence gave him no particular pleasure they were nevertheless lucky to get him; Hueffer, for one, thought highly of him and he himself recognized certain qualities. 'If I were an editor I should probably accept his work without reading it. As a prose writer I grant him first place among the younger men.'

As a result of a visit to 10 Church Walk of a young woman active in the feminist movement of the day Pound was brought into touch with *The New Freewoman: An Individualist Review* which was founded by Harriet Shaw Weaver and Dora Marsden in June. Beginning 15 August Pound was given charge temporarily of the paper's literary department. This first issue in which he collaborated contained a selection of his 'Contemporania', which had already been noticed by Rebecca West, and an article by her on 'Imagisme'. When he wrote to Henry James asking whether he had anything to contribute James replied that he had no charming little pieces on hand that might be suitable for a journal calling itself *The New Freewoman*; he invited Pound to watch out lest he end up as 'Bondsman'.

Miss Lowell meanwhile had established herself in a suite at the Berkeley Hotel in Piccadilly and invited Pound to dinner. 'Figure to yourself a young man arrayed as "poet",' she wrote to Harriet Monroe, 'and yet making the costume agreeable by his personal charm; a sweep of conversation and youthful enthusiasm which keeps him talking delightfully as many hours as you please; the violence of his writings giving way to show a very thin-skinned and sensitive personality opening out like a flower in a sympathetic circle, and I should imagine shutting up like a clam in an alien atmosphere.' Eleven years older than Pound Miss Lowell thought that 'all sorts of developments' might be expected of him and was inclined to believe that his 'chip-on-the-shoulder attitude' would disappear in time. Pound for his part described her to Miss Monroe as 'pleasingly intelligent'. He arranged for her to meet Yeats, took her to tea at South Lodge and on behalf of *The New Freewoman* asked for her poem 'In a Garden' which had appeared in the July issue of *Poetry*. He later included it in his anthology *Des Imagistes*.

In *The New Freewoman* of 1 September he published a review of Frost's *A Boy's Will*, making it also the occasion of an attack on the American literary scene: 'There is another personality in the realm of verse, another American, found as usual, on this side of the water, by an English publisher long known as a lover of good letters. David Nutt publishes at his own expense *A Boy's Will*, by Robert Frost, the latter having long been scorned by the "great American editors".' Although he and Frost were by now estranged Pound did not hesitate in praising the other's verse. It was a 'little raw' but underneath the infelicities was the tang of the New Hampshire woods. 'This man has the good sense to speak naturally and to paint the thing, the thing as he sees it.'

On 22 October, at 10 Church Walk, Pound had his photograph taken by the photographer Alvin Langdon Coburn. As Pound was recovering from an attack of jaundice he posed in his dressing-gown. He was very pleased with one of Coburn's exposures which in 1916 he used as frontispiece to *Lustra*. Mr Shakespear thought it looked like the portrait of 'a sinister but very brilliant Italian'. Mrs Langley said it was the only photograph which had ever done him justice and as she was moving out of the room she offered, with increasing embarrassment ('I hope you won't be offended, sir'), the opinion that 'it *is* rather like the good man of Nazareth, isn't it sir?'

With Dora Marsden and Harriet Shaw Weaver attending to the feminist and philosophical contents of *The New Freewoman* Pound was left free to run the literary section more or less as he liked. He took the opportunity to insert into its pages two essays of his in which he attempted to put some of his ideas in order. The first was 'The Serious Artist', published in three instalments between 15 October and 15 November. Very clearly in this essay Pound sets out to show that the arts have a place in the community and can be justified because they are a science 'just as chemistry is'. Where chemistry studies the composition of matter, the arts 'give us a great percentage of the lasting and unassailable data regarding the nature of man, of immaterial man, of man considered as a thinking and sentient creature'. From medicine, he says, we learn that man thrives best when duly washed, aired and sunned; from the arts we learn that one man differs from another and that they do not resemble each other as do buttons cut by machine. It follows from this that an artist who 'falsifies his report', for whatever reason, is no better than a doctor or scientist who falsifies his, and should be punished or despised in proportion to the seriousness of his offence. Pound goes on to say that the 'touchstone of an art is its precision'. In the case of writing it shows in the way an author controls the energy seeking outlet and says just what he means 'with complete clarity and simplicity' and using the smallest possible number of words. Poetry he regarded as something like *maximum efficiency of expression*, taking into account that in verse the 'thinking, word-arranging, clarifying faculty must move and leap with the energizing, sentient, musical faculties'. It is, he says, the difficulty of 'this amphibious existence' which keeps down the number of good poets.

On the difference between poetry and prose he says that certain poignant verse has a passionate simplicity 'which is beyond the precisions of the intellect'. As perfect as fine prose it is in some way different; for without violating prose simplicity it goes beyond the clear statement of an observer and brings the intellect into contact with 'the passionate moment'. Whereas in fine prose the intelligence has found a subject for its observations, in the verse something has 'come upon' the intelligence. 'The poetic fact pre-exists.'

In this same essay Pound shows signs of a more positive interest than before in economics and social affairs. This new turn is discernible in some of his letters of the previous year, in one of which he expresses the hope that the President 'really means to smash the trusts'. It shows also in the article, 'Troubadours – Their Sorts and Conditions', published in the October 1913 issue of the *Quarterly Review*. There he speaks of a corrupt press and monopoly and of the fact that there exists always in some form or other a 'conspiracy of ignorance and interest'.

The second essay, which appeared on 15 November was a review of Allen Upward's *The Divine Mystery*. Accepting Upward wholeheartedly as the final word on folk-lore and the history of religions Pound found in him two things of great importance in the development of his own ideas: a scientific explanation of genius which seemed to accord with and place in their universal context his own ideas on the subject and secondly a kind of scientific rule for the measurement of religious ideas. At the head of the review he gave a long passage from the beginning of the book, concerning the 'lord of the thunder'. One day while 'resident' in Nigeria Upward had seen the 'lord of the thunder' going dressed in his wizard's robe to a nearby town to call down the thunder from heaven. After he had danced his special dance before the king and his people it thundered for the first time in many days. The 'secret of genius', says Upward, 'is sensitiveness. The Genius of the Thunder who revealed himself to me could not call the thunder, but he could be called by it. He was more quick than other men to feel the changes of the atmosphere; perhaps he had rendered his nervous system more sensitive still by fasting or mental abstraction; and he had learned to read his own symptoms as we read a barometer. So, when he felt the storm gathering round his head, he put on his symbolical vestment and marched forth to be its Word, the archetype of all Heroes in all Mysteries.'

For Pound it seemed that here as in a nutshell was an explanation at once scientific and wide enough to account for a great deal of religious and artistic phenomena. Not only had Upward traced the gradual recognition of the sun, of the 'life-giving Helios', and the growth of religion and superstition from the thunder-maker to the idea of the messiah, he had shown how so many of the detestable customs of modern life had their roots in superstition. At every point he seemed to bring matters long hidden into the clear. Thus the ecclesiastical inter-pretation of the Bible was a sham; thus those who upheld what they were pleased to call the 'sacrament' of marriage were merely perpetuat-ing the laws of slave concubinage; thus 'the charming pastoral figure of Jesus' was left in a better light by Upward than by the advocates of the religion the Nazarene was accused of founding. By presenting 'simple fact after simple fact' Upward with his 'sense of major relations' had exposed the unutterable silliness of all the canting fools by whom Pound had ever been plagued. 'If one has been "reared in the Christian faith" and been forced to eat at the same table with ministers and members of the Y.M.C.A., it is pleasant to know for certain just what part of their conversation is pure buncomb.' Upward, with his mind balanced by nature and a knowledge of the Chinese classics, was 'a focus': 'The enlightenments of our era have come to him. He has seen how the things "put together".' Far from being an impious book *The Divine Mystery* was the work of one of the 'devoutest men of the age' who simply insisted that the real God was 'neither a cad nor an imbecile'. In Upward, in other words, he had found a key with which to free those ideas and feelings about science and religion that had been forming in his mind without his being able to bring them into focus. Now he could employ them in his thought and work.

Before Pound had found a publisher for his anthology of Imagist poetry he received a visit from John Cournos bearing a letter from a new American periodical called *The Glebe* whose editors were searching for contributors. Pound offered them the anthology which by early November they had accepted for publication as soon as possible.

In November *Poetry* published a large group of poems by Pound in his new style. In a number of them we see him reaching towards his ideal of 'maximum efficiency of expression':

The tricksome Hermes is here;
He moves behind me
Eager to catch my words
Eager to spread them with rumour. . . .

('Surgit Fama')

She passed and left no quiver in the veins, who now
Moving among the trees, and clinging
                              in the air she severed,
Fanning the grass she walked on then, endures. . . .

('Gentildonna')

You who can know at first hand,
Hated, shut in, mistrusted:

Take thought:
I have weathered the storm,
I have beaten out my exile.

('The Rest')

The poems from which these extracts are taken were later published in
Lustra, as were the following which first appeared in the December
1913 issue of the *Smart Set*:

As a bathtub lined with white porcelain,
When the hot water gives out or goes tepid,
So is the slow cooling of our chivalrous passion. . . .

('The Bath Tub')

'It rests me to converse with beautiful women
Even though we talk nothing but nonsense,

The purring of the invisible antennae
Is both stimulating and delightful.'

('Tame Cat')

Thanking his mother in November for a birthday present of money
he said he would buy four luxurious undershirts, or rather that he had
planned to do so until a 'bloody guardsman' stole his luxurious hat from
the cloak-room at the Cabaret Theatre Club off Regent Street. If it
was not returned he might have to divert some of the money to buy a
new one. The Cabaret Theatre Club, also known as the Cave of the
Golden Calf, was run by Strindberg's second wife, Freda. Decorated in
violent colours and designs by Wyndham Lewis and other artists it was

one of London's first night-clubs and the only one, according to Pound many years later, which admitted 'impoverished artists'. For those lucky enough to be accepted at Freda's table the food was free. In speaking to Pound of the club she explained that it was her need of money that had caused her to take up prostitution 'in this particular form'. On another occasion he saw her wave a customer away from her table saying as she did so that sleep with him she would, but talk to him, never: 'One must draw the line *somewhere*.'

In the same letter to his mother Pound said that he seemed to spend most of his time attending to other people's affairs, such as weaning 'young poetettes' from obscurity into the pages of 'divers rotten publications' and besieging the Home Office to allow the American poet Harry Kemp, a stowaway, to remain in England.[1] One of his 'poetettes' was Frances Gregg, a friend of Hilda's, whom he had known in Philadelphia in 1906. In October 1913 he conceded that she had written 'a permissible poem' and told her to get in touch with *Poetry*. His other news for his mother included the fact that Aldington and Hilda had been 'decently married' a week or two before and the statement that Jacob Epstein was a great sculptor: 'I wish he would wash, but I believe Michel Angelo *never* did, so I suppose it is part of the tradition.'

In November Pound and Yeats went to spend three months at Stone Cottage, Coleman's Hatch, in the Ashdown Forest, Sussex, where they were looked after by two sisters, the Misses Wellfare. The idea was for Pound to act as Yeats's secretary. Yeats spent much of his time attempting to correlate Lady Gregory's Irish folk-lore with myths and religious stories from other countries – an exercise which carried on over several winters helped to strengthen Pound's belief in the importance of myth. In the course of a row with Harriet Monroe in November over the contents of *Poetry* and other matters, Pound resigned in Hueffer's favour, only to have Hueffer resign, according to Pound, in his favour, with the result that by 8 December Pound was once again the magazine's foreign correspondent. At the same time Yeats suggested to Miss Monroe that of the £50 awarded to him as a prize by *Poetry* £40 might go to Pound: 'I suggest him to you because, although I do not really like with my whole soul the metrical experiments he has made for you, I think those experiments show a vigorous imaginative mind. He is certainly a creative personality of some sort, though it is too soon yet to say of what sort. His experiments are perhaps errors, I am not certain; but I would always sooner give the laurel to vigorous errors than to any orthodoxy not inspired.' Harriet Monroe announced in the January 1914 issue of *Poetry* that she accepted Yeats's suggestion: 'And she does this with the more pleasure as it enables her to acknowledge her high appreciation not only of Mr Pound's poetry, but also of his disinterested and valuable service as foreign correspondent of the magazine.'

With the money from *Poetry* Pound bought two small statues 'from *the* coming sculptor, Gaudier-Brzeska', and a new typewriter. Pound and Olivia Shakespear had met Henri Gaudier-Brzeska, aged twenty-one, while wandering about looking for new work at an art show at the Albert Hall earlier in 1913. Standing in front of one of the young Frenchman's works Pound had pretended to be in hopeless difficulty in his attempt to pronounce the second part of his name. Suddenly the sculptor himself darted from behind a pedestal and pronounced it for him. It turned out later that his real name was Henri Gaudier; the Brzeska had been added because he was living with Sophie Brzeska, a Polishwoman much older than himself whom he referred to as his sister. Pound visited the sculptor's studio under a railway arch at Putney and Gaudier-Brzeska came to Church Walk and the Cabaret Theatre Club and on at least one occasion heard Rummel play at the Shakespears'. The two men became friendly and the following year Gaudier-Brzeska cut a large head of Pound in marble supplied by the sitter. As he chiselled one day he told Pound: 'You understand it will not look like you, it *will . . . not . . . look . . .* like you. It will be the expression of certain emotions which I get from your character.'

In Pound's collection of works by Gaudier-Brzeska is a pen drawing of an old wolf, given to him by the artist after reading the poem on Piere Vidal who ran mad 'as a wolf' through the mountains of Cabaret. The inscription reads:

> *a mon ami Ezra Pound*
> *en admiration de 'Piere Vidal Old'*
> > *H. Gaudier-Brzeska*

At Stone Cottage in December 1913 Yeats spoke to Pound of the writings of an unknown Irish author by the name of James Joyce who was living in Trieste. On 15 December Pound explained to Joyce that he acted for a number of magazines in England and America and asked to see some of his work. Eleven days later, before Joyce had had a chance to reply, Yeats unearthed Joyce's poem 'I Hear an Army Charging' and Pound wrote immediately asking for permission to include it in his anthology *Des Imagistes*. Permission was granted early in January and thus began one of the most important literary associations of the time. *The New Freewoman* had with the coming of the New Year changed its name to *The Egoist*. In the issue of 15 January Pound printed a long letter from Joyce about the troubles he had encountered in finding a publisher for his book of short stories, *Dubliners*, and soon afterwards

Pound persuaded Harriet Shaw Weaver to run Joyce's novel, *A Portrait of the Artist as a Young Man* as a serial in *The Egoist*.

Des Imagistes appeared as the February 1914 number of *The Glebe*. On 2 March the same sheets bound in blue cloth board were issued as a book by Albert and Charles Boni of 96 Fifth Avenue, New York, and in April by the Poetry Bookshop in London. Four of Pound's contributions were derived from translations of Chinese poems which he had found in the works of the Sinologist H. A. Giles. They included 'Liu Ch'e':

> There is no sound of foot-fall, and the leaves
> Scurry into heaps and lie still,
> And she the rejoicer of the heart is beneath them.
> A wet leaf that clings to the threshold.

and 'Fan-piece for Her Imperial Lord':

> O fan of white silk,
>   clear as frost on the grass-blade,
> You also are laid aside.

NOTES

1 Pound met Kemp in Laurence Gomme's bookshop in New York in 1910; he was bundled off home again despite Pound's efforts which included a call by Pound and Hueffer on the American ambassador Walter Hines Page.

X Ernest Fenollosa
1913/1915

During the second half of 1913, at the home in London of the Bengali poetess, Sarojini Naidu, Pound met an American widow, Mrs Mary Fenollosa. After reading Pound's 'Contemporania' and possibly other poems Mrs Fenollosa decided that he was the one to whom she could entrust the literary remains of her late husband Ernest Fenollosa. Son of a Spanish musician and a young woman from Salem, Massachusetts, Fenollosa studied at Harvard and in the 1870s became an instructor in rhetoric at the Imperial University in Japan. He so loved the arts of Japan and fought so strongly for them at a time when many Japanese had eyes only for the West and westernization that eventually he was appointed Imperial Commissioner of Art in Tokyo. In addition to his work of conservation and the assembling of a personal art collection which is now in the Boston Museum of Fine Arts, he studied Chinese and Japanese literature under Japanese instructors: Mori, Ariga, Hirai and Shida for Chinese and Umewaka and Hirata for the Japanese Noh drama. After his death in 1908 Mrs Fenollosa saw to the publication in 1911 of his two-volume *Epochs of Chinese and Japanese Art* and began to look for a suitable person to take charge of his literary papers. Her introductory note to the book on art shows that she was hostile to academic experts; it may have been this, as much as anything else, which caused her to think of Pound as the one best fitted to act as literary executor. Some of the material, I think, she handed to Pound personally, other material she posted in London – this was towards the end of 1913 – and in November 1915 she sent a further packet from Alabama. In a letter to John Quinn on 17 May 1917 he said that after three weeks' acquaintance, Mrs Fenollosa had not only given him a free hand to edit and publish the material but the right to any profit plus £40 to go on with. Altogether there were about sixteen notebooks containing notes on Far Eastern literature, draft translations of Chinese poetry and Noh dramas, and an essay by Fenollosa on 'The Chinese Written Character as a Medium for Poetry'.

It was Pound's understanding when he received the bulk of the material from Mrs Fenollosa in 1913 that her husband wanted it handled as 'literature' rather than as 'philology'. He took the notebooks with him to Stone Cottage and worked on them there during the winter of 1913–14. He began first on the Noh dramas, the delicate blend of words, actions and music which thrived in Japan some four hundred years earlier, and on 31 January 1914 he sent to Harriet Monroe a translation by Fenollosa of the play *Nishikigi*; Pound's part had been to edit and polish the literal version made by Fenollosa under the supervision of his Japanese masters. It was published in *Poetry* in May:

> SHITE [Hero, ghost of the lover]
> There is at the root of hell
> No distinction between princes and commons;
> Wretched for me! 'tis the saying.
>
> WAKI [a priest]
> Strange, what seemed so very old a cave
> Is all glittering-bright within,
> Like the flicker of fire.
> It is like the inside of a house. . . .
>
> TSURE [ghost of the woman]
> Our hearts have been in the dark of the falling snow,
> We have been astray in the flurry.
> You should tell better than we
> How much is illusion,
> You who are in the world.
> We have been in the whirl of those who are fading.

In an attempt to counteract claims that the Imagists were revolutionaries Pound contributed to the January 1914 number of *Poetry* a short essay called 'The Tradition' in which he said that tradition was a beauty to be preserved, not a set of fetters to bind us. In attempting to preserve this beauty we returned to origins and this was invigorating because it was a return to nature and reason. 'The man who returns to origins does so because he wishes to behave in the eternally sensible manner. That is to say, naturally, reasonably, intuitively.' Although the essay said nothing profound about tradition and nothing about the connection between tradition and the individual, it enabled Pound to score at least one good point against the false traditionalists of the day: 'To say that such and such combinations of sound and tempo are not proper, is as foolish as to say that a painter should not use red in the upper left hand corners of his pictures. The movement of poetry is limited only by the nature of syllables and of articulate sound, and by the laws of music, or melodic rhythm.' Even if this did not exhaust the matter it did answer those who valued the sonnet or the quatrain for its own sake regardless of the merits of the verse it enclosed.

On Sunday, 18 January, Pound was among the committee of poets who called to pay tribute to Wilfred Scawen Blunt, aged seventy-four, mainly it seems on account of Blunt's irascible opposition to the British Empire and its institutions. Pound's account, published in *Poetry* in March, said that the committee – W. B. Yeats, T. Sturge Moore, Frederic Manning, Victor Plarr, F. S. Flint, Richard Aldington and Ezra Pound – had presented to Blunt in token of homage a reliquary carved in Pentelican marble by the 'brilliant young sculptor' Gaudier-Brzeska, ornamented with a female nude recumbent and an inscription, 'Homage to Wilfred Blunt'. Pound included John Masefield's name on the list but it seems that he did not attend the presentation, perhaps because he objected to Blunt's politics. The committee, Pound said, 'had proposed a large dinner of honour, but Mr Blunt pleaded age as an excuse and preferred to receive the committee in private. This he did with great charm, regaling us with the roast flesh of peacocks at Newbuildings, a sixteenth-century defensible grange in Sussex.' Pound is said to have composed and declaimed to the company the following verse:

> Because you have gone your individual gait,
> Written fine verses, made mock of the world,
> Swung the grand style, not made a trade of art,
> Upheld Mazzini and detested institutions
>
> We who are little given to respect,
> Respect you, and having no better way to show it,
> Bring you this stone to be some record of it.

Another of Pound's occasional verses appeared early in 1914 in a large book entitled *Chippewa County, Wisconsin, Past and Present*. Although dated 1913 it was published in Chicago in 1914. In addition to the history of the county and biographical sketches it contains the reminiscences of grandfather Thaddeus Pound 'while on a visit, from his home in Chicago, to his friends in Chippewa Falls in the summer of 1913'. Thaddeus died the following year, aged eighty-one. His grandson's contribution appeared in the chapter devoted to the Indians: a forty-four line poem in imitation of Longfellow entitled 'Legend of the Chippewa Spring and Minnehaha, the Indian Maiden'.

On 20 January Pound wrote to Harriet Monroe protesting against the substitution of the name 'Bêl' for Christ in Aldington's 'Lesbia':

And Picus of Mirandola is dead;
And all the gods they dreamed and fabled of,
Hermes and Thoth and Christ are rotten now,
Rotten and dank.

'If Mr Aldington believes more in Delphos', he said, 'than in Nazareth, I can see no reason for misrepresenting his creed.' On 22 January he attended a lecture by Hulme, 'Modern Art and its Philosophy', arranged by the Quest Society and delivered in the Kensington town hall.[1] Shortly before Yeats sailed on 28 January to spend two months in America, Pound carefully pasted Amy Lowell's address in his address-book and asked him to call on her if possible. Seeing that she wrote poetry and was interested in Imagism, Pound was hoping that her money might in some way be harnessed to the cause of genuine art.

In *The Egoist* of 2 Feburary he published two articles signed 'Bastien von Helmholtz'. One of them, 'John Synge and the Habits of Criticism', opened with a quotation: ' "She was so fine, and she was so healthy that you could have cracked a flea on either one of her breasts", said the old sea captain bragging about the loves of his youth.' He referred to this again many years later in *The Pisan Cantos* as an example of precise definition. The second article by Bastien von Helmholtz was called 'The Bourgeois': 'The bourgeoisie is a state of mind . . . the stomach and gross intestines of the body politic and social, as distinct from the artist, who is the nostrils and the invisible antennae.' In the following issue of the paper (16 February) he published an article on 'The New Sculpture' in which he granted that Hulme in his Quest Society lecture had been 'quite right' in saying that the difference between the new art and the old was not a difference in degree but a difference in kind, but elsewhere in the article he declared the lecture 'wholly unintelligible'. The same issue contains a letter to the editor signed Baptiste von Helmholtz. The purpose of it was to point out that by some slight error the article, 'The Bourgeois', in the issue of 2 February had been attributed to his brother, Bastien, whereas in fact he (Baptiste) was the author. Also in the issue of 16 February was an 'Essay in Constructive Criticism', by Ezra Pound, this time hiding under the name of 'Herrmann Karl Georg Jesus Maria'. The subject was golf; the idea, to poke fun at the British love of amateurs in the arts:

Of course you know, or, if you don't know, you jolly well ought to know that it's a jolly difficult job to introduce a sporting page into a quiet literary review like *The Egoist*. However golf is golf and as I have noticed – for I look about a bit and see a lot of things that you and your likes would never think of seeing – I have noticed, I was about to say, and will say in the run of a page or so that golfers get jolly narrow-minded and get into clubs and pay no attention to the great mass of people . . . And any way there are a lot of silly golfing prejudices to be got rid of before we can chat comfortably together . . . and that reminds me of a prejudice of my own about a chap who used to use pink clubs. Always hated that chap for using pink clubs but now by jingo after all these years, and I think it is a crying shame that even I had to wait ten years to get over that prejudice and find out what a fine game he plays – just my sort of game. He don't play golf, he just gives the impression of it. . . Beautiful form, of course not much direction – THANK GOD! not much direction – doesn't get his ball into the holes but that is a rather silly thing to do with a golf-ball anyhow.

On 23 February Pound began a series of letters to Amy Lowell in which he tried to persuade her to put money into *The Egoist* and make it livelier and more influential, or later to finance a magazine. Behind this was the hope that he might end up with a paper or magazine to do what he liked with, and also with a salary as editor. But Miss Lowell declined because there would be too big a loss of money before such a publication could possibly pay its own way. *Poetry and Drama* for March published eight new poems by Pound including 'Coitus':

> The gilded phaloi of the crocuses
> are thrusting at the spring air.
> Here is there naught of dead gods
> But a procession of festival . . .

Another of them was 'Alb^tre', the idea for which first came to him in Paris a year or two before. The woman was a friend of Rummel's brother:

> And the delicate white feet of her little white dog
> Are not more delicate than she is,
> Nor would Gautier himself have despised their
> contrasts in whiteness
> As she sits in the great chair
> Between the two indolent candles.

In Chicago on 1 March the guarantors, contributors and editors of *Poetry* gave a dinner in honour of W. B. Yeats. In his address of thanks Yeats warned American poets against the vices of sentimentality, rhetoric and '"moral uplift"' which he found were still favoured in the ordinary American magazines. These vices, against which the Rhymers' Club had rebelled some twenty years earlier, still existed in America, he said, because culturally Americans were still too far from Paris:

It is from Paris that nearly all the great influences in art and literature have come, from the time of Chaucer until now. Today the metrical experiments of French poets are overwhelming in their variety and delicacy. The best English writing is dominated by French criticism; in France is the great critical mind.

. . .

I would have all American poets keep in mind the example of François Villon.

We rebelled against rhetoric, and now there is a group of younger poets who dare to call us rhetorical. When I returned to London from Ireland, I had a young man go over all my work with me to eliminate the abstract. This was an American poet, Ezra Pound. Much of his work is experimental; his work will come slowly, he will make many an experiment before he comes into his own. I should like to read to you two poems of permanent value, 'The Ballad of the Goodly Fere' and 'The Return'. This last is, I think, the most beautiful poem that has been written in the free form, one of the few in which I find real organic rhythm. A great many poets use *vers libre* because they think it is easier to write than rhymed verse, but it is much more difficult.

The announcement in March of Pound's engagement to Dorothy Shakespear was reported in the *Philadelphia Evening Bulletin* of 24 March under the heading, 'Phila. Poet to Wed Abroad'. 'The announcement yesterday of the engagement of Ezra Pound, the young Philadelphia poet who was "discovered" several years ago in England, to Miss Dorothy Shakespear, the twenty-year-old daughter of Mr and Mrs Hope Shakespear, of Brunswick Gardens, London, has aroused a great deal of interest in literary and university circles. The wedding is to take place, 18 April, in London . . . He became acquainted with Miss Shakespear shortly after he moved to London, and the announcement of his engagement was not a surprise to his parents.' The following day the *Bulletin* sent a reporter to Wyncote to interview the poet's mother; the result, published on 26 March, opened with the heading, 'Poet in Love Song Extols His Bride', and a quotation from 'Canzon: To Be Sung beneath a Window':

> Man's love follows many faces,
> My love only one face knoweth;
> Towards thee only my love floweth,
> And outstrips the swift stream's paces.

Pound, the story said, had been hailed in England as 'one of the world's great poets'; Kipling had placed such an estimate on him, saying also that the young man's lyrical gifts were of the highest. The poet's mother was naturally very proud of his career; concerning his approaching marriage she said: 'My son has known Miss Shakespear for some years. Although I have not yet met her, we were waiting for the "inevitable". I do not know, definitely, whether members of the family will attend the wedding, but it is probable that instead we shall await the return of my son and his bride from their honeymoon and then visit them in London. I've been trying to persuade my boy to visit me in Wyncote, but his work and his close alliance with men of note in the literary and art world of London have thus far prevented his coming here for an extended stay.' She had been advised in a recent letter, she said, that Brzeska, the noted exponent of the new art of sculpture, was chiselling a head of her son in marble. She thought that his introductory note on Tagore, published in *Poetry* more than a year before Tagore won the Nobel Prize, was one of his strongest writings: 'It indicates a splendid personal knowledge of and intimacy with Tagore.'

All indications reaching Philadelphia were that the wedding would take place at the bride's home in Brunswick Gardens on 18 April. Accordingly the *Philadelphia Inquirer* published a story on 18 April saying, 'In London, England, tonight, Ezra Pound, the world-famous young American poet and critic, was married to Miss Dorothy Shakespear . . .' There were no details, the paper said, because 'with the true eccentricity of real genius' the poet had not disclosed the name of the officiating clergyman, nor the number of guests, nor the names of the members of the bridal party. All that Isabel Pound could tell the *Inquirer* was that Ezra had taken his wedding very much as a matter of course. She had received a formal invitation a fortnight before and she knew that her daughter-in-law belonged to 'a distinguished English family' but she did not know a single thing about her gown, nor about her bridesmaids nor the guests.

Actually the marriage ceremony took place at about a quarter-past ten on Monday morning, 20 April, at St Mary Abbots: the bride did not wear a wedding-dress but a coat and skirt and there were only about six guests – most of them members of the bride's family. Although Yeats in New York told his father in March that he had to 'hurry home for Ezra Pound's marriage', Dorothy Pound had no recollection, when I asked her in 1967, that he had attended the ceremony. According to the marriage entry at St Mary Abbots, Pound was twenty-eight, and Dorothy Pound, twenty-seven. The witnesses were the bride's father, Henry Hope Shakespear, and her uncle, Olivia's brother, H. T. Tucker. For their honeymoon they went to Stone Cottage where Pound continued his work on the Noh dramas. They called on Wilfred Scawen Blunt who welcomed them in Arab robes, drank champagne mixed with water and took them for a drive in a small wagon. They planned to continue their honeymoon the following winter in Spain but the First World War intervened and they did not get to the Continent until 1919 when they went on a walking-tour of Provence. With a wedding cheque Dorothy Pound bought a piece of Chinese jade. Her interest in the Orient went back some years to the time when an old relative after retiring from the Indian service had gone on a world-trip and had brought back a number of Chinese pieces; and there was another relative with some Japanese prints. Out of this contact she had developed an interest in jade. After a while she grew tired of the wedding piece and Edgar Jepson ('lover of jade' in *The Pisan Cantos*) offered to take it from her and in its place found a small beautifully-carved horse which never lost its power to charm.

Pound had left his room at 10 Church Walk shortly before the wedding and had taken a small dark flat just around the corner – number 5 Holland Place Chambers. The couple made their home there for the next five years. Some of the furniture Pound had made himself, but the most treasured item was a clavichord made by Arnold Dolmetsch. T. S. Eliot said many years later that in the largest room Pound cooked, by artificial light, and in the lightest but smallest room, which was inconveniently triangular, he did his work and received his visitors. The Aldingtons lived on the same floor. Some mornings Pound and his wife would walk along the Row, watching the horses and riders and occasionally meeting acquaintances: Colonel Jackson, an elderly Victorian who spoke good French and R. B. Cunninghame Graham, who went by mounted, 'an ear and the beard's point showing'.

Friends or acquaintances who lived not far away during the years Pound was at Holland Place Chambers, included the painter Edward Wadsworth who had a place in Kensington Church Street near Notting Hill Gate; Edmund Dulac, artist and illustrator, who lived off Holland Park Road; Wickham Steed, who had a flat not far from Dulac; Annette Hullah, a friend of Colonel Jackson's, who had a large collection of material relating to Provençal poetry, including reproductions of the Milan manuscripts – she had a flat in a narrow lane not far from Holland Park House – and George Sauter, a Bavarian painter, an admirer of Bismarck and friend of Whistler, who lived in or near Holland Park Road.

The tailor who was responsible for Pound's clothing at this stage, clothing which was unusual in cut and colour and attracted a good deal of attention, was Cotton of Holland Street, with occasional visits during moments of prosperity to another by the name of Poole. He possessed during the early years of his marriage a grey topcoat which apparently he deemed unnecessarily subdued. To remedy the matter he and

Dorothy went to a nearby shop which dealt in semi-precious stones and there had cut three large square buttons made of *lapis lazuli*. When they ate out, it was usually at Belotti's restaurant at 12 Old Compton Street, where the cook knew his job and where they were waited on by a 'half-cracked' waiter by the name of Angelo. It was, Pound maintained, the cheapest clean restaurant in London. The owner, Belotti, had worked at the Ritz or some such establishment, before opening a restaurant of his own, and as a result he had stories to tell, if you were interested, about the rich and the famous. Pound introduces him into canto 80, in *The Pisan Cantos*, both for the fact that he had read the inscription, 'There is no darkness but ignorance', beneath the statue of Shakespeare in Leicester Square, and because of the trouble he had gone to in order to import two ounces of saffron for a risotto during the First World War.

Pound's literary affairs continued unabated in the weeks before the wedding and throughout the 'expectable disturbances of such a season'. Thus we find him on 28 March writing a long letter to Harriet Monroe, insisting that the Fenollosa translation of *Nishikigi* must on no account be held aside and replaced by inferior work, and instructing her in various other aspects of her job as editor of *Poetry*; we find him also in correspondence with Amy Lowell, still hoping to run a paper or a quarterly with her; and again, writing to Harriet Monroe to get money for a young poet, married, with a child, who was said to be on the point of starvation, having got into financial trouble while starting his own magazine: 'The last I had of him was to send him a telegraph order to buy food, then he disappeared, ashamed to ask for more, and I heard nothing until his wife found my address among his papers and wrote from Leicester.' At the same time, he continued to publish a stream of articles in *The Egoist* and *The New Age*. One of these was a piece on Allen Upward in *The New Age* of 23 April – important as the point at which he attempted to find a definite place within society for the author and the artist. Earlier, in 'The Serious Artist', he had said that the arts were a science, just as chemistry is, because they gave us a great percentage of the 'lasting and unassailable data' regarding the nature of man; but now he went further, and, in summarizing Upward's position, proposed that the arts be given a concrete place inside the social system. 'I must needs', he said, 'make a partial summary of certain things that he [Upward] stands for, or that he appears to stand for; certain conclusions which I draw more or less from his books':

1. That a nation is civilized in so far as it recognizes the special faculties of the individual and makes use thereof.

1a. Corollary, Syndicalism. A social order is well balanced when the community recognizes the special aptitudes of groups of men and applies them.

2. That Mr Upward's propaganda is for a syndicate of intelligence; of thinkers and authors and artists.

2a. That such a guild is perfectly in accord with Syndicalist doctrines. That it would take its place with the guilds of more highly skilled craftsmen.

3. That Mr Upward 'sees further into a mile-stone, etc.', I mean that his propaganda is for the recognition of the man who can see the meaning of data, not necessarily as opposed to, but as supplementary to, the man who is only capable of assembling or memorizing such data. NOTE. – This latter sort of man is the only sort now provided for by the American University system. I cannot speak for the English.

And so, almost inexorably, the young aesthete from Philadelphia was brought by temperament and by his American heritage of 'practical' thought and 'science for everybody', to the point where he was ready to embrace the ideal of the artist serving a society in which the parts ('aptitudes') functioned as in a machine. In so far as there was a single factor which governed his thought for the next forty years and the direction he took in both poetry and politics, it was this ideal of the artist's place in a smoothly functioning society. The artist was at once the 'intelligence' and 'the nostrils and the invisible antennae' of society: his job was not propaganda in the crude sense but to act as society's guide; sensing danger before his less gifted fellows, just as the 'lord of the thunder' sensed the approaching storm, his job was to define it if he were poet or novelist, in clear language free of habit and superstition. Although for his ideas on society he was largely dependent on Upward and the Guild Socialism of *The New Age* he was not a Guild Socialist and there is no evidence that at this stage he considered the possibility of a guild society run by and for human beings: he wanted a smoothly functioning apparatus in which artists had a visible role as 'intelligence' and 'antennae'.

Pound's growing interest in society as a whole was accompanied by a growing interest in the arts of painting, sculpture and decoration. This was in part a natural development but not unconnected with the increasing attention being paid to modern art in *The New Age* and *The Egoist*. In December 1913 and during the first half of 1914 there was a war of words in *The New Age* over Epstein and modern art, involving Hulme, Anthony Ludovici, Walter Sickert, Wyndham Lewis and others. The paper also carried numerous reproductions of drawings and paintings by Epstein, Gaudier-Brzeska, Wyndham Lewis, David Bomberg, Edward Wadsworth, William Roberts and C. R. W. Nevinson, some of them accompanied by Hulme's annotations.

With activity going on all around him, in favour of what was new, Pound was unable to resist participating in it and in *The Egoist* of 16 February 1914 he published his first piece on art, 'The New Sculpture', devoted to Gaudier-Brzeska and Epstein. After a long period in which, he said, the arts had been humanist and had tried unsuccessfully to lead and persuade an 'unbearably stupid' humanity, the artist had at last been aroused to the fact that the war between him and the world was a war without truce. That the only remedy, in fact, was slaughter: 'The artist has been at peace with his oppressors long enough. He has dabbled in democracy and he is now done with that folly. We turn back, we artists, to the powers of the air, to the djinns who were our allies aforetime, to the spirits of our ancestors.' With the connivance of these spirits the artist was ready to take over: 'The aristocracy of entail and of title is decayed, the aristocracy of commerce is decaying, the aristocracy of the arts is ready again for its service . . . and we who are the heirs of the witch-doctor and the voodoo, we artists who have been so long the despised are about to take over control.' He continued his art criticism in *The Egoist* of 16 March with a review of an exhibition of sculpture and painting at the Goupil Gallery; part of this review, dealing with Jacob Epstein, was reprinted by Epstein in his book *Let There Be Sculpture* in 1940.

Pound was spending more time now with Wyndham Lewis, the belligerent author and painter, who having joined Roger Fry's Omega Workshops in July 1913 and soon afterwards having broken completely with Fry, was ready to lead the aristocracy of the arts in its fight to 'take over control'. Pound and Lewis had met first in 1909, probably in the Vienna Café, after Hueffer had published them both in *The English Review*. Their first meetings seem to have been enveloped in wariness and suspicion, with Lewis almost certainly to blame, for while Pound was sometimes more wary than need be, his sensitivity was as nothing compared with Lewis's which was incredible. Laurence Binyon, it appears, had taken Pound to the Vienna Café, which was in New Oxford Street not far from the British Museum, and there had met Sturge Moore in company with Lewis. If Pound's memory was accurate when he came to write *The Pisan Cantos*, Binyon and Moore stood back and urged each his respective 'bulldog' into the fray, or at any rate stood back and watched. This was not a good start and although they saw one another occasionally during the next three years I know of no evidence that they played any part in each other's career during this time. In 1914, however, with interest in the 'new art' rising, and both dedicated to perfection in art, they took up arms together against the reign of mediocrity – despite Lewis's feeling that Pound's ideas were rather old-fashioned.

In the spring of 1914 they joined with Hulme in presenting on behalf of the Quest Society in the Kensington town hall an evening on modern poetry. Many years later Miss Kate Lechmere, who knew the three of them, gave her impressions of the evening. Hulme was not a good lecturer apparently and his delivery was mumbled and indistinct. Lewis, too, was inaudible, his head buried in his notes. Only when Pound stepped forward, completely self-possessed, she thought, in his velvet coat and red tie, was the evening saved from being a complete failure. He was witty, urbane and fluent and in a mid-American nasal twang he snarled some of his own and Hulme's verses. Such a voice seemed to clown verse rather than read it, Miss Lechmere said, but an otherwise unfortunate evening was made memorable.

In the spring of 1914 Miss Lechmere also backed Lewis in the establishment of the Rebel Art Centre at 38 Great Ormond Street, Queen's Square, London, W.C. From this headquarters Lewis issued prospectuses, called in Pound, Gaudier-Brzeska and others to lecture, and there, and in his studio in Fitzroy Street, began to edit the first issue of his large magazine, *Blast*. This new movement, of which *Blast* was the official organ, was by Pound named Vorticism, with Pound and Lewis its chief publicists. Whatever reservations he still had about some of Pound's ideas Lewis had by now accepted him as a friend and when Pound and his wife called at the Centre at tea-time on Saturdays Lewis would express his confidence by inviting him into the back-room to see his latest paintings. They were kept locked in the back-room for fear of imitators and Mrs Pound told me her husband was at that time the only one allowed to see them. The advent of *Blast*, which was still two months away, was announced on the back of *The Egoist* of 15 April in an advertisement which proclaimed: 'End of Christian Era.'

The aggressiveness which caused Lewis to lead other members of the Rebel Art Centre in an assault on one of Marinetti's meetings, was almost responsible in the literary field for an event of similar magnitude. Lascelles Abercrombie, one of the Georgian poets, had written somewhere in favour of a return to Wordsworth as a source of inspiration. Into this inevitably dull and platitudinous situation Pound added some ginger. 'Dear Mr Abercrombie,' he wrote, 'Stupidity carried beyond a certain point becomes a public menace. I hereby challenge you to a duel, to be fought at the earliest moment that is suited to your convenience . . . Yours sincerely, Ezra Pound.' Abercrombie was a little perturbed, it is said, when news reached him of Pound's skill at fencing, but he took heart when he remembered that the choice of weapon lay with the party challenged. He suggested that they should bombard each other with unsold copies of their own books – a brilliant solution which saved Abercrombie from the rapier and no doubt caused Pound to call off the whole thing, lest he suffer the embarrassment of finding his own arms full and his opponent weaponless.

In addition to these more strenuous affairs Pound continued with his poetry and his day to day tasks, the latter including articles and snippets for *The Egoist* and the writing of material and securing of contributions for *Poetry*. In addition to Fenollosa's *Nishikigi* the May number of *Poetry* included a dozen poems by Yeats and Pound's review of Yeats's *Responsibilities* (Cuala Press, 1914). From what Pound remembered when I spoke to him about *Responsibilities* some years ago, it seems likely that he chose, or helped Yeats to choose, that title. In his review of the book in *Poetry* he said that Yeats being 'assuredly an immortal' there was no need for him to recast his style to suit new doctrine, meaning Imagism; but there was, nevertheless, 'a manifestly new note in his later work', in some of which he replaced inversion with 'prose directness'. For the June issue of *Poetry* he secured Hueffer's long poem 'On Heaven', which he described in a letter to Harriet Monroe on 23 May as 'the most important poem in the modern manner' and in a note in the June issue as 'the best poem yet written in the "twentieth century fashion".' In the perspective of mid-1914 this opinion may have seemed justified in view of the poem's relaxed tone and unhurried directness:

> I sat about
> And played long games of dominos with the *maire*,
> Or passing *commis-voyageurs*. And so
> I sat and watched the trams come in, and read
> The *Libre Parole*, and sipped the thin, fresh wine
> They call Piquette
>
> . . .
>
> And that day there was no puncturing of the tires to fear;
> And no trouble at all with the engine and the gear;
> Smoothly and softly we ran between the great poplar alley
> All down the valley of the Rhone.
> For the dear, good God knew how we needed rest and
> to be alone.

In his review of Hueffer's *Collected Poems* in the same issue as 'On Heaven' Pound said that it was Hueffer who in the face of 'a still Victorian press' had fought for good writing as opposed to the 'opalescent word, the rhetorical tradition'. He found him significant and revolutionary because of his insistence upon clarity and precision: 'in brief, upon efficient writing – even in verse.' When some fifteen years later Pound was preparing the abortive edition of his collected prose he made a point of placing the date, 1914, against his original praise of 'On Heaven'. Whether this was in extenuation of its extravagance or to draw attention to the early date of his good judgement, I do not know.

Blast, 'A Review of the Great English Vortex', came out on 20 June, a delight to some, outrageous to others. It was 12½ inches by 9½ inches, with the title in large capitals on a calliope pink cover. Its typographical exuberance (large type, many words in capital letters, etc.) was used to blast such people or things as Marie Corelli, 'Sentimental Gallic Gush', Thomas Beecham, his pills and his opera, the Meynells, the Bishop of London, 'Sentimental Hygienics', and Sidney Webb; it was also used to convey such sentiments as:

> Curse abysmal inexcusable middle-class
> (also Aristocracy and Proletariat).

And to bless many things held dear by the Vorticists themselves, including the music-halls and Brigit Patmore. The most important contribution by far was Lewis's 'Enemy of the Stars', which, were it not for one or two other passages by Lewis himself, and sections of Joyce's *Ulysses*, might be considered unique in English:

> The Earth has burst, a granite flower, and disclosed the scene.
> A wheelwright's yard.
> Full of dry, white volcanic light.
> Full of emblems of one trade: stacks of pine, iron, wheels stranded.
> Rough Eden of one soul, to whom another man, and not Eve, would be mated.
> A canal at one side, the night pouring into it like blood from a butcher's pail.
> . . .
> The stars shone madly in the archaic blank wilderness of the universe, machines of prey.
> Mastodons, placid in electric atmosphere, white rivers of power. They stood in eternal black sunlight.
> . . .
> He sprang from the bridge clumsily, too unhappy for instinctive science, and sank like lead, his heart a sagging weight of stagnant hatred.

There were also a number of manifestos by Lewis containing such declarations as: 'Dehumanization is the chief diagnostic of the modern World', 'Human insanity has never flowered so colossally', and

> Our Vortex is not afraid of the Past: it has forgotten its existence.
> Our Vortex regards the Future as as sentimental as the Past.
> . . .
> Our Vortex rushes out like an angry dog at your Impressionistic fuss.
> Our Vortex is white and abstract with its red-hot swiftness.

Most of the other contributions were innocuous in comparison. There were a dozen poems by Pound, full of such expressions as 'You slut-bellied obstructionist' and 'As for you, you will rot in the earth'. One of them began, 'With minds still hovering above their testicles', and ended:

> They complain in delicate and exhausted metres
> That the twitching of three abdominal nerves
> Is incapable of producing a lasting Nirvana.

The first line and the last two were cancelled in ink or crayon in many copies, for fear of prosecution.

Dorothy Pound, an unlikely warrior in such a ferocious campaign as the Vorticists had launched, took the war into the enemy's camp by prominently displaying a copy of the magazine on her way from Kensington to Tottenham Court Road. It was a Monday, and Pound, having attended Orage's weekly tea in Chancery Lane, would be waiting to take her to Belotti's. As she stepped down from the bus two urchins looked in amazement at the magazine, at the lady, and then at one another, saying: 'Blawst? *Blawst?*'

G. W. Prothero, editor of the *Quarterly Review*, was so upset by *Blast* that on 22 October he answered a proposal of Pound's as follows:

Dear Mr Pound,
  Many thanks for your letter of the other day. I am afraid that I must say frankly that I do not think I can open the columns of the *Q.R.* – at any rate, at present – to any one associated publicly with such a publication as *Blast*. It stamps a man too disadvantageously.
                    Yours truly,
                    G. W. Prothero.
Of course, having accepted your paper on the *Noh*, I could not refrain from publishing it. But other things would be in a different category.

In *The New Age* of 16 July Orage praised Lewis's 'Enemy of the Stars' as an 'extraordinary piece of work', but the other literary contributions he found disappointing. It was characteristic of the period, he thought, that the new school could muster so few works to exemplify its principles. He came close to stating the truth of the matter, that there were in fact no Vorticists except Wyndham Lewis.

Writing in *The Egoist* of 1 July, as Bastien von Helmholtz, Pound declared that 'One would, of course, hate to abolish that picturesque relic "The Lords", though the thought of being even slightly controlled by a body containing bishops is both painful and ridiculous.' Under his own name, in the issue of 15 July he reviewed Joyce's *Dubliners*, published that day by Grant Richards. Joyce's prose, he said, was clear and hard and free from sloppiness. Although he dealt with subjective things he presented them with such clarity of outline that he might be dealing with locomotives or builders' specifications. His most engaging merit, Pound thought, was that he carefully avoided telling a lot of things that the reader didn't want to know. He was also a realist: 'He does not believe "life" would be all right if we stopped vivisection or if we instituted a new sort of "economics". He gives the thing as it is.' He believed that *Dubliners* together with *A Portrait of the Artist as a Young Man* which was then running in *The Egoist* in serial form, were such 'as to win for Mr Joyce a very definite place among English contemporary prose writers'. In a review of *Blast* in the same issue Richard Aldington said that Pound's contributions were quite unworthy of him, because he could not write satire. 'Mr Pound is one of the gentlest, most modest, bashful, kind creatures who ever walked the earth; so I cannot help thinking that all this enormous arrogance and petulance and fierceness are a pose. And it is a wearisome pose.'

On 28 June 1914 the Archduke Franz Ferdinand, heir to the throne of Austria, and his wife, were shot and killed while driving through the streets of Sarajevo in Bosnia. Thus began the series of events leading to the outbreak of the European war in August. Among those who went to the war in 1914 was Gaudier-Brzeska who shortly before the outbreak attended a dinner given by Ezra and Dorothy Pound for some of their friends at Leber's restaurant in Holland Park Avenue. Also among the guests was Colonel Jackson who combined with his distinguished manners a certain heartiness which Pound maintained was pre-Victorian. The colonel complimented Gaudier-Brzeska on his decision to fight for his country if war came. As for himself, aged about eighty, he proposed to cook for the army of Ulster, if they would have him, and prove the soundness of his maxim that good soup makes good soldiers.

Accompanied by a large motorcar and a chauffeur, Amy Lowell returned to London and the Berkeley Hotel in July 1914 in time to attend the dinner given by the Vorticists on 15 July at the Dieudonné restaurant in Ryder Street, St James's, to celebrate the first issue of *Blast*. At the same restaurant two days later Miss Lowell gave an 'Imagist Dinner', attended by Ezra and Dorothy Pound, Richard Aldington and H. D., John Gould Fletcher, Allen Upward, John Cournos, Flint and Hueffer, and possibly by Gaudier-Brzeska. The meal consisted of:

Hors d'Oeuvres Norvégienne
Consommé Sarah Bernhardt
Bisque de Homards
Filets de sole Lucullus
Cailles en Gelée aux Muscats
Selle d'Agneau Richelieu
Canetons d'Aylesbury a l'Anglaise
Petits Pois aux Laitues
Jambon d'York au Champagne
Haricots Verts Maitre d'Hôtel
Bombe Moka   Friandises   Dessert
Café

Upward and several others present made fun of Miss Lowell's stoutness and drew attention to the line, 'not the water, but you in your whiteness, bathing', in her poem 'In a Garden', in *Des Imagistes*; and to cap it off, Pound carried in from an adjoining salon, where it had been placed under a leak, a circular tub, clearly large enough for Miss Lowell to bathe in. He set it down in front of her and announced that *Les Imagistes* were about to be succeeded by a new school, *Les Nagistes*.

Miss Lowell was in London for a purpose, which was to propose a second Imagist anthology larger than the first, for which the contributors would each select their own poems; and Miss Lowell would arrange for the book to be published by a large and recognized publisher. Pound saw this proposal as the certain end of all that he had hoped to achieve when he coined the name and invented the movement. Under a name which stood, he maintained, for 'hard light and clear edges', for 'a certain clarity and intensity', Miss Lowell would set up a new and wider movement with lower standards. He refused to participate, which may have been a relief to Miss Lowell, and suggested that since free verse seemed to be the only bond between the contributors she had in mind, she should call the anthology *Vers Libre*, with a subtitle: 'an anthology devoted to Imagisme, vers libre and modern movements in verse.' But she persisted and when she left for America in September she had the five contributors she wanted: Richard Aldington, H.D., John Gould Fletcher, F. S. Flint and D. H. Lawrence, with herself the sixth. On behalf of the group she signed a contract with Houghton,

Mifflin & Company of Boston for the publication of three anthologies which appeared in 1915, 1916 and 1917 under the title, *Some Imagist Poets*.

Understandably Pound was annoyed and he named the new movement *Amygisme*. He was still further annoyed and felt justified in his suspicions about Amy Lowell when in October 1914 he discovered that her publisher in America, in advertising her book *Sword Blades and Poppy Seed*, was saying: 'Of the poets who today are doing the interesting and original work, there is no more striking and unique figure than Amy Lowell. The foremost member of the "Imagists" – a group of poets that includes William Butler Yeats, Ezra Pound, Ford Madox Hueffer – she has won wide recognition for her writing in new and free forms of poetical expression.'

Looking at the quarrel now it is clear that in the matter of literary principle Pound was in the right. But there is a passage in a letter which Amy Lowell wrote to Harriet Monroe soon after her return to America in 1914, which indicates that Pound's resistance was not all based on his concern for the purity of Imagism. 'Do you remember', she wrote, 'Ezra was very anxious to run the *Mercure de France*?' The letter continued:

He came to me at once as soon as I got to London, and then it transpired that he expected to become editor of said 'Review' with a salary. I was to guarantee all the money and put in what I pleased, and he was to run the magazine his way. We talked over the cost of expenses, and we both thought that $5000 a year was the least that such a magazine could be run on. As I have not $5000 a year that I can afford to put into it, I based my refusal upon that fact, and it was most unfortunate that Ezra apparently did not believe it. Like many people of no income, Ezra does not know the difference between thousands and millions, and thinks that anyone who knows where to look for next week's dinners, is a millionaire, and therefore lost his temper with me completely, although he never told me why, and he accused me of being unwilling to give any money towards art.

Irrespective of whether this is an accurate account of the matter it seems likely that money or the manner in which Miss Lowell chose to spend her money entered into their quarrel.

Homer and Isabel Pound arrived in London in July and went to stay at 48 Langham Street where their son had lived during his first year in England. After about a month Homer had to return to work in Philadelphia but Isabel took a flat in Holland Place Chambers and stayed on for six weeks or more.

The First World War had begun and England was now involved. As the war continued there was food rationing and the unpleasantness of air-raids; but the worst of it, Dorothy Pound told me in 1967, was the noise of the anti-aircraft guns in the grounds of the barracks just across the road from their flat.

In the *Fortnightly Review* for 1 September Pound published a long article called 'Vorticism' in which he tried to give his Imagism a philosophy and to show that Imagism and Vorticism were really the same thing. Imagism, he said, was not symbolism; and whereas the symbolist's symbols had a fixed value, the Imagist's images had a variable significance. Since the beginning of bad writing, writers had used images as ornaments. The point about Imagism, Pound said, was that it did not use images in this way: 'The image is itself the speech. The image is the word beyond formulated language.' Further on he linked the image with Vorticism, saying that it was not an idea but a radiant node or cluster: 'it is what I can, and must perforce, call a VORTEX, from which, and through which, and into which, ideas are constantly rushing.'

During a discussion with a young Harvard graduate, Conrad Aiken, Pound asked for news of poetry in America. When Aiken mentioned Edward Arlington Robinson, Pound said yes but that was old stuff; wasn't there anyone in Boston or thereabouts who was writing something different? Aiken admitted that there was a young gentleman, a philosopher actually, who had done some very peculiar work. Aiken had already offered some of it to Harold Monro for *Poetry and Drama* but Monro had rejected it as absolutely insane. The poet's name was Thomas Eliot. In the spring of 1914 he had left Harvard, where he was an Assistant in Philosophy, to continue his studies at Marburg in Germany. Forced by the war to leave Germany he went to London and about 22 September 1914 he called at Pound's flat in Holland Place Chambers – a rather prim and quiet young man who dressed in keeping with his serious station. With Dorothy Pound present they had tea and talked. On 22 September Pound wrote to Harriet Monroe to say that an American by the name of Eliot had called and seemed to have 'some sense'. On 30 September he wrote again: 'I was jolly well right about Eliot. He has sent in the best poem I have yet had or seen from an American. *Pray God it be not a single and unique success.*' Eliot had taken the poem back to get it ready for the press; Pound would send it on to her in a few days.

The poem was 'The Love Song of J. Alfred Prufrock' which Eliot had begun in 1910 and finished about a year later. What amazed Pound was that Eliot had actually 'trained himself *and* modernized himself *on his own*'. The rest of the promising young writers had done one or the other, he told Harriet Monroe, but never both (and 'most of the swine have done neither'). It was such a comfort, he said, to meet a man and not have to tell him to wash his face, wipe his feet, and remember the date on the calendar. Pound sent 'Prufrock' to *Poetry* in October, saying 'Here is the Eliot poem. The most interesting contribution I've had from an American. P. S. Hope you'll get it *in* soon.' He sent off another of Eliot's poems to H. L. Mencken, one of the editors of the *Smart Set*: 'I enclose a poem by the last intelligent man I've found – a young American, T. S. Eliot.' He was worth watching, he told Mencken, because his mind was ' "not primitive".'

Continuing throughout with his work on the Fenollosa notebooks Pound published in the October *Quarterly Review* a long selection from Fenollosa's notes, including the two plays, 'Kinuta' and 'Hagoromo':

> The stag's voice has bent her heart toward sorrow,
> Sending the evening winds which she does not see,
> We cannot see the tip of the branch.
> The last leaf falls without witness.
> There is an awe in the shadow,
> And even the moon is quiet,
> With the love-grass under the eaves.
>
> ('Kinuta')

In 'Hagoromo', given beautiful material to work on, he was able to bring to a high pitch the poetic prose he had tried without much success to write years before and had published in *A Lume Spento* and *A Quinzaine for This Yule*. Parts of 'Hagoromo' are not unlike some of the free verse in *The Cantos*:

Nor is this rock of earth overmuch worn by the brushing of that feather-mantle, the feathery skirt of the stars: rarely, how rarely. There is a magic song from the east, the voices of many and many: and flute and sho, filling the space beyond the cloud's edge, seven-stringed; dance filling and filling. The red sun blots on the sky the line of the colour-drenched mountains. The flowers rain in a gust; it is no racking storm that comes over this green moor, which is afloat, as it would seem, in these waves.

In the notebooks Pound came across a great number of Chinese poems by Li Po and others which Fenollosa had copied out as part of his university studies in Tokyo. After brushing in the Chinese characters Fenollosa had written first a phonetic transcription (using the Japanese pronunciation of the Chinese), then a character-by-character translation into English, and finally a translation or attempted explanation of each line as a whole. Selecting those that seemed best suited to his purpose Pound began to work Fenollosa's translations into English poems. He was so excited as the job progressed that he kept going across to the Aldington's flat to read out to them the results, which were indeed remarkable. In a poem called 'The River Merchant's Wife' Fenollosa had worked out the opening six lines as follows:

> My hair was at first covering my brows (child's method of
>   wearing hair)
> Breaking flowers I was frolicking in front of our gate
> When you came riding on bamboo stilts (you – ride on –
>   bamboo-horse – come)
> And going about my seat you played with the blue plums
> Together we dwelt in the same Chokan village
> And we two little ones had neither mutual dislike nor suspicion.

In the first line Pound thought he would use the American word *bangs* to describe the girl's hair but Dorothy Pound protested and said the word was *fringe*. He eventually found a way of avoiding both:

> While my hair was still cut straight across my forehead
> I played about the front gate, pulling flowers.
> You came by on bamboo stilts, playing horse,
> You walked about my seat, playing with blue plums.
> And we went on living in the village of Chokan:
> Two small people, without dislike or suspicion.

Another poem, 'Exile's Letter', was translated by Fenollosa thus:

> (If you) ask me how much I regret the parting
> I would answer that my sorrow is as much as the falling
>   flowers of spring
> Struggling with one another in a tangle.
> Words cannot be exhausted
> Nor can the feelings be fathomed
> So calling to me my son I make him sit on the ground for a
>   long time
> And write to my dictation
> And sending them to you over a thousand miles we think of
>   each other at a distance.

Pound transformed this into:

> And if you ask how I regret that parting:
> It is like the flowers falling at Spring's end
>   Confused, whirled in a tangle.

What is the use of talking, and there is no end of talking,
There is no end of things in the heart.
I call in the boy,
Have him sit on his knees here
        To seal this,
And send it a thousand miles, thinking.

In October 1914 Pound came across the free verse of Edgar Lee
Masters and for a time was at the centre of a small stir in favour of
Master's work. He directed Harriet Monroe to get some of it for *Poetry*
and wrote two articles in 1915 – one for *The Egoist* and the other for
Reedy's Mirror in St Louis, Missouri. Macmillan & Company imported
from America some copies of Masters' *Spoon River Anthology* and
Hueffer published 'a fine review of it'. Pound printed some of his work
in *Catholic Anthology* but soon lost interest when Masters refused to
tighten his style; in November 1916 he wrote that Masters had 'gone
off into gas'.

In Chicago, towards the end of October 1914 Miss Monroe received
her copy of 'The Love Song of J. Alfred Prufrock' and was disappointed
to find that it was not what she had expected. She had very definite
ideas about American superiority and she wanted her American poets
to exemplify this superiority in rousing verse like Nicholas Vachel
Lindsay's 'The Firemen's Ball' which had appeared in the July *Poetry*:

They are hitched, they are off,
They are gone in a flash,
And they strain at the driver's iron arm.
Clangaranga, clangaranga,
Clang, clang, clang. . . .

To the September issue of *Poetry* she herself had contributed a poem on
'The Giant Cactus of Arizona', which in the desert stands 'Like time's
inviolate sentinel'. So naturally she was disappointed when she found
that Eliot had betrayed his heritage into the hands of the very cosmo-
politanism which American civilization was destined to overcome.
Pound was so disgusted when early in November he received her letter
objecting to 'Prufrock' that he could manage only seven words in reply:
'Your objection to Eliot is the climax.' But later the same day weary
resignation turned to something like fury and he wrote a second letter:
'No, most emphatically I will not ask Eliot to write down to any
audience whatsoever. I dare say my instinct was sound enough when
I volunteered to quit the magazine quietly about a year ago.' Neither
would he send her Eliot's address in order that he might be insulted.
This was on 9 November. Ten weeks later she was still objecting and on

31 January Pound was patiently explaining to her that 'Prufrock' did not go off at the end. It was a portrait of failure and it would be false art to make it end on a note of triumph: 'a portrait satire on futility can't end by turning that quintessence of futility, Mr P. into a reformed character breathing out fire and ozone.'

While this struggle was going on, Pound was attempting to launch in London a College of Arts with the following among its faculty members: Gaudier-Brzeska, Wyndham Lewis, Katherine Heyman, John Cournos, Edward Wadsworth, Arnold Dolmetsch, Edmund Dulac, Alvin Langdon Coburn and of course Pound himself. The first announcement of the college was an article by Pound in *The Egoist* of 1 November 1914. Nine days later he sent a proof of the college prospectus to Harriet Monroe; the leaflet was printed at the Complete Press in London and copies distributed towards the end of November. It was called 'Preliminary Announcement of the College of Arts' and made its appeal to American students who because of the war were unable to study on the Continent. The college offered them 'contact with artists of established position, creative minds, men for the most part who have already suffered in the cause of their art'. The cost of instruction for a year would vary from £20 to £100 depending on how much the student wished to do himself and how much he wished to have done for him. The prospectus drew attention to the fact that Arnold Dolmetsch's position in the world of music was 'unique' and music lovers so well aware of it that there was no need to proclaim it. Painting and sculpture, it said, would be taught by the most advanced and brilliant men of the decade, but instruction in 'representative painting' would also be available to the student interested in 'earlier forms of the art'. The aim of the college was 'an intellectual status no lower than that attained by the courts of the Italian Renaissance'.

The idea of a 'super-college' had been in Pound's mind since before he wrote the booklet *Patria Mia*; it now appeared as if he might be able to put his idea into action. He sent a bundle of prospectuses to his parents who were now back in Wyncote and towards the end of 1914 wrote to his mother: 'Ask Dad to send those notices of the Col. of Arts to the Press. How many more does he want?' But the war which had seemed to offer him unexpectedly the opportunity he had been waiting for, placed too many obstacles in the way and the college was abandoned without ever having existed except on paper.

His enthusiasm for Dolmetsch was the result of a recent visit to the Dolmetsch home:

I found myself in a reconstructed century – in a century of music, back before Mozart or Purcell, listening to clear music, to tones clear as brown amber. And this music came indifferently out of the harpsichord or the clavichord or out of virginals or out of odd-shaped viols, or whatever they may be. There were two small girls playing upon them with an exquisite precision . . . one steps into a past era when one sees all the other Dolmetsches dancing quaint, ancient steps of sixteenth-century dancing. One feels that the dance would go on even if there were no audience.

Pound continued to publish articles on art during the second half of 1914 – one on Wyndham Lewis in *The Egoist* of 15 June, 'An Authorized Appreciation' of Wadsworth in the issue of 15 August and his explanation of 'Vorticism' in the *Fortnightly Review* of 1 September: 'In the "eighties" there were symbolists opposed to impressionists, now you have vorticism, which is, roughly speaking, expressionism, neo-cubism, and imagism gathered together in one camp and futurism in the other.' In so far as it was an art movement futurism was a kind of accelerated impressionism, 'a spreading, or surface art, as opposed to vorticism, which is intensive'.

Early in November he attended a Rodin exhibition at the South Kensington museum. It was good of its kind but it looked 'like muck' after one had got one's eye in on Epstein's 'Babylonian austerity'. Even the work of Gaudier-Brzeska who was only twenty-two was much more interesting than Rodin's. Accompanied by Coburn he went in November to see an exhibition of Modern Spanish Art at the Grafton gallery. This was quite definitely 'MUCK' and the preface to the catalogue as silly as the show itself, 'all anchored about 1875 and amateurish'. Picasso, he noted, was not even mentioned in it. The only work in the show which stood out was that of Nestor Martin Fernandez della Torre who seemed to be trying to combine Van Gogh's 'hardness' with the splendour of Seville or of the Renaissance period. Although the war was beginning to make a difference to things, the Vorticists were still in evidence: Lewis when not decorating Hueffer's study at South Lodge was editing a second number of *Blast* for which Gaudier in France was preparing an essay on sculpture.

In the December issue of *Poetry* Pound published a review of Frost's *North of Boston* in which he described him as an honest writer writing from his own knowledge and emotion and not simply picking up the manner which magazines were accepting at the moment and applying it to topics in vogue. He had dared to write, and for the most part with success, in the natural speech of New England – a spoken speech very different from the 'natural' speech of the newspapers and of many professors. 'His book is a contribution', Pound said, 'to American literature, the sort of sound work that will develop into very interesting literature if persevered in.'

Early in December Pound sent typescript copies of some of his

Chinese poems to Gaudier who by this time was fighting in the trenches. Two of them were war poems which his growing feeling of involvement in the war perhaps helped him to shape. 'Song of the Bowmen of Shu' was a song of Chinese soldiers fighting barbarian tribes in the wilderness far from home; they were hungry and thirsty, wondering when they would be allowed to return to their own country:

> The enemy is swift, we must be careful.
> When we set out, the willows were drooping with spring,
> We come back in the snow,
> We go slowly, we are hungry and thirsty,
> Our mind is full of sorrow, who will know of our grief?

The other was 'Lament of the Frontier Guard':

> By the North Gate, the wind blows full of sand,
> Lonely from the beginning of time until now!

On 18 December Gaudier wrote to Pound that 'The poems depict our situation in a wonderful way.' Two days later Pound informed his family that he had put together a good little book from Fenollosa's notes and on 30 December he told them that Elkin Mathews had agreed to publish the book, to be called *Cathay*, in March.

Pound continued to attract trouble from many quarters and to meet it with a headlong rush. In August 1914 the New Zealand magazine *The Triad* attacked the 'mordant pen' of 'Mr Isaiah Ounce' for its part in promoting the new poetry. Reviewing *Blast* in October the magazine spoke of the Vorticists as lunatics and of the 'perverted drivelling' of the 'deplorable and ridiculous Mr Ezra Pound'. On 21 December Pound sent off a counter-blast – a letter justifying his position; it was published in the March 1915 issue, at the beginning of an article 'Mr Ezra Pound and Vorticism' by one of the magazine's editors, Frank Morton, who appears to have tampered a little with Pound's spelling and punctuation. Pound's way of meeting the charges was to appear to rejoice in them. It was, he said, an 'excellent and honourable thing' to be condemned in company with Cézanne and Picasso. As for the claim that he was 'a charlatan and deceiver of women' (a reference to Harriet Monroe), how was it, he asked, that he had been accepted by such a 'male and mature' editor as Courtney of the *Fortnightly Review*?

During the first months of war Pound had been impressed by the 'fine sight' of troops flocking to Europe from 'the four corners of Empire' and by news of May Sinclair working for the Red Cross in Belgium. In the courtyard of the Royal Academy Wadsworth, Augustus John 'and nearly everybody' were drilling for home defence and in a huge studio building in Chelsea he found that every man save a sculptor who made monuments had volunteered; but still he viewed it from the outside and was content to quote Charles Ricketts, a man of the 1890s and a friend of Yeats, who said: 'What depresses me most is the horrible fact that they can't *all* of them be beaten.' In writing to Harriet Monroe in November he said the war was possibly a conflict between two forces almost equally detestable: 'Atavism and the loathsome spirit of mediocrity cloaked in graft.' But one did not really know for the thing was too involved. His thoughts were directed to what would happen to civilization after the war had been won: 'One wonders if the war is only a stop-gap. Only a symptom of the real disease.'

Not until Hulme went and Gaudier began to report the horrors of trench warfare did the war touch him personally. By February 1915 he was furious with the Germans and trying to stir up American interest in the Allied cause. In a letter sent to Hessler on 9 February he spoke soberly of the land being full of 'armed men about to die for their country' and on the 18th he sent Mencken a war poem for the *Smart Set*: 'I did it this morning. I think it has some guts, but am perhaps still blinded by the fury in which I wrote it, and still confuse the cause with the result.' It was never published.

On 12 February he was correcting the proofs of *Cathay* and in *T.P.'s Weekly* of 20 February he published an article called 'Imagisme and England' in which he linked Imagism with material he had discovered in the Fenollosa notebooks. He discussed first the 'two sorts of poetry' which to him were the 'most interesting, the most *poetic*'. There was lyric poetry, in which sheer melody seemed as if it were just coming over into speech; and there was poetry in which painting or sculpture seemed as if it were just forcing itself into words. 'The second sort of poetry is as old and as distinct [as the first], but until recently no one had named it. We now call it *Imagist*, it is not a new invention, it is a critical discrimination.' As for Chinese, 'it is quite true', he said, 'that we have sought the force of Chinese ideographs *without knowing it*'. He discounted talk about the unsuitability of English for the purpose of translating Chinese: 'I have now by me the papers of the late Ernest Fenollosa, sometime Imperial Commissioner of Art in Tokyo. He certainly knew more about this matter than anyone else whose opinion we are likely to get at. In his essay on the Chinese written character he expressly contends that English, being the strongest and least inflected of the European languages, is precisely the one language best suited to render the force and the concision of the uninflected Chinese.' The first of the Fenollosa-Pound Chinese poems to appear in print was 'Exile's Letter', in the March number of *Poetry*:

> With boats floating, and the sounds of mouth-organ
>   and drums,
> With ripples like dragon-scales, going grass green
>   on the water. . . .

Cathay was published by Mathews on 6 April, a thirty-two page booklet in heavy tan paper wrappers, price 1s. The title-page says 'Translations by Ezra Pound, for the most part from the Chinese of Rihaku [Japanese for Li Po], from the notes of the late Ernest Fenollosa, and the decipherings of the Professors Mori and Ariga.' The book is so justly famous for the new note it brought into English verse that it is easy to overlook its strong traditional roots. Some at least of the pleasure comes from the way a decidedly English idiom is used to convey a fresh subject with which it had not previously been associated:

> This boat is of shato-wood, and its gunwales are cut magnolia,
> Musicians with jewelled flutes and with pipes of gold
> Fill full the sides in rows, and our wine
> Is rich for a thousand cups.
>
> . . .
>
> And heard the five-score nightingales aimlessly singing.
>   ('The River Song')

On the last page of the booklet was a note signed E.P. in which he said he had not come to the end of Fenollosa's notes by a long way, nor was it entirely perplexity that caused him to cease from translation. He felt that if he gave the poems with the necessary breaks for explanation, and a tedium of notes, it was 'quite certain' that the personal hatred in which he was held by many, and the *invidia* which was directed against him because he had dared openly to declare his belief in certain young artists, would be brought to bear first on the flaws of such translation, and would then be merged into depreciation of the whole book: 'Therefore I give only these unquestionable poems'.

In a review of *Cathay* on 29 April *The Times Literary Supplement* said 'Mr Pound has kept to the reality of the original because he keeps his language simple and sharp and precise. We hope he will give us some more versions of Chinese poetry.' Hueffer was enthusiastic in his review in *The Outlook* of 19 June. If these were original verses, he said, then Pound was the greatest poet of the day – which was a reference apparently to complaints that the poems contained more of Pound than of the Chinese originals. He described them as 'things of a supreme beauty' which in a sense only backed up a theory and practice of poetry that was already old: 'the theory that poetry consists in so rendering concrete objects that the emotions produced by the objects shall arise in the reader – and not in writing about the emotions themselves.' *Cathay* was like a door in a wall, opening suddenly upon fields of an extreme beauty, and upon a landscape made real by the intensity of human emotions. 'Beauty is a very valuable thing', he said; 'perhaps it is the most valuable thing in life; but the power to express emotion so that it shall communicate itself intact and exactly is almost more valuable. Of both these qualities Mr Pound's book is very full.'

Writing in *The New Age* of 5 August Orage welcomed the book but noted 'in the vers librists' a tendency to confine themselves 'to the elementary emotions of elementary people'. He was inclined to the view that *Cathay* contained the best and only good work that Pound had yet done; at any rate such a judgement might be defended. As in the case of 'The Seafarer', he said, the thoughts contained in the Chinese poems were of a very simple character. The imaginary persons were without subtlety and almost, one might say, without mind. 'But it cannot be the case that only simple natures can be the subjects of poetry; or that "naturalness" belongs to them alone.' The extension of the directness and simplicity, the veracity and the actuality aimed at by vers librists into subtler regions than the commonplace was advisable, he said, if they were not to keep in the nursery of art.

NOTES

1 Published in *Speculations*, 1924.

XI Joyce and Eliot
1915/1917

Pound and his wife spent the winter of 1914–15 with Yeats at Coleman's Hatch. In January, while following up material he had found among the Fenollosa papers, Pound began to read Confucius, probably Pauthier's French translation of the 'Tschoung-Young'. His mother and father had been interested for years in the work of some of the Christian missionaries in China and he had read a little Confucius as early as July 1907; he had also had some contact with Chinese thought through Upward; but now, in his enthusiasm for Fenollosa, he began to pursue the matter more seriously.

In a letter which appeared in the 16 January issue of an American magazine, *The Dial* – not yet the famous *Dial* of the 1920s – he held up to ridicule an American editor who in 1912 or 1913 had referred to Henri de Regnier and Remy de Gourmont as young men whose work was unknown to him. Pound did not mention that until about January 1912 their work was unknown to him also. But what annoyed him still more was that the editor did not show any desire to rectify 'this lacuna in his mental decorations'. In their effort to bequeath a heritage of good letters to America, men like Henry James had been forced to work abroad; and it was the same, he said, for the younger generation: 'after years of struggle, one by one, they come abroad, in search of good company and good conversation, or send their manuscripts abroad for recognition', and 'find themselves in the pages even of the "stolid and pre-Victorian *Quarterly*" before "hustling and modern America" has arrived at tolerance of their modernity'.

He also took up again the cry for a Renaissance. Beginning with the February issue of *Poetry* he published three instalments under the title, 'The Renaissance', in which he suggested that the new awakening might find its inspiration in China. He called for the development of a criticism of poetry based on world-poetry, on the work of maximum excellence, and for the subsidy of individual artists and writers, such as would enable them to 'follow their highest ambitions without needing to conciliate the ignorant *en route*'. When a civilization was vivid, he said, it preserved and fostered painters, poets, sculptors, musicians, architects; when it was dull and anaemic it preserved only 'a rabble of priests, sterile instructors, and repeaters of things second-hand'.

There was similar talk in a series called 'Affirmations' which ran in *The New Age* in seven instalments from 7 January to 25 February. There were 'new masses of unexplored arts and facts' pouring into the 'vortex' of London, he wrote, which 'cannot help but bring about changes as great as the Renaissance changes, even if we set ourselves blindly against it. As it is, there is life in the fusion. The complete man must have more interest in things which are in seed and dynamic than in things which are dead, dying, static.'

But so much needed doing and so much needed attacking before he could have his Renaissance that he was unable to handle with due propriety the multitude of necessary details and in his letters and his prose showed signs of lapsing more and more into a private language. He jumped from one point to another and seldom explained himself. Such prose became a habit.

He was writing meanwhile some of his most effective short poems. In the December 1914 issue of Harold Munro's *Poetry and Drama* he published 'Ione, Dead the Long Year':

> Empty are the ways of this land
>
> Where Ione
>
> Walked once, and now does not walk
> But seems like a person just gone.

To *Poetry* of March 1915 he contributed a group of poems which included 'The Spring':

> And wild desire
> Falls like black lightning.
> O bewildered heart,
> Though every branch have back what last year lost,
> She, who moved here amid the cyclamen,
> Moves only now a clinging tenuous ghost.

Another was 'Provincia Deserta', a longer poem than the others, which tells of his walk through Provence in the summer of 1912 but in such a way that the facts of a particular journey are blended by poetry with the Provence of the troubadours. It is a genuine poem of evocation and gentle regret, in Pound's best vein, and perhaps the only one of his poems of which we can say that it was a forerunner of *The Pisan Cantos*.

Through March and April Pound was busy lecturing Harriet Monroe, acting as unpaid literary agent for Joyce, Cournos and others, and attempting with some success to draw in John Quinn as one of the patrons of his Renaissance. Quinn bought work by Gaudier and Lewis and later was of assistance to Joyce. Pound also sought his aid in raising money in America for a new monthly or quarterly magazine of the arts which Pound would edit according to his own ideas. He thought at one stage that he would be having his fare paid to America to enable him to make final arrangements for the new publication and in September 1915 he asked Joyce whether, in addition to creative work, he would consider contributing a regular survey of current Italian literature, but Joyce replied that he preferred to stick to his creative work. Pound composed a prospectus for the new magazine but failed to raise the necessary money.

His other activities at this time included the sending of a circular letter to 'various young writers in the U.S.', urging them to fight for the removal of the tariff on books and to engage in other civic activities; he was also attempting, but without success, to arrange for the publication in a serious magazine or learned periodical of Fenollosa's essay on the Chinese written character. In June 1915 he told his old teacher Felix Schelling (whom he had met by accident in the British Museum the year before) that the essay contained 'a whole basis of aesthetic' but that the 'adamantine stupidity of all magazine editors' was delaying its appearance. In later years he was particularly hard on Paul Carus whose various books on Chinese thought and writing were published by the Open Court Publishing Company in Illinois. He sent the essay to Carus for publication in his magazine, *The Monist*, but he rejected it; thereafter Pound always spoke of him contemptuously. In an article in *The Criterion* of October 1935 he wrote: 'The effects of his [Fenollosa's] vision were sabotaged right and left, and the small group of men comprising "the learned world" will some day feel a disgust for Paul Carus in particular.'

On 18 April 1915 Pound sent Mencken a long poem in couplets, 'L'Homme Moyen Sensuel', for publication in the *Smart Set*: 'My business instinct, such as it is, makes me think the most advantageous thing all round would be to boom it as THE satire, "best since Byron". New York is accustomed to a new Keats and a new Shelley once a fortnight and one might vary the note.' The poem had its moments:

> Still we look toward the day when man, with unction,
> Will long only to be a *social function*,
> And even Zeus' wild lightning fear to strike
> Lest it should fail to treat all men alike. . . .

Pound was hoping that readers of the *Smart Set* would like it and that he would be asked to contribute verse satire on a regular basis. 'If it goes,' he told Mencken, 'I can turn you out an instalment every two or three months.' But the editors of the *Smart Set* denied their readers the opportunity to enjoy even the first instalment and 'L'Homme Moyen Sensuel' was not published until September 1917 in *The Little Review*. As a result perhaps of his friendship with Victor Plarr or because of an affinity with the 1890s Pound rested a moment from Renaissance, Vorticism and satire to publish in the April *Poetry* a review of Plarr's *Ernest Dowson*. It is clear from the tone that he felt there was something attractive about Dowson, 'a young Englishman enamoured of many things French', and about Plarr, 'an Alsatian, half refugee from the war of '70, a survivor of the senatorial families of Strasbourg'. The memoir of their friendship, he said, was 'charming'. He thought perhaps that Plarr was right and that some writers had borne too heavily upon the supposed luridity of Dowson's career, 'which was in all truth pastoral enough, a delicate temperament that ran a little amuck towards the end, an irregular man with nothing a sane man would call vices'.

With the publication by Houghton, Mifflin in Boston and by Constable in London of Amy Lowell's *Some Imagist Poets*, Imagism gained a wider public and became the subject of uninstructive argument in both England and America. *The Egoist* of 1 May was a special Imagist number. In addition to articles on individual poets and their work, including 'The Poetry of D. H. Lawrence' by Olivia Shakespear, it contained Flint's 'The History of Imagism' in which he said that Hulme, as ringleader of the 1909 group, had insisted on 'absolutely accurate presentation and no verbiage'. There had been also a lot of talk and practice, Storer leading it chiefly, of what they called 'the Image'. Having differed with Pound over the Amy Lowell anthology Flint treated him as an interloper who had got his ideas from the 1909 group and who had done little since then except invent the term *Imagisme*. This led to a bitter exchange of letters between Pound and Flint in July with Pound saying that Flint's history was 'BULLSHIT' and that the drive for current simple speech had come from Hueffer; and with Flint denying that Hueffer was as important as Pound maintained and listing some of Pound's shortcomings: 'You had the energy, you had the talents (obscured these by a certain American mushiness), you might have been generalissimo in a compact onslaught: and you spoiled everything by some native incapacity for walking square with your fellows.'

In America, Conrad Aiken, writing in the *New Republic* of 22 May, accused the Imagists of being a mutual admiration society and found their work lacking in force: 'They give us frail pictures – whiffs of windy beaches, marshes, meadows, city streets, dishevelled leaves;

pictures pleasant and suggestive enough. But seldom is any of them more than a nice description, coolly sensuous, a rustle to the ear, a ripple to the eye. Of organic movement there is practically none.' Arguments about Imagism and the publication of Imagist books continued on both sides of the Atlantic for several years.

There seems to have been a temporary break in Pound's relations with *The Egoist* at this time and practically nothing of his was published there during 1915. He sought another outlet and in May 1915 hopefully began negotiations to take over the editorship of a weekly called *The Academy*. When this came to nothing he took up again the idea of establishing a new fortnightly similar to the *Mercure de France* and began to cast about among his correspondents for assistance. From New York the lawyer John Quinn reported that there was a chance of capturing *The Forum* but the scheme evaporated when the magazine's sponsor Mitchell Kennerley decided to sit tight.

Pound's struggle on behalf of Eliot's poetry, which had begun the moment in September 1914 that he had recognized something of its superior quality, was neutralized during the first few months of 1915 by Harriet Monroe's stubbornness. After six months and numerous letters he wrote wearily at the end of a letter of 10 April: '*Do* get on with that Eliot.' Finally, in June, she capitulated, but not without a small gesture of defiance in the process. The June number of *Poetry* opened with two poems by Arjan Syrian and there followed poems by Bliss Carman ('Ah, traveller, hast thou nought of thanks or praise'), Dorothy Dudley ('I have seen an old street weeping'), Georgia Wood Pangborn ('Some brighter thing than sunlight touched the sea'), William Griffi ('Once more the crimson rumour'), Skipwith Cannell ('The lean grey rats of hunger'), and at last, tucked away safely at the end of the verse contributions, 'The Love Song of J. Alfred Prufrock' by Mr T. S. Eliot, 'a young American poet resident in England, who has published nothing hitherto in this country'. It was in fact Eliot's first appearance in print since 24 June 1910 when the Class Ode which he had delivered at his Harvard graduation ceremony was published in the *Harvard Advocate* and reprinted the same day in the *Boston Evening Transcript* and *Boston Evening Herald*.

With the aid of a Sheldon Travelling Fellowship Eliot had gone to Oxford in September 1914 to continue his post-graduate studies at Merton College, under F. H. Bradley's disciple Harold Joachim, a Greek scholar with whom he studied the *Posterior Analytics*. He wrote to Pound from Merton on 2 February 1915, enclosing a copy of 'Portrait of a Lady' (composed about 1910) and saying that he had received a Christmas card from the lady in question, bearing the 'ringing greetings of friend to friend at this season of high festival'. He thanked

Pound for having introduced him to the Dolmetsch family among whom he had recently passed one of the most delightful afternoons he had ever spent, listening to them play old music and watching them dance old dances. He had been reading some of Pound's work lately, he said, and had enjoyed the article on the Vortex: 'I distrust and detest Aesthetics, when it cuts loose from the Object, and vapours into the void, but you have not done that.'

Eliot published further poems in *Blast, Poetry* and *Others* during 1915 and 1916 and began slowly to acquire a small place in the literature of the day. He left Oxford in 1915 and in July married his first wife, Vivien Haigh-Wood. After a trip home in the summer of 1915 he took up school-teaching: at High Wycombe Grammar School at £140 a year plus one meal a day, and later at Highgate Junior School where the stipend was £160 plus dinner and tea. Between 1916 and 1918 he also delivered extension lectures on French and English literature at Oxford and the University of London and evening lectures on Victorian literature at the County Secondary School, High Street, Sydenham, S.E.26, under the auspices of the London County Council. He also continued for a time with his philosophical studies. In April 1916 he completed his dissertation 'Experience and the Objects of Knowledge in the Philosophy of F. H. Bradley – A thesis submitted in partial fulfilment of the requirements for candidates for the doctorate of philosophy at Harvard University.' He sent it to Harvard and about two months later received word from one of his teachers that the Division of Philosophy accepted it 'without the least hesitation' and that Professor Josiah Royce acclaimed it 'the work of an expert'. Eliot had been marked out by his teachers for a post in philosophy but thanks largely to Pound, who gave him encouragement and helped him with editors at the right moment, he remained in London, began to publish criticism and was saved for poetry.

Although the Rebel Art Centre had closed in the autumn of 1914 Lewis brought out a second issue of *Blast* in July 1915. Among a group of poems by Pound was a short piece, 'Our Contemporaries', which alluded to an experience of Rupert Brooke's in Tahiti. The poem, which did not mention Brooke by name, had been written while he was still alive, but its appearance in *Blast*, of all places, after his death in April, brought on much criticism of Pound's bad taste. Pound had always regarded Brooke as the best of the Georgian poets and I doubt whether he foresaw the fuss that resulted. Forced to defend himself he pointed out that *Blast* had been due to appear in December 1914, months before Brooke's death, and that some of the blame therefore was Lewis's. It is difficult to say anything about the affair now except that the poem which caused it was so bad as to be quite unworthy of the occasion. Any blame should have fallen on Pound for having written it and Lewis for not having rejected it. In a letter to an American acquaintance, Milton Bronner, on 21 September 1915 Pound wrote of Brooke at some length:

I am very sorry that Brooke is dead, he was the best of the younger English, though Eliot is certainly more interesting.

Brooke flocked with the stupidest set of Blockheads to be found in any country, i.e. the Abercrombie, Drinkwater, New Numbers assortment and that certainly did not promise much for him, still he was infinitely better than his friends.

Whether he was better than Aldington I don't know. I am afraid that Aldington's head will petrify, but then English heads do.
. . .
Brzeska's death is, so far, the worst calamity of the war. There *was* a loss to art with a vengeance. In Brooke's case I think it was more the loss of a charming young man. I can't see that he has done or would have done much that Eliot won't do better.

Gaudier-Brzeska had been killed in action on 5 June at Neuville St Vaast. His manifesto, 'Vortex', written in the trenches, was published in *Blast*:

This war is a great remedy.

In the individual it kills arrogance, self esteem, pride.

It takes away from the masses numbers upon numbers of unimportant units, whose economic activities become noxious as the recent trade crises have shown us.

His views on sculpture, he said, remained unchanged; he would derive his emotions solely from the arrangement of surfaces and he would present them by the arrangement of surfaces, 'the planes and lines by which they are defined'. Soon after news of Gaudier's death reached London Pound began to prepare a memorial volume.

Because of the war Joyce had moved first to Venice and then to Zurich. He wrote to Pound in June to say that he was hard up and Pound began at once to stir up interest among those with power to influence the Royal Literary Fund. Indefatigable in the cause of a writer in whom he had faith Pound prodded Yeats and answered questions, wrote to Joyce for details of his position and did all else he could to push the matter forward as quickly as possible. The result was a grant of £75 and when Joyce wrote to thank Yeats in September the latter replied: 'I am very glad indeed that "The Royal Literary Fund" has been so wise and serviceable. You need not thank me, for it was really Ezra Pound who thought of your need. I acted at his suggestion, because it was easier for me to approach the Fund for purely personal reasons. We thought Gosse (who has great influence with the Fund people, but is rather prejudiced) would take it better from me. What trouble there was fell on Ezra.' The money and the recognition implied gave Joyce a certain measure of peace and helped him to go ahead with the Bloom episodes of *Ulysses* on which he was then working.

But not content with this, Pound continued his efforts for Joyce in all directions: he acted as literary agent (even after J. B. Pinker had the job officially), wrote a long article boosting Joyce's play *Exiles* (the article was published in the February 1916 issue of *The Drama*, Chicago), offered to send Joyce books, gave him advice about how to live cheaply, and even turned doctor and prescribed for Joyce's eye trouble. In print, in letters and by word of mouth he proclaimed Joyce one of the best contemporary authors and said that *A Portrait of the Artist as a Young Man* was as permanent a novel as those of Stendhal and Flaubert. In *Poetry* of April 1916 he declared that he was 'by far the most significant writer of our decade'.

In June 1916 Pound secured Joyce a grant of £2 a week for thirteen weeks from the Incorporated Society of Authors, Playwrights and Composers, passed on to Joyce a gift of £20 from his friend Lady Maud Cunard, and by constant activity in the right quarters was responsible for the Asquith government granting Joyce £100 from the Civil List. Lady Cunard had helped, it seems, by lending Joyce's works to Edward Marsh.

On 14 July 1915 the *Boston Evening Transcript* published a letter from Pound in which he called one of its reviewers a liar for having said that Robert Frost was the only American poet of the generation who 'unheralded, unintroduced, untrumpeted' had won the acceptance of an English publisher on his own terms. Pound described his own experience with Elkin Mathews several years before Frost's arrival in England and also his part in promoting Frost's work, and it is difficult not to sympathize with his irritation when one thinks of his struggle and all that he had done for other writers; but it was a foolish letter and showed signs of persecution complex: 'from the beginning, in my pushing Frost's work, I have known that he would ultimately be boomed in America by fifty energetic young men who would use any club to beat me.'

When in August he heard of a new booklet of poems by Robert Bridges he wrote for permission to publish some of them in *Poetry*. Bridges replied that the booklet was privately printed but allowed him to quote two of the poems in full in a short review published in October.

Both poems were 'very good', Pound said in a letter to Harriet Monroe, and the cadence of one of them was 'exquisite'. Some years later he recalled how Bridges when going through *Personae* and *Exultations*, at a time when Pound was trying to use modern speech, had been delighted with the younger poet's archaisms: 'We'll get 'em all back,' he exclaimed, 'we'll get 'em *all* back.'

By early September 1915 John Lane (The Bodley Head) had accepted the memoir he was preparing on Gaudier and on the 12th Pound 'sent to the press' a new collection of recent poetry called *Catholic Anthology*, a reply perhaps to Amy Lowell's *Some Imagist Poets*. He was also busy writing letters in connection with his proposed magazine and in early September spoke of going 'down town' and buying two modern pictures on behalf of a collector, presumably Quinn. He volunteered for war service, but was not accepted. Later, after America's entry into the war, he sought Quinn's assistance in finding service with the Americans in France, in which country, he said, neither his profession nor appearance would be against him. These efforts were, however, unsuccessful.

In his letter of 21 September to Milton Bronner, Pound said that from his own point of view 'Exile's Letter' and 'The Seafarer' were worth about as much as anything he had done. He did not expect to improve on 'Exile's Letter'. He thought that England had been in a state of coma since before the war and said it was 'possible to put up an American literary team – Eliot, Orrick Johns, Edgar Lee Masters, Maxwell Bodenheim, Williams and H.D. – which would beat anything England could show among the new generation. But he went on to point out that the gods were no respecters of national boundaries and named Arnold Dolmetsch, Gaudier and his Japanese friend Michio Itow as proof that they bestowed intelligence where they chose. In discussing the Fenollosa papers he told Bronner: 'I should probably have gone to China if I hadn't married', although he doubted whether China today was the China he cared about.

In this same letter Pound mentioned that he had started work on his long poem, *The Cantos*: 'I am also at work on a cryselephantine poem of immeasurable length which will occupy me for the next four decades unless it becomes a bore.' It was not at this stage called *The Cantos* nor was he clear in 1915 about the form it would take.

In October Pound wrote two articles on Remy de Gourmont, recently deceased. Although they had never met, Pound had been in touch with him by letter. De Gourmont contributed an article on Lautréamont to *The Egoist* in 1914 and in June 1915 he offered to co-operate in Pound's plans for a new magazine to maintain communications between New York, London and Paris. The aim of the *Mercure de France*, he told Pound, 'has been to permit any man, who is worth it, to write down his thoughts frankly – this is a writer's sole pleasure. And this aim should be yours.' The first of Pound's two articles appeared in the *Fortnightly Review* of 1 December and the other in the January 1916 issue of *Poetry*. In his efforts to lead the 'party of intelligence', as he called it, to a new Renaissance, he took De Gourmont as a guide: 'It is foolish, perhaps, to say that a man "stands for all that is best in such and such a country". It is a vague phrase, and the use of vague phrases is foolish, and yet Remy de Gourmont had in some way made himself into a symbol of so much that is finest in France that one is tempted to apply some such phrase to him.' Paul Claudel, he said, was merely a craze, and Francis Jammes, after four beautiful books to his credit, had 'gone *gaga* over catholicism'. From De Gourmont alone there proceeded a personal, living force, better described perhaps, as a 'personal light'. He hoped that this same intelligence was at last stirring in English literature: 'With the appearance of James Joyce and T. S. Eliot, and the more "normal" part of Mr Wyndham Lewis's narrative writings, one may even hope that intelligence shall once more have its innings, even in our own stalwart tongue.'

Partly as a result of Pound's work on the Japanese Noh plays and his friendship with a young Japanese, Michio Itow, then living in Pound's old room at 10 Church Walk, there was a rush of interest in things Japanese. Pound was extremely fond of Itow and in September 1915 remarked that all Japanese except Itow seemed detestable. On another occasion he excepted also a 'pleasant' young Japanese who played a large bamboo flute. Beside Church Walk was a fence shutting out St Mary Abbots graveyard. A neighbour, Mrs Tinkey, had her worst suspicions confirmed when she caught Itow trying to entice her cat over the fence. Itow wanted it for the purpose of clearing out some mice but Mrs Tinkey was certain that he intended to use it for oriental cooking. Pound was obviously fascinated by Itow and in his article on De Gourmont in the *Fortnightly* he reported a conversation he had had with him in a bus: 'I am, let us say, in an omnibus with Michio Itow. He has just seen some Japanese armour and says it is like his grand-father's, and then simply running on in his own memory he says: "When I first put on my grandfather's helmet, my grandmother cried . . . because I was so like what my grandfather was at eighteen."' Towards the end of October 1915 Itow gave some performances for Pound and his friends of Noh dancing, dressed in a costume specially reconstructed for the event by Edmund Dulac and Charles Ricketts.

Yeats was stimulated by the Noh to write plays himself in a similar form, beginning with *At the Hawk's Well*, parts of which he dictated to Pound while they were at Coleman's Hatch together in January 1916. With the help of Itow, Dulac and Ricketts the play was staged in

Lady Cunard's drawing-room on 2 April. According to Michael Reck, a friend of Pound's who talked to Michio Itow in Japan in the 1950s, Itow was not a Noh dancer when he left Japan for Europe. But hearing about it in London he quickly visited the appropriate libraries and learnt enough to be accepted as such.[1] In 1916 he performed 'traditional' Japanese dances to the accompaniment of poems pieced together by Pound from the notes of Masirni Utchiyama. Itow went to the United States and in January 1923 he staged, for the benefit of members of the Thursday Evening Club, the Noh play, *Hagoromo*. In the printed programme it was advertised as: 'Japanese Noh Drama Given for the First Time outside of Japan, Staged by Michio Itow.' He spent the years between the wars in Hollywood and when Reck spoke to him he was a rich old man famous throughout Japan as the proprietor of dancing-girl establishments. One of the things which most impressed Yeats in 1916 was that Itow in his dedication to his profession used to visit the London Zoo and there learn to imitate the movements of birds and animals.

Soon afterwards Pound met another Japanese, a young painter, Tami Koume, who told him that at the age of about six he had danced the role of a spirit (called a 'tennin') in the play *Hagoromo*. He could still remember the wing movements which he was able to repeat for Pound who said later that they were the most beautiful movements he had ever seen on or off the stage. He believed that Koume knew and understood an aspect of Noh that 'no mere philologist' could discover from a text-book. When in the 1920s Pound went to Paris he held a show of some of Tami Koume's paintings, one of which permanently decorated a wall of his flat there. Later when he moved to Italy the painting was transferred to a friend's flat in Venice. At one stage Pound had in mind to visit Koume in Tokio but the painter was killed in the Japanese earthquake of 1924.

In October 1915 Elkin Mathews published a collection called *Poetical Works of Lionel Johnson*, with a preface by Pound in which he refers to himself as the editor of the book. He did not check the text but merely added a few unpublished poems to a collection of already published work; he and Dorothy also read the proofs. Pound was not much interested in Johnson, despite the connection with his mother-in-law, but Mathews paid him for the job and he was able to find in some of Johnson's work an imagistic clarity. When in 1915 Mathews offered sheets of the collection to the Macmillan Company in New York they accepted but asked Mathews to remove Pound's preface from their copies. Pound wrote to Bronner on 25 September that this was a fairly good indication of America's 'irritation and resentment at having had a poet born within her geographical boundaries'. Mathews also deleted the preface from the second English impression published in 1917, apparently because Pound quoted some harsh comments by Johnson on Arthur Symons, William Watson, Richard Le Gallienne and Francis Thompson, all of whom had been published at one time or another by Mathews and three of whom were alive in 1915.

Early in November when Pound counted up his earnings for the year from November 1st 1914 to the end of October 1915 he found that they came to only £42 10s.[2] This was the lowest they had reached for some years and Pound claimed that it had been brought about by Prothero and others who objected to his association with *Blast*. He maintained that they punished him on his pocket because he had dared to discern a great sculptor and a great painter, namely Gaudier and Lewis, in the midst of England's 'artistic desolation'; but more likely they were simply stodgy gentlemen who objected to all the noise and to his use of the word 'testicles'.

Although Pound was short of money for years to come and often worried by the thought of where to go for his next cheque, he was generally not desperate. Dorothy Pound had an annuity of £150 and paid her own way – and there were times no doubt when her money tided them both over lean periods.

In *Poetry* of November 1915 Pound published a long poem on Bertran de Born, 'Near Perigord':

> Bewildering spring, and by the Auvezere
> Poppies and day's eyes in the green émail
> Rose over us; and we knew all that stream,
> And our two horses had traced out the valleys
> . . .
>
>   And great wings beat above us in the twilight,
> And the great wheels in heaven
> Bore us together. . . .

As a meditation on history and on the power of art to preserve what has gone, it is interesting, and there are fine passages, but none of the rest matches up to the superb ending:

> And all the rest of her a shifting change,
> A broken bundle of mirrors . . .!

In the same issue he published 'Villanelle: The Psychological Hour' with its firmly-paced opening:

> I had over-prepared the event,
>   that much was ominous.

> With middle-ageing care
>> I had laid out just the right books.
> I had almost turned down the pages.

In November Pound had three cables from Quinn about his new magazine, one of which indicated 'fair hopes of success'. He was very pleased with the way Lane was bringing out his book on Gaudier but was annoyed to be mixed up in 'a lot of petty intrigue' about the disposition of the sculptor's artistic remains, whether or when certain pieces would go to the nation, and so on. He had recently made a 'fine haul' of old Greek books, including a 'fairly rare' edition of the Emperor Julian. Towards the end of November he was 'ploughing through' William Roscoe's *The Life and Pontificate of Leo the Tenth, With a dissertation on the character of Lucretia Borgia*. 'The Borgias couldn't possibly have been *so* wicked', he wrote to Joyce, 'or their contemporaries would have been *much* more shocked.'

Pound's *Catholic Anthology* was published by Mathews in November bound in grey paper boards with a design in black by D.S. (Dorothy Shakespear). It was the first appearance in book-form of any of Eliot's verse and Pound often said that it was for the sake of the Eliot poems that he published it. One or two authors he included because he could not avoid it. One of these was Harriet Monroe in whose 'Letter from Pekin' banality is carried to heroic lengths. The main points of interest, apart from the finished products of Eliot, Yeats and Pound, are the long poem by Williams, 'The Wanderer', in which we see him near the beginning of his struggle to present contemporary America in verse, and poems by Harold Monro which show that he was one of the most readable poets of the period.

About the beginning of December Pound began to plan a new prose book, put together from his articles of the past five years and to be called *The Half Decade*. The title was later changed to *This Generation*. His idea was to show that the present decade in France and England was quite different from the 1890s but just as interesting. The book would treat of what was new in France during the past fifteen years and in England during the past five or six years. It would be informal, with the articles and reviews interspersed with an occasional letter or 'a touch of incident'. He thought it would have some permanent value as a first-hand record of literary and artistic events in the two capitals.

So important was the job facing the 'party of intelligence' that Pound tried to persuade his casual correspondents in America to act as agents for the publication of his books and to attend to clerical or similar matters in New York. Thus on 13 December 1915 he suggested to

Bronner that he might, if passing the door of the John Lane Company in New York, enquire about the possibility of an American edition of *Catholic Anthology*; he might also mention to them Pound's proposed book, *The Half Decade*, for if the John Lane Company in New York wrote to London about it, this might influence John Lane in London to do the English edition. If Lane refused it, but some other American firm published it, he told Bronner, then he was sure that Douglas Goldring would be glad to circulate the book in England. Goldring, a contributor to *Catholic Anthology* and formerly sub-editor of Ford Hueffer's *The English Review*, was trying to become a publisher but could not afford to bring out a work like *The Half Decade*.

Pound was also in touch with the Yale University Press about the publication of his Fenollosa material; in December they seemed 'well disposed toward Fenollosa', but nothing came of it. His earlier plan for a small book on Arnaut Daniel, for which Ralph Fletcher Seymour in Chicago had printed a handsome prospectus, had fallen through, but he was still working on Provençal and was thinking that maybe he would do a larger book on the troubadours as a whole.

On 16 December he wrote an eighty-four line poem, 'To a Friend Writing on Cabaret Dancers', which he sent almost immediately to Harriet Monroe. He thought it was the 'best thing' he had done for a long time but Miss Monroe rejected it as too outspoken. She feared prosecution, Pound said in January 1916, because he had used the word 'whore' instead of 'the refined Americo-Wellso-New Statesman-New Republic' term, 'prostitute', in the line: 'The prudent whore is not without her future.' The poem had to wait for his next book *Lustra*.

By mid-December Pound had drafted the first three cantos of his long poem and was working on canto 5. In a letter of 18 December 1915 he warned Homer that he had better begin reading Browning's *Sordello* to prepare himself for the 'big long endless poem' with which he was then struggling. Such preparation was necessary, he said, because it alluded much to Browning's poem. It should be two months before he was ready to send home a copy of the cantos already written; one of his reasons being that he did not want to muddle his mind in the fifth canto by typing the first three.

Once more Pound and his wife joined Yeats at Coleman's Hatch where the air was cleaner and there were no Zeppelin raids. Pound wrote to Joyce on 12 January 1916 that he was down in the country because he could not afford London: he was behind in his accounts but hoped to catch up. At this time he was a little weary of Joyce and his affairs and may have been suggesting indirectly that Joyce could not hope to rely on him indefinitely. Taking it in turns to read aloud Pound and Yeats worked their way through Landor's *Imaginary*

Conversations – a vital experience for Pound who thereafter regarded Landor as of first-rate importance.

During the winter of 1915–16, or possibly the previous year, the pastoral serenity of the poets' cottage was disturbed by the police who informed Pound and also his wife who was American by marriage that as Coleman's Hatch was within sixteen miles of the sea they were 'Aliens in a Prohibited Area' and so required to report regularly to the nearest police station. This they did, but at the same time Yeats and Pound sent letters all over the land in an attempt to have the nuisance removed. Most of the letters were composed by Pound in what he judged to be the other's epistolary style, were typed by him, and then signed by Yeats. One went to Robert Bridges who was asked to declare to the police that Ezra Pound was Ezra Pound. He entered into the spirit of the affair by asking what proof there was that the request came from the real Pound and Yeats – but on re-examining the letter, he was able to say, on the evidence of its appearance and style, that it was definitely the work of Ezra Pound. Finally Hueffer's friend, C. F. G. Masterman, recently a junior member of Asquith's cabinet, sent a telegram to the police and the matter was dropped. It was probably in company with Masterman that Lloyd George once waited on Pound in the courtyard outside 10 Church Walk, but for what purpose I have never been able to establish.

Due largely to Pound's efforts Harriet Shaw Weaver in January 1916 accepted Lewis's novel *Tarr* for serial publication in *The Egoist*, after numerous unsuccessful attempts to have it issued as a book by a regular publisher. It was about this time that Pound's chances of getting his own magazine seemed brightest but the money was not forthcoming. He had discovered meanwhile a publisher in New York, John Marshall, who was willing to publish *The Half Decade* ('No! not "the half-decayed",' Pound wrote) which by then he had re-titled *This Generation*. By March terms were being drawn up and Pound spoke of the work as already assembled, but I am not sure whether John Marshall actually had the whole or only a part in his possession. Pound had by this time submitted the typescript or a description of *Lustra* to Elkin Mathews who accepted it for publication in the autumn.

In a letter to Bronner early in 1916 Pound attacked Amy Lowell's Imagists as a 'public nuisance': they would have been just as much a nuisance, he said, even if he had not invented the term Imagism and he could not accept any responsibility for their actions. 'The people who interest me at present are Lewis, Joyce, Eliot.' He denied Bronner's suggestion that he had a persecution mania and explained his conduct thus: 'A lot of people know damn well that if I got a grip on things there'd be no place for their kind of tosh and they naturally don't want me to get a grip.' The letter contains some interesting opinions about Hueffer's shortcomings as a writer, which Pound did not air in public: 'Now about Hueffer's work. It is precisely what you say, too flabby, too easy, too lacking in intensity. But for all that it is sane and whole, and no man was ever harmed by reading it. That is to say he is right, but through a certain lack of intensity he fails to satisfy.' His best work was a book half done, he said, which he could not get him to finish. He did not say what book it was.

In letters to various correspondents about this time Pound said that Francis Meynell, a well-known Catholic, had protested to Mathews against the title *Catholic Anthology* and had threatened him that he would not sell a copy. Pound feared that the book had been boycotted and towards the end of February 1916, while he was still in the country with Yeats, he told Bronner that if there had been any reviews he had not seen them; he thought it possible that 'mouse Mathews' had been terrified into not sending out copies for review. Pound said that despite the threats copies had been sold – but they cannot have been very many, for as late as 1936 some of the original five hundred copies were still available at the original price, 3s. 6d.

Exasperated by the long and continuing fight to find publishers for Joyce's *A Portrait of the Artist* and Lewis's *Tarr* Pound committed his thoughts to writing: the result was published in *The Egoist* of 1 March under the title 'Meditatio'. He made no plea, he said, for smuttiness or unnecessary erotic glamour but it was essential for the writer to have the same freedom and privilege as the scientist in reaching for truth. Otherwise, what was the use of anything? He reserved his strongest words for the Christian churches, perhaps ten per cent of whose activities were not wholly venal. People like himself, he said, who in normal mood had no concern with churches were too apt to presume that all such pother had long since been settled. But in fact there were thousands of prim, soaped little Tertullians opposing enlightenment, entrenched in their bigotry, sterile save perhaps in the production of human offspring whereof there was already a superabundance.

Busier than ever with the affairs of others, now that so many were away at the war, Pound wrote on 9 March to the American reviewer Kate Buss that his week had been spent (1) in finally ('let us hope') dealing with Gaudier's estate, (2) getting a Vorticist art show packed and started for New York, (3) making a selection of letters by Yeats's father, for publication in a small book, and (4) bothering 'a good deal' about the production of Yeats's play, *At the Hawk's Well*. Not surprisingly he was a little sharp with Joyce in a letter of 16 March, by which time it may have penetrated his consciousness that Joyce had a remarkable capacity for concentrating attention on Joyce's needs: 'I will try to get time', he wrote, 'to look into your affairs in a few days. I have never been so hurried in my life, as during these weeks just after return to town, with all sorts of accumulations.' He said Joyce ought to be in London as it was next to impossible to conduct a career by post.

Nevertheless he was unflagging in Joyce's cause: he persuaded Harriet Shaw Weaver to handle the English issue of *A Portrait of the Artist* and late in March withdrew *This Generation* and asked Marshall to publish the American edition of *Portrait* in its place. Marshall agreed but soon afterwards retired from publishing and the book was finally brought out by Huebsch.

Pound's *Gaudier-Brzeska: A Memoir* ('Including the published writings of the sculptor, and a selection from his letters with thirty-eight illustrations, consisting of photographs of his sculpture, and four portraits by Walter Bennington, and numerous reproductions of drawings') was published by John Lane in London and by the John Lane Company in New York on 14 April. Among those who admired it was Miss Ella Abbott who had the tea-shop around the corner in Holland Street; she afterwards bought a number of copies to give to her friends as Christmas presents. The sculptor Henry Moore once spoke of the liberating effect of this book when he read it in the 1920s. While Roger Fry's *Vision and Design* drew his attention to African and pre-Columbian carving, the Pound book brought the age-old art of direct carving into relation with Vorticism and modernist aesthetics. In 1918 Pound wrote a preface for the catalogue, which he compiled, of the Gaudier memorial exhibition at the Leicester galleries, Leicester Square, in May and June of that year.

In April 1916 Pound began a teacher-pupil correspondence with a young poetess, Iris Barry, who lived in Birmingham. He had seen some of her work in *Poetry and Drama* and asked if she had any more that might be suitable for *Poetry*. From a bundle she sent he selected a few and by the end of the month they were on their way to Harriet Monroe. He later sent a group to *Others* which was being edited by Alfred Kreymborg in collaboration with William Carlos Williams. In July Miss Barry visited London and they went for a walk together on Wimbledon Common, Pound talking the whole time in a variety of accents punctuated by dramatic pauses, diminuendos, and strange exclamations. After her return to Birmingham he conducted a correspondence course in 'KOMPLEAT KULTURE'. 'Catullus, Propertius, Horace and Ovid are the people that matter. Catullus most. Martial somewhat. Propertius for beautiful cadence. . . .' 'Charles D'Orleans and the Pleiade. And Burns is worth study as technique in song rhythms. But I don't think this is the main line. Théophile Gautier is, I suppose, the next man who can write.' 'As I said Sunday, I suppose

Flaubert's *Trois Contes*, especially "Coeur Simple", contain all that anyone knows *about* writing.' 'Everybody has been sloppily imitating the Elizabethans for so long that I think they probably do one more harm than good. At any rate let 'em alone.' '. . . the Roman poets are the only ones we know of who had approximately the same problems as we have. The metropolis, the imperial posts to all corners of the known world.' 'Spanish, nothing. Italian, Leopardi splendid . . . but not essential as a tool. Spain has one good modern novelist, Galdos.' 'If you are panting for the Frenchmen, they are, with all sorts of qualifications and restrictions, Rémy de Gourmont, De Régnier (a very few poems), Francis Jammes, Jules Romains, Chas. Vildrac, TRISTAN CORBIÈRE, Laurent Tailhade, Jules Laforgue, (dates all out of order), Rimbaud.'

In August he told her to send on some plays she had, as he was supposed to be meeting Edward Knoblock whom he had heard was 'the Gawd of the British theatre'. He had something of his own to offer and also Joyce's play *Exiles*, 'but if he is to be harnessed I may as well have any stray bits of twine handy'. He met Knoblock in September but none of the work was accepted.

Out of the correspondence a friendship developed and Pound urged her to leave Birmingham for good and continue her studies in London, which in 1917 she did; she got a job with the Ministry of Munitions, became an assistant librarian at the school of Oriental Studies, a film editor in Fleet Street and later librarian of the Museum of Modern Art in New York and curator of its film library. In October 1930 she contributed an article on 'The Ezra Pound Period' to an American magazine *The Bookman*, in which she described Pound as she had known him in London. On Thursdays there was a weekly meeting at a Chinese restaurant in Regent Street:

Into the restaurant with his clothes always seeming to fly round him, letting his ebony stick clatter to the floor, came Pound himself with his exuberant hair, pale cat-like face with the greenish cat-eyes, clearing his throat, making strange sounds and cries in his talking, but otherwise always quite formal and extremely polite. With him came Mrs Pound, carrying herself delicately with the air, always, of a young Victorian lady out skating, and a profile as clear and lovely as that of a porcelain Kuan-yin.

Sometimes present was Edgar Jepson who used to pass around the table pieces of jade which Pound would finger 'long and lovingly'. Around the table also

went the story of Miss Lowell's amazing descent upon London, of the opening of London's first night club by Madame Strindberg with her troop of little monkeys, of what young Nevinson [a vorticist Futurist] had said to

193

annoy in the Café Royal, of Saint Augustine and his mother's death, of Rihaku and Catullus, of Keats and the *Edinburgh Review*, of the big munition works which (so rumour had it every month or so) had been blown up by Zeppelin bombs overnight. Mixed in would be someone's account (Pound's, I think) of a row of houses discovered intact in Earl's Court outside the front door of each of which was a pair of stone dogs, large as life and no pair alike or even of the same species.

Early in 1916 Pound delivered the typescript of *Lustra* to Elkin Mathews who apparently sent it to the printer, Clowes, without properly reading it. In May Pound received from Yeats a letter which said that both Mathews and Clowes, having read the poems in proof, were horrified. Yeats agreed with them about the 'violent' poems but not the indecent ones. He thought that a man should be allowed to be as indecent as he liked. In a letter to Pound on 31 May Mathews described three of the poems as 'very nasty'. They were 'Meditatio':

> When I carefully consider the curious habits of dogs
> I am compelled to conclude
> That man is the superior animal. . . .

'Phyllidula':

> Phyllidula is scrawny but amorous,
> Thus have the gods awarded her,
> That in pleasure she receives more than she can give. . . .

and 'The Patterns':

> Erinna is a model parent,
> Her children have never discovered her adulteries. . . .

Mathews considered that the parody, 'Ancient Music':

> Winter is icummen in,
> Lhude sing Goddam

was blasphemous; the poem to Atthis:

> I long for thy narrow breasts,
> Thou restless, ungathered

he described as 'anything but delicate'. Pound consulted Augustine Birrell and J. B. Pinker who appear to have taken his side and to have agreed that there was no similarity, as Mathews had suggested, between *Lustra* and D. H. Lawrence's *The Rainbow* suppressed the previous year. He had written proof, he told Mathews, that the Home Office was well disposed toward him. And in reply to Mathews's statement that not only men but also ladies came into his shop, Pound said that before sending the typescript for publication he had submitted it to 'four perfectly well-bred women' and had sought their advice about what to include.

After much argument the printing firm agreed to supply a private edition of two hundred copies, containing all the poems except four, 'which they decline,' said Mathews in a letter of 10 June, 'to print in any form whatever'. The four were 'Ancient Music' and:

Nine adulteries, 12 liaisons, 64 fornications
   and something approaching a rape
Rest nightly upon the soul of our delicate friend Florialis. . . .
        ('The Temperaments')

And the whores dropping in for a word or two in passing. . . .
        ('The Lake Isle')

Suddenly discovering in the eyes of the very beautiful Normande
   cocotte
The eyes of the very learned British Museum assistant.
        ('Pagani's, November 8')

The private edition, issued in September, was private in name only, for Mathews sold it to anyone who specifically asked for it. The normal edition, published under Mathews's imprint in October, was identical with the first except for the omission of nine poems and the changing of the title 'Coitus' to 'Pervigilium'. The book was dedicated to V.L., short for Vail de Lencour, a Provençal *nom de plume* chosen by Pound for Brigit Patmore.

The critics varied considerably in their opinions about it: *The Observer* and the *Daily Chronicle* praised it but others disapproved, including the *Times Literary Supplement* of 16 November:

We have already praised the translations of Chinese poetry which are reprinted in this book. Most of Mr Pound's original poems are in the same loose form, but he has not learned from his Chinese originals, and from his success in translating them, what kind of matter his form requires to justify it. The Chinese poems are full of content and of a content interesting to everyone. . . But in Mr Pound's original poems there is seldom this

compensation. In matter he seems to have taken Catullus for his model. He expresses any chance whim of his own, any liking, or more often dislike, that he happens to have experienced. Catullus does this too, but in concise and regular verse; Mr Pound does it in the loose verse of 'The River Merchant's Wife'.
. . .
His verse is not ordinary speech, but he aims at the illusion of ordinary speech; and, although this illusion gives an air of liveliness to his poems, it seems to us to be bought at too high a price. Certainly the original poems as well as the translations show that he has talent – one can read them all with some interest – but why should he use it to express so much indifference and impatience? Why should he so constantly be ironical about nothing in particular? . . . One suspects a hidden timidity in this air of indifference, as if Mr Pound feared above all things to give himself away.

During the first half of 1916 Pound continued his work on the Fenollosa notebooks – the Chinese poems and the Noh material – and continued his search for a magazine or publisher to bring out the essay on the Chinese written character. Four new Fenollosa-Pound translations of Chinese poems appeared in *The New Age* of 22 June, including 'Old Idea of Choan':

> Night birds, and night women,
> Spread out their sounds through the gardens.

and 'Sennin Poem', with its brilliant 'image' of the birds:

> The red and green kingfishers
> flash between the orchids and the clover,
> One bird casts its gleam on another.

The four translations were included in the 'Cathay' section of *Lustra*. He had also prepared a small book of Noh plays which was published by the Cuala Press, Churchtown, Dundrum, in the County of Dublin, Ireland, on 16 September. The plays were 'From the Manuscripts of Ernest Fenollosa, Chosen and Finished by Ezra Pound', and there was an introduction by Yeats. Sometime before June 1916 Yeats introduced Pound to the agent, Watt, who took a larger collection of Fenollosa material to Macmillan who accepted it immediately and within three days Pound had a favourable contract.

About June he received from The Committee of One Hundred in Newark, New Jersey, a pamphlet advertising a series of prizes totalling $1,000, for poems on Newark and its two hundred and fiftieth anniversary. The committee planned to publish the best of the poems submitted

in a volume to be called *Newark Anniversary Poems*. He wrote out
some seventy lines of free verse under the title, 'To a City Sending Him
Advertisements', which opened with these questions:

> But will you do all these things?
>   You, with your promises,
>   You, with your claims to life,
> Will you see fine things perish?
> Will you always take sides with the heavy;
> Will you, having got the songs you ask for,
>   Choose only the worst, the coarsest?
> Will you choose flattering tongues.

Unmoved, the committee awarded first prize to Clement Wood's 'The
Smithy of God':

> I am Newark, forger of men,
> Forger of men, forger of men. . . .

Pound was not among the first three but was awarded one of the ten
special prizes of $50 each. When the poems were published in 1917
the committee said: 'That philosophic iconoclast, Ezra Pound, earlier
exponent of the Imagist School of Poetic Palpitation, writing from
London, assaulted our civic sensibilities in a poem of violence directed
at the head, heart, and hands of Newark. Of his poem, one of the
judges remarked that it is "Captious, arrogant, hypercritical, but has
some merit". Another judge cast it into the discard. But it won a prize
and fits snugly into the rationale of the present volume. Also there is
food for thought in our London poet's catechistic cadences.'

Pound had a week at the seaside in July 1916 but was glad to get
back to Kensington and the pleasures of metropolitan society, such as
the occasion when he heard Thomas Beecham read free verse poems in
which the rhythm was 'so faint as to be almost imperceptible'. He read
them, Pound said later, 'with the author's cadence, with flawless
correctness'. When Augustine Birrell took up the same book the effect
was quite different: he read 'with the intonations of a legal document,
paying no attention to the movement inherent in the words before
him.' In August he began translating the libretto of Massenet's
Cinderella for the Thomas Beecham Opera Company. With the money
from this he was hoping, he told Joyce, to pay off some of his debts, but
it would by no means start him 'in the ways of opulence'. One of the
consolations of the job was free seats at the opera – good seats, for on
one occasion he sat between Balfour and a duchess. Also in August he

succeeded in selling in New York 'a lot of pictures' by Lewis, Wadsworth and other vorticist painters. With this matter off his mind and Joyce now in receipt of a Civil List grant Pound thought he might devote the next six months to his own interests. 'All life's blessings except loose change seem to have been showered upon me', he wrote to Joyce, 'it behooves me to remedy that deficiency at once.' He tried to get work in Fleet Street writing articles or reviews for some of the more popular papers; in this he was apparently unsuccessful but in October he published an article on art and the war in *Vogue* and reviewed William Morton Fullerton's *The American Crisis and the War* in the *Times Literary Supplement* of 19 October.

Since reading Landor the previous winter he had been wondering if he might not present his ideas in the form of dialogues and prose sketches. As a start he translated twelve dialogues of Fontenelle which were published in *The Egoist*, beginning on 1 May 1916, and were issued in October the following year as a small book. Towards the end of August 1916 he did a prose sketch, 'Jodindranath Mawhwor's Occupation', on India and the Indian attitude to sex, which was the first of a series of such pieces published in 1917 in *The Little Review*.

By mid-November 1916 his days were 'dotted' with book reviews, but he found that each paper, after professing itself delighted with what he had written, and promising more work in the future, did nothing more about it. Also in November he read the proofs of the Macmillan book on the Noh drama and wrote to Felix Schelling about the possibility of the University of Pennsylvania giving a lead to the rest of America by establishing a fellowship for 'creative ability, regardless of whether the man had any university degree whatsoever'. He had in mind for such a fellowship two poets whose work he feared would stay imperfect through lack of culture. They were Carl Sandburg and Orrick Johns who needed a year in a library, 'with a few suggestions for reading and no worry about their rent'. He took the opportunity to comment on the behaviour of another of his teachers, Cornelius Weygandt, whose interest in contemporary literature, he told Schelling, seemed typical of America. 'That is to say he wrote to me for free copies of my books, just after he had come into a comfortable inheritance and at a time when I was working my own way on the edge of starvation.'

By the end of the year Pound had finished the Massenet libretto and on 1 January 1917 he had a pleasant surprise when Beecham ('a good fellow') paid him not in pounds as proposed but in guineas, but the libretto was never used. Early in 1917 Macmillan published *'Noh' Or Accomplishment*, 'A Study of the Classical Stage of Japan by Ernest Fenollosa and Ezra Pound'. In a note at the beginning Pound said:

'The vision and the plan are Fenollosa's. In the prose I have had but the part of literary executor; in the plays my work has been that of translator who has found all the heavy work done for him and who has had but the pleasure of arranging beauty into the words.' Although dated 1916 the book was not published until 12 January 1917. There was a long and favourable review in the *Times Literary Supplement* of 25 January in which Pound's part was specially praised.

Upon seeing a new American magazine with high ambitions, called *The Seven Arts*, Pound sent them in January Fenollosa's essay, 'The Chinese Written Character as a Medium for Poetry', but once again he was unsuccessful. His faith in the essay remained, however, unshaken; it seemed, in fact, to grow. From its being, in 1915, a most enlightening work which provided 'a whole basis of aesthetic', and in 1916 a very good theory for poets to go by, it had by 1917 become 'one of the most important essays of our time', 'basic for all aesthetics', and Fenollosa was beginning to look like an Imagist and a Vorticist.

In January John Quinn wrote to say that he had enjoyed *Lustra* and offered to find a publisher for it in the United States, despite the fact that he had failed earlier to place it with Macmillan in New York; he also began to take an interest in *This Generation* which was still unplaced. It was about this time that Charles Granville, who had been sent to prison in connection with the failure of Swift & Company in 1912, made a new start in literature with a magazine called *The Future*. After his release he had called one day on the Pounds at Holland Place Chambers; he was down-and-out and they gave him a meal and £5. When later he started his new magazine he invited Pound to contribute and the first of a number of articles and reviews published there by Pound during the next two years was an article in praise of Crabbe's 'exactness' in the issue of February 1917. One day while Pound was in Granville's outer office Granville came out and offered to introduce him to G. K. Chesterton who was inside. At this stage in his career Pound was unable to mention Chesterton without lapsing into abuse and so he declined the offer. Chesterton, it appears, had written somewhere that if a thing was worth doing it was worth doing badly; from the moment he heard this it was the end of Chesterton as far as Pound was concerned. He also disliked Chesterton's religion which represented all that was worst in Catholicism – a subject on which he had grown eloquent since reading the sermon in Joyce's *Portrait of the Artist*. But despite these almost uncontrollable feelings he suspected that he might like Chesterton personally if ever he met him and one day when he saw him in the street in Kensington he was almost tempted to stop and introduce himself. Chesterton had alighted from a taxi, leaving the door open behind him. When Pound came along he was bending over some old books on display outside a bookshop and there was no room to pass between bulky author and open door. Pound was going to speak but decided not to; he drew the door towards him, passed through the opening, and continued on his way.

Huebsch in New York had brought out *Portrait of the Artist* on 29 December 1916; on the following 12 February The Egoist Ltd issued in England copies imported from New York. Pound's first review appeared in the February issue of *The Egoist* under the heading, 'James Joyce: at Last the Novel Appears'. A number of qualified judges, he said, has acquiesced in his statement of two years ago that Joyce was an excellent and important writer of prose. It was 'hard, clear-cut, with no waste of words, no bundling up of useless phrases, no filling in with pages of slosh'. The last few years had seen the gradual shaping of a party of intelligence not bound by any central doctrine or theory; it was impossible to define accurately the work of these new writers by applying tag-names from old authors, but in order to give a general impression that was nothing more than an approximation, he would say that Joyce 'produces the nearest thing to Flaubertian prose that we have now in English, just as Wyndham Lewis has written a novel which is more like, and more fitly compared with, Dostoievsky than is the work of any of his contemporaries. In like manner Mr T. S. Eliot comes nearer to filling the place of Jules Laforgue in our generation.' Both Joyce and Lewis, he said, had met with all sorts of opposition; if Eliot probably had not yet encountered very much opposition it was only because his work was not yet very widely known. Towards the end of the review he declared that 'the obstructionist and the provincial' were everywhere and in them alone was the permanent danger to civilization. Clear, hard prose was the safeguard, for the mind accustomed to it would not be cheated or stampeded by 'national phrases and public emotionalities'.

NOTES

1 Michael Reck, *Ezra Pound, A Close Up*, New York, 1967.
2 He kept his accounts from birthday to birthday.

XII   The Little Review
1917/1918

After the book on Japanese drama had been well received by the reviewers Pound went to Watt with a new proposal for Macmillan. It was for a ten-volume anthology of world poetry, to contain all the inventive work from Homer and the early Chinese down to 1916. Greek, Latin and other European poetry would be given in the original language with a translation opposite; oriental poems would be represented by translations where such translations were of literary interest. When Watt asked for an outline of the plan Pound sat down at an office typewriter and made a list of some three hundred items with comments. Watt was amazed at this feat and barely glanced at the list before sending it immediately to Macmillan. He had not seen that it contained the statement, 'It is time we had something to replace that doddard Palgrave.' Within two days Pound received a hurried note from Watt asking him to call at once. Macmillan, he said, had rejected the proposal; and pointing to Pound's comment about the doddard asked him didn't he know that the whole fortune of Macmillan & Co. was founded on Sir Francis Turner Palgrave's *Golden Treasury of English Songs and Lyrics*? Thereafter Pound was convinced that Macmillan had refused the idea because of their investment in Palgrave; any other possibility, such as a doubt about the project itself, does not seem to have occurred to him. With Macmillan ruled out he tried the Oxford University Press who professed interest in the idea but said the outlay would be too great for wartime. He took up the matter with them again during the early 1920s but without success: if they did anything in the international line it 'would be more in the nature of gems'.

In February 1917 Pound spoke at the opening of an exhibition of 'vortographs' and paintings by Alvin Langdon Coburn at the Camera Club, 17 John Street, Adelphi, Strand, W.C. 'Vortographs' were the result of a bringing together of Vorticism and the camera, which had been made possible by the invention late in 1916 of an instrument called the vortescope. The inventors were Pound and Coburn and the main part of the vortescope was Pound's old shaving-mirror. Thus armed the vortographer could 'make summer of London October' and achieve various sub-marine and other effects. To the exhibition catalogue Pound contributed a note on 'The Vortographs' and another entitled 'The Camera Is Freed from Reality'. Among those present at the exhibition was George Bernard Shaw; the two met and got on well together. In Paris in 1923 Pound and D. Murphy attached the vorte-scope to a movie-camera but Pound resigned in the face of better results obtained by Léger and Man Ray.

By March *Poetry* had received Pound's first three cantos. He hoped that Harriet Monroe might print them in one batch accompanied by Jean de Bosschère's long article on him which was then appearing in *The Egoist*. In April she wrote that she would have to string them out into three numbers. He replied on 24 April that the price she had offered for them was satisfactory – 'Only for gawd's sake send it along as soon as possible.' By the time the cantos appeared in the issues of June, July and August Pound had become dissatisfied with them and had already revised and reduced them for the American editions of *Lustra* which came out later in the year. Eliot was the only person, he told Harriet Monroe, who had proffered criticism of the cantos instead of general objection. For the April number of *Poetry* he sent a review of the anthology *Wheels* in which he said that both Sacheverell and Edith Sitwell showed promise, 'the latter using alternate ten- and six-syllable lines with excellent rhythmic and tonal effect but with an inexcusable carelessness as to meaning and to fitness of expression'.

Since January 1915 Pound had been in regular communication with John Quinn, nurturing him as a patron for himself and others and helping him to find paintings and sculpture for his rapidly growing collection housed in his flat on Central Park West. Within two months of Quinn's first letter, when he was considering buying Epstein's *Birds,* Pound wrote: 'for God's sake get the two that are stuck together, not the pair in which one is standing up on its legs.' Epstein assured Quinn that he was getting the two birds stuck together and went on to suggest that Pound should mind his own business – although in fact Quinn had sought Pound's advice. When Gaudier died at the front Quinn asked Pound to buy as much of his work as possible; he also ordered twenty copies of *Blast* and began to buy work by Lewis. Later in 1915 when Pound cabled that Lewis, recently enlisted in the army, needed money to pay debts, Quinn immediately cabled £30. He also helped in numerous other ways with publishers and art galleries and offered $750 a year as subsidy to any journal in which Pound chose to interest himself.

Early in 1917 Quinn undertook to bring out the American private edition of *Lustra* and placed the trade edition with the New York publisher Alfred A. Knopf. He also continued to take an active interest in Joyce's affairs and as a collector gave Pound £8 for a copy of *A Lume Spento*. Although Pound did not get the magazine of his own that he had been working for, Quinn joined with him in a scheme to take over a section of an already existing American periodical, *The Little Review*, run by Margaret Anderson and Jane Heap.

What he wanted, Pound told Margaret Anderson, was 'a place where I and T. S. Eliot can appear once a month (or once an issue) and where Joyce can appear when he likes, and where Wyndham Lewis can appear if he comes back from the war.' Quinn agreed to assist the magazine for two years, paying Pound $750 a year – $300 of it for his editorial duties and $450 for his contributors. Quinn later increased his own backing, secured $400 each from three New York patrons, Otto Kahn, Max Pam and Mrs James Byrne, and from time to time provided Margaret Anderson and Jane Heap and also Pound with additional funds out of his own pocket. By the end of March 1917 Pound was the magazine's London Editor and for the May issue had sent a series of imaginary letters by Lewis, part one of a prose satire by Eliot called 'Eeldrop and Appleplex' and his own sketch, 'Jodindranath Mawhwor's Occupation'. He also contributed an editorial in which he said that if any human activity was 'sacred' it was the formulation of thought in clear speech; any falsification or evasion in this activity was evil. He saw no reason for concealing his belief that the two novels by Joyce and Lewis, and Eliot's poems, were not only the most important contributions to English literature of the past three years but that they were practically the only works of the time in which the creative element was present, which in any way showed invention or 'progress beyond precedent work'. As he did not want to risk losing the money he received from *Poetry* he refrained for the present from publishing any verse in *The Little Review* under his own name; but he did send for the May number a translation of Laforgue signed John Hall:

> And I am sliced with loyal aesthetics.
> Hate tremolos and national frenetics.
> In brief, violet is the ground tone of my phonetics.

Eliot's 'Eeldrop and Appleplex' was a satirical account of the differences in temperament between Pound and himself:

Then Eeldrop and Appleplex would break off their discourse, and rush out to mingle with the mob. Each pursued his own line of enquiry. Appleplex who had the gift of an extraordinary address with the lower classes of both sexes, questioned the onlookers, and usually extracted full and inconsistent histories: Eeldrop preserved a more passive demeanor, listened to the conversation of the people among themselves, registered in his mind their oaths, their redundance of phrase, their various manners of spitting, and the cries of the victim from the hall of justice within.

When the crowd dispersed Eeldrop and Appleplex retired to their rooms, Appleplex to enter the results of his enquiries into large notebooks filed according to the nature of the case and Eeldrop to smoke reflectively. As a practical step towards increasing the magazine's circulation Pound took copies around to Miss Abbott's tea-shop: Miss Abbott subscribed and placed a placard advertising the magazine in a prominent position in the shop.

The June issue of *The Little Review* (now sub-titled 'A Magazine of the Arts, Making No Compromise with the Public Taste') contained a large group of new poems by Yeats, including 'The Wild Swans at Coole' and 'The Collar-Bone of a Hare', and a letter from Joyce to say that he hoped to send something very soon – 'as soon, in fact, as my health allows me to resume work'. He had been having fresh trouble with his eyes and was under the care of a doctor.

During the next six months *The Little Review* published poetry by Eliot and Yeats, a play by Lady Gregory, a prose piece, 'Improvisations', by William Carlos Williams which begins characteristically, 'Fools have big wombs', a play by Arthur Symons, translations from the Chinese by Arthur Waley, and several pieces in Lewis's most ferocious vein, one of which, 'Cantleman's Spring Mate', caused the October issue of the magazine to be suppressed in the United States.

Writing to Margaret Anderson about Quinn's financial support Pound said that Quinn was not mean with his money as she seemed to think; he spent a good deal on the arts and only a year earlier had wanted Pound to take £120 a year for himself in connection with his work on *The Egoist*. 'The point is that if I accept more than I *need* I at once become a sponger, and I at once lose my integrity. By doing the job for the absolute minimum I remain respectable and when I see something I want I can ask for it.' It would appear from this letter that it was Pound and not Quinn who fixed the amounts to be made available to *The Little Review* or convinced Quinn to accept his estimate of the magazine's needs.

In the spring of 1917 Pound approached Mathews with a small collection which he and Eliot had put together from Eliot's poems. Mathews was unwilling to take a risk on such a slim newcomer containing only a dozen poems; he imposed conditions and asked for an advance payment. Pound refused and turned to Harriet Shaw Weaver, persuading her to lend him the Egoist imprint if he could raise enough money to cover the cost of printing. As a result T. S. Eliot's first book, *Prufrock and Other Observations*, was published in London by The Egoist Ltd sometime in June 1917 in an edition of five hundred copies. A review by Pound appeared in the June issue of *The Egoist* under the title 'Drunken Helots and Mr Eliot'; it was in part a reply to Arthur Waugh who in a review of *Catholic Anthology* in the October 1916 *Quarterly Review* had laboriously likened the work of Pound and Eliot to the drunken slaves of classic custom exhibited before the sons of the household as a warning against such 'ignominious folly'. Pound declared that Eliot at once took rank with the five or six living poets whose English one could read with enjoyment. 'I have read the contents of this book over and over, and with continued joy in the freshness, the humanity, the deep quiet culture.'

In a more careful review for the August *Poetry* he said that after much contemporary work that was merely factitious, much that was good in intention but impotently unfinished and incomplete, and much whose flaws were due to sheer ignorance which a year's study or thought might have remedied, it was a comfort to come upon complete art, naive despite its intellectual subtlety, lacking all pretence. The reader who compared Eliot's work with anything written in French, English or American since the death of Jules Laforgue would find nothing better and he would be extremely fortunate if he found much half as good. Pound said he had read most of the poems many times; he had last read the whole book at breakfast time from flimsy proof-sheets; his verdict after these '"test conditions"' was the unqualified admiration of one genuine poet for another: '"confound it, the fellow can write."'

In 1917 while he was assistant-editor of *The Egoist* (a £1 a week post which he owed to Pound's recommendation and held until 1919) Eliot joined Lloyds Bank at £120 per annum. He was twenty-eight when he joined and was employed in the Colonial and Foreign Department at 17 Cornhill. Some years later the department moved to Stafford House, 20 King William Street, and was still there in 1925 when he left the bank to go into publishing. One of his tasks at Lloyds was to compile information on the economies of foreign countries for inclusion in the bank's periodical reports on foreign affairs.

He and Pound saw a good deal of each other between 1917 and 1921, for despite differences of temperament, attitude and methods they both wanted to bring back good writing into English poetry. Eliot recognized Pound's grasp of technical questions and in his poetry especially was only too happy to consider his advice.

Free verse and Imagism had once seemed to Pound to hold out some hope but it had become increasingly clear to him that despite any demarcations he may have tried to erect through Imagism, free verse lately had run wild. 'It is too late to prevent *vers libre*,' he wrote in an article on Arnold Dolmetsch in *The Egoist* of July 1917, 'but, conceivably, one might improve it.' What was needed perhaps was a counter-current and Pound and Eliot decided they might try to provide it. There is a brief account of their decision in Pound's 1932 essay on Harold Monro: 'That is to say, at a particular date in a particular room, two authors, neither engaged in picking the other's pocket, decided that the dilutation of *vers libre*, Amygism, Lee Masterism, general floppiness had gone too far and that some counter-current must be set going. Parallel situation centuries ago in China. Remedy prescribed "Émaux et Camées" (or the Bay State Hymn Book). Rhyme and regular strophes.' The result of this decision, Pound said, was his own series of poems, *Hugh Selwyn Mauberley*, published in 1920, and a number of poems by Eliot, including 'The Hippopotamus' and 'Sweeney among the Nightingales', which appeared in *The Little Review* and other magazines between 1917 and 1919. Years later Eliot wrote: 'Half of the work that Pound did as a critic can be known only from the testimony of those who benefited from his conversation or correspondence. At a certain moment, my debt to him was for his advice to read Gautier's *Émaux et Camées*.' In the same way Eliot was responsible for Pound's sudden interest in 1917 in Laforgue's sophistication. Pound's translation of Laforgue appeared in the May issue of *The Little Review* and his first essay on Laforgue in the November *Poetry*. In 1925 Pound was under the impression that a warning he had delivered in 1916 was in some measure to blame for what he termed 'the extreme caution' of Eliot's criticism. 'I pointed out to him in the beginning', Pound wrote in a letter to Henry Allen Moe, 'that there was no use of two of us butting a stone wall; that he would never be as hefty a battering ram as I was, nor as explosive as Lewis, and that he had better try a more oceanic and fluid method of sapping the foundations.' But what struck him most in 1917 was Eliot's 'unusual intelligence': 'Eliot has thought of things I had not thought of', he told Margaret Anderson, 'and I'm damned if many of the others have done so.'

In a letter to Iris Barry on 27 July 1916 Pound had said that if she could not find any decent translations of Catullus and Propertius he supposed he would have 'to rig up something'. It was the same letter in which he had spoken of the Roman poets as 'the only ones we know of who had approximately the same problems as we have. The metropolis, the imperial posts to all corners of the known world.' Here possibly was the origin of his *Homage to Sextus Propertius* – an idea which may have taken fire while he was considering how to supply a guide to Propertius and some of the characteristics of his verse for one who had no

Latin. The work was dated by the author 1917 but was probably not finished until the middle of 1918 at the earliest and was not published until the following year. It was not a direct translation but an approximation and a re-arrangement: a personal statement, by Pound's Propertius or by Pound, which places the joys and trials of female company and the inspirations to be derived from love, above imperial police-work. It is in free verse but among the most firmly controlled surely that has ever been written and was possibly intended as an example of how the job should be done, to be displayed in conjunction with the rhyme and regular strophes of *Mauberley*:

> Annalists will continue to record Roman reputations,
> Celebrities from the Trans-Caucasus will belaud Roman
>   celebrities
> And expound the distentions of Empire,
> But for something to read in normal circumstances?
> For a few pages brought down from the forked hill unsullied?
> I ask a wreath which will not crush my head.
>   And there is no hurry about it;
> I shall have, doubtless, a boom after my funeral,
> Seeing that long standing increases all things
>   regardless of quality.

It seldom falls below this level and is sometimes higher; it is a delightful work, as fresh now as ever, though more notable for the wording and the brilliance of individual passages than for any progression or profundity. It reads as the work of a very talented poet enjoying himself in the role of Sextus Propertius, but there is no sign of a guiding intelligence which sees how to draw parts into a whole.

During the first half of May 1917 Pound corrected the proofs of the American editions of *Lustra* and in or near Charing Cross Road bought for a guinea Pierre Bayle's *Dictionnaire historique* in four large folios; for five shillings a few days later he picked up six volumes of *Poètes François jusqu'à Malherbe* containing some troubadours he had been seeking. He was hoping to go on with his Provençal studies now that he had found a musician, a 'cellist with an incapacitated arm, who could help him with the twelfth-century music.

It was at this stage that Pound began to have doubts about the turn his work was taking. While Joyce and Eliot were already producing work that was of the modern world he was playing behind ancient masks, translating Arnaut Daniel again, and in his early cantos worrying out aloud about the construction of a suitable 'rag-bag' in which to stuff the 'modern world' but obviously happier when dreaming about the past and his own explorations into the past by way of Venice. His problem was that in his ideas he had consciously developed a modernist programme which seemed to run counter to the ideas and feelings of his sensitive self out of which came his poetry.

But untiring always, whatever his doubts, he continued by various means to help Joyce and in the June issue of *The Egoist* published a large collection he had made of extracts from reviews of *A Portrait of the Artist*. In June he met Davray of the *Mercure de France* who was in London on government business; he told him about Joyce and Davray promised to write something when he had time off from his national work.

Much of July and August Pound spent in the British Museum working on a study of 'Elizabethan Classicists' which appeared in *The Egoist* in five instalments beginning in September. He was also collecting from current newspapers and periodicals extracts which he believed to be patently idiotic and was publishing them in a long series in *The New Age* entitled 'Contemporary Mentality'. In a commentary on books in the August *Little Review* he attacked Tagore's popularization and said: 'Another man who stands in peril is Edgar Masters. He did a good job in *The Spoon River Anthology*. What is good in it is good in common with like things in the Greek Anthology, Villon and Crabbe: plus Masters's sense of real people.' The book however needed rewriting if Masters wanted his work to last as Crabbe's *The Borough* had lasted. He tried in August to entice Mencken into *The Little Review* with any material which was too strong for the *Smart Set*; he also became involved with Joyce and Quinn in a comedy of errors over the whereabouts of a typed copy of *Exiles*, in the process of which he received from Quinn a cable seeking last-minute changes in *Lustra*. Quinn did not like the word 'thrice' in one poem and in 'The Seafarer' wanted to change 'full oft' to 'often' – which would have been banal and completely out of keeping with the poem. In addition to minor tasks such as putting together a copy of Lewis's *Tarr* and sending it to New York for the American edition by Knopf, he was preparing a collection of his own prose for publication in America. It consisted of a number of pieces rescued from *This Generation* plus reviews, articles and prose sketches of the past two years, including his notes on the Elizabethan Classicists in *The Egoist*. It was published by Knopf the following year under the title *Pavannes and Divisions*.

Beginning with the September *Little Review* he published a series of 'Imaginary Letters', the continuation of a feature started by Lewis which owing to the war he was unable to maintain. For Pound it was an opportunity to continue with the Landor-type prose sketches of the previous year. There were eight letters altogether, signed by a Mr

Walter Villerant who is attempting, without much success, to educate his women friends.

Writing to Lewis about the series in the summer of 1917 Pound said: 'Mr Villerant has written some letters for Sept., Oct. and Nov. to keep the "reader" in mind of the existence of the Burn family.' Lewis's letters were by William Bland Burn to his wife; Villerant's first few letters were to the same lady who in the process becomes the ex-Mrs Burn. 'This literary rape and adultery is most underhanded and scandalous', Pound said. His continuation of the series was interrupted by two further contributions from Lewis the following year. The series ended with the November 1918 issue and all Pound's letters were collected in a small book, *Imaginary Letters*, published by Caresse Crosby's Black Sun Press in Paris in October 1930.

In September 1917 we find him writing to Margaret Anderson to justify work by John Rodker and Iris Barry which he had sent to *The Little Review* and staking his 'critical position, or some part of it' on a belief that both would produce something worthwhile in the future. On the 7th he asked Edgar Jepson to call and discuss working together on a spy-detective story he had thought of, but nothing seems to have been written.

Beginning on 19 September John Quinn began to distribute the sixty copies of the private American edition of *Lustra* which contained additional material: the four poems left out of the English private edition, a poem of the previous year called 'Impressions of François-Marie Arouet (de Voltaire),' a selection of poems from earlier books, and 'Three Cantos of a Poem of Some Length'. The trade edition published by Knopf on 16 October was identical in contents except for the omission of 'The Temperaments.' Two copies reached Pound on 14 November and he wrote immediately to Quinn that he was delighted with the look and the feel of them. In January 1918 Knopf issued in connection with the publication of *Lustra* a small book called *Ezra Pound His Metric and Poetry*. The anonymous author was T. S. Eliot whose typescript Pound had corrected and edited the previous April before sending it to Quinn; Pound also compiled the 'Bibliography of Books and Partial Bibliography of Notable Critical Articles by Ezra Pound'. The idea for such a book had been suggested to Knopf by Quinn who agreed to pay four-fifths of the cost. Pound said that Eliot was the one best suited for the job but he insisted that it be published anonymously so that he could go on booming Eliot's work unhandicapped by too much mutual praise. Quinn sent one hundred copies of the book to Pound and kept two hundred for distribution himself. Pound appreciated the money and energy that Quinn was spending and when copies of *Ezra Pound His Metric and Poetry* arrived in London he wrote to him: 'I am delighted with the format, you certainly have done me proud . . . if America finally decides to pay my rent, it will be your doing.' Although extremely busy as a lawyer Quinn obviously enjoyed immensely his part in the world of literature; he insisted on reading the proofs of the works that passed through his hands, made suggestions to the authors about style and punctuation, and innumerable suggestions to the publishers about type and printing. He applied the same drive to his practice of financial law and was in great demand by the Federal Government as well as banks and insurance companies. For his work on behalf of the Custodian of Alien Property during and after the war he received a fee of $174,000.

On 22 November 1917 Pound began to contribute art criticism to *The New Age* under the name B. H. Dias and on 6 December music criticism under the name William Atheling. To his father he wrote on 24 January 1918: 'Am doing art and music critiques under pseudonyms, paying the rent. Rather entertaining. NOT to be mentioned. It may be I have at last found a moderately easy way to earn my daily. Bloody queer what a man will do for money.' His art notes continued for two and a half years, his music notes for nearly three years.

On 18 August 1917 Joyce collapsed in Zurich from an attack of glaucoma and his eyes had to be operated on a week later. When Pound received the news in September he attempted to hasten advances and other payments for Joyce and in a letter of encouragement to Mrs Joyce on 10 September said he was trying to raise other money by offering for sale some autograph manuscripts he possessed of King Ferdinand and Queen Isabella of Spain, dated 1492. A fortnight earlier he had told Quinn that the letters were in his father's safe: he asked him to put them on the market and said that if they brought more than a thousand dollars he would put half into *The Little Review*. From Locarno where he had gone to recuperate Joyce wrote to Pound: 'It is useless to go into the subject of my physical and financial collapse in August. As regards the former what is done is done. I cannot see very well even yet but the sight gets better. About the latter I owe you and Miss Weaver very much for your prompt kindness. But for you I should have been derelict.'

In 1917 or 1918 Pound wrote a reference for Eliot when he applied for a commission in the United States Navy. He chose the navy because as a youth he had sailed expertly in a small cat-boat off the coast of Massachusetts. 'This is to state', Pound's letter ran, 'that Thomas S. Eliot, now resident at 31 West Street, Marlow, Bucks, employed in Lloyds Bank, 17 Cornhill, London, has been known to me for some years. He is a loyal American-born American citizen, and a man fit for positions of trust.' He signed himself Ezra Pound, M.A., American Citizen, and added a note: 'Born Hailey, Idaho, 1885, son of Homer L.

Pound, asst. assayer U.S. Mint, Philadelphia, son of Hon. T. C. Pound of Wisconsin, of American parentage and descent.' Eliot applied but was turned down as medically unfit. Pound later asked Quinn to cable London in support of a new application by Eliot to join the U.S. Intelligence Service abroad: Quinn did so and Eliot was offered an appointment as Chief Yeoman with Navy Intelligence, to be followed by an early commission. But red tape intervened and the Armistice finally put an end to the matter while he was still waiting to join.

There were merrier moments also in the affairs of Pound and his friends. In October 1917 Yeats, aged fifty-two, married a friend of Dorothy's, Georgiana Hyde-Lees, who was much younger than her husband. As he was leaving for his honeymoon Yeats asked Pound to send a telegram about the wedding to Lady Gregory at Coole Park. But suddenly reflecting upon the nature of the event and the breadth of Pound's creative faculties and epistolary style, he thoughtfully added: '*Not* one that will be talked about in Coole for the next generation.'

During the second week in December 1917 Pound was working hard to finish his new Arnaut Daniel translations for publication by the Rev. C. C. Bubb who had a private press in Cleveland, Ohio, but although Pound sent his typescript it apparently went astray and the publication did not materialize. He was relieved when in December the art critic P. G. Konody of whom he had seen a good deal since 1909 was able to get Lewis out of the trenches and appointed as a war artist for the Canadian War Records Office. About 19 December he received from Joyce the first chapters of his new novel, *Ulysses*. In his letter of acknowledgement he praised the work in one of his American dialects: 'Wall, Mr Joice, I recon' your a damn fine writer, that's what I recon'. An' I recon' this here work o' yourn is some concarn'd litterchure. You can take it from me, an' I'm a jedge.' He went ahead immediately with plans for its publication as soon as possible in serial form in *The Little Review*, now sub-titled 'The Magazine that is read by those who write the others'.

By the end of December Pound had completed a group of Provençal translations called 'Homage à la langue d'Oc' and a group of satirical poems on contemporaries called 'Moeurs Contemporaines'. He sent them, together with one of his recent Daniel translations, to Harriet Monroe who rejected them as too frank. In the poem about Mr Hecatomb Styrax whose ineptitudes had 'driven his wife from one religious excess to another', she objected to the word 'virgo' in:

> has married at the age of 28,
> He being at that age a virgin,
> The term 'virgo' being made male in mediaeval latinity. . . .

Another poem she thought 'unprintable' was the Provençal translation, 'Vergier':

> 'Lovely thou art, to hold me close and kisst,
> Now cry the birds out, in the meadow mist,
> Despite the cuckold, do thou as thou list,
> So swiftly goes the night
>   And day comes on.'

Her comment was, 'lovely, but – frank'. After she had rejected both groups he felt free to send them to *The Little Review* where they were published in May 1918; 'Homage à la langue d'Oc' was reprinted in *The New Age* of 27 June and both lots included in his next book of verse, *Quia Pauper Amavi*.

Some of Pound's friends in London greatly admired the Provençal translations and Lewis writing from France on 16 January 1918 told him that the painter Helen Saunders had described them as 'very fine'. 'If they are all as good as the one I read,' Lewis said, 'you are on the point of producing an important book.' Encouraged by this reception he was full of plans during the next few months for reviving the music of the troubadors and the art of setting words to music, which had almost completely lapsed, he thought, after Campion and Waller. At the end of January he wrote enthusiastically to Quinn of going ahead with the work despite the fact that Rummel was in Paris; some of it would have to be done by letter, but a new start was now possible because he had found a singer, Raymonde Collignon, with the right vocal equipment and intelligence to sing the old music: 'It means a new start on the whole thing . . . and probably the resurrection of as much of it as is worth while.' Pound had mentioned Raymonde Collignon in one of his concert reviews signed William Atheling in *The New Age* of 3 January and he published a note on her work in the March *Little Review*. At the Aeolian Hall on 27 April she sang some of the Rummel-Pound troubadour songs of 1911–12 and the event was recorded by William Atheling in *The New Age* of 16 May. One night on his concert-round he heard the manager of the Wigmore Hall, a man named Pearson, explaining the wartime change of name from Bechstein Hall to Wigmore Hall: 'Vigmore', he said with a faint smile, 'is French for Bechstein.'

In February 1918 *The Little Review* was given over to Pound's sixty-one page 'Study in French Poets' in which he discussed and quoted from Laforgue, Corbière, Rimbaud, De Gourmont, De Régnier, Verhaeren, Vielé-Griffin, Stuart Merrill, Tailhade, Jammes, Moréas, André Spire, Vildrac and Romains. The time when the intellectual affairs of America could be conducted on a monolingual basis was over, he said, and he offered no apology for printing most of the number in French. The intellectual life of London was dependent on people who understood the French language about as well as their own and America's part in contemporary culture was based chiefly upon Whistler and Henry James, both familiar with Paris. 'It is something of a national disgrace', he declared, 'that a New Zealand paper, *The Triad*, should be more alert to, and have better regular criticism of, contemporary French publications, than any American periodical has yet had.' If the reader familiarized himself with the work of Gautier, Baudelaire, Verlaine, Mallarmé, Samain, Heredia, and of the authors quoted in his 'Study', he would have a pretty fair idea, he thought, of the sort of poetry that had been written in France during the last forty years, and, for what his opinion was worth, he would know most of the best of it. 'After Gautier', he said, 'France produced, as nearly as I can understand, three chief and admirable poets: Tristan Corbière, perhaps the most poignant writer since Villon; Rimbaud, a vivid and indisputable genius; and Laforgue, – a slighter, but in some ways a finer "artist", than either of the others.' Where Laforgue, out of infinite knowledge of all the ways of saying a thing, found the right way, Rimbaud, when right, did the right thing because he simply couldn't be bothered to do it any other way. But Corbière, he thought, was the 'greatest poet of the period'. Also in February he published in *Poetry* some of his recent conclusions under the title, 'The Hard and Soft in French Poetry'. By hardness he meant a quality which in poetry was nearly always a virtue: 'I can think of no case where it is not.' By softness he meant an opposite quality which was not always, however, a fault. 'One tends to conclude that all attempts to be poetic in some manner or other defeat their own end; whereas an intentness on the quality of the emotion to be conveyed makes for poetry.'

The Little Review began its long serialization of Joyce's *Ulysses* with the publication of 'Episode I' in March. Publication continued with few breaks until the issue of September–December 1920 when the United States Post Office intervened on account of 'obscenity'. *The Egoist* printed five small selections in 1919 until the printer called a halt. Pound himself had moments of doubt occasionally about the style and the contents and edited slightly some pages before sending them to *The Little Review*; nevertheless he defended the method and the overall impact: 'I can't agree with you about Joyce's first chapter', he wrote to Quinn. 'I don't think the passages about his mother's death and the sea would come with such force if they weren't imbedded in squalor and disgust.'

In the March 1918 issue of *Poetry* Pound attacked Edmund Gosse's

Life of Swinburne as the attempt of 'a silly and pompous old man' to present a man of genius, an attempt necessarily foredoomed to failure. He acknowledged that in one of his positions of trust under the British government Gosse had fulfilled his functions with great credit and fairness – a reference to Joyce's Civil List grant; but the attack was clearly the result of Gosse's failure to assist a second time after Joyce's collapse in August 1917. According to a letter Pound sent to Mrs Joyce at the time Gosse professed willingness to help but said that his connection had ended when Asquith left office and that he was 'unacquainted with the present Prime Minister'. In 1924 Gosse wrote to Louis Gillet in an attempt to prevent any discussion of Joyce's work in the *Revue des Deux-Mondes.* Joyce, he said, was not without talent, but he was literary charlatan of the extremest order whose *Ulysses* was obscene and anarchical: 'There are no English critics of weight or judgement who consider Mr Joyce an author of any importance.'

In the fuss over the indecency of Joyce's work in 1918 Pound generally took the line that it was foolish to run too close to the law as it stood on matters that were not worth the trouble; but he was convinced that false delicacy and a refusal to see and to record things clearly were a menace. And he even thought, he told Quinn, that the international situation in 1918 was in no small measure due to the English and American habit of keeping 'their ostrich heads carefully down their little silk-lined sand-holes'.

Possibly as a result of the poem which appeared in the Newark anniversary book in 1917, Homer Pound the following year arranged for his son to write a series of articles for the *Newark Sunday Call.* For his first article Pound recast a piece which he published in the April 1918 issue of the *Future;* it appeared in the *Sunday Call* of 21 April under the title 'Henry James – The Last Phase'. Perhaps because he was too 'highbrow' for its readers the paper terminated the series after the first article

As well as his work for *The Little Review, The New Age, The Egoist* and *Poetry* Pound was now contributing fairly regularly to the *Future,* not only articles and book reviews but also poetry. The first three cantos appeared there during the first half of 1918, but considerably reduced from their first publication in *Poetry* and bearing makeshift titles. Two sections of the original canto 1 appeared in the February issue as 'Passages from the Opening Address in a Long Poem'; about eighty lines from canto 2 in the March issue as 'Images from the Second Canto of a Long Poem'; and a passage from canto 3 in the April issue as 'An Interpolation Taken from the Third Canto of a Long Poem'.

In March meanwhile The Egoist Ltd had published a second edition of *Portrait of the Artist* printed this time in England. For Pound it was a victory in the war against the old publishing houses: a turning point, he thought, because it now seemed that the 'lovers of good writing' had at last begun to break free of the regular publishing system. He turned these thoughts to flamboyant account in the May *Future*: 'Despite the war, despite the paper shortage, and despite those old-established publishers whose god is their belly and whose god-father was the late F. T. Palgrave, there is a new edition of James Joyce's *A Portrait of the Artist as a Young Man*. It is extremely gratifying that this book should have "reached its fourth thousand", and the fact is significant in just so far as it marks the beginning of a new phase of English publishing, a phase comparable to that started in France some years ago by the "Mercure".' The actual output so far was small: a few brochures of translations, Eliot's *Prufrock*, Joyce's *Portrait*, and Lewis's *Tarr* (announced), but he had it on good authority that at least one other periodical would start publishing The Egoist Ltd's authors after the war, 'so there are new rods in pickle for the old fat-stomached contingent and for the cardboard generation.' Turning to the *Portrait* he pointed to its method of 'swift alternation' between subjective beauty and external sordidness: 'It is the bass and treble of his method. And he has his scope beyond that of the novelists his contemporaries, in just so far as whole stretches of his keyboard are utterly out of their compass.'

In an article on 'The New Poetry' in the June issue of *Future* he spoke of 'a new French vitality among our younger writers of poetry', of whom Eliot was 'the most finished, the most composed'. The cold sardonic statement of Eliot's 'The Hippopotamus' was of the school of Gautier and 'Conversation Galante' was in the manner of Laforgue; but there was a great deal, he said, in the rest of his poetry which was personal and in no wise derivative either from the French or from Webster and Tourneur – just as there was in 'The Hippopotamus' a great deal which was not from Gautier.

In New York Alfred Knopf published *Pavannes and Divisions*, dedicated 'To John Quinn', on 29 June; it was advertised on the front of the dust-jacket as 'a collection of the best prose written by Mr Pound during the last six years . . . On the whole a unique collection, a book out of the common run and a summary of most of the important artistic interests of our time.' It included 'Jodindranath Mawhwor's Occupation' and several similar sketches; the twelve dialogues of Fontenelle; 'A Few Don'ts by an Imagiste' (1913), with additional comments; 'The Serious Artist' (1913); 'Mr Hueffer and the Prose Tradition in Verse' (1914); 'Remy de Gourmont' (1915–16); and more recent pieces such as his article on Crabbe.

The August *Little Review* was a 'Henry James Number', edited by Pound. He himself contributed three articles, parts of which came from earlier pieces in *The Egoist* and *Future*; other contributions were Eliot on 'The Hawthorne Aspect', Ethel Coburn Mayne on 'Henry James (as seen from the Yellow Book)', Orage on 'Henry James and the Ghostly', John Rodker discussing 'The Notes on Novelists', and James's former secretary Theodora Bosanquet on 'The Revised Version'.

Continuing with the line of study he had begun with his notes on the Elizabethan Classicists, Pound contributed a new series called 'Early Translators of Homer' to the August, September and October issues of *The Egoist* and soon afterwards three more articles on translators of Aeschylus. The September article, on Andreas Divus, included a translation by Pound of Divus's Latin translation of Book XI of the *Odyssey*. It was at this stage called canto 3; altered slightly and added to, it later became canto 1.

In September *The Little Review* published an article by Edgar Jepson, 'The Western School', which was an attack on such American poets as Vachel Lindsay, Edgar Lee Masters and Frost. Whether or not Pound commissioned the article in the first place, I do not know, but there is no doubt that he encouraged Jepson in his task and did all he could to make it as effective as possible. It was offered first to *Poetry* whose rejection of it was mentioned by Pound in a note to the article in *The Little Review*. In a letter published in the November *Little Review* Harriet Monroe said it had not been rejected because of its 'lack of flattery', as Pound had alleged, but for 'its cheap incompetence'. As a supporter of the 'Western School' she naturally was annoyed; but probably what stung more than Jepson's descriptions of shoddy workmanship and 'lumbering fakement' was his claim that amongst all the 'wamblings and yawpings' of recent American poetry he had found 'a real poet', T. S. Eliot, who was 'the very fine flower of the finest spirit of the United States'. Jepson replied to the indignation aroused by his article in a letter to the February–March issue 1919. 'Neither Harriet Monroe nor any of her supporters', he said, 'made any attempt whatever to counter a single one of my criticisms, to demonstrate that the punk I said was punk was not punk.' William Carlos Williams agreed that Jepson's strictures were 'in the main well-merited', but the praise of Eliot as an *American* poet so annoyed him that he began to formulate his own independent view of American poetry which was published in his book *Kora in Hell* in 1920.

On 19 September 1918 the *Times Literary Supplement* published a long review of Pound's *Pavannes and Divisions*: 'He says that he takes no great pleasure in writing prose about aesthetic, and that one work of art is worth forty prefaces. But he continues to write prefaces and prose about aesthetic as if he liked doing it; and we confess we like reading him.' He had learning, the reviewer said, a grasp of principle, and a strong, wilful taste of his own: 'We could annotate nearly every page of the book with eager agreement or dissent. This means that it is worth reading. You may wish that you had Mr Pound before you in the flesh, to tell him what you think of him; but that, no doubt, is exactly the effect he wishes to produce on you.'

In a review in *The Egoist* of November-December Eliot wrote: 'Whether we agree or not with his opinions, we may be always sure that in his brief and fugitive utterances he is not to be diverted on any pretext from the essential literary problem, that he is always concerned with the work of art, never with incidental fancies.' More pronounced, he said, than his enthusiasm for particular writers was his 'enthusiasm for good writing'.

Pound lunched with H. G. Wells in October, the first time he had seen him for six years, although more recently Wells had published a favourable review of *A Portrait of the Artist* and in other ways had helped to spread Joyce's name. 'I think you would like Wells', Pound wrote to Joyce in November. 'His remarks on Q. Victoria's monument before Buckingham Palace I shall reserve for some future prose work of my own.' He used them in canto 42, published in 1937:

> 'And how this people CAN in this the fifth et cetera
>   year of the war, leave that old etcetera up
> there on that monument!' 'H.G.' to E.P. 1918.

When in November the war ended and the crowds gathered and surged in the London streets, Pound caught a cold walking through the drizzle watching: he was particularly impressed when in Piccadilly he found himself within a few feet of King George's open carriage which was without escort except for a couple of policemen. To Quinn he wrote: 'Poor devil was looking happy, I should think, for the first time in his life.' Forty years later he included the item in canto 105:

> George Fifth under the drizzle,
> as in one November
> a man who had willed no wrong.

In the November *Little Review* Pound published nine poems, in some of which we see a new effort to create a poetic world of his own; poems in which he tries to solidify the intangible:

Lapped in the gold-coloured flame I descend through the aether.
The silver ball forms in my hand,
It falls and rolls to your feet.

('Rose White, Yellow, Silver')

I have wrapped the wind round your shoulders
And the molten metal of your shoulders
bends into the turn of the wind. . . .

('Concava Vallis')

The same issue contained Ben Hecht's 'Pounding Ezra': 'In fact my complaint against Ezra is that, having attracted me time and again with the promise of delightful cerebral embraces, he is forever bidding me adieu with no more than a languid handshake – a suave, a fastidious, an irreproachable, but still a handshake . . . he has always about him the air of a mimic . . . He does not present to me a style – but a series of portrayals . . . To me Pound remains the exquisite showman minus a show.'

More perhaps than at any other time in his career Pound in 1918 lived the life of a literary journalist caught up in the mechanism of deadlines, proof-sheets and printing-houses. In addition to his editorial work and articles for *The Little Review* and his art and music criticism for *The New Age* he reviewed numerous books in *Future* under the heading 'Books Current'. Among those he discussed, though sometimes only very briefly, were: *The Turkish Empire, Its Growth and Decay* by Lord Eversley; *The Crescent Moon* by F. Brett Young; *My Adventures as a German Secret Service* by Capt. Horst von der Goltz; *A New Study of English Poetry* by Sir Henry Newbolt; *On Heaven and Other Poems* by Ford Madox Hueffer. In September he devoted most of his space to a review of Lewis's *Tarr*, published by The Egoist Ltd in London and by Knopf in New York, but also mentioned *The People's Palace* by Sacheverell Sitwell, a young man 'presumably on the right track'; in October he reviewed at some length Lytton Strachey's *Eminent Victorians*:

Mr Strachey's study of Manning is particularly valuable in a time when people still persist in not understanding the Papal church as a political organization exploiting a religion; its force, doubtless, has come, through the centuries, from men like Manning, balked in political careers, suffering from a 'complex' of power-lust. . . It is, indeed, difficult to restrain one's growing conviction that Mr Gladstone was not all his party had hoped for. . . Gladstone was decidedly unpleasant.

In November he reviewed the following: *Oriental Encounters* by Marmaduke Pickthall; *Studies in Literature* by Sir Arthur Quiller-

Couch; *Exiles* by Joyce; *The Sheepfold* by Laurence Housman; and *170 Chinese Poems* by Arthur Waley. Pound did not apparently dislike this busy life at the time and was pleased when 'the owner of the *Manchester Guardian*' said that William Atheling's criticisms were 'brilliantly written'; Pound hoped the *Guardian* might consider employing him in its own columns, better paid than *The New Age*'s, but he does not seem to have heard any more about it.

In Wyncote Isabel Pound was a member of the Woman's Club where often to an audience that included Mrs Cyrus H. K. Curtis, Mrs George H. Lorimer and Mrs J. B. Stetson, Jr, she read her son's latest poems. On 27 November 1918 Mrs Van Court read a poem of her own:

> Mrs Pound was early with us
> Mother of the famous Ezra;
> Living far away in London
> Writes his verses weird and witty. . . .

Early in December Isabel reported to the Club on a meeting of the 'Drama League' and on the 11th used information from her son's letters and books to present a talk on 'Art and Artists in England during the War'.

The money Pound had raised for *The Little Review* was due to run out in April 1919 and he had not succeeded in finding any more; by the middle of December, however, he was hoping to start a new quarterly in England, for which some of the money had already been promised. When Marianne Moore sent him a group of poems in December he asked her whether she would prefer to wait for his new quarterly ('I think the poems too good to print without paying for them') or have them published in *The Little Review*, sooner, but probably without payment. She replied that she would wait for the quarterly; she recalled that 'In 1911, my mother and I were some months in England and happening into Elkin Mathews's shop, were shown photographs of you which we were much pleased to see. I like a fight but I admit that I have at times objected to your promptness with the cudgels.' The day after his letter to Miss Moore, Pound wrote to Harriet Shaw Weaver that his series of articles on early translators of Homer and Aeschylus were not altogether worth the booklet she proposed to issue: 'They were hurriedly concluded', he said, 'during the week I thought I was to be rushed out to Persia', and while he did not think they were spoiled, he did not feel they were quite final. He would prefer that the money be spent on a book like *Prufrock*, by some new poet. 'I believe I have one in sight.' He meant Marianne Moore and in 1921 her first book, *Poems*, was published by The Egoist Ltd.

As his year of greatest activity with *The Little Review* drew to a close Pound was still worried by his failure so far to find a voice and a poetry to match his ideas. He had rash moments, he told Joyce on 12 December of believing that the gift of immortality lay within his reach. But he was better perhaps at 'digging up corpses of let us say Li Po, or more lately Sextus Propertius' than in preserving 'this bitched mess of modernity'.

XIII Major C. H. Douglas 1918/1921

In *The New Age* office in 1918 Pound met Major C. H. Douglas who had come to Orage with the claim that he knew what caused economic depressions and how they could be avoided. Drawing upon his own experiences with the cost accounting methods of modern industry Douglas explained to his listeners that industry in general created prices faster than it distributed the power to buy; he had a scheme, he said, whereby the system could be healed and private property protected without inflation, government debt, collectivism or any other form of authoritarianism. Douglas had already expressed some of his ideas very badly in Holbrook Jackson's *The Organizer* (1917) and in December 1918 published a further article in *The English Review* edited by Austin Harrison. Orage drew out Douglas's ideas in conversation and Pound and others joined in. Pound suggested, he said later, that if what Douglas said was right then 'any government worth a damn' could pay dividends instead of collecting taxes. It was agreed that Douglas seemed to have found a solution to the problem of instituting an economic democracy to match political democracy. Orage helped Douglas with his prose style and the first of his articles published by *The New Age* appeared on 2 January 1919; his first book, *Economic Democracy*, began to appear serially in June, and a second book, *Credit-Power and Democracy*, the following February. Thus Pound was drawn into what later became well known as Social Credit.

He had for some time been preaching 'contempt for the mob' and saying that there was no respect for mankind 'save in respect for detached individuals'. His position on art was that there was no common denominator between the little that was good and the waste output that was dull and mediocre. As for politics, the intelligent man's job was to fight the 'dominant imbecilities of his time', whether aristocratic or democratic, 'mono-tyrannic or demo-tyrannic'. The value of a writer, he had said, was proportionate to the clarity and precision of his statement; to the closeness of correspondence between his statement and fact. Now, through Douglas, he saw the possibility of an economic freedom that would allow him to have, within a society of individuals, free from the pressure of the credit system, the art he so desperately wanted.

All around him he saw evidence of the falsity in society against which, he believed, there was only one sure weapon, namely clear thought expressed in clear words. This falsity pervaded the established publishing system and the newspapers. Against both he had been voicing his anger and contempt for some years, although occasionally he felt he would be able to do more good by getting control of a newspaper section or supplement than by publishing his work in literary magazines. About August 1918, during a fit of such hope, he composed an article for the eyes of newspapermen, entitled 'The Highbrow – How He Looks on American Newspapers', which was published soon afterwards in a newspaper journal, *PEP*. Generally, however, he saw journalism as something opposed to literature and was confirmed in this view one Sunday evening at Wickham Steed's flat, when Steed or Arthur Clutton-Brock explained to him that the aim in journalism was to write in such a way that the reader would find what he was looking for. Whether this was an exaggeration for the purpose of explanation, I do not know, but Pound certainly seems to have taken it as a plain fact. Another source of information on the corruption of society was his father-in-law, Mr Shakespear, who as a solicitor used to curse Lloyd George for laws so badly or so vaguely worded that lawyers could not understand them.

But where once Pound had seen the solution in terms of clarity of expression only, he now under Douglas's influence began to consider whether there was not another cause of all this corruption – false credit. I do not think that in 1919 he had fully made up his mind: for a year or more while Douglas's articles were appearing in *The New Age* he had other matters to think about which were of more immediate concern and it was not until the end of 1919 that he was able to consider his own ideas in the light of Douglas's.

His life as a literary journalist continued meanwhile in an atmosphere of expectancy now that the war was over; there were schemes in the air for a new quarterly and a new weekly, old faces to be seen again as soldiers came back from the war, and news from Paris and Switzerland of new art movements and manifestos. In January 1919 he put together a new prose collection entitled *Instigations* which Knopf was to bring out the following autumn. Late in January when a show of work by Lewis opened at the Goupil Gallery in London, Pound and Lewis independently made a list of the works each thought that Quinn would want. They pooled their recommendations and eventually Quinn bought seven drawings for £245. He had sent his *Propertius* to Harriet Monroe who said she was unable to take all of it but agreed to pay him ten guineas for four of its twelve sections. With the February issue of *Poetry* he ceased to be its foreign correspondent – a position he had held for more than six years. He continued his round of the concert-halls and art galleries for *The New Age,* but all the while looking for an opportunity to take Dorothy on their long-awaited trip to the Continent unavoidably postponed in 1914.

For a time Pound moved in the circle that had gathered about Frank Rutter's magazine *Art and Letters* and about the Sitwells. To the magazine he contributed an article on De Bosschère and another later on Arnaut Daniel, but he does not seem to have been happy in such company. Sir Herbert Read who was a witness to meetings between Pound and the Sitwells doubted if Pound ever really understood such typical English eccentrics. Years later he said that the Sitwells' rejection of British philistinism was as absolute as Pound's but they wished to concentrate their forces on the home front and were indifferent to some things in which he was deeply interested. Another trouble apparently was that the Sitwells were apt to make fun of him: 'indeed, it was very difficult for anyone to take him seriously in person (and it was his *persona* that he used to project)', Sir Herbert wrote. 'Apart from his exotic appearance, he rattled off his elliptic sentences with a harsh nasal twang, twitched incessantly, and prowled round the room like a caged panther. He was not made for compromise or co-operation, two qualities essential for any literary or artistic "movement".'

Pound continued to act as editor and go-between for the serial publication of *Ulysses* and made the February–March issue of *The Little Review* into a tribute to Remy de Gourmont. His own contribution was nineteen pages of notes and observations under the heading 'De Gourmont: A Distinction (Followed by Notes)'. In it he contends that 'Gourmont prepared our era; behind him there stretches a limitless darkness'. He explains this by saying that De Gourmont was intensely aware of differences of 'emotional timbre' and this awareness was his '"message".' Where Henry James was concerned with the social tone of his subjects, De Gourmont was concerned with 'their modality and resonance in emotion' and recognized the right of individuals to *feel* differently. He had passed the point, according to Pound, where people take abstract statements of dogma for enlightenment and had moved into an era in which an idea has little value apart from 'the modality of the mind which receives it'. The French magazine *Intransigeant* of 23 April noted the tribute with pleasure and said that Pound had handled the subject with passion and originality. Although Pound continued to contribute to *The Little Review* he had now ceased to be London editor and the job was taken over by John Rodker.

The four sections of *Homage to Sextus Propertius* selected by Harriet

Monroe appeared in the March *Poetry*; three of these plus three other sections were published in *The New Age* between 19 June and 28 August. The poem was attacked immediately by Professor William Hale, in *Poetry* and in the *Chicago Tribune*: like some others since, Hale thought that it was simply an inaccurate translation and was able to give instances where the English diverged from the Latin; but Pound denied that there was ever any question of a translation: 'My job', he told Orage, 'was to bring a dead man to life, to present a living figure.'

In May Pound and his wife managed to overcome post-war restrictions on travel and left London for Paris and the south of France. Their difficulties before leaving were described by Pound eight years later in an attack on passports in the New York *Nation*:

The war produced, if not a new ruling class, at least a new zealous bossiness. I had my first meeting with the new civic order during the armistice. I was living in London. I was told that I 'could not go to France unless I had business'. I naturally had business . . . My wife could not possibly accompany me unless she were ill. I naturally produced doctors' certificates. I could not move about in France; I must go to one place and stay there. At this point I was rescued by an elderly intelligent official from another department who took two hours off and swore to several contradictory statements in a manner showing great familiarity with the mind-ersatz of officialdom.

In Paris they stayed for a day with Miss Ida Lee Mapel, a lady from Virginia who had a flat there. Pound had met Miss Ida and her sister Miss Adah during his visit to Spain in 1906. From Paris Pound and his wife went to Toulouse where they found prices comparatively low. They stayed at 13 rue St Ursule and while there Pound received and corrected the proofs of *Quia Pauper Amavi*. Much of the time they carried rucksacks on their backs and explored Provence on foot. They visited Nîmes, Arles and Avignon in May and later went to the Pyrenees. Some of the time they slept in the open. When they arrived at Foix they had been some days walking; the flags of many nations were hanging from the central tower and they heard the news that the peace had at last been signed at Versailles. One day while in the Pyrenees Pound walked to the site of Mount Segur, the Provençal castle destroyed at the time of the Albigensian crusade (1208–33). A few miles from the Spanish border a French officer on horseback rode up behind him and asked him where he was going. When Pound explained that he was on his way to Mount Segur the officer told him to continue, explaining that he was on the lookout for French deserters.

While they were in Provence Pound received from Joyce the 'Sirens' episode of *Ulysess* and passed it on for publication. He did not think it was up to the standard of the rest and on 10 June he wrote to Joyce from Toulouse explaining that the episode was difficult to follow and suggesting that Joyce insert a few signposts. For *The New Age* Pound wrote a long series called 'Pastiche, The Regional', which was published in eighteen instalments, beginning with the issue of 12 June and continuing until 20 November. It was in the form of loose meditations on the problems he saw facing the artist in the modern world, with illustrations drawn from history, contemporary England and his own experiences in Provence at the time of writing. Mainly it was directed against provincialism in all its forms: 'Clemence Isaura endowed the local literary society of Toulouse a century after the troubadour vein was exhausted. The funds still insure her celebrity; but the form of endowment is typical of provincialism. It rewards not the best work submitted, but the best local product. The Jeux Floraux are in result as dull as any other high school performance, despite their six centuries of history. The capital, the vortex, is that which draws intelligence into it, not that which builds up a wall for its own "protection".' Provincialism of time, he said, was as damned as provincialism of place: 'our evils come in great part from the fact that we are governed by men who take count of too few of the facts, as the poverty of modern art movements lies in the paucity of the mental reference of the artists.' In both art and politics this paucity resulted in 'febrile stirs and excursions' because artist and legislator alike had no knowledge of the history of their subject and were unable to place in perspective whatever came their way.

In his own search for points of reference Pound had recently visited the House of Commons while it was in session and had been paying more attention to the daily run of politics. He worked some of this into the series: 'It is the curse of our contemporary "mentality" that its general concepts have so little anchor in particular and known objects; that, for example, in a legislative body (read House of Commons) trying to make laws about coal, there is only one man who knows how coal lies in the rock.'

Back in Paris Pound found himself in trouble again with officialdom as soon as he entered the American consulate.

There the vice-assistant-second-sub categorically forbade me to return to my home in London. I said: 'I live there', and suggested that he ask the assistant-first-vice or some one higher up concerning the regulations. He disappeared behind a partition, and returned with a request that I 'get a letter' from my employer, evidently knowing no strata of life save one where *everyone* has an employer. It was next suggested that I find some sort of 'reference' for myself. Every American I had known in Paris before the war had left. I knew no one save the ambassador whom I had met two days before . . . I stepped into a taxi and drove round to the embassy. The embassy dealt with the consulate, and I proceeded about my lawful occasions.

Pound and his wife returned to London in September, the month in which *The Little Review* began to publish Fenollosa's 'The Chinese Written Character as a Medium for Poetry'. The rest of the essay followed in the issues of October, November and December. Its appearance was for Pound an important event, for it was no bare philological document, he believed, but a study of the fundamentals of all aesthetics. Fenollosa he regarded as a forerunner who had explored 'many modes of thought' which had since been fruitful in recent poetry and painting.

In October Pound was appointed drama critic of *The Outlook*, which was a well-paid job of the kind that for years he had been searching for. He published two pieces of criticism, signed M. D. Adkins, in the issues of 11 October and 18 October and was then fired. 'Have had two opulent weeks', he told Quinn, 'as dramatic critic on *The Outlook*, and have been fired in most caddish possible manner.'

About 4 October John Rodker at his newly-established Ovid Press completed work on a private printing of forty copies of Pound's *The Fourth Canto* which were distributed gratis by the author. It contains some of his most beautiful lines:

> The valley is thick with leaves, with leaves, the trees,
> The sunlight glitters, glitters a-top,
> Like a fish-scale roof,
> > Like the church roof in Poictiers
> If it were gold.
> > Beneath it, beneath it,
> Not a ray, not a slivver, not a spare disc of sunlight
> Flaking the black, soft water;
> Bathing the body of nymphs, of nymphs, and Diana,
> Nymphs, white-gathered about her, and the air, air,
> Shaking, alight with the goddess,
> > fanning their hair in the dark. . . .

Later in October *The Egoist* published his *Quia Pauper Amavi* containing his recent translations from Provençal, the sketches of contemporaries entitled 'Moeurs Contemporaines', cantos 1, 2 and 3 (still differing radically from the final texts of three or four years later), and the 'homage' to Propertius. He had offered it originally to Elkin Mathews who was anxious to do another book of his poetry, but when Mathews suggested that he omit both the Propertius and the 'Moeurs

Contemporaines' he took it to *The Egoist*. He did however come to an agreement with Mathews for the publication the following year of all the early poems he wished to keep in circulation.

Pound's faith in Joyce was completely restored when in September or October he received the 'Cyclops' episode; he told John Quinn on 25 October that it was perhaps the best thing Joyce had done. The parody of styles had never been handled better, even by Rabelais, and he added: 'Our James is a grrreat man.'

Although Pound was moving deeper into politics it was still with independence in mind: independence for the artist in his work, independence for the 'party of intelligence' in its fight against stupidity, and independence for an aristocracy of taste whose function was to be a model of how to live. In the fifteenth instalment of 'The Regional', published in *The New Age* of 30 October, he said that at least two factors in the 'social question' had been insufficiently recognized or defined. The failure of many revolutionary parties was due, he claimed, to their failure to recognize that luxury, despite the fact that it was abused, had a function in the 'social machine'. It was futile to think of sacking the West End; the function of the West End was to 'set a model for living', the luxury of one age becoming the convenience of the next. His second point, which owed much to Douglas, was the desirability of over-production. It was, he maintained, the duty of a sane manufacturing system to overproduce every luxury which tended to increase the comforts and amenities of existence; to overproduce until these things were within every man's reach. The function of an aristocracy was largely to 'criticize, select, castigate luxury, to reduce the baroque to an elegance'. A fine model of life, as here envisaged, had, he said, its value, and any real system of sociology, as opposed to a doctrinaire system, must recognize this value and its nature. He concluded his series, 'The Regional', with the words: 'Universal peace will never be maintained unless it be by a conspiracy of intelligent men.'

On 13 November he began a new series entitled 'The Revolt of Intelligence' which ran for ten instalments, the last on 18 March 1920. He was fed up with 'suffrage, vegetarianism and eugenics' and what in 1918 he had called 'fabian crankist unhumanizing kulturbunds' which regarded man as a unit to be dealt with by committees. 'I have no interest in any country as *a nation*', he wrote in the third instalment of 'The Revolt of Intelligence', published on 18 December 1919. 'The league of *nations* appears to me about as safe and inviting for the individual as does a combine of large companies for the employee. The more I see of *nations*, the more I loathe them; the more I learn of civilization, the more I desire that it exist.' In the fifth instalment

(8 January 1920) he warned that a League of Nations backed up by force was a danger because every local conflict would tend to become a world conflict. It was perilous also because the power would be in the hands of a small committee appointed by 'Governmental inner cliques in each nation' and would lead to further recession of power away from the people.

In the midst of these concerns he was still struggling with the early cantos. Writing to his father in December 1919 he said he had 'done cantos 5, 6, 7' and each was 'more incomprehensible than the one preceding it; I don't know what's to be done about it'. On 13 December he told Quinn that he suspected the cantos were getting 'too too too abstruse and obscure for human consumption'. It was about this time also that he drafted cantos 14 and 15, sometimes called the 'hell cantos', which are a splendidly written if sometimes hysterical denunciation of the established order in England. Some of it is simply clever abuse but there is mastery and poetry in it as well:

> howling, as of a hen-yard in a printing-house,
>   the clatter of presses,
> the blowing of dry dust and stray paper,
> foetor, sweat, the stench of stale oranges. . . .

He expressed his mounting dislike of British civilization in an article, 'The Curse', published in the January issue of a London magazine entitled *The Apple (of Beauty and Discord)*. Museums, which were the highest achievement of the age, were also, he said, a pest, because too often they were a tomb rather than a school. 'And the utter condemnation of today's British civilization, if any more condemnations were needed, might be found in the fact that uncountable excellent things are housed in a horror like the "Victoria and Albert".' What he wanted was a living civilization in which beauty was a part of everyday life: 'Instead of a bit of jade in a box, why should I not have a doorway fit to look at?'

Pound was still advising Quinn on his art purchases and on 6 February 1920 after a visit to an exhibition of work by Epstein at the Leicester Galleries he recommended four works – busts of Margaret Epstein and Gabrielle Saonne, a full-length 'Christ', and 'American Soldier'. Quinn eventually bought the Saonne bust and the 'American Soldier'; he refused the 'Christ' largely because the face reminded him of Woodrow Wilson whom he detested.

Early in 1920 Pound became angry at attacks against *Quia Pauper Amavi*. It had been reviewed favourably by Eliot in the *Athenaeum* and Hueffer (who had changed his name to Ford Madox Ford) in

Piccadilly. But in *The Observer* of 11 January Robert Nichols spoke contemptuously of it and concluded with the statement that 'In himself Mr Pound is not, never has been, and, almost I might hazard, never will be a poet.' The paper published letters from Pound and Lewis later in the month, together with replies by Nichols to both. There was a further unfavourable review in the *Spectator* of 7 February.

Pound was composing, meanwhile, his series of poems, *Hugh Selwyn Mauberley*, in which he was attempting to summarize his position and his attitude to England in more stringent verse than he had written hitherto, some of it in rhyme. He showed the work to Eliot who thought that the second poem in part II was not as clear as it might be; after making some adjustments Pound sent it back with a note saying 'Cher T: Now, 'n' be DAMN this thing mUST be comprehensible ????!!!!' Although intellectually he was in a transition period he was still hoping to remain in London. In March he began to write drama criticism for the *Athenaeum* under the initials T. J. V. and in his first eight weeks he published eighteen reviews of the theatre and ballet, plus a review, signed J.L., of Major Douglas's *Economic Democracy*. In the issue of 23 April he reviewed Gogol's *The Government Inspector* playing at the Duke of York's Theatre. Complaints were lodged and on 7 May the magazine expressed regret that the review contained words 'which might be construed as imputing to Miss Mary Grey want of ability in her profession of an actress'.

Through the efforts of Eliot and Quinn he was appointed in March a correspondent for the American magazine, *The Dial*, which had recently been taken over and transformed by two wealthy men, Scofield Thayer and James Sibley Watson, Jr. '*The Dial*', Pound told T. E. Lawrence, who had asked his advice about a career in journalism, 'is an aged and staid publication which I hope, rather rashly, to ginger up to something approaching the frenetic wildness of *The Athenaeum*.' In his six-page letter of acceptance on 24 March Pound lectured the editors of *The Dial* on literature and criticism and sought their attitude to Fenollosa; he also offered them four cantos and said he could probably be counted on to provide two cantos a year for publication in future. After seeing a copy of the letter Quinn advised Pound to act always with 'tact and discretion' in his dealings with the magazine. Pound's salary as correspondent was $750 a year.

On 25 April Pound's *Instigations* was published by Boni & Liveright, New York. It was dedicated, 'To My Father Homer L. Pound'. It had been sent originally to Knopf, who rejected it, and was then taken up by Boni & Liveright. It collected his recent notes on modern French poetry, Henry James and Remy de Gourmont, the *Egoist* series on translators from the Greek, reviews of Eliot, Joyce and Lewis, his recent essay on Arnaut Daniel together with his new translations of that poet, and a number of lesser pieces. It also marked the first book publication of Fenollosa's 'The Chinese Written Character as a Medium for Poetry', edited, with notes, by Pound.

Towards the end of April or early in May Pound and his wife left London for a holiday in Italy. By 3 May they were at the hotel Pilsen-Mannin, Venice, where they intended to stay until the 30th but within a few days Dorothy Pound became ill and they decided that the air would be better for her at Sirmione. Before they left however Pound began his experiment in autobiography, 'Indiscretions', which was published in *The New Age* in twelve instalments, beginning 27 May. They reached the hotel Eden at Sirmione about 13 May and Pound continued his efforts, begun in Venice, to arrange a meeting with Joyce who was now back in Trieste. He described to him the advantages of Sirmione and the blueness of the lake ('I have never found anything quite up to it save in the Capri grotto') and to convince him of the colour sent one of Dorothy's recent water-colours. Owing to train strikes, Joyce's hesitancy and Pound's inability to write a clear letter and then wait, there was three weeks of indescribable confusion before Joyce accompanied by his son Giorgio finally arrived on 8 June. Pound met them at Desenzano station and they drove across to Sirmione; Joyce thought Pound was 'a miracle of ebulliency, gusto, and help', and 'a large bundle of unpredictable electricity', while Pound, in a letter to John Quinn on 19 June described Joyce as pleasing: 'after the first shell of cantankerous Irishman, I got the impression that the real man is the author of *Chamber Music*, the sensitive. The rest is the genius; the registration of realities on the temperament, the delicate temperament of the early poems. A concentration and absorption passing Yeats's – Yeats has never taken on anything requiring the condensation of *Ulysses*.' Joyce stayed two days at Sirmione during which he listened to Pound's advice and decided to leave Trieste for Paris. Joyce dreaded thunderstorms and while he was at Sirmione there was a particularly fierce one: he was, Dorothy Pound told me, 'very nervous'. When I asked her what she had thought of him on that first meeting, she replied, 'Irish, very Irish'.

The May–June issue of *The Little Review* had appeared meanwhile with an article by Pound on W. H. Hudson which contained his fiercest attack so far on the established order and his fiercest defence of the individual genius:

A bloated usury, a cowardly and snivelling politics, a disgusting financial system, the sadistic curse of Christianity work together, not only that an hundred species of wild fowl and beast shall give way before the advance of industry, i.e. that the plains be covered with uniform and verminous sheep, bleating in perfect social monotony; but in our alleged 'society' the same tendencies and the same urge that the bright plumed and fine voiced species of the genus anthropos, the favoured of the gods, the only part of humanity worth saving is attacked. The milkable human cows, the shearable human sheep are invited by the exploiters, and all others regarded as caput lupinum, dangerous: lest the truth *should* shine out in art, which ceases to be art and degenerates into religion and cant and superstition as soon as it has tax-gathering priests: lest works comparable to the Cretan vases and Assyrian lions *should* be reproduced or superseded.

Two books by Pound were published in London in June: *Hugh Selwyn Mauberley* and *Umbra*. *Mauberley* was published by Rodker's Ovid Press in an edition of two hundred copies. If *Propertius* was the victory of a certain technical bravado over the tendency of words to stray when given a little freedom, *Mauberley* was an exploration of some of the possibilities of restriction and syncopation. He establishes equilibrium by setting speech-type rhythms and emphases and figures against fairly tight forms, neither being able to overcome the other, but one against the other to maintain constant tension.

> For three years, out of key with his time,
> He strove to resuscitate the dead art
> Of poetry. . . .

The run-over from the second to the third line does not disrupt the form; it does justice to both the natural fall of the words and the form simultaneously. The second run-over is different from the first:

> to maintain 'the sublime'
> In the old sense. Wrong from the start –

As recorded in the ear the 'art' of the first includes an almost imperceptible pause, followed by a quick leap to the words 'Of poetry'. Almost like a springboard being forced down and then let go. With 'sublime', on the other hand, the ear records a long and smooth diminuendo, followed by a graceful scooping up of the phrase 'In the old sense', which is neatly deposited to rest. The phrase, 'Wrong from the start –' completes the quatrain, while holding it ready for the beginning of the next:

> No, hardly, but seeing he had been born
> In a half savage country, out of date. . . .

In section X, a 'traditional' cadence is followed by several lines of syncopation and counter-rhythm; the result justifies the risk:

> Unpaid, uncelebrated,
> At last from the world's welter
>
> Nature receives him;
> With a placid and uneducated mistress
> He exercises his talents
> And the soil meets his distress.

If any section of *Mauberley* is better known than the rest it is the 'Envoi (1919)', with its beautiful echo of Waller's song, 'Go lovely rose':

> Go, dumb-born book,
> Tell her that sang me once that song of Lawes
> . . .
> When our two dusts with Waller's shall be laid,
> Siftings on siftings in oblivion,
> Till change hath broken down
> All things save Beauty alone.

Mauberley draws together as much of the European scene as Pound was able to hold within a single work. It tells of 'old lies and new infamy' and 'usury age-old and age-thick', and of an age which demanded an image 'Of its accelerated grimace', which demanded

>   chiefly a mould in plaster,
> Made with no loss of time,
> A prose kinema, not, not assuredly, alabaster
> Or the 'sculpture' of rhyme.

The poem succeeds because despite its ambiguities, some of them serious, the poet embodies his feelings in the texture of it: the anger, the loathing, the discriminations and the beauty are transformed into poetry where we are free to share them with the poet without necessarily sharing his views.

The other book which came out in June, *Umbra*, was published by Mathews. It was a collection dear to Mathews's heart, 'The Early Poems of Ezra Pound', further described on the title-page as 'All that he now wishes to keep in circulation from "Personae", "Exultation", "Ripostes", etc. With translations from Guido Cavalcanti and Arnaut

Daniel and poems by the late T. E. Hulme.'[1] Into the selection from *Ripostes* Pound inserted a previously unpublished poem of 1912, 'The Alchemist', subtitled 'Chant for the Transmutation of Metals':

> Under night, the peacock-throated,
> Bring the saffron-coloured shell,
> Bring the red gold of the maple,
> Bring the light of the birch tree in Autumn
> Mirals, Cembelins, Audiarda,
>   Remember this fire.

After Mathews's death in 1922 Pound wrote to Mrs Mathews: 'Whatever has been done since, I shall not forget that he was the first who accepted my work when I landed in London – sans sous – and these beginnings count for more than the middle steps of the journey.'

About the middle of June 1920 the Pounds left Italy for Paris; conditions in Italy were chaotic and transport apparently difficult to find. 'I came out of Italy on a tram-car', he wrote to Quinn, 'and reckon the next man will come out in a cab.' In Paris he helped the Joyce family to settle in when they arrived from Trieste on 9 July and he secured for *The Dial* some unpublished writings by De Gourmont which he himself translated; they were published under the title 'Dust for Sparrows' ('Things Thought, Felt, Seen, Heard, and Dreamed') in nine instalments beginning with the September issue. He also secured manuscripts or promises of contributions from a number of other French writers. Well pleased with himself he returned to London where he had writing-paper printed giving 5 Holland Place Chambers as the magazine's London address, and announcing in a column at the side that in addition to 'inedited writings of Remy de Gourmont' *The Dial* had already received 'either acceptable manuscripts or promises of collaboration from' Julian Benda, Marcel Proust, Benedetto Croce, Miguel Unamuno, W. B. Yeats, Paul Valery, Ford Madox Hueffer, T. S. Eliot, James Joyce, Wyndham Lewis, Louis Aragon, and numerous others. Another reason for his buoyancy was that he thought he was returning to his position as drama critic of the *Athenaeum*, especially as the editor, John Middleton Murry, had been in touch with him by letter while he was in Paris; but soon after he got back to London he received an additional communication to the effect that he was fired. He was very angry and said he would not have wasted the fare back to London had he been informed, as he thought he should have been, before he left Italy. In a letter to Joyce on 2 August he said the job had brought him £10 a month and had been the 'chief cash reason' for his return to England.

But although his position was difficult it was not desperate. He had his connection with *The Dial* which had begun to publish both his poetry and his prose; he was still music critic for *The New Age* and had been writing articles recently for journals in France and Spain; and he received other sums, such as ten guineas for poems published in Sir Henry Newbolt's anthology of modern verse. Also there were small amounts coming in from his books. Between 25 April and 30 June Boni & Liveright had sold three hundred and eight copies of *Instigations* and Pound's royalty of fifteen per cent, amounting to $138.60, was paid into his account with the Jenkintown Trust Company on 11 November.

During the final months of 1920 he considered what to do next. His regard for the individual genius, 'the favoured of the gods', was as high as ever, but Douglas had introduced a new factor which began to place him at the mercy of contemporary events. If things were happening he had a desire always to participate; the difficulty now was to decide where they were happening most. He thought of returning to America; he thought of taking up medicine but had not the funds necessary for four or five years' study; in the end he came to the conclusion that 'The Island of Paris', as he titled his Paris reports to *The Dial*, was the one live spot in Europe and he decided to live there, perhaps for a year, perhaps for good.

His admiration for the city's intellectual and artistic life is everywhere visible in the three 'Island of Paris' reports published in October, November and December. He speaks of his visit the previous June when he sought there 'a poetic serum to save English letters from post-mature and American letters from premature suicide and decomposition'. Valery, he says, 'bears unquestioned the symbolic and ghostly plaid shawl of Mallarmé', and 'the young and very ferocious are going to "understand" Guillaume Apollinaire as their elders "understood" Mallarmé'. He sees new life springing up among the dadaists with their attacks upon journalism and sanctimoniousness in the presence of the arts; he notices also that they are beginning to attack the 'international financiers'. Also he was impressed by Julien Benda; he had read his article 'L'Eternelle Idole' in *Le Figaro* of 9 March 1920 and reviewed *Belphégor*, Benda's defence of 'intelligence' against 'feeling', in the *Athenaeum* of 9 July 1920, under the initials B.L. He admired particularly Benda's 'hardness' and clarity which seemed to promise no doubt a mental vigour in Paris such as he had not been able to find in England. In 1966 Dorothy Pound put the matter concisely: the London climate, physical and mental, did not suit Ezra; he was searching for 'mental life' and thought he would find it in Paris.

On 10 December 1920 Boosey & Company in London published

Five Troubadour Songs by Pound in collaboration with Agnes Bedford, a professional musician. In addition to the Provençal texts the book contained English words by Pound, or adapted by him from Chaucer, together with music for voice and piano accompaniment. The 'Proem' was signed by both Ezra Pound and William Atheling: 'Two of the lyrics are pastiche; in the case of Faidit's lament for Coeur de Lion, the subject matter is definite, here I have made a condensation of the original poem, and interpolated certain data which would have been known to Faidit's audience, but of which the modern auditor may require some glose or reminder.'

When the Pounds left London Miss Bedford took over their flat in Holland Place Chambers and helped Pound with technical matters when later he composed operas.

By Christmas 1920 he and Dorothy were living in a flat at 70 *bis* rue Notre Dame des Champs. In *The New Age* of 13 January 1921 Pound published 'Axiomata', his 'intellectual will and testament' on leaving England, the themes of which were the mental constriction he felt in England and the dangers of 'Belief' as a paralysis or atrophy of the mind. Orage commented in the same issue: 'Mr Pound has shaken the dust of London from his feet with not too emphatic a gesture of disgust, but, at least, without gratitude to this country. I can perfectly well understand, even if I find it difficult to approve. Mr Pound has been an exhilarating influence for culture in England: he has left his mark upon more than one of the arts, upon literature, music, poetry and sculpture; and quite a number of men and movements owe their initiation to his self-sacrificing stimulus; among them being relatively popular successes as well as failures. With all this, however, Mr Pound, like so many others who have striven for the advancement of intelligence and culture in England, has made more enemies than friends, and far more powerful enemies than friends. Much of the Press has deliberately closed by cabal to him; his books have for some time been ignored or written down; and he himself has been compelled to live on much less than would support a navvy.' Soon after Pound arrived in France the Paris edition of the *New York Herald* published the following interview:

Mr Ezra Pound has just arrived in Paris from London. He says that after a visit of several months to the Riviera he will return here to remain indefinitely. His reason is that he finds 'the decay of the British Empire too depressing a spectacle to witness at close range' . . . Having a number of pleasant memories of England in the last ten years, he finds that he can retain them more easily by being away now.

With regard to present conditions in England, Mr Pound declared that he looks upon credit control as the focus of power, and that he can see no economic improvement without revision of the credit system. He holds that, money should not be available to non-essential industries until necessities are provided for, and that free credits would work out to better advantage than the high rates of interest, which contribute to the present low production both in England and America.

'England is largely insensitised,' Mr Pound continued, 'suffering from the same poison that exists in German kultur and in the American university system, and which aims at filling the student's head full of facts to paralyse him with data instead of developing his perspicacity. I suppose the word sensitive gives an impression of femininity. And yet any scientist is anxious to have his instruments highly sensitised. It is one result of the war which had its most serious effect in this weakening of civilization. . . .'

'The situation is evident in the fact that England has not yet noticed the one contribution to creative thought which has been made in five years. It is found in C. H. Douglas's book published some months ago, *Economic Democracy*. The underlying idea is elaborated in Mr Douglas's new book, *Credit-Power and Democracy*. He is working to frustrate both the extreme revolutionists and the Junker party in England, which is just as stupid as that formerly existing in Germany, as well as foreign capital, which is indifferent to the undermining of the Empire, even to the point of bringing about another war, so long as its own ends are served. That sort of thing is obviously not given much publicity under the present censorship.'

Asked what his own plans are, Mr Pound said that he will keep clear of England and devote himself to his study of 12th-century music . . . He is also writing a long poem, although he says that he realises that one should not write long poems in the 20th-century. He is accompanied by Mrs Pound and they intend to return here in April.

It was about this time that he first encountered the work of Jean Cocteau whose *Poésies 1917–1920* he reviewed in *The Dial* of January 1921. In the process he claimed that Cocteau wrote a poetry that belonged to the city intellect and he went on to air a view which may have had some effect on Eliot when later that year he began to write his long poem *The Waste Land*. 'The life of a village is narrative,' Pound wrote, 'you have not been there three weeks before you know that in the revolution et cetera, and when M. le Comte et cetera, and so forth. In a city the visual impressions succeed each other, overlap, overcross, they are cinematographic.' One of the distinguishing marks of *The Waste Land* is the succession of scenes and impressions, crossing and overlapping.

NOTES

1 Killed in action on 28 September 1917.

1. *above* Cheltenham Military Academy
group, c. 1897
Pound is in the centre, two below the
moustachioed clergyman
(Free Library of Philadelphia)

2. Close-up of Pound
(Free Library of Philadelphia)

3. The Jenkintown home
(Free Library of
Philadelphia)

4. The house in
Fernbrook Avenue
(Free Library of
Philadelphia)

5. The ruins of the
Wanamaker mansion
after the fire, 1907
(Free Library of
Philadelphia)

6. *above* A house-party at the home of Wilfrid Scawen Blunt 18th January 1914: Victor Plarr, Sturge Moore, W. B. Yeats, Blunt, Pound, Richard Aldington, F.S. Flint (Humanities Research Center, University of Texas)

7. Dorothy Pound (Walter Benington)

8. Pound in 1916
(Humanities Research Center, University of Texas)

9. Portrait of Pound by Wyndham Lewis
(Humanities Research Center, University of Texas)

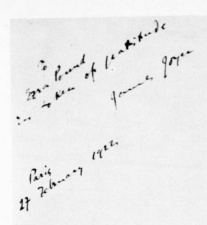

ULYSSES

10. The inscriptions to Pound by James Joyce and T. S. Eliot for
Ulysses and 'The Waste Land'
(Mary de Rachewiltz)

For subscriptions, etc., refer to F. B. Neumeyer, 70, Charing Cross Road, W.C. 2.

HE DIAL.

Edited by Scofield Thayer.

W. 13th St. New York.

Agency—

5, HOLLAND PLACE CHAMBERS,

LONDON, W. 8.

ʼill print during 1920-21 the
inedited writings of

Y DE GOURMONT;

s already received either acceptable
script or promises of collaboration
from

en Benda
rcel Proust
edetto Croce
guel Unamuno
B. Yeats
Valery
d Madox Hueffer
S. Eliot
es Joyce
adham Lewis
de Bosschère
Pound
Charles Cros
illy"
ert Mockel
re Spire
Morand
Sinclair
s Aragon
andre Arnoux
Giraudoux
and Divoire
ard Aldington
re Salmon
ppe Soupault
C. Williams
a Loy
V. de Lubicz Milosz
nila Savitzky
Vanderpyl
ur Symons
asel Arlen
.

BUT Bleeding Christ ! Mr Walpole :
        That is
precisely what you shouldn't have done ;
and which if you didn't you shouldn't
dash my hopes by professing to have
accomplished.

        The Dial for the past months
has been too confounded dull to be born,
it has been no better than the London
Mercury , or the Athanaeum or a dozen and
one of these other mortuaries for the
entombment of dead fecal mentality.

        One hopes , with a flicker
aroused by my past month in Paris , as
witness the opposite column of names) to
have in time a paper which an intelligent
being can read.

        And in the hope that your
politeness has got the better of your
candid opinion , I shall be very glad if
you help in labour of making it so.

*Only do make it suitable
to the 1920·21 Dial, and
to last years or last months.*

E. P.

Ezra Pound

30/7/1920

11. Letter to Hugh Walpole, 30th July 1920 (Humanities Research Center, University of Texas)

12. Decorative title-page to 'The Fourth Canto' (Humanities Research Center, University of Texas)

THE FOURTH CANTO

PALACE in smoky light,
Troy but a heap of smouldering boundary stones,
ANAXIFORMINGES! Aurunculeia!
Hear me. Cadmus of Golden Prows!
The silver mirrors catch the bright stones and flare,
Dawn, to our waking, drifts in the green cool light;
Dew-haze blurs, in the grass, pale ankles moving.
Beat, beat, whirr, thud, in the soft turf
            under the apple trees,
Choros nympharum, goat-foot, with the pale foot alternate;
Crescent of blue-shot waters, green-gold in the shallows,
A black cock crows in the sea-foam;

And by the curved, carved foot of the couch,
        claw-foot and lion head, an old man seated,
Speaking in the low drone . . . :
            Ityn!
Et ter flebiliter, Ityn, Ityn!
And she went toward the window and cast her down,
        "All the while, the while, swallows crying:
Ityn!

        "It is Cabestan's heart in the dish."
        "It is Cabestan's heart in the dish?
        "No other taste shall change this."
And she went toward the window,
            the slim white stone bar
Making a double arch;
Firm even fingers held to the firm pale stone;
Swung for a moment,
            and the wind out of Rhodez
Caught in the full of her sleeve.
        . . . the swallows crying :

Itys

Ityn!

Bi

13. Homer Pound on his 80th birthday at Rapallo
(Free Library of Philadelphia)

14. Dorothy Pound, 1958
(Free Library of Philadelphia)

15. Pound in Rome,
March 1941
(Associated Press)

16. Cages at the
Disciplinary Training
Centre, Pisa, where
Pound was held, 1945

17.   Pound with his grandchildren Patricia and Walter de Rachewiltz, in the
grounds of the de Rachewiltz castle, near Merano, July 1958

18.   Pound revisits Fernbrook Avenue in June 1958
(Free Library of Philadelphia)

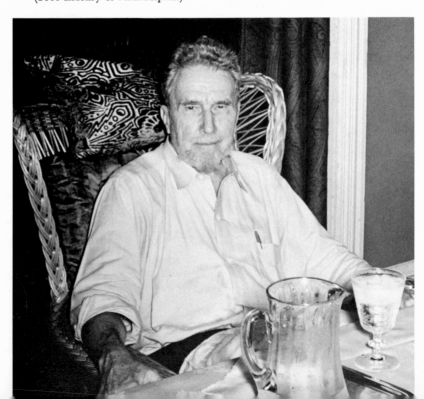

19. Pound in February 1966
(Carpanini)

20, 21. Pound at Sant' Ambrogio, April 1969
(Carpanini)

XIV Paris
1921/1924

Pound and his wife spent the first three months of 1921 at St Raphael on the Côte d'Azur between Cannes and St Tropez, staying for part of the time at least at the Hotel Terminus. While there he corresponded with Flint on Imagism, maintaining still, though their tone now was more friendly than in 1915, that Flint's work had more in common with impressionism than with his own Imagism which concentrated on hardness and condensation. Of the early days of Imagism he said that it was only by rather overbearing arrogance that he had managed for a few months to coerce the movement into a semblance of unity. It had been justified, he thought, because 'poetic English' was dead and Imagism drew attention to the necessity for good writing – compression and greater emotional energy. From St Raphael he also wrote to William Carlos Williams to say that he would consider a lecture tour of the United States if the money involved was sufficient to give him a year of leisure afterwards. With the money guaranteed he would listen to the stern voice of duty and return to save as much of America as was ready to be snatched from the yawning maw of gum shoes and the Y.M.C.A. 'I went to Newcastle year before last for one lecture – I suppose coming to U.S. would be like doing that for a year???' His emphasis on the money aspect possibly was caused by the news, received shortly after his arrival in France from London, that *The New Age* could not continue to pay for regular contributions.

Early in 1921 the energetic but irascible Quinn found that he could no longer bear the demands of artists and others on his time, money and energy and he finally exploded. When Joyce cabled that he was in 'financial difficulties' Quinn paid up, but cabled back: 'Do not cable me again on any subject.' When Pound sent a brief letter asking him to pass on a message to Michio Itow in New York Quinn lectured him on how busy he was for ten hot-tempered pages. When Pound feared that his connection with *The Dial* might be ending he asked Quinn to see about a job for him as correspondent of *The Century*. Quinn replied: 'I am glad that I was able to land you with *The Dial* for a year, but because I got that idea and carried it out that is no reason why you should expect me to be your literary agent with the Century.' He was angry because he now disliked the work he had bought from Wyndham Lewis and Epstein and thought that he had been a victim of Pound's bad taste. Complaining to Joyce about the demands of his friends he said that of them all Pound was 'the worst and most persistent'. Despite his anger Quinn later made enquiries at The Century but there was nothing suitable for Pound.

Back in Paris in April the Pounds went to their flat at 70 bis rue Notre Dame des Champs. It was on the ground floor and looked into a courtyard and garden. They brought over their books, paintings and sculpture from London and Pound made the furniture: a low tea-table put together from packing-cases and painted scarlet, another table, long and narrow, made of rough boards, and two large armchairs made of rough boards and canvas. There were also several couches. Here he worked on his first opera, 'Le Testament', based upon incidents in the life of François Villon; for his arias he used ballades and rondeaux by Villon in the original French, which were held together by spoken passages in English, some translated from Villon and some written by Pound. To Agnes Bedford who was helping him with the opera he wrote: 'Find Cocteau and Picabia intelligent. Fools abound but are less in one's way here, or at least for the moment.' Joyce's new chapter, 'Circe', was, he told her, 'enormous – megaloscrumptious – mastodonic'. Joyce had given him the 'Circe' and 'Eumaeus' sections on 16 April. 'Great stuff', Pound told his family on 20 April and again a few days later, 'a new Inferno in full sail'. But he was no longer able to send them to New York for publication in The Little Review because in February the Society for the Prevention of Vice had successfully prosecuted the editors, Margaret Anderson and Jane Heap, for publishing the 'Nausicaa' episode. After this, Huebsch and Boni & Liveright lost interest in bringing out Ulysses in book form, but early in April, Sylvia Beach, a young American woman who ran the Shakespeare & Company bookshop, at 8 rue Dupuytren (later at 12 rue de l'Odeon), asked Joyce if she might have the honour of publishing the book in Paris, and he agreed.

Both Pound and his wife went frequently to Miss Beach's shop where Pound, always available for carpentry or woodwork, mended a cigarette box and a chair; Dorothy Pound, anxious about the difficult location of the shop, drew a map which Miss Beach had printed on the back of her library circular. When Shakespeare & Company took over the publishing of Ulysses Pound was active in collecting subscriptions, among them one from Yeats, but he could not break down George Bernard Shaw's resistance. There was a 'long and wordy war' between them with Shaw declaring that it was much too expensive (signed copies,

350 francs; copies on *vergé d'arches*, 250 francs; and those on linen paper, 150 francs). Shaw terminated his side of the correspondence with the words: 'I take care of the pence and let the Pounds take care of themselves.' Not satisfied with this Pound continued his side of the argument in public, by declaring in the June 1922 issue of *The Dial* that Joyce's picture of Dublin was 'so veridic that a ninth-rate coward like Shaw (Geo. B.) dare not even look it in the face.'

Pound also helped Joyce in other ways more practical, as when in London he entrusted Eliot, accompanied by Wyndham Lewis, with a large brown paper parcel to be delivered to Joyce in Paris. In *Blasting and Bombardiering* (1937) Lewis left an account of the delivery which Eliot said later was perfectly remembered; an account which must be given in Lewis's own words:

Eliot now rose to his feet. He approached the table, and with one eyebrow drawn up, and a finger pointing, announced to James Joyce that *this* was that parcel, to which he had referred in his wire, and which had been given into his care, and he formally delivered it, thus acquitting himself of his commission.

'Ah! Is this the parcel you mentioned in your note?' enquired Joyce. . . .

James Joyce was by now attempting to untie the crafty housewifely knots of the cunning old Ezra. After a little he asked his son crossly in Italian for a penknife. Still more crossly his son informed him that he had no penknife. But Eliot got up, saying 'You want a knife? I have not got a knife, I think!' We were able, ultimately, to provide a pair of nail scissors.

At last the strings were cut. A little gingerly Joyce unrolled the slovenly swaddlings of damp British brown paper in which the good-hearted American had packed up what he had put inside. Thereupon, along with some nondescript garments for the trunk – there were no trousers I believe – a fairly presentable pair of *old brown shoes* stood revealed. . . .

In April 1921 Pound wrote to Lewis that he was 'taking up the *Little Review* again, as a quarterly'. He contributed half a dozen items during the next twelve months but the only one of interest was his short article on Brancusi, to accompany reproductions of some of the sculptor's works, in the issue of autumn 1921. He had become friendly with Brancusi and occasionally visited his studio, which was remarkable, Pound thought, for its peace and quiet. Sometimes he was invited to a meal cooked by Brancusi's own expert hand.

Among the steady stream of visitors to see Pound was Alfred Kreymborg, formerly of *Others*, and now editor of a new magazine called *Broom*.[1] According to Kreymborg, Pound immediately delivered a lecture on how to run *Broom* and when a list of potential contributors was brought out he crossed off one name after another, usually with a brief remark as to why, until there were few left.

When Pound attended a performance of Debussy's *Pelléas et Mélisande* ('that mush of hysteria') he was encouraged, he told Miss Bedford, to tear up the whole era of harmony and write his own opera for 'two tins and a washboard'. Ignorance held no further terrors, he said, if *Pelléas* was the result of what was called musical knowledge. He was further encouraged by the fact that people endured Satie's *Socrate* despite its being 'damn dull' and that Georges Auric was out for even less system than he himself. He had not been able to exclude violins altogether and he supposed that eventually the opera would include a few chords. A few days later he wrote again to say that he wanted nothing to interfere with the words, 'or with the utmost possible clarity of impact of words on audience'. Given the action on stage for the eye, and the song, how much of the actual orchestration, he asked her, did the audience hear, and how much therefore was really necessary.

When Scofield Thayer of *The Dial* came to Paris in July Dorothy Pound was visiting England and Pound was staying at a hotel in the rue des Saintes Pères. 'When one arrives at his hotel', Thayer wrote in a letter, 'one usually learns from the young lady that Mr Pound is *au bain*. But the young lady consents to go upstairs to see Mr Pound and to inquire if Mr Pound will see guests. Mr Pound receives, beaming and incisive.' Thayer found him awkward and sometimes self-conscious in public places but decided that he had a fine imagination and was surprised to find that at close quarters he was fairer in his judgements than his correspondence or books had given him to believe. At Thayer's hotel, the Continental in the rue Castiglione, Pound met E. E. Cummings who had first begun to attract attention with a group of seven simple but startlingly fresh poems in *The Dial* of January 1920. When later that night they walked together through the streets of Paris Cummings (aged twenty-six) was charmed, he said many years later, by the other's kindness, and found him 'wonderfully entertaining'.

Another visitor to Paris in July was John Quinn who had recovered from his earlier anger. Pound seemed to be fairly hard-up and Quinn offered to lend him $200, but Pound said no, things would improve. When by 22 October they had not done so, he wrote to Quinn that he was ready to accept; Quinn sent $250 and told him not to worry about paying it back.

In *The Dial* for August Pound published three cantos and in the 'Literary Review' of the *New York Evening Post* of 13 August a survey of the Paris literary scene dealing largely with Picabia. He had taken to Picabia's writings as well as his designs and was hoping to devote a section to him in a book called *Four Modern Artists* – the others being Brancusi, Picasso and Lewis – but the book was never written.

In August Miss Bedford went to Paris for a holiday and to help

Pound with his opera. Although they made progress Pound discovered that hunting around with one finger on a keyboard instrument was not perhaps the best method of composition, so he bought a bassoon. Even friends who were well disposed towards his musical efforts were hard put to justify this expenditure, in view of the 'deep rumblings and tootings' which ensued. Rodker, who enjoyed the opera when he heard it, was unable to say the same thing about the bassoon; the sounds were so strange, he said, that he could not gauge how far they fell short of what was expected of them. Lewis was not so kind. 'Dear Miss Bedford,' he wrote after a visit to Paris, 'was it you who stimulated Pound to the purchase of a BASSOON? And if so, do you think that is an action justified by the facts of existence, as you understand them?'

Pound continued meanwhile to publicize the theories of Major Douglas; he reviewed *Credit-Power and Democracy* in the summer issue of the American magazine *Contact* (with which Williams was associated) and for the August–September issue of *Les Écrits Nouveaux* in Paris he wrote an article, 'Le major C.-H. Douglas et la situation en Angleterre'. The editor explained to his readers that it was not a translation from English but had been written by the author in French: 'Nous avons respecté les savoureux exotismes de cet article écrit directement en francais. . . .' Large extracts from it were published in *Progrès civique* of 10 September under the title, 'La réforme du crédit est la clef de toutes les autres'. One day in the rue des Saintes Pères Pound picked up a leaflet advertising subscriptions to a papal loan. He interpreted this as evidence of Vatican involvement in the machinations of the bankers and he included it among material for a special issue of *The Little Review* devoted to credit control and banking; the magazine's editors reported later however that they had misplaced the material and the issue never appeared.

In 1921 Pound was interviewed by Clara Whiteside, whom he had known in Philadelphia, for *Youth*, 'A Magazine of the Arts'. The interview was published in October: '"Any country which is afraid of thought in whatever form it may be expressed is not a habitable country", was Ezra Pound's answer, when I asked him what was his opinion of America and whether he intended to return in the near future.' He told Miss Whiteside that for his activities on behalf of high standards in American art he was being attacked 'as un-American' and 'the most vigorous of my attackers is my dear friend, that Dago-emigrant, Bill Williams (who is about the best thing left in America)'.

During 1921 Pound had translated Remy de Gourmont's *Physique de l'amour; essai sur l'instinct sexuel*, under the title *The Natural Philosophy of Love*, and had written a postscript dated 21 June 1921 in which he expressed his agreement with de Gourmont that there is a

241

connection between 'la copulation complète et profonde et le développe-
ment cérébral'. Not only was this suggestion both possible and probable
but it was more than likely that the brain itself was, in origin and
development, only a 'sort of great clot of genital fluid held in suspense
or reserve'. Man, he said, was really 'the phallus or spermatozoide
charging, head-on, the female chaos . . . Even oneself has felt it,
driving any new idea into the great passive vulva of London, a sensation analogous to the male feeling in copulation.' Creative thought, he
said, was an act like fecundation, although the thought once born and
separated from the brain that begat it led an independent life much
like a member of the vegetable kingdom, 'blowing seeds, ideas from
the paradisal garden at the summit of Dante's Mount Purgatory,
capable of lodging and sprouting where they fall'. In describing man's
ability to develop 'new faculties', Pound gave, as examples, the mystics
('for what there is to them') and a friend of his in London, B. C.
Windeler, a wool-broker, 'who suddenly at 3 a.m. visualizes the whole
of his letter-file, three hundred folios; he sees and reads particularly the
letter at folder 171, but he sees simultaneously the entire contents of
the file, the whole thing about the size of two lumps of domino sugar
laid flat side to side'. He distinguished between creative male thought
and the thought of woman, 'the conservator, the inheritor of past
gestures'. She was clever and practical but not inventive. A third
category of thought was abstraction which was simply a 'dead or
laborious form of compilation'.

The Natural Philosophy of Love, including the translator's postscript, was published by Boni & Liveright on 10 August 1922. In some
copies was a slip containing an 'Important Notice': 'This work is
supplied to the Bookseller on condition that all discretion shall be used
in its sale or distribution.' The first English edition was published by
the Casanova Society in 1926 and in both countries there were
numerous later impressions and new editions.

On 8 December 1921 Boni & Liveright published Pound's *Poems
1918–21*, containing 'Three Portraits and Four Cantos'. The three
'portraits' were (1) *Homage to Sextus Propertius*, (2) 'Langue d'Oc' and
'Moeurs Contemporaines', and (3) *Hugh Selwyn Mauberley*. Worrying
still about the form his work was taking he hoped perhaps to give some
shape or direction to it by bringing these four groups of poems together
under a single heading, 'Three Portraits'. The four cantos were nos. 4,
5, 6 and 7, all differing, the last but slightly, from the final versions.

On 9 May 1921 Eliot had written to Quinn that he had 'a long poem
in mind and partly on paper'. During the summer he was in touch
with friends about a new magazine which he was to edit, but suddenly
he collapsed and had to take a rest cure at Margate and Lausanne

during the autumn. His difficulties were increased by the fact that his wife who had developed an internal complaint which aggravated her nervous temperament to hysteria, needed frequent treatment. Her mental unbalance and subsequent behaviour caused him much worry.

While resting after his collapse he completed the draft of his long poem, *The Waste Land*, and in Paris he took it to Pound for advice. Pound studied the forty pages – most of it typed, the rest in Eliot's own hand – and they then discussed it by letter. Following these discussions and Pound's markings and marginal comments on the draft itself, Eliot deleted a number of long passages. From part one he took out a fifty-four line account of a low-life evening in London ending at sunrise. From part three he deleted several sections: a sixty-nine line pastiche of Pope describing a fashionable lady having breakfast in bed and attending to her toilet, another about a Lady Katzegg's patronage of the arts, and a section on London. In part four he cancelled seventy-one lines describing the voyage and shipwreck of a fishing schooner.

Correspondence between the two men during the winter shows that by the end of 1921 Eliot had completed the poem except for any tidying up that remained following the cuts and Pound's suggestions as to choice of word or phrasing. In a letter of 24 December Pound wrote: 'Complimenti, you bitch. I am wracked by the seven jealousies, and cogitating an excuse for always exuding my deformative secretions in my own stuff, and never getting an outline.'

Pound and Eliot met several times on the Continent in 1919 and the 1920s: in Provence when they spent several days walking in the country around Excideuil, Eliot with a rucksack on his back, and another time in Verona, where at the Café Dante they drew up a 'programme' for Eliot's proposed new magazine, which to Pound's annoyance Eliot later failed to implement. Also present in Verona was Bride Scratton; she and Pound were very close at this period and saw a good deal of each other. In Paris he took her to Brancusi's studio where they watched the sculptor at work on a column. She returned to England and in 1923 was divorced by her husband who named Pound as co-respondent. Left with two children to bring up she had a difficult time during the late 1920s. She and Pound corresponded and he helped and encouraged her with her writing. In canto 29, written about 1928, he mentioned the occasion when she was present in Verona, but without naming her; in canto 78, written in 1945, he recalled the scene again, using the name by which he addressed her, Thiy, and also touched on his discussion with Eliot about his magazine:

> So we sat there by the arena,
>   outside, Thiy and il decaduto

the lace cuff fallen over his knuckles
considering Rochefoucauld
but the program (Cafe Dante) a literary program 1920 or
thereabouts was neither published nor followed

Pound and Mrs Scratton continued to correspond occasionally during the 1930s. Ever since their first meeting together in London they had shared the idea of building a temple to the true religion; in 1938 Pound wrote twice to tell her that 'after twenty years' waiting' Brancusi was at last 'building his temple in Indore' and that the stone column of which she saw 'the small start' in Paris had been set up at Jargu in Roumania. This idea of the temple merged with other symbols and ideas – the line, 'To build a dream over the world', the references in cantos 4 and 5 to Ecbatan 'City of patterned streets', and the story of that same Ecbatan, city of the legendary king of the Medes, Deïoces, as translated in G. Rawlinson's *History of Herodotus* (1880) – and eventually was transformed into the beautiful line, 'To build the city of Dioce whose terraces are the colour of stars', on the opening page of *The Pisan Cantos.*

About the beginning of 1922 Eliot returned to work at Lloyds Bank but by February Pound was worried that he was on the verge of another collapse. On 21 February he wrote to Quinn's friend and assistant, Mrs Jeanne Robert Foster: 'Eliot produced a fine poem (19 pages) during his enforced vacation, but has since relapsed. I wish something could be found for him, to get him out of Lloyds Bank'. By 12 March he had devised a plan, given the title 'Bel Esprit' by the American writer Natalie Barney , which called for the co-operation of working authors and enlightened patrons in raising money on Eliot's behalf, to enable him to leave the bank and to concentrate on writing. The idea was to find thirty donors willing to give £10 a year 'for life or for as long as Eliot needs it'. He believed that once the scheme started it would be possible to do the same for other writers or even to raise money for worthwhile American poets like Williams or Marianne Moore to visit Europe.

About mid-March he circulated carbon-copies of a typed notice explaining the scheme and pointing out that during his recent conva-lescence in Switzerland Eliot had written 'a masterpiece; one of the most important 19 pages in English'. Before the end of the month he had leaflets printed which announced that Aldington, May Sinclair and Pound were among the initial life subscribers and gave the names of the treasurers as R. Aldington, Malthouse Cottage, Padworth, Reading, Berks, and Ezra Pound, 70 *bis* rue Notre Dame des Champs, Paris. According to the leaflet Eliot was earning £600 a year at the bank but the work was exhausting and left him little energy for writing. It described *The Waste Land* as 'a series of poems, possibly the finest that the modern movement in English has produced, at any rate as good as anything that has been done since 1900, and which certainly lose nothing by comparison with the best work of Keats, Browning or Shelley'. Pound also wrote an article on the project which was published in *The New Age* of 30 March under the title 'Credit and the Fine Arts'. This article is interesting in the perspective of Pound's intellectual development because it shows him employing Douglas's ideas about the importance of leisure and the desirability of freeing as many as possible from unnecessary work and releasing more energy for invention and design. This 'Bel Esprit' was aimed at freeing Eliot from work that others could do, so as to leave him time in which to do the creative work he was suited for. 'The only thing one can give an artist', Pound wrote, 'is leisure in which to work.' The article is also interesting because it contains the first published reference to *The Waste Land*: 'Rightly or wrongly some of us consider Eliot's employment in a bank the worst waste in contemporary literature. During his recent three months' absence due to a complete physical breakdown he produced a very important sequence of poems: one of the few things in contemporary literature to which one can ascribe permanent value. That seems a fairly clear proof of restriction of output, due to enforced waste of his time and energy in banking.'

The scheme, which had been concocted without Eliot's knowledge, soon began to cause anxiety: 'I think you will agree', Eliot wrote to Aldington on 30 June, 'that the method proposed by Ezra is rather bordering on the precarious and slightly undignified charity. At the bank I am at least independent of the people whom I know, and a doubtful income, which I should be obliged to attempt to double by literary work would not be of the slightest advantage from anyone's point of view.' By the end of the year, a garbled version of the scheme had been discussed, much to Eliot's annoyance, in the *Liverpool Post* and Eliot began to receive anonymous gifts – on one occasion, four postage stamps; also he had to contend with his family in America, including his brother Henry, who were indignant at the whole idea. Pound kept on with the scheme until well into 1923 but Eliot refused to take the money and 'Bel Esprit' collapsed.[2]

On 4 January 1922 Pound signed an agreement with Horace Liveright, of Boni & Liveright, by which he was to receive a minimum of $500 a year for translating from French into English:

Mr Liveright agrees from this date 4 January 1922 until 24 January 1924 to pay to Ezra Pound the minimum of five hundred dollars yearly as an advance on whatever translations from French into English Mr Pound shall make at Mr Liveright's request. Mr Pound undertakes to translate such books as Mr Liveright chooses to the best of his ability and with reasonable promptitude. The rate of payment to be computed roughly on that paid for the translation of Gourmont's 'Physique de l'amour'. Mr Pound is not to forfeit right to said five hundred dollars should Mr Liveright fail to select or accept any French works for translation and publication.

It is further understood that Mr Pound will probably be unable to undertake more than one thousand dollars worth of translation in any one year.

Mr Liveright agrees not to demand Mr Pound's signature on the translation of any work that Mr Pound considers a disgrace to humanity or too imbecile to be borne.

According to Charles Norman, to whose book, *Ezra Pound*, I am indebted for this document, figures afterwards added to it show that Pound received $500 in all. The only book he seems to have translated under the agreement was Edouard Estaunié's *L'Appel de la route* which was published by Boni & Liveright in November 1923 under the title *The Call of the Road*. According to the dust-jacket the translation was by Hiram Janus but in 1923 in their autumn catalogue the publishers unmasked him: 'Ezra Pound, who is responsible for its exquisite English translation calls it one of the most thrilling stories of adventurous mystery that he has ever read.'

Ulysses was published by Shakespeare & Company in February and Joyce gave Pound an inscribed copy:

> *To*
> *Ezra Pound*
> *in token of gratitude*
> *James Joyce*
> *Paris*
> *27 February* 1922

After his initial efforts towards the formation of 'Bel Esprit' Pound left Paris on 27 March for Italy and when on 5 April he wrote to Lewis about the scheme, and why Lewis could not expect to benefit from it, he was in Siena. To the spring issue of *The Little Review* he contributed several short comments and a satirical squib in verse, all signed Abel Saunders; he also contributed a calendar which helps to confirm that he had maintained his early interest in astrology, magic and the occult, such as we find in the references to spirits and the Talmud in some of his early verse and in the letter he wrote to his mother in 1910 for exact information about the hour of his birth. Working from this and similar information he decided that the Christian Era had ended at midnight on 29–30 October, 1921: the world was now living in the first year of a new pagan age called the Pound Era.

After touring central Italy Pound went to Venice; from there on 6 May he wrote to Mrs Foster in New York to find out how much *Vanity Fair* would pay Eliot for *The Waste Land*. Quinn took up the matter with the editor, Frank Crowninshield, but the magazine was not interested. Eliot had already written to Thayer in January, asking how much *The Dial* would pay, but in four months no commitment had been entered into by the magazine.

Pound's 'Eighth Canto' appeared in *The Dial* for May, but he was not satisfied with it; before publishing it in book form in 1925 he removed the first fourteen lines, in their place wrote three new lines, and re-numbered it canto 2; and later when correcting the proofs for the book he added two more lines. Of the fourteen deleted he abandoned all except a few phrases used later in canto 7.

His 'Paris Letter' in the June issue of *The Dial* was a review of *Ulysses*. 'All men', he said, 'should "Unite to give praise to Ulysses"; those who will not, may content themselves with a place in the lower intellectual orders.' Joyce had taken up the art of writing where Flaubert had left it, attaining in *Ulysses* a greater efficiency, a greater compactness, than Flaubert in *Bouvard et Pécuchet*. The book was, he said, 'an epoch-making report on the state of the human mind in the twentieth century (first of the new era)'. It was uncensored, just as the 'foecal analysis, in the hospital around the corner, is uncensored', and no one but a Presbyterian, he declared, would contest the utility of the latter exactitude. And he added that a great literary masterwork was made for minds quite as serious as those engaged in the science of medicine. Several times in the review he mentioned Thomas Jefferson whom he was now studying, Eliot having presented him with his own set of the 'Memorial' edition of Jefferson's works. Pound also wrote a review of *Ulysses* in French, which was published in the *Mercure de France* on 1 June under the title 'James Joyce et Pécuchet'.

Halfway through the year Eliot was seriously short of money. Pound explained the position to Kate Buss who placed details before the Authors' Club in New York. On 28 June the club transferred to Pound, on Eliot's behalf, an emergency grant of $200.

Pound returned to Paris early in July and immediately began to organize in his flat a show of paintings by his Japanese friend, Tami Koume, later killed in an earthquake. On 8 July he wrote outlining his plans for *The Cantos* to Felix Schelling. He said that in the first eleven cantos, which were a 'preparation of the palette', he was getting down all the colours or elements that he would need in the course of the work – some of them, he admitted, 'perhaps too enigmatically and abbreviatedly'. He hoped to bring them into some sort of design and architecture later. 'Having the crust to attempt a poem in 100 or 120 cantos long after all mankind has been commanded never again to attempt a poem of any length, I have to stagger as I can.' *The Waste Land*, he thought, was the justification of the modern movement or experiment since 1900.

Pound meanwhile had met a young American journalist, Ernest Hemingway, whose prose style he admired for its new approach to the problem of clarity; he also admired his American tough-guy manner and his skill at sport. One day when Lewis rang the bell at Pound's flat he got no answer so he opened the door himself: 'A splendidly built young man, stript to the waist, and with a torso of dazzling white, was standing not far from me. He was tall, handsome, and serene, and was repelling with his boxing gloves – I thought without undue exertion – a hectic assault of Ezra's. After a final swing at the dazzling solar plexus (parried effortlessly by the trousered statue) Pound fell back upon his settee. The young man was Hemingway.' Pound went over Hemingway's manuscripts and gave him advice about getting rid of superfluous words. Hemingway introduced Pound to another American journalist, William Bird, who had bought an old hand press and housed it on the Île Saint-Louis with the intention of publishing good books in small editions well printed and tastefully designed. About the beginning of August 1922 Bird asked Pound to supervise a series of prose booklets; he agreed and wrote immediately to Williams to see if he had anything suitable, about fifty pages long. As well as Williams and himself, he was hoping to include Ford Madox Ford, Eliot, Lewis, B. C. Windeler and Hemingway. His own contribution was a reprint of the articles published in *The New Age* in 1920 as 'Indiscretions; or, Une revue des deux mondes'.

As he strove to work out a view of life suitable to the new pagan era, in which there would be no place for 'coercive ideologies', the capitalist state, or for monotheism either Christian or Jewish, he began to place more emphasis upon the biological aspect of life and upon literature as a science. In his 'Paris Letter' in the September *Dial* he said: 'with Flaubert, with the writer of first magnitude there is no answer, humanity being what it is, and the given character moving inside its own limitations there is *no* easy way out; the given situation has arisen, and will continue to arise; the impasse is a biological impasse.' Hence, he said, the idea of literature 'assuming the duties of a science'. He thought that good poets had always believed this, but that the light had also come to a few prose authors.

Scofield Thayer could not make up his mind about *The Waste Land* when he saw a typescript in the summer of 1922, so *The Dial*'s managing-editor, Gilbert Seldes, took the initiative and called a meeting between Horace Liveright of Boni & Liveright, John Quinn, representing Eliot, and himself for *The Dial*. As a result Thayer and Watson agreed to publish the poem in the November issue at the rate of $20 a page (a total of $260) and also to present Eliot with the *Dial* Award for the year worth $2000. They agreed also to take three hundred and fifty copies of the Boni & Liveright first edition to be used in a *Dial* subscription campaign. The first publication of the poem was reserved for the first issue of Eliot's own magazine *The Criterion*, due to appear in October; when the time came he delayed copies to American subscribers so that *The Dial* would have it first in the United States. When on 21 September Eliot wrote to Quinn approving of the scheme he said his only regret, which might seem in the circumstances 'either ungracious or hypocritical', was that the *Dial* Award should come to him before it had been given to Pound. 'I feel that he deserves the recognition much more than I do, certainly "for his services to Letters", and I feel that I ought to have been made to wait until after he had received this public testimony.' When Quinn offered to buy the original draft of *The Waste Land* Eliot refused, preferring to present it to him instead; but he allowed him to buy for $140 a notebook containing all his early poetry, much of it unpublished. In his letter of 21 September Eliot referred to Pound's editing: 'In the manuscript of *The Waste Land* which I am sending you, you will see the evidences of his work, and I think that this manuscript is worth preserving in its present form solely for the reason that it is the only evidence of the difference which his criticism has made to this poem.' He expressed the wish however that the suppressed portions would never be printed. For many years the typescript was thought to have been destroyed or lost but has since come to light in the New York Public Library.

In praising *The Waste Land* in the December *Dial* Edmund Wilson took the opportunity to say that he much preferred Eliot's poetry to Pound's. Eliot was annoyed and wrote to both Seldes and Wilson to say that he resented being praised at Pound's expense, as he was infinitely in his debt as a poet, as well as a personal friend. 'I sincerely consider Ezra Pound,' he told Seldes, 'the most important living poet in the English language.' The Boni & Liveright edition of the poem, incorporating for the first time Eliot's 'Notes', was published on 15 December. In the copy he sent to Pound, Eliot wrote:

for E.P.
miglior fabbro
from T.S.E.
Jan 1923

In 1925 when Eliot published his *Poems 1909–1925* he made public this inscription by adding to *The Waste Land* the dedication 'For Ezra Pound *il miglior fabbro*', which has remained there ever since.

Towards the end of 1922, before the Pounds left Paris to spend several months in Rapallo, they had dinner with Yeats and his wife and the Joyces. Pound also prepared, for free distribution, a printed notice stating that under the editorial direction of Mr Ezra Pound, The Three Mountains Press was about to issue the following books: *Indiscretions* by Ezra Pound; *Women and Men* by Ford Madox Ford; *Elimus* by B. C. Windeler; *The Great American Novel* by William Carlos Williams; *England* by B. M. G.-Adams, and an unnamed book by Hemingway. Pound's contribution, *Indiscretions*, was published in March 1923 in an edition of three hundred copies and was dedicated 'To A. R. Orage at whose request this fragment was first hitched together'. In a postscript he explained that the works of the other five authors formed a series: 'They have set out from five very different points to tell the truth about *moeurs contemporaines*, without fake, melodrama, conventional ending.' Hemingway's contribution came out in 1924 under the title *In Our Time*. In order of preparation it was his first book, but by the time Bird got to it in 1924 another expatriate American, Robert McAlmon, had already published another small book containing three stories and ten poems.

In *The Criterion* of January 1923 Pound published an article, 'On Criticism in General', which was a rough sketch of his later work, *How To Read*. He drew attention to his favourite stylists in literature, Flaubert, Gautier, Rimbaud, Laforgue, etc., and also mentioned what he believed were the three components of the art of poetry: *melopoeia* (the handling of the musical properties of words), *phanopoeia* (the evoking or defining of 'visual phenomena' by means of words), and *logopoeia* (the playing upon the meanings, usages and implied contexts of words). Although Pound had retired from the English world of letters he was unable to remain silent on the state of English culture. When in 1922 Harold Monro circulated three questions about poetry in the modern world, Pound replied briefly to the questions and then attacked 'modern civilization and the British literary world'. When Monro asked him to contribute to *The Chapbook* Pound told him to bring the periodical to Paris first and there try to collect 'a real team of contributors'. He then compared Monro with Eliot. 'Eliot may be in the act of sinking beneath the Londonian slough – but after all he has . . . been associated with some form of activity. Blast, Little Review, etc.' The trouble with Monro was that he had never had 'a programme' and was always trying to draw in second-rate work. During 1923 he did, however, allow Monro to reprint an early poem, 'An Immorality', as a large broadside with decorations by Paul Nash.

After several months in Rapallo, the Pounds, accompanied by Hemingway and his wife, visited Grossetto and other small towns in central Italy; about the middle of February 1923 the Pounds went to Sicily with Yeats and his wife. Pound was now more restless than ever. For one thing he did not feel at home in Paris, the atmosphere of which he likened to 'the indisputable enervation of Proust'. Not surprisingly he felt attracted to D'Annunzio, the writer who was also a man of action, and he spoke about the need for vigour and assertion, for 'some sort of courage, or at least ebullience that throws a certain amount of remembered beauty into an unconquered consciousness'. Although during the past two years he had reviewed Cocteau's *Poésies 1917–1920* and Guy-Charles Cros' *Pastorales Parisiennes* he had no great interest in recent French poetry, not even in Apollinaire or Valery; his interests now were in other directions. In *The New Age* of 16 March 1922 he had published a review in praise of Dr Louis Berman's *Glands Regulating Personality* and for the next few years he kept in touch with Berman's progress through such works as 'A Crystalline Substance from the Parathyroid Glands that Influences the Calcium Content of the Blood', reprinted from the Proceedings of the Society for Experimental Biology and Medicine, 1924.[3] His concern about the encroachment of the bureaucracy on the life of the individual is reflected in occasional letters he wrote to the newspapers complaining about the introduction of passports. The first was a letter headed 'Oh, Those Passports' in the Paris edition of the *New York Herald* of 22 July 1920 which was followed during the next few years by similar protests in the Paris edition of the *Chicago Tribune*.

During his visits to Italy he had been gathering information about Sigismondo Malatesta (1417–68), Niccolò d'Este (1384–1441), and other Italians of the fourteenth and fifteenth centuries and had begun to write cantos to celebrate these personalities who by will-power had impressed themselves on events. One of the libraries he visited was the Malatestine Library at Cesena where the librarian Manlio Dazzi made a great impression on him, as we see in the article, 'Possibilities of Civilization: What the Small Town Can Do', which was published in the July 1936 issue of *The Delphian Quarterly* (Chicago):

My research into the life of Sigimundo Malatesta took me to Cesena and from the library to a concert, managed by the librarian. The programme was composed of music of the highest quality. . . .

Both that concert and the librarian have taught me a good deal. M. T. Dazzi is probably less known to the outer world than Dazzi the sculptor; his name does not appear in heavy advertising. Let me take his record as showing what a man can do outside a big city and without any pretentions to upsetting the history either of his age. or of letters.

Firstly: M. T. Dazzi has probably rectified learned opinion of Mussato. At any rate Dante's contemporary, a dramatist and historian, is better known because Dazzi started being interested in him some years ago, and is still editing him for a very learned and encyclopedic collection.

Secondly: The Malatestine Library in Cesena, a unique monument to the culture of the best decades of the Renaissance, is in better condition because Dazzi was once its librarian.

Thirdly: Cesena showed me how to have first rate music in a small town.

By May 1923 William Bird had agreed to publish a book of cantos – a limited edition with large clear type on large pages and with the capitals specially designed for the occasion by the American artist Henry Strater, whose preliminary sketches immediately won Pound's approval. The book would, he told Kate Buss on 12 May, be of 'UN-RIVALLED magnificence': 'It is to be one of the real bits of printing; modern book to be jacked up to something near level of mediaeval mss. No Kelmscott mess of illegibility.'

About May Pound ceased to be Paris correspondent of *The Dial* and was replaced by Paul Morand whose 'Turkish Night' he had translated for the issue of September 1921. In his letter to Kate Buss he said that he had been 'sacked', and suggested that 'Public laments over this might be useful'. He did not think there would be any unless they were 'engineer'd or faked' by his friends. He had been asked to contribute to *Vanity Fair*, he told her, but he refused to write 'the kind of assininity' published in that magazine. 'If any of you people exiled in America wants news from the front you'll have to organize a demand.'

A young American pianist and composer George Antheil arrived in Paris in June and at a tea soon afterwards met Pound; they became interested in each other's music, with Antheil helping Pound to get his opera down on paper and Pound advertising Antheil's music in a book called *Antheil and The Treatise on Harmony*. In an article in the Sunday Magazine of the *Chicago Tribune* Antheil said that Pound had been a musician from the beginning and that the transfer from poetry to music was natural. Pound introduced him to his friend Olga Rudge, an American violinist, aged twenty-eight, who had lived most of her life in Europe. Pound had heard her play at one of the last concerts he had attended before leaving London and William Atheling had noted her performance in *The New Age* of 25 November 1920.

In July Pound published four cantos in *The Criterion*. They were entitled 'Malatesta Cantos', with the subtitle 'Cantos IX to XII of a Long Poem'. Convinced now that his task was to write about actual events in history he composed these cantos out of notes taken from history books and in some cases from original documents consulted during the past two years in Italian libraries. In places he gave translations of entire letters as well as long quotations in Italian and Latin. He was not yet completely satisfied with these cantos nor the shape of the work as a whole, and he revised and re-numbered them cantos 8 to 11. One of the Malatesta cantos referred to Pius II as a 's.o.b.'. Richard Aldington who was editor of *The Criterion* in Eliot's absence deleted this expression, in deference, he wrote later, to Catholic sensitivity, and because he did not think it urbane to refer in this way to a pope. 'Whereupon', said Aldington, 'Ezra promptly transferred the epithet to me by mail.' Needless to say Pius II has continued to be a s.o.b. in the canto's subsequent appearances.

Joyce was now planning a new work eventually titled *Finnegans Wake*. When Pound heard about it in the summer of 1923 he had become so engrossed in the satirical aspect of *Ulysses* that he took it for granted the new book would be similar. 'J.J. launched on another work', he wrote to his father in August, 'Calculated to take the hide off a few more sons of bitches.' When a sample typescript reached him in 1926 he wrote to wish Joyce every success but admitted that he could make nothing of it whatever: 'nothing short of divine vision or a new cure for the clapp can possibly be worth all the circumambient peripherization.'

Pound continued to lead a busy life in Paris and to attend the teas and parties, the concerts and readings, that were a part of the social and literary life of the time. He met Harriet Monroe for the first time when she arrived on holiday and also Margaret Anderson and Jane Heap of *The Little Review*. He saw Gertrude Stein a few times but they did not get on together; he also met Gurdjieff and sampled his cooking: 'Gurdjieff made Persian soup, bright yellow in colour, far more delicate – you might say Pier della Francesca in tone, as compared with a bortch (tinted Rembrandt). If he had had more of that sort of thing in his repertoire he could had he suspected it, or desired it, have worked on toward at least one further conversion.' One of Gurdjieff's 'conversions' was Orage who had left *The New Age* in September the previous year and in October had entered Gurdjieff's institute at Château Prieuré, near Fontainbleau. One day walking in the street Pound met Djuna Barnes accompanied by Edmund Wilson. She introduced the two men but they did not meet again and never corresponded. When John Quinn arrived in Paris in September the Pounds held a reception for him and in due course he was prevailed upon to back a new magazine edited by Ford, to be called *Transatlantic Review*. Quinn was already very ill and died in July the following year, aged fifty-four.

During the summer of 1923 Pound was occupied also with the

series of prose booklets he was supervising for William Bird. In September Bird wrote from Venice with suggestions about the design of the Hemingway book which Pound forwarded to Hemingway at the *Toronto Star* office in Canada. Bird said that when he returned to Paris he had a week's more work to do on Mrs Scratton's book, *England*, and would then be able to start on the Hemingway. He also planned to begin work soon on a prospectus for the book of cantos. Apparently by this time Pound had decided to spend some months in Italy during the following year, for Bird said that as Pound would not be available to correct the proofs of the cantos they had better meet before he left Paris and go over the typescript together 'to get it as near as possible letter perfect'. It would appear that Bird was hoping to include detailed glosses in smaller print beside the main text, but the idea was not carried through.

Now that he had finished his opera Pound was planning to continue as a composer; he was often in the company of George Antheil and Olga Rudge, and was composing music for the violin. There were some complaints to the police about the noise he was making at the piano but when he explained that he was a composer of music the Commissaire apparently was satisfied and allowed him to continue. On 11 December at the Salle du Conservatoire Olga Rudge played Pound's 'Sujet pour violon (resineux)', in a programme that included also Faidit's 'Plainte' for the death of Richard Coeur de Lion, copied by Pound from a manuscript in the Ambrosian Library, and two sonatas by Antheil for violin and piano.

When the first issue of Ford's *Transatlantic Review* appeared in January 1924 it included work by Pound: 'One Canto' (no. 13) and 'Another Canto' (first half of no. 12). Beginning with the February issue Pound contributed notes on music which in October that year were collected in the book, *Antheil and The Treatise on Harmony*. They included excerpts from William Atheling's *New Age* reviews, selected by Agnes Bedford, with 'Marginalia Emitted by George Antheil'. In April while Pound was still away in Italy Bird issued a large prospectus for the book of cantos, with the opening of canto 4 as a specimen. From 22 to 29 November an exhibition of specimen pages of the edition was held at the Shakespeare and Company bookshop.

To the spring issue of the German magazine *Der Querschnitt* Pound contributed an article, 'Le Prix Nobel', dealing with the award of the Nobel Prize to Yeats. The article was 'Specially Written for *Der Querschnitt*' and was accompanied by a translation into German. It is disjointed, composed mostly of asides but the main idea seems to be that 'if the award had not gone to Mr Yeats it should have been given to his most distinguished compatriot, the author of *Ulysses*'. He suggests that if next time the prize cannot be awarded to Joyce as an Irishman it might go to him as 'representative of the republic of letters, or of the Heimatlos [the homeless, or exiles]; who are, at this moment, as respectable a collection of writers as is found in any one country'.

Pound's health was not good at this time and during the spring of 1924 he had trouble with his appendix but managed to have it treated without an operation. 'Am reviving slowly', he wrote to Yeats from the Hotel Windsor, Assisi, on 8 May. William Carlos Williams and his wife had arrived in Europe in January and spent the next four months touring France, Italy and Austria. They did not see Pound until he arrived back in Paris in May or June. When Williams called on him Pound described his appendix trouble and then, according to Williams, talked at length about the history of music, musical notation and various other technical matters. On 19 June Pound wrote to Yeats about the possibility of arranging a concert by Antheil in Ireland: 'We are giving a show of his and my music here on July 7th.' He pointed out also that the Theatre Beriza was interested in putting on his own opera:

I don't know whether you have ever grasped the fact that I have made an opera out of Villon's text; I mean all the words sung, save about twenty used as connecting links, are taken strophe by strophe from Villon's testament. It ought ultimately to be a french national fete; as Villon is their only possible substitute for Homer. The thing needs

    4 bass voices

    2 tenors

    2 contraltos, and a very small orchestra,

minimum, 2 cellos, 2 bassoons, 1 trombone, percussion, one fiddle, oboe, saxophone, etc., anything from 8 to 16 instruments for small house.

I guarantee that the drama is O.K.; greek model, one act, and final tableau; but the play is O.K. and reinforces the sung text.

I insist on masks; the decor can be almost any old thing, one set with a drop curtain, that lifts, and comes down again, a few feet behind a few properties that are hidden by it during the main act.

At least masks for Villon, his mother, and the aged whore; i.e. the main characters. The minor characters and crowd don't matter.

This show is the best thing I have *finished* up to the present. Possibly less important than the cantos; yes, certainly less important than they ought ultimately to be. . . .

ANNY HOW, there it is. IF I come over, is the Abbey available; and are there any means for production. I DO NOT want operatic voices, I want a few singers who can understand the text.

In a postscript he wrote: 'If you really want to be of use, you might try and get me a real Irish passport (i.e. passports for both D. and myself) and thus free me from degrading contact with the sons of bitches who represent the infamous Wilsonian tyranny and red tape.'

At the Salle Pleyel on 7 July Olga Rudge played two pieces by Pound, 'Fanfare, Violin and Tambourin' and 'Fiddle Music, First Suite'. She also accompanied the tenor Yves Tinayre in two songs from his opera: 'Mort, j'appelle' and 'Je renye amours'. The violin accompaniment was specially written for the occasion, and was not, according to Pound, an attempt to condense or to represent the orchestration of the opera. Also on the programme of 7 July were two sonatas for violin and piano, and a string quartet, by Antheil. A reproduction of the manuscript of Pound's 'Fiddle Music' was published in the August issue of the *Transatlantic Review*.

Pound had grown tired of Paris and was now ready to leave there for good. It was not simply a question of culture ('France has no writer of first magnitude', he wrote) but also of personal taste. He liked to be in everything and spent a good deal of time at parties, night-clubs and cafes; but not being a drinker he did not always feel at home, especially among the hard-drinking Americans. 'I have been drunk only three times in my life', he told me in 1959, 'each occasion memorable.' There was also his feeling that the important things were happening elsewhere. Mary Colum has described how he asked her and her husband Padraic Colum to go with him to a lecture on Soviet Russia by the American journalist Lincoln Steffens. Pound listened with 'rapt attention', his eyes fixed on the speaker's face, and after Steffens was finished he rose to his feet and addressed the audience on Social Credit, 'to which', she said, 'he had tried to convert Arthur Griffith and through him the new Irish state'. Things were also happening in Italy where Mussolini had come to power following the 'march on Rome' in October 1922. I doubt whether at this stage Pound saw Italy in terms of politics but he had found during his recent visits that the atmosphere there was more to his liking than that of France. In October the Pounds left Paris for Rapallo which was to be their home for the next twenty years.

NOTES

1 The first issue was published in November 1921.
2 Two years later Pound wrote in a letter to Henry Allen Moe of the Guggenheim Foundation that 'Bel Esprit' had been 'a dismal nerve-wracking failure for everyone concerned', but said that in Paris it had led to a group of Frenchmen 'subsidizing Paul Valery, a man of less interest than Eliot, but the best they've got at the moment'. Valery was a man of 'perfect artistic probity' and he was very glad he was being supported.
3 Pound persuaded Joyce to consult Berman when the doctor visited Paris in 1922 and Joyce underwent endocrine treatment for his arthritic back.

XV   Rapallo
1924/1929

Rapallo is a small town on the Riviera di Levante, seventeen miles from Genoa; it faces a bay which also contains Santa Margherita Ligure and Portofino. Behind Rapallo the land rises steeply to hills and mountains covered with vines, olives and woods, and from the hill-paths the view below, of cypress, red-tiled roofs and the sea, is classically mediterranean. For a time the Pounds lived in hotels but soon found a small flat five floors up on the roof of the Albergo Rapallo on the sea-front; their entrance was in the Via Marsala and their address Via Marsala 12. There was a lift to their flat but a few days after they moved in it stopped working and remained permanently out of order; to get to their flat thereafter they had to climb more than a hundred steps. From their rooftop terrace they looked south, over the sea. On 23 March each year, Mrs Pound told me, the swallows would fly directly overhead, on their way to two nearby streams where they rested before flying north again.

By November 1924 Pound had drafted cantos 18 and 19 and in Rapallo was busy with later cantos. About the middle of December he and his wife went to Sicily for several months, visiting Taormina, Siracusa and Palermo. *A Draft of XVI Cantos of Ezra Pound for the Beginning of a Poem of some Length* ('now first made into a Book with Initials by Henry Strater') was published by the Three Mountains Press, Paris, towards the end of January 1925. The edition consisted of ninety copies: a few on Imperial Japan paper, autographed by the poet, at 1600 francs, fifteen on Whatman paper at 800 francs, and seventy on Roma paper at 400 francs. There were also a few 'proof' copies, some of which, on poor quality paper were bound and in June 1925 at the author's request sent to Homer Pound, Ford, Miss Bedford and Mrs Scratton. On 26 December 1924 Pound wrote to Bird from Taormina not to send a copy, as arranged, to Thomas Hardy. He thought Hardy might die at any moment and he did not want the 'hell' cantos, dealing with England as he saw it in 1919, to fall into the wrong hands until there were enough 'later chants' available to bring them into proportion with the whole.

To the January 1925 issue of *Der Querschnitt* Pound contributed a series of 'Definitions'. A good state, he said, was one which 'impinges least upon the peripheries of its citizens', and the function of the state was to 'facilitate the traffic' (the circulation of goods, water, coal, power) and to prevent the citizens 'from impinging on each other'. The aim of state education, he claimed, had been to prevent people from discovering that the classics were worth reading and in this it had been almost wholly successful. He said it was the duty of an aristocracy 'to educate its plebs'; failure to do so meant its own bloody destruction. History presented no more imbecile a series of spectacles than the conduct of aristocracies – without whom, however, civilization was impossible.

Back in Rapallo after his holiday in Sicily Pound wrote in February to Henry Allen Moe, secretary of the newly established John Simon Guggenheim Memorial Foundation in New York, congratulating him: 'As nearly as I can judge from the terms of your announcement', he said, 'your endowment represents a new phase. You really want the goods delivered.' When Moe replied, inviting his suggestions, Pound obliged with a five-thousand word letter dated 31 March:

Wyndham Lewis, I consider without exception the best possible 'value' for your endowment, and *the* man most hampered by lack of funds at the moment. Acquaintance with his published work can give you but a very partial idea of why I recommended him.

His work in *design* is, I can not say more important than his *capacity* for writing, but the two capacities very nearly of equal importance. His published writings have flaws due to hasty composition between his work as a painter. His mind is far more fecund and original than let us say James Joyce's; he had at the time of publishing *Tarr* or *The Enemy of the Stars* a less accomplished technique, BUT he has invented more in modern art than any living man save possibly Picasso.

. . .

I can say, from my own seventeen years' experience (since 1908) that whenever I have been offered money or had a chance to make it, *even though* the offer or chance came from someone in sympathy with my general aim; that any sum over $75 or $100 has always been offered on condition that I *interrupt* my *main* work and spend my time on stuff of secondary or tertiary importance. The same is I think true of Lewis. In my case I have existed by a series of accidents, and for a long time I managed by writing articles at $5 a piece, in order to write about something that didn't interfere with my work or study. I mean by giving up all thought of placing ANYTHING at $50 to $75, or even at $25.

It is a mistake to think that there is a career in creative or inventive activity; or that things get better as one goes on. I remember in 1909 going to the bank with Yeats, he was going to draw his last £5, and that was from an advance payment for a play he didn't finish till eight or nine years later.

There had been a 'great hullabaloo about Joyce', he said, but Lewis had the 'most diversely inventive and "volcanic" mind' of anyone he knew in Europe or America and if he had to buy the next five or ten years' work of either man with his eyes shut he would choose Lewis's. He was trying to obviate some of Lewis's difficulties, he told Moe, by urging Tauchnitz to publish him on the Continent, but he did not know that this would suit either party, as Tauchnitz could pay very little for the rights of a cheap Continental edition and there was always the possibility that such an edition might depreciate the value of English publication.

For Eliot he recommended that the foundation give him an endowment for life with pension to his widow in case he predeceased her, which was 'highly unlikely'. He also recommended a grant of between $1500 and $2000 a year for three years for Antheil, to enable him to give up the concert platform and to concentrate on composing. The support he had already received was on condition that he became a concert pianist: 'Parenthesis, not the first time I have seen such reduction. Back in 1910, Paderewski offered to put Walter Rummel on as pianist, Rummel said no, he wanted to compose. Paderewski did not press the matter. Rummel was a person of interest until the war, etc etc finally reduced him to the status of pianist; he now fills the Albert Hall in London, and gets a sapphire tie-pin each year from the Belgian Royal Family. The last time I heard him his playing had every possible skill and no interest.' Marianne Moore, he suggested, was less important than Eliot, Lewis or Antheil, but the foundation might provide the money for her to travel to Europe. He described her work as 'meritorious and sincere . . . no sham, no pretense,' whereas the work of Edgar Lee Masters and Amy Lowell was to a large degree fake, 'not necessarily conscious fake, but full of stuff that even they in their most alive moments would recognize as not up to the mark.'

He told Moe that he did not think that Williams needed a grant from the foundation, as his wife's family had money, but perhaps a word from Senator Guggenheim or a member of the foundation committee might awaken his father-in-law to the fact that if Williams took an occasional longer vacation from being a country doctor it would not be simply loafing. Apart from subsidies to artists he thought there were several other matters the committee should look into. For one thing they could 'stimulate communication between the subsidized'. He himself, he said, was constantly hampered in his work by lack of touch with scientists and men of affairs. 'I am extremely glad to be out of the maelstrom of literary London and artistic Paris, with leisure to do my own job. But I should be glad if any travelling appointees of your committee are in Europe to help them find what they want and to promote better understanding and *communication* between art and science, and between the various arts.' Painting, he believed, had 'gone to hell' by being cut off from architecture and architects had grown stupid from not getting condensed results from other artists. He also tried to draw the foundation into his campaign, which had been going on now for some years, against subsection 211 of the United States Penal Code which, he said, lumped together 'smutty postcards, contraceptive and abortion-producing instruments AND "the classics".' Thirteen years later Pound told Archibald MacLeish that not one of his nominees had ever had a fellowship except Antheil who, as the result of an approach by Pound to Otto Kahn, received help when it was too late – not when Pound nominated him or signed his recommendation papers but 'after he was messed up'.

In the spring of 1925 the first issue of a new magazine, *This Quarter*, edited in Europe by Ernest Walsh and Ethel Moorhead, was dedicated to 'Ezra Pound who by his creative work, his editorship of several magazines, his helpful friendship for young and unknown artists . . . comes first to our mind as meriting the gratitude of this generation.' There were also tributes from Joyce and Hemingway.

Joyce's was generous but couched in the language of formal recommendation which he used to cover the fact that he was not really interested in the work of his contemporaries: 'He helped me in every possible way in the face of very great difficulties for seven years before I met him, and since then he has always been ready to give me advice and appreciation which I esteem very highly as coming from a mind of such brilliance and discernment.' Hemingway wrote: 'So far, we have Pound the major poet devoting, say, one-fifth of his time to poetry. With the rest of his time he tries to advance the fortunes, both material and artistic, of his friends. He defends them when they are attacked, he gets them into magazines and out of jail. He loans them money. He sells their pictures. He arranges concerts for them . . . He advances them hospital expenses and dissuades them from suicide. And in the end a few of them refrain from knifing him at the first opportunity.' Of Pound's opera he said that it was 'a very fine opera': 'But I feel about Ezra and music something like about M. Constantin Brancusi and cooking. M. Brancusi is a famous sculptor who is also a very famous cook. Cooking is, of course, an art but it would be lamentable if M. Brancusi would give up sculpture for it or even devote the major part of his time to cookery. Still, Ezra is not a minor poet. He has never been troubled by lack of energy. If he wants to write more operas he will write them and there will be plenty of force left over.'

The Autumn-Winter issue of *This Quarter* contained cantos 17, 18 and 19 (for which he was paid, according to Miss Moorhead, £40) and a bibliographical note by Pound in which he said: 'I suppose the best friend I ever had in an editorial office was A. R. Orage, through twelve years of almost continual disagreement.' There was also a letter about Pound from Aldington, dated 19 June 1925: 'He has wide knowledge, with strange gaps of ignorance, especially when he leaves the one subject he really knows – i.e. poetry. Possibly his credulity in matters of occultism and economics, for example, is due to a complete lack of the philosophical training so conspicuous in T. S. Eliot.'

Walsh died soon afterwards and Miss Moorhead, distressed by what she regarded as Pound's neglect of Walsh's poetry, in a later issue of the magazine withdrew the earlier dedication: 'I herewith take back that dedication. I have said before that Ernest Walsh was disillusioned about Ezra Pound before he died. *We* take back our too-generous dedication.' While it may be true, as Miss Moorhead suggested, that Pound cooled to them when they did not follow his advice about the editing of *This Quarter*, there is evidence to suggest that he helped Walsh financially on one occasion when he was ill in Paris; just as, about the same time, he gave financial and other aid to the poet Cheever Dunning and went to a good deal of trouble, also during the 1920s, to raise money for Emanuel Carnevali suffering from an incurable illness in Bologna. In Dunning's case he even convinced himself that his poetry was better than it really was and pushed it on Harriet Monroe and Mencken. Dunning's 'Shadows' was published in *Poetry* in 1925 and included by Pound in his 1932 anthology *Profile*:

> Lo, my shadow started like a restless flame;
> Started, stood forth like a bas-relief emergent,
> Bulked into a statue, a body swift and urgent,
> Came and stood beside me and brushed the roadside grass,
> While I shook and waited till the dream should pass.

Pound tried to find a publisher for Dunning's collection of poems, *The Four Winds*, but without success. In sending them to Mencken in February 1925 to see if he could do any better Pound explained that Dunning was forty-seven – the first case he had met, he said, where a poet had done mediocre and submediocre work up to such an age and 'then pulled the real thing'. Eliot did not like them, 'but then he don't see either Yeats or Hardy'. In the case of Carnevali (who wrote in English) Pound and his wife contributed money of their own when he was desperate, and Pound, with the assistance of Harriet Monroe, arranged for some of his hospital expenses to be paid from America.

Writing to R. P. Blackmur on 26 March 1925, Pound deprecated 'stray bits of curiosity' about the cantos while there were still more to come. But if Blackmur wanted to be of use, as he had offered, then he might try to find a publisher for some of Pound's uncollected prose, including his 'Paris Letters' to *The Dial*. Pound also suggested that in his prose he had 'outlined a new criticism or critical system' and hinted that someone might publicize it in an essay, a Ph.D. thesis or a book.

In June William Bird joined with Robert McAlmon, who was married to Sir John Ellerman's daughter, Winifred, to publish a three hundred and thirty-eight page book entitled *Contact Collection of Contemporary Authors*. Contributors included Djuna Barnes, Norman Douglas, Ford, Hemingway, H.D., Joyce, Mina Loy, McAlmon, Gertrude Stein, Edith Sitwell, Williams, and Pound, who was represented by the first sixty lines of canto 20.

Pound and Olga Rudge meanwhile had become attracted to each other and in July they went to Bressanone, just north of Bolzano in the Italian Tyrol, where on 9 July at the Bressanone hospital Miss Rudge gave birth to a daughter christened Maria. At the hospital was a peasant woman, Frau Marcher, whose baby had died at birth; she agreed to take Maria Rudge and to bring her up on her farm at Gais, a village not far from Bruneck nearby.

On 24 August Pound wrote to Bird from Rapallo that he had taken a copy of *A Draft of XVI Cantos* to Cesena and suitably inscribed had placed it in the Malatestine Library. In September Pound became annoyed at being an authors' agent, possibly as the result of a letter he had received from Joyce about the proofs of material sent to *This Quarter*. Pound wrote a letter to the Paris edition of the *Chicago Tribune* where it appeared on 3 September: 'Sir: May I avail myself of your sometimes hospitable letter column to state that I have no editorial connection with any current periodical; and that I am not a receiving station for manuscript, typescript, drawings, photographs or other paraphernalia, accompanied or unaccompanied by return postage (French, Guatemalian, or Etats Unisien).'

During the next fifteen months Pound published only one article (four pages on Antheil in *The Criterion* of October 1926) and four letters to the editor. It was his most unproductive period since 1908, as far as publication was concerned, although 1926 was his biggest year musically. At the Sala Sgambati, Via di Ripetta, Rome, on Thursday 6 May Olga Rudge gave a concert with Alfredo Casella at the piano. On the programme were two works performed publicly for the first time: Eric Satie's 'Choses vues à droit et à gauche' and Pound's 'Hommage Froissart'. On Saturday 19 June Pound was in Paris for the first public performance of Antheil's *Ballet Mécanique* at the Théâtre des Champs-Elysées. There was a riot when the nine pianos (including a player-piano operated by the composer), electric bells, xylophones, loud-speakers and whistles began to play accompanied by the whirring of an aeroplane propeller which sent a stream of cold air through the shouting throng. It was said afterwards by witnesses that Pound played an heroic part in the attempt by Antheil's supporters to shout down the rioters and to give the work a chance to be heard.

On Tuesday 29 June Pound's opera *Le Testament* was given its first performance at a concert at the Salle Pleyel. Although this was not a performance of the whole work but of a selection, it is generally regarded as the *première*. The invitation said:

M. et Mme. Ezra Pound
vous invitent à une audition privée

Paroles de Villon
Arias and fragments from an opera
LE TESTAMENT
Texte de Villon   Musique par Ezra Pound
à la Salle Pleyel
22, Rue Rochechouart
Le Mardi Soir
29 Juin 1926
(à 9 heures 15)

PROGRAMME
(probablement)

Hommage ou ouverture	cornet de dessus
Et mourut Paris	ténor et violon
Je plains	ténor et violon
Mort j'appelle	ténor et violon
Motif	
False beauté	ténor, violon et clavecin

Yves Tinayre, ténor – Olga Rudge, violon
Paul Tinayre

Heaulmière	les mêmes
Motifs de la foule, mélange	violon, clavecin et cuivres
Si J'ayme et sers	basse et cuivres
Frères Humains	ensemble

Robert Maitland, basse – Yves Tinayre, ténor
Olga Rudge et Paul Tinayre, et cuivres

Paul Tinayre's part in the performance was to play a huge medieval horn with deep rich notes which had cost Pound a great deal of trouble to find. A small pamphlet with the French text was issued on the evening. A fortnight later, on 12 July, Robert Maitland sang four songs from the opera at the home in Paris of Mrs Christian Gross. On 10 September at the American Hospital in Paris, Dorothy Pound gave birth to a boy, Omar Shakespear Pound. Soon afterwards he was given into the care of his grandmother, Olivia Shakespear, and brought up in England.

During the autumn of 1926 Pound began to plan a new magazine which he himself would edit and control. He wrote to Hemingway, Cummings, Rodker and others in search of contributions and in November received the typescript of Rodker's short novel *Adolphe 1920*. 'Mr Rodker, who admires your products', he wrote to Hemingway on 20 November, 'has himself sent in printable mss; at least, not in puffik shape, but bloody good for the most part, and not like every damn other mss. in every damn other review.'

The previous winter Pound had contemplated legal action against an American publisher, Samuel Roth, who in his magazine *Two Worlds* was taking advantage of the bad American copyright law to pirate the work of authors in Europe. He found that legal action would be too costly but forced Roth to stop advertising Pound as one of his collaborators. But in the summer and autumn of 1926 when Roth began to publish *Ulysses*, without authorization, Pound refused to do more than offer Joyce, somewhat coldly, advice about how to write letters of protest to the newspapers. And in December when writers from all over the world signed a petition of protest Pound refused to participate. It was not Roth's fault, he told Joyce in a letter dated 25 December 1926, but was due to the infamous state of the American law which not only tolerated robbery but encouraged unscrupulous adventurers. What Pound wanted apparently was for Joyce to lead a general campaign against the evils of the copyright and pornography laws; but Hemingway advised Joyce that Pound's idea was 'moonshine' and Joyce did not take it any further. Later when Roth claimed that Pound, acting as Joyce's agent, had authorized him to publish *Ulysses*, Pound formally denied the charge at the American Consulate in Genoa and agreed to give evidence if it were needed.

Pound still had in mind to visit the United States. In a letter of 30 November he told Harriet Monroe that he had no strong objection at the moment to such a visit even though he would be horrified by what he saw. As for a lecture tour, the question was simply one of payment: 'I can not afford to do it on the cheap. If I blow all that energy, I have got to have a few years free from worry after it.' Pound mentioned that he had written an article on machines and was on the way 'more or less' towards a book on *Art and Machines*, 'both plastic and acoustic phase'. Answering her question whether authors were any better off abroad than in America, he said that England gave small pensions and in France even 'a ninth rate slob like Claudel gets a job as ambassador'. In Italy authors got jobs in libraries, not highly paid, but comfortable and respectable. On the subject of politics he said: 'I personally think extremely well of Mussolini', with whom it was impossible to compare the last three American presidents or British prime ministers without insulting him. If the intelligentsia did not think well of him it was because they knew nothing about '"the state"' and government and had no particularly large sense of values.

The Communist periodical in New York, *New Masses*, published in December 1926 a letter from Pound headed 'Pound Joins the Revolution': 'I find five numbers of *New Masses* waiting for me here on my return from Paris, and have read most of the text with a good deal of care. For the first time in years I have even gone so far as to think of making a trip to America; so you can take the blame for that if for nothing else.' He asked them to send him John Reed's *Ten Days that Shook the World* and Scott Nearing's *Dollar Diplomacy*; he had been vaguely interested in Nearing ever since his student days when rumours went around concerning the reasons for Nearing's departure from the University of Pennsylvania.

On 22 December Boni & Liveright published *Personae The Collected Poems of Ezra Pound* ('Including *Ripostes, Lustra, Homage to Sextus Propertius, H. S. Mauberley*'). Although it claimed to be an edition of all Pound's poems except *The Cantos* as yet unfinished, it was actually a selection by the author, assisted possibly by Williams and other friends, of the poems he wanted to keep in print. Except for the inclusion of a few unworthy poems the collection was an excellent one; it has sold steadily for forty years and seems certain to remain the most widely read of all Pound's books.

Pound wrote to Joyce on 2 January 1927 reporting that the first number of his new periodical, *The Exile*, had been sent to the printer. His tone was friendlier than it had been in December, but Joyce, who liked to have Pound supporting his work, was upset by his continuing casualness towards *Finnegans Wake*. Joyce did not value Pound as a critic but as a supporter who had fought for him from the beginning and it unnerved him now to find that Pound was not much interested in his new work. 'It is possible Pound is right,' he wrote to Miss Weaver on 1 February, 'but I cannot go back. I never listened to his objections to *Ulysses* as it was being sent him once I had made up my mind but dodged them as tactfully as I could. He understood certain aspects of that book very quickly and that was more than enough then. He makes brilliant discoveries and howling blunders. . . .' That same month he told Miss Weaver how he had submitted to Pound some poems from the collection published later as *Pomes Penyeach*; Pound had handed them back a few days later saying that they belonged in the family bible or in the family photograph album. In answer to a direct question from Joyce he had said no, he did not think they were worth publishing. Pound praised instead his new discovery, Cheever Dunning, which unsettled Joyce and sent him in search of Dunning's work; having found some and read it he was much relieved and decided he could disregard Pound's advice about publishing his poems. He wrote to Miss Weaver: 'It was only after having read Mr Dunning's drivel which Pound defends as if it were Verlaine that I thought the affair over from another angle.' He was glad to discover that Miss Weaver shared his views about Dunning, even though like Pound she had her doubts about Joyce's latest prose work, which she called his 'Safety Pun Factory'.

In February 1927 Pound arranged to have printed in the United States at least twenty-five copies of a three-column broadside containing part of canto 20 and part of Rodker's *Adolphe*; the aim was to secure American copyright for the first number of his magazine, due to be published in France in the spring. His application for copyright was rejected on the grounds that the broadside submitted was neither a book nor a periodical, so he was forced to publish later issues of the magazine in the United States.

On 19 February Olga Rudge, George Antheil and the pianist Daniel Amfitheatrow gave a concert of works by Mozart and Antheil at the Sala Capizucchi in Rome. Afterwards Miss Rudge secured an audience with Mussolini. According to Pound in a letter to Bird on 4 March Mussolini preferred the classics to contemporary music but Miss Rudge did what she could to pave the way for an Antheil audition with him later. When Amfitheatrow spoke contemptuously of Antheil's use of the piano as a percussion instrument, Mussolini took the wind out of his sails, Pound said, by declaring, 'So it *is*'.

Pound had been negotiating with the Chicago publisher, Pascal Covici, from whom on 21 March he received a cable: WILL PUBLISH ANTHEIL AND ADOLPHE AND MACHINE ART ALSO MAGAZINE THIRD ISSUE PLEASE RUSH COPY OF ANTHEIL AND OTHER MANUSCRIPTS WHEN READY. On 14 September that year Covici published a new edition of *Antheil and The Treatise on Harmony*, 'With Supplementary Notes'. The notes were two short pieces on Antheil – one which appeared in *The Criterion* the previous year, and another, 'Workshop Orchestration', about the possibility of orchestrated factory noises, which was published in the March 1927 issue of *New Masses*. The book on 'Machine Art', part of which had been sent to *This Quarter* and was still among the belongings of the late Ernest Walsh, was probably never completed.

Pound took up the matter again in 1931 but that was only to write a short introductory note to fifteen photographs of modern machinery published in the winter 1931–2 issue of *The New Review*.

The question of a lecture-tour of the United States was still in the air. On 28 March 1927 he received a letter about it from Ford who was at Toulon: 'I spoke to Lee Keedick [a lecture tour agency] with empressment of your lecturing in the U.S.A. I certainly think you ought to do so, now, or at any rate the autumn being the moment, for your star there is on the wax. I have hopes then that we might go there together – or at any rate togetherish as to boats – in September.' Although Pound never returned for such a tour he continued to be interested for some time to come and had correspondence on the subject with the Leigh-Emmerich Lecture Bureau Inc. in 1928.

In his publicity campaign for Antheil, Pound got in touch with Sisley Huddleston and other Paris journalists about a riot which was said to have followed a concert by Antheil in Hungary. The Paris edition of the *New York Herald Tribune* of 10 April carried a story headed 'A Riot of Music', in which the following information was given 'on the authority of Ezra Pound': 'Two hundred and fifty Socialists were arrested after his last concert there . . . The temperamental Hungarians expected the *Ballet Mécanique* and when given the milder side of Antheil began discussion with the classikers. The discussion continued through the night, ending in a row at the opening of Parliament . . . Two hundred and fifty arrests.'

The first of four issues of the magazine *The Exile*, edited by Pound, was published in Paris in the spring. While Pound handled the editorial work, Dorothy Pound helped with the business side of the magazine and kept a list of subscribers. In addition to a part of canto 20 and a large extract from Rodker's *Adolphe 1920*, it included a poem by Hemingway, as follows:

NEO-THOMIST POEM

The Lord is my Shepherd,
I shall not want him for long.

With the following editorial comment by Pound: 'Mr Hemingway's poem refers to events in what remains of the French world of letters.' In his comments on the political situation in America Pound said that the state ought to be a convenience, not an infernal nuisance. He took the view that detailed emendment of an evil situation was usually preferable to revolution and he thought it unlikely he would be joining any revolutions. He wondered, however, whether there was any mental activity in America outside the revolutionary and communist elements. 'Both Fascio and the Russian revolution are interesting phenomena; beyond which there is historic perspective.' The capitalist imperialist state had to be judged, he said, not only in comparison with unrealized utopias but with past forms of the state such as the feudal order and the small city states both republican and despotic; and this meant comparison either as to social justice or such permanent products as art, science and literature.

He also attacked economists who failed to distinguish between transient goods (fresh vegetables, battleships and fake art), durable goods (well constructed buildings, intelligent afforestation), and permanent goods (scientific discoveries, works of art, classics). The artist, he claimed, was always far ahead of any revolution, or reaction, or counter-revolution, or counter-reaction, and no party platform ever contained enough of his programme to give him the least satisfaction. 'The party that follows him wins; and the speed with which they set about it, is the measure of their practical capacity and intelligence.'

Some of Pound's political ideas at this time were based upon 'tips' received from Mencken; but 'tips' uttered only under pressure from Pound who then used them in a way that the other would hardly have understood, for the two men were of widely differing temperaments. Theoretically Pound was able to classify Mencken's type of mind: 'The perfect Manichean', he wrote in 1939, 'very tiresome to a serious character like the undersigned, but simpatico.' He was quite unable however to enter into the element of common sense in Mencken's 'cynicism'. With the result that for more than a decade they addressed letters to each other in vain. Thus Pound urged Mencken to take action to improve the United States Congress, whereupon Mencken replied that Pound had no idea, living in Europe, how bad it really was: come on home, he told him, and see the circus, it is 'twenty times as bad as you suspect'. For Pound, as he himself pointed out in *The Exile*, this decay was not something to be enjoyed as a spectacle but a matter for action. And where Pound wanted a president who would be a man of action as 'interesting' as Lenin or Mussolini, Mencken merely rejoiced that Hoover would win the coming election – a ninth-rate country, he said, deserved a ninth-rate president.

In a letter to his father on 11 April Pound admitted that his cantos so far were obscure: 'Afraid', he said, 'the whole damn poem is rather obscure, especially in fragments.' As an aid he suggested that it was 'rather like, or unlike subject and response and counter subject in fugue', and he gave three headings under which the poem might be considered: (1) The 'live man' going down into the world of the dead, (2) The 'repeat' in history, and (3) The 'magic moment' or moment of metamorphosis, the 'bust through' from the everyday world into the divine or permanent world of the gods.

In September Pound was working on a translation of Cavalcanti's canzone 'Donna mi prega' and perhaps on his essay on the poet, entitled 'Medievalism'. When he asked Joyce about the meaning of Cavalcanti's phrase 'natural dimostramento', Joyce replied: 'I cannot find the phrase you ask about either in Father Rickeby's enormous edition of Aquinas or in the French one I have. The scholastic machinery of the process of thought is very intricate . . . These philosophical terms are such tricky bombs that I am shy of handling them, being afraid they may go off in my hands.' Also in September Pound was in touch with Glen Hughes, of the University of Washington, Seattle, who apparently wanted Pound to write his literary autobiography for publication in a series entitled 'University of Washington Chapbooks'. Pound refused the offer but gave Hughes some information for a projected history of Imagism. With Hughes obviously interested in publishing some of his work in the series Pound began to make, with the aid of existing translations, a new English version of the 'Ta Hio' of Confucius; he had finished it by 17 October when he wrote to Aldington: 'I have offered Hughes my new version of the TA HIO which I hope is Capo Lavoro. It has a introduction, and is in any case badly needed in English or Murkn . . . I had been meditating doing the job for some years, but couldn't face doing the whole four classics [of Confucius], and had no place to plant twenty pages of typescript.' He had suggested to Hughes, he said, that he follow the Confucius with a reprint of Fenollosa's essay on the Chinese written character, especially as his collection, *Instigations*, in which the Fenollosa had been included, was now out of print. If Hughes published these two works he might translate another Confucian book, 'The Invariability', which later he was to call 'The Unwobbling Pivot'. Hughes accepted the 'Ta Hio' which appeared on 10 April 1928 as *Ta Hio The Great Learning*, 'Newly rendered into the American Language by Ezra Pound'. There was no introduction by Pound, only a few lines of explanation about 'The Confucian Classics'. His introduction he had deleted because on reflection he considered it a 'bloody impertinence' to use Confucius as the occasion for an attack on bureaucracy and 'a curse on American State Dept. and the Wilson-Harding Administrations, etc'. He did not, he told Hughes, want to distract attention from Confucius by raising such irrelevant issues as the state of America, the perversion of the American constitution, the collapse of Christianity, and the 'goddamnability of all monotheistic Jew, Mohammed, Xtn. buncomb'. He approached Hughes about the possibility of a new edition of the Fenollosa material on the Noh, corrected by a suitable Japanese scholar who understood the subject; if guaranteed correct in every detail such a book, he believed, could become a standard work, and if Hughes was not able to publish large books he might take the proposal to Harper or Scribners. But nothing came of the idea, nor did Hughes bring out the Fenollosa essay, and the *Ta Hio* was the only one of Pound's books published by the University of Washington Book Store.

The Exile number two, the appearance of which had been delayed by the transfer of the magazine to Covici in Chicago, was finally published in the autumn of 1927. 'But for Mr Covici undertaking to print this second issue', Pound wrote, 'the editors would have desisted.' Copies of the first issue, on their way from France to the United States, had been held up by the customs in New York, because they were incorrectly dated. In the second number he quoted a correspondent's account of a New York customs official's reaction to the magazine: 'Say, the fellow that wrote that stuff in your magazine must be a narcotic fiend! Nobody has thoughts like those except under the influence of drugs! We don't want stuff like that here – we're going to have to defend our women and children against the Bolsheviks pretty soon!!' The second number contained work by Dunning, Carl Rakosi, McAlmon, and a chapter from Joe Gould's now legendary 'Oral History', the product of a man who made a profession of being an educated tramp and whose most famous remark perhaps was, 'I have delusions of grandeur; I think I am Joe Gould'. Pound in his editorial, 'Prolegomena', declared that the drear horror of American life could be traced to two damnable roots: (1) The loss of all distinction between public and private affairs, and (2) The tendency to mess into other people's affairs before establishing order in one's own. The principle of good, he said, had been enunciated by Confucius: it consisted in establishing order within oneself. The principle of evil consisted in messing into other people's affairs. 'Against this principle of evil no adequate precaution is taken by Christianity, Moslemism, Judaism, nor, so far as I know, by *any* monotheistic religion. Many "mystics" do not even aim at the principle of good; they seek merely establishment of a parasitic relationship with the unknown.' He allowed that the early Quakers may have had some idea of the good principle but he had no early Quaker texts from which to find out. Under the title 'Modern Thought' he gave the following quotations:

We are tired of government in which there is no responsible person having a hind-name, a front name and an address. (*Mussolini*)

The banking business is declared a state monopoly. The interests of the small depositors will be safeguarded. (*Lenin*)

The duty of being is to persevere in its being and even to augment the characteristics which specialize it. (*De Gourmont*)

People are not charming *enough*. (*McAlmon*)

In 1927 Wyndham Lewis disturbed the world of modern letters by exposing what he considered to be the faults of his contemporaries – first in an article, 'The Revolutionary Simpleton', in the February issue of his magazine *The Enemy*, and then at greater length in his book *Time and Western Man* published in September. Lewis's criticisms were sometimes unfair but often brilliant and perceptive; among those attacked were Joyce, Pound, and Hemingway. Joyce admitted that it was the best hostile criticism his work had received; Hemingway waited thirty years and had a well-publicized revenge in his memoirs, *A Moveable Feast*. In Pound's case there was no sharp break in their friendship but a further cooling in a relationship which had been strained for several years, as witness a note of Pound's in 1925: 'There are some matters in which you really do behave like, and *some* lines in this letter of yours in which you really do write like, a God damn fool.' Pound's patience was remarkable in the face of some of Lewis's statements in *Time and Western Man*, especially as Lewis had placed his finger on a weak spot which had worried Pound himself only a few years before. Lewis maintained that there was still a gap between Pound's feeling for the past and his fire-eating utterances on contemporary affairs; he was both 'a man in love with the past' and 'a sort of revolutionary simpleton'.

'There is nothing', Lewis wrote, 'that he intuits well, certainly never originally. Yet when he can get into the skin of somebody else, of power and renown, a Propertius or an Arnaut Daniel, he becomes a lion or a lynx on the spot.' As a man he had found him true, disinterested and unspoilt. 'He has not effected this intimate entrance into everything that is noble and enchanting for nothing. He has really walked with Sophocles beside the Aegean; he has *seen* the Florence of Cavalcanti; there is almost nowhere in the Past that he has not visited . . .' But where the Present was concerned, Lewis said, it was a different matter; he was extremely untrustworthy where that was concerned. Of Pound's versification he wrote: 'Now a kind of mock-bitter, sententious *terseness* characterizes most of Pound's semi-original verse, and even mars some of his translations . . . It is the laconicism of the strong silent man. Were he a novelist, you would undoubtedly find the description "He broke off" repeatedly used. In his verse he is always "breaking off". And he "breaks off", indeed, as a rule, twice in every line.'

The coolness between the two men did not last for long and by 1931 Pound was attempting to enlist Lewis in a campaign for the betterment of education.

In his war against passport regulations Pound had been content to write letters to the newspapers, but with the matter showing no sign of improvement after eight years, he wrote an article, 'The Passport Nuisance', which was published in the New York *Nation* of 30 November 1927. The American official and executive group did not, he claimed, desire the comfort and convenience of the American individual, nor did the normal American have any idea how he should or could deal 'with any executive infamy'; this was part, he believed, of the price Americans paid for having their national capital 'tucked away in a corner'. The English, who did most things badly, were at least able to get at their rulers: 'Someone takes little Whiff or old Jiblet out on a golf-links and wrings his figurative neck; someone knows so-and-so and the matter gets a few moments' attention. Anything causing inconvenience to ten or twenty thousand literate people can be got on the floor of the House of Commons in, I should say, forty-eight hours. In the United States this could only happen if the issue affected some very large organized business.'

In October 1927 Pound received a letter from Dr James Watson asking him to accept, for his services to literature, *The Dial* Award for the year. Pound replied on 20 October that it would be impossible for him to accept an award except for his cantos or his verse as a whole. Watson agreed to this, and in the issue of January 1928 made the following announcement:

The Dial Award for 1927 was recently offered to Mr Ezra Pound, and we are most happy to announce that he accepted it – with this proviso: 'It is impossible for me to accept an award except on Cantos or on my verse as a whole. ... 'It would be stupid to make the award on prose-basis as my prose is mostly stop-gap; attempts to deal with transient states of murky[1] imbecility or ignorance.' We agreed to the proviso without hesitation, indeed we had never any different notion about it.

. . .

When he was foreign editor of *The Little Review*, *The Little Review* was the most interesting magazine of a quarter century.

. . .

What Mr Pound perceives he gives value to. Without any of the antics of generosity, he is the most generous of contemporary writers.

. . .

Apart entirely then from the influence of his verse, we can assert that Mr Pound is one of the most valuable forces in contemporary letters.

The same issue of *The Dial* in which the announcement appeared contained part of canto 27 and a review by Eliot of *Personae*, under the heading 'Isolated Superiority'. No one living, he said, had practised the art of verse with such austerity and devotion; and no one living had practised it with more success. Pound had had 'an immense influence', but no disciples, and for the absence of the latter he was to be felicitated. The review ended with a question, 'What does Mr Pound believe?' which was the subject of mild contention between the two men for some years to come.

There was another favourable review of *Personae* in *The Times Literary Supplement* of 5 January, written by Richard Aldington. Although it was not hard, he said, to produce examples of crudity and uncertain taste in the collection, it was also easy to produce examples of delicate emotion and poetic felicity; in the case of his original 'reworking' of Propertius, the wilful anachronisms and not always wilful misreadings of the text should not blind the reader to the curious successes and quaint energy of the poems. 'And in Envoi (1919), built upon a hint from Waller, Mr Pound once more huddles on his singing-robes, and takes his leave with a beautiful stanza, just to show that he can do it when he chooses.' The review did not please Pound who would have preferred something more direct, with fewer qualifications, but Aldington defended it as the means best adapted to bring about a revival of interest in Pound's work in England.

Pound invested the $2000 from *The Dial* Award. In sending money to John Cournos who recently had undergone an operation, he said: 'Investment of Dial prize is due to yield about one hundred bucks per annum. The first 100 has already gone, discounted in three lots, one ten guinea S.O.S. earlier this week, and from most unexpected source. I think you better regard the enclosed as advance payment for something to be written for *Exile*, when the skies are clearer. No hurry. What have you on hand unsaleable elsewhere?' On the subject of operations he told Cournos he had had 'four slits' made in his own anatomy during the past fifteen months: 'Do you want any advice from the experience?'

A year later Pound was again helping Carnevali. He told Harriet Monroe that Carnevali's expenses were $40 a month; his assets, including the $5 monthly he received from Miss Monroe, were $15 a month. McAlmon had been paying his bills for about four years but could not continue. He was trying, he said, to get a grant from the Authors' League; he thought perhaps that Miss Monroe might be able to stir up some American patroness to take over from McAlmon.

Pound was working ahead steadily with his cantos and was planning a new instalment in book form. In December 1927 John Rodker issued a prospectus for a limited edition of cantos 17 to 27, reproducing two sample pages – the opening of canto 21 and the opening of 25.

Homer Pound was due to retire from the U.S. Mint in June 1928 and he and Isabel were looking forward to a long holiday in Rapallo beginning later that year. On 20 February the *Philadelphia Evening Bulletin* published an interview with Homer; included was a recent letter from his son: 'Dear Dad: . . . Article on Guido in March *Dial* . . . Hughes printing *Ta Hio*. Am looking at empty apartments here for you. Kitty Heyman having success with Scriabin concerts in Paris. Olga stopping off at Santa Margherita, goes on to Paris.'

Yeats and his wife, George, so liked Rapallo when they went there for Yeats's health that in February 1928 they decided to take a flat there. On 23 February Yeats wrote to Olivia Shakespear: 'Ezra and Dorothy seem happy and content, pleased with their way of life, and Dorothy and George compare their experience of infancy and its strange behaviour.' Next day he wrote to Lady Gregory: 'Ezra Pound has been helping me to punctuate my new poems, and thinks the best of all is a little song I wrote at Cannes just before I was ordered to stop work.' He wrote to her again two months later: 'He [Pound] has most of Maud Gonne's opinions (political and economic) about the world in general, being what Lewis calls "the revolutionary simpleton". The chief difference is that he hates Palgrave's *Golden Treasury* as she does the Free State Government, and thinks even worse of its editor than she does of President Cosgrave. He has even her passion for cats and large numbers wait him every night at a certain street corner knowing that his pocket is full of meat bones or chicken bones.'

In March 1928 Pound heard from Hemingway that he had had an accident. He sent his sympathy on 11 March, but how 'the hellsufferin tomcats', he asked, 'did you git drunk enough to fall upwards thru the blithering skylight?'

Pound's writing-paper which earlier had been headed with his name and address only, now displayed, in small print at the top, the additional words: 'res publica, the public convenience.'

He was now working on a complete edition, in Italian, of the works of Cavalcanti, with plates showing some of the principal manuscripts, and other editorial apparatus. From the explanatory matter he selected a section dealing with medieval thought and sent it to *The Dial* where it appeared in the March 1928 issue under the title, 'Mediaevalism and Mediaevalism (Guido Cavalcanti)'. In this he wrote that we appeared to have lost 'the radiant world where one thought cuts through another with clean edge, a world of moving energies *"mezzo oscura rade"*, *"risplende in sè perpetuale effecto"*, magnetisms that take form, that are seen, or that border the visible, the matter of Dante's *paradiso*, the glass under water, the form that seems a form seen in a mirror, these realities perceptible to the sense, interacting, *"a lui si tiri"* untouched by the two maladies, the Hebrew disease, the Hindoo disease, fanaticisms and excess that produce Savonarola, asceticisms that produce fakirs, St Clement of Alexandria, with his prohibition of bathing by women'.

Eliot had left Lloyds Bank in August 1925 and had joined the publishing firm of Faber & Gwyer. As a result of efforts by Aldington and Eliot to give Pound a new start in England, Faber & Gwyer undertook to publish his *Selected Poems*, 'Edited with an Introduction by T. S. Eliot', which came out on 23 November; Eliot left out *Homage to Sextus Propertius* because he thought it would trouble too many readers, but otherwise it is an almost perfect selection unburdened by a number of inferior poems which the author allowed into the 1926 *Personae*. The only serious omission, apart from *Propertius*, was the 'Ballad of the Goodly Fere'. Like *Personae*, *Selected Poems* has been reprinted at frequent intervals. Pound tried to interest Faber & Gwyer in his Cavalcanti book but without success.

The third number of *The Exile* was published in the spring of 1928; it included Yeats's 'Sailing to Byzantium', part of canto 23 (with this explanatory note: 'The opening of this canto is too obscure to be printed apart from the main context of the poem'), and twenty pages from a long poem by a young American poet Louis Zukofsky. When Dorothy Pound, who was fond of cats, read Zukofsky's lines:

> The prowl, our prowl,
> Of gentlemen cats
> With paws like spats. . . .

she made an ink drawing of three cats which Pound forwarded to the poet. In his editorial comment in number three Pound said: 'Quite simply: I want a new civilization.' There was no need for it to be much different from the best there had been in the past, as long as it was as good. He found space for a swipe at passports and despatched contemporary France with the same stroke: 'We refuse to recognize France as a contemporary part of civilization so long as kow-tow to paper forms, faddle of passports and *cartes d'identité* remains an integral part of the outward manifestations of her internal imbecility.'

In the 18 April issue of the *Nation* Pound continued his effort to stir up civic and artistic action in America, with an article entitled 'Where is American Culture?' Not only had the citizens of the United States shown, he said, a displeasing incapacity to maintain the civic institutions left to them by their forerunners but did not, save in matters of immediate utilities, show a capacity for intelligent individual opportunism. With the result that such institutions as the Carnegie and Morgan libraries and the Julliard and Guggenheim Foundations did not know how to go about their tasks and spent large sums to no real cultural effect. 'It is not that I am a crank; it is simply that the American millionaire is not serious in this matter of the arts.'

By May Pound was in Vienna where he attended a concert by Olga Rudge accompanied at the piano by a Fräulein Krause, saw the Russian film 'The End of Petersburg' and a German '"abstract" or Gestalt' film, 'Die Simphonie der Grosse Stadt Berlin', both of which he praised, and discussed politics with Count Albert von Mensdorff-Pouilly-Dietrichstein and other survivors of the Austro-Hungarian Empire. Count Mensdorff was an agent in Europe for the Carnegie Endowment for Peace; out of their conversations emerged the following letter, drafted jointly, and signed by Mensdorff:

Minoritenplatz 3, Vienna 1,
June 18th, 1928

Professor Nicholas Murray Butler,
Chairman of the Executive Committee,
Carnegie Endowment for Peace,
New York City.

Sir,
On page 67 of your Year Book of 1927 the wish is expressed for suggestions and collaboration of thought. This gave me the idea that I might venture to suggest certain points as worth while some study, considering the causes of war, which it might be perhaps more useful to go into carefully than to investigate the effects of war.

Some of these causes are:
1. Intense production and sale of munitions; the whole of the trade in munitions and armaments might be subjugated to contemporary, not retrospective investigation via trade channels.
2. Overproduction and dumping, leading to trade rivalries and irritation.
3. The intrigues of interested cliques.
All these are general and constantly active forces toward war.

The letter contained four additional points about international law, in which Pound had little part except perhaps for the suggestion that the principles of international law be 'summarized by clear statement'. On 20 August when Pound was back in Rapallo Count Mensdorff's secretary sent him a copy of the Carnegie Endowment's reply. It was a polite acknowledgement, stating that the suggestions were being forwarded to the appropriate Endowment officials. For Pound it was one more piece of evidence against the American foundations and for years to come he attacked Nicholas Murray Butler on every possible occasion.

In July 1928 *The Dial* published Pound's translation of Cavalcanti's 'Donna mi prega' under the heading: 'Donna Mi Prega by Guido Cavalcanti with traduction and commentary by Ezra Pound: Followed by notes and a consideration of the Sonnet.' The translation was strange but compelling:

> Because a lady asks me, I would tell
> Of an affect that comes often and is fell
> And is so overweening: Love, by name.
> E'en its deniers can now hear the truth,
> I for the nonce to them that know it call,
> Having no hope at all
>   that man who is base in heart
> Can bear his part of wit
>   into the light of it. . . .

In July, with Glen Hughes coming to Europe to gather material for a book on Imagism, Pound and Aldington exchanged letters on the early history of the movement, in the hope that they and Flint might be able to present a common front to the inquiring historian. In Aldington's view Hulme was to be regarded as a 'distant ancestor' and Pound the inventor of Imagism. The 'movement' had been formed, at Pound's suggestion, by Pound, Aldington and H.D., meeting in a tea-shop; the immediate aim had been to launch H.D. The first Imagist anthology, he said, had been Pound's idea. In a second letter on 14 August Aldington said that in all essentials they were in agreement; he was inclined however to give more credit than Pound to Amy Lowell for her part in the affair. 'Amy did put over Imagism by giving innumerable lectures and readings – i.e. she advertised, chiefly herself, but us too. I have MS. of her lecture on me somewhere, and she had others on you, H.D., Fletcher . . . She was a mixed blessing.' Hughes spent the winter of 1928–9 in Europe and Pound was among those he interviewed. His *Imagism and the Imagists* was published by the Stanford and Oxford university presses in 1931. Although he gave Pound much of the credit that was his due, Hughes treated Amy Lowell's group as the movement proper.

On 24 July 1928 Pound wrote to Hemingway about the possibility of Herbert Herlitschka, whom he had met in Vienna, translating Hemingway into German. Next day he wrote to Marianne Moore in her capacity as editor of *The Dial*; he had read Eliot's recent article on Irving Babbitt and proposed that he be allowed to answer in *The Dial*.

He would advocate, he told her, a form of polytheism instead of the usual monotheistic idiocies. When finally he did write his reply it appeared not in *The Dial* but three years later in *The New Review* in Paris.

A Draft of the Cantos 17–27 was published by John Rodker in London in September 1928, in an edition of about one hundred copies. The initials were designed by Gladys Hynes. In addition to seventy copies, most of them for sale at five guineas each, the following special copies were advertised but not all disposed of according to plan: four copies on vellum, three for sale at fifty guineas each, five on Imperial Japan paper at twenty guineas, and fifteen on Whatman paper at ten guineas.

The fourth and final issue of *The Exile* was published by Covici Friede, New York, in the autumn. Contributions included forty pages of poetry and prose by William Carlos Williams, under the title 'The Descent of Winter', poetry and prose by Zukofsky, McAlmon on Gertrude Stein, and poetry by John Cournos and Carl Rakosi. Pound contributed forty pages of prose, most of it on politics. 'Practical men like Lenin and Mussolini', he said, 'differ from inefficients like Otto Bauer in that they have a sense of time.' He mentioned two sources for his information on Russia: Reed's *Ten Days that Shook the World* and Lincoln Steffens's lecture or lectures in Paris. 'Apart from the social aspect he [Lenin] was of interest, technically, to serious writers. He never wrote a sentence that has any interest in itself, but he evolved almost a new medium, a sort of expression half way between writing and action.' And this was as definite a creation as the Napoleonic code. But what interested Pound most, as the sure sign of Lenin's 'lucidity', was his declared attitude to bureaucracy. 'Giving it as nearly as possible in the words Steffens used on his return from Russia, Lenin had said: "All that is the political department, and it is to be got rid of as soon as we can".' Enlarging upon this theme Pound declared that bureaucrats were a pox. 'If we must have bureaucrats by all means let us treat them humanely; let us increase their salaries, let us give them comforting pensions; let them be employed making concordances to Hiawatha, or in computing the number of sand-flies to every mile of beach at Cape May, but under no circumstances allow them to do anything what bloody ever that brings them into contact with the citizen.' The bureaucrat should be treated with every consideration and when ultimately he died should not be replaced. The qualifications of the ideal official were that he should be lazy, timid, have nice manners, no power, and a good deal of intelligence. The higher officials, Pound said, should be grounded in the *Ta Hio* and *Analects* of Confucius. For the ideal state there was one final rule: 'no Christian should ever be permitted to hold executive office.'

Pound also contributed notes on the city of the future, in which the streets would 'follow the stream line or speed line, not a set of blocking and checking right-angles'. Flats would be designed and placed for the maximum of air and light, office towers would have parking-space for motor-cars in the basement, and to the north of the city there would be a huge wind-wall made of light vitreous matter; it would be left open in summer 'like the slats of a blind' and closed in winter. He also announced in large print that he wanted 'a properly equipped palazzo in which to restart civilization' and also 'a few more serious jews'.

Back in his stride again after some years of hesitation and perplexity he began to contribute regularly to *The Dial* and once again to offer his work to a wider public. The first of seven instalments of *Igor Stravinsky* by Boris de Schloezer, translated from the French by Pound, was published in *The Dial* for October; in the November issue he published his only long article on his friend Williams, entitled 'Dr Williams' Position'. He noted that Williams's father was half English and half Danish and his mother a mixture of Spanish and French with possibly a remote Jewish connection. 'At any rate he has not in his ancestral endocrines the arid curse of our nation. None of his immediate forbears burnt witches in Salem, or attended assemblies for producing prohibitions. His father was in the rum trade; the rich ichors of the Indes, Hollands, Jamaicas, Goldwasser, Curaçaos provided the infant William with material sustenance. Spanish was not a strange tongue, and the trade profited by discrimination, by dissociations performed with the palate.' From this secure ingle Williams, he said, was able to look out and see America as something exterior and interesting. Where Pound became angry with America Williams was able to examine it with calm. 'And by just this susceptibility on my part Williams, as author, has the no small advantage . . . Where I see scoundrels and vandals, he sees a spectacle or an ineluctable process of nature. Where I want to kill at once, he ruminates, and if this rumination leads to anger it is an almost inarticulate anger, that may but lend colour to style.' Williams, he said, had but one fixed idea: he started where a European would start, treating America as a subject of interest to be inspected and analysed. Pound quoted, as a key to his work, Williams's statement 'All I do is to try to understand something in its natural colours and shapes.' On 6 November Williams wrote from 9 Ridge Road, Rutherford, New Jersey:

Dear Ezrie: Nothing will ever be said of better understanding regarding my work than your article in *The Dial*. I must thank you for your great interest and discriminating defence of my position. Without question you have hit most of the trends that I am following with the effect that you have clarified

my designs on the future which in turn will act as encouragement and
strength for me.

. . .

But I am touched by the sobriety of your review, that is what I set out to say
meaning to add that I am going on as best I can and that you have helped
me there also. You also have grown older – without loss. In fact I like your
writing in what you have said of me as well as anything I have seen of
yours in prose.

Homer and Isabel Pound arrived in Rapallo for their holiday but
they liked it so well and the cost of living was so low that they decided
to remain there. The furnishings at 166 Fernbrook Avenue were
auctioned and a neighbour, Mrs Van Court, sent the silver and portraits to Rapallo. The house itself was auctioned in July 1930.

Towards the end of November the Yeatses moved into a flat at Via
Americhe 12 where Yeats finished a small book for the Cuala Press,
entitled *A Packet for Ezra*, in which he described Pound's activities on
behalf of the cat population of Rapallo and his attempt to explain his
cantos. 'Sometimes about ten o'clock at night', Yeats wrote, 'I accompany him to a street where there are hotels upon one side, upon the
other palm-trees and the sea, and there, taking out of his pocket bones
and pieces of meat, he begins to call the cats.' Of the *Cantos* he said:

For the last hour we have sat upon the roof which is also a garden, discussing
that immense poem of which but seven and twenty cantos are already
published. I have often found there brightly painted kings, queens, knaves,
but have never discovered why all the suits could not be dealt out in some
quite different order. Now at last he explains that it will, when the hundredth
canto is finished, display a structure like that of a Bach Fugue. There will be
no plot, no chronicle of events, no logic of discourse, but two themes, the
Descent into Hades from Homer, a Metamorphosis from Ovid, and mixed
with these, mediaeval or modern historical characters.

Richard Aldington was now living with Brigit Patmore and in 1928
they visited Rapallo. Pound had been of assistance to them earlier in
Paris and when they headed south he found rooms for them in a small
hotel in Rapallo. In the January 1929 issue of *The Dial* Pound
reviewed Aldington's *Remy de Gourmont*; he took the opportunity to
summarize his views on honesty of thought and the book trade:

We cannot afford to lose sight of his [De Gourmont's] value, of his significance as a type, a man standing for freedom and honesty of thought, a type
rarer than the 'general reader' imagines, for the general reader does not
know, and I doubt if even men of letters realize until they have been on
their job a long time (say twenty years as a minimum) how many well

known and so called 'critical' writers pass their whole lives in, and how many entire periodicals are given over to, the production of statements agreeable to editors, agreeable to the book trade (in the widest sense of the term, publishers, printers, bookshops) but having nothing whatever to do with thought, civilization, or honesty.

Later in January he published in three instalments in the *New York Herald Tribune Books* a long prose piece, 'How To Read, or Why', apparently written some months earlier. It was an account of his conclusions 'after twenty-five years of examination of comparative poesy' and included a sketch of 'a method', like the loose-leaf system in accountancy, which would get rid of dead material and preserve the 'live items'. The idea was to apply to literature 'a little of the common-sense' of current physics and biology and for the instructor in literature to choose specimens which contained the known 'procedures' and 'discoveries'. 'To tranquillize the low-brow reader, let me say at once that I do not wish to muddle him by making him read more books, but to allow him to read fewer with greater result.' Great literature, he said, was simply language charged with meaning to the utmost possible degree, and it was ascertainable that this charging had been done by several clearly definable sorts of people: (1) The inventors, writers who had discovered a process or processes, (2) the masters, who had been able to assimilate and co-ordinate a large number of previous inventions and bring the whole to fullness, (3) the diluters, who had followed the inventors or masters, producing something of lower intensity, (4) the writers who had done more or less good work in the more or less good style of a period (he suggested Wyatt, Donne, Herrick), (5) the masters of *Belles Lettres*, like Longus or Prévost, who had not invented a form but had brought some mode to a very high development, and (6) the starters of crazes, writers who had launched a wave of fashion which had subsided and left things as they were.

For a sound and liberal education in letters, he said, the student should master the following minimum basis: all of Confucius (in Chinese or Pauthier's French version), all of Homer (with Latin crib or Hughes Salel in French), Ovid, Catullus and Propertius (using as reference Golding's *Metamorphoses* and Marlowe's *Amores*), a Provençal song book (with a glance at the Minnesingers and Bion), Dante (plus thirty poems by his contemporaries, mostly by Cavalcanti), 'Some other mediaeval matter . . . and some general outline of history of thought through the Renaissance', Villon, Voltaire's critical writings (with a dip into his prose contemporaries), Stendhal (at least a book and a half), Flaubert (and the Goncourts), Gautier, Corbière and Rimbaud.

Pound also dealt briefly with the question which had occupied his mind for years and was to occupy it still more in the future – the 'function' of literature in the state. This function, he said, had nothing to do with coercing or emotionally persuading or bullying people into accepting a certain set of opinions; it had to do rather with the clarity and vigour of any and every thought and opinion, with maintaining the cleanliness of the tools and the health of the very matter of thought itself. The individual could not think and communicate his thought, the governor and legislator could not act effectively or frame their laws, without words, and the solidity and validity of these words was in the care of the despised *litterati*. 'When their work goes rotten – by that I do not mean when they express indecorous thoughts – but when their very medium, the very essence of their work, the application of word to thing goes rotten, i.e. becomes slushy and inexact, or excessive or bloated, the whole machinery of social and of individual thought and order goes to pot.'

After appearing in the *New York Herald Tribune Books* of 13, 20 and 27 January 1929, 'How to Read, or Why' was published as a small book, *How To Read*, by Desmond Harmsworth, London, in December 1931.

For 1929 Pound drew up a programme of 'civic' action and had copies made which he circulated among his correspondents in America, especially the young. It was also published in the March issue of the magazine *Blues* in Columbus, Mississippi. It consisted of three points which Pound claimed were civic not political:

1. Government for utility only.
2. Article 211 of the Penal Code to be amended by the twelve words: *This statute does not apply to works of literary and scientific merit.*
3. Vestal's bill or some other decent and civilized copyright act to be passed. Footnote: instead of everybody's going to New York, ten or a dozen bright lads ought to look in on the national capital. We need several novels in the vein of Hemingway's *The Torrents of Spring* dealing not with helpless rural morons but with 'our rulers' and the 'representatives of the people'.

Because he received letters from aspiring writers who kept him in touch with their quarrels with the established publishing system Pound believed that he was as well informed about America as he would be if he lived there. He did not hesitate to prescribe for the country's ills nor to enlist the aid of his correspondents in the fight against them. As his correspondence grew he began to think of himself more and more as a leader having a part to play in the affairs of his country. This sense of being a man of affairs crops up in other contexts.

One day in Rapallo Aldington noticed that Pound had vanished; when he saw him next day he asked him where he had been and Pound 'answered importantly that he had been "in conference" with Antheil'. It was about this time that Antheil wrote, under the name Stacey Bishop, a detective story called *Death in the Dark* which Faber published in 1930. Pound is mentioned in it as the ideal professional poet of the day.

The Pounds did most of their entertaining in the restaurant of the Albergo Rapallo. Early in March 1929 they gave a dinner there for Yeats to meet another Nobel Prize winner, Gerhart Hauptmann, who lived for some months each year at Rapallo. Also living there at this time was Basil Bunting whom Yeats described as 'one of Ezra's more savage disciples'. He was from the north of England, a determined and independent young man whose verse Pound admired. In Paris he had been a sub-editor on Ford's *Transatlantic Review*. On one occasion returning home drunk he had entered the wrong building and Pound had had to extricate him from gaol. After the Pounds went to Rapallo he had followed, and he stayed there, on and off, for some years. The celebration of Burns' Night was much to Bunting's taste and on a number of occasions he and Pound imported haggis to Rapallo. Later Bunting went to the Canary Islands where apparently he got into financial difficulties. Pound wrote to Rabindranath Tagore to see if he could arrange a grant for him from the Roerich Museum:

Do you think you could interest him (Prof. Roerich) in Basil Bunting, who is an excellent poet, and wants to know more Persian, and is now broke in the Canary Islands. I think Bunting is about the only man who did six months jail as a conscientious objector during the armistice, i.e. after the war was over, on principle that if there was a war he wouldn't go (Quaker) . . . Bunting has done what I think a very good condensation of Cho Mei, and writes Persian very beautifully (I mean as far as the handwriting goes. I don't know any, so I can't tell whether it is correct). He has no money, and simply will not melt himself into the vile patterns of expediency.

In the spring of 1929 the Aquila Press at 15a Lenthall Place, Gloucester Road, London S.W.7 agreed to publish Pound's edition of Cavalcanti in December 1929, to be followed in the autumn of 1930 or spring of 1931 by his collected prose works in one volume and a translation by him of 'the Odes of Confucius'. I know of no evidence that Pound took any steps towards the translation but he did begin to assemble his prose writings, revising and correcting his magazine articles and books and also inserting footnotes and additions.

It may have been about this time that he wrote an essay, which he hoped to publish as a small book, on 'The Music of Beowulf'. He had heard this music at a concert given in London by the Kennedy-Frasers some years earlier. They had found it in the outer Hebrides where it was entitled 'Aillte'. During the concert Pound racked his mind to think where it fitted. 'It wouldn't go to the Seafarer. Two lines fitted a bit of the Beowulf, then the next wouldn't fit. I skipped a line of the Beowulf, and went on. The Kennedy-Frasers had omittted a line of the music at that point because it didn't seem to them to have an inherent musical interest.' This description is from his *ABC of Reading* published in 1934. But in writing his booklet on 'The Music of Beowulf' he allowed himself to be side-tracked and before he had explained the purpose of the essay he veered off to discuss 'snivelling war profiteers, abject lackeys' and 'an England scared out of its nether garment by the terror of anything likely to cause thought'. As a result the essay appears never to have been finished, but if it was, it was never published.

Pound was continuing with his cantos and about this time sent copies of nos. 28, 29 and 30 to Mrs Scratton; there is a reference near the end of canto 29 to the time they were in Verona together ('And another day or evening toward sundown by the arena'); also it is possible that the 'dear Dennis' mentioned at the end of canto 28, apparently the actor Dennis Wyndham, was a mutual acquaintance.

In April 1929 Yeats wrote to Sturge Moore about an author in whom Pound had become interested, the German anthropologist Leo Frobenius, head of the Research Institute for *Kulturmorphologie* at Frankfort. 'Ezra Pound has just been in. He says "Spengler is a Wells who has founded himself on German scholarship instead of English journalism". He is sunk in Frobenius, Spengler's German source, and finds him a most interesting person. For Frobenius suggested the idea that cultures (including arts and sciences) arise out of races, express those races as if they were fruit and leaves in a preordained order and perish with them.' It would seem from this that Pound had already begun to read Frobenius; he appears to have bought the seven-volume *Erlebte Erdteile* about a year later and also the section published separately as *Paideuma* which he was soon to consider Frobenius's most important work.

Pound was still not feeling well and in the summer of 1929 visited London to see a doctor. He stayed at 169 Sloane Street, S.W.1, and attended a doctor in Gower Street for tests.

His circle of correspondents in the United States continued to grow. In 1929 he received a letter from Upton Sinclair at Long Beach, California. Sinclair was already well known for his inquiries into some of the less savoury aspects of 'capitalist society' and had begun to publish his own books apparently with some success. He had read something of Pound's in 'the Tribune', probably 'How to Read', and asked if he might send him two of his own works, *Money Writes* and *Mammonart*. Pound agreed and they corresponded for some years. He also began to collaborate with a Harvard group, including Lincoln Kirstein and R. P. Blackmur, who were publishing the magazine *Hound and Horn*, sometimes referred to by Pound as 'Bitch and Bugle'. The collaboration did not last for long, however; his cantos 28, 29 and 30 appeared in the issue of April–June 1930 and the editors showed some interest in a plan he put forward for the publication of a series of books: Cocteau's *Le Mystère Laic* (translated by Olga Rudge, with revisions by Pound), Chirico on the technique of painting, an English translation of Frobenius's *Paideuma* (which he considered the most important work in the series), and his own *How To Read*. But the plan did not come to anything and during the next few years he contributed only one article to the magazine and a few letters to the editor.

Pound did not manage, then or later, to find a publisher for *Paideuma* but the Cocteau appeared in the Boston magazine *Pagany*.

Despite the increase in his correspondence with America he was not satisfied with the results so far achieved and decided to buy if possible a printing-press. He wrote to Williams on 2 December 1929 asking him to send advertisements of small, simply operated presses such as were used by some business houses. 'Damn it, I oughtn't to have to bother', he told Williams, but the rest of the world was so lazy he thought he might as well look into the matter. I do not know how much further he took it, but he did not buy one.

NOTES

1 Pound had possibly written 'Murkn', meaning American; it is given as 'Murkn' in *The Letters of Ezra Pound*.

XVI The Cantos
1930/1934

Pound's edition of Cavalcanti was not published as planned in December 1929. A sample copy containing the first thirty-two pages and filled out with blank leaves was bound up, but after fifty-six pages of the edition had been printed the Aquila Press failed. Pound managed to rescue the pages already printed and decided to complete the job at his own expense. He handed over the printing of the Italian text and apparatus to the Edizioni Marsano in Genoa and arranged for the reproductions of the manuscripts to be done in Germany.

In *The Criterion* for January 1930 he published an article on Horace, written from fifty pages of notes which he had taken in the British Museum some twelve years earlier while doing his articles for *The Egoist* on translations from the classics. He was not interested in Horace and was merely using up his notes; his boredom in putting the article together may have inspired his letter on 'Criterionism' in the October–December issue of *Hound and Horn* in which he complained of Eliot's interest in 'dead and moribund writing'.

Among visitors to Rapallo during January 1930 was Louis Untermeyer and his wife. Pound had been in touch with him in 1914 when he had hoped that Untermeyer might know of some way to raise funds for *The Egoist*. Towards the end of December 1929 Untermeyer wrote that he was coming to Rapallo and on 2 January Pound advised him about accommodation:

Dear L.U.

The Casino is better at twice the price, can't be done on licherchoor alone, but if you are representing the family banking house, by all means don't deprive etc . . .

The Europa is, I think the worst placed hotel in Rap. Savoia much better (I usually send comfortable bourgeois there, cook not so good this year as two years ago). The Moderno was good enough for Vail-Guggenheims. (No reports on present cuisine available.)

There are others at a few lire less per diem.

Bristol has an aussicht and also the Verdi if you want to study english pathology. both comfortable. (save for mentality of the denizens.)

On the hole should suggest Savoia or Moderno unless you want eyetalyan ammosphere in which case the Marsala and Rosa Bianca are both on the sea front. but lack drawrin rooms. However; licherary gents have survived 'em and a front room in the Marsala gets all the sun there is.

As a result of the Untermeyers' visit the firm of Harcourt, Brace in New York became interested in Pound's *How To Read* which they asked him to expand from fifteen thousand words to fifty thousand. However Pound did not like the contract they offered, which, if not intended for fraud, he told Untermeyer, 'was certainly admirably designed to permit the publisher to swindle the author', and the matter was dropped. Pound typed out for Untermeyer a brief autobiography in which he said: 'in 1930 P was able to state that NO american publisher had *ever* accepted a book on his recommendation! No am. univ. or cultural institution had ever invited him to lecture (this despite his double qualification as author and man of learning) nor had he ever been invited to serve on any jury of awards to art, music or literature, nor had any fellowship to a writer ever been made on his recommendation.' This was not a complaint, he added, but an observation 'helping one calculate the state of intelligence in certain quarters'. By 1920, he said, 'he had been excluded from every review or weekly paper in England except *The New Age*'. As for the accuracy or inaccuracy of his scholarship this question could best be settled by someone who had tried to find an error in his life of Sigismundo Malatesta in the cantos or in his edition of Cavalcanti. In March 1930 Pound advised Untermeyer on his translations of Heine and included in his letter a recent translation of his own of 'Diese Damen', as an example of how it might be done:

> Our talk, I think, turned on the art of verse
> And when my hunger was relieved
> I thanked them for the honour
> That I thus from them received.

The two men continued on good terms for a while but Pound was dissatisfied with the poems of his which Untermeyer chose for his *Book of Living Verse* and he soon became hostile.[1]

In February and March 1930 Pound was in touch with E. E. Cummings about material he was helping to gather for an American number of the magazine *Variétés*; he was particularly anxious to have a photograph of a Cigar Store Indian as he believed that these wooden statues used to advertise cigars were comparatively unknown in Europe. On 25 March he acknowledged receipt of two photographs: 'One piece nicotine refined woodlady, 2 views, recd.'

In April Yeats wrote to Lady Gregory: 'Ezra Pound arrived the other day, his first visit since I got ill – fear of infection – and being warned by his wife tried to be very peaceable but couldn't help being very litigious about Confucius who I consider should have worn an eighteenth-century wig and preached in St Paul's, and he thinks the perfect man.'

Pound contributed to the April *Criterion* an article, 'Epstein, Belgion, and Meaning', in which he claimed that writers were laggards compared with scientists because they clung 'to modes of expression and verbal arrangement sprung from, and limited by, scholastic logic'. In mid-April Mary Howell, a correspondent for the Paris edition of the *Chicago Tribune*, interviewed Pound at Rapallo; the story carried the dateline, Rapallo, 18 April, and was published the following day under this headline:

Pound Paints Peccadilloes of Pedants
In Money Murdered Marts of Learning
Lean Limbs of Science
Pin Pain on Poet
In Italian Idyll

Pound told the *Tribune* of efforts made by Jefferson, Washington and John Quincy Adams to lay the foundation of civilization in the United States; he also praised Andrew Carnegie as being sincere in his desire to civilize America but said that the Carnegie Peace Foundation was run by a type of academic impervious to the present: 'Nothing will persuade those people to study the *causes* of war'; all they did was to study writers who wrote three hundred years ago or the effects of war on Chile. He declared that in America there were no institutions functioning at maximum efficiency except the banks: 'We do not have to spend hours cashing a cheque.' He praised Lincoln Steffens and the Frenchman Albert Londres as expert journalists and declared that if the university system made no provision for the 'unusual man', as had been claimed by a professor from the University of Pennsylvania, then the university system was dead.

Pound went to Frankfort for the first performance of Antheil's opera, *Transatlantic (The Peoples Choice)*, given at the Frankfort Opera House on Sunday 25 May. Both words and music were by Antheil who was now widely known as 'the bad boy of modern music'. It included sections in 'Jazz' and a mingling of scenery with film sequences. I have not been able to find any comment by Pound but before the performance he called on Frobenius and insisted that he attend; afterwards, according to Pound's account in *Guide to Kulchur*, the German said: 'Not satiric, naive', and added that it was 'Wrong to use royal instruments for proletarian music. . . .' Alfred Einstein wrote a report published in *The New York Times* on 22 June:

The new opera, 'Transatlantic', by the young American composer George Antheil, which was given its first hearing a few days ago at the Frankfort Opera House, is lacking in two essential things. First, it tells nothing new about America. . . Secondly, its creator is quite unable to compose opera either in the old or in any other concept of the word. Further, and I am constrained to speak my mind candidly, though it pains me to. He is quite unable to compose anything whatever. . . Above all, this music has no style. . . There was much applause after the first and last acts and little dissent.

By 26 June 1930 Pound was staying at no. 779 on the Zattere, Venice. During the 1930s it became a custom for Dorothy Pound to visit London during the summer to stay with her mother and to see Omar; at the same time Pound and Olga Rudge went to Venice where they spent part of the time with their daughter.

A Draft of XXX Cantos was published by the Hours Press, Paris, in August, in an edition of two hundred and ten copies, including ten signed by the author. The signed copies cost five guineas each and the others £2. There were also two copies on vellum not for sale. The initials were designed by Dorothy Pound.

When this book was published Pound was forty-four and had been working on his cantos for fifteen years and planning them for longer. As early as his articles of 1912 grouped together in *The New Age* under the title 'Patria Mia' he had expressed a desire to 'find out by a study of historical evidence what sort of things endure, and what sort of things are transient; what sort of things recur; . . . to learn upon what the forces, constructive and dispersive, of social order, move; to learn what rules and axioms hold firm and what sort fade, and what sort are durable but permutable. . . .' By the end of 1915 he was at work on the early cantos but had not solved the problems associated with the large work that he had in mind. When on 17 March 1917 he wrote to Joyce about the cantos he was rather diffident: 'I have begun an endless poem, of no known category. Phanopoeia or something or other, all about everything. . . I wonder what you will make of it. Probably too sprawling and unmusical to find favour in your ears. Will try to get some melody into it further on.' This was written about the time he sent the first three cantos for publication in *Poetry* but even before they had appeared he was revising and reducing them.

One of his difficulties had been to find a form elastic enough to hold the material he wanted to include. By adopting eventually a certain type of free verse he solved all his problems at once, although it took him some time to realize this.

During his London years he had written two different kinds of free verse, one of which progresses by an inward music which is made of both the sound and the meaning of the words simultaneously:

> And wild desire
> Falls like black lightning.
> O bewildered heart,
> Though every branch have back what last year lost,
> She, who moved here amid the cyclamen,
> Moves only now a clinging tenuous ghost.
>
> ('The Spring')

More irregular but still held together by its inner music is 'Albâtre':

> Nor would Gautier himself have despised their contrasts in
>   whiteness
> As she sits in the great chair
> Between the two indolent candles.

The other type of free verse moves by the accretion of words, phrases and lines; a good example is 'Effects of Music Upon a Company of People':

> Their souls like petals,
> Thin, long, spiral,
> Like those of a chrysanthemum, curl
> Smoke-like up and back from the
> Vavicel, the calyx,
> Pale green, pale gold, transparent,
> Greens of plasma, rose-white,
>   . . .
> Woven the step,
> Woven the tread, the moving.
> Ribands they move,
> Wave, bow to the centre.
>   . . .
> Their soul, moving beneath the satin,
> Plied the gold threads,
> Pushed at the gauze above it.
> The notes beat upon this,
> Beat and indented it;

Rain dropped and came and fell upon this,
Hail and snow,
My sight gone in the flurry.

It was this latter type which he adopted in the cantos; it was elastic
enough to hold the materials that he wanted to include and also
enabled him to keep the work moving by a process of accretion. When
he wanted to include something, he had only to add it to what was
already there; and the music, similarly, was a music of phrase added to
phrase, of line added to line, without inner progress or development.

Early in his life Pound had dedicated himself to the writing of a
masterwork and later decided that it should take the form of an 'epic'
about history and civilizations. But the trouble was that the 'epic' was
born of the desire to write a masterwork rather than of a particular
living knowledge which demanded to be embodied in art. At no stage
was he clear about what he was trying to do and further confusion was
added when in the wake of Joyce and Eliot he decided that his 'epic'
would have to be modern and up to date. Although he had no intellectual grasp of the work to be made he was determined nevertheless to
write it. Thus persisting against the virtue of his art he lost any chance
he may have had to pause and rethink the whole project and went on
piecing together an endless row of fragments. Some cantos and some
fragments contain high poetry and there is much that is humorous or
otherwise interesting; but in so far as the work asks to be taken as a
whole it verges on bluff.

Canto 1 is a translation of an extract from Homer, the descent of
Ulysses into the underworld; canto 2 introduces Robert Browning and
Sordello for a brief, enigmatic moment, but is mostly about the sea
and metamorphosis, with an account, taken from Ovid, of Dionysus'
journey to Naxos, during which the crew of the ship attempts to kidnap
the god who causes leopards to appear, entwines the ship in vines, and
turns the sailors into dolphins. The poet himself enters the poem for a
moment at the beginning of canto 3:

I sat on the Dogana's steps
For the gondolas cost too much that year. . . .

But otherwise cantos 3, 4, 5, 6 and 7 are composed mostly of extracts
from Pound's reading: the Cid at Burgos, images of Provence, Diana
and her nymphs, echoes of Sappho, Aldington, and Catullus, and brief
interludes of medieval and Renaissance history. For a moment in canto
7 he describes his search for traces of his own earlier visits to France and
breaks into a different kind of verse (not unlike his 'Portrait d'une
Femme' of 1912):

> We also made ghostly visits, and the stair
> That knew us, found us again on the turn of it,
> Knocking at empty rooms, seeking for buried beauty;
> But the sun-tanned, gracious and well-formed fingers
> Lift no latch of bent bronze, no Empire handle
> Twists for the knocker's fall; no voice to answer.

Cantos 8 to 11 are his life of Sigismundo Malatesta. By quoting from documents and describing or listing incidents and people in Malatesta's life Pound attempts to register his idea of Malatesta as a ruler who in a small town wanted civilization and by intelligence and will-power got it. Among those whom he drew to Rimini were Pisanello, Pier della Francesca and the architect Battista Alberti. Pound particularly liked a letter he wrote to one of the Medici seeking a master painter (apparently Pier della Francesca) for life; not only did he promise the painter a set sum and security but sufficiently understood the creative process to say that the artist would not be obliged to be continually working:

> And for this I mean to make due provision,
> So that he can work as he likes,
> Or waste his time as he likes. . . .

Canto 12 deals with 'Baldy Bacon', the jobber whom Pound met in New York in 1911, and also with an enterprising Portuguese who made a fortune by buying a cargo of ruined maize that nobody else wanted and using it to fatten pigs. The canto ends with a racy story about a hard-drinking sailor which John Quinn told to a bankers' meeting when he got tired of their primness and propriety.

Canto 13 is devoted to Confucius and provides translations of a number of Confucian maxims about human nature, self-knowledge and self-control; and it is possibly meant also to throw light upon the true basis of social order. When his disciples all give different answers to a question about how they would like to spend their time, Kung (Confucius) is not disturbed:

> Kung smiled upon all of them equally.
> And Thseng-sie desired to know:
> 'Which had answered correctly?'
> And Kung said, 'They have all answered correctly,
> 'That is to say, each in his nature.'

Thought or meditation are only beneficial, according to Kung, if they are directed towards useful action; thus his anger at the sight of Yuan Jang sitting by the roadside 'pretending to be receiving wisdom':

And Kung said
     'You old fool, come out of it,
'Get up and do something useful.'

On the question of social order and politics Kung said:

     'If a man have not order within him
'He can not spread order about him;
'And if a man have not order within him
'His family will not act with due order;
     'And if the prince have not order within him
'He can not put order in his dominions.'

Confucius said nothing, according to Pound, of the 'life after death'.

The two cantos which follow (nos. 14 and 15) describe Pound's 'hell', which is full of 'malevolent stupidities', 'vice-crusaders, fahrting through silk, waving the Christian symbols', slum owners, usurers, philologers 'obscuring the texts with philology', monopolists, 'obstructors of knowledge, obstructors of distribution', and so on. It seems likely that Pound intends a contrast between the calm of Confucius and the agitation and filth of the Western 'hell':

     and the laudatores temporis acti
claiming that the shit used to be blacker and richer
and the fabians crying for the petrification of
     putrefaction,
for a new dung-flow cut in lozenges,
the conservatives chatting,
     distinguished by gaiters of slum-flesh, . . .

Canto 16 begins with a description of an earthly paradise which contains Pound's heroes and then switches to the Franco-Prussian war, Lord Byron, and the war of 1914–18; it ends with a long section about the Russian revolution.

Cantos 17 to 23 display a great variety of subject-matter including a beautiful description of an earthly paradise, a description of Venice, a brief dissertation on Kublai Khan's monetary system, examples of business fraud, an account of Pound's visit to see Emil Lévy at Freiburg in 1911, a section in which Niccolo d'Este, delirious, thinks of the death of Roland, a long and superb description in the same canto (20) of the 'lotus eaters', references to Thaddeus Pound building a railway in the wilderness, Jefferson as a civilizing influence, and descriptions of scenes apparently witnessed by the young Ezra in Gibraltar in 1908.

Canto 24 deals with the history of the Este family in the fifteenth century, cantos 25 and 26 with documents relating to the history of Venice. Cantos 27, 28 and 29 continue to present items from history and Pound's own experience and reading, interspersed with brief and sometimes beautiful passages of nature description. The final canto in the book begins with a 'compleynt' by Artemis against 'Pity', and after several brief interludes, including one dealing with type-cutting by Francesco da Bologna during the Renaissance, it ends with the death of a Borgia pope, Alexander VI, in 1503.

Using the set of Jefferson's works presented to him by Eliot, Pound was now composing new cantos dealing largely with American history.

In one of his attempts to come to terms with teachers of English in the United States, Pound contributed an article on 'Small Magazines' to the November issue of the College edition of the *English Journal* published in Chicago. It is interesting to note that in it he spoke both as a European ('we Europeans') and 'as an American'. In describing his London years he wrote: 'A movement for the purgation of poetic writing occurred from 1908 till 1914. Later Mr Eliot added certain complexities.' Of *The Little Review* he wrote: 'From 1917 to 1919 the *Little Review* printed all that Mr Wyndham Lewis produced; it printed nearly all that either Mr Eliot or I produced. It wrote itself almost immediately into the history of European letters by publishing the opening chapters of *Ulysses*. It published work by Yeats, Lady Gregory, John Rodker. So far as one could gather, it was regarded as widely erratic and unbalanced.' As for *Blast*, he thought that Lewis had got 'a great deal more of a world-map of his own intentions' into the two volumes, than anyone had taken the trouble to notice. At this time he contributed a number of letters to the editors of various newspapers and periodicals, including the *Chicago Tribune* in Paris. Typical was one published in the *Tribune* in November 1930, signed E.P. He attacked the *Atlantic Monthly*, *Harpers* and *Scribners* and then turned to 'the American Academy and Institute' which not only functioned less than the French Academy, he said, but acted as 'obfuscatory impediment in opposition to an acceptance of international criteria'. They had never, he claimed, committed any act for the advancement of either art or letters, even when simple action was as obvious as in the case of the struggle for civilized copyright in America or the abolition of section 211. The *Tribune* of 11 November carried a story from Mary Howell, with the dateline, Rapallo, 10 November, and headed 'Ezra Pound in "Best Novels" Dispute Says Few Words For Henry James'. In replying to a *Tribune* writer, Waverley Lewis Root, Pound said: 'James definitely entered the main stream of international literature.'

In 1930 and 1931 he contributed items in Italian to a magazine called *L'Indice* published in Genoa; he also contributed to a communist-inspired magazine called *Front* published in Albuquerque, New Mexico. In the December 1930 issue he published his 'Credo':

Mr Eliot who is at times an excellent poet and who has arrived at the supreme Eminence among English critics largely through disguising himself as a corpse once asked in the course of an amiable article what 'I believed'.

Having a strong disbelief in abstract and general statement as a means of conveying one's thought to others I have for a number of years answered such questions by telling the enquirer to read Confucius and Ovid. This can do no harm to the intelligent and the unintelligent may be damned.

Given the material means I would replace the statue of Venus on the cliffs at Terracina. I would erect a temple to Artemis in Park Lane. I believe that a light from Eleusis persisted through the middle ages and set beauty in the song of Provence and of Italy.

I believe that post-war 'returns to Christianity' (and its various subdivisions) have been merely the *gran' rifute* and, in general, signs of fatigue.

I do not expect science (mathematics, biology, etc.) to lead us back to the unwarrantable assumptions of theologians.

I do not expect the machine to dominate the human consciousness that created it.

In his attempt to influence events in the United States Pound was now beginning to write to Senators and Congressmen. On 9 December 1930 Bronson Cutting answered his inquiry about the literacy of the Senate: 'As for "literacy", I don't suppose you are interested in people like Moses and Brigham and Dan Read, who sin against the light. That leaves Borah and Norris and La Follette and Hiram Johnson and Tydings and Wheeler and Walsh of Montana and I suppose Dwight Morrow, and not much else.' The following March and April he got into correspondence with Senator Smith Brookhart of the Committee on Interstate Commerce. 'Your speech against Meyer', he told him, 'seems to me very important. Parts of it at any rate seem to me the most important historical document of the period I have come upon.' Eugene Meyer was at the time one of the most important Governors of the Federal Reserve banking system; Pound placed an extract from Brookhart's speech at the end of canto 33. He was now being drawn into the world of political propaganda and in February contributed a piece called 'Open Letter to Tretyakow' to *Front*. It was an attempt to deal fairly with Russia while at the same time doubting whether 'anything like the Russian revolution is possible, advisable or necessary for either the U.S.A. or for Western Europe. . . For example: you can not "introduce" a village tractor in a community where each farmer already has a tractor of his own.' He saw no need for a revolution in the forms and mechanisms of government in America; what he wanted was a social and intellectual revolution. The trouble with America was that 'the American people are too hog lazy and too unfathomly ignorant to use the mechanism they have inherited to better economic and intellectual advantage.'

Since settling in Rapallo Pound had continued to visit Paris regularly where he was well known among the Americans for his letters to the *Chicago Tribune* and as a frequent subject in the literary gossip columns. Wambly Bald, in his column 'La Vie de Bohème', in the *Tribune,* considered him to be a newsworthy subject, keeping readers informed of his movements and reporting on his literary projects real or rumoured.

On one of his trips to Paris Pound took his parents to see the flat in which he had lived in the rue Notre Dame des Champs; and they too, because of their son, were sometimes mentioned in the American press in Paris: 'Mr and Mrs Homer Pound,' said a report in the *Chicago Sunday Tribune* of 2 November 1930, 'who have recently taken up residence in Rapallo, in order to be near their distinguished son, Ezra Pound and his wife, visited Genoa, the House of Columbus and the old cathedral. They were at tea at the Genoa Press Club.' In 1931 or thereabouts they moved into the flat which the Yeatses had occupied in the Via Americhe. In mid-May 1931 two men posing as beggars gained access to the flat and robbed the Pounds of jewellery said to have been worth five thousand dollars.

On 2 April 1931 Gino Nibbi wrote to Pound from 166 Little Collins Street, Melbourne, seeking a poem or an essay for his magazine *Stream.* In August 1931 the magazine announced that 'Ezra Pound, in a letter to the Editors, has granted *Stream* the Australian rights of publishing any of his new work. A selection of Mr Pound's recent writings will be presented shortly.' His 'Credo', reprinted from *Front,* appeared in the September (and final) issue.

In July 1931 he contributed three cantos (nos. 31, 32 and 33) to *Pagany;* the first two deal mainly with Jefferson, being extracts from his correspondence, the third contains about thirty extracts from the letters or writings of John Adams, Jefferson, Marx, Senator Brookhart, Lord Howard de Walden, etc., dealing with such subjects as the perversion of history, child labour and the American banking system. It would appear, from a letter that Pound wrote to Mrs Scratton about this time, that this section of the work is devoted to just men and lawgivers. He was probably thinking of the cantos when he contributed the following note on obscurity to the August–September–October issue of *The New Review:* 'The "poem" should theoretically, in its final stage of composition, swallow its own notes . . . Certain kinds of depth are obtainable only I suppose with a concision that produces an apparent obscurity. The test is probably: precision. If the phrase is exact the obscurity grows steadily less with increased attention from the reader. As with Guido's "luce rade". If however the expression is inexact, the longer and more intensely the reader considers it, the less he respects the author.'

The BBC periodical *Radio Times* published on 23 October 1931 an account of 'the fantastic history of François Villon, around whom Ezra Pound has written Monday's and Tuesday's "melodrama".' This was advance publicity for a broadcast performance on 26 October, repeated the following night, of his opera *Le Testament*. This was a complete performance, largely rearranged for violin accompaniment.

The opera opens outside a brothel next to St Julian's Cathedral, with the police completing preparations to capture Villon and his associates. The scene then shifts to the interior of the brothel where Villon, drinking, has a premonition of his fate and sings of death; friends enter and urge him to escape from Paris, but he refuses and makes his will. After the old whore, Heaulmière, has sung a lament for old age and vanished charms the scene is interrupted by Gallant come to visit one of the girls. Villon's mother is seen on her way into the Cathedral to pray and afterwards a priest emerges and attempts to enter the brothel, but the way is barred by the brothel-keeper who sings loudly of the joys of his trade. When Gallant emerges he is subdued and sings accordingly, after which Villon and his friends return to their drinking, toasting one another and departed friends, and finally collapsing on the floor. The police rush in and arrest them and the scene then shifts to a windy hill-top where the criminals sing a song of comradeship from the gallows.

The critics were sharply divided in their opinions. The *Manchester Guardian* thought it was 'one of the best plays the BBC has given', but the *Sunday Referee* declared: 'Of all the clotted nonsense, *The Testament of François Villon* stands supreme. For an hour we had to listen to the quintessence of stupidity forming a mottled muddle of alleged poetry and synthetic histrionics.' John Rodker wrote:

On the evening of October 26th the National programme broadcast the Villon of Ezra Pound, and on the 27th a further performance was sent out by the London Regional stations. The voices came through with what I imagine must have been almost their full weight. There was a quite unusual power of evocation in the phrasing, the appropriateness of the music to the text, and the simplicity of the performance. There were few stage directions, but enough to call up clear pictures always, and the interpolation of colloquial American to connect the poems was an admirably effective device to secure continuity. . . This, one thought, is what singing ought always to have been, and perhaps will be again. . . I see in these performances every reason for Villon taking an honoured place in the repertory of opera.

After the critics had had their say the *Radio Times* commented: 'The disagreement of critics, both public and private, as to the merits of the recent radio-play production, *The Testament of François Villon*, has been both prolonged and heated. That a play of this character, with music of so strange an order as Ezra Pound's and a convention so extraordinary as that of making the vagabonds of fourteenth-century Paris talk in the dialect of Chicago racketeers, should have met with wholehearted approval from every listener, was scarcely to be expected. *The Testament* was an experiment . . . the path of the experimentalist is thorny . . . the first attempts at a novel technique are at best groping.'

In Paris on 5 December 1931 Olga Rudge and the pianist Renata Borgatti gave a concert at 52 avenue de la Motte-Picquet, at which Miss Rudge performed Pound's 'Sonate "Ghuidonis" pour violon seul' (Lirico – Larghetto – Allegro – Maestoso).

The following summer Pound drafted a second opera entitled *Cavalcanti*; it was in three acts with the words taken from poems by Cavalcanti and Sordello. The BBC considered the possibility of a performance in the spring of 1933 but did not go ahead with it; there was a report in the *Chicago Tribune* of 13 December that year which said: 'It is expected that a new opera by Ezra Pound will shortly be produced', but it was never performed.

During 1931 Pound was a regular contributor to *The New Review*, 'An International Notebook for the Arts Published from Paris', and edited by Samuel Putnam and Peter Neagoe. In the winter issue 1931–1932 he published a long article, 'Terra Italica', which was his first and only extended statement on religion and his answer both to Eliot's question about his beliefs and to Eliot's Christianity.

It was a long tribute to paganism, especially the mysteries of Eleusis, which he believed had persisted into the Middle Ages, shining forth in the song of Provence. Further on he referred briefly to such 'disgusting or distressing' aspects of modern life as 'sadistic maniacs judging cases in British law courts', and such 'curious or diverting' phenomena as religious superstitions and stigmata in Italy, and ended by praising anthropology as an 'extremely satisfactory' aspect of modern life, giving as an example Frobenius's 'profoundly satisfactory account of the old chief who "was so foine and so healthy" that he was convinced that his soul should go into the soil of Africa and enrich the crops at his death. And you find Pitt-Rivers' account of the equally fine old Maori who would not have his people corrupted by the vile practices of British marriage, than which he could conceive nothing worse.'

On 21 December 1931 Pound wrote to Joyce asking whether the kissing of the Blarney Stone had been originally a fecundity ritual; Joyce replied that he did not think so. From about this time Pound began to date his letters according to the Fascist calendar; thus the letter to Joyce bore, in addition to the normal date, the words 'Anno X', meaning the tenth year of Fascism.

Always desirous of helping young writers who seemed to be following a satisfactory path Pound had become interested in Zukofsky. Since the time when Pound had published his work in *The Exile* Zukofsky had tried various ways of life, including teaching at the University of Wisconsin. By the end of 1931 he had become 'secretary' of a new publishing venture. Pound not only kept in touch with him by letter but sent his friends to see him when they went to America. He sent Basil Bunting and the two poets formed a firm friendship; he also sent Lauro de Bosis who invited Zukofsky to a concert in New York of early Italian music. Pound had apparently told him that Zukofsky was 'the only intelligent man in America'. When later de Bosis flew over Rome dropping anti-Fascist leaflets he is said to have been pursued by Italian Air Force planes; he flew out to sea and was never seen again.

Zukofsky wrote a long article on Pound and the cantos, part of which was published in *The Criterion*. The whole article was published in an Italian translation in *L'Indice* and in a French translation in *Echanges*. In 1931 Pound wanted Zukofsky to visit Europe and was annoyed that he himself did not have the money at the time to pay his fare. 'How badly', Pound wrote to Williams, 'does Zuk want to git to Yourup? And how badly ought he?' If in Williams's judgment he would benefit by a 'breathing spell', Pound wondered whether he and Williams together might be able to manage the fare. Pound told Zukofsky that the £50 he had received from the BBC for his opera was useful but not enough 'to wipe out all indebtedness'. One reason for his shortage was the money he had spent on printing his Cavalcanti, published by Edizioni Marsano towards the end of January 1932 under the title *Guido Cavalcanti Rime*. It was described on the title-page as 'pieced together from the ruins', and the date was given according to the Fascist calendar. About five hundred copies were printed on four different kinds of paper and the price was seventy-five lire. Pound's name did not appear in it, only the initials, E.P. The book was dedicated to his friend Manlio Dazzi, who had eaten, he said, at the 'Dodici Apostoli' restaurant in Verona and had helped him with the editing. On 24 December 1932, writing to the Anglo-Austrian critic, Joseph Bard, whom he had met several years earlier, Pound described the final stages of the printing: 'I left Genova at 5.03, having made final corrections with the type on the machine. The other eight pages had just been printed on one side and were waiting to be run thru on the reverse.'

On several occasions since leaving the University of Pennsylvania both Pound and his father had taken up with the university, but without success, the question of the doctorate to which he believed he was entitled. He now submitted the Cavalcanti in lieu of the thesis which he had never completed but the university explained that he had still not fulfilled all the requirements and unless he did so they could not give him his doctorate.

In search of material for his cantos Pound had been reading *The Diary of John Quincy Adams* 1794–1845, 'American Political, Social and Intellectual Life from Washington to Polk', edited by Allan Nevins and published by Longmans, Green & Company, New York, London and Toronto in 1928. As he went through it he made pencil-marks in the margin against numerous passages, from which later he composed canto 34. These passages if placed together amount to thirty-four pages; in the canto Pound reduced them to eight pages. He provides no clear narrative and it is difficult to sort out the facts, but the canto does perhaps convey a sense of Adams's varied life and interests. There are errors in Pound's transcription and sometimes he conveys an erroneous impression by giving only part of a statement; occasionally he fails to record relevant material which does not agree with his own view of Adams, American history and economics. This canto was first published in *Poetry* in April 1933.

Because of his growing interest in American history he had become interested in Martin Van Buren who was president of the United States from 1837 to 1841. He wrote to William Wadsworth for information and in April 1932 received a reply which gave details of Van Buren's *Autobiography*, written about 1860 at Sorrento and published for the first time in 1920 as part of the Annual Report of the American Historical Association for 1918. Pound bought a copy later that year and began to compose canto 37 from it, as he had canto 24 from the *Diary*. The Van Buren canto was published in the March 1934 issue of *Poetry* under the title ' "Thou Shalt Not", Said Martin Van Buren,' which is from the opening line of the canto: ' "Thou shalt not", said Martin Van Buren, "jail 'em for debt".'

In 1929 Pound had sent a brief tribute for inclusion in a book, *Omaggio a Modigliani*, published in Milan by Giovanni Scheiwiller in 1930. Pound had not known Modigliani and could not write a memoir as requested, nor did he know his work except in reproductions, so he limited himself to the statement that 'Premature death of Modigliani removed a definite, valuable and emotive force from the contemporary art world.' Although of Swiss descent the publisher of the book,

Scheiwiller, was an Italian employed by Hoepli, a large firm of publishers and book distributors. In his spare time he himself was a publisher and during the 1930s brought out work by a number of distinguished artists and writers. In late May 1932 he published Pound's *Profile*, 'An Anthology Collected in 1931'. The edition was limited to two hundred and fifty numbered copies at $3 each, and was, according to Pound in a note at the front, 'A collection of poems which have stuck in my memory and which may possibly define their epoch, or at least rectify current ideas in respect of at least one contour.' The contents included a poem by Arthur Symons, two by Padraic Colum, one by Joyce, four by Williams, three by Ford, two by Walter de la Mare, five by Hulme one by Yeats, three by Eliot, five by Marianne Moore, two by Archibald MacLeish, one each by Zukofsky and Bunting, two groups of poems taken from the Communist paper *New Masses*, and six by Pound.

In the summer of 1932 Pound was invited to lecture at an international gathering in Florence, to which originally Joyce had been asked. In regretting that he was unable to accept Joyce mentioned that his friend Pound had translated the great Florentine poet Cavalcanti and suggested that he be invited instead. Pound was delighted to receive his invitation. 'Merejkowsky, Stefan Zweig, Pirandello, yours very truly and some lesser lights,' he told Zukofsky, 'are asked to orate at the gran Fiera del Libro in Firenze this month, representin' internashunal licherchoor. . . Me first offishul honours.' He also told Zukofsky that he had been to Rome where he had had an amiable talk with Marinetti; he had come back loaded with Futurist and Fascist literature.

In 1932 Pound was encouraged by Zukofsky's new publishing career to prepare again for an edition of his collected prose. The programme apparently called for the co-operation of several small publishing groups in the United States and France. It began in June 1932 with the publication at Le Beausset, France, of a volume called *Prolegomena I*, containing *How to Read* and chapters one to four of *The Spirit of Romance*, plus a new chapter five – his article 'Psychology and Troubadours' from the October 1912 issue of Mead's *The Quest*. This book was to have been followed by others containing the rest of Pound's prose but the publishers went out of business. In New York, the Objectivist Press, with Pound, Williams and Zukofsky on its advisory board, considered the same or a similar scheme for the publication of Pound's collected prose in twenty volumes, as well as an enormous folio containing *How to Read* and part of *The Spirit of Romance*; but this idea expired in the planning, although the Objectivist Press did survive long enough to publish Williams's *Collected Poems 1921–31* in 1934.

Orage was back in London after some years in America and in 1932 launched a new periodical *The New English Weekly*. Although it never achieved a position like that held earlier by *The New Age* it numbered among its contributors T. S. Eliot, Dylan Thomas, Lawrence Durrell, Allen Tate, Bonamy Dobrée, Basil Bunting, George Orwell. Orage approached a number of his former writers asking for their co-operation; Pound responded and the first of his contributions, 'Swelling of the Occiput', was published in the issue of 16 June. During the next eight years he contributed more than one hundred and eighty items – verse, articles and letters to the editor. Also in 1932 he began to contribute to the Rapallo newspaper *Il Mare*, publishing more than sixty items during the next seven years. At the same time he was continuing with his letters to the press, most of them to the Paris edition of the *Chicago Tribune* and the *New York Sun*. Many were devoted to economics. On 22 June 1932 he wrote to the *Tribune* (the letter was published on the 25th):

I should feel more competent to form a judgment not so much of Mr Small's economic scholarship as of the soundness of his judgment and the incisiveness of his economic perception if he would give a clear statement of his conclusions on the following questions:

1. What effect does he think the drastic shortening of the working day would have on the distribution of purchasing power?

2. Does he think it necessary or advisable that there should be enough 'money' or liquid credit to move *all* available and proximately producable goods?

3. What distinction does he draw between having 'enough' money, credit etc., and 'inflation'?

If by chance he has not defined a dissociation of ideas re this third subject he will find a very able and lucid statement by R.H.C. in *The New English Weekly* for the 16th of this month.

R.H.C. was a pseudonym used by Orage in *The New Age* which he carried over into his new paper; the statement to which Pound refers was the following, which several times he quoted in his own economic writings: 'Would you call it inflation to print tickets for every seat in a theatre, regardless of the fact that the house had hitherto been always two-thirds empty simply because no tickets had been printed for the greater number of seats?'

To the July issue of *The Criterion* Pound contributed an obituary article on Harold Monro, a good-natured piece in which he followed to some extent Eliot's editorial suggestions, with the result that he kept fairly close to his subject, with only occasional asides about the 'intellectual health of England', the Russian revolution 'and the later fiscal calamities'. It was a tribute to Monro's honesty and also an attempt to do justice to his poetry. In mentioning that it was Monro who had published the English edition of the original Imagist anthology, *Des Imagistes*, Pound said he could no longer remember why Monro's own work had not been included in it, 'unless it was that I had called him a blithering idiot or because he had clung to an adjective. Either at that time or later he certainly wrote poems that measured up to that standard, or at any rate without reconstructing the standard or re-examining the actual text, one remembers them as attaining the level desired. It may have been that I was strict, at that time, to the point of fanaticism.' Although Monro was slow, his mind was not wholly closed and his tendency, according to Pound, was steadily toward a definite image and clear speaking in a contemporary idiom. As an example of his work and of his humanity he quoted from 'Hearthstone':

> I want nothing but your fireside now.
> Friend, you are sitting there alone I know,
> And the quiet flames are licking up the soot,
> Or crackling out of some enormous root:
> All the logs on your hearth are four feet long.
> Everything in your room is wide and strong
> According to the breed of your hard thought.

During the summer of 1932 Ford made one of his several visits to see Pound in Rapallo. On one occasion when Olga Rudge was present to take notes they had a conversation about writing; after Pound had added a touch here and there it was published in *Il Mare* of 20 August in an Italian version by Miss Rudge and later in English in *Pavannes and Divigations* (1958).

Pound: What are the most important qualities in a prose writer?

Ford: What does 'prose writer' mean? The Napoleonic Code or the Canticle of Canticles?

Pound: Let us say a novelist.

Ford: (In agony) Oh Hell! Say philosophical grounding, a knowledge of words' roots, of the meaning of words.

Pound: What should a young prose writer do first?

Ford: (More and more annoyed at the inquisition) Brush his teeth.

Pound: (Ironically calm, with serene magniloquence) In the vast critical output of the illustrious critic now being interviewed (changing tone) . . . You have praised writer after writer with no apparent distinction (stressing the word 'apparent' nearly with rage). Is there any?

Ford: There are authentic writers and imitation writers; there is no difference among the authentic ones. There is no difference between Picasso and El Greco.

Pound: Don't get away from me into painting. Stick to literary examples. . . .

When Ford heard that Farrar & Rinehart in New York were planning to bring out *A Draft of XXX Cantos* he conceived the idea of putting together a pamphlet of tributes to Pound by distinguished authors, to be issued at the same time as the book. In August he wrote to John Farrar: 'I hear you are publishing Ezra's cantos in the fall. I hope you will do well with them, for, as you know, the book is of very great importance and Ezra has been working at it for a very long time. I am trying to get up some sort of a campaign in its favour because Ezra is not half as much recognized as he ought to be in his own country.' At his villa at Cap Brun on the outskirts of Toulon Ford received testimonials from fifteen of Pound's friends or supporters, among them Joyce, Williams, Eliot, Hemingway, MacLeish, Allen Tate, Hugh Walpole and Hilda Doolittle. The pamphlet was published the following March by Farrar & Rinehart under the title *The Cantos of Ezra Pound: Some Testimonies by Ernest Hemingway, Ford Madox Ford, T. S. Eliot, Hugh Walpole, Archibald MacLeish, James Joyce, and Others.*

Hemingway in his tribute wrote: 'Any poet born in this century or in the last ten years of the preceding century who can honestly say that he has not been influenced by or learned greatly from the work of Ezra Pound deserves to be pitied rather than rebuked. . . The best of Pound's writing – and it is in the Cantos – will last as long as there is any literature.' Joyce once again managed to praise Pound without saying very much about his work. He was very glad, he said, to hear that Pound was at last to be published in a befitting form in his own country. 'Last year I tried to arrange in London a publication by subscription of his collected prose writings. For some reason the scheme fell through.' Nothing could be more true than to say that 'we all owe a great deal to him. But I most of all surely. It is nearly twenty years since he first began his vigorous campaign on my behalf and it is probable that but for him I should still be the unknown drudge that he discovered – if it was a discovery.' *A Draft of XXX Cantos* was published by Farrar & Rinehart on 15 March 1933 and the English edition by Faber & Faber on 14 September of the same year. Early in 1933 Ford was short of money and Pound with characteristic generosity sent him a cheque.

As well as recent articles by Pound written in Italian *Il Mare* was also publishing some of his earlier prose translated by two of his protégés – Lina Caico and Edmondo Dodsworth. Lina Caico's translation of 'A Study of French Poets' appeared in eleven instalments between 3 September 1932 and 15 July 1933; Dodsworth's translation of his article 'Vorticism' was published in four instalments from 18 February to 6 May 1933.

At Pound's suggestion Zukofsky had been invited by Harriet Monroe to edit an 'Objectivists' number of *Poetry* which appeared in February 1931. It did not include work by Pound who gave over to younger poets the space offered him. Among the contributors were Basil Bunting, Charles Reznikov, Robert McAlmon, Kenneth Rexroth, Zukofsky and Williams. Using the 'Objectivists' number as a basis Zukofsky edited *An 'Objectivists' Anthology*, published during the summer of 1932 by a publishing enterprise known as 'To', the same which had recently brought out Pound's *Prolegomena*. It was dedicated to Pound who 'is still for the poets of our time the most important'. Additional contributions included Eliot's 'Marina' and two poems by Pound, one of them beginning 'Gentle Jheezus sleek and wild'. Pound said later that this was an error on Zukofsky's part; it should have been: 'Jazzing Jheezus, sleek and wild.'

In the autumn of 1932 Pound sent Zukofsky his fare to Europe – a cheque for $112 on his account with the Jenkintown Trust Company. Zukofsky did not cash the cheque but asked Pound if he might keep it as a souvenir. Pound replied: 'I imagine if you wish to give free rein to sentiment and "frame it" that honour and safety would be both sa'sfied by cutting a long V into the right-hand end (eliminating the series number and the figures of the amount; but conserving date and signature and the written sum). You could return the V to me.' Zukofsky's poem celebrating the gesture was published in *Il Mare*, accompanied by a Latin translation of it by Bunting.

Zukofsky visited Europe the following year when Pound, Williams and the Hungarian musician, Tibor Serly, contributed to his expenses. Bunting met him at Genoa and took him to Rapallo where they had lunch with the Pounds at the Albergo Rapallo. Zukofsky stayed with Homer and Isabel Pound but had his two main meals with the Buntings; he had tea every day with Ezra and Dorothy Pound at their flat.

Pound's high regard for the Fascist government of Italy prompted him in 1932 to join with F. Ferruccio Cerio in preparing a film scenario on the history of Fascism. It was privately printed in Rapallo on 21 December 1932, probably for use in stirring up interest in the proposed film. It is not clear what part, if any, Pound had in planning the actual scenario; according to the title-page he was responsible for adapting it for foreign consumption. For the most part the text was printed in three columns and there were a number of notes in the third column about changes necessary before the film was sent abroad. However, it was never made.

In his search for facts on contemporary history Pound was now reading such books as *Mercanti di Cannoni*, about armament manufacturers and their influence, and in January 1933 he wrote to William Bird asking his opinion about a claim in *Mercanti di Cannoni* that much of the Paris press was in the pay of an armament group known as the Comité des Forges. Because of the economic depression and unemployment and the apparent inability of anybody to do anything about it, there was a great deal of this type of literature in circulation, and Pound, in his desire to stay abreast of events, began to read some of it and fell under its influence.

On 15 January 1933 he wrote to Hemingway from Rapallo to thank him for an offer of assistance: 'Thanks fer kind offer. Me earnin capacity still remarkably low, but credit still good at the eat-house. . . Thanks all the same.' Later in the letter he mentioned *Mercanti di Cannoni* and wondered whether Hemingway knew of any publisher in the United States who might be interested in it, as he had a 'sort of option' on it. He said that Mussolini was 'gettin on wiff his job' and that now Hemingway would find Italy more pleasing.

When Pound refused to join an anthology edited by William Rose Benét, in which the authors would choose their own poems and comment on them, Benét cabled that he would pay more, if the fee was not high enough. Pound replied on 23 January that he was refusing to participate because of the harm done by the *Saturday Review of Literature*, with which Benét was connected, and because he thought the anthology, with its comments by the authors, was just one more effort to shield the public from what was written on the page. 'I think I should forgo the $25 for the sake of critical integrity.'

Pound went to Rome and on 30 January 1933 had an interview with Mussolini at the Palazzo Venezia. It was for Pound an important day, for the event matched his highest expectations. Not only was he able to present to the head of the Italian government a list of proposals for monetary and economic reform but to glimpse what appeared to be his greatness of mind. It seems, for example, that Pound either took with him, or had sent along earlier, a copy of *A Draft of XXX Cantos*. Mussolini glanced at a passage here and there, or perhaps the author pointed out some lines of which he was particularly fond. Appropriately, as a famous statesman having his first meeting with a distinguished American poet, Mussolini remarked that he found the work, or the passage, 'divertente', meaning entertaining. Pound seems to have taken this as a serious comment indicating that in a flash the statesman had seen through to the heart of the matter – the liveliness and strong flavour of the work – which was at once a proof of Mussolini's brilliance and of the fact that the cantos were meat for strong men and men of affairs. Another example of what seemed to Pound the high quality of Mussolini's mind was provided when the poet mentioned that he was trying to put all his ideas in order. The Duce asked, 'Why do you wish to put your ideas in order?' Pound replied, 'For my poem', by which he meant his cantos. This question of Mussolini's, Pound said in *Guide to Kulchur* written four years later, was a sign of his ability to carry his thought 'unhesitant to the root'. And on the same page he wrote: 'Mussolini a great man, demonstrably in his effects on event, unadvertisedly so in the swiftness of mind, in the speed with which his real emotion is shown in his face, so that only a crooked man could misinterpret his meaning and his basic intention.'

Pound did not succeed in meeting Mussolini again but at that first and only interview was completely captivated and often referred to him thereafter as 'Muss' or 'the Boss'. He also kept a scrapbook of his life and activities and on the wall of his flat in Rapallo hung the official notice which had come from Rome granting the interview.

The fact that Mussolini had seemed to grasp one of the dimensions of the cantos was proof not only of his superiority among the statesmen of the day but among the intellectuals as well. With his 'swiftness of mind' he had beaten 'the aesthetes' in their own field. This swiftness and the Fascist government's public works programme were praised soon afterwards in the opening lines of canto 41:

'Ma qvesto,'
said the Boss, 'è divertente.'
catching the point before the aesthetes had got there;
Having drained off the muck by Vada
From the marshes, by Circeo, where no one else wd. have
    drained it.
Waited 2000 years, ate grain from the marshes;
Water supply for ten million, another one million '*vani*'
that is rooms for people to live in.

One immediate effect of his meeting with Mussolini was to strengthen his determination to reach inside the government of the United States and to play a part in moulding the future. 'I am more concerned', he wrote to the monetary reformer, Arthur Kitson, towards the end of 1933, 'with getting ideas into the heads of a few men near the centre of power in the U.S. than with saving England, which seems to me the blackest country in Europe, and the last where any intellectual or economic progress is likely to occur.'

During February 1933 Pound began work on two books – *ABC of Economics* and *Jefferson and/or Mussolini*. He was not too busy however to write numerous letters as well, some for publication, some for private consumption, and most of them on economics and politics. He still did not like the League of Nations any better than in the 1920s and on 27 February after one of its decisions he wrote a letter which was published in the Paris *Chicago Tribune* of 13 March:

The damned and drivveling hypocrisy of the League of Nations shows up neatly in the simultaneous rebuke to Nippon and the full steam ahead order for selling guns. The real righteousness shining in primal purity.

Can you follow the lead of some of the old home papers and print a few comparative figures showing at least which sections of the international *mitrailleuse* combine are getting which gobs of gravy?

The embargo just sure would lift at this moment when the 'need' (O blessed word) for powder is rising.

Pound had recently tried various designs for his writing-paper. For a time he had at the top a reproduction of a drawing of himself by Wyndham Lewis; later he used a portrait by Gaudier, executed when he was cutting his marble bust of Pound; he also tried various mottoes, such as 'A tax is not a share' and the Fascist slogan, 'Liberty is a duty, not a right'. The Gaudier bust which for years had stood in Violet Hunt's garden on Campden Hill was brought to Rapallo and placed beside Pound's table in the Albergo Rapallo. It was later carried up to his flat and placed on the roof outside, with its eyes facing seaward.

On 15 March 1933 Ulisse Gobbi, rector of the Luigi Bocconi University – an economics and commercial university in Milan – began to issue invitations to a series of lectures to be given by Pound from 21 to 31 March. Pound's name had been put forward by a citizen of Rapallo, Angelo Sraffa, a jurist and professor at Milan University who had helped to organize the Bocconi. When Pound asked whether there were any specifications about subject-matter, Sraffa, according to Pound in 1958, replied: 'Whatever gives you the least trouble.' The lectures were delivered in English under the general title, 'An Historical Background for Economics'. The first, at half past five on Tuesday afternoon, 21 March, was entitled 'Introduction. Forms of thought in two different systems. Why or how a poet came to be drawn into economic discussion.' Wednesday, at 5.30 p.m.: 'Problems that have been there. Economics for Mohamed, Kublai Khan, the middle ages.' Thursday, at 5.30 p.m.: 'The transition.' Friday, at 5.30 p.m.: 'Economic ideas of the early and constructive American presidents: Jefferson.' Saturday, at ten in the morning: 'John Quincy Adams.' Monday, at 5.30 p.m.: 'Martin Van Buren.' Tuesday at 5.30 p.m.: 'The "new" economics in England.' Wednesday and Thursday, at 5.30 p.m.: 'Conclusions.' Friday, at 5.30 p.m.: 'What literature has to do with it – The function of good writing in the State.'

One of his aims, Pound told his audience, was to combat the idea prevalent at the time that economics was a dry subject and also to show that without a knowledge of economics it was impossible to understand the working of modern history and modern life. He traced the history of banking from the Temple of Delphi and claimed to discover the principles of economics in the sayings of Confucius. Many problems thought to be exclusively modern were to be found, he said, in history, and to illustrate this he gave examples of capitalist behaviour in the Roman Empire. In order to show that it was possible for poetry to have an active part in economics and the study of history he read from his cantos. After discussing economic life during the Middle Ages, with particular reference to the banks of Florence, he spoke of the economic ideas of the early presidents of the United States, whose constructive spirit, he said, with illustrations from Jefferson, was closely related to the spirit of Fascist Italy.

Referring to recent economic crises Pound said the cause was in the deficiency of purchasing-power in comparison with the abundance and possibilities of modern productivity; this deficiency was at the root of contemporary decay and it was this point precisely which 'demo-liberal' economists refused to see and to understand.

Some of the material used by Pound in his lectures came from his book, *ABC of Economics*, which was published by Faber & Faber on 16 April. It was not issued in America until 1940. On the dust-jacket it said: 'Mr Ezra Pound was asked to deliver ten lectures in an Italian university – on economics, not on the mummified muses. This is his necessary evisceration and clarification of the subject; a concise introduction to "volitionist economics".' In a note at the beginning Pound said that his aim was to express the fundamentals of economics so simply and clearly that even people of different economic schools and factions would be able to understand each other when they discussed them. In his desire for simplicity and clarity he reduced the economic problem to four points:

There are four elements; and it is useless trying to function with three:
1. The product.
2. The want.
3. The means of transport.
4. AND the certificates of value, preferably legal tender and 'general', in the sense that they should be good for wheat, iron, lumber, dress goods, or whatever the heart and stomach desire.

He did not, however, stick to terminological questions but branched out into history and politics, with a discussion of different types of government and of some aspects of the class-system. One of the points he made was that 'the brains' of a nation ought to be employed in discerning 'what work is most useful, what work is less necessary and what is desirable even though not strictly necessary'.

Also in April Pound published in the magazine *Symposium* (Concord, New Hampshire) a review of Douglas's *The Secret International: The New and the Old Economics* and of *Mercanti di Cannoni*; he continued during the rest of the year to write numerous letters to the newspapers, on economics and the armaments industry, and in the November issue of the magazine *Harkness Hoot* (New Haven, Connecticut) published an article, ' "Abject and Utter Farce",' in which he praised the work of the Union of Democratic Control, a left wing organization devoted to peace and the control of armaments. On 10 April the singer Raymonde Collignon wrote from London to thank him for a cheque he had sent to help tide her over a difficult period; she mentioned that on 20 May she would be singing some of Pound's music over the BBC and asked him for an English translation of the song 'Tos temps serai' from his opera, *Cavalcanti*. Pound refused, pointing out that his music was meant to fit Sordello's original words and not some other text.

Writing in the College edition of *The English Journal* for May, in an article entitled 'Past History', Pound summarized his association with Joyce and criticized Joyce's later work:

if you ask me whether I believe that Joyce in 1933 is alive to the world as it is, a world in which technocracy has just knocked out all previous economic computations, and upset practically all calculations save those of C. H. Douglas; a world in which the network of French banks and international munition sellers is just beginning to be expressable on the printed page; in which class-war has been, or is as I write this, simply going out of date, along with the paddle-wheel steamer, and replaced by a different lineup or conflict, I must answer that Mr Joyce seems to me ignorant of, and very little concerned with these matters.

Knowing that money was still something of a problem Hemingway sent Dorothy Pound a cheque for £20, for some of her own sketches which had reached him in Cuba; in thanking him on 25 April she said she had meant them as a gift but would keep the money in their 'Literature and Arts Fund' as a 'long loan'. Hemingway wrote to Pound that he did not think much of Mussolini. Replying on 29 April Pound said that on that subject Hemingway was 'all wet'. Mussolini had informed him that the Fascist government did not step in before people had been given a chance to handle things themselves. The government first of all asked contending parties to try to come to an agreement; if the fools could not do so after three weeks' talk, then the government took a hand in the matter. Pound told Hemingway about his lectures in Milan which had been well reported in the Italian daily press ('as distinct from muzzle that would have been applied in Britain'). His *ABC of Economics* had been published in London where the *Evening Standard*, he said, had piously wished that other economists would make a like effort to liven up the subject.

Earlier in April Pound had received a copy of Cummings's *Eimi*, a long and extremely individual account of a visit to Russia. Pound was greatly taken with it and later placed it with *Ulysses* and Lewis's *The Apes of God* as one of the great books of the century. In recommending it to Hemingway, Pound said that he understood the reason he was now being attacked in Russia was that he had told the Russians they would not be doing themselves any harm by allowing Cummings to pay them a visit. Apparently Pound had helped Cummings to get a visa from the Russian embassy in Paris.

In another letter to Hemingway at the end of April 1933 Pound reported that F. V. Morley of Faber & Faber was delighted to have got a copy of *ABC of Economics* 'into' the Bank of England. As to his second book, *Jefferson and/or Mussolini*, he did not think that Hemingway would approve of it, 'but at least', he said, 'I don't advocate boy scouts for America', meaning that he did not recommend for his own country the Fascist system as such, with its uniforms and other trappings.

Hemingway replied on 22 July. Where Pound was 'a natural patriot', he was not, and he hated the whole conception of the state 'with a small or a big s'. His only wish, he said, was to be let alone. Nobody had any business doing things to people for their own good or for the good of any collection of individuals formed as a state. After describing himself as a sincere friend and admirer of Pound, he turned to the subject of influence and the part that Gertrude Stein had played in his own development. He had written *The Sun Also Rises* in six weeks ('one of its principal defects'), starting it on his birthday, 4 July, in Madrid, and finishing it in Paris on 6 September, without sight nor sound of Miss Stein. It was from Pound that he had learnt more about 'how to write and how not to write', he said, than from any son of a bitch alive and had always said so. He had had some good advice from Gertrude Stein in conversation but much rubbish as well. He had kept her in Ford's magazine *Transatlantic Review* when it nearly drove Ford crazy. It would be a big day when he wrote his memoirs.

Pound did not let up; in his replies in August he said his reason for writing about economics was 'to reduce the amount of state machinery to a minimum'. Whereas Jefferson had been against government because all the governments of his day were a nuisance, Mussolini had changed all this by turning government 'into a plus, a useful machine'. On 29 September he wrote that while other countries were talking, Italy was acting: there were new houses, grain growing where there had been swamp and smokeless trains. Referring apparently to property or investments in America, Pound said he thought that it would be advisable for him to 'get everything out of America'. Some months earlier he had looked at some land in Italy but so far had not done anything about it. In another letter he asked Hemingway if he knew any way he might be able to make money writing songs for American election campaigns.

Another friend who was subjected to political and economic propaganda was Yeats. He went to Rapallo in 1933, according to his account the following year, to get Pound's advice about some of his latest verse. But Pound refused to talk about anything except Douglas and the fact that all modern statesmen except Mussolini and Hitler were more or less scoundrels. They were dining at Yeats's hotel and Pound agreed to take away with him Yeats's poems. When he returned them to the hotel the following day his only comment was 'putrid'. Yeats was pleased when the play from which the verse was taken afterwards proved to be one of his most successful pieces. Pound 'may have been right to condemn it as poetry', Yeats wrote to Olivia Shakespear, 'but he condemned it as drama.'

Pound had written most of his *Jefferson and/or Mussolini* during February 1933 and had sent the typescript to his agent, but after six months he had not found a publisher for it; this was disappointing for him because he thought that a book on such a topical subject as Mussolini would not only find a publisher quickly but sell well. During August and September he wrote to the British Union of Fascists asking for their support in having it published but to no avail. It was not published until 1935.

On 14 September 1933 Faber published *A Draft of XXX Cantos* and on 12 October Pound's *Active Anthology*, the aim of which, he said, was to present an assortment of writers, mostly ill-known in England, in whose work a development appeared to be taking place, 'in contradistinction to authors in whose work no such activity has occurred or seems likely to proceed any further'. Contributors were: Williams, Bunting, Zukofsky, Aragon (translated by Cummings), Cummings, Hemingway, Marianne Moore, George Oppen, D. G. Bridson, Eliot, and Pound, who was represented by a selection from the cantos made by John Drummond, a young Englishman with whom he had recently been in touch and who had published an article on the cantos in *The New English Weekly*. There was also a note on the cantos by Zukofsky. When later Zukofsky did not respond favourably to Pound's economic ideas, and suggested they were the result of insufficient knowledge, Pound was not pleased. And when Zukofsky sent a group of poems for his comments Pound replied that his next anthology would be of poets who were conscious of the economic problem and Zukofsky would not be in it.

Under the pressure of social disintegration during the 1930s periodicals of all kinds appeared and disappeared with great frequency and Pound could nearly always be relied on to contribute; any platform was acceptable that would allow him to propound his economic views. Typical of the time was a small paper called *The Outrider* published in Cincinnati, Ohio, with the sub-title, 'A Journal for Literates'. In its first issue, dated 1 November 1933, it said in an editorial note: 'If there is a living man to point to as symbolic of all that has happened (both good and bad) in the evolvement of letters since the turn of the century, it is Ezra Pound. If America generally does not know him we can only refer to the English *Who's Who*, where the recital of his attainments runs over a solid column of agate type. Suffice it to say that, no matter who or what one reads, especially in contemporary French, German and Italian, the influence of his many-sided talent is bound somewhere to emerge.' And in the same issue was an article by Pound, 'The Master of Rapallo Speaks', in which he asked readers to consider the superiority of Douglas's plan over Marxism. The evils of the capitalist system proceeded from 'Insufficient purchasing power' and 'Rotten distribution of what purchasing power there is'. Whereas the Marxist was interested in public ownership on a large scale, Douglas was more specific and sought public ownership and management of the nation's money, believing that this did away with the need for public ownership in general. He also contributed a letter to the first issue, in which he listed the following books as necessary for an understanding of contemporary life: Douglas's *The Monopoly of Credit* and *Economic Democracy*, Fenner Brockway's *The Bloody Traffic*, Corbaccio's *Mercanti di Cannoni*, René Crevel's *Les Pieds dans le Plat*, Irving Fisher's *Stamp Scrip*, a play called *Marchands de Canons*, and a book, *L'Abominable Venalité de la Presse*.

He did not confine himself, however, to new journals; if established periodicals or newspapers would have him, then he would write for them. He wrote to the *New York World Telegram* ('Presenting Some Thoughts on Fascism') and began a series of letters to the London *Morning Post*; for *The Criterion* of July 1933 he wrote an article called 'Murder by Capital'. In this he said that Mussolini was the first head of state in recent times to perceive and to proclaim quality as a dimension in national production. As for the capitalist states, they had failed to make the best use of the best writers and artists and in their place had erected an 'enormous and horrible bureaucracy of letters' which almost uninterruptedly had sabotaged intellectual life. 'As for proposed remedies, C. H. Douglas is the first economist to include creative art and writing in an economic scheme, and the first to give the painter or sculptor or poet a definite reason for being interested in economics; namely, that a better economic system would release more energy for invention and design.'

As a popular resort among the literary Rapallo continued to attract the attention of the newspapers. On 13 December 1933 the *Chicago Tribune* in Paris published an account of some permanent residents and of recent comings and goings:

Basil Bunting, the poet, has taken his wife and child to the Canary Islands, where they will make their residence. . . The Max Beerbohms keep very much to their white villa on the Ambrogian hill. . . Fritz von Unruh, the German poet, who has a villa at Zoagli, is working on a drama with an Italian background. His *Verdun* created a great furore in Paris and was banned by the Hitler government. Von Unruh, who received the highest decorations of the German Army, is dedicating his life to disarmament and world peace. . . It is said that Mr and Mrs William Yeats will not return to Rapallo, as Yeats' work keeps him in Dublin. The Homer Pounds are occupying his beautiful home, which is filled with original Blakes, Burne-Jones and Gordon Craigs. . . Gordon Craig is still in Paris, although his villa is always open, with its marvellous collection of theatrical books and works. . . Mrs Edith Wharton motored from Florence to Genoa and left the following morning for Cannes.

Through all his campaigning for economic and political reform (he contributed more than one hundred items on these subjects to periodicals during 1934) Pound went on writing his cantos which he now regarded as all of a piece with his economic concerns – an instrument through which he would help to make the future. A new instalment of the work, under the title *Eleven New Cantos* (nos. 31 to 41), was published by Farrar & Rinehart on 8 October 1934 and by Faber the following March. Eight of the eleven dealt with questions uppermost in his mind – Jefferson, Quincy Adams, Van Buren, Mussolini, the armament industry; and no. 38 contained a summary of Douglas's theory about the deficiency of purchasing-power. On questions of history he expressed himself with customary verve, remarking of the Emperor Franz-Josef that he was a lousy old bewhiskered son of a bitch of whom nothing good was recorded. Two cantos stand out amongst the politics, history and economics; they are nos. 36 and 39. The first was a new translation of Cavalcanti's 'Donna mi prega':

A lady asks me
     I speak in season
She seeks reason for an affect, wild often
That is so proud he hath Love for a name. . . .

The canto ends with some fragmentary speculation by Pound about copulation and clear thinking, from which it appears that Aquinas thought with his 'head down in a vacuum' and Aristotle with his 'not quite in a vacuum'. Canto 39 deals with the sexual mysteries:

> Dark shoulders have stirred the lightning
> A girl's arms have nested the fire,
> Not I but the handmaid kindled
>   Cantat sic nupta
> I have eaten the flame.

In theory Pound was completely happy with his involvement in current affairs and lost no opportunity to denigrate mere 'aesthetes' who did not understand the purposes of epic poetry like the cantos or the new world that was in the making. He suffered however from a feeling of being out of things; so much so that in 1934 he wrote a long letter in which he accused Bruce Richmond, editor of *The Times Literary Supplement*, of being a moral coward 'who has hidden behind anonymity for twenty years and never opened his mousy paper to my critical work'.

NOTES

1 *The Book of Living Verse* was published by Harcourt, Brace in 1932 and the English edition by Collins in 1933 under the title *The Albatross Book of Living Verse*.

XVII   Music
1933/1936

The idea of holding concerts in Rapallo came to Pound from his experience in Cesena years earlier when he had attended a concert organized by Manlio Dazzi, in which local and visiting musicians had taken part. The two who formed the nucleus in Rapallo were Olga Rudge and the German pianist Gerhart Münch. They began in the summer of 1933 with performances in the Theatre Reale of all the Mozart sonatas for violin and piano. In a programme note in Italian Pound described the sonatas as comparable in music to Dante's *Paradiso* in literature. Basil Bunting reviewed the concerts in a front-page article in *Il Mare* for 1 July. On 12 July Münch performed music by Scriabin in a private home, placed at the disposal of Rapallo music lovers by Father Desmond Chute who had come to live in Rapallo during the 1920s.

There was so much interest in the summer performances that the local authorities granted Pound the use of the Rapallo town hall for future events and he began to organize concerts known as 'Concerti Tigulliani', after the bay of Tigullio on which Rapallo is situated. Not only was the hall more suited to chamber music than the Theatre Reale but it was available free, except for staff expenses; since the responsibility for raising the necessary funds fell on Pound, this was an important consideration. Among those who agreed to back future concerts were Homer Pound, Dorothy Pound, Natalie Barney and Fr Chute. The organizing committee consisted of Pound, Basil Bunting and a German resident by the name of Haas – the three of whom, said advertisements, had been professional music critics on journals in large European cities and offered their guarantee of the high quality of performers and programmes. When towards the end of 1933 Bunting left for the Canary Islands he was replaced by Mrs Ephra Townley who had had experience organizing concerts in Paris.

The first full season opened on 10 October 1933 with the violinists Olga Rudge and Luigi Sansoni and the pianist Münch, in a programme which included sonatas by Corelli, Bach and Debussy. For the second concert, on 14 November, the three musicians were joined by the cellist Marco Ottone for a programme which included sonatas by Purcell Bach and Boccherini; the third concert, by Rudge, Sansoni and Münch on 5 December, included a Bach concerto for two violins and piano and a sonata by Ravel.

The programmes were chosen, according to Pound, to illustrate the 'ideogrammic method' of criticism, outlined by Fenollosa in his essay on the Chinese written character and said by Pound to be the basis of his *How To Read*. He discussed the Rapallo concerts in his *ABC of Reading*, published by George Routledge in May 1934 and in America by Yale University Press the following September. 'A series of coincidences', he wrote, 'has permitted me (1933) to demonstrate the *How To Read* thesis in a medium nearer to poetry than painting is.' He then gave the programmes for 10 October and 5 December and commented: 'There was nothing fortuitous. The point of this experiment is that everyone present at the two concerts now knows a great deal more about the relations, the relative weight, etc., of Debussy and Ravel than they possibly could have found out by reading ALL the criticisms that have ever been written of both.'

As time went on the committee was able to buy a piano and there was support from residents, both Italian and foreign. There was encouragement also, Pound said in a note published in *Il Mare* of 8 January 1938, from the organization for Fascist Culture and the local tourist office.

Pound was in touch with the Scottish musicologist W. Gillies Whittaker and in December 1933 received from Oxford University Press a copy of their recent printing of Whittaker's edition of the sonatas of the seventeenth-century composer William Young. They were played in Rapallo in 1934, in advance of the 'first' performance given under Whittaker at Oxford. The Mozart sonatas were repeated and there were performances also of the sonatas of Bach, Pergolesi and Purcell. On three consecutive afternoons in a private house Münch played the complete *Wohltemperierte Clavier*. From time to time Pound introduced outside musicians, such as the Gertler Quartet, the Hungarian-American composer Tibor Serly, the singers Chiarina Fino Savio and Lonny Mayer, the pianists Renata Borgatti and Luigi Franchetti, and the New Hungarian Quartet. Programmes between 1934 and 1940 included the New Hungarian Quartet playing Bartok and Haydn, Lonny Mayer singing Telemann and Hindemith, Olga Rudge and Gerhart Münch playing Bach, Debussy, Stravinsky, Pergolesi and Satie, Chiarina Fino Savio singing Alessandro Scarlatti and other Italian composers of the sixteenth, seventeenth and eighteenth centuries, and Renata Borgatti playing Bach, Mozart, Ravel and Debussy.

Pound not only did most of the organizing but sent out reviews and announcements to the American papers in Paris and wrote articles for periodicals in England and America. He also wrote numerous stories and announcements for *Il Mare*, some of which were reprinted separately as advertisements. 'Fanned by his disinterested and unflagging enthusiasm', wrote Desmond Chute years later, 'rare and unforgettable little concerts sprang up according to the frequency and incidence of performers. One remembers blocks of music. *Block* in this context was a great word with Ezra: not only did he insist at rehearsals on "blocks" of light and shade in the performance of old music, he also demanded integrated and consecutive programmes.' Rhythm was another matter upon which he held very definite ideas. 'The chief component of the grand style in composition or execution', he wrote at this time, 'consists in the maintenance of the same velocity for a sufficient period.' Decadence sprang from fear of monotony, which led to constant variations of tempo. In the case of orchestral playing the conductor's job was 'to give the beat' and those failing to do so ought to be assassinated.

As usual Pound's interest in the Rapallo concerts did not stop at organizing and publicity, and when Münch was short of money it was to Pound that he applied for a loan. Although Pound was happiest when doing something, preferably something associated in his mind with the world of the future, nevertheless he swam and played tennis regularly and sometimes for relaxation read detective stories. Both he and Dorothy Pound were fond of Edgar Wallace whom they occasionally read in French. He was unable to relax for long, however, without connecting his relaxation with economics. In reading Dorothy L. Sayers he began to think that it would be better if she gave some of her time to the larger 'crimes' in the world of economics and government and he wrote to her accordingly; in reply she said she did not think there was enough element of mystery in what he proposed, whereupon he explained as follows:

No my dear Gal: That iz where you go wrong. I wrote the first life of Zaharoff, before the Berlin bloke, and I assure you there is PPPPlenty of mystery, and now that the *Express* is tellin' London that Sir Basil loves roses, there are a lot more mysteries.

Fitzgerald (Sinn Fein revoluter, etc) that I have known from youth, had to trace a certain influence through a series of five holding companies.

We are under a secret and dangerous REAL govt. High 'permanent officials' lunch *a trois* and get shocks. Balfour and Zaharoff being 'Arthur and Basil' long long long before the pub knows anything about the mysterious greek.

There is plenty of detective work, and a lot more exciting than merely the Duckesses trinkets.

Also the human nature, when one gets it direct from blokes sitting in on the actual source of state policies, is good and plenty.

Nothing was more important now than the quick spread of the 'new economics' and to this end he was willing to use any means to hand. For example, he gave Graham Seton Hutchison permission to use, in his novel *Blood Money*, extensive quotations from *ABC of Economics*. The novel was published in London in 1934, under the pseudonym Graham Seton; the passages from the *ABC* occur towards the end, without acknowledgment of their source.

Pound was now writing dozens of letters each week, most of them on economics. The monetary reformers he wrote to included Professor Irving Fisher, Arthur Kitson, Gladys Bing, Douglas, Sir Montagu Webb, W. K. Bardsley, Miles Hyatt and Crate Larkin. He wrote also to men like Nicholas Murray Butler and the banker James Paul Warburg, and twice during 1934 to President Roosevelt. In one letter he corrected a misprint – the omission of the word *not* – in the American edition of the president's book *On Our Way*. As a result the president inserted and initialled the word in his own copy and the error was corrected before the book was published in London by Faber & Faber. He also sent the president a facsimile of the private money issued many years earlier by Thaddeus Pound's Union Lumbering Company in Chippewa Falls. He explained to the president as follows:

Lest you forget the nature of money/i.e. that it is a ticket. For the govt. To issue it against any particular merchandise or metal, is merely to favour the owners of that metal and by just that much to betray the rest of the public. You can see that the bill here photod. has SERVED (I mean by the worn state of the note).

Certificates of work done. That is what these notes were in fact/before the bank swine got the monopoly.

For Professor Fisher he would go through the manuscript of a book and make suggestions; to others he would write seeking clarification of economic terminology or a concerted drive against the Carnegie Endowment for Peace; to a young man in America who preferred Communism to Douglas he would attempt to explain that the two were not incompatible: 'There is no reason why Douglas economics shouldn't be used by communists, any more than Ford tractors are incompatible with Russia.' He was prepared to discuss literature only with certain correspondents who were doing some necessary job. In 1934 he began a series of letters in which he assisted Laurence Binyon with his verse translation of Dante; he also began a series with W. H. D. Rouse about his prose translation of Homer. When a young American poet, Mary

Barnard, wrote to him, he encouraged her to translate Sappho and discussed prosody and sound values at some length. In the case of friends like Hemingway, Joyce and McAlmon, however, he criticized their work because they refused to consider the importance of economics. Nor was he interested in sickness in any of its forms, but in health. 'Lot of psychic bellyache *not* a problem any longer', he wrote to McAlmon, 'any more than man being melancholy for lack of a pill. Just as damn silly as dying of thirst in an attic because some kid has turned off the water from the basement.' People too lazy to examine the facts were not intelligent enough, he said, to write interesting books and were 'reduced to bulls and memoirs depending on personalities'.

On 24 May 1934 Routledge published his *ABC of Reading* which he intended as a text-book. On 27 September Faber published *Make It New*, a four-hundred-page collection of some of the best of his earlier literary prose which he had been enticed to prepare by one of the directors of Faber, F. V. Morley. Pound wanted Faber to publish books on the 'new economics' but he could not resist Morley's sense of humour; not only had Eliot made a veritable fortune out of his *Selected Essays*, Morley told him, but was in line for a bishopric as well. The only new essay was the first, an introductory piece entitled 'Date Line' which he wrote in January 1934. It opened with a list of the various kinds of criticism and included a survey of some of the major literary events during his London years; but it was political also: 'From Harding to Hoover, no clean thing in power. And heaven knows Wilson's stink was sufficient.' A little further on he gave the date as 'the year XII of the present era' and said: 'In the year XII where are we? We are in the epoch of Stalin, Gesell, C. H. Douglas and of Il Duce, with Mr Roosevelt still a more or less nebulous figure . . . Mussolini a male of the species, and the author of this year's *consegna* [consignment or delivery].' Still answering Eliot's question about what he believed, Pound wrote: 'I believe the *Ta Hio*. When a dozen people have convinced me that they understand that so lucid work, I may see reason for accepting a more elaborate exposition.' The American edition of *Make It New* was published by Yale University Press the following March.

On 15 August 1934 the *Gazzetta del Popolo* published an interview with Pound conducted by Gino Saviotti, who referred to him as 'the poet economist'. Pound mentioned, among other things, debasement of the coinage by Philippe le Bel, R. McNair Wilson's recent book on money, *Promise To Pay*, and Binyon's translation of the *Inferno*. He pointed out that during the Middle Ages a distinction was made between *partaggio* and usury: the former a sharing-out of the fruits of work done in collaboration and the other a 'corrosive interest' representing no increase 'in useful and material production of any sort'. And in an attack upon gold as the basis of monetary issue he declared with great emphasis: 'It is unjust that a man who has a cow and another who has a plough cannot exchange without leave of a third who has metal.'

In a letter to Hemingway during 1934 Pound suggested that he indulge in 'a little mass action', by which he meant a campaign by Hemingway, MacLeish, Williams 'and five or six young huskies' against the Carnegie Endowment. That was in March. In August he wrote again; this time it was to say that since Hemingway had admitted that Pound had helped him during the early stages of his writing career, he might now give thought to the idea that after fifteen years examining economics Pound might be able to do the same for those trying to 'find their way' about that subject. He also doubted whether the Roosevelt Brains Trust contained the best brains in America. As he himself knew things which some of those on government boards did not, he indicated that he would be willing to return home if asked. 'Might be as easy for you to push me over on Washington, as to push me into front page of *Esquire*' – this latter remark referring to the fact that Pound had been invited to contribute to *Esquire*, by the editor, Arnold Gingrich, who had given Hemingway as a reference. Pound said that Roosevelt's bluff ought to be called; he ought to be asked why he did not call home the 'best brains' from abroad. 'What the hell is the use', he asked, 'of foozlin fer another ten years when the job could be fixed an' we could then turn our minds to something more interestin.'

According to Charles Norman, Hemingway wrote later to the lawyer Julien Cornell that in Paris in 1934 Joyce had asked him to come along to dinner with Pound because he was convinced that Pound was 'mad' and was 'genuinely frightened of him'. Throughout dinner, Hemingway said, Pound spoke 'very erratically'.

He now seemed to regard himself as a central office for the correlation of important economic and other information. In August 1934 he had forms printed in Rapallo containing eight questions with space for replies; these he sent out to bankers, politicians, writers and others in England, the United States and other parts of the world:

VOLITIONIST ECONOMICS

Which of the following statements do you agree with?

1. It is an outrage that the state shd. run into debt to individuals by the act and in the act of creating real wealth.

2. Several nations recognize the necessity of distributing purchasing power. They do actually distribute it. The question is whether it shd. be distributed as favour to corporations; as reward for not having a job; or impartially and per capita.

3. A country CAN have one currency for internal use, and another good both for home and foreign use.

4. If money is regarded as certificate of work done, taxes are no longer necessary.

5. It is possible to concentrate all taxation onto the actual paper money of a country (or onto one sort of its money).

6. You can issue valid paper money against any commodity UP TO the amount of that commodity that people want.

7. Some of the commonest failures of clarity among economists are due to using one word to signify two or more different concepts: such as, DEMAND, meaning sometimes WANT and sometimes power to buy; authoritative, meaning also responsible.

8. It is an outrage that the owner of one commodity can not exchange it with someone possessing another, without being impeded or taxed by a third party holding a monopoly over some third substance or controlling some convention, regardless of what it be called.

Answer to E. Pound,
Via Marsala, 12/5,
Rapallo,
Italy.

The answers he received varied considerably. Some agreed with him, others argued or suggested that the questions were loaded in favour of his own views.

As well as publishing three books of his own during 1934 Pound contributed to two anthologies and wrote a preface for a book of poems. For *Negro Anthology*, edited by Nancy Cunard and published by her in conjunction with Wishart & Co., London, he wrote a short note on Frobenius; to Parker Tyler's anthology *Modern Things*, published in New York by the Galleon Press, he contributed a part of canto 34; and for George Oppen's book of poems, *Discrete Series*, published by the Objectivist Press, New York, he wrote a two page preface. It seems that about this time the Objectivist Press again considered the possibility of publishing Pound's collected prose. To the material he had brought together several years earlier he now added more recent pieces, including his preface to *Active Anthology* and his review of T. A. Sinclair's *A History of Classical Greek Literature*, published in *Time and Tide* of 10 November 1934 under the title 'Dust Upon Hellas'. During one of his bursts of activity associated with the collected prose Pound wrote a four-page note on Gerard Manley Hopkins and a number of other notes and comments aimed at filling gaps in his published work.

Among visitors to Rapallo in 1934 was James Laughlin, aged twenty, who was on leave of absence from Harvard. Born on 30 October 1914 in Pittsburgh he belonged to a family with an interest in the huge Jones and Laughlin steel company. At boarding school, at Choate, in Connecticut, he studied English under the poet and translator Dudley Fitts who introduced him to Pound's poetry and further stimulated his interest by showing him letters he had received from Pound in Rapallo. Later Laughlin went to Harvard and in Paris on leave of absence in 1934 he wrote to Pound asking if he could come and see him. Back came a telegram, 'Visibility High', and Laughlin journeyed south to study at what was known as the 'Ezuversity'. He lunched and dined regularly with the Pounds at the Albergo Rapallo, took brisk afternoon walks with Pound, and spent a good deal of time in Pound's small study in his rooftop flat. And sometimes, after tea, Dorothy Pound would take him into her small room and read to him from the works of Henry James.

Encouraged by Pound, Laughlin began to edit the literary section of the American Social Credit paper *New Democracy*; the section was called 'New Directions', and included Pound and Williams among its contributors. Again at Pound's instigation Laughlin started a publishing house, giving it the name New Directions. Whenever practicable he accepted Pound's advice and one of the first authors he published was Williams, who in those days was having difficulty in finding a publisher for some of his books. The venture grew into New Directions Inc., and is today Pound's American publisher.

One thing in particular that struck Laughlin during his visits to Rapallo during the 1930s was Pound's love of the cinema. Whenever Laughlin went with him Pound sat in the front row upstairs with his feet on the balustrade.

In the London *Morning Post* of 20 March 1934 Pound published a letter 'on Fascism and the British Press'. It was noticed by a retired Italian naval officer, Ubaldo degli Uberti, who drew it to the atttention of Italians in the *Giornale di Genova*, under the title 'Foreign Lies Contradicted by a Foreigner'. When on 9 April Pound published in the Paris edition of the *Chicago Tribune* an article, 'Mussolini Defines State as "Spirit of the People",' Ubaldo degli Uberti translated it into Italian for the Milan periodical *Quadrante* and it was reprinted in *Il Mare* on 16 June. A friendship developed between the two men and they often discussed Pound's ideas on usury and his fight against the 'international financiers', whom he called the usurocracy.

Among the many articles and letters which Pound published in 1934 were several pieces on literature, including an amusing and sometimes informative review of A. E. Housman's *The Name and Nature of Poetry* in the January *Criterion*: 'This volume reaches me with a friend's note stating that it has "upset a lot of the Cambridge critics". My first hope was, naturally, that the upset had occurred in the highest possible seas and at furthest possible from any danger of rescue.' In *The Criterion* for April he published a review of Binyon's translation of the *Inferno*; it is harder to follow than the Housman review but contains some interesting insights. Another literary piece, 'Mr Eliot's Solid Merit', was published in *The New English Weekly* of 12 July. It is amusing in isolated paragraphs and concludes: 'As Mr Eliot is a younger man than I am, I see no reason why he should lie down on his achievements, or why cantankerous observers should despair of his further utility.' In all three articles he took the opportunity to attack abominated names: Milton and Dryden in the pieces on Housman and Binyon, Ben Jonson and *The Times Literary Supplement* in the Eliot.

However, most of his writings in 1934 were on economics or politics, and included reviews of such books as James Paul Warburg's *The Money Muddle* and Paul de Kruif's *Hunger Fighters* ('a just record of heroisms that have solved vital problems of food production'). De Kruif worked for the American government and for a year or more was bombarded by Pound with letters suggesting that he turn his attention to the real causes of poverty. De Kruif later introduced Pound to the Secretary of Agriculture, Henry A. Wallace. Another man in the American government with whom Pound was in touch was W. E. Woodward, a journalist and historian who sat on several of Roosevelt's advisory boards dealing with business and insurance. Pound sent Woodward items on economics to pass on to the president. In apologizing for his failure to do so, Woodward explained, according to Pound, that it was Roosevelt who always did all the talking.

Although there was much discussion of monetary reform, things were not moving quickly enough for Pound. When in December 1934 he was asked to write an article on Joyce he refused and in a letter said: 'There is too much future, and nobody but me and Muss/and half a dozen others to attend to it.' Writing in January 1935 to an Anglican clergyman, the Rev. Henry Swabey, he said: 'I want (privately) news of state of opinion, etc., in let us say Durham (which is a place like another). Being out here, I have more time to reflect on such items than blokes in an office can . . . spill out what you think and you may serve me as an extra eye. I need about 400.'

Impelled by his sense of mission Pound continued in the same way during 1935. He published one book and two pamphlets, all dealing with economics and politics, and contributed one hundred and fifty items to newspapers and periodicals. He began to write the 'American Notes' for *The New English Weekly* and a series called 'Ez Sez: Being Some Pithy Promulgations' for the *Santa Fé New Mexican*. He corresponded with C. K. Ogden in an unsuccessful attempt to fire the 'Basic English' circle with enthusiasm for Frobenius and Fenollosa.

The previous year he had used the columns of *The New English Weekly* in an attempt to arouse Eliot's interest in these two authors, but Eliot in his reply had found himself unable to respond with any warmth. He did not think much of Fenollosa except for his part in Pound's *Cathay*; as for Frobenius, he appeared to be a typically unpleasant example of the modern mind.

Pound also wrote numerous editorial suggestions to *New Democracy* and *Esquire* in America and to *The New English Weekly* and other periodicals in England; he also kept up a steady stream of advice to the various monetary reform sects. He assisted the Hungarian-Italian economist Odon Por with an article published in the February 1935 issue of *Civiltà Fascista* and translated some remarks by Mussolini which Homer Pound sent to the *Herald-Telegram* in Chippewa Falls where they appeared on 5 March. Under his son's influence Homer had become a convinced monetary reformer; his writing-paper bore a notice which proclaimed that leisure was 'spare-time free from anxiety', and when Zukofsky seemed to be straying too far from the path of righteousness Homer wrote to him: 'Ezra had me read your book of poems and I must confess that it seems to me you could spend your time and talents on a much more needed Message to the world. Put your book aside, take up Social Credit, get in touch with *New Democracy* 55–5th Ave., New York.'

If in retrospect Pound's vast correspondence now begins to take on some aspect of a nightmare, it is well to remember that the times in which it was conducted were something of a nightmare also; and if his letters were sometimes arrogant or foolish and say little for his sense of proportion or sense of reality, they nevertheless testify to his zeal and energy. To Paul de Kruif he wrote, 'If Roosevelt thinks he can borrow the nation out of debt, he is a fool. And if he knows he can't and goes on as if he could, he is a traitor. Do send me items, and also criticize what I say, I want to make a just estimate, based on facts.' The reference to 'items' is interesting, for it illustrates his belief that knowledge is the result of a collection of facts or nuggets of information; he had great faith in snippets of 'news' supplied by his correspondents and thought that he had as good an idea of what was going on in America as the inhabitants. To Senator A. H. Vandenburg he wrote: 'War is caused by finance, not by guns. Your committee is doing fine work, but so far as the press lets one learn anything, no sign that it has got down to bedrock.' Then followed the suggestion that Vandenburg might investigate the Carnegie Endowment. To Senator W. Borah: 'I don't hold ANY theories about money that I am not ready to drop if anyone can and will stand up and show that I am in error. Eden is the son-in-law of the Westminster Bank, so THAT mystery is largely explained.

It has taken me a shameful time to find this out. Father-in-law, Sir Gervase Beckett, haven't had time to trace what that means in detail.'

Needless to say, many recipients did not welcome his letters, or if they did at the outset soon grew tired of them. There were others of whom Pound grew tired when they refused to take the action he assigned to them. About the only American politician who earned his admiration was George Holden Tinkham, a wealthy Republican congressman from Boston, who years before had fought to keep the United States out of the League of Nations. Pound wrote to him in March 1935:

The Hon. G. H. Tinck: I am very glad to read (*Santa Fé New Mexican*) that you mean to show up the Carnegie Endowment. The Rockefeller, I know less about but would be glad of details. More power to your elbow.

Butler deserves no pity. Those buzzards have spent half a million a year taxed out of the people and they have steadily avoided exposing or investigating the economic causes of war.

All these big endowments feed a bureaucracy, and what they do toward the 'purpose' avowed or 'intended' by their founders, is not always clear.

As I am doing a weekly column on American affairs which does percolate back into American offices, I should be glad to have congressional record for days when you get going.

Tinkham wore a beard and travelled the world; he and Pound met later in Italy and in 1939 Pound wrote to the *Boston Herald* putting him forward as a candidate for the Presidency.

To W. E. Woodward he wrote in 1935: 'Down at bottom there is difference between the good guy and the louse. A few men wantin' to go straight would get us a decent mechanism without a helluva lot of stalling.' To Babette Deutsch: 'The whole game of publishing in America is so foetid and the sloth of writers so great, and the refusal to consider any ideas until 20 years late so damnable, and the supine acceptance of the N.Y. gang control of distribution so placid. And the dastardly lack of co-operation on the part of American writers who make professions of appreciating my work so really disgusting, that my patience has long since been exhausted.'

At the time of the 'Abyssinian crisis', when Italy's case was before the League of Nations, he wrote to the English journalist, A. S. Elwell Sutton:

My point being that the League was born rotten/ continued as an assembly of bank pimps, as foreseen by Orage. No honesty; either of intention or of procedure. A packed jury and a judge interested in the case, is mere skunkery.

I wouldn't trust the League with a 3 quid common magistrate's decision. Retreat of power FROM the people.

I come to an American journalist who don't care a rap about Italy and he says 'British sportsmanship? In 54 years I have NEVER seen it.'

I think your 'WE' is just upper claws jargon, or as Yeats said years ago, 'England is the only country where a man will lie WITHOUT being paid for it.' Which he elaborated: certain opinions get whispered around as the 'right thing'.

Week after week, month after month, the letters poured forth. To John Masefield: 'I have chucked a good many literary scruples, and I hold you responsible at least to think for 24 hours on your responsibility in the face of crass ignorance and of crass falsification.' To Senator J. P. Pope: 'Thanks for your letter. What I want you to do is to tear right through the activities OF the munitions makers INTO the financial forces that drive on the gun-buzzards.' To Lady Buchanan: 'Either you people start thinking now, or your bloomink empire will follow the Austria of '59. State of mentality is very similar. And mere noise and swish sentiment wont help matters for very long.' To Senator Borah: 'Very astute speech by Roosevelt at Atlanta. Three years Social Credit hammering and he now admits that the mass of American people eat third class diet because they have not the purchasing power to get more and better food.' However, in pointing a way out Roosevelt offered a false dilemma: 'the dirty old clothes of England, DOLE based on pity (or fear the starved will get nasty) AND public works on fascist model. The dilemma is false. The second question on my Volitionist list is not faced.'

Orage had died on 6 November 1934 and to *The Criterion* of the following April Pound contributed an article, 'In the Wounds (Memoriam A. R. Orage)', in which he attempted to explain Social Credit and the ideas to which Orage 'devoted the last fifteen years of his life'. It also contains several pleasant glimpses of their association in the days of *The New Age* and a reminder of the fact that Pound had always been much more impressed by England and English politics than his Americanism had generally allowed him to admit: 'Orage wrote in the British Empire. Even I am old enough to remember a time when the Empire was very efficient. I think it was efficient probably because it could make use of a great number of half-wits (bureaucracy) admirably controlled by a very much smaller number of johnnies who were manifestly ALL THERE.'

Of Orage's literary criticism he said: 'For twenty-three years I don't think that either of us ever took the other seriously as a critic of letters, and now thinking of it in retrospect, I wonder how far the difference of view was a mere matter of the twelve years between us.'

In an obituary notice in *The New English Weekly* Eliot described Orage as 'the best leader-writer in London', and, in the days of *The New Age*, 'the best literary critic of that time in London'.

It was probably about this time that the Pounds were visited by a Miss Tseng, a Chinese Christian with a school for girls in central China. She was staying in Rapallo with a friend of Dorothy Pound's, an Englishwoman by the name of Miss Madge who later taught music at the school in China. One afternoon when the two women came to tea Pound sat on his rooftop terrace with Miss Tseng and asked her to translate from a small 'book' of Chinese poems which belonged to his parents; it was made of silk and each poem was accompanied by a painted scene. Miss Tseng obliged and Pound took notes. From the notes he later wrote canto 49 which has a resonance such as is not to be found in any other of the cantos and contains some of the most striking lines in the whole work:

> Evening is like a curtain of cloud,
> a blurr above ripples; and through it
> sharp long spikes of the cinnamon,
> a cold tune amid reeds.
> . . .
> Sun up; work
> sundown; to rest
> dig well and drink of the water
> dig field; eat of the grain. . . .

When it came out in *The Fifth Decad of Cantos* in 1937 Dorothy Pound sent a copy to Miss Tseng. After the 1939 war she and her brother founded a university on Formosa.

If monetary reform was often the cause of disagreement in the 1930s, in at least one case it had the opposite effect, being the lenitive which reconciled Pound to G. K. Chesterton. Beginning in November 1934 Chesterton began to publish Pound's articles in *G.K.'s Weekly*. On 10 May 1935 they had lunch together in Rapallo and Pound discovered that he liked him. 'G. K. Chesterton here yesterday,' he wrote to Irving Fisher at Yale, 'also finds nothing to contradict in as much social credit as I advocate.' On 30 May Chesterton published Pound's *Child's Guide to Economics* which had previously been turned down by the *Morning Post*. When towards the end of the year Chesterton had some kind words to say about Pound over the BBC, Pound wrote to thank him, enclosing his sheet of Volitionist questions for Chesterton to answer: 'They have served', he told him, 'to correlate present state of opinion. I don't make out whether there is actually something in Douglas that holds you up, or whether you are working as I am, towards a decent system, but feel the need of something less technical, i.e. some less technical formulation if one is to get it into enough heads for it to take action . . . I should like to see Belloc again, can't make out if his ideas change with state of his liver. At any rate I take it we are all three definitely against Shaw, Wells etc. paucity of perception.' Two years later in a long article on Jefferson and Adams he spoke of Chesterton's whole life as a protest against the 'impoverishment' of the Encyclopaedists and the Enlightenment, and ten years later in his *Pisan Cantos* he summoned up the ghost of an earlier and better England with the words, 'Chesterton's England of has-been and why-not'.

The two pamphlets which Pound published in 1935 were *Alfred Venison's Poems* and *Social Credit: An Impact*, both brought out by Stanley Nott who had begun to publish Social Credit books and pamphlets from 69 Grafton Street, Fitzroy Square, London. Alfred Venison, 'The Poet of Titchfield Street', had burst into print in *The New English Weekly* of 1 February 1934 with 'The Charge of the Bread Brigade', based on Tennyson's 'The Charge of the Light Brigade'. Beginning with his second offering later that month each poem was accompanied by a letter signed A.V. (composed anonymously by Orage): 'Your printing of my little piece about the Hunger Marchers has encouraged me to send you another. They come to me while I'm pushing my rabbit-barrow down Titchfield Street. I don't claim to be as educated as some of your other poets; but I attend night school and pick up a bit of the dictionary that way. It would tickle my missus to see this new bit in print.' The new bit was 'The Neo-Commune':

> Manhood of England,
> Dougth of the Shires,
>   Want Russia to save 'em
> And answer their prayers.
> Want Russia to save 'em,
> Lenin to save 'em, Trotsky to save 'em
> (And valets to shave 'em)
> The youth of the shires.

Another was a lament for 'Old Kate' the charwoman:

> She died on the job they tells me,
> Fell plump into her pail.
> Never got properly tanked as I saw,
> And never got took to jail,

Just went on a sloshin'
And totin' up scuttles of coal,
And kissin' her cat fer diversion,
God rest her sloshin' soul.

Twenty of them were published by Nott as a pamphlet in April 1935. There was no mention of Pound's connection with Alfred but the poems were later added to a new edition of his *Personae*.

The other pamphlet, *Social Credit: An Impact*, was published in May; it was a lively digest of his ideas on money, Social Credit and monetary history, and included historical material gathered recently in Siena, which he also used in cantos 42 and 43. The pamphlet was dedicated 'To the Green Shirts of England', a group of Social Crediters led by John Hargrave, author of the novel *Summer Time Ends*. The Green Shirt movement had come into being with the London Hunger March of 30 October 1932; its forebears, according to Hargrave, were Douglas Social Credit and the Kibbo Kift movement, this latter founded in 1920 'to counteract the ill-effects of industrialism' by encouraging boys to take up woodcraft and hiking. As their following grew the Green Shirts took the message of monetary reform out into the streets, with marches and public meetings. In addition to reams of advice Pound also gave the movement publicity in his writings and helped with the composition of marching songs. About May 1935 he donated a flag which members embroidered with the poet's name.

Among the many monetary reform pamphlets in Pound's possession at this time was *Correspondence between Montagu Norman Governor of the Bank of England and The Green Shirt Movement for Social Credit from May 14, 1934 to April, 1935*, issued by the movement from its office at 44 Little Britain Street, E.C.1, in 1935. The first letter had been delivered by a squad of Green Shirts who had marched from Green Shirt headquarters to the Bank of England at 12 noon on 14 May 1934. Although the movement claimed, with some reason, to be descended from Douglas, it was looked upon with great suspicion by Douglas and the purer Social Crediters; and in fact the so-called monetary reform movement of the 1930s was composed of numerous warring sects and individuals. The only person who seems to have had a good word and an illimitable supply of advice for all of them was Ezra Pound; he wanted to combine the good points of each – a desire not shared usually by the reformers themselves who naturally thought that their own particular solution was the right one. These squabbles and his attempts to reconcile the irreconcilable and to get the various groups to clarify their terminology took up a great part of his time between 1934 and 1940.

Pound was not alone among literary men in his support at this time for monetary reform and Social Credit; other pamphleteers who contributed to the same series included Herbert Read, Storm Jameson and Bonamy Dobrée.

In July 1935 Stanley Nott published *Jefferson and/or Mussolini*. In a foreword dated April 1935 Pound wrote: 'The body of this ms. was written and left my hands in February 1933. 40 publishers have refused it. No typescript of mine had been read by so many people or brought me a more interesting correspondence. It is here printed verbatim, unaltered. . . It is printed as record of what I saw in February 1933.' The book contains many interesting observations which bear the mark of Pound's intelligence, but it is more remarkable for what it ignores than for what it includes and by its abrupt style and lack of construction inevitably did more harm than good to the cause for which Pound was fighting, namely a better understanding in England and America of what Mussolini was doing.

In Pound's view the fundamental likenesses between Jefferson and Mussolini were probably greater than their differences. Jefferson had taken part in, and had helped to shape, the American revolution; Mussolini was similarly shaping the Italian revolution, 'driven by a vast and deep "concern" or will for the welfare of Italy, not Italy as a bureaucracy, or Italy as a state machinery stuck on top of the people, but for Italy organic, composed of the last ploughman and the last girl in the olive-yards'. Things being what they were in Europe Pound believed that a strong Italy was necessary, especially in view of the fact that Germany was 'epileptic', with 'lots of crusted old militars yelling to get back "the Kaiser" and lots more wanting pogroms'. In praising Mussolini, Pound called him a genius and said: 'I don't believe any estimate of Mussolini will be valid unless it *starts* from his passion for construction. Treat him as *artifex* and all the details fall into place. Take him as anything save the artist and you will get muddled with contradictions.' The notion of a ruler constructing a work of art out of people is not a happy one, whichever way we look at it; I can only suppose that in his anger at people who thoughtlessly criticized Mussolini, Pound got carried away and did not know what he was writing. For no matter what aspects he embraced of Fascism or Nazism, he never, so far as I have been able to discover, accepted the idea that people are there to be used by the government for purposes of its own, artistic or otherwise. As the war of 1939 drew nearer his politics became increasingly ambiguous, but generally he seems to have favoured the individual rather than the state. Certainly he did not advocate Fascism as such for the United States, or for any country probably except Italy, although he did favour a general application of the corporate state ideal of men being represented in parliament by one of their own trade or profession rather than by geographic area, as in England or America at present.

Among those who reviewed *Jefferson and/or Mussolini* favourably was William Carlos Williams, in the issue of *New Democracy* for 15 October. The Liveright Publishing Corporation brought out an American edition in January 1936.

On a number of occasions during the 1930s Pound attended the Salzburg Festival where he heard performances under Bruno Walter and Toscanini. 'The aesthetic pleasure of hearing Bruno Walter play Mozart', he wrote in the essay 'Civilization', published in *Polite Essays* (1937), 'is about what one would derive from seeing a bust of Mozart carved in sausage.' He also heard Toscanini conduct Verdi's *Falstaff* and Beethoven's *Fidelio*. 'To hear any other man conduct these operas would probably be intolerable.' He admitted that the 'beastly Beethoven' contributed to the development of the opera: 'Let us by all means know it. Let us have the perfect rendering which leaves Ludwig no possible alibi. It is NOT a pleasant way of passing an evening but it is immeasurably instructive. It shows what poor Ludwig suffered.'

His protest at the performance itself was more specific. James Laughlin, who was there, told me in 1967 that at one interval Pound sang out, 'What can you expect of a man who had syphilis'. There was a buzz of disapproval from the audience some of whom apparently thought he was referring to Toscanini.

As for Verdi, his *Falstaff* was 'vindication of his drive toward making a unity out of that heteroclite chaos of stage, orchestra and cater-wauling. Everything in it fits and belongs. It needs Toscanini BUT it is second rate music.'

After the Salzburg Festival Pound and Miss Rudge, accompanied by Laughlin, went to Gais to see their daughter Mary.

During one of his visits to Austria at this time Pound visited the small town of Wörgl, near Innsbruck, which had issued its own money. He had first heard about it in Claud Cockburn's newsletter *The Week*, in the early 1930s. He mentioned it briefly in canto 41, a single line which can have meant nothing to his readers at that time and must be puzzling to most of his readers today. He wrote about it again in the pamphlet *What is Money For?* in 1939: 'Unterguggenberger, the Austrian monetary reformer, used work as a measure, "Arbeitswert", 10 schillings' worth of work. That was o.k. in a mountain valley where everyone could do pretty much the same kind of work in the fields.' Three years later in a booklet, *Carta da Visita*, written in Italian, he said: 'In the early 1930s the small Tyrolean town of Wörgl sent shivers down the backs of all the lice in Europe, by issuing its own

Gesellist money (or rather the Gesellist variety of Mazzinian money). Each month every note of this money had to have a revenue stamp affixed to it of a value equal to one per cent of the face-value of the note. Thus the municipality derived an income of twelve per cent per annum on the new money put into circulation.' The town had been bankrupt, according to Pound, but in less than two years everything had been put right. 'All went well until an ill-starred Wörgl note was presented at the counter of an Innsbruck bank. . . The plutocratic monopoly had been infringed. Threats, fulminations, anathema! The burgomaster was deprived of his office, but the ideological war had been won.' We get something of the flavour of his visit to Wörgl in *The Pisan Cantos*. The Burgomaster, Unterguggenberger, was out chopping wood when Pound arrived, but he spoke to Mrs Unterguggenberger:

> the state need not borrow
> as was shown by the mayor of Wörgl
> who had a milk route
> and whose wife sold shirts and short breeches
> and on whose book-shelf was the Life of Henry Ford
> and also a copy of the Divina Commedia
> and of the Gedichte of Heine
> a nice little town in the Tyrol in a wide flat-lying
> valley
> near Innsbruck and when a note of the
> small town of Wörgl went over
> a counter in Innsbruck
> and the banker saw it go over
> all the slobs in Europe were terrified
> 'no one' said the Frau Burgomeister
> 'in this village who cd/write a newspaper article.

Pound's fascination with Unterguggenberger's notes, based upon the ideas of the German reformer Silvio Gesell (1862–1930), was not shared by strict Social Crediters who did not think it sound economically and regarded it as more likely to aid authoritarianism than 'economic democracy'. This did not, however, deter Pound, who at every available opportunity praised Gesell and urged others to do likewise; he contributed also to the Gesellite paper, *The Way Out*, published by Leo Fack in San Antonio, Texas.

In September 1935 Pound prodded two Italian writers, Carlo Izzo and Aldo Camerino, into establishing a new literary 'movement', based upon Pound and Fenollosa, and numbering Pound, Zukofsky, Laughlin and the English poet and writer on economics, J. P. Angold, among its ten members, who were to circulate their compositions and ideas among one another for comment; Pound, the final recipient, would then collate their observations. In November he contributed to the *Kingswood Review* (Salem, Oregon) an article, nominally a defence of the Social Credit government elected in Alberta, Canada, but really publicity for a new book:

The English attacks on Aberhart's victory reduce themselves to saying that Aberhart will NOT BE ALLOWED to put his ideas – or Douglas' ideas – into practice.

. . .

The smoke screen will be still more cleared away by a book now in press by Montgomery Butchart called *Money*. Herein he has collected the thought of the best English minds from 1640 to the present.

It is an absolutely basic, noncontroversial volume that ought to be in every high school curriculum.

It gathers the clearest thought of the best minds – Berkeley, Hume, Larranaga, the saints of economic honesty, great names and forgotten fighters.

We have at last the overwhelming evidence that honest thought about money has come time and again, independently and without collusion to certain *sane* and *clear* perceptions.

Too much emphasis has been put on Douglas' innovation and too little on the century-old common sense that is summed up in his economics.

Money, by M. Butchart; Stanley Nott, publisher, 69 Grafton Street, London, W.1. – in press as I write this but published by the time it gets into print.

For the next twenty years or more Pound continued to praise and recommend Butchart's book as necessary background for the study of economic history.

Italy had attacked Ethiopia in October 1935 and Pound rushed inevitably to Italy's defence – out of sympathy for Italy but also because of his dislike of the League of Nations and of what he believed, with some reason, to be the hypocrisy of the British press. There is little doubt that the madness which impelled Mussolini to attack was the same madness which impelled Pound to rush to his defence and impelled ill-informed humanitarians or malicious propagandists to rise up in defence of Abyssinian innocence.

In his attempt to explain Italy and Fascism to the British world Pound contributed in less than a year more than twenty articles to *The British-Italian Bulletin*, a supplement to *L'Italia Nostra*, an Italian newspaper in London. The first was published on 27 December 1935 during the controversy over 'sanctions' against Italy by the League of Nations. 'Twelve years I lived in London,' he began, 'four years in

Paris, and twelve have I lived in Italy, each time from my own free choice. I deny an American Editor's statement that I represent the Italian point of view. If my point of view is not international and organic or structural, I believe that no international point of view can exist, or that there are few men who can claim it with greater right.' After stating his belief that empires decay at the top and in the middle (by which he meant, apparently, the British Empire), he went on to suggest that usury was the root of ruin, of decay, and of 'all scarcity economics', and to say that Europe had lost the distinction between *usura* and *partaggio*, usury and fair sharing. He believed, he said, that the men who were crying out for the starving of Italy represented the same errors, the same weaknesses of mind, which had caused the 'sanctioning' of great masses of the English, French and American population. An England which listened to the facts of the 'NEW ITALY' or of the Loeb Chart of Plenty compiled by forty experts for the United States Government, could not cry out for the strangulation of Italy. 'I believe that the whole constructive force of the new organization of the Corporate State is unknown in England, or so little known and so utterly misunderstood that it might just as well never have been heard of.' England and Italy both needed education, he said; England as to the facts of the 'new Italy' and Italy as to the English and American ignorance of nearly everything that had happened in Italy for a decade. Italy would be able to tell her story to the outer world only when she had become infinitely more aware of the prejudices and pre-conceptions existing in other countries about Italian affairs:

England and America, the plain men in those countries, do not know, and can not be expected to know of such men as Carlo Delcroix. They can not be expected to get the *feel* of the new Italy, or to hear the sincerity of Delcroix' speaking in private, 'But we have no intention of doing any *harm* to their Empire,' meaning the British Empire.

The best of Italy is not in print. The best I have had in Italy I have had *viva voce*.

Italy believes in 'Libertà Economica, con responsibilità civica,' economic liberty, and civic responsibility. It is this *Civic* Responsibility, this sense of responsibility, every man to himself *and* to the nation, that has been lost in both England and America. Therein is the decline of democracy.

A strong Italy is the keystone of Europe for peace, for the good life, for civilization.

No man living has preserved the Peace of Europe as often as has Benito Mussolini.

It was typical of Pound that he should mention Carlo Delcroix as a man worth knowing about and then not say who he was – a blind and maimed war veteran who was a minister in Mussolini's government. The article ended:

Justice implies a balance, total weight against total weight. It does not mean catching someone out on a technicality. The mass of humanity in most of Abyssinia will be better under the Duce's rule, than under that of the Negus.
The facts are ascertainable.

This was easier to say than to illustrate. But, whatever the rights or wrongs of Pound's opinions, the truth of the matter is that intellectually he was now at the mercy of the pseudo-system of thought, which, with his rare zeal, he had manufactured out of Fenollosa and bits and pieces of information and learning. He had convinced himself that he possessed a method which enabled him to recognize the meaning of things without having to submit to any discipline or go through any process of abstract thought. In practice it meant no more than that he picked up information from old books, newspapers, monetary reform pamphlets, etc., and meditated upon them, using, within the limits of his nineteenth-century heritage, the method of abstraction which he claimed to despise. With a mind as brilliant as Pound's at work it was inevitable that some of the results should turn out to be stimulating and worth while; but there was nothing new about his method and his results were worth while just in so far as they clarified or co-ordinated information or ideas upon an already existing basis.

Many of his errors however were due to simple ignorance; the ignorance of a man now imprisoned inside his own dreams of a better world. When F. S. Flint wrote for *The Criterion* a technical article against Douglas's theory Eliot sent it to Pound for his comment. Pound replied in a rage that Flint (pigeonholed in his mind under *Imagism*) had no right to discuss a subject like algebra which was far above him. But as Flint was a mathematician employed in the statistics division of the Ministry of Labour he had at least as much right as Pound to an opinion on Douglas's formula on costs and purchasing-power.

And so he continued from 1935 into 1936: writing a summary of monetary economics 'for the Plain Man', organizing concerts, skimming through newspapers, pamphlets and books looking for evidence of usurocratic tyranny, contributing to little papers like *The Rocking-Horse* (Madison, Wisconsin) and to magazines like *Esquire*, composing cantos, writing letters to the *Morning Post* and advising one of its editors, Robert Hield, on English politics and foreign affairs, publicly and privately defending Italy and Fascism, and all the while offering advice to monetary reformers, editors of literary magazines and individual authors. When Christopher Hollis published his book on history and money, *The Two Nations*, Pound immediately informed his correspondents; but whether his method of informing them was the one best suited to his object is doubtful. 'Is the *Post* facing Hollis' *Two Nations*', he wrote to Robert Hield, 'or trying to sort out his one error?' Instead of explaining what he meant, he left it hanging in the air. To Hollis he wrote: 'I thought the book very lively. The only error right at the start, your talking about prices being stable when they were steadily declining as measured by metal. That I touched in my American Notes in *New English Weekly*.'

Nothing was too big for him to undertake: he wrote to John Cournos about the possibility of Communists adopting Douglas and set out to save the Catholic Church from its baser elements by drawing attention to its better side: 'The archbishop of Costanza, Mons. Pisani', he wrote to a priest in London, 'has just sent me a very beautiful book. The adjective may surprise some people who do not expect to find it applied to a treatise on economics; but Sac. L. P. Cairoli has treated *Il Giusto Prezzo nel Medio Aevo* with such lucidity of spirit that I, a pagan, find no other adjective for it.' He asked the priest's assistance in finding a Catholic publisher for it in London: 'I am, as per enclosed carbon, advocating an english edition for the propagation of the Faith among a great number of people who would never open a book ostensibly on religion.' Although the subject of the Just Price during the Middle Ages was a difficult one, about which a great deal had been written, Pound did not hesitate to single out this unknown book printed at the 'Pessina' printing works, Merato, in 1913.

No wonder, as he hammered away at his typewriter, he often discomforted those he was trying to help:

London, January 7, 1936

Dear E.P.,

Pending engaging a whole-time secretary to correspond with you, I suggest that you concentrate on the subject of taxation as a form of modern highway robbery combined with iniquitous interference with the freedom of the individual.

Yours ever,
C. H. Douglas

If much of what Pound was doing at this time is of little interest now, this is not true of his activity on behalf of the works of Vivaldi. Not only did he organize concerts and lectures in Rapallo but in 1936 he sent Olga Rudge to Turin to compile a catalogue of Vivaldi material in the National Library there. This was the beginning of a new wave of interest in the composer's work, leading to the large-scale studies and performances which Miss Rudge helped to organize several years later at the Accademia Musicale Chigiana in Siena.

Pound's part-in the revival may be seen as twofold. He played the leading part as organizer in the early stages, but more important in the long-run probably was his constant support and encouragement of Olga Rudge. To her he communicated his enthusiasm and helped her to overcome various obstacles, with the result that she carried out a difficult and arduous programme of research that was beyond Pound himself.

At the Vivaldi concerts held in Rapallo in 1936 and for the next few years, Pound lectured on the composer's work; he also wrote articles which were published in *Il Mare* and in England and the United States. Miss Rudge also wrote a number of articles for *Il Mare* and such periodicals as *The Delphian Quarterly*, *The Listener* and *Music and Letters*.

But even Vivaldi concerts were not free from economics and at one of his talks in April 1936 he drew attention to the gulf separating the Rapallo concerts from those held in the large cities – centres of usury, he called them, where avidity governed almost every manifestation of art. Pound and some of his friends shared in the national hysteria that accompanied the Italian campaign in Abyssinia and they began to dream of Rapallo as a centre of the new culture. In 1936 both Pound and Gerhart Münch published articles on this subject in *Il Mare*, with an eye to the possibility of official support for a centre of advanced studies at Rapallo. Pound also published his views on the proposed erection of a new building for the Fascists of Rapallo; such a building, he wrote in *Il Mare* of 2 May 1936, might house a library accessible to tourists and other outsiders, which would help them to understand 'the New Italy'.

In March 1936 Stanley Nott published Fenollosa's *The Chinese Written Character as a Medium for Poetry*, 'An Ars Poetica With Foreword and Notes by Ezra Pound'. After twenty years struggle, on and off, by Pound, this was its first separate publication in book-form. It included an appendix in which Pound ('a Very Ignorant Man', he said) commented on the meaning of certain Chinese characters. The Fenollosa was the first in a new 'Ideogramic Series' edited by Pound; the second was *Ta Hio, the Great Learning*, published in May 1936 – an English edition of Pound's translation brought out in 1928 by Glenn Hughes in Seattle; the third volume in the 'Ideogramic Series' was to have been a reprint of William Carlos Williams's *In the American Grain* (first published in 1925), but Stanley Nott went out of business before it could be printed. At Pound's urging it was brought out by New Direction in 1939.

Among Pound's many contributions to newspapers and periodicals in 1936 were two new cantos, nos. 45 and 46. Canto 45, published in the February issue of the English monetary reform journal, *Prosperity*, is a chant against usury:

> with usura, sin against nature,
> is thy bread ever more of stale rags
> is thy bread dry as paper,
> with no mountain wheat, no strong flour
> with usura the line grows thick
> with usura is no clear demarcation
> and no man can find site for his dwelling.
> Stone cutter is kept from his stone
> weaver is kept from his loom
> . . .
> Came not by usura Angelico; came not Ambrogio Praedis,
> Came no church of cut stone signed: *Adamo me fecit*.
> Not by usura St Trophime
> Not by usura Saint Hilaire,
> Usura rusteth the chisel
> It rusteth the craft and the craftsman
> It gnaweth the thread in the loom. . . .

Canto 46, first published in the March *New Democracy*, is a confused heaping together of personal observations and what Pound regarded as 'evidence' against the usurers; the pleasure to be derived from it does not repay the considerable research necessary to discover what it is about.

Throughout 1936 his correspondence continued without a pause: to Douglas on the need for clear terminology and a nucleus of well-read intellectuals within the Social Credit movement; to Herbert Read on the need to liven up the literary pages of *The New English Weekly*; to Hemingway in an attempt to stir his interest in Burton Hendrick's *Life and Letters of Walter Hines Page* (he could review it himself, he said, 'but nobody would print it', and besides, 'I do NOT reach the electorate'); to Alberto de Stefani about a conference on economics which Professor Camillo Pellizzi wanted Pound to attend; to Harold Nicholson on the British press: 'Can you get the idea that never has the human brain been so besotted with tons of print, every morning all that print to keep England's mind OFF the truth;' and to Hewlett Johnson, the 'Red Dean' hinting that the Church of Rome was doing more than the Anglican Church about 'the evils of usury'.

But not for a moment did he lose sight of America and the need for monetary knowledge in the schoolbooks. 'For a REAL text book', he wrote to Senator L. J. Frazier of Dakota, 'I should suggest starting with Woodward [*A New American History*] and letting the School Authorities, say two or three of your best men prepare a text on that plus the vital remarks of Jefferson, Jackson, Van Buren, Lincoln. And then submit the result to a committee, international, say Odon Por, Christopher Hollis and (to hell with modesty) me. To see that the essentials were there and that no nonsense had crept into the simplification.' A real book of that sort, he said, would then spread from Dakota to other parts of the United States and the next generation would not be as ignorant as the present one. 'This is a long war and only persistence will win it.'

In 1936 he drew up a new literary manifesto which he sent to Williams and others in the United States for their signature; so far as I know it was never issued. The 'Proem' read: 'In the intellectual climate of Ford Madox Ford's *English Review* and later of the Rebel Art Centre in Ormond Street (founded by Wyndham Lewis, and gathering Gaudier-Brzeska, Ed. Wadsworth, W. Roberts), forerun by Ernest Fenollosa; a renovation has been accomplished in part.'

MANIFESTO

The steps of the renovation of writing were (and of right should be)

1. the clamping of the word to the individual object (for the purpose of poetry).

2. the clamping of word to groups of objects; not necessarily of the same species, that is to say the ideogrammic method (for the purpose of poetry).

The third step essential to the health of prose and to the communication and life of all thought is the demarcation of generic terms.

We are faced and engulphed by a society and red-herring press which does not know and which refuses to distinguish a *tax* from a *share*. We are faced by a boiled stew of professional scribblers which refuses all healthful exercise in terminology, which soddenly ignores the whole discipline of dialectic as it existed vigorously from Scotus Erigena through Grosseteste and Albertus Magnus.

If our contemporaries are mentally paralyzed to the point of not seeing the difference between such obvious phenomena as Property and Capital, between Fruit and Corrosive, how in the name of earth and heaven are they to dissociate more delicate and complicated domains? How dissociate anything more complicated than a pig and an ashcan?

WE DEMAND a more trenchant orthography.

We also demand, concretely, a reform of the text books and a clean teaching of history.

We demand from the New Deal as much respect for the printing press as for mural decorations and orchestras. That is we demand that the same facilities be given verbal formulation as are now being given pictorial and musical formulation. We demand that a reasonable number of linotype machines be placed at the disposition of men capable of using them for something better than mere material gain and/or obfuscation of others.

WE ASSERT that the direction of the will is the dominant factor; and not the inertia of chaos.

In 1936 Pound contributed a number of articles on music to *The Listener,* having discovered a sympathetic young man on its staff who apparently shared some of his own views on that subject. Together they planned a series of attacks on the various kinds of music to which Pound objected, including Gregorian Chant, but the BBC made some alterations in its staff arrangements and the articles were never published, probably never written.

XVIII Politics and Economics 1937/1939

In February 1937 Pound entered into correspondence with Morley of Faber & Faber about a new prose book. It would be well, thought Morley and his colleagues, if instead of writing another short work like *ABC of Reading* Pound published his ideas on literature and culture at some length. Pound's first thought was to call the book *The New Learning*, but from the beginning Morley saw it more as a 'guide', and so it was given the title *Guide to Kulchur*. In a letter to Morley in February Pound described it as 'Wot Ez knows, all of it, fer 7 and sax pence'. He would, he explained, introduce certain contrasts between the Orient and the Occident and would also mention the racial elements in culture. He predicted that these aspects might not please Eliot (called 'Possum'): 'An how you gwine ter keep deh Possum in his feedbox when I brings in deh Chinas and blackmen?? He won't laak fer to see no Chinas and blackmen in a bukk about Kulchur.'

The name 'Possum', which Eliot had apparently given himself, belonged to a private game between the two men, into which Morley was sometimes admitted; the game was conducted in the language of Uncle Remus. For Christmas one year Eliot sent Pound a copy of C. P. Nettels's *The Money Supply of the American Colonies before 1720*, published by the University of Wisconsin in 1934. The book was inscribed:

> *Rabbit from Possum*
> *for Canto XCI*
> *Noel Noel!*

But not all was so light-hearted. The deplorable state of the world exerted on Pound a pressure to act which he found irresistible. But action was called for on so many fronts that he was all but swallowed by his own correspondence and became absorbed in a world of make-believe over which he ruled according to laws of his own devising. In a letter of 25 March 1937, written while he was working on *Guide to Kulchur*, he discussed theology. St Thomas Aquinas he described as an empty noise in a bungless barrel, propagator of a 'kind of NON-thought that one would expect of the class dunce'. St Augustine was a 'drunken African', by which he meant that he was drunk on Platonism. 'Might as well', he commented, 'try to anchor all thought to Marx or 1918 as to these dumb bunnies.' Two days later he wrote to Edwin Muir to thank him for a review of one of his monetary works. 'I wonder if it would clarify discussion if I could get a few more writers to understand that I believe in an economic truth, which several honest men and groups approach (I mean approach in understanding).' Douglas's diagnosis was good, he said, but Gesell also had seen a lot and so had the Canonists of the Middle Ages. To reinforce this last point he added, 'vide Cairoli, *Prezzo Giusto nel Medioaevo*'. It is not clear how Muir was to consult this rare book, unknown even in Italy, of which there was no translation available in English. It is as if he was not writing to inform Muir but to create a propaganda for his own work of saving Europe and America. 'One can't wait', he told Muir, 'for the stupidest men or stupidest milieu.'

In April he wrote to Fr F. H. Drinkwater about the possibility of an English edition of the Cairoli but nothing ever came of it. As Fr Drinkwater had written on money and Social Credit Pound turned to the question of enlivening *The New English Weekly*: 'You might revive the *New Eng. Weekly* if you could turn a hose on 'em without their suspecting I had suggested it.' On 10 July he wrote to Tinkham about economics and a monetary bill then before Congress; he also sent a small book, his own recent condensation of the *Analects* of Confucius. On 19 October he thanked Vincent Vickers for a copy of his pamphlet *Finance in the Melting Pot*. A director of Vickers Ltd for twenty-two years and of the Bank of England for nine years, Vickers had become a monetary reformer. Pound tried to arrange a meeting between him and Tinkham, at the Savoy in London, in an effort to draw the wealthy Tinkham into monetary reform. 'You might', he told Vickers, 'have a very great influence if you tackled him man to man. He represents an America that has only too greatly ceased to exist.' Both then and later Tinkham successfully eluded capture.

Another of Pound's correspondents was the Englishman Arnold Leese who was fanatically anti-Jewish and thoroughly deserved the sometimes loosely used label, 'anti-semite'. So suspicious was he, that when he saw the Gaudier portrait on Pound's writing-paper, he wondered if Pound had any Jewish blood. Pound assured him that he had none and sent him a list of his family's racial strains. Leese was interested in monetary reform as well as Jews and Pound attempted, without much success, to educate him in the former. Extreme even among extremists, Leese regarded Mussolini as a tool of the Jews and Sir Oswald Mosley as a 'Kosher Fascist'.

343

Although literature was still important to Pound, his list of priorities was very much his own and his opinion of a writer sometimes depended on whether that writer mentioned money or economics. It would sometimes appear that he maintained an interest in such figures as Homer, Dante and Shakespeare, and in some lesser men, by convincing himself that they were really poet-economists. In 1937 he considered writing a Life and Times of Max Beerbohm, if the amount of money offered was high enough, but generally he took the view that he should discuss only writers of importance. When Eliot asked him to write something on Robert Bridges for *The Criterion* he refused because Bridges was not worth his attention and a note by Pound on Bridges, he said, would be a falsification of values.

Among the literary magazines he assisted at this time were *Broletto*, published in Como, and Ronald Duncan's *Townsman* (London). To both he contributed items of his own and also gave editorial advice and helped to get contributions from others. He also got into correspondence with a Japanese poet, Kitasono Katue, editor of a literary magazine *Vou* in Tokyo. He was a great admirer of Pound's work and between 1936 and 1940 published translations of some of his poetry, an abridged translation of *ABC of Reading* and a translation of the essay 'Mediaevalism' from *Guido Cavalcanti Rime*, a copy of which Pound sent to Tokyo soon after he first heard from the Japanese poet.

Pound in his turn thought very highly of the *Vou* poets; he saw them as heirs of the Orient that had been opened up to him years before by Fenollosa, Michio Itow and Tami Koume, although in fact Kitasono Katue was a modernist who had no interest in Noh drama or the old Japan. Pound wrote an introduction to a group of *Vou* poems translated into English. He sent the poems and his introduction to the magazine *Globe* in Milwaukee, to which he contributed articles on politics and economics during 1937 and 1938. The *Vou* poets were so important, he told the *Globe*, that he regarded the poems as a news item rather than as a mere literary matter and he thought it would be an enormous loss to the magazine if it did not take this opportunity to be first in introducing them to the outside world. On the same day 11 March 1937, he told Katue that the poems were splendid and that they gave him his first clear idea of what was going on in the '*new* Japan'. It was Surrealism, he said, without 'the half-baked ignorance of the French young'. When the *Globe* refused the poems Pound sent them to Ronald Duncan who published them in the first issue of *Townsman* (January 1938), with Pound's introduction: 'All the moss and fuzz that for 20 years we have been trying to scrape off our language, these young men start without it. They see the crystal set, the chemical laboratory and the pine tree with untrammeled clearness. . . I know that nowhere in Europe is there any such vortex of poetic alertness. Tokio takes over, where Paris stopped.' The poems were not without thought, he warned, but the Japanese poet 'has gone from one peak of it to another faster than our slow wits permit us to follow before we have got used to his pace'. On 12 March 1937, the day after he wrote this introduction, Pound composed chapter twenty of *Guide to Kulchur* which includes a statement of poetics by Kitasono Katue and some comments on it by Pound. The statement was in reply to a question from Pound, who then used it to support his remark, at the beginning of chapter twenty, that 'A civilized man is one who will give a serious answer to a serious question.'

Another periodical to which Pound contributed at this time was *The Delphian Quarterly* in Chicago, edited by Mary W. Burd, recipient of numerous letters of advice from Pound on subjects ranging from music to Mussolini. 'In trying to understand me,' ran a typical letter, 'for god's sake don't try to mix Italy and Germany. They are not the same. . . My economic knowledge is independent of ANY political view.' Although she disapproved of Pound's political ideas she published a number of his articles on economics, music and education. At this stage of his career almost everything he wrote was about economics or at some point turned in that direction. In 'Reorganize Your Dead Universities', published in the April 1938 issue of *The Delphian Quarterly*, he discussed for a while the impact of photography on the study of old music and the literatures of Persia, Bengal and China; but eventually he got down to the real business of the article: 'Following Aristotle, Hume, Berkeley and Anthony Trollope my first step in any enquiry is now economic. I look to the cost and the profits. Your American periodicals are now full of peace advertisements, one before me says war costs 25,000 dollars per corpse. I want to know WHO gets the 25,000 dollars. That question seems to me to be elementary criminology.'

In June 1937 Nancy Cunard distributed from Paris her questionnaire on the Spanish Civil War, addressed to 'Writers and Poets of England, Scotland, Ireland and Wales'. The replies were published as a book, by the *Left Review*, London, in December, under the title *Authors Take Sides on the Spanish War*. Pound's reply appeared under the heading, 'Neutral?' In a letter to Nancy Cunard in June he explained why he did not think much of the questionnaire nor those who had signed it, such as Aragon, Auden, Spender and Pablo Neruda. 'Your gang are all diarrhoea', he told her. For fifteen years he had been telling people that the root of the trouble was money, but like Stalin they were too stupid to look. 'Personally I am against taking sides in a sham conflict.' Some months later he received a request for assistance from a pro-Franco organization called the Friends of National Spain, formed in London in 1937 to 'combat the flood of propaganda from Valencia and Moscow' and to place before the British public 'the real facts about the present disastrous conflict in Spain'. He again refused to take sides, pointing out to the society that its letter did not touch upon the all-important question of economics: in fact, 'Nicholas Butler himself could not have penned a more evasive document.' If the society dared not publish the economic truth about Spain, then it would publish no truth at all about Spain. And if it did not know the economic truth, then its pretence of diffusing facts was 'hollow and fraudulent'. From other letters he wrote at this time it would appear that he regarded the war as a 'sham conflict' because the real forces behind it were the international usurers and the manufacturers of armaments.

Pound's knowledge of Chinese had been increasing steadily since his English version of the *Ta Hio* published in 1928. With the aid of translations by others he had recently made a digest, in English, of the *Analects* of Confucius, which was published as a small book by Scheiwiller in June 1937, under the title *Confucius, Digest of the Analects*; Pound's part was not mentioned except in the colophon. He also included the digest as chapter one of *Guide to Kulchur*. In August and September 1937 he spent six weeks studying Confucius and Mencius. One of the first fruits was his long essay 'Mang Tsze (The Ethics of Mencius)' in *The Criterion* of July 1938, in which he explained what he had done: 'During August and the first half of September 1937, I isolated myself with the chinese text of the three books of Confucius, *Ta Hio*, *Analects* and *Unwavering Middle*, and that of Mencius, together with an enormously learned crib but no dictionary. You can't pack Morrison or Giles in a suitcase. When I disagreed with the crib or was puzzled by it I had only the look of the characters and the radicals to go on from. And my contention is that the learned have known too much and seen a little too little.' The essay contains, in addition to some translations from Mencius, a number of statements about economics, philosophy and religion. He was concerned mainly to advertise the sanity of the Confucian system as interpreted by Mencius and to attack the 'semitic component in Christianity'. The ethic of Confucius and Mencius, he said, was a Nordic ethic; Christianity on the other hand had been tainted by 'semitic insanity', 'semitic immoderation', and by Greek hair-splitting. In illustration of the fact that straightforward and honest men have arrived repeatedly at the same answers in ethics, he drew attention to a similarity between the 'nine fields system' of agriculture in ancient China and the system of *ammassi* (grain pools) in Italy under Rossoni – one of Mussolini's ministers with whom Pound had once discussed Gesell. It is clear from this essay that in his Confucianism he had found a confirmation of his earlier philosophical efforts, in which he had been influenced by the natural sciences of the nineteenth century; it is clear also that in some of his ideas he was close to the Nazi movement in Germany. He was in no sense a simple follower of Nazism but philosophically he was moving in the same direction and in some of his writings about paganism he began to call for a truly European religion unpolluted by semitic influences.

Two other books by Pound came out in 1937: *Polite Essays*, published by Faber on 11 February, and *The Fifth Decad of Cantos*, published by Faber on 3 June and by Farrar & Rinehart in New York on 29 November. Eliot helped Pound to select the contents of *Polite Essays* which contained a number of recent literary articles and a few earlier pieces including *How To Read*, his 1914 essay, 'Mr Hueffer and the Prose Tradition in Verse' and an extract from the chapter on Dante in *The Spirit of Romance*. Throughout these pieces, including several which introduce economics and politics, there is much that is true, much that needed saying and still needs saying; but unfortunately it is rendered almost useless by Pound's lack of attention to essential detail and his inability to reason closely from point to point.

In the other book were cantos 42 to 51, a group in which we see reflected the poet's desire to explain history and have thrust upon us the proof of his inability to do so; a group which contains all the elements of the undertaking as a whole: history and pseudo-history, passages well-written alongside passages ill-written, incoherence alongside just observation, banality and platitude interspersed with moments of quickness and lucidity, and lines here and there of great beauty which remind us of the gift he was neglecting in the pursuit of his obsessions.

Some of Pound's friends, including Joyce and Hemingway, maintained a certain reserve, as the only means of avoiding unpleasantness; for Pound was not content usually to let economics and politics rest, even where his friends made it clear that they had no wish to hear about Mussolini's housing programme or his draining of the marshes near Circeo.

One of those who had remained closer was Ford; in 1937 and 1938 he made an effort to help Pound by finding him a post at Olivet College in Michigan where he himself lectured for part of the year. In February 1937 he wrote to Pound from Paris:

In short, you are invited to stroll for eight months of a year – or several years – about the philosophers' groves of Olivet. I personally give a couple of lectures a week to classes because I like lecturing. You would not have to if you did not want to. You would be conferring obligation if you talked to any youth or youths you thought intelligent. There the duties would – or could – stop. The real point is that you would have complete leisure to write whilst

347

earning a living wage. They pay me slightly less than a living wage but would pay you more. They also pay boat fares from Europe and back.

If he went to Olivet he would have an orchestra at his disposal and also a good library and would have 'a working, model educational machine to play with'. Pound was happier, however, in the New Italy, where, as he told C. H. Douglas in November 1937, a writer by the name of Zappa had recently contributed to the newspaper *La Stampa* a series of articles on international finance. 'What other country', he asked, 'could have run 'em in a daily paper?' In March 1938 Ford was still trying to get a clear answer; from Paris he wrote: 'Dear God, Father Divine. . . I know that Your awful face must be veiled to the lesser mackerel nuzzling between Your toes in the ooze . . . But in this case it would be a convenience if Your Divinity would communicate directly to this l.m.' It may be, of course, that Ford was painting too rosy a picture of life at Olivet and that Pound knew this; but another difficulty seems to have been that Pound was not interested unless he could continue while at the college to preach Social Credit and Mussolini. A week later Ford wrote again from Paris: 'Do exercise a little imagination and try to understand the situation. I am an *extremely* sick man and your incomprehensible scrawls are a torture to me – to read and to have to answer. Get the waiter at your hotel to write your letters for you; he will at least write comprehensible dog-English. Your 1892 O. Henry stuff is wearisomely incomprehensible by now.' He was offering to give up his job at Olivet in Pound's favour 'because you have been making noises about universities for a long time and it would give you a chance really to do something. . . They have already a press at Olivet. They print a paper. They would no doubt do any necessary scholastic printing you needed. But they probably would not print Mussolini-Douglas propaganda for you. They might. But it would be up to you to persuade them. . . .' The college, he said, paid him $150 a month, roughly $1500 a year, and he made a further $1200 by lecturing in the neighbourhood. 'You will probably want more than that salary . . . and, anyhow, you should ask more on principle.' Pound would probably turn the college into a disastrous sort of hell, but it was his duty, Ford said, to tell him that the job was available and that the college authorities wanted him because they admired him as a poet and a teacher. 'Please again: If you want to ask any more questions get someone to put them into comprehensible English.'

On 6 May 1938 Pound wrote to the president of the college, Dr Joseph Brewer, that he would not be coming to Olivet for the winter; any idea that he might be, was due to the imagination of his dear friend Ford. He then offered this explanation of his position:

As to Italy, Douglas, etc., I am not engaged in propagating theories. I am trying to break down the mania for swallowing absolutely false news as facts.

An atmosphere wherein Aristotle, Hume, and St Ambrose are suppressed, for example. Where ignorance is maintained on principle etc., etc., is not conducive to efficient study of anything.

Fifteen thousand a year would be insufficient bribe, for example if it means suppressing the registered facts of chinese history from 1766 B.C. or denying the existence of Jefferson, Van Buren and J. Adams.

These are topics which I was permitted to lecture on in Milan at the Bocconi, and which were reported in the press at a time when they were supposed to be in complete opposition to the views of the government in Rome. I shouldn't care to surrender this kind of freedom to any board of trustees.

Certain facts are facts and certain lies are lies. This is different distinction from that between one theory and another, or between one policy and/or expediency and another.

One reason why Pound was not much interested in the post at Olivet was that he was no longer short of money, as he had been earlier; also he may have felt that the college was not important enough, and too far away from the main centres, to be of any real use to him in the important work he had before him. And there was another reason which contributed to keep him in Italy and that was his collaboration with the Hungarian-Italian economist Odon Por and his recent success in having monetary articles published in *Rassegna Monetaria*, a serious journal of monetary economics published in Rome. This was further proof of Fascist Italy's hospitality to living thought. Although he was still a follower of Douglas, and still making efforts to 'educate' the Social Crediters, he did not share Douglas's dislike of Fascism and began to support, with articles and advice, Sir Oswald Mosley's movement in England. His connection with the 'English Fascist Party' was proudly brought out in an article, 'Attività tigulliana all'estero', published in *Il Mare* of 18 December 1937; it was either written by Pound or at his instigation, as it contains, among other things, a continuation of his one-sided feud with George Bernard Shaw – the same which erupted at the time of the first publication of *Ulysses*.

Pound's first article for the Mosley movement, on Social Credit, was published in the *Fascist Quarterly* of October 1936; he continued to contribute after the movement changed its name to British Union and the magazine became, in January 1937, the *British Union Quarterly*. Between 1937 and 1940 he also published numerous articles in Mosley's newspaper *Action*. It is clear from Pound's letters and writings that he did not want the world to become Fascist, in the sense that he did not want it to adopt Fascist uniforms or other mere paraphernalia of

Fascist government; in the case of the United States, and, I think, of England he was in favour of democracy, but he believed that some Fascist ideas, which were above party politics and could be applied universally, were part of the future and he did not want to be left behind. Also, he indulged in wishful-thinking and believed that the Fascists would soon introduce some, at least, of the monetary reforms that were dear to his own heart. To what extent, exactly, he deluded himself on this point, I cannot say, but he continued to write and to act as if monetary reform was about to be put into effect in Italy and Germany at any moment. What may have helped to keep him in this state was the continuing propaganda in both countries against international finance.

It was this desire to move with history, and the thought that by moving with it he might be able to change it, that caused him to work with Mosley's party. He knew that it favoured a corporate state system like that in Italy and he could see that it was 'on the march', so he moved in step with it in the hope that it would carry into English public life some of his own ideas on money, culture and religion.

In March and April 1938 he helped A. Raven Thomson, a Mosley official, to revise his pamphlet *The Coming Corporate State*; about a month later Thomson edited and rearranged Pound's *What is money for?* to make it suitable for British Union readers, and it was published in April 1939 by Mosley's Greater Britain Publications. This tuppeny pamphlet, designed as 'A sane man's guide to Economics', contained Pound's threefold definition of money as: (1) a measure of value, (2) a means of exchange, and (3) a guarantee of future exchange. But economics led to politics and we see the difficulty in which he had landed himself by trying to choose, from above, the good points of various opposed systems: for the systems which had the most good, according to Pound's standards, based largely on monetary reform, were the Fascist and Nazi systems. Mussolini and Hitler did not talk, they acted; being essentially naive he smiled upon them as efficient and constructive: 'Usury is the cancer of the world', he wrote, 'which only the surgeon's knife of Fascism can cut out of the life of the nations.'

Pound did not see proofs of *What is money for?* and discovered after it was already out that the definition of money was not as tight as he would have liked and he later changed the first point to read 'measure of price'. He kept in touch with the Mosley party until 1940 but it is impossible to say whether he had any impact on it; what is certain is that owing to his strange and fragmentary style of letter-writing, which was not without a touch of humbug, there were moments of misunderstanding. During an exchange of letters on monetary reform the pace became too hot for his correspondent who in June 1938 wrote:

'What do you mean by "Ta Hio"? Is it a tax on money? If so, I think it need only be adopted in an emergency.'

Continuing with his cantos Pound had decided to include large sections from Chinese history, taken from Moyriac de Mailla's *Histoire Générale de la Chine, ou Annales de cet Empire* (Paris, 1777–85). As was his method generally in composing cantos, he copied extracts from de Mailla into his notebooks, translating and paraphrasing as he went, and later incorporated these into cantos 53 to 61. One evening in 1938, after he had copied out a passage from de Mailla dealing with the visit of a Tartar ruler to a Chinese emperor, Pound went to the cinema where he saw a newsreel on a visit of Hitler to Italy. It showed a group of Italian submarines which in honour of the German leader's visit dived and then surfaced simultaneously – a manoeuvre which Ubaldo degli Uberti told Pound was very dangerous. Pound entered this in his notebook, next to the passage on the Tartar's visit to the emperor. When he came to write canto 64 he placed a very abbreviated reference to the submarine manoeuvre alongside his account of the Tartar episode, because apparently he saw a similarity between the event in ancient China and Hitler's visit to Mussolini.

After the section on China he drafted ten cantos (62 to 71) on John Adams, lawyer, diplomat and second president of the United States. The material was taken from *The Works of John Adams* (Boston, 1852–65) and the ten cantos were in 'rough typescript' by February 1939.

When their daughter Mary was twelve Pound and Olga Rudge sent her to 'La Quiete', a school for young ladies in Florence. Pound wanted her to be a writer and began to train her for such a career and to procure her an audience. When at the age of twelve or thirteen she wrote an article, 'The Beauty of the Tirol', dealing with the Italian Tirol, where she had been brought up, Pound translated it from Italian into English and sent it to Kitasono Katue; he translated it from English into Japanese and in 1938 it was published in a Japanese magazine for girls called 'Girls' Circle'. One interesting memory which his daughter has from this period is of a train journey, after her summer holidays, when her father accompanied her from Venice back to the Tirol. There was a foreign priest sitting in the same compartment and having no European language in common he and her father conversed in Latin.

In 1938 Pound became a member of the National Institute of Art and Letters in the United States. Many of his letters during the next few years were to the Institute or its members, urging action to convert it into what he could regard as a live organization. Thus on 14 February 1938 he wrote to the secretary, Henry Seidel Canby:

A job, and I think the first job for a serious Institute is the publication in convenient form of the thought of John Adams, Jefferson and Van Buren.

That kind of thing is particularly the sort of thing an Institute could and should do.

Creative genius can not be made obligatory of members, but intellectual responsibility can, and in fact when it is not, the Inst. is a mere sham and fake, worthy of the mental state of an America who tolerated the era of Wilson/Coolidge and Hoover.

The disgusting torpidity of American Universities is a subject for Institute's attention.

Note again my demand for a bulletin, even if only four pages monthly wherein each member when so inclined shall have right to print 10 lines in parliamentary language.

Can these points be raised at March dinner?

He wrote in similar terms to such members of the Institute as Archibald MacLeish, Felix Schelling, Van Wyck Brooks and Claude G. Bowers. As author of *Jefferson and Hamilton* Bowers was one of the few modern historians in good odour with Pound, who often recommended the book as a true account of the struggle between Jefferson and Hamilton. When he received a reply from Bowers he was surprised to learn that he was United States ambassador to Spain. Bowers's letter was dated 10 May 1938, from San Jean de Luz in France; in it he referred to 'the atmosphere of incredible hate' in Spain, a phrase which Pound later worked into his cantos. In his reply of 13 May Pound wrote:

Muy Senor Mio: I hadn't the ghost of an idea you were a damnbassador. I begin to feel like old Scawen Blunt: 'all the boyes growin up to be bishops and viceroys.'

If the damn red knew any economics, or if they would attack the concession hunters who hang onto Franco. Anyhow I have to try to keep my head, and I don't think Europe ever intended Russia to hold Barcelona. I do think the red volunteers have ALL been had, quite definitely to keep the gun market going.

Took 18 months to get a quotation from Jefferson into North American Review, I suppose the monetary light was too bright.[1]

The Institute could and should use its powers to awaken American universities, especially in introducing valid work, both mislaid and contemporary into their curricula. It could also stimulate reprint of basic American writings, notably those on which our republic is founded (note the statesmanlike pomp of phrase, probably necessary to move the Canbys).

Lenin, Trotsk, Marx, Stalin, editions of 100,000 at 10 and 25 cents. Jefferson, Van Buren, J. Adams unobtainable, or at 15 dollars.

After the fall of Barcelona, mebbe a few of us could start sacking the palace of the Insteroot, and putting in a few dynamos. I wonder who holds the purse, and pays the rent and where it comes from.

On 4 June Pound replied to a letter from Van Wyck Brooks about the internal organization of the Institute and the contents of its library:

Dear Van W. B.: Yours of 25th May. Our first need if we are to act as a body, is inter-communication. There is a paid secretary, under Canby. Whoever holds the post should be capable of sending out a few pages of mimeographed report, quarterly or monthly. Every member to have a right to ten lines in such reports. Naturally most members will not, at the start avail themselves of this privilege.

We are supposed to be the elite. If the library doesn't contain our books what does it contain?

The mimeograph bulletin should contain current information re *our* publications. At present there is no life in America because whenever a serious essay appears it is hidden in some mag. with a circ. of 400.

Among the many other letters he wrote during 1938 were several to the Italian poet Carlo Izzo about his translation of canto 45, a series to Laurence Binyon containing long and detailed comments on the proofs of Binyon's English translation of Dante's *Purgatorio*, a letter to his old teacher Dr Shepard urging him to use Binyon's translation of Dante in place of the Temple Classics edition for introducing students to the *Divina Commedia*, advice to Ronald Duncan about *Townsman* and about Duncan's own poetry and drama, and a note to Kitasono Katue in which he speaks of his admiration for Max Ernst.

Although Pound had been friendly with Binyon during his first year or two in London he did not begin to correspond with him until 1934 when he wrote to congratulate the English poet on his translation of the *Inferno*. Binyon was at Harvard at the time, lecturing on Oriental Art. Pound reviewed the translation enthusiastically and urged Binyon to go on with the rest of the *Commedia*. Binyon sent him the proofs of the *Purgatorio* and on 27 September 1938 wrote that the book was at last out. Pound published two reviews immediately: one in the *New English Weekly* of 29 September and the other in Italian in the October *Broletto*.

In the autumn of 1938 Pound received from John Crowe Ransom an announcement about his proposed new magazine, *The Kenyon Review*. In his reply of 15 October Pound welcomed the newcomer, but with caution, suggesting that he had better see the first issue before 'looking into my owne heart and typing'. In respect of the announcement that the review would publish 'complete essays', Pound questioned whether it would be a good thing to constrain an author to always produce a 'complete essay' when that author had already published a good deal of serious work. A writer, like a physicist, should be allowed, he thought, to publish brief addenda to his already existing work. I do not know if Pound sent any contributions to the magazine but none of his work was published there.

The only book by Pound that came out in 1938 was *Guide to Kulchur*. Copies were bound, ready for publication in June, when Faber & Faber decided that some passages were possibly libellous. At least fifteen offending pages were excised and new ones printed and pasted in; new sets of pages were also printed for copies of the book not yet bound. Here are some of the changes. On page 93, Gilbert Murray ceased to be 'unspeakable' and appeared simply as 'the Genevan pacifist', Pound admiring neither his translations from the Greek ('upholstered and straw-filled') nor his views in favour of the League of Nations. On page 131, one of President Roosevelt's economic experts was transformed from a 'shark' into a 'dogfish' and the words in italics removed from the following sentence: 'As an example of this time-spirit in this latter vein, one of Roosevelt's gang, now happily ex-, in a slimily flattering preface drew F.D.'s notice to F.D.'s greatness and then slithered from a discussion of dollars into one of pure numbers, as if *no cheating or substitution had occurred*.' Instead of these words three dots were inserted: 'from a discussion of dollars into one of pure numbers, as if . . .' On the same page, with reference to another economist, unnamed, the word 'mendacity' was deleted and also the sentence, 'This kind of thing is hired'. On page 158, in commenting on Spanish civilization, he wrote: 'A few chaps in Madrid read Rémy de Gourmont. These litterati were neither numerous enough, vigorous enough nor sufficiently "all round" men to "save Spain". Among the signal shirkers I think we may list Sr. Madariaga.' This reference to Salvador de Madariaga, inserted because Madariaga, after a brief correspondence some years earlier, had been unwilling to support Pound's programme of reform, was omitted from the published version.

On page 190, 'the gang of punks, pimps and cheap dudes now ruling England' was trimmed to read 'the gang now ruling England'. On page 195, in an outburst against the Church of England, he mentioned a letter sent to him by 'a colonial parson' – most likely a man in Queensland, Australia, who wrote to him about monetary reform. The letter, according to Pound, described Cosmo Lang, Archbishop of Canterbury, as 'probably the wickedest man who ever sat in the seat of St Augustine'. This statement was replaced by another which said: 'a colonial parson (who can't be unique in his convictions) writes me privately in such a manner that I can't print what he says without danger of libel.'

The book was finally published on 21 July; it was dedicated 'To Louis Zukofsky and Basil Bunting strugglers in the desert'. On 11 November James Laughlin issued it in America under the title

Culture, using sheets imported from England. Although it contained many fine insights and flashes of humour, the book was typical of Pound at this period, in that the material was not sifted and sorted and drawn together into a reasoned discourse. In place of the consistency which we naturally look for, in a book of this kind, he introduced once again his 'ideogramic method'. In practice this meant that a chapter could be about anything he chose, that it could start or end anywhere, and that any subject could be placed, without explanation, beside any other.

Much of *Guide to Kulchur* was put together while he wrote, according to what material was at hand. Pound might say that this was the whole point of his Confucian philosophy and 'ideogramic method', that they enabled him to draw together whatever came under the heading of culture; but in the light of reason the method disappears and we are left with a brilliant slipshod display of uncoordinated items of varying quality. Chapter 48, for example, was composed by putting together (1) a brief note on Doughty's *Arabia Deserta* about the disadvantages of 'life in the open' even when compared with 'the hell of mercantilist industrialism', (2) a quotation about bankers from Wu Yung's *The Flight of an Empress* followed by some sketchy observations arising out of the book's other contents, (3) quotations on usury from Appian and Cicero and (4) a few comments on monetary ignorance, credit and a growing awareness of monetary economics among the young. *The Flight of an Empress* ('Told by Wu Yung') was published by Faber in February 1937 while Pound was writing his *Guide*. In reading it he placed a pencil mark against a passage on page 283 dealing with the strategy of Chinese bankers in getting a hold on provincial governors; he copied this passage into chapter 48 of his book and then commented very briefly on a few other items from Wu Yung. Next he copied out two long quotations on usury, from Appian and Cicero, which had arrived in the post that same day from a student in England. These excerpts, he said, showed that young men were getting back to a sane state of curiosity and were reading the classics in search of 'living material': 'Given enough of this it shd. within a few decades be impossible for us to have secretaries of the Treasury and infamous Chancellors of Exchequers who dare not and/or cannot define money, credit, or property.' He closed the chapter with criticism of Roosevelt, a statement that 'Communism with its dictatorship of the proletariat is merely barbarous and Hebrew', and a definition of credit. Numerous other chapters were put together in the same way; the result was a book which failed to be either a guide to culture or an intelligible account of the poet's beliefs and ideas.

Pound's mother-in-law, Olivia Shakespear, a widow for some years, died in London in October 1938. Some weeks later Pound went to London, on behalf of his wife, to settle matters connected with the estate and to see Omar. He entertained freely and held dinner-parties for Eliot, Lewis and other friends. He wanted badly to see a Noh play performed in a theatre and to this end Ronald Duncan persuaded Ashley Dukes to lend them the Mercury Theatre. Benjamin Britten produced a musician who could play gongs and another of Duncan's friends, Henry Boys, suggested a female dancer by the name of Suria Magito. One afternoon, with Duncan as audience, Pound recited one of his own Noh translations while the girl danced.

Pound made a number of visits to Kensington Garden Studios, 29 Notting Hill Gate, where Lewis painted his portrait in oils. He returned to Rapallo early in December; on 17 December Lewis wrote that he would send photographs of the painting as soon as it was finished. It had, he said, already aroused 'a quite unusual amount of approval' and he himself thought it was '*very* good'. However, an artistic problem remained to be solved before he could complete it – and he made a small sketch for Pound showing the space to be filled and then another giving a possible solution. In his reply towards the end of December Pound advised Lewis to leave the portrait as it was: 'Ef you must diddle an MONKEY with problumbs you take a GNU canvasss or paper and you do a ABstrakk dEEsign, but don't do piddlin round like Velasquez/ three hosses hooves whaar one orter be/and messin up the paint in that thaaar north west corner.' The portrait now hangs in the Tate Gallery and is one of Lewis's best-known works.

Still as generous as ever, Pound helped Lewis by buying drawings. In his letter of 17 December Lewis thanked him for 'the welcome fiver' and said that for the £20 he had 'now so generously disbursed' he could have either early or recent drawings.

By December 1938 Pound had decided to visit the United States the following year. With Europe drifting towards war he wanted to play his part in keeping the peace between Italy and the United States and also thought it was time that he went personally to see American leaders, to point out to them the road to economic sanity and if necessary to accept an advisory post and to spend some months at least each year in his own country.

Although he was an enthusiastic supporter of Mussolini and Fascism, and, to a lesser extent, of Hitler, Pound was quite clearly in favour of traditional democracy in the United States, even if he did insist upon statements or beliefs of some of the American founding fathers to the point where he became unorthodox. If he wanted to see established in America one or two Fascist ideas it was only to make the traditional system work more efficiently. Thus, when he urged representation in

Congress according to trades and professions, rather than representation according to geographic area, he was not, I think, urging this because it was to be found in Fascism but as a means of carrying out better the original democratic ideas of Jefferson and Adams.

In 1938, a young man in Boston, William Fitzgerald, began a series called 'Reactionary Pamphlets'. The first, by Fitzgerald himself, was called *Art and Interference* and was published in Boston that same year. It began in satirical vein: 'Wanted at once – a "national" culture in good condition for purposes of protection against subversions of marxist internationalists, Jews and such', and then went on to speak of a re-estimation of society in the light of an older, fresher America. When Fitzgerald invited Pound to contribute to the series he immediately produced a piece called 'National Culture: A Manifesto'.

In it he argued that since the American Civil War when the usurocracy had come to power it had been necessary for individual Americans 'to emigrate in order to conserve such fragments of American culture as had survived'. Obviously he counted himself as one of the chief among these. The essay was severe with contemporary America, both its art and politics, but underneath there was pride in his American heritage. He was against the United States simply following Europe in matters of art and culture or praising bad work because it was produced at home; he wanted an America that was content with nothing but the best and he wanted it to be based upon the 'civic order' that existed at the time of Jackson and Van Buren and upon the monetary section of the constitution: 'I mean to say there is one point in the constitution which has not been tried and which the infamies infesting the White House for the past decades do not and dare not try: namely the right of congress to determine the value of money.' He made it clear also that he did not believe in 'equality' in the modern sense: 'There is no more equality between men than between animals. Jefferson never thought that there was.' The equality Pound believed in was 'Equality before the law courts, equality in the sense of there being no insurmountable obstacles imposed by arbitrary classification and arbitrary limits of categories. Liberty: to do that which harms not another.'

'Reactionary Pamphlets' went out of business before Pound's essay could be published and it remained in typescript until it was included in the collection *Impact* in 1960; but together with some of his other writings and letters it shows that it was in the spirit of an American who wanted to reform the United States in accordance with what he believed were Jeffersonian principles that Pound prepared to return home in 1939.

Letters continued to flow, meanwhile, from Rapallo, offering advice, encouragement and criticism. 'Keep at it', he wrote on 13 January 1939 to Senator Borah, an important American spokesman on international affairs who wanted to keep the United States out of European quarrels. He disliked war, he told the senator, but if it was going to be, then the practical move was to keep it out of Europe – and in this letter and in many others he wrote at this time he used the slogan, 'no more war west of the Vistula', by which he meant that the main European powers, Italy, England and France, and also perhaps the United States, should take common action to divert Germany's warlike instincts in the direction of Russia.

On 26 June 1938 he had told J. Leo Coupe of Hamilton College that Dr Hjalmar Schacht, head of the German banking system under Hitler, had recently 'emitted a truth far more "liberal" than any republican sec. of treasury would have emitted since the assassination of Lincoln'. Five months later he had changed his mind about the German banker. 'Your friend Schacht,' he wrote to Tinkham on 10 December 1938, 'after having come clean with an honest definition of money, has now flopped.' In speaking of Schacht's 'having come clean' he may have been thinking of a statement in 1937 in which the banker referred to economics in terms of 'Goods that are needed' – a quotation which Pound copied into canto 52:

'Goods that are needed' said Schacht (anno sedici)
commerciabili beni deliverable things that are wanted.

When on 13 January 1939 he wrote to Tinkham about his trip to England he said: 'Bloke who had been in their secret service, with reference to the "City" said he could buy any of the big politicians, except Chamberlain. He also had the dope on all the communist leaders, some of the lower men honest, but the rest definitely paid by Russia for military espionage.' As for the American constitution, it was, he told Tinkham, an 'admirable document betrayed by every damned administration since Andy Johnson'. He thought Tinkham would make a good president and wrote accordingly to the *Boston Herald*; the letter was published on 7 February: 'Can't you people do anything better with Uncle George Tinkham than to send him back into Congress? I mean, it's all right for the next year or so, but in 1940 an exclusive mansion in Washington will have need (and how!!) of a new tenant . . . no other eastern Republican would pull ten votes west of the Mississippi and it is time we had something AUTHENTIC in the White House.'

Also in February Pound replied to some enquiries from the American poet and critic Hubert Creekmore about the obscurity and form of his cantos. There was no intentional obscurity, he told Creekmore, but there was 'condensation to maximum attainable'. He also explained that it was impossible to make 'the deep' as quickly comprehensible as the shallow. 'As to the *form* of *The Cantos*: All I can say or pray is: *wait* till it's there. I mean wait till I get 'em written and then if it don't show, I will start exegesis.' He did not, he said, have an 'Aquinas-map' to guide him: 'Aquinas *not* valid now.'

On another occasion, writing to the American poet Delmore Schwartz, he pardoned the lack of structure in the work by saying that after all the *Divina Commedia* had practically no narrative or plot and was merely 'a walk upstairs'. Schwartz, an admirer at the time of much of Pound's work, refused to accept this. The literal fact was, he said, that Dante's poem was about a man lost in a dark wood where he met various animals and then a great poet's ghost. Schwartz went on to explain how the story expressed Dante's ideas, and how, for example, the exaltation towards the end of the *Purgatorio* was from the very nature of the story – the fact that Dante was about to meet Beatrice.

In his hurry to reduce everything in the world of knowledge to a few pungent phrases Pound compiled in 1938 an *Introductory Text Book* for the study of American history. It consisted of four chapters which I give in full:

CHAPTER I

'All the perplexities, confusion, and distress in America arise, not from defects in their constitution or confederation, not from want of honour and virtue, so much as from downright ignorance of the nature of coin, credit, and circulation.' *John Adams*.

CHAPTER II

'. . . and if the national bills issued, be bottomed (as is indispensable) on pledges of specific taxes for their redemption within certain and moderate epochs, and be of *proper denomination* for *circulation*, no interest on them would be necessary or just, because they would answer to every one of the purposes of the metallic money withdrawn and replaced by them.' *Thomas Jefferson* (1816, *letter to Crawford*).

CHAPTER III

'. . . and gave to the people of this Republic THE GREATEST BLESSING THEY EVER HAD – THEIR OWN PAPER TO PAY THEIR OWN DEBTS.' *Abraham Lincoln*.

CHAPTER IV

'The Congress shall have power; To coin money, regulate the value thereof and of foreign coin and to fix the standards of weights and measures.' Constitution of the United States, Article I Legislative Department, Section 8, page 5. Done in the Convention by the unanimous consent of the States, 7th September, 1787, and of the Independence of the United States the twelfth. In witness whereof we have hereunto subscribed our names.

George Washington.
President and Deputy
from Virginia.

There followed a brief note in which Pound explained that Douglas's proposals were 'a sub-head' under the main idea in Lincoln's sentence and that Gesell's plan was a 'special case' under Jefferson's general law. He also recommended a number of books by Douglas, Gesell, Butchart and others.

Altogether the *Introductory Text Book* occupied three small pages of a leaflet that was privately printed for the author by Bonner & Company of London in 1939. Pound had received copies by March when he began to enclose them with letters. An Italian translation was published in *Il Mare* of 8 April, preceded by a signed note in which Pound said that attacks on Fascist Italy were based not only on falsehood but on fetid ignorance of the history of the United States and of the principles of its founders.

On 13 April 1939 Pound sailed from Genoa aboard the Italian liner *Rex*, on which he occupied a first-class suite, and arrived in New York on 21 April. He said in a newspaper interview twenty years later that he had booked to travel second-class but had been given the suite for $160 because the ship was empty. He had taken, he said, only one suitcase and a rucksack and had not needed porters; he had spent only $5 over and above his fare.

It was his first trip home since 1911. It seems that the critic Gorham Munson, an expert on Social Credit with whom Pound had been associated for some years, sent a cable to the ship advising him to give economic but not political views to the press; but when New York reporters came on board he lay back in a chair with legs outstretched and spoke on politics as well as economics and literature. 'Nothing but devilment', he was reported as having said, 'can start a new war west of the Vistula. I'm not making any accusation against anyone. But the bankers and the munitions interests, whoever and wherever they may be, are more responsible for the present talk of war than are the intentions of Mussolini or anyone else.' He said that Mussolini had a mind with the 'quickest uptake' of any man he knew of except Picabia – adding that 'Picabia is the man who ties the knots in Picasso's tail'. This referred to the fact that in Paris in 1921 or 1922 Picabia, who was known for his wit, picked up a sheet of paper one day when Pound was visiting him and quickly drew a few lines; he showed it to Pound with a remark to the effect that this was Picasso's latest style.

Pound told the reporters that he regarded the literature of 'social significance' as 'pseudo pink blah'. The men who were worth anything today were 'writing about money, the problem of money, exchange, gold and silver'. He indicated that he did not think much of Joyce's later work which was retrogressive; Hemingway was 'a good guy' but owing to his stand on Spain he did not think he wanted to meet him personally at the moment. The one poet he cared to name was Cummings.

Immediately on leaving the ship he went to Cummings's flat in Patchin Place. While in New York he stayed with John Slocum to whom he had been introduced by James Laughlin in Austria four years earlier. Before the end of April he went to Washington and remained there for about a fortnight discussing monetary reform and politics with senators, congressmen and government officials. Introduced by Paul de Kruif, whose books he had reviewed a few years earlier, Pound met the Secretary of Agriculture, Henry A. Wallace, to whom he pointed out the virtues of a smoothly functioning money and credit system based upon the nation's productive capacity and under some form of national control. Others with whom he discussed monetary reform included Senators Byrd and Bankhead and Congressman J. Voorhis, a monetary reformer who the previous year had used in a speech in the House the quotation from John Adams which Pound later used as chapter one of *Introductory Text Book*. Pound believed that the nation would benefit if Congress were broadcast and he asked Voorhis to bring this forward in the House as soon as possible. With Senator Burton Wheeler, later a leader of the movement to keep America out of the war, he discussed President Roosevelt; he later quoted Wheeler as saying that Roosevelt had packed the Supreme Court with justices who would declare constitutional anything that he did. This conversation is referred to also in canto 100:

> 'Has packed the Supreme Court
>> so they will declare anything he does constitutional.'
>>> Senator Wheeler, 1939.

When he saw Senator Borah he apparently discussed his desire to serve in some official capacity; he later quoted Borah as replying: 'I am sure I don't know what a man like you would find to do here.' Pound took this as a comment on the sad state of the country and a few years later he used it in canto 84, together with a snatch of Bankhead's conversation on Roosevelt:

> 'an' doan you think he chop an' change all the time
> stubborn az a mule, sah, stubborn as a MULE,
> got th' eastern idea about money'
>> Thus Senator Bankhead
> 'am sure I don't know what a man like you
>> would find to *do* here'
>>> said Senator Borah
> Thus the solons, in Washington,
>> on the executive, and on the country, a.d. 1939

While in Washington he took his *Introductory Text Book* to the Library of Congress, to find out whether any other students of American history had been able to bring together in this way four famous presidents – Washington, Adams, Jefferson and Lincoln. Five years later he gave this account of his visit in a pamphlet written in Italian:

One day, thinking of the trouble it had cost me to unearth these four 'chapters', I asked the head of the American history department of the Library of Congress if there existed a history of America, whether in one volume or in ten, that contained these four chapters or the substance of them.

After reflecting for a while he replied that so far as he knew I was the first to have brought together and in relation to each other the four great names of the greatest presidents of the Republic.

He also visited the head of the Japanese department of the Library, Dr Shio Sakanishi, who arranged for him to see a film of the Noh play *Aoi No Uye*; he was greatly impressed by 'the sound of the singing and the crescendo of excitement as the hero rubs his rosary with ever faster rattling of beads against beads'. Dr Sakanishi caused him 'a good deal of anguish' when he insisted that something which Pound had found in one of Fenollosa's translations of the Noh plays was not in the original.

In March Pound had written to William Cowley, the president of Hamilton College, with suggestions about the teaching of economics and history; he had enclosed a copy of his *Introductory Text Book*. From Washington he wrote again in April asking why he had not been told whether these matters were being covered at Hamilton. I do not know what the president said in reply to this advice but by early May, while he was still in Washington, Pound had entered into discussions with Cowley about taking an honorary doctorate at the college in June.

Ford Madox Ford, who was living in a small and ill-furnished flat at no. 10 Fifth Avenue, wrote to Allen Tate on 3 May: 'Carlos Williams saw Ezra by accident in Washington the other day. He says the author of the Cantos seems very mild and depressed and fearful. That is all I know about him. He has made no sign to me.' Pound was depressed because he was not having the success in Washington that he thought he might have, either with regard to monetary reform or in finding an advisory position through which he might place his knowledge of Europe, history and economics at the service of his country. The ideas he had for the building of a better America seemed to be falling on deaf ears or to be doomed to suffer transformation in the machinery of political compromise, machinery now thoroughly suspect owing to Roosevelt's disregard for the constitution. Although disappointed he does not seem to have lost faith in the American system, not entirely at any rate, for he continued to believe that the nation could be saved from the degradation into which it was falling by a new application, in line with modern conditions, of the political wisdom and principles of Adams, Jefferson and the constitution. At the same time he tended to fix blame for the nation's ills on Roosevelt and the sinister figures at work behind him. This might not have done any great harm to Pound had he kept it within the realm of politics or the speculative sciences which bear upon it; but transformed within a mind now bent on reducing everything to a gist or a few sentences, Roosevelt and the bankers who supported him were no longer considered as men but as a virus to be eliminated so that the national bloodstream might be healthy again.

He continued to worry about the possibility of war in Europe and one day in May he had lunch with the Polish ambassador, Count Patocki, warning him against Winston Churchill whom he considered dangerous. 'God help you', he told the ambassador, 'if you trust England.'

While he was in Washington or soon after he left, Pound wrote an article for the *Capitol Daily* which was published in the issue of 9 May. It appeared on the front page under the heading, 'Ezra Pound on Gold, War, and National Money'.

When he returned to New York early in May he began to call regularly on such friends as Ford and Tibor Serly and to visit the Museum of Modern Art where Iris Barry was curator of the film library. He saw his old friend Katherine Heyman and met Zukofsky again; he met Marianne Moore for the first time, although they had corresponded on and off for twenty years; he had lunch one day with Mencken. When he saw that Gorham Munson's flat at 66 Fifth Avenue included a huge studio he began to wonder whether it might not be possible to hold evenings there devoted to the arts. Although they never took place it is clear that he was still hoping to stir up new life in the arts in New York – with the intention I suspect of spending some of his time each year in that city if only he could make it habitable. At all times he seems to have dressed casually, his shirt open at the neck.

With copies of *Introductory Text Book* and *What is Money For?* he visited Fordham University, in the Bronx. There he discussed the Church's attitude to economics with two Jesuits, Fr Moorhouse Millar and a Fr Murphy. Father Millar read through *What Is Money For?* and according to Pound, in a letter the following year, 'was good enough to express interest and to catch a couple of slips', these slips due to the fact that he had not seen the proofs. In another letter he described Fr Millar as 'one of the serious characters I saw in U.S.'.

From New York he went to Cambridge, Massachusetts, where he stayed with the poet Theodore Spencer, an Assistant Professor of

English at Harvard. As well as defeating Spencer at tennis Pound had a talk with the head of the Economics Department and acceded to a request from the English Department to read from his own work in a lecture-room in Sever Hall. For Professor Frederick Packard of the Department of Speech he recorded on 17 May for the Harvard Vocarium Series the following poems: 'Sestina: Altaforte' and 'The Seafarer' (during which he accompanied himself on two kettle-drums), part six of *Homage to Sextus Propertius*, 'Cantico del sole', sections from *Hugh Selwyn Mauberley* and cantos 17, 30, 45 and 58. Among those he met at Cambridge was Archibald MacLeish, now Librarian of Congress, who contributed an article on Pound to the June issue of the *Atlantic Monthly*.

Another visit he made was to New Haven, Connecticut, to see James Angleton who published the *Introductory Text Book* in the first issue of his magazine *Furioso* (Summer 1939). He also visited a correspondent who lived in Greenwich, Connecticut, and wrote an article, 'The Cabinet of a Dream, and Congress Should Go on the Air', which was published in the issue of 13 July of the newspaper *Greenwich Time*. On another occasion he visited Williams at his home in Rutherford, New Jersey, and stayed the night. At Robert's restaurant, East 55th Street, New York, where Mencken had taken him for lunch, he was host to Cummings and his wife, who at Pound's request brought along Max Eastman and his wife. According to Charles Norman, Eastman described Pound as 'attractively curly-headed, almost roly-poly, and with lots of laughter in the corners of his eyes'. When inevitably the subject of Italian Fascism was brought up Eastman suggested that as a non-Italian Pound probably escaped the regimentation which was the essence of the system, adding that he did not think Pound would greatly enjoy being regimented himself. To which, says Norman, Pound made the following reply: 'Fascism only regiments those who can't do anything without it. If a man knows how to do anything, it's the essence of Fascism to leave him alone.'

About 9 June he went to Clinton, in Upper New York State, to receive his honorary doctorate from Hamilton. Whatever feelings there may have been about some of his political utterances, the college was obviously glad to welcome such a famous son; he had kept in touch with Ibbotson and others, and in its March issue the *Hamilton Alumni Review* had printed an unsigned review of *Guide to Kulchur* which said that like all his writings the book was 'intensely personal': 'He is infuriated by cowardice, by cringing, by mental corruption. His book is an irritant, stinging the reader into consciousness of abuses hidden by custom, by convention, abuses which are part of the folklore or current ideology, never tested.'

Pound stayed at the home of Edward Root who had been a fellow-student at the college and was now a teacher. When interviewed by the *Utica Observer-Dispatch* Pound put in a word for Tinkham as a possible Republican candidate for the presidency the following year and spoke 'fiercely' about England. When he discovered that a fellow-guest, Charles A. Miller, was a banker who had served under Roosevelt, he talked to him at length about Douglas and monetary reform. He played a good deal of tennis on the college courts; one of his partners was Olivia Saunders, the daughter of Professor A. P. Saunders who in Pound's time had been Dean of the college. She wrote later to Charles Norman:

I have a vivid recollection of playing one or two doubles matches in Clinton with him because he was the most individualistic partner I ever played with. When we were receiving I was instructed to stand in the middle of the baseline and take any balls which might get by him. He placed himself in the middle of the court at net and was such an agile and fiery tennis player that few balls got back to me. When he served he did the same thing, served, got to the net midcourt and returned almost every ball, I again standing on the baseline in the middle of the court.

Pound and Miss Saunders 'won easily'.

On 12 June Pound attended the Hamilton commencement exercises in the same chapel where thirty-four years earlier he had received his Ph.B. On this second occasion he was awarded the honorary degree of Doctor of Letters for having led 'a full life of significance in the arts'. Also awarded an honorary degree was the journalist H. V. Kaltenborn who was the main speaker at the alumni luncheon in the Commons afterwards. While discussing the differences between democracy and dictatorships he spoke of the 'doubtful' alliance between Germany and Italy, whereupon Pound asked loudly what he meant by 'doubtful'. Pound was not satisfied with Kaltenborn's explanation and in the heat of the exchange began to praise Mussolini; Professor Saunders, who was sitting next to Pound, tried to calm him, but the wrangle developed, said witnesses, into an uproar and President Cowley intervened firmly to restore order. After Kaltenborn had finished, Pound described, according to the *Utica Daily Press*, the difficulty he had experienced in obtaining the writings of John Adams – it had taken him, he said, seven years – whereas the works of Marx and Trotsky were readily available in selections costing ten to twenty-five cents. 'It is my conviction that you ought to be able to purchase the thoughts and writings of America's founders as easily and cheaply as you can those of subversive propagandists.' In closing he recommended his *Introductory Text Book* as required reading.

It was a sad and disappointed man who left Hamilton for New York and who a few days later went to the pier to board the *Conte di Savoia* for the trip back to Genoa, leaving behind him hopes and plans for America and himself which two months earlier had quickened the outward journey.

On shipboard (I do not know whether it was going, or on the way home) Pound heard for the first time the name Wiseman – a name which was to colour much of his thinking during the next few years. It was at table, and a diplomat present mentioned that Wiseman, a banker, was a man of some importance behind the scenes in the United States. Pound was intrigued that he had never heard of the man and soon afterwards wrote to a friend in England asking him to find out some details of his life. It turned out that Wiseman was an Englishman who had been head of British Intelligence in the Western hemisphere; more recently he had joined the New York banking firm of Kuhn, Loeb & Company, one of the giants of 'international finance'. Here then was evidence, according to Pound's way of thinking, of a sinister link between the highest powers in England and the usurers in New York and it was obvious too that Wiseman was in some way connected with the effort to bring in America on the side of England, in the struggle against Germany.

On 29 June Ford died at Deauville in France and Pound wrote an article which was published in the August issue of the London magazine *Nineteenth Century and After*. To Lewis he wrote on 3 August: 'I have buried pore ole Fordie in (of all places) *The XIXth Century and After*. Only hole left. And an inadequate oration as they had room for "under 1500" and by the day after the day, etc. An I think you make a beau geste and putt a penny on the ole man's other eye. No one else will.' Pound's article was called 'Ford Madox (Hueffer) Ford; Obit' and was aimed at showing his own debt to Ford, as well as Ford's special contribution to modern writing:

I have put it down as personal debt to my forerunners that I have had five, and only five, useful criticisms of my writings in my lifetime, one from Yeats, one from Bridges, one from Thomas Hardy, a recent one from a Roman Archbishop and one from Ford, and that last the most vital, or at any rate on par with Hardy's.

. . .

And he felt the errors of contemporary style to the point of rolling (physically, and if you look at it as mere superficial snob, ridiculously) on the floor of his temporary quarters in Giessen when my third volume displayed me trapped, fly-papered, gummed and strapped down in a jejune provincial effort to learn, *mehercule*, the stilted language that then passed for 'good English' in the arthritic milieu that held control of the respected British critical circles, Newbolt, the backwash of Lionel Johnson, Fred Manning, the Quarterlies and the rest of 'em.

And that roll saved me at least two years, perhaps more. It sent me back to my own proper effort, namely, toward using the living tongue (with younger men after me) though none of us has found a more natural language than Ford did.

This is a dimension of poetry. It is, magari, an Homeric dimension, for of Homer there are at least two dimensions apart from the surge and thunder. Apart from narrative sense and the main constructive, there is this to be said of Homer, that never can you read half a page without finding melodic invention, still fresh, and that you can hear the actual voices, as of the old men speaking in the course of the phrases.

It is for this latter quality that Ford's poetry is of high importance, both in itself and for its effect on the best subsequent work of his time. Let no young snob forget this.

The four other hints mentioned at the beginning of this extract refer to: (1) Yeats's lyrics of the 1908 period, some of which 'stripped English poetry of its perdamnable rhetoric', (2) a warning from Bridges against the use of homophones, (3) a brief comment by Hardy on *Homage to Sextus Propertius* which showed that Hardy had his eye on the subject matter rather than the manner, and (4) a warning from an Italian archbishop, to whom he showed one of his articles on money, against trying to pack too many points into a single article.

However disappointed Pound may have been at the failure of his American visit he was not one to sulk, for there was always the future to think of and much work to be done. American education was full of 'syphilis' and her intellectual life full of 'dryrot'. Also, the nation's economy, under the Roosevelt administration, was shaky, and from about the end of July 1939 onwards he turned increasingly, in his investments, towards Italian government bonds rather than American industrial shares. His fears were heightened when in August Tinkham wrote to say that if there was a war Roosevelt would do everything in his power to draw America into it, because politically it was the only thing that could save him. As usual, Pound's method of meeting the situation was peculiarly his own. For example, he had become greatly attached to Willis A. Overholser's *A Short Review and Analysis of the History of Money in the United States*, published in Libertyville, Illinois, in 1936; in particular it contained material about the chicanery of the usurers in the United States in the 1860s. In September 1939 Pound wrote to Douglas McPherson, editor of a proposed new magazine called *Pan*, that 'The *only* American book that *needs* reading is Overholser's *History of Money in the U.S.*' Also needed, he told him, was a sixty- to eighty-page selection of gists from the works of Adams, Jefferson, Van Buren, Jackson and Johnson.

When Christina Foyle asked him to become a patron of the Book

Club, London, he wrote in October in similar vein, listing as important such authors as Gesell, Trollope, Cummings and Eliot, and recommending such books as Lewis's *Tarr* and his own Cavalcanti (I suppose he meant the large edition of 1932); he then suggested a selection from the works of Adams, Jefferson, etc., and pointed out the need for 'a little real history, say Overholser's *Hist. of Money in the U.S.*, as supplement to Woodward's *New American History* or Bowers' *Tragic Era*'. He went on to say that Douglas's *Economic Democracy* was 'of as general an interest' as Marx's *Das Kapital* and that *Money*, edited by Montgomery Butchart, ought to be on every high school student's bookshelf.

When in September the war started in Europe he began a letter-writing campaign to keep America out of it, for it had been caused, he told Congressman Voorhis on 13 September, by 'international usury' and by England's barefaced attempt to embezzle the mandated territories formerly belonging to Germany. 'This war is no place for boys', he said, 'especially American boys.' If anyone wanted to 'boom steel', they ought to be able to rig the market without actual American participation in carnage. He hoped that Voorhis would teach his constituents and at least part of the House the 'choice facts' that Overholser had printed in his booklet.

For Pound the war was a confirmation of all his views on politics and economics; and the more he heard from America the darker the picture grew. On 30 September Tinkham wrote that Roosevelt would 'stop at nothing' to involve the United States in the war and about the same time he had a letter from Mencken saying that the president would find some way of entering the fight.

Among contributors to *The New English Weekly* whose work Pound had admired was the poet J. P. Angold. Not only did he include economics in his verse but wrote articles on the subject as well. In a letter to Voorhis, dated 24 October, Pound said that Angold, 'the best of England's younger poets', had joined up or been conscripted; it was damn nonsense that such a man should get shot 'for profits on gold exchange'. Angold was killed on active service with the Royal Air Force in 1943.

He wrote to R. McNair Wilson on 25 October that the war would be for the profit of Russia who had already received 'an enormous slice' and would no doubt receive more. The following day he wrote to Cummings asking him to do his bit to prevent Americans being sent to Europe to fight for interest on British loans.

But characteristically he wrote also to a number of English correspondents on the importance of farmers and farm products to national defence and suggested that England should put back under cultivation as much land as possible.

With the American situation daily growing worse he began to consider another visit to the United States in the spring of 1940. In October he wrote to Tibor Serly, for whom he had recently made an English version of the words of Moussorgsky's song, 'The Flea', that if he got to New York in 1940 they might be able to publish some of Vivaldi's music, worked out from Pound's reductions of the original scores. He also told other correspondents in America that he might return.

By 8 December he believed, as he told Douglas, that if the American people went on refusing to read the Congressional Record they would wake up one morning to find that the government had handed over all real power to a committee appointed by Roosevelt or his successor. 'And with the aid', he added, 'of nice young men who meant well.'

While this fight had been going on, on the political front, Pound had been witnessing the first real flowering of his efforts on behalf of Vivaldi. For in September (from the 16th to the 21st) the Accademia Musicale Chigiana, of which Olga Rudge was secretary, held at Siena a Vivaldi week with some of Italy's leading musicians taking part. In a sense the whole enterprise was due to Pound's earlier enthusiasm, to Olga Rudge's compilation of a Vivaldi catalogue, published by Count Chigi in the series 'Note e Documenti', and finally to her organizing ability at the Accademia. Among the works performed were some which Pound, after his discovery of the possibilities of microfilm, had had photographed at the Library of Congress in Washington and at the Sächsische Landesbibliothek in Dresden.

Pound had finished his cantos on China and John Adams (nos. 51 to 71) which by September 1939 had gone to Faber in London and by November were in proof. As he thought about future cantos he decided that he would have to consider questions of belief and philosophy; and he began to acquaint his correspondents of this fact and to cast around for ideas that might fill the gap. Writing to Douglas McPherson in November he said that in the main his economic work was now done and although he would have to go on condensing and restating his ideas he could 'depute the rest to Overholser'. He himself had now passed on to 'questions of belief'. It is not irrelevant to point out that this idea of Overholser as deputy was not shared by Overholser who as far as I can make out was an unwilling ally.

One of Pound's main points was that Europe needed a purely European religion unpoisoned by Jewish or other non-European elements, and on 7 August he had sent an essay on this theme to Douglas Fox in New York, in the hope that Fox would translate it into German and perhaps find a publisher for it in Germany. There, he believed, it would receive serious attention. As in much of his correspondence at this time he insisted in the essay that Christianity was composed of 'very mixed elements' and that the 'valid elements' were European. The only vigorous feasts of the Church, he maintained, were grafted onto European roots having to do with the sun, the grain, the harvest, and Aphrodite. Pound could recognize paganism when he saw it and not unnaturally turned in the direction of Germany: 'The function of Germany, as I see it, in the next forty years' art is indispensable. Nowhere else is there enough force toward a purgation. The Italians are too easygoing. Spain is African and Christian, and you cannot trust Christianity for ten minutes.' Towards the end of 1939 there was much in his letters about the god Pan, the relation between coition and clear thought, and the need to sort out the various elements in Christianity.

With these ideas turning over in his mind it is not surprising, when we think of the propaganda that was in the air, that Pound's attitude towards the Jews took a turn for the worse. He had inherited the anti-semitism of the East Coast American, directed against the coarseness and habits as well as the supposed racial traits of Jewish immigrants; but this was possibly not much more than a faint sense of superiority, unpleasant perhaps but not necessarily dangerous. If later he developed stronger feelings, especially against the Jewish religion and its infil-tration of Europe, they did not prevent him from trying to see the matter fairly, even after his interest in economics had brought him into contact with usurers who were Jews. About 1935 he held for a time a theory that organized anti-semitism might be the hidden war of Swiss Protestant dynasties against the Rothschilds, whom they had never forgiven for breaking into their banking monopoly. 'Usurers have no race', he wrote in the *New English Weekly* in November 1935. 'How long the whole Jewish people is to be sacrificial goat for the usurer, I know not.' In *Guide to Kulchur* he wrote that Meyer Anselm, founder of the Rothschild dynasty, 'had, let us say, a purpose, a race (his own race) to "avenge". He used the ONLY weapons available for a tiny minority, for a lone hand against organized goy power, pomp, mili-tarism, rhetoric, buncombe.' And in an article in the *British Union Quarterly* in 1938 he said, 'international usury contains more Cal-vinism, Protestant sectarianism than Judaism'.

I do not think that he was always right, either in his facts or his ideas, nor does he appear always to have been consistent; but a study of his sayings on the subject during the 1930s shows that he made conscious efforts to be fair, only lapsing occasionally when some item of news or gossip touched off an explosion of anger. In *What Is Money For?* he distinguished between 'prejudice against the Jew as such' and 'the suggestion that the Jew should face his own problem'. He also said that the tendency to usury had been recognized and stigmatized from the time of the laws of Moses and indicated that he was prepared to respect the individual Jew who observed this law but not the one who while claiming to observe it went on robbing other men by usury. But at the same time the pamphlet contained crude references to 'Jews-papers' and to an England in which pictures were 'put in the Jew dealer's cellar under a black and iniquitous inheritance tax'.

By the end of 1939 he was taking an unhealthy interest in Jewish participation in any activity whatsoever and when he read in *Il Regime Fascista* for 24 November a story about Jewish control of news-distributing agencies he was further confirmed in his belief about the power of usury. Isolated by the war he spent more and more time reading anti-Jewish tracts and articles, some of which, sent earlier from America and England, he had never or barely opened. Typical of these was the eight-page pamphlet *Britain & Jewry* published by Greater Britain Publications. It attacked 'Jewish Finance', declared that Communism was Jewish, and advocated Sir Oswald Mosley's solution that 'the Jews must be found a land of their own', preferably Madagascar.

There is no doubt that by the beginning of 1940 Pound was isolated in several senses. He was cut off in the physical sense, for even though the war was still only in an early stage and America still neutral, he was geographically with the 'Axis' powers; sides were already forming and Pound was in Italy defending the Italian and German point of view. He was also isolated in the sense that he was imprisoned in a world of his own – a man with a mission to change the world both culturally and economically. At times he had his doubts about the Nazis, and even about the Fascists, but he had the future to think of.

NOTE

1 Ezra Pound, 'The Jefferson-Adams Correspondence', *North American Review*, Winter, 1937–8.

XIX   The War Years
1939/1943

For several years Pound had been seeking an opportunity to meet George Santayana the Spanish philosopher and former lecturer at Harvard who since the 1920s had lived in Italy. Santayana's secretary and assistant, Daniel Cory, had been seeing Pound on and off at Rapallo since about 1930 and it was no doubt as a result of his remarks that Pound felt the desire to arrange a meeting. When he made his first attempt in 1937 Santayana was busy and did not want any distractions; in July he wrote, 'For heaven's sake, dear Cory, do stop Ezra Pound from sending me his book', and a few days later, after he had been apprised of the philosopher's attitude, Pound let the matter rest; but on 4 January 1939, while on a visit to Rome, he called on Santayana at the Hotel Bristol. 'He is taller, younger, better-looking than I had expected', wrote Santayana to Cory the following day. 'Reminded me of several old friends (young, when I knew them) who were spasmodic rebels, but decent by tradition, emulators of Thoreau, full of scraps of culture but lost, lost, lost in the intellectual world. . . On the whole we got on very well, but nothing was said except commonplace. . .' Santayana mentioned Rimbaud and was pleased when Pound singled out the poem 'Au Cabaret-Vert', for this was one of his favourites. Two of the things which impressed him were the great mop of wavy hair and the beard: 'His beard is like a painter's and his head of hair (is it a wig?) like a musician's.'

In the autumn of 1939 after a holiday at Cortina d'Ampezzo Santayana went to stay at the Hotel Danieli in Venice and on 30 November sent a postcard to Pound at the Hotel Anglo-Americano, via Quattro Fontane, Rome: 'I have finished *The Realm of Spirit* and apart from proof-reading shall be free to amuse myself with other things. I had thought possibly of going to Rapallo, with a prospect of seeing you and perhaps getting Cory to go there also . . . but I shall be glad to see you anywhere.' This was good news for Pound who in his search for material for his cantos saw Santayana as the man best-fitted to answer his questions about belief and philosophy. In his reply from Rapallo on 8 December he said that having dealt with 'money in history' he now had to tackle 'philosophy or my "paradise"' and badly wanted to talk with some one who had thought a little about it. There were 'one or two gropings' in his Cavalcanti notes and one or two Chinese texts he would like Santayana to consider. He hoped to be in Venice on 26 or 27 December. Santayana sent a postcard to Rapallo on 13 December: 'I shall certainly be here on the 26th and 27th . . . But you must not count on my philosophy to answer your questions, because questions are apt to imply a philosophy and don't admit of answers in terms of any other; so that you had better find your answers for yourself. But you might show me some of the beauties of Venice, which I have very likely missed all my life.'

After the meeting Pound wrote enthusiastically to Eliot: 'Had a lot of jaw with Geo. Santayana in Venice, and like him. Never met anyone who seems to me to fake less. In fact I gave him a clean bill.' He had, he said, 'fed him the Cavalcanti' and all was nice and cordial at the Hotel Danieli.

So buoyed up was he by their talk that he began to consider a long essay on the philosopher Scotus Erigena whose work he had recently bought. He told Eliot that if he could get hold of recent publications about Erigena he could 'write quite a chunk'.

By the middle of January 1940 Pound was no longer seeking the philosopher's advice but engaged rather in instructing him in Fenollosa's 'ideogramic method'. On the 15th Santayana wrote from Venice that the Fenollosa essay had given him his first glimpse of what 'Chinese hieroglyphics' were and how they were composed. He did not think much of the essay apparently for he wished there had been more about the Chinese signs and 'less romantic metaphysics'. He went on to discuss the signs and Confucius for several paragraphs, ending: 'You see I am floundering in your philosophy, badly but not unpleasantly. I am sending you Fenollosa back in the same envelope.' Santayana obviously saw no point in continuing the discussion: he recognized Pound's right to his ideas about Fenollosa and Confucius and paid him the compliment of dealing with them at some length; at the same time he tried to draw the matter to a close. Pound having got started, however, was now brimming over with missionary zeal; not only did he like Santayana, not only did he see him as a possible convert to the 'ideogramic method' and perhaps even to monetary reform but also as an active participant in the building of the 'New Learning'. In a letter about some of his ideas he mentioned his belief in a mode of thought based upon mental leaps connecting 'things' or 'particulars', as opposed to 'abstract thought'. On 20 January Santayana replied: 'This musn't go on for ever, but I have a word to say, in the direction of fathoming your potential philosophy. . . When you ask for jumps and other particulars, you don't mean (I suppose) *any* other particulars, although your tendency to jump is so irresistible that the bond between the particulars jumped to is not always apparent? It is a mental grab-bag. A *latent* classification or a *latent* genetic connection would seem to be required, if utter miscellaneousness is to be avoided.'

Following consultations with Faber, Pound wrote in February asking Santayana to collaborate with Eliot and himself in writing a book on 'the Ideal University, or The Proper Curriculum'. He quoted Eliot as saying that 'It is he [Santayana] who adds just the spot of respectability that makes the book queer whereas if you and me didn't have him I don't say we couldn't make the book just as queer, but the public wouldn't be so surprised.' He assured Santayana that he had no such designs on his quiet when he entered the Hotel Danieli in Venice and apologized that the project savoured of revivalism: 'I plead the missionary sperrit: GUILTY!' The whole idea, he said, arose out of his transmission to Eliot of a story of Santayana's about Henry Adams and the teaching of history at Harvard and a remark by Santayana to the effect that it did not matter, in education, what books were read so long as everybody read the same books. Santayana, who was still at the Danieli, replied on 7 March:

Dear E.P.: No, it is impossible for many reasons that I should accept the honour of collaborating with you and T.S.E. on a subject, about which I have no ideas. It is impossible materially at this moment because I have seven critical essays about my philosophy to reply to, nine more coming, and the proofs of the *Realm of Spirit*, in two editions, to read. And it would always be impossible morally because you and T.S.E. are reformers, full of prophetic zeal and faith in the Advent of the Lord; whereas I am cynically content to let people educate or neglect themselves as they may prefer. . .

I don't remember my Henry Adams anecdote further than that he said history couldn't be taught. If I have embroidered on that, you or Eliot are welcome to use my fancy-work as a text. But you, you must preach the sermon.

The Henry Adams anecdote appeared later in Santayana's autobiography *Persons and Places* which was published in New York in 1944 after the manuscript had been smuggled from Rome to the United States by way of Padraic Colum and the Vatican. Santayana tells how in Washington many years earlier a friend 'took me to see Mr Henry Adams, with whom he was on very friendly terms. "So you are trying to teach philosophy at Harvard", Mr Adams said, somewhat in the gentle but sad tone we knew in Professor Norton. "I once tried to teach history there, but it can't be done. It isn't really possible to teach anything". This may be true, if we give very exacting meanings to our terms; but it was not very encouraging.' When Pound recounted the story five years later in *The Pisan Cantos* he made it refer to Harvard in particular, whereas in *Persons and Places* it seems to refer to teaching in general.

On 28 January 1940 Faber published *Cantos LII-LXXI* dealing with Chinese history and John Adams. It would appear that at this point Pound was planning to write only one more book of cantos, for in a letter to a correspondent in Hailey, his birthplace, he said: 'my best stuff is in *Cantos*. 1 to 71 (so far pubd) & complete as it stands. Tho' there's a final volume to be done.' Also included among his 'best stuff' were *Personae* (1926 collection), *Guide to Kulchur, Ta Hio* and *Make It New*; in what he called the 'second category' were *ABC of Economics, ABC of Reading* and the pamphlet *Social Credit: An Impact*. Soon after copies of *Cantos LII-LXXI* arrived in Rapallo from London Pound gave one to his wife with the inscription 'D.P. her copy'. Inserted in his own hand, near the date 11 February 1940, were the words:

> *To build up the city of Dioce*
> *(Tan Wu Tsze)*
> *Whose terraces are the colour of stars*

This beautiful image, which went back to the letter he wrote to Bride Scratton thirty years earlier ('To build a dream over the world'), appeared again later on the opening page of *The Pisan Cantos*:

> To build the city of Dioce whose terraces are
> the colour of stars.

Here glowing in the dark of a world gone mad, this constellation reminds us not only of a true poetic self long suppressed but of the beauty of the dream of a better world which lay beneath his obsessive harping on certain economic, political and cultural themes.

The American edition of *Cantos LII-LXXI* was published by New Directions on 17 September 1940. Earlier when James Laughlin saw the text for the first time he thought that readers might be puzzled by some aspects and he suggested to the author that perhaps a preface would help; Pound did not think so and in February 1940 provided this explanation of the text, together with his answer to Laughlin's claim that some of his language and some of his ideas might prove offensive to other people:

Dear Jas: Cantos 52/71 can NOT have a preface in the book. Cover gives ample space for blurb. The new set is not incomprehensible. Nobody can summarize what is already condensed to the absolute limit. The point is that with Cantos 52/71 a NEW thing is.

Plain narrative with chronological sequence. Read 'em before you go off half-cocked.

All institutions are judged on their merits, idem religions. No one can be boosted or exempted on grounds of being a lutheran or a manichaean. Nor can all philosophy be degraded to status of propaganda merely because the author has one philosophy and not another. Is the Divina Commedia propaganda or not?

From 72 on we will enter the empyrean, philosophy, Geo. Santayana etc. The publisher can not expect to control the religion and philosophy of his authors. Certain evil habits of language etc. must be weighed, and probably will be found wanting.

When six months later the American edition came out, there was an envelope pasted inside the back cover, containing a pamphlet, *Notes on Ezra Pound's Cantos: Structure and Metric*; the greater part was taken up with general notes on the cantos by James Laughlin, signing himself 'H.H.', followed by two pages on the versification, by 'S.D.' (Delmore Schwartz).

Pound did not return home in the spring of 1940 as he had planned; but there was no falling off in his concern for America's future. He was in touch with Ernest Minor Patterson, president of the American Academy of Political and Social Science in Philadelphia; on 6 February he wrote enclosing a cheque for life membership: 'I shall probably annoy you or the secretary or a few fellow members by excess activity during the first few months, and then sink into the normal inactivity of academicians.' There and then he took the opportunity to mention the 'appalling lack of handy compendia of the thought and aims of the American founders', compared with the accessibility of cheap editions of Marx, Lenin, Trotsky and Stalin. Made a life-member of the Academy on 23 February he was soon asking for co-operation by members in the defining of economic terms and the study of other problems facing the United States and the world. To the editor of *The Annals* of the Academy he wrote asking whether space might be devoted to the following matters:

1. Among the first rights of a man or nation is the right to stay out of debt.
2. (ref. Brooks Adams, an author whom the American universities have for 30 years refused to face).

Dumping is an hostile act, whether it be dumping of wheat or of gold. Any attempt to force a nation to take a useless or at least unnecessary commodity like gold is a move towards war.

cordially yours

P.S. Are you touching problem of American responsibility for present war?

This postscript was due to his belief, expressed in a letter of 5 February to Senator Styles Bridges, that Britain's attitude to Germany was governed largely by the fact that she received encouragement from 'Americans saying "we are behind you".'

About this time he had a similar burst of activity with respect to the National Institute of Arts and Letters, writing to members to get aid for Joe Gould, to whip up 'committees of correspondence' and to suggest that Eliot and Santayana be appointed European members.

As for his other correspondence during 1940, it was so extensive that I can give only a rough idea of it. There were letters to Pearl Buck about the war ('The war is mainly for money lending and three or four metal monopolies'); and one to Lester Littlefield dealing with America's attitude to high quality in the arts ('The point being the country won't feed its five or ten best writers'). To the historian Charles Beard he wrote asking him to start a series of volumes of 'gists' of the thought of the American founders, beginning with chapter twelve of Beard's *Economic Origins of Jeffersonian Democracy*, dealing with Taylor of Caroline; he also wrote that the true function of the House of Representatives, were the country at all conscious, would consist mainly in determining the value of the dollar as measured in an index of essential commodities. In a letter to Mencken he stated his attitude to Fascism in relation to the United States: 'as I said and az wuz printed while I was in America, the danger for the U.S. is not fascism, the danger is in getting a god damned tyranny with none of the humanizing and constructive elements of the corporate state. No guilds, no representation of every man by someone of his own trade, no checking of monopolies and price ramps, no tribunal where a man can take a case of economic injustice, etc.' He said further that he had compared all the rival systems and correlated as many facts as had been humanly possible; he had not been 'sold' on any one sect but had dug out some of the horse-sense that was common to the four best systems and also the principles that had established dynasties in China.

When he received a request from the editors of a book containing biographies of Catholic authors, asking whether he was a Catholic, he replied on 5 February: 'It is up to you. The late Pope was pleased that I remembered to send him my *Make It New*, but he played safe and "marvelled" at my "versatility".' He had immense respect for what he believed to be the true work of the Church, but could not support an institution that was too cowardly to preach its own doctrine and acted as a mere lackey to international usury. Until Pacelli (Pius XII) damned the men who had caused the war and branded it largely as a crusade for money-lending and metal monopoly, he would have to remain, he said, among the 'doubtful adherents'.

In the hope of having his Cavalcanti translations published in England in a bilingual edition he wrote to Ernest Rhys (11 February) to see if J. M. Dent would be interested; this was in an attempt to keep open as many lines of communication with England as possible. The book was not published. To the United States ambassador in Rome he wrote (27 February) that his concern was mainly for the people of England ('part of which contains some of the finest human material in Europe') who did not want the war and had not been allowed to vote on it. He did not think that England could exhaust Germany and the result could be 'infinite harm' to the English people. On 12 March he told Pearl Buck that he did not enjoy sitting with his hands tied and all American newspapers closed to news of Europe. 'Even Mencken can't get my news into the *Baltimore Sun*.' The aim of those who governed both England and France, he told Tinkham (22 March), was to crush 'all the decent life of gentry, or anyone with income from 400 to 2000 sterling'. He also suggested an amendment to a monetary bill put forward by Voorhis; the bill, which died in the legislative process, called for reforms if and when a state of emergency arose. 'Nine to 12 million unemployed ought to be enough emergency', Pound remarked, 'without waiting for external complications.'

The same day he wrote to Zukofsky praising a translation he had made of a poem by Catullus. 'Mebbe if you an' the kumrad an' ole Ez and basil keep at it, we'll evolve a style of the period that will give the Catullian ferocity. Estlin clicked in his "Dirge".' 'Kumrad' and 'Estlin' both refer to the same person, E. E. Cummings, whom Pound called Kumrad or Comrade because of his trip to Russia, and whose full name was Edward Estlin Cummings; the ferocity of his sixteen line poem 'Dirge' greatly pleased Pound:

> vive the millenni
> um three cheers for labor
> give all things to enni
> one buggar they nabor
>
> (neck and senecktie
> are gentleman ppoyds
> even whose recta
> are covered by lloyds

Pound later included the poem in his 1942 pamphlet *Carta da Visita*. In the same letter to Zukofsky he said that the test of poetry was: 'can Ez read it?' and secondly, 'can he read it with approval and/or pleasure?' And he added, referring apparently to the composition of verse: 'as

Kreymborg learned about chess: when you see a good move? NO, don't make it, look for a better one.'

Also on 22 March he wrote to Dr G. B. Mathews, of the Dies investigating committee in Washington, saying that since their conversation in Washington the previous May he had pestered him 'singularly little', but he could not resist drawing his attention to crumbs of enlightenment available in the annual report for 1939 of his old friend the Carnegie Endowment for International Peace. These included a statement on page 6 that the time had passed for the discussion of so-called national problems, as there were no longer any such problems of outstanding consequence, and a record on page 63 of $355,149.77 ('seventy-seven cents', Pound noted) spent 'on going to Bogota and other places where you could neither start a world war nor stop one'. This attitude towards national problems, as against international problems, was consistent with Pound's belief, derived from his Confucianism, that the place to begin reforms is at home and that men unwilling to begin at home distract attention from the fact by becoming internationally minded.

One of his chief worries was the 'provincial ignorance' of his friends and allies, which on 24 March necessitated a long letter to A. L. Gibson, a Social Crediter in Sheffield, pointing out that Douglas was hopelessly wrong in his remarks about Mussolini in the *Social Creditor* of 9 March.

In the first place M. never was a blacksmith. His father was, his mother was a school teacher, he was a school teacher. His father was a socialist blacksmith with some sort of political training. M. grew up in that argumentative milieu, he then went to Switzerland, attended univ. lectures and was in the most cosmopolitan intelligentzia, along with rhoosians etc. But not a provincial italian milieu. He then went to Paris and read like hell. . . Probably no man in Europe with a more thorough grounding in the study of sociology or whatever you want to call it. As editor of the *Avanti* and *Popolo d'Italia* he had Odon Por for his London correspondent. He knew German and French, and when he came into power learned English.

In the same letter he said that the 'purchasing power of labour' might be considered the crucial test of any civilization; in this respect both the United States and Russia had failed.

Other letters included one to Senator R. A. Taft offering advice about Republican strategy in the elections, one or more to an English member of parliament on getting land back under cultivation, and one to Burton Wheeler trusting that he (Wheeler) would get due credit for his efforts to 'keep young America from being slaughtered'. In many of his letters, containing as they certainly did various points about current affairs that were worth consideration, he had the disconcerting tendency to insert statements about such topics as the betrayal of America by bankers in 1863 – this manipulation of the currency during the Civil War being 'the cardinal fact' of American history. Whether he was right or wrong this sort of thing was hardly reassuring if his correspondents did not see (and Pound did not help them) how this was connected with the events of 1940.

Although the previous year he thought that he had come to the end of his monetary researches and could concentrate on the refining of his monetary terms and definitions, the discovery of two books during 1940 gave him new facts with which to support his ideas. They were: Davis Rich Dewey's *Financial History of the United States* first published in New York in 1903 and Brooks Adams's *Law of Civilization and Decay* first published in London in 1895, revised edition in New York in 1897. He seems to have read the Dewey, or part of it, during the second half of March 1940; on the 30th he wrote to the author congratulating him on his achievement, seeking clarification on several points, and probing to discover whether Dewey had any knowledge of the material in Overholser's booklet. On 2 April he wrote to Voorhis enclosing a quotation from the Dewey, about John Calhoun in 1814, 'in support' of the Voorhis bill on credit. Dewey probably did not realize 'his own kinks', Pound told the congressman, and added that he did not trust his 'tendencies', by which he meant, I think, that the historian did not lay bare sufficiently the workings of the usurocracy in American history.

The next day he wrote exultantly to Douglas:

Dear Doug: Another bung knocked out of the anti-dividend buggars. National dividend was paid by the U.S. in 1837. It was paid by the National Govt. to the states, i.e. the individual states, and not to individuals, but it was none the less paid.

Vide D. R. Dewey, *Financial History of the U.S.*, pp. 220/221 (12th edition).

There was a bit of wrapping, and it was called 'deposit'. Benton remarking 'in name a deposit, in form a loan, in essential design a distribution'.

Twenty-eight million was paid, and Dewey remarks 'an outright gift'. Some even claimed that 9 million more was due the states.

'to this day not a dollar has been called for' I.E. the loan fiction never invoked.

It is thaar in black and white 'Distribution of the Surplus'.
. . .

The distribution was made after Jackson had paid off the nat. debt. No more interest payments, so govt. had surplus from revenue.

Note: the use made of money by the states.

Massachusetts distributed it to towns. Boston used it for current expenses, Salem built Town Hall, Groton repaired a bridge.

State of Maine made a per capita distribution.

Here was proof that Douglas's idea of Social Credit, of national dividends to be distributed to the people once a surplus had been achieved, was not so far-fetched after all. Pound used this material and gave prominence to other aspects of Dewey's book in a pamphlet he published in 1944 on the 'Economic Nature of the United States'. The book could, he said there, be of help to students already prepared to understand the importance of the facts listed in it, but it perhaps lacked 'total candour'. These same themes, of paying off the national debt and distributing the surplus, he continued to sound in his writings and letters after the war was over.

On 24 July 1940 Pound wrote to Dewey asking him couldn't he set some of his graduate students the task of discovering from whom the United States had been buying gold at $14.33 an ounce above the 1932 price. This also was a constant theme with Pound during and after the war – that Roosevelt (or his Secretary of the Treasury, Morgenthau) had, between 1932 and 1939, paid out more than was necessary, donating millions of dollars belonging to the American people to the gold merchants. He does not seem to have considered that when the American government increased the price of gold to $35 an ounce it was attempting to implement a policy of economic recovery, perhaps a poor one, but one nevertheless which had the support of some sincere experts and at the time may have looked to be the only way out, the only way to restore confidence. This is worth saying because in Pound's account it appears simply as a swindle.

The second book which he discovered in 1940, Brooks Adams's *Law of Civilization and Decay*, was important for the information it provided on the part played by usury and money in the rise and fall of countries and civilizations. Brooks, brother of Henry Adams, and direct descendant of John Adams, maintained (more or less) that at times of economic competition the capitalist and usurer become predominant in society and the producer of goods falls into debt and servitude. We can imagine with what excitement Pound read an historian who in chapter eleven, 'Modern Centralization', told his story largely in terms of the Rothschilds, the Barings and the Lloyds and summed up modern history in the sentence, 'Probably Waterloo marked the opening of the new era, for after Waterloo the bankers met with no serious defeat.' A few pages further on Adams described the method of the usurocracy:

Perhaps no financier has ever lived abler than Samuel Lloyd. Certainly he understood as few men, even of later generations, have understood, the mighty engine of the single standard. He comprehended that, with expanding trade, an inelastic currency must rise in value; he saw that, with sufficient resources at command, his class might be able to establish such a rise, almost at pleasure; certainly that they could manipulate it when it came, by taking advantage of foreign exchange. He perceived moreover that, once established, a contraction of the currency might be forced to an extreme, and that when money rose beyond price, as in 1825, debtors would have to surrender their property on such terms as creditors might dictate.

Pound seems to have received the book early in May 1940, for in a letter of the 9th, to Jorian Jenks, an Englishman interested in economics and agricultural reform, he said: 'By the way, great book by Brooks Adams, very slow in reaching me, as was published 1897. *Law of Civilization and Decay*.' Writing again two days later he declared that it was a pity he didn't start reading it sooner as there was 'a whale of a lot' in it. Drawing lessons from it he said: 'Roman Empire flopped because of low price of grain, egyptian dumping etc. Usury buggared that empire, but low price of grain was basic part of usury syphilis.' On 15 May he recommended it to Douglas and on 1 June to Eliot; and in his 24 July letter to Dewey he remarked that there had been no adequate recognition of Brooks Adams even after forty years.

In addition to *Law of Civilization and Decay* Pound also read Adams's *The New Empire* (New York, 1902) and *The Theory of Social Revolutions* (New York, 1913) about the same time; he worked him into an article he published in the *Japan Times* of 12 August 1940, into his pamphlets published in Italy during the war and into some of his broadcasts over Rome Radio; after the war he continued to use his ideas and to find comfort in the fact that Adams had preceded him in the struggle against usury. About 1940 he also read Henry Adams's *The Degradation of the Democratic Dogma* published in New York in 1919 with a long introduction by Brooks. Although Pound rejoiced in their attacks on plutocracy he was too optimistic a spirit to fall in with their pessimism: either Henry's gloomy certainty that the universe was a 'machine' in the process of running down, or Brooks's belief in history as determined by inexorable laws. On page 105 of *The Degradation of the Democratic Dogma* Brooks wrote: 'and the flesh is, in a general way, incarnated in the principle of competition, which, rooted in the passions of greed, avarice, and cruelty, is apt to prevail to an unendurable degree unless restrained by law.' This was too much for Pound. Beside the words, 'unless restrained by law', he pencilled a large 'NO'. And when Adams went on to say that 'it is to regulate and restrain competition that human laws have been and are still devised', Pound pencilled emphatically the words, 'NO: EDUCATION', meaning that man could be saved by education.

In his letter of 1 June to Eliot, Pound said that he was continuing with his cantos but not exclusively; he still had material to 'chew and digest' including an item about silver-mines which was now concurring with Erigena's statement, 'Omnia quae sunt, lumina sunt', translated a few years later in canto 74, in *The Pisan Cantos*, as 'all things that are are lights'. There is no sign in the canto of the silver-mines. As Faber wanted another book from him, he suggested to Eliot that he might do a commentary on Dewey's *Financial History* but nothing came of the idea.

America, improved by intelligent acceptance of those worthy aspects of other systems which were not incompatible with the true basis of American democracy, was never far from his thoughts. 'Waal as to ole Ez hiz rightness', he wrote to Cummings and his wife Marion on 8 June. 'Do we perceive a tenDENcy to perceive that the choice is between a republican (in the old sense) with strong executive form of govt (at least as strong exec. as Tommy Jeff) *with* an organic insides wherein every bloke is represented by a bloke of his own trade or profession. And on the other an bloody 'and a dictatorship by and for usura, run by figureheads working for money lenders?' A bit of 'classy curiosity' about the government's purchase of gold was called for, he told them, but whether he could crystallize his own thoughts on the subject he did not know.

In September 1940 Pound made an attempt to return to America. 'Great excitements last month', he wrote to Kitasono Katue on 29 October; 'thought of going to U.S. to annoy 'em, but Clipper won't take anything except mails until Dec. 15. So am back here at the old stand.' He was glad, he said, that he did not get as far as Portugal and get stuck there. He went on to speak of the 'curious letch' of Americans to try to start or restart civilization in the United States, there having been some there until 1863. And he added, 'I should *still* like to'.

This concern over America is one side of the coin; but there is another and darker side which appears in some of his articles of 1940. Because of his isolation he was now more inclined than ever to publish in any paper or magazine that would have him. Writing as one who by virtue of his life of art and search for information was qualified to build bridges between nations and cultures he contributed articles on cultural subjects and the war to the *Japan Times* and *Japan Times Weekly* and in Italy to the *Meridiano di Roma*. In the *Japan Times* of 22 July 1940 he spoke of the 'essential fairness' of Hitler's war aims, as outlined in an interview on 14 June; taking Hitler's victories into consideration he considered the aims mild. Churchill he described as 'senile' and a mere 'shopfront' for the Rothschilds and others of their kind. On the question of the true American heritage, now in danger, he looked to Japan, he said, to educate that country by reminding it of the facts of American history and economics. His continuing drift towards the Nazi viewpoint is visible in a *Japan Times* article of 12 August in which he wrote: 'Democracy is now currently defined in Europe as "a country governed by Jews".'

He hammered on the same subjects in the *Meridiano di Roma*; to the issue of 24 March 1940 he contributed an article on 'The Jews and this War', in which he combined monetary history of the kind to be found in Overholser, with information only recently discovered in an anti-semitic book published in England.[1] The book leant heavily on revelations about Jewish community life said to have been published in Russia during the nineteenth century by Jacob Brafman, a Jew turned Christian. According to Pound's article Jewish communities are controlled by a central authority called the Kahal and it was this organization that was behind the war, partly in order to control nickel production. An English translation of the article was published in paraphrase in the May 1940 issue of *News from Germany*, put out by H. R. Hoffman, first in Starnberg, Bavaria, and later in Munich.

Pound received *News from Germany* regularly throughout the war; there is no evidence that he read it very carefully except occasionally when it dealt with monetary economics or music, and I do not think that he was taken in by its crude propaganda or the propaganda of its sister publications, such as *German Art and Culture*, which later in a fairly typical article in September 1940 said: 'Since Rubens always stressed the old and close allegiance of Flanders to the German folk and cultural realm, German authorities in Belgium will honour the famous painter. . .' But when *News from Germany* put out a special edition on 9 November with an English translation of 'The Fuehrer's Speech in Munich on November 8th 1940', Pound went through it with eyes alert for monetary news and marked with a green crayon the following passage: 'We then experienced that the gold countries suffered shipwreck with their currencies, while we, the non-gold State, maintained our currency. . . Now began the international fight against us with all means from within and from the outside. . .'

Another Italian journal to which he contributed was the *Giornale di Genova*, where on 13 April, under the heading 'Nego' (I deny), he attacked 'a rabble' of bankers, taking care to note that they included Aryans as well as Jews, and proclaimed the right of a nation to control its own purchasing-power; he also took the opportunity to declare that the Democratic party in the United States was a usurers' party which aimed to increase the national debt. A week later (20 April) he appeared on the front page of *Libro e Moschetto*, a journal of Fascist groups in the universities, published in Milan. The article was called

'Historical Parallels': it began by drawing attention to Mussolini's powerful intuition and the duty of the studious section of the population not only to obey but also to savour the high intellectual value of Fascism in action and to analyse and respect the wisdom of the Duce. Then he turned to the points in common between the Fascist and American revolutions, all of them to do with money or debt. American prejudice against Fascism was due, he said, to ignorance of American history and to terminological confusion. At one point in the article he mentioned Italian proposals for money based on work, such as he himself had been suggesting – which may explain a passage in his 29 October letter to Kitasono Katue in which he spoke of culture being 'facilitated by Ez' system of economics, now the programme of Ministers Funk and Riccardi. Tho' I don't spose they knew it was mine.'

The war was now in its second year and although the United States was not yet directly involved, the government was quite frankly backing England. In his appeal for a true understanding of the facts behind the war, Pound was taking the 'Axis' side and slipping further and further away from a true understanding of America's position. Living in a dream-world he did not realize this, although sometimes he seems to have been aware of his isolation. There are plaintive appeals in some of his letters of 1941 for news of Ronald Duncan, Eliot and others. On 18 January 1941 he wrote to Cummings – a man ever suspicious of organizations and movements – urging him to make use of the National Institute of Arts and Letters:

Estmbl Estlin: I not suggested you attend meetings of Dorcas Society. H. James never did, neither have I, but them bogies has money to strew and unless a few decent enter, how strew it on lil Joe Gould or other whereupon strewage would etc. Also consider the sec's prose a cameo fer preservation, but can't guarantee that my sense of cameo is unyvussul.

If nobuddy ever stick finger in hole in dyke, water flood etc. Metaphwore as you like; but do keep to original for the preembroidered moment. Waaal naow it wouldn't be degeneration fer you and the burly WyndDAMN to meet. I know you are Robespierre pewer etc, but I am contagious, at least to point of wishing larger editions and sales of *Apes of God* and *Eimi*, whereof I a month past blurrbed. Further sales of *Ulysses* can do Joyce no practical good. Or as was said: Brit. Public 'can stand only one poet at a time. They are standing Tennyson now' (meaning then in Bull Yeats' young).

yrs trewly Polonius

I still hanker after news re say Fox and young Duncan or other members of the human race as distinct from. Remarkable thing that the planet is still inhabited at all.

Ever hopeful about the fruits of action he wrote to the Institute on 15 May outlining a programme:

The Institute should stand for continual curiosity as to the nature of MAXIMA standards of excellence in all the arts.

To that end, the members including the worst should be placed in prison until they have read at least the main demands of my published criticism, let alone other critical demands of at least equal critical merit.

There has been plenty of encouragement of commercial efficiency. We need a little looking forward, a little courage in facing facts and ideas, and even in contemplating art that is not immediately and speedily remunerative.

He was, as he told Eliot, still writing cantos, or lines and passages to be inserted later when he found subject-matter for a new section. In March he sent a passage to Kitasono Katue, which he described as 'Lines to go into Canto 72 or somewhere':

> The sexton of San Pantaleo plays 'è mobile' on his
>   carillon
> 'un' e due . . . che la donna è mobile'
>   in the hill tower (videt et urbes)
> And a black head under white cherry boughs
>   precedes us down the *salita*.

'All of which shows', he commented to Kitasono, 'that I am not wholly absorbed in saving Europe by economics.' A longer passage written about the same time and destined for the same section of the work was published in the January 1942 issue of the New York magazine *Vice Versa*.

By the middle of 1941 letters from abroad were few; one that arrived in July was from William Carlos Williams. Pound replied:

Siena, as from Rapallo, July 14

Dear Bull: Thanks fer them kind words and herewith a memoranDUMB for yr consideration.

What no one seems to remember is the damage done to England during the Napoleonic wars by simply being cut off from ALL contemporary thought. Same goes for the U.S. now. I note it in *Hika* and other magazines. Not only gross ignorance of thought on the Axis side of the line. . . BUT gross ignorance of Irish thought and of English thought.

They have heard of Douglas because I told 'em 23 years ago or 21 years or 20 or whenever. BUT they are bone ignorant of 20 years English thought on guilds that preceded it.

Whole masses of geo-political thought ignored. The Acad. of Soc. and Pol. Sci. is ham ignorant. Even Bolchevism was not discussed, basic fact that no one was really communist, not in Europe or the U.S., but the capitalists did not open their papers to serious analysis of communism.

The whole occident wants homesteads or an equivalent, plus defence of purchasing power of labour, especially agricultural.

What is the sense of *Hika* giving only one side?

The opposition that you indicate is TIME LAG, or at least you better figure out how far there is any real opposition and how far it is Time lag and nowt but time lag.

I should be delighted for any items you thinks wd guide me in the labyrinth.

Shd welcome yr ideas as to what I ought to think about our native land and its rulers. Naturally you object to thinking about its govt and prefer to consider the anthropomorphology and composition of the humus and subsoil, but you keep on exposin that the outcroppins result from etc or are symptoms of.

Waaal, more power to yr bloody elbow.

In June and July Pound translated into English the first volume, entitled *Moscardino*, of the four-volume novel, *Il romanzo di Moscardino*, by the Italian, Enrico Pea. In a short and unexpected letter he informed Pea of his proposal; highly gratified to hear from this famous man whose name had been cropping up recently in Italian literary circles, Pea gave his permission and soon afterwards ('almost before he could have received my reply to his letter') Pound arrived in Viareggio for consultations. The first sight that Pea had of him was jumping out of a taxi at the entrance to the café where Pea used to work. The Italian took to him immediately, on account of his 'air of civility', his general appearance and 'lively bearing'. 'The original pale copper of his somewhat dishevelled hair', Pea later wrote, 'was mingled with the grey due to his years. And the beard, though it covered his chin but sparsely, gave length to his slightly Mephistophelean features.'

Pound would not let Pea take the small case in his left hand. 'Inside the café, when he opened it on the marble-topped table, the half-moon of a typewriter's bars made its appearance. The metal clips held a sheet of paper on the roller, and on it were already listed words in the Versilia dialect that occurred in *Moscardino*.' They set to work immediately, with Pea explaining their meaning and Pound typing the English equivalents. Afterwards when they began talking about other things, Pea mentioned that he had lived in Egypt as 'a workman, manufacturer and merchant'. Pound asked him for information on the social life of the ordinary people: to what extent, for example, the fellaheen were exploited by the Jews, Greeks and English. 'I was able to tell him how I had made iron-bound wooden chests for the Ottoman Bank, for the shipment of gold sovereigns overseas; and, when the Anglo-Egyptian Bank sumptuously renewed its premises, opposite the Bourse in Rue Sherif Pasha, how I had supplied the desks of red mahogany at a price of £60 each. I was not competent to discourse with him about "High Finance", which he inveighed against, as he said it was the cause of all the wars in the world.'

Apparently Pound had finished his translation, or the first draft, by the third week in July, for on the 23rd he wrote to Williams:

Waaal ole Cock: I have just translated an excellent novel (or short novel) by Enrico Pea, god knows when the trans. can get published.[2] By contrast I am wondering if you ever read H. James *American Scene*, pubd 1907. Also strikes me that H.J. was another damn immigrant like you, or son of an immigrant, hence the continuity of effort between you. I neglected to ask whether you had ever decently read H. J. collected.

I should appreciate a little communication. No reason why civil life should be totally suspended.

Pound had read *The American Scene* years earlier when he was living at Holland Place Chambers in London; if, as appears likely, he read it again in 1941, he cannot fail to have been impressed by James's superior attitude to the Jews in New York and his reflections on their effect on culture – more proof of the desperate situation of the old America which Pound was attempting to preserve.

Pound and Pea met 'frequently' in 1941 as Pound travelled to and fro between Rapallo and Rome. 'I have a vivid memory', Pea wrote, 'of what proved to be his last departure. I went along with him to the station. We found the barrier already closed, and the train beginning to move off. Pound lost no time in farewells. Taking a firm grip on the handle of his typewriter with his left hand, he took a flying leap over the barrier and jumped onto the moving train with all the ability of an American cowboy who vaults onto the back of a fleeing horse.'

Between 1941 and 1943 Pound's daughter, Mary, lived with her mother in a small house at Sant' Ambrogio, above Rapallo, where Pound had heard the sexton playing 'La donna è mobile'. Breathtaking in its beauty this hillside plunging into the sea far below provided much of the sea, cliff and hill-path imagery of the cantos. With his daughter now growing up Pound took her education in hand: he gave her books to read, set her the task of translating Thomas Hardy's *Under the Greenwood Tree* and his own *Cathay* into Italian, and also spent many hours with her, over a period of two years, helping her to translate his cantos into Italian. Recalling this period a quarter of a century later she wrote:

I think he made me do over the first line of canto 10 at least twenty times – we spent two years over twelve cantos: a sign of my slowness, of course, but also of Pound's thoroughness and patience. . . Sometimes Pound rewrote entire pages in Italian indifferent to Italian contemporary verse. His Italian was quarried from the classics, Dante and Cavalcanti, and such vigorous writers as Tozzi and Pea, and modulated by the speech his fine ear caught in the streets.

To encourage her in the work on Hardy he showed her three letters he had received from the famous novelist twenty years earlier in London and on one of his visits to Pea he took along her Italian version for his comments. Pea sent it back with corrections and a note of encouragement.

Under her father's eye she also translated some of Frobenius from German into Italian and the introduction of Pound's '*Noh*' *or Accomplishment* (1917) from English into Italian. This latter was published in the *Meridiano di Roma* of 19 April 1942.

After completing his translation of *Moscardino* during the summer of 1941 Pound began translating Confucius into Italian, with the help of Alberto Luchini. The opening chapter of the *Ta Hio*, which he now called *Ta S'eu* or *Dai Gaku*, appeared in the *Meridiano di Roma* of 26 October under the title 'Studio Integrale'. In a letter of 3 November, to Mrs Virgil Jordan (the Viola Baxter of his student days at Hamilton), he said: 'I am . . . making a real translation of Confucius' Ta S'eu (wrongly spelled Ta Hio, by the frogs whom I followed in earlier edtns/. . . Have just finished the Italian draft/ and a bloke, called Luchini is supposed to put it into real Italian.' The complete translation – Chinese text, with the Italian below – was published in Rapallo early in 1942 as *Studio Integrale*, perhaps in pursuance of his programme of university reform mentioned in his pamphlet *Carta da Visita* published in Rome in December 1942. There he wrote: 'A reform of the universities could be effected, in my opinion, by the infusion of certain known facts condensable into a few pages. Confucius, Mencius,[3] the anthology compiled by Confucius of poems already ancient in his time. A dozen Chinese poets, and a general idea, at least, of the nature of the ideogram as a means of verbal and visual expression. This vitalizes.' The reform called for such other measures as the study of Homer, the instilling of a 'proper sense of the maxima of poetry', and in history the teaching of 'a synthesis not inferior to that of Brooks Adams', but the basis obviously was to be Confucius and China. Later on in *Carta da Visita*, under the heading 'Good Government', he said: 'I believe the most useful service I could do would be to put before you, every year, a few lines of Confucius, so that they might sink into the brain.'

Another work by Pound published in Italy in 1941 was *What Is Money For?* which appeared in the *Meridiano di Roma* of 27 July, done into Italian by a friend, Olivia Rossetti Agresti. A daughter of W. M. Rossetti she had been assistant to David Lubin when before the First World War he had founded an international organization for the protection of agriculture and later she had been an interpreter at the Versailles Peace Conference. She had first been drawn to Pound's work by his defence of Mussolini during the Abyssinian war.

In September 1941 the Institute of Graphic Arts at Bergamo published Pound's translation of Odon Por's book, *Italy's Policy of Social Economics 1939–1940*. His reason for translating it, he once told me, was with the intention of having it distributed in America, as a step towards keeping the peace between that country and Italy, but the translation had been published too late to be of use in this way. What he had hoped, I think, was that Americans of goodwill, when they saw the constructive features of Italy's programme, would have been more sympathetic towards Fascism.

Pound himself saw the programme as a big step in the direction of Social Credit. On page 136 of *Italy's Policy of Social Economics* he inserted this footnote: 'The family allowances provisions approach steadily nearer and nearer to C. H. Douglas's Social Credit principles. They do not constitute, obviously, a national dividend per capita as Douglas proposes, but they are definitely consumer credit. On Feb. 11, 1941, they were extended far beyond the working class and made to include college graduates, sons and daughters of professional men, who weren't yet earning their own livings.'

If Italy was proving amenable to the best thought, America was not. In 1940, for example, when he published in the issues of the *Meridiano* for 24 November and 1 December the points he had placed before Mussolini at their meeting in 1933, both issues, according to Pound in his 1944 pamphlet *Oro e Lavoro*, were excluded from the United States mails. It seemed to him that official America did not want the American people or any section of them to hear what was going on abroad. In January 1941 when the opportunity arose to broadcast regularly over Rome Radio, in a programme directed at the English-speaking world, he took it. But whatever the immediate irritants were that made him accept, the desire to broadcast was not new: for some years he had been thinking about the importance of radio as a means of communication in the modern world and according to statements he made in letters to an American friend, Harry Meacham, in 1957 and 1958, he arrived at the Italian microphone only after a struggle. In one of the letters he said: 'It took me, I think it was, TWO years, insistence and wangling etc to GET HOLD of their microphone. . . .'

We may safely assume then that when he began to broadcast from studios in the Via Asiago, Rome, he was irritated by America's refusal, especially during the past few years, to accept his ideas, and, at a higher level, he saw himself to be carrying out his mission as a man of truth. The fact that he needed the money he was paid for the broadcasts may also have entered into his decision; certainly it may have contributed to his decision to continue broadcasting later on, when America and Italy were at war and money must have been short. It would seem that he received 350 lire for scripts he wrote and broadcast himself and 300 lire for those he wrote for others; in 1945 his lawyer Julien Cornell said in a letter that he had received only about $17 for each broadcast.

Another factor which may have hardened his mind towards official America was the intervention on 12 July 1941 of the Department of State, which on that day instructed the American embassy in Rome to limit Pound's passport for return to the United States only. According to the U.S. Department of Justice this action appears to have followed an alleged report in the American press that Pound had expressed a desire to return to the United States for the purpose of collecting his American and British royalties – the implication being that he intended to take them back with him to Italy, but of this I have found no definite evidence.

All that emerges with any certainty is that from 12 July onwards the State Department was anxious for Pound to return to America and stay there. What Pound did about it at this stage I do not know, but a State Department memorandum of 11 October 1941 refers to him as a 'pseudo-American', indicating that perhaps tempers had become frayed.

Pound continued to broadcast; one of his talks took place at twelve minutes past six in the evening on 7 December 1941, the day on which the Japanese bombed Pearl Harbor. For twelve minutes Pound rambled on about Confucius, the state of England, monetary reform, and the Jews. 'Roosevelt is more in the hands of the Jews', he said, 'than Wilson was in 1919.' As for Fascism as a means of saving the United States, he commented: 'Lord knows I don't see how America can have Fascism without years of previous training.' The best way to begin saving the country, he said, was through monetary reform.

According to Charles Norman he later went to see Reynolds Packard, Rome correspondent for United Press. Packard and his wife were preparing to leave: the United States, they told him, was at war.

After Pearl Harbor Pound 'retired' from Rome to Rapallo to think over his position. What happened during the next month or so is not clear. There are stories, told by Packard and others, that he had an argument with an American official in Rome and that he was refused permission to board the last train carrying Americans from Rome to Lisbon. I have read in an article by an Italian friend, Francesco

Monotti, that Pound and his wife made preparations to leave Italy, handing over their Gaudier drawings and sculpture and other works of art to Ubaldo degli Uberti for safe-keeping; and I have heard that either early in 1942 or later Pound was prepared to leave by the Clipper but was offered instead a passage on a steamer going to Portugal; this he declined on the ground that it would be too risky. His daughter told me in November 1966 that she remembered him coming to Siena to say goodbye to her and her mother before leaving for America but something prevented his departure. I have also heard that on another occasion both Olga Rudge and his daughter might have gone with him but again something happened.

One of the few pieces of evidence that I have seen dealing with these uncertain days is a report from New York published in the *Philadelphia Evening Bulletin* of 5 June 1942: 'Nancy Horton, American woman who returned Monday from Italy . . . says Ezra Pound, American poet who has been broadcasting Italian propaganda, was refused permission to leave Italy aboard a diplomatic train carrying other Americans. Miss Horton said Pound told her that George Wadsworth, U.S. Chargé d'Affaires in Rome, had informed him he could not return to the United States.' A report on 'The Medical, Legal, Literary and Political Status of Ezra Weston (Loomis) Pound', issued by the Library of Congress in 1958, said that in 1941 Pound's passport 'was extended for six months only, to compel his return'. It is possible that by the time the Chargé d'Affaires made his alleged statement the passport had expired.

Another difficulty perhaps was that his mother and father, now old, were still living in Rapallo – at Villa Raggio, Sestiere Cerisola, where Homer, bed-ridden, read books on the Red Indians and the American West, and Isabel, still active, absorbed her mental nourishment from such works as Alice Roosevelt Longworth's *Crowded Years*. On one of his visits to his father in January 1942, or thereabouts, Pound read to him a few pages from the Loeb edition of Aristotle. On another occasion when Homer wanted something to read Pound took him some Henry James. After a while Homer became deeply interested and began to read aloud to Isabel. As the sentences rolled on, Isabel began to fidget: 'Don't read all that,' she said, 'just tell me what happens!'

Homer had fallen out of bed and broken his hip, and was in no condition to travel. If Pound left Italy at this time it was fairly certain that he would not see his parents again; and in fact Homer died in hospital soon afterwards – not so much from his injury, Dorothy Pound told me, but from shock caused by a carelessly-placed hot-water bottle.

But whatever happened about his proposed return to America the crucial fact is that on 29 January 1942, with the United States now at war with Germany and Italy as well as Japan, he resumed his broadcasts over Rome Radio. It would appear that some days before the broadcast he had already made up his mind to stay and had applied to the Italian authorities accordingly, for about 26 January, after he had left Rapallo for Rome, the authorities in Rapallo received word that the Pounds had been granted permission to stay on there for the duration of the war.

Whereas his earlier broadcasts had been introduced by a simple announcement, on 29 January he was preceded by an elaborate preamble: 'Rome Radio, acting in accordance with the Fascist policy of intellectual freedom and free expression of opinion by those who are qualified to hold it, has offered Dr Ezra Pound the use of the microphone twice a week. It is understood that he will not be asked to say anything whatsoever that goes against his conscience, or anything incompatible with his duties as a citizen of the United States of America.' For Pound the statement about freedom of expression for those qualified to hold an opinion was a proof of Fascism's insight; the statement about his not being asked to go against his conscience or say anything incompatible with his duties as an American he regarded as proof of his innocence of treason and he continued to cite it as such years afterwards.

Pound continued to broadcast, at least twice a week, until July 1943. The contents of his talks varied greatly. Sometimes he abused Roosevelt or urged monetary reform, sometimes he read cantos or talked about his literary friends – Joyce, Cummings, Lewis, Eliot. On 14 May 1942 he discussed Louis-Ferdinand Céline; on 6 July he analysed 'the disease behind modern art'. He spoke in a variety of accents, American and English, grunted and exclaimed, and sometimes jumped about from point to point in such a way that he must have been extremely difficult to follow.

All the old themes were mentioned: usury, the American constitution, the betrayal of America during the Civil War, Brooks Adams, Confucius etc. When a BBC commentator referred to the Japanese as jackals who had only recently emerged from barbarism, Pound listed some of the Noh plays and commented: 'These are Japanese classical plays, would convince any man with more sense than a peahen of the degree of Japanese civilization.' Sometimes he was Ezra Pound the scourge of the usurocracy, at other times a simple small-town American philosopher.

The Jews were a favourite subject: the Jews who were behind Roosevelt, the Jews who were ruining England, the Jewish religion. The latter had a law, he said on 4 May 1943, but not an ethical system; the main purpose of the law was to 'provide fines, payable to a gang or tribe of allegedly religious superiors, who seem to have had no particular ethical status'. He asked why Christ was crucified, and answered: 'He was crucified for trying to bust a racket.' He was not in

favour of harming 'the small Jew', it was the big men he was after –
the Rothschilds, Sassoons and Sieffs in England, the Warburgs, the
Schiffs, Baruch and Morgenthau in the United States. 'Don't start a
pogrom,' he said on 30 April 1942, 'that is, not an old style killing of
small Jews. That system is no good, whatever. Of course, if some man
had a stroke of genius, and could start a pogrom up at the top . . . there
might be something to say for it. But on the whole, legal measures are
preferable. The sixty kikes who started this war might be sent to
St Helena, as a measure of world prophylaxis, and some hyper-kikes or
non-Jewish kikes along with them.' You cannot blame it on the small
Jew, he said on 16 May 1943, 'for he is in most cases as damned a fool
and as witless a victim as you are'.

The reference above to 'prophylaxis' recalls another theme running
through the talks – an obsession with intellectual 'health' and a horror
of 'disease', derived from his paganism. 'Health is more interesting than
disease', he declared on 6 July 1942, 'health is total.' And later in the
same broadcast: 'Health is cruel', or seems cruel to the bacillus. 'A man
who is totally healthy don't worry about bacillus.' He urged his
listeners to 'think about health' while waiting for his next talk. Not
unconnected with this theme was his expression of agreement with
Hitler, in his talk of 18 May 1942, on the application of eugenic theory
to humans as well as cattle. Pound incidentally did not get this idea
from Germany but from John Adams, nineteenth-century 'progres-
sives' and other earlier sources.

Much of what he said was sound, but he was seldom sound for more
than a sentence or two at a time; and if he had good things to say, for
instance about the importance of local control as opposed to too much
centralization, he also said many things that were foolish or worse.
Sometimes he would play the seer and manufacture connections to suit
his theories, as on 13 April 1942 when he said: 'in London I did try to
make a few people see why the printed matter on sale in that city would
finally kill off the inhabitants. Witness Dunkirk.' Here, and in other
broadcasts, we see him dealing in partial truths and formulating ideas
far beyond his actual knowledge.

In some of his talks he predicted with accuracy some aspects of the
post-war situation when the United States would have to face Russia.
On 8 March 1942 and in other broadcasts he spoke frankly of his
inability sometimes to think and write clearly. 'I lose my thread at
times, so much that I can't count on anyone's mind.' On 6 and 7 July
1942 he said:

There is so much that the United States does not know. This war is proof of
such vast incomprehensions, such tangled ignorance, so many strains of

unknowing, I am held up, enraged by the delay needed to change the typing ribbon, so much is there that ought to be put into young America's head. I don't know what to put down, can't write two scripts at once. The necessary facts, ideas come in pell-mell, I try to get too much into ten minutes. Condensed form is all right in a book; saves eyesight. The reader can turn back and look at a summary. Maybe if I had more sense of form, legal training, God knows what, I could get the matter across the Atlantic, or the bally old Channel.

Whatever his intentions were, some of his words must have sounded highly treasonable coming from an enemy station in wartime. 'You are at war for the duration of the Germans' pleasure', he said on 3 February 1942, 'You are at war for the duration of Japan's pleasure.' On 16 April 1942: 'For the United States to be making war on Italy and on Europe is just plain nonsense, and every native-born American of American stock knows that it is plain downright damn nonsense. And for this state of things Franklin Roosevelt is more than any other one man responsible.' His enthusiasm for what he called 'the just price' seems to have run away with him on 26 May 1942: 'Every hour that you go on with this war is an hour lost to you and your children. And every sane act that you commit is committed in homage to Mussolini and Hitler. Every reform, every lurch toward the just price, toward the control of a market, is an act of homage to Mussolini and Hitler. They are your leaders, however much you think you are conducted by Roosevelt or told by Churchill. You follow Mussolini and Hitler in every constructive act of your government.' And on 28 June 1942 he told Americans: 'You are not going to win this war. . . You have never had a chance in this war.' In other broadcasts he pointed out that there was a struggle going on against international lending – a war, he said in one of them, in which he himself had been engaged for twenty years; and in various ways he made it clear that in this war he was on the side of Italy and Germany against usury and the betrayal of the true American heritage.

Camillo Pellizzi, of the Institute of Fascist Culture, who was connected with Pound in his broadcasting activities, wrote in an Italian newspaper in 1953 that the Fascist authorities were puzzled and suspicious:

in Rome, those in authority in the regime more than once asked me these questions: 'But what does the fellow want? Can we be really sure that there isn't a code of some sort in what he says? Can you guarantee that he is not a spy?' They credited me, I don't know how correctly, with a particular understanding of the Anglo-Saxon man and mentality; and since they couldn't explain to themselves the phenomenon of this distinguished

American man of letters who was in wartime engaged in polemics over Rome Radio against Roosevelt and usury, who acted in a clearly disinterested manner . . . and who would not let them change a comma in the texts he prepared for transmission; because of all this they wanted some sort of proof from me that Pound was not a spy, but I added that it would require an entire university course given by someone more competent than I to explain to the Italian mind that a man like Pound, indubitably an American patriot motivated by a proud conscience should feel an irresistible impulse to talk over the radio.

The authorities may, as Pellizzi says, have been suspicious; I think it is in the nature of things that they should have been; but his testimony, valuable as it is, does not tell the whole story: for Pound entered into his job as broadcaster with the same zeal he had always brought to any subject that claimed his attention. He wrote messages for others to read, slogans for a war of nerves against England, advised on how to present propaganda and even suggested that a chair be established to enable him to teach this art – but whether these things occurred after America had entered the war, I cannot be certain. Judging by the indictment drawn up against him by the American government in 1945, some at least of these activities took place after the country was at war. That he was useful to the Italian propagandists is borne out by the fact that they used him in chats with other speakers. From the text of one of these, heard on 12 May 1943, it appears that there had been a similar broadcast the night before without Pound having realized that he was on the air.

One night Pound put in a friendly reference in one of his broadcasts to William Carlos Williams, who was not at all pleased when he heard about it next day from his wife, who had been acquainted with the news by a teller at a local bank. When later he was visited by the FBI he was thoroughly exasperated by Pound's behaviour. But Pound's mind was so constituted, his idea of the world so divorced from reality, and his belief in what he was doing so firm, he would have been incapable, I think, of grasping beforehand how such consequences might follow upon a friendly reference in a radio talk.

In the United States the Federal Communications Commission had begun to monitor his broadcasts as early as 7 December 1941, perhaps earlier; and copies exist in the Library of Congress and National Archive of one hundred and twenty-five broadcasts delivered between 7 December 1941 and 25 July 1943. These activities were first brought to the attention of the Department of Justice in April 1942 and soon afterwards the FBI began a closer enquiry. As a result he was indicted for treason by a Federal Grand Jury in the United States District Court, District of Columbia, on 26 July 1943. When he heard the news (over the BBC, according to one account) Pound wrote a long letter, dated 4 August 1943, to the Attorney General of the United States, Francis Biddle, and took it to the Swiss Legation in Rome for delivery to America. 'I do not believe,' he wrote, 'that the simple fact of speaking over the radio, wherever placed, can in itself constitute treason. I think that must depend on what is said, and on the motives for speaking.' He claimed that he had not spoken to the troops and had not suggested that the troops should mutiny or revolt; the idea of free speech became a mockery if it did not include the right of free speech over the radio. 'I have not spoken with regard to *this* war', he said, 'but in protest against a system which creates one war after another. . . .' And to support his case he named Arthur Kitson and Brooks Adams and spoke of the course of events from the foundation of the Bank of England (1694) to the Treaty of Versailles. By way of explanation he told the Attorney General that he had taken out a life membership in the American Academy of Social and Political Science in the hope of obtaining fuller discussion of some of these issues. But he did not find the Academy ready for full and frank expression of certain vital elements in the case: 'this may in part have been due to their incomprehension of the nature of the case.'

Throughout this difficult period Pound continued to write articles for the *Meridiano di Roma*; between January 1942 and September 1943, when Rome fell to the Allies, he contributed more than thirty items on literature, Jewry, economics, history and religion. Typical was the article of 1 November 1942. It began and ended as a tribute to Giulio Del Pelo Pardi whose work as an inventor of agricultural equipment and historian of agriculture placed him, Pound said, at the forefront of 'contemporary totalitarian philology'. But most of the article was devoted to the problem of reforming the Catholic Church by bringing it into line with Roman paganism, and in attacking, by various routes, the poison of Judaism. True religion, he maintained, was from agriculture; the Hebrew religion, on the other hand, with its deity who was a shark and a monopolist, was the religion of the 'butchers of lesser cattle'. These 'butchers' were tribes who rather than hunt wild beasts, fattened cows and sheep and then killed them at leisure, with no danger to themselves. In the course of the article he also managed to attack the syllogism and abstract thought, especially in theology, revise the early history of the Church, and describe 'that fool Milton' as an Anglican Hebrew. Some of the phrases and ideas from the article occur in *Carta da Visita* (December 1942) and much of the material appeared again in his letters and writings after the war. Another article (20 December 1942) was entitled 'Ideas and Books for the Axis Victory'. It was largely devoted to *La Sibylle*, by the Polish classical scholar

Thaddeus Zielinski, who held that Catholicism was a Greek rather than a Semitic religion. It too was an important subject for Pound after the war.

During the period of his broadcasts Pound was in touch occasionally with Santayana; he visited him, sent him some Brooks Adams to read, and wrote letters about philosophy. Santayana in turn sent Pound a copy of his *Realm of Spirit* and made an effort to clarify his notions for him but sometimes was stumped: 'I can't reply to your suggestions and diagrams,' he wrote from the Grand Hotel, Rome, in January 1941, 'because I don't understand them.' On 29 July 1942, after he had moved to the clinic of the Sisters of the Little Company of Mary, at number six Via Santo Stefano Rotondo, Rome, Santayana explained what he had meant by an expression he had used in *Realm of Spirit* and commented on Adams's *Emancipation of Massachusetts*. He had learnt a good deal from it about Boston colonial history, which was much more agitated than he had imagined it; he had been interested also in Adams's theory of historical materialism but did not think the material chosen to illustrate it was much more than 'anti-clerical propaganda – out of date even in 1886!' If the motive power in history was always industrial, as Adams claimed, why, Santayana asked, didn't the author explain the industrial motive of his own liberalism? If Pound had a 'theoretical' book by Adams, he would be glad, he said, to see it.

For several years Pound went back and forth between Rapallo and Rome, staying while in the capital at the Albergo d'Italia in the Via Quattro Fontane. In his search for material for his talks and articles he read the newspapers, listened to the BBC, searched through books and pamphlets on monetary reform and other subjects, and even read mimeographed copies of radio talks by other commentators on Rome Radio, marking salient points with a red crayon. In Rapallo he would read his talks to Olga Rudge and his daughter before taking the scripts to Rome; for a time he also gave the scripts to Dorothy Pound to read, but stopped doing so, she told me, when she mentioned to him that because of the jumps he made they were sometimes hard to follow. It was apparently during this period that Pound gave a talk to an economic congress in Pisa. Watching the audience, he wrote to R. McNair Wilson in 1953, he saw that they took in what he said about 'No economic science without clear terminology, no science without clear definitions', but were less attentive when he got to Gesell. 'Of course they promised to print the remarks, but never did.' He also told McNair Wilson that when he published an article on Gesell, Senator Bevione answered him seriously, suggesting that he write a book on the subject.

In 1943 when the Germans, building coastal defences, moved the

Pounds out of their flat on the seafront, it was thought best to send Mary Rudge back to her home at Gais in the north, so that Dorothy Pound could move into the small house at Sant' Ambrogio, where Pound, his wife and Olga Rudge lived for the rest of the war. Mrs Pound told me that she and Miss Rudge took it in turns to cook; Miss Rudge did most of the shopping because of the two she spoke the better Italian.

NOTES

1 L. Fry, *Waters Flowing Eastward* (19—).
2 Pound's translation of *Moscardino* was first published in the annual *New Directions* (no. 15) in December 1955.
3 The *Book of Mencius*, he said elsewhere in the pamphlet, 'is the most modern book in the world'.

XX   Out of the Ruins
1943/1945

Early in September 1943, as the Allied armies prepared to invade Italy, and Badoglio, who had replaced Mussolini, agreed to capitulate, Pound was on one of his visits to the capital. During the final days there was chaos and many of those who were connected with the government fled north by car, having made provision for such an emergency. Pound, who had not, suddenly found himself alone with nowhere to go. How many hours or days he lived in this uncertainty I do not know, but after refusing to take shelter with the Degli Uberti family he borrowed from them a knapsack, a road map, and a pair of heavy walking boots, with the intention of heading out of the city to the north. At midday on 8 September – the day on which capitulation was announced – he rang the doorbell at the flat of a friend, Naldo Naldi, whose wife was English; this seems to have been his last call before leaving Rome.

In an unpublished account written some years later, Naldi described how at first when the doorbell rang he and his wife hesitated: they had no idea who it might be. When they opened the door, in walked the poet carrying his knapsack. He was not upset, said Naldi, but calm and resigned; he explained his position in short sentences, speaking part of the time to the wife in English. When she asked what they could do for him, he said there was nothing he wanted, but later he admitted he was hungry and gratefully accepted two eggs – then unprocurable in Rome – together with tea and some bread. Into his knapsack they put an egg, fruit, a tea-bag and the rest of the bread. He had not come for food, he explained, but to see a friendly face and to get some information on the best way to leave the city. Naldi marked his map for him and they said goodbye; he was very upset as he shook Mrs Naldi by both hands. The husband accompanied him along the street for a short distance. 'At the corner', he wrote, 'I showed him the right way to go. He shook my hand, without speaking. It is difficult to find the right words when things are so enormously complex. I watched him go off, his stick striking the footpath regularly . . . I did not see him again.'

Pound left Rome by the Via Salaria; he passed by the township of

Fara Sabina to Rieti, sleeping under the stars. In what appears to be a reference to this in the pamphlet *Oro e Lavoro*, published in Rapallo the following spring, Pound gave the date of his leaving Rome as 10 September. Later he managed to board a train going north. It is said that on one occasion during the journey the train was so crowded he gave up his seat, got out, and continued for part of the way again on foot. Another account says that he ran into trouble with some German military authorities and it was because of this that he left the train. Probably it was during his flight that he was helped by Carl Goedel, an official in the English section of Rome Radio who soon afterwards went to work for the Salò Republic in Northern Italy. Goedel is mentioned on the second page of canto 78, in a passage which deals with Pound's journey northwards and the fall of Fascism; he is brought in again on the first page of canto 79:

> (to Goedel in memoriam)
> Sleek head that saved me out of one chaos. . . .

In a letter written in October 1966 Mrs Pound recalled the period in these words: 'E.P. was in Rome when it was taken and he walked out (in a pair of Degli Uberti's heavy boots, many years later restored to owner) along the only road going north not infested by troops – spent a night in the open and with some peasants – got to a junction where there was a train going north with a herd of the dismantled Italian army. . .' In an article published in 1966 his daughter said that during the long journey he slept in farms, in dormitories, and in the open, receiving food from kindly women on the way. Altogether Pound travelled more than 450 miles, arriving at Gais, his daughter said, 'one late afternoon, exhausted, his feet all blisters'. In the safety of his daughter's foster-family he was at last able to rest.

But the situation in the Italian Tirol was no less chaotic than in the south, for the war had afforded the German-speaking section of the population the opportunity to display its Pan-Germanism and to sever, as it thought, its connection with Italy. A few days after Pound's arrival at Gais two Tiroleans with rifles – members of the local Home Guard – called at the house, apparently with the intention of arresting him. By their calculation Pound was some sort of enemy; but one of them, a wood-carver, was fascinated by the poet's head, and the interrogation drifted to other things. They decided to allow him to stay until his feet had healed, suggesting that he then go to Germany, or – a guide could be provided – over the mountains into Switzerland. He filled in his time at Gais by doing odd jobs around the house: he repaired a chicken-coop and also stairs leading from the stable to the upper-floor and barn. From Gais he sent a letter to Olga Rudge at Sant' Ambrogio, who went down immediately to Rapallo, where Dorothy Pound was staying, to give her the news. They knew from the letter, Mrs Pound told me, that he was safe and that he had slept in the open, but it gave no details of what had happened.

Two years later he included glimpses of Gais and the Italian Tirol in his *Pisan Cantos*: in nos. 77 and 78 he recalled 'the long lazy float' of the tall banners carried by the Tiroleans in religious processions and in 77 mentioned a girl he had seen there who had been brought up by the same woman as his daughter:

> And Margherita's voice was clear as the notes of a clavichord
> tending her rabbit hutch

While there he also saw, or heard of, examples of maladministration or dishonesty of a kind that accounted, he thought, for the fall of Fascism:

> cut down the woods whose leaves served for bedding cattle
>   so there was a lack of manure
>
> (canto 77)

After several weeks he returned to Rapallo by way of Lake Garda and Milan. Mrs Pound, in her letter of October 1966, says that he had 'various adventures' along the way, mentioning two Japanese with a volume of Confucius whom he came across in a restaurant in Milan. It is likely that he took the opportunity while passing around Lake Garda to make contact with the new Italian Republic then in the process of being formed at the small town of Salò, on the southern shore of the lake, by remnants of the Fascist regime.

Back in Rapallo he was soon working again: composing cantos, translating, and writing pamphlets, articles, manifestos and posters – all in Italian. Among the works he translated into Italian was an unpublished book on economics by J. P. Angold called *Lavoro e Privilegi* ('Work and Privilege'). Because of the wartime paper shortage the translation was closely typed to the edges on thirty large sheets; the typing was not done by Pound but later he made corrections and additions in his own hand. It was never published. In November 1943 he began to contribute to a newspaper, *Il Popolo di Alessandria*, published at Alessandria which lies between Genoa and Turin. Some thirty-five of his articles appeared there during the next sixteen months, dealing with usury, banking, the race question, Confucius, etc. Another Italian paper he contributed to at this time was *L'Idea Sociale*, also published at Alessandria.

But not content with newspaper articles and pamphlets as a means of drumming certain fundamental truths into people's heads, he also composed posters and a manifesto. The posters were printed, probably at the author's expense, in two sizes: approximately thirteen inches by twenty-seven inches and strips two and a half inches by nineteen inches. On the strips were such maxims (in Italian) as 'The archer who misses the bullseye turns and seeks the cause of his failure in himself' and 'The unmixed functions without end, in time and space without end', both of them from Pound's translation of Confucius. Another strip carried a message from Cavalcanti, 'Fashions a new person from desire', and there was one which read, 'So live that your children and their descendants will be thankful'. The larger posters, also in Italian, were on economics: 'Of the liberals we ask: Why are usurers all liberals? A Nation that will not get itself into debt drives the usurers to fury.' Although obviously printed for posting on walls and perhaps for distribution among friends and organizations, I have no evidence that they were so used.

In a letter to his lawyer, Julien Cornell, in October 1948 Pound made reference to what was apparently his success in introducing Jefferson to Fascist circles. 'Jefferson', he wrote, 'was finally quoted on fascist posters.' But whether these were official posters or posters which Pound supplied, for example to local Fascist organizations, I do not know.

Early in 1944 two manifestos were issued signed by Pound and a small group of Italian writers. The first appeared in *Il Popolo di Alessandria* for 27 February and also as a broadside; signed by Gilberto Gaburri, Ezra Pound, Edgardo Rossaro, Giuseppe Soldato and Michele Tanzi, it bears every mark of Pound's authorship. Calling themselves 'Gli scrittori del Tigullio' ('Writers of the Tigullio', after the gulf of Tigullio, on which Rapallo is situated) they first saluted the other writers of Italy and then immediately launched into a declaration beginning 'The live thought of the epoch is permeated by the fascist spirit'. With or without label the fascist intellect was visible in various countries: if Frobenius was not a textbook in Germany, yet his attitude was none the less totalitarian; Zielinski, the manifesto said, had sought to liberate Christianity from judaic dregs; and Cruet was similarly following Fascism in the legislative sphere. In fact a little of Fascism was to be found everywhere and it was even possible to speak of Confucius as the philosopher of Fascism; at the same time, however, Italy and Mussolini were essential elements. The perspicacity of Fascism, the 'scrittori del Tigullio' declared, was visible in the programme of the new Salò Republic, in which a distinction was drawn between the rights *of* property and the right *to* property. They also claimed that every truly 'live' writer outside the Axis countries was either openly in favour of Fascism or attacked 'our common enemies' in such a way that dull and anti-fascist writers dared not take up the challenge. The manifesto included the statement, 'The treasure of a nation is its honesty', which is also to be found in Pound's *Oro e Lavoro* and a declaration of the group's 'faith', namely that 'Liberty is a duty'. Some of these points, including those dealing with property and with liberty as a duty rather than a right, are taken up again in the *Pisan* section and later cantos. A second manifesto issued by Pound and three Italian writers later in 1944 bears little evidence of his authorship.

At Sant' Ambrogio he also wrote two cantos in Italian: they have the war for background and deal largely with Italians he had known, including Marinetti and Dazzi. He sent copies of them to his daughter who by the end of 1943 was working in a German military hospital at Cortina D'Ampezzo; sometimes he would also send copies of *Il Popolo di Alessandria* containing his articles. The two cantos (nos. 72 and 73) have not been published unless unnoticed in some Italian newspaper or magazine during the war.

In one of her letters from the hospital Mary Rudge told her father about a boy, then aged 23, who lived not far from her at Gais. Sent home from the hospital blind he did not approve of his father letting the old cows get so thin he could count their ribs with his fingers. Pound recalled this in canto 76:

> 'both eyes, (the loss of) and to find someone
> who talked his own dialect. We
> talked of every boy and girl in the valley
> but when he came back from leave
> he was sad because he had been able to feel
> all the ribs of his cow. . . .'

During 1944 and early 1945 Pound was in touch with officials of the Salò Republic, some of whom he called on at Lake Garda; his pamphlet *Oro e Lavoro*, possibly published at his own expense, was largely an attempt to lead the republic in the direction of monetary reform. In a letter to R. McNair Wilson on 26 November 1956 Pound said that the Salò government had published an Italian translation of Arthur Kitson's pamphlet on the 'Bank Conspiracy'. He was referring to Kitson's *The Bankers' Conspiracy* (London, 1933) which was published in Italian in May 1944 under the title *La storia di un reato* ('Story of a Crime'). This work came out under the imprint of the 'Casa Editrice delle Edizioni Popolari' in Venice — the same publishing house that handled six of Pound's own books and pamphlets in 1944 and 1945. Whether the republic backed the publishing house or only certain books is not clear; but it does seem likely that Pound was closely connected with the venture. If the republic had not been destroyed, he told McNair Wilson, 'one might have had at least an effective or active publishing machinery'. The six works by Pound printed by 'Edizioni Popolari' were: *L'America, Roosevelt e le cause della guerra presente* ('America, Roosevelt, and the Causes of the Present War'), a pamphlet published during the first half of 1944; *Introduzione alla natura economica degli S.U.A.* ('Introduction to the Economic Nature of the United States'), a pamphlet published in June 1944; *Testamento di Confucio* ('Testament of Confucius'), a republication in July 1944 of the Italian text of the bilingual edition of 1942; *Orientamenti* ('Orientations' or 'Bearings'), a one hundred and forty page book of political and economic articles printed in September 1944; *Jefferson e Mussolini*, a one hundred and twenty page book printed in December 1944; and *Ciung Iung L'Asse che non vacilla* ('Chung Yung, The Unwobbling Axis)', an Italian version by Pound of *The Unwobbling Pivot* of Confucius, published in February 1945.

The first two pamphlets, along with *Oro e Lavoro*, have been published since in English; so have the Confucius translations; but *Orientamenti* and *Jefferson e Mussolini* have not. Except for the first article, 'Nego', from the *Giornale di Genova* of 13 April 1940, *Orientamenti* consisted entirely of articles originally published in the *Meridiano di Roma* between 1939 and 1943. The printing of the book was completed towards the end of September 1944 and a few copies were distributed – one to the author and a few for review. Before the book was published the printer or publisher in Venice decided that the time was not propitious for the distribution of such material and almost the entire edition was destroyed. Donald Gallup, in his *Bibliography of Ezra Pound*, says: 'Only a small number of copies escaped destruction: although efforts were made at the time to secure additional author's copies, none was forthcoming.' Pound did not see proofs of the book and as a result there were numerous misprints. Looking through it and finding numerous fanatical references to Jews and Jewish bankers and to such groups as 'Baruch-Wiseman-Morgenthau-Roosevelt', and references also to most of his other political and economic themes, all expressed in the usual inflammatory language, we understand, even if we do not altogether approve, the action of the Venetian book-burner.

Jefferson e Mussolini was a rewriting by Pound in Italian of his earlier book, *Jefferson and/or Mussolini*, first published in 1935. Soon after the printing of the Italian version was completed in December 1944 it suffered the same fate as *Orientamenti*. Donald Gallup writes: 'Only a few copies escaped: one copy had been sent to Mussolini, although none had been sent to the author, and a few other copies had apparently been distributed for review.'

The Italian version of *The Unwobbling Pivot* (*L'Asse che non vacilla* in Pound's Italian) was actually published in February 1945 and copies were sold, but most of the edition was burned immediately after the Liberation because the word 'asse' means 'axis' and it was apparently taken to be Axis propaganda.

In Rapallo there had been the usual wartime hardships but not much evidence of the war itself: there was some low-level bombing and on one occasion a church and an orphanage were hit and an old priest killed; another day when Dorothy Pound visited Isabel she found her sweeping up glass from shattered windows, indignant at such unseemly conduct. Although money was once again scarce, Pound had a credit with the Bank of Chiavari and they were able to cover such essential expenses as family-tax. As for the Italian government bonds which he had bought some years earlier, these became worthless with the fall of Fascism.

I do not know what Pound thought about his predicament in 1945 as the Allied armies advanced into northern Italy and the war in Europe drew towards its close; but apparently there was some speculation even in the Salò Republic, for in the republic's Armed Forces magazine *Gladio* of 15 March 1945 Marco Ramperti praised him for his courage and defended him for his broadcasts over Rome Radio. Years later in *Il Nazionale* of 4 September 1955 a writer by the name of Damaso Riccioni said that he had met the poet at Lake Garda in 1944 with Serafino Mazzolini, Foreign Minister of the Salò Republic. Pound had defended himself against accusations that the broadcasts were wrong and according to Riccioni spoke of being guided by an interior light and claimed that his ideas were above warring factions and that eventually his own countrymen would have to admit that he was right. Riccioni's article may not be an accurate account of Pound's views but it does suggest that even then his conduct was under discussion.

Whatever he may have thought about it himself the fact is that he had been the subject of numerous cables and letters between Washington and the United States forces in Europe and Africa ever since the indictment of July 1943. His photograph and a description had been distributed and the Attorney-General Francis Biddle asked to be notified promptly if Pound was taken into custody.

The poet's final article at this time appears to have been a piece on economics published in *L'Idea Sociale* of 9 April 1945, after which he occupied himself at Sant' Ambrogio translating the *Book of Mencius*; he was at work on this – at the end of April or early in May – when two partisans came to the front-door with a tommy-gun. According to

Mrs Pound, in her letter of October 1966, he had attempted to give himself up to the Americans earlier: 'E.P. went to town to give himself up, as having lots of information about Italy which could be of use.' But nobody understood him, she said, and he was sent away.

Now the partisans took him for questioning, accompanied by Olga Rudge who insisted on staying with him. Dorothy Pound was away at the time paying her weekly visit to Isabel in Rapallo; she returned about six o'clock in the evening to find both Pound and Miss Rudge gone; it was five months before she saw her husband again. There are conflicting reports about what happened next: one says that he escaped from the partisans and gave himself up to the Americans in Genoa; but Pound's lawyer Julien Cornell said in an affidavit in November 1945 that Pound gave himself up to an American negro soldier whom he found with a partisan group and that at Pound's request the negro took him to an American post at Lavagna, a small town not far south of Rapallo. On 17 May an American Military Intelligence report said that Pound had been in the custody of the Counter Intelligence Centre at Genoa since 3 May; two days later a report to Allied headquarters in Italy said that 'Dr Ezra Pound', captured by partisans on 3 May, was in the custody of the Counter Intelligence Centre at Genoa and that an FBI agent had obtained a signed statement from him and was in possession of pertinent documents. The agent was probably a man by the name of Amprim, mentioned by Pound in letters later: Pound got on well with him and spoke freely about his aims in broadcasting. He also identified transcripts of some of his broadcasts and possibly other material. Apparently Amprim or some other FBI agent examined Pound's typewriter and found that the letter 't' was out of alignment; in this way the FBI traced some of his wartime writing.

On 8 May while under arrest in Genoa Pound was interviewed by an American journalist, Edd Johnson, whose story appeared the following day in the *Philadelphia Record* and *Chicago Sun*. It is possible that part of what Pound told Johnson disappeared in the mechanics of journalism, but the words published certainly have the true Poundian ring:

There is no doubt which I preferred between Mussolini and Roosevelt. In my radio broadcasts I spoke in favour of the economic construction of Fascism. Mussolini was a very human, imperfect character who lost his head.

Winston believes in the maximum of injustice enforced with the maximum of brutality.

Stalin is the best brain in politics today. But that does not mean that I have become a Bolshevik.

He also described Hitler as a martyr: 'Like many martyrs, he held extreme views.' He did not think that he would be shot for treason, he told his interviewer, and would rely on the American sense of justice. It was characteristic of him that he was less concerned with his own position than the importance of the information and shrewdness he had to offer the post-war world: 'If I am not shot for treason, I think my chances of seeing Truman are good.'

Obviously the army did not know what to do with its prisoner and finally the matter was passed to the Allied Commander, Field Marshal Alexander, who on 21 May informed the War Department in Washington that Pound was in custody and that the investigation into his activities had been completed; he asked what he should do with him. Next day came instructions that Pound be transferred without delay to the American Disciplinary Training Centre at Pisa: 'Exercise utmost security measures to prevent escape or suicide. No press interviews authorized. Accord no preferential treatment.' Handcuffed and led to a jeep the prisoner 'naïvely' believed, according to Cornell's November affidavit, that he was on his way to an aerodrome and the United States; but actually, by official blunder or design, he was headed for a camp that held the toughest criminals of the American army in the Mediterranean area. He was delivered to the camp on 24 May and held there as a military prisoner for six months.

The DTC, as it was called, was outside Pisa, on the road to Viareggio; it consisted of a barbed-wire stockade surrounded by fourteen guard-towers and at night illuminated by glaring lights. Inside were medical and dental sections, mess-halls, areas where the ordinary prisoners pitched their 'pup tents', and several rows of wire and concrete cages – the solitary confinement and death cells. The night before Pound arrived, acetylene torches were seen as engineers reinforced one of the cages with heavy 'airstrip' steel, a fact which immediately caused the new prisoner to be held in awe: what manner of man was this who was so resourceful as to render insecure cells that had hitherto proved inviolable. But it was not fear of Pound breaking out, apparently, which led to these precautions, but fear that Fascist commandos might break in and rescue him.

Dressed in an army 'fatigue' uniform – but without belt or shoe-laces, to prevent suicide – he paced the concrete floor of his tiny cage which gave no adequate shelter from rain, sun or dust from a nearby road. At first he slept on the floor with blankets but later was given a 'pup tent'. No one was supposed to speak to him but gradually surreptitious words were passed when meals were delivered or the lavatory bucket emptied. He was allowed several books – Confucius and a bible – and also writing paper and pencil or pen; to keep fit he played tennis with himself, fenced and shadow-boxed.

But despite his efforts to stay healthy and keep a hold on himself, after about three weeks of hot sun, dust and isolation he was stricken, according to Cornell, with violent and hysterical terror: 'He lost his memory. He became desperately thin and weak until finally the prison doctor feared for him.' From the cage he was removed to a tent in the medical compound where he had an army cot and a packing-case for furniture; later another packing-case and table were added. Although he was now given proper medical treatment he was kept isolated as much as possible and only allowed to visit the doctors after the other prisoners had left. It was September before he recovered from his attack. When word spread that he had run rings around the camp psychiatrist he became something of a hero. Gradually the men in the medical section allowed him to talk and before long he was telling them about usury and the American constitution. His daily exercises now became a feature of camp life: he took a brisk walk which gradually wore a circular path in the grass of the compound and with a broom-stick played imaginary games of tennis, billiards, baseball etc. But if conditions now were easier they were still far from perfect and his tent offered little protection from rain or cold. A member of the staff, Robert Allen, noted that his request for more blankets was delayed for a week while an officious corporal pondered the matter. Another staff member, John Gruesen, went to Rome to see Santayana, and carried with him a salutation from Pound. According to Charles Norman, Santayana was shocked to hear of Pound's plight: he expressed admiration for his work and hoped that he would be judged as a poet and helper of artists and that his confusing entry into alien disciplines would be understood and forgiven. When Gruesen reported on his trip Pound was delighted to hear that Santayana was well and had a good word for him.

Late at night the medical men allowed Pound to use the dispensary typewriter: he wrote letters for other prisoners – several, it has been said, for men about to be executed – and typed out English versions of several books of Confucius, working largely from his own earlier publications in Italian. For months his family did not know where he was or what had happened to him, but eventually he was allowed to write to his wife. There being no organized transport down the coast from Rapallo and with money short and petrol rationed, Mrs Pound spent ten days searching before she finally found a seat in a car going to Viareggio. Wearing a mackintosh which had belonged to Homer, she arrived at the camp on 3 October – his first visitor after five months' of imprisonment. When she told the guard at the gate who she was, he rang through on the sentry-box telephone: 'Tell Uncle Ez his wife is here to see him.' Their meeting took place in an office with guards present. At one point she handed her husband a slip of paper containing a number of ideograms from Confucius; the guards would not allow her to take it back again. She was given a meal at the camp and left about 6 o'clock in the evening for the return trip to Rapallo. This she managed with the help of an unknown Italian doctor who took her to his home at Massa Carrara where his wife gave her soup and hot milk and she stayed the night before moving north again next morning.

On 17 October Pound received a visit from Olga Rudge and Mary who travelled from Rapallo in an army jeep. Mrs Pound made a second visit on 3 November in a truck full of New Zealand army footballers. Miss Rudge and her daughter were planning a second trip but Pound was taken to the United States before they could arrange it. Omar Pound, who was in the American army, also visited the camp, but arrived the day after Pound's departure; he was the first to know that Pound had been taken to America and went immediately to Rapallo to tell his mother.

Meanwhile, news of Pound's predicament and an impending trial had reached James Laughlin in America and in September he asked a friend, Julien Cornell, an experienced lawyer, to defend him. Also in September Pound received a letter about his defence from his late father-in-law's firm, Shakespear & Parkyn, of John Street, Bedford Row, London. In a long reply dated 5 October Pound said he was glad to see from the firm's writing-paper that John Street had not been bombed out of existence. Regarding his defence he wrote that he had not been sending Axis propaganda but broadcasting his own ideas, the nucleus of which was in books by Brooks Adams published forty years earlier. He also discussed Douglas, the British Labour Party, freedom of speech in Italy, and the question of 'the re-education of Europe'. Observing that his own programme was now being put into effect 'all over the place', he was obviously confident that he still had a part to play in world economic and cultural affairs. He was particularly anxious to know whether Eliot at Faber & Faber was ready to publish his new versions of Confucius as 'the only basis on which a world order can work'. The Chinese Empire, he told Shakespear & Parkyn, offered during its great periods the only working model that could possibly serve in the post-war period: 'This may sound a large order, but we have come through a very large war. And someone has got to use adult intelligence in dealing with the world problem.' As Dorothy Pound, an American by marriage, was unable at this stage to obtain release of her money in England, Pound asked whether he had any royalties at Faber that could be sent to her.

On 9 October Arthur Moore, Pound's legal representative at Shakespear and Parkyn, wrote to Laughlin that he was troubled with the thought that in the face of advice Pound might try to handle his own defence. He had urged him, he said, not to attempt to address the court but to allow himself to be represented by the best possible Counsel.

Another difficulty with which I am confronted is the matter of finance. Dorothy in one of her letters to me states she is prepared to spend her last penny in the defence of her husband, but all her investments and funds in this country are in the hands of the official Custodian of Enemy Property . . . I was informed by this official that release could be obtained provided I obtained confirmation from American sources in Italy that Dorothy claimed protection as an American citizen, and that there was no charge of any description filed against her personally. I asked Dorothy to obtain this, and she informs me the American Consul at Genoa has informed her her status as an American citizen has 'lapsed' as she has not renewed her Passport since 1941.

He wondered whether Archibald MacLeish might be able to help in straightening the matter out. And he went on: 'I am only therefore in a position to say that any fees which Mr Cornell may charge could only be paid by Dorothy as and when her money is available, for she has ample to meet the costs, but if it will help matters I should be prepared to undertake that any costs would eventually be met, and if required I would make a personal remittance on account for this purpose.'

Hungry for news of the outside world Pound spent much of his time at the camp reading the army newspaper *The Stars and Stripes* and the magazines *Time* and *Newsweek*; also novels and memoirs. He was also writing poetry and in his letter of 5 October to Shakespear & Parkyn he said: 'can you ask Mr Eliot whether Faber will be ready to print another volume of Cantos?' At night in September, October and November when the other patients had left the dispensary and he was free to go there and use the typewriter, he sometimes sat typing this new batch of verse from notes entered during the day into a series of Italian school exercise books. As he typed he hummed to himself in a high-pitched tone, swearing 'well and profusely', said Robert Allen, whenever he made a mistake. When he had finished a sizable amount and had made numerous pencilled additions he would send the parcel to Dorothy Pound, who would pass it on to his daughter for re-typing. The fresh typescript would then be sent back to the camp.

Altogether he composed eleven new cantos – one hundred and twenty pages – in this way. They are confused and often fragmentary; and they bear no relation structurally to the seventy earlier cantos; but shot through by a rare sad light they tell of things gone which some-how seem to live on, and are probably his best poetry. In those few desperate months he was forced to return to that point within himself where the human person meets the outside world of real things, and to speak of what he found there. If at times the verse is silly, it is because in himself Pound was often silly; if at times it is firm, dignified and intelligent, it is because in himself Pound was often firm, dignified and intelligent; if it is fragmentary and confused, it is because Pound was never able to think out his position and did not know how the matters with which he dealt were related; and if often lines and passages have a beauty seldom equalled in the poetry of the twentieth century it is because Pound had a true lyric gift.

Out of a life of bright achievement and miserable failure he rescued the rare pieces and the broken columns, transforming them as with the pale light of a late afternoon in autumn. *The Pisan Cantos* are a man of sixty remembering, against a background of life in the Disciplinary Training Centre at Pisa, with a charitable Negro prisoner ('doan you tell no one I made you that table') taking his place alongside a memory of Cunninghame Graham riding in the Row in 1914. With an ear for voices and an eye for the telling image or phrase, he recorded memories of his early visits to New York and his first visit to Europe with his Aunt Frank; he remembered the stones of Venice and the house there ('the hidden nest') belonging to Olga Rudge; he also remembered London and Paris and his dead companions – Yeats, Ford, Hulme, Joyce, Newbolt, etc. Dreaming of his celestial city, 'now in the mind indestructible', he mentioned monetary reform and justice and voiced his hatred – though with less rancour now and in a more mellow tone – of usury and usurers. Inspired by association of ideas or words, as he recalled the past and what might have been, he inserted glimpses of the Pagan Mysteries and Christianity and quoted as they came to mind, borne upon what murmuring wind that blew through the camp, the words, phrases and lines of poets and writers past and present.

Often he quoted from his own versions of Confucius, on which he was then working. Thus, in canto 74, 'To study with the white wings of time passing', is from the *Analects* of Confucius (1.I.); in canto 74, 'and for three months did not know the taste of his food,' is from the *Analects* (3.XXV, 7.XIII, and 15.X); in canto 76, 'and in government not to lie down on it', is from the *Analects* (13.I); and in cantos 79 and 80, 'to get it across e poi basta' and 'To communicate and then stop', are from the *Analects* (15.XL).

One day, remembering Enrico Pea, he inserted a few lines of what Pea had told him in 1941 about the red mahogany bank desks in Egypt; at the same time he sent the novelist a 'treasured message' reminding him of their conversation. Another day he found Morris Speare's *The Pocket Book of Verse* on a lavatory seat, containing poems he was glad to re-read; he worked this incident into canto 80. In four different cantos he recalled Tinkham – his meeting with him in Venice and scraps from his letters in 1936; in canto 77 he remembered how Arthur Kitson had told him in a letter that many years earlier he had built a marine light on the hilltop at Portofino, across the bay from Rapallo.

The opening line of the Pisan section, 'The enormous tragedy of the dream in the peasant's bent shoulders', appears to be the fusion of a line, perhaps unconsciously remembered, from Joyce's *Ulysees* ('The movements which work revolutions in the world are born out of the dreams and visions in a peasant's heart on the hillside') and the idea, recently expressed in his own pamphlet, *L'America, Roosevelt e le cause della guerra presente*, that the war was 'part of the secular war between usurers and peasants, between the usurocracy and whomever does an honest day's work with his own brains or hands'. Sometimes, as in this case, the essence is contained in the words on the page, despite their brevity or the lack of accompanying explanation; but in some other cases the words are too few or too lifeless to convey what the poet has grasped and the reader is left with a puzzle, unenlightening even if solved. Much of the information we need to buttress our reading of many passages is not contained anywhere in the cantos but in *Guide to Kulchur* and other books; some of it is not in any of his books but only in his letters or in his biography or the books he had read; and some is nowhere but in the poet's head.

But in *The Pisan Cantos*, unlike earlier sections, the bad passages are seldom tiresome and if we read on we are sure to be rewarded. For, stript of all but himself and his one mastery, control of speech, he created a world which astonishes and delights, whether it be by sudden shock:

> all things that are are lights

and

> there was a smell of mint under the tent flaps
> especially after the rain

or by straggling procession, in which dignity and solemnity are matched with neat disorder:

> Lordly men are to earth o'ergiven
>   these the companions:
> Fordie that wrote of giants
>   and William who dreamed of nobility
>   and Jim the comedian singing:
>   'Blarrney castle me darlin'
>   you're nothing now but a StOWne'

413

One of the high points of *The Pisan Cantos* is the ending to canto 81, beginning:

What thou lovest well remains,
                                        the rest is dross
What thou lov'st well shall not be reft from thee
What thou lov'st well is thy true heritage. . . .

What Pound loved well he drew together in these eleven cantos; not the least of his loves, although he seldom could bring himself to admit it, was England:

and the Serpentine will look just the same
and the gulls be as neat on the pond
and the sunken garden unchanged
and God knows what else is left of our London
    my London, your London

                                        (canto 80)

In a written explanation to the camp censor, who may have suspected some kind of hidden message, Pound said that the cantos contained nothing in the nature of cypher or intended obscurity. They did however contain allusions and references to matter in the seventy-one cantos already published, many of which allusions and references could not be made clear to readers unacquainted with the earlier sections. There was also, he said, extreme condensation in the quotations, and he gave as example the words 'mi-hine eyes hev' ('Mine eyes have') in canto 80. They referred 'to the Battle Hymn of the Republic as heard from the loud speaker. There is not time or place in the narrative to give the further remarks on seeing the glory of the lord.' In like manner citations from Homer or Sophocles were brief and served to remind the ready reader that we were not born yesterday. The Chinese ideograms were mainly translated or commented on in the English text; at any rate they contained nothing seditious. He concluded: 'The form of the poem and main progress is conditioned by its own inner shape, but the life of the D.T.C. passing OUTSIDE the scheme cannot but impinge, or break into the main flow. The proper names given are mostly those of men on sick call seen passing my tent. A very brief allusion to further study in names, that is, I am interested to note the prevalence of early American names, either of whites of the old tradition (most of the early presidents for example) or of descendants of slaves who took the names of their masters. Interesting in contrast to the relative scarcity of melting-pot names.'

XXI   St Elizabeths Hospital 1945/1958

Five months having passed since Pound's arrival at Pisa and no word having been received from Washington, the American army in Italy began to worry about what to do with him. On 22 October a message was sent to the War Department saying that unless instructions were received soon they would release him. At this the bureaucratic machine began to move and in early November Pound read in *Stars and Stripes* that a number of Italian wireless technicians who had been present at his broadcasts were to be flown to the United States to testify as government witnesses at his trial. By now the case was being handled at the highest level and on 15 November the United States Attorney General, Tom C. Clark, wrote to the Secretary of War asking for Pound to be returned in the custody of the War Department, to arrive if possible in Washington, D.C., on 19 November. Next day a message from Washington to Italy said that he was to be taken 'on highest priority on regular flight leaving Rome 17 November and arriving US 19 November'. He was to be 'transported under military guards until relinquishment to federal authorities in US' and it was important that the aircraft make its first landing in the United States at Bolling Field in the District of Columbia. This last was because in the case of crimes committed outside the United States jurisdiction was in the district to which the defendant was first brought. Delivery to Bolling Field would avoid complications and enable him to be tried immediately in Washington.

On the night of 16 November Pound was sitting in the dispensary reading Joseph E. Davies's *Mission to Moscow*, from time to time commenting on its contents to the young man in charge. The door opened and two young officers entered; they told Pound to get his personal belongings together as he was about to be flown to Washington. According to Robert Allen, the poet handed the book to the 'Charge of Quarters' and asked him to thank all the medical personnel for their kindness. 'He then walked to the door of the prefab, turned and, with a half-smile, put both hands around his neck to form a noose and jerked up his chin.' He travelled to Rome in a jeep and handcuffed was taken aboard a waiting aircraft. Recalling the occasion for McNair Wilson thirteen years later he wrote that the Provost Marshal in charge was delighted to discover afterwards that the man 'he kicked out of the front seats reserved for the captive and guard' was the French ambassador. The ambassador's wife was amused later by the 'AMOUNT of armed force' required to receive the handcuffed prisoner in Washington. When he stepped from the plane it was night-time on 18 November; he was wearing baggy coat and trousers, an American army 'sweatshirt' and outsize army shoes, and carried a hat, heavy overcoat and small case.

He was taken to the District of Columbia gaol and next day appeared before Chief Judge Bolitha J. Laws; when he asked permission to act as his own counsel he was told that the charge was too serious for that. Returned to the gaol he was visited there for two hours on the morning of 20 November by Julien Cornell who the following day wrote to James Laughlin:

I found the poor devil in a rather desperate condition. He is very wobbly in his mind and while his talk is entirely rational, he flits from one idea to another and is unable to concentrate even to the extent of answering a single question without immediately wandering off the subject. We spent most of the time talking about Confucius, Jefferson and the economic and political implications of their ideas. I let him ramble on, even though I did not get much of the information which I wanted, as it seemed a shame to deprive him of the pleasure of talking, which has been almost entirely denied to him for a long while.

He felt that the poet was still under 'a considerable mental cloud': 'For instance, he kept talking about the possibility that powerful government officials with whom he had no acquaintance whatever might interest themselves in his case if they could be persuaded of the soundness of his economic views. He said that whether or not he is convicted he could be of tremendous help to President Truman, because of his knowledge of conditions in Italy and Japan.'

Cornell told Laughlin that he had discussed with Pound the possibility of 'pleading insanity' and the poet had no objection; he had also explained to him that he had not yet made up his mind whether he would handle the defence – it would depend somewhat on the course it would take – although he was quite willing to arrange for it and act as adviser. In a postscript he said: 'Pound wants you to publish his translations of Confucius, which are ready, and also a new volume of Cantos, some of which I believe he sent out from prison in Italy. He seems to think the Confucius is world shaking in its import and should be published immediately.'

416

In his cell on 25 November Pound had a serious attack of claustrophobia and spent the night in the gaol infirmary. On 26 November a new indictment, in place of the original one of 1943, was returned against Pound in the District of Columbia, because there was some question as to the sufficiency of the available evidence to sustain the charges in their original form, owing to the requirement in the American constitution of two witnesses to each overt act of treason. When next morning Cornell saw Pound at the gaol he found him in 'a state of almost complete mental and physical exhaustion'. After spending about an hour with him reading over the Pisan cantos the lawyer explained to him that he was to be arraigned that afternoon and would have to plead to the indictment. 'When I asked him whether he wanted to stand mute or would prefer to enter a plea', Cornell wrote in a letter of 6 December, 'he was unable to answer me. His mouth opened once or twice as if to speak, but no words came out. He looked up at the ceiling and his face began to twitch. Finally he said he felt ill and asked if he could not go back to the infirmary.'

In the afternoon the courtroom was crowded and Pound sat quietly, his hands folded and his eyes downcast, while Cornell explained that he was not in a fit condition to plead; the lawyer asked Judge Laws to enter a plea of not guilty for him. The charges against him were numerous and detailed: not only was it claimed that he did 'knowingly, intentionally, wilfully, unlawfully, feloniously, traitorously and treasonably' adhere to the enemies of the United States, namely the Kingdom of Italy and its military allies, and that he gave 'aid and comfort' to these enemies, but specific charges were made which indicate that the Department of Justice had detailed evidence of his wartime activities.

Among other things he was said to have accepted employment from Italy as a 'radio propagandist' and to have composed 'texts, speeches, talks and announcements' for broadcasting; to have counselled and aided Italy and its military allies by advocating to Italian officials ideas and thoughts which he believed would be 'useful to the Kingdom of Italy for propaganda purposes in the prosecution of the said war'; to have taken part in activities intended to persuade citizens and residents of the United States 'to decline to support the United States in the conduct of the said war' and to weaken or destroy confidence in the American government and the integrity and loyalty of the country's allies; and to have attempted to strengthen the morale of the Italian people in support of the war against America. Other points made in the charges were that he attempted to cause dissension and distrust between America and her allies and asserted in his broadcasts that the war was an economic war in which the U.S. and its allies were the aggressors; also that he attempted to create racial prejudice in the United States, that he urged Americans to read European publications rather than the American press, that he said Italy was the natural ally of the U.S. and that the 'true nature of the Axis regime' had been misrepresented to the American people.

Cornell told the court that Pound was in urgent need of medical care and asked that he be moved immediately from the gaol to a hospital; that same day Judge Laws directed that he be transferred to a hospital 'for examination and observation and for treatment, if found necessary'. Writing to A. V. Moore on 29 November Cornell explained what had been happening and assured him that Pound's friends in the U.S. were anxious to help him. 'Among those I know to be concerned, in addition to Mr MacLeish, are Ernest Hemingway, H. L. Mencken and E. E. Cummings. In addition, he has two very old and good friends living in Washington, Ida and Adah Lee Mapel, who have known him for 40 years, and they have been to see him and will continue to visit him regularly.'

Ida and Adah Lee Mapel were the two old Virginia ladies whom Pound had first met in Spain in 1906; he and Dorothy had stayed at Miss Ida's flat in Paris during their first post-war holiday in 1919. They visited him regularly in gaol and later in hospital and regularly sent Dorothy news: she described them to me later as 'two old ladies not used to having friends in gaol'. They were, she said, invaluable.

Pound's expenses were mounting but at the time Mrs Pound's funds in England were still blocked and the poet's account with the Jenkintown Trust Company, Jenkintown, Pennsylvania, was in the hands of the Custodian of Alien Property. However the immediate financial problem was met unexpectedly on 29 November when Cornell called on E. E. Cummings and his wife at their home in Patchin Place, New York. He was about to leave when Cummings walked across to his desk and searched through some papers; he handed the lawyer a cheque for one thousand dollars from an art gallery, saying that he had sold one of his paintings and did not need the money: 'Please take it and use it for Ezra.' Although it was intended as a gift rather than a loan Mrs Pound insisted on repaying Cummings when her funds were later released.

Pound was admitted to Gallinger Hospital in Washington on 4 December and was later examined by four doctors – three representing the government and the fourth chosen by Cornell. They were Dr Winfred Overholser, Superintendent of St Elizabeths Hospital, a Federal government asylum for the insane; Dr Marion King, Medical Director of the United States Health Service; Dr Joseph Gilbert, chief psychiatrist at Gallinger Hospital; and Cornell's choice, Dr Wendell Muncie, among other things Associate Professor of Psychiatry at the Johns Hopkins Hospital, Baltimore. They examined Pound together and separately over more than a week and on 14 December reported unanimously to Judge Laws that he was 'insane and mentally unfit for trial': 'At the present time', they wrote, 'he exhibits extremely poor judgment as to his situation, its seriousness and the manner in which the charges are to be met. He insists that his broadcasts were not treasonable, but that all of his radio activities have stemmed from his self appointed mission to "save the constitution". He is abnormally grandiose, is expansive and exuberant in manner, exhibiting pressure of speech, discursiveness, and distractibility. In our opinion, with advancing years his personality, for many years abnormal, has undergone further distortion to the extent that he is now suffering from a paranoid state which renders him mentally unfit to advise properly with counsel or to participate intelligently and reasonably in his own defence.'

A week later Cornell's motion for bail was denied and Pound was committed to St Elizabeths Hospital. But this was not the end of the matter: the government's lawyers said, according to the *New York Herald Tribune* of 22 December, that he might be feigning insanity and that they would ask for a public hearing. Army psychiatrists who had examined him a month ago in Italy had found, they said, that he was sane, although he might be suffering temporarily from claustrophobia.

At St Elizabeths, Pound was placed in Howard Hall, a ward with locked doors and barred windows, and surrounded by a very high wall; the other inmates were lunatics. Pound began to refer to it as the 'hell-hole'. Not only did his claustrophobia return but he was visited by the fear of going mad; he also became concerned in January 1946 about the world's ignorance and the task of education that still confronted him. But if conditions were difficult and the outlook for the future bleak he was kept going by faith in his cause and his belief that he was right. On at least one occasion his 'clear conscience' was the occasion of great happiness despite his surroundings. 'I remember', he wrote to McNair Wilson in April 1958, 'a moment of quite irrational happiness in the hell-hole.'

Determined to go further into the question of his mental state, the Attorney General's office applied to the court for a further hearing and on 16 January the motion was granted. The actual hearing took place on 13 February in a crowded courtroom. In his book *The Trial of Ezra Pound*, published in New York in 1966, Cornell said that on the day he was worried about Pound: 'He was very nervous about the trial and I was afraid he might blow up. I told him that I would not put him on the witness stand, and he did not need to do anything but listen to the proceedings.'

The four doctors who earlier had declared him insane had examined

him further in St Elizabeths. Called before the court they were subjected to detailed questioning by two government lawyers and Cornell,
the former attempting to break their testimony. But the doctors
remained firm: Pound was unable to reason properly, in the sense that
he was unable to stick to the point, and suffered from an accumulation
of delusions about the world and his own powers which inside his mind
had become, according to Muncie, systematized and embedded; as a
result he would be unable to consult with a lawyer in meeting the
charges against him.

During the afternoon session while Dr Overholser was being
questioned, a government lawyer, Isaiah Matlack, asked: 'Did he give
you in his general history anything about his belief in Fascism?' At the
mention of Fascism Pound jumped to his feet and shouted: 'I never did
believe in Fascism, God damn it; I am opposed to Fascism.'

Dr Overholser had with him in court a briefcase containing reports
on Pound by a number of young doctors on his staff at St Elizabeths.
The previous day he had told Cornell that the doctors disagreed with
his own finding; they thought Pound was merely eccentric and wanted
to see him tried and convicted. Overholser said he would take the reports
with him to the court and produce them if asked, explaining why he disagreed with them. At one stage during the hearing Matlack asked him
if he had received opinions from doctors on his staff: Overholser said
yes, he had them in his briefcase; but he was not asked to read them.

After a brief summary and explanation by Judge Laws the jury
retired; they returned after only three minutes to announce a verdict
of 'unsound mind'. The poet was then committed to St Elizabeths
Hospital, but under American law liable, if restored to sanity, to be
brought before the court for trial.

In June 1946 Dorothy Pound succeeded in having her passport
renewed and sailed from Genoa for the United States and Washington,
where she stayed with the Mapel sisters until she found a room near
the hospital. She had been to see her husband three times when on
14 July she wrote to Cornell saying that he was very nervous and jumpy:
'I believe his wits are really very scattered, and he has difficulty in
concentrating for more than a few minutes.' Judging from the letter
Pound was anxious for news of the outside world but did not trust the
newspapers to supply his need; also he was not sure that Cornell understood his case or the relevance of his economic teachings. From letters
and the testimony of the doctors it would seem that Pound was living
in a world at times far removed from reality. For one thing he kept
insisting that when he 'gave himself up' in May 1945 it was with the
intention of assisting the American government in the difficult post-
war period, but he had been betrayed by the British Secret Service or the

Communists; he also insisted that his new versions of Confucius provided the only solid foundation on which to build a new world.

Pound was aware that he was ill and believed that he could never
get well while at Howard Hall; those who visited him were appalled at
the conditions in which he was confined. Mrs Pound suggested that he
might be moved to a private sanatorium but on 15 July Cornell pointed
out to her that this could only be done by obtaining bail or dismissal of
the charges. 'I discussed this question', he said, 'with Mr Eliot, Mr
Laughlin and others a few weeks ago and all were agreed that such an
application should not be made at the present time because of public
clamour which would arise in opposition.'

On 29 January 1947 Cornell made an application for bail, pointing
out to the court that the law was silent on the question of what should
be done with a person who having been committed to St Elizabeths
Hospital was judged to be permanently insane but not in need of
hospital treatment. When Overholser testified that the poet was still in
need of care but would benefit by removal from Howard Hall, a
compromise was reached by which the Judge and the Attorney General
overrode hospital regulations and allowed him to be moved to the
Chestnut Ward, a more pleasant section of St Elizabeths where he had
a room with a view over the Potomac River. In the dark and sometimes
noisy ward outside was an alcove where he was allowed to entertain
visitors. He moved into his new quarters on 4 February 1947 and Mrs
Pound was able to spend several hours with him each day instead of the
fifteen minutes allowed in the 'hell-hole'.

Because Pound was considered an 'incompetent person' Mrs Pound
was appointed 'committee' to act for him and to take charge of his
estate. In December 1947 she discussed with her husband and Cornell
the possibility of obtaining his release and of their returning to Italy if
conditions were suitable or going to Spain. As a result Cornell applied to
the District Court on 11 February 1948, in the name of Mrs Pound,
for a writ of habeas corpus. He pointed out that after several years of
treatment it was Overholser's opinion that Pound would never recover
his sanity and never be fit to stand trial; at the same time the doctor
described his condition as mild and said that he would benefit by being
released. Cornell then went on to describe the strange situation whereby
a man who had been charged with a crime but not tried was in danger
of being confined for life because 'he had not sufficient mental capacity
to meet the charge'. When in March the court refused to issue the
writ Cornell immediately appealed: he explained to Mrs Pound that
the appeal might be difficult and might have to go as far as the Supreme
Court but he thought there was a good chance of success. On 13 March
Mrs Pound wrote to the lawyer: 'Please withdraw the appeal at once.

My husband is not fit to appear in court and must still be kept as quiet as possible; the least thing shakes his nerves up terribly.' There the matter rested for ten years, until April 1958 when with the government's consent the indictment was dismissed.

During his first few years in St Elizabeths Pound read newspapers and magazines and any books that came his way and drew support from the visits of his wife and friends. Dorothy Pound visited the hospital almost every day for twelve years, providing him with a good listener who could also see to his various wants – subscriptions to magazines, writing materials, etc. Among the first to visit him, early in 1946, were E. E. Cummings and his wife, the photographer Marion Morehouse. A snap she took (against the regulations) shows Pound leaning back in a U.S. Government chair, a wry expression on his face, a carnation in his buttonhole. Another early visitor for whom Pound was extremely thankful at the time was the poet Charles Olson who had covered the court hearings for *The Partisan Review*; he defended Pound in the Winter issue, 1946, and was frequently in touch with him during the next few years. According to Cornell, the 'most faithful and concerned' of Pound's friends was Eliot who each year on lecture-tours or business trips to the United States called on Pound and also met Cornell and others to discuss his welfare. His efforts had begun on 16 May 1945 as soon as he heard of his being taken into custody and quite early when there was still the possibility of a trial he wrote to leading literary figures asking them to sign an appeal on Pound's behalf should he be found guilty. After a visit to the hospital in November 1948 he attempted to have certain restrictions lifted on Pound's freedom of movement in the grounds and suggested that it might be a good thing if he were moved to some other building where he would not be among patients so visibly insane as those in the Chestnut Ward. Cornell referred the matter to Overholser who replied: 'he has at the present time far more privileges than any other prisoner in the Hospital. He is on a quiet ward, has a room by himself and is allowed a good deal of latitude in the way he occupies himself . . . I can assure you that we shall do everything within reason for the comfort of Mr Pound, but in spite of his being a well-known author, I question whether I should put myself in the position of giving unusual privileges to him over and above those which he already enjoys.'

Other support came in the form of letters from Olga Rudge, his daughter Mary, now married to an Italian, and a few old friends such as Olivia Rossetti Agresti. Miss Rudge salvaged, or re-translated from Italian, the conversation between Ford and Pound at Rapallo in 1932 which at the time she had published in *Il Mare*. Her English version appeared in *The Western Review* in the Autumn of 1947 and later was included in the book *Pavannes and Divagations*. In January 1948 Miss Rudge had a small booklet printed in Siena, where she still worked for the Accademia Chigiana, containing six of his wartime broadcasts. It was called '*If this be treason . . .*' and was distributed to those who might be interested in Pound's case and be able to help. The broadcasts were on Cummings, Joyce, modern French literature (including Celine), canto 45 and Wyndham Lewis and *Blast*. In October 1948 she drew up, for signature by responsible citizens of Rapallo, a statement dealing with Pound's activities there before and during the war:

The undersigned having known the American writer Ezra Pound in Rapallo where he resided from 1923 declare that to their knowledge he took no part in Fascist activities in this town. He was never present at the local meetings or enrolled in the Fascist organizations.

He was always considered as an American citizen, a friend of Italy, openly sympathizing with certain Fascist principles relating to political economy and in the fight against Communism which he held to be a danger to the United States themselves. During the war Mr Pound continued to reside in Rapallo and from the tenor of his life it was evident that not only was he not benefitting from any special privileges but was suffering privations and economic hardship. The fact being evident that he had never acted from hope of gain enabled him to maintain the respect even of those among his fellow townsmen who disagreed with his political opinions.

Mr Pound's activity during the long years of his residence in Rapallo was always artistic and cultural as shown in his literary criticism and writings on political economy.

He always behaved with correctness and has never demonstrated anti-semitism.

Among those who signed were doctors, shopkeepers, waiters, priests, peasants, municipal and bank employees, a lawyer, a painter and an editor. The final signature was the mayor's, a man by the name of Maggio, said to have been well known as an anti-Fascist; he added a note saying that he signed 'in consideration of the good that Mr Pound had always done in Rapallo'. Miss Rudge also continued the work he had carried out in his *Guido Cavalcanti Rime* and in 1949 published in Siena, as number nineteen in the series 'Quaderni dell' Accademia Chigiana', three canzoni not included in that book.

Life in St Elizabeths was not always easy and there were many distractions such as blaring wireless and television sets and wandering or curious patients in the ward; but, as always, Pound made the best of it and despite the feeling sometimes of isolation and being neglected eventually established there a 'Pound Centre' with world-wide ramifications. There was plenty to keep his mind active, including hostility in some newspapers, controversy over his work and his legal position, and the publication during 1946 and 1947 of some of the *Pisan Cantos* in such magazines as *The Quarterly Review of Literature* (canto 84, in the summer of 1946), *The Rocky Mountain Review* (canto 77, summer 1946), *The Yale Poetry Review* (canto 83, 1947), and *Sewanee Review* (canto 74, January–March issue, 1947). Also, his versions of *The Unwobbling Pivot* and *The Great Digest* of Confucius, which he considered so important, were published by Laughlin in the Winter 1946–7 issue of *Pharos*, and his version of four chapters from Mencius in the Autumn 1947 issue of *New Iconograph* (New York).

In 1946 Random House of New York, in the person of Bennett Cerf, decided to delete twelve poems by Pound from a new edition of their *Anthology of Famous English and American Poetry*, edited by William Rose Benét and Conrad Aiken. In their place it was decided to publish a note that the publishers, overruling Aiken, flatly refused to include a single line by Pound. But before the book could be published a storm of argument blew up and on 16 March 1946, in the *Saturday Review of Literature*, Cerf admitted that he was wrong. Finally, after letters from Cornell, Random House paid three hundred dollars for the twelve poems and to accompany them inserted a brief note, approved by Pound, in which they mentioned the controversy and conceded that 'it may be wrong to confuse Pound the poet with Pound the man'.

It was not long before Pound was seeking an outlet for his economic and political ideas and in 1948, a young man by the name of Dallam Simpson, began to publish at Galveston, Texas, a small Poundian leaflet called *Four Pages*, with Henry Swabey its representative in England. The first issue, published in January 1948, after consultations with Pound about contents and format, contained a statement by Cummings: 'Since you ask me, I'd love to experience a universe of individual human beings; where-and-when the privacy of each individual was honoured – not merely respected – by every', and an item from Olivia Rossetti Agresti bemoaning the effect of orthodox economics on Italy and England; there was also an unsigned item almost certainly by Pound: 'The defeated British would rather be taxed 45 per cent, or more, of their gross income, than 12 per cent of what they do not spend within a month of getting. That gives one the measure of the mental squalor of the nation from which we derived our official language, and which supplied us until recently, with the backbone of our reading matter.' The opening part of the statement was a typically Poundian way of saying that the British preferred income tax to Gesell's stamp scrip money; under this latter, money not spent by the end of each month would be taxed one per cent (twelve per cent per year).

Four Pages continued for several years and numbered Basil Bunting and the late Duke of Bedford (who was a monetary reformer) among its contributors. The issue of October 1950 contained an unsigned piece by Pound in which he discussed Gesell and government control of money, declared that Alexander Del Mar's 'thirty volumes may be taken as preface to whatever anyone may henceforth write on such subjects', and followed this with the statement that 'the mystery of his occultation from 1900 until his death in 1926 has yet to be unveiled'. To the fourth number of the leaflet he contributed a short literary item – a translation of 'Going South', by an Italian friend Felice Chilanti.

In 1955 he helped to establish a similar leaflet called *Strike* which was edited in Washington by another of his young visitors, William McNaughton. During 1955 and 1956 Pound contributed about sixty short items on economics, politics and education.

But let us return now to the 1940s. After Dorothy Pound had left Rapallo for America, Isabel Pound, now an invalid, journeyed to the Italian Tirol to live with her granddaughter Mary at Schloss Neuhaus, Gais. She died there on 9 February 1948, aged 88. Speaking to me of her husband a few years ago Dorothy Pound said: 'Ezra got his charm from Homer, his push from Isabel.' In 1958 Pound remarked in conversation that he had never appreciated his mother or what she had done for him in the way of up-bringing until she was dead.

On 30 July 1948 Laughlin published *The Pisan Cantos*; the Faber edition followed on 22 July 1949 but with a number of omissions and expurgations. In canto 74, for example, Faber deleted a reference to King David as 'the prime s.o.b.' and a few pages further on took out the words 'Churchill's backers' in the following:

and if the packet gets lost in transit
        ask Churchill's backers
where it has got to

A few pages further on again, in the same canto, they removed the following passage about Will Lawrence and the Duke of Windsor:

and sd Mr Kettlewell looking up from a
pseudo-Beardsley of his freshman composition
   and speaking to W. Lawrence:
                      Pity you didn't finish the job
while you were at it"
    W.L. having run into the future non-sovereign Edvardus
on a bicycle equally freshman
            a.d. 1910 or about that

In canto 77 where Cocteau's housekeeper refers to Jacques Maritain as a priest in disguise, Faber replaced the name Maritain by 'M . . .' and in canto 80 deleted the line about the bidet in the following:

> Pétain defended Verdun while Blum
> was defending a bidet

Although not universally praised *The Pisan Cantos* was well received or sympathetically reviewed in numerous important newspapers and journals in the United States; but on 20 February 1949 when the Library of Congress announced that the book had won the first annual award of the Bollingen Prize for poetry, a new storm broke. The prize of one thousand dollars was for the best book of American verse for the year, chosen by the Fellows in American Letters of the Library of Congress, at the time consisting of Conrad Aiken, W. H. Auden, Louise Bogan, Katherine Garrison Chapin, T. S. Eliot, Paul Green, Robert Lowell, Katherine Anne Porter, Karl Shapiro, Allen Tate, Willard Thorp, Robert Penn Warren and Leonie Adams. In recommending the award to Pound the Fellows were aware that objections might be raised and defended their choice in advance by pointing out that they had been asked to select the best book among those eligible: 'To permit other considerations than that of poetic achievement to sway the decision would destroy the significance of the award and would in principle deny the validity of that objective perception of value on which civilized society must rest.'

Argument broke out immediately in the daily papers and continued for more than a year in literary magazines and journals of opinion. One of the Fellows, Karl Shapiro, who voted against Pound in the balloting, told the other judges that he had done so 'in the belief that the poet's political and moral philosophy ultimately vitiates his poetry and lowers its standards as literary work'. But his main reason, he wrote in the May 1949 issue of *The Partisan Review*, was that he was a Jew and could not honour an anti-semite. There was a certain amount of laughter in the popular papers about poetry and madness: 'He started out to be a bard and ended up barred', 'Pound went from bad to verse and won $1000', 'Ezra was so unbalanced he wouldn't even hang straight'. But the more serious comment, when it was not about the difficulty of modern poetry, was divided generally between those who saw it as a blow struck for Fascism and anti-semitism and those like Dwight Macdonald who believed that it was one of the brightest and most civilized things that had happened in America for some time.

Fresh fuel was added to the blaze in June 1949 when Robert Hillyer ('Pulitzer Poetry Prize winner and president of the Poetry Society of

America') wrote a particularly heated series of articles for the *Saturday Review of Literature*; this caused the newspapers to join in again, forced the Librarian of Congress, Luther Evans, to reply, and in August resulted in the government deciding that poetry was too hot to handle and that in future it would have nothing to do with the Bollingen prize, which was taken over by Yale University.

One of the Fellows who voted for Pound, Allen Tate, later defended the choice in the *Partisan Review*: he said that even if Pound had been a convicted traitor it would not alter the fact that in his concern for language he had performed 'an indispensable duty to society'. Like Eliot, Tate had taken an interest in Pound's welfare and had discussed the matter with Cornell in New York, despite the fact that Pound was not very enthusiastic about him or his work. Shortly after the judges' decision, but before it had been made public, Tate visited Pound at St Elizabeths, accompanied by another Fellow, Theodore Spencer, with whom Pound had stayed during his 1939 visit to Harvard. In a letter of 4 July 1966 Tate told me that Pound virtually ignored Spencer. He handed Tate a slip of paper on which he had written the names of twelve men, such as could be entrusted no doubt with important literary and educational work in the future. When Tate asked why he had not included Marianne Moore in the list Pound replied: 'We couldn't have a woman among the twelve.' Tate carried away the distinct impression that Pound was unbalanced. As far as I have been able to judge Pound did not actively dislike him and in St Elizabeths was pleased to number him among his friends; he also urged some of his correspondents to write to him as to a person of some importance. I think that generally he regarded Tate as a man who was on the right side but not active enough in the pursuit of Poundian goals. Certainly there is evidence that during this period Pound could turn suddenly, even against good friends, when they seemed to be getting too much of the limelight or were slow in falling in behind him in his fight to reform the universities and the monetary system.

It was about this time that Pound began to translate the 'Odes' of ancient China, assisted sometimes by Veronica Sun, a Chinese girl who was a student at the Catholic University in Washington. She would sit opposite him with the Chinese text while he read out his translations; her job was to warn him when he was straying too far from the original, but I was once told that she was sometimes reluctant to do this, as she thought it a breach of good manners for a young student to correct a great poet. A high-born Chinese, she was considered haughty by Pound and some of his other visitors; she is listed in one of the later cantos.

Life at the hospital entered a new phase about 1950 when *The Hudson Review* in New York began to publish and promote his work, and also, at his instigation, published Jaime de Angulo's 'Indians in Overalls', which in a letter to Hemingway in 1957 he described as 'possibly the only bit' of American prose 'from outside our li'l circle.' (De Angulo was an anthropologist and his 'Indians in Overalls' a neatly written account of the language and ways of the Pit River Indians among whom he lived.) Pound's version of the Confucian *Analects* appeared in the Spring and Summer issues of *The Hudson Review* in 1950 and his version of Sophocles' *The Women of Trachis* in the Winter issue, 1953–4; between 1954 and the end of 1956 they also published seven of the later cantos. Another step in the dissemination of his work and ideas was the publication in England and the United States in 1951 of Hugh Kenner's *The Poetry of Ezra Pound* which introduced him to a new generation, made converts of, or attracted anew, some of the old generation, and initiated a new era in Pound studies. An upsurge of interest also occurred in England as the result of Peter Russell's activities. He not only edited a collection of essays on Pound, published in 1950, but formed an 'Ezra Pound Society', published some of Pound's work and publicized some of his ideas in his magazine *Nine*, and gave prominence to his books and ideas through the lively booklists he distributed in connection with this new and secondhand book business at Tunbridge Wells. Between 1950 and 1952 he brought out English translations of Pound's four wartime pamphlets, under the titles, *A Visiting Card*, *America*, *Roosevelt and the Causes of the Present War*, *Gold and Work* and *Introduction to the Economic Nature of the United States*, and also new editions of the earlier pamphlets in English – *Social Credit*: *An Impact* and *What is money for?* With assistance from Pound he established The Pound Press which in 1953 published a new edition of *ABC of Economics*.

It was at this time also that D. D. Paige, who in 1948 had been granted access by Olga Rudge to Pound's papers in Rapallo, edited *The Letters of Ezra Pound 1907–1941*; the American edition was published by Harcourt, Brace & Company in October 1950 and the English edition by Faber in March 1951. Although only a selection it contained much interesting information on a crucial period in English letters and pleased also by its flashes of brilliance and humour and came as a revelation to many for whom previously Pound had been just a name or a closed book.

Pound had by now discovered the nineteenth-century American historian Alexander Del Mar and was once again taking notes for his cantos. Born in New York in 1836 Del Mar became a mining and civil engineer and for a short time in the 1860s was Director of the U.S. Bureau of Statistics. In 1872 he represented the United States at the International Statistical Congress in Russia and four years later was appointed Mining Commissioner to the U.S. Monetary Commission; he wrote a number of books and articles on the history of money and the precious metals. Soon Pound was referring to him as a great historian and finally as America's greatest historian, whose work had been made to disappear by the usurocracy or a combination of the usurocracy and a mindless or corrupt education system. One of Pound's main points at this time was that there could be no civilization without local control of local purchasing-power. He had first been struck by this idea while reading Brooks Adams in 1940. 'Throughout Alexander of Macedon's empire', he wrote to Douglas in that year, 'many cities retained right of coinage, struck imperial tetradrachma by their own authority and for own convenience. Maintained standard long after Alex's death. Hence of course a bit of civil life.' When he discovered support for the idea in Del Mar he was soon informing his correspondents and jotting it in one of his notebooks for use in the cantos.

Now that he was back at work on the poem he was reading or skimming through numerous books, tracts and articles on history, current events, philosophy, natural science, etc., and began corresponding again with Santayana in Rome. Although unable to understand or decipher much of what Pound wrote Santayana answered when he could; but it was no use: Pound was once again in full stride and the patient pen of the old Spanish philosopher was powerless against such a headlong rush. Pound had developed a theory about 'the intelligence working in nature', reverence for which formed, he said, 'a tradition that runs from Mencius, through Dante, to Agassiz, needing no particular theories to keep it alive'. When he spoke to Santayana of this 'intelligence', which enabled the cherry-stone to produce a cherry-tree rather than an oak, Santayana replied on 17 February 1950: 'somehow it possesses a capacity to develop other cherries under favourable circumstances, without getting anything vital wrong. That is "intelligence" of an unconscious sort. I agree in "respecting it". (It would be fussy to object to your word intelligence to describe that potentiality in the cherrystone).' Pound was irritated by Santayana's use of the word 'unconscious', but apparently he took the letter to mean that the philosopher had accepted his idea and henceforth could be counted as one of its supporters, for if I interpret correctly this is what he is saying in the following passage in canto 95:

'O World!'
        said Mr Beddoes.
'Something *there*.'
        sd/ Santayana.
Responsus:
        Not stasis/
        at least not in our immediate vicinage.

One of the early visitors to St Elizabeths, who did not tire of Pound's obsessions or quarrel with him, was a young law student, T. D. Horton, who continued to visit him throughout the 1950s. With John Kasper, a bookseller, Horton began a publishing venture called the Square Dollar Series, the aim of which was to publish little known works which Pound said were essential for every student. The series boasted an advisory committee consisting of Otto Allen Bird (University of Notre Dame), James Craig La Driere (Catholic University of America), L. R. Lind (University of Kansas), Herbert Marshal McLuhan (University of Toronto) and Norman Holmes Pearson (Yale); but most of the advising was done by Pound who also composed or inspired the 'blurbs' and advertising material. All six books in the series were sold for one dollar; they were: Fenollosa's *The Chinese Written Character* (in the same volume as Pound's *The Unwobbling Pivot* and *The Great Digest*); *The Analects* of Confucius, translated by Pound; *Gists from Agassiz* selected by John Kasper; *Barbara Villiers or A History of Monetary Crimes* by Del Mar; *Bank of the United States* by Thomas Hart Benton; and Del Mar's *Roman and Moslem Moneys*. Agassiz was the nineteenth-century Harvard naturalist, Louis Agassiz, famous in his day as a teacher; he was also an opponent of Darwin. Thomas Hart Benton was a nineteenth-century senator who in the 1850s published an account of his political life under the title *Thirty Years' View: or A History of the Working of the American Government 1820 to 1850*; it was from this book that the Square Dollar text was drawn.

On an advertising leaflet for the series Pound wrote:

The boredom caused by 'American culture' of the second half of the XIXth century was due largely to its being offered as 'something like' English culture, but rather less lively; something to join Tennyson in 'The Abbey' perhaps, but nothing quite as exciting as Browning, or Fitzgerald's Rubaiyat. . . . Square Dollar is starting with American writers who can hold their own either as stylists or historians against any foreign competition whatsoever. Agassiz, apart from his brilliant achievements in natural science, ranks as a writer of prose, precise knowledge of his subject leading to great exactitude of expression.

The Square Dollar books were, he said, 'A set of texts intended to foster the spirit of reverence for the intelligence working in nature' and also 'Basic education at a price every student can afford'. The leaflet announced that Confucius and Del Mar were 'now required reading in a number of major colleges and universities' and went on to say that Del Mar was America's greatest historian: 'He made great progress from Mommsen, and corrected Thorold Rogers. Along with Louis Agassiz and Leo Frobenius, he builds upon Alexander von Humboldt's "art of collecting and arranging a mass of isolated facts, and rising thence, by a process of induction to general ideas",' this latter acknowledged as a quotation from 'K. Bruhns'. It was announced that 'The basic sections of Blackstone necessary to a well balanced study of the humanities will be published as soon as possible', but they never appeared. Other items published by Kasper & Horton under Pound's guidance were a small pamphlet containing the text of the American constitution, a fourteen-page chapter from Del Mar called *History of Netherlands Monetary Systems*, and *A Study of the Federal Reserve* by Eustace Mullins – another regular visitor to St Elizabeths during the 1950s. Kasper & Horton also appear to have had a hand in the publication by Dallam Simpson in 1950 of *Poems* by Basil Bunting; or if not connected with the actual publication seem to have taken the book over soon afterwards.

John Kasper withdrew from Kasper & Horton to join the fight to maintain segregation of negroes and by 1956, when he was still in his twenties, was executive Secretary of the Seabord White Citizens Councils of Washington D.C. Stimulated largely by Pound's ideas on race and the Jews Kasper built much of his propaganda on Poundian lines and based one of his booklets on *Blast*:

> JAIL NAACP, alien, unclean, unchristian
> BLAST irreverent ungodly LEADERS

Apparently gifted as a public speaker he toured parts of the South stirring up his audiences against 'racial integration', the Jews and the Supreme Court. In Tennessee he became editor of the *Clinton-Knox County Stars and Bars*, described on its front page as 'A Nationalist-Attack Newspaper Serving East Tennessee'. In its first issue (8 February 1957) it announced that it was 'For local control of local purchasing-power' and 'Against interest-slavery' and its first leader was a previously published statement by Pound: 'The right aim of law is to prevent coercion, either by force or by fraud.' In another leader it criticized Clare Boothe Luce for not responding, while ambassador to Italy, 'to the countless pleas of Italian intellectual, religious, academic and political leaders demanding the immediate release from an 11-year political imprisonment of Ezra Pound'. He was described as 'America's greatest poet, man of letters, and leader in the life-death struggle against deadly usury, national and international'. What Pound wanted, the paper declared, was 'freedom from ruinous taxation and the right to issue circulating currency against available goods and work done, instead of the present infamy of interest-bearing bonds which benefits only the jew-bankers in New York and Washington.' Other contents included a review of Claude Bowers's *The Tragic Era* by one who had read Pound's *Jefferson and/or Mussolini* and a reprint of 'The River Merchant's Wife' from *Cathay*.

Kasper finally was sent to gaol for his stirring up of strife in Tennessee and the newspapers and magazines gave considerable attention to his connection with Pound. While there is no evidence that Pound told Kasper to go and do the things he did, there is plenty of evidence that he used him for his own purposes during the early 1950s and was a contributing factor in his later excesses. By the time Kasper began to visit St Elizabeths Pound had Jews on the brain and was tireless in his efforts to warn selected correspondents of their infiltration. There is little doubt that in attacking 'desegregation' Kasper thought that he was carrying on Pound's work and attacking Jewish power.

But, as always, Pound was fighting on many fronts. He inspired or helped to draw up a manifesto on 'the neglect of the Greek and Latin classics' and the need 'to maintain language in a healthy condition', which was signed by at least ten university professors, including Hugh Kenner and Marshal McLuhan; he helped to form an organization called the Defenders of the American Constitution, the president of which was a retired Lieutenant-General of the Marine Corps, Pedro del Valle; and even wrote the long 'blurb' on the back of the dust-jacket of a new enlarged edition of *Guide to Kulchur* published by New Directions in August 1952:

'Kulch', or Ez' Guide to Kulchur, so specified in the English contract was an interim account of (in the Jamesian phrase) 'where in a manner of speaking we had got to,' that is, culturally. There are phrases both of Yeats and of Santayana to show that E.P. was not alone in this search for a cultural basis or location. He had begun by examining the limited area first approached in *The Spirit of Romance* (1910) [re-issued in London and New York in 1953]. It is perhaps unfortunate that several decades of the American professoriate, spoon-fed on aestheticism, have assumed that every departure from the received ideas of their period is an eccentricity, especially when it, the departure, has been based on examination of facts not included in their undergraduate studies. They had not read Alexander Del Mar at all, few were familiar with Brooks Adams, almost none had even looked at the parts of Aristotle, Locke, Berkeley, Hume, etc., first collected and correlated by Montgomery Butchart as check on crank writing. None of them had noticed either the method of historiography followed in the Malatesta cantos, or the methodology in the Genova paleographic edition of the Cavalcanti *Rime*, and they seldom hesitated to write of what they did not know in the same tone and with the same cockiness with which they treated books they had actually read.

He went on to say that some subjects – by which he meant money and banking in history – were so dangerous that the historian Charles

Beard had been forced to 'hide them under a vast mass of documentation', and he also criticized the American foundations and endowments for failing to follow where Pound had beaten a path – a familiar theme in his letters at this time and even worked into the cantos.

Continued interest in Pound's work led to the publication by Faber and New Directions of *The Translations of Ezra Pound* in 1953 and of *The Literary Essays* (edited with an introduction by Eliot) in 1954. In addition Laughlin brought out a new edition of *The Great Digest & The Unwobbling Pivot*, with the Chinese text opposite the English. In England it was issued by Peter Owen Ltd. Also in 1954 Harvard University Press published his translation of the three hundred 'Odes' of ancient China under the title *The Classic Anthology Defined by Confucius*. The book was published on 10 September; on the 23rd *The Chinese World* (San Francisco) celebrated the 2,505th anniversary of the birth of Confucius by printing a message from Pound ('Kung is to China as water to fishes') and a review of *The Classic Anthology*:

Earlier this month, the Harvard University Press honoured Confucius by publishing Pound's complete translation of Shih Ching, which the American poet re-entitled as *The Classic Anthology Defined by Confucius*. This is the best 'singing version' of the most ancient anthology of Chinese folk poetry put into any western language so far. Pound's translation, entirely rhymed, can be put immediately into songs like the 305 ballad-poems the Chinese first sang 3,000 years ago. For this brilliant rendition in English, Mr Pound has been hailed by Achilles Fang of Harvard as the 'Confucian poet!'

Many of Pound's versions read beautifully and some are a triumph technically; but the book is very uneven and there are a number of lapses and blemishes; there is also a certain sameness about many of the poems which makes us feel that a selection would have been preferable. Pound however told me in conversation in 1960 that he had translated all three hundred of the poems because Confucius had said or implied that each one was essential to the collection as a whole. For the reader who finds it difficult to appreciate the sentiments of many of the poems, with their etiquette and politics derived from the pre-dawn of the human intellect, it is the many lyric passages which are the most pleasing. Of these there is a great variety; sometimes he uses a simple skipping rhythm:

Plucking the vine leaves, hear my song:
'A day without him is three months long.'

Sometimes he echoes a ballad or song:

> He waited me by our gate-screen,
> > come by, come by.
> His ear-plugs shone so florally,
> > come by,
> on white silk tassels airily,
> > come by, come by.

There are also poems making use of more modern devices, as when he rhymes chopped and uneven lines:

> Twixt door and screen
> at moon-rise
> I hear
> Her departing sighs.

or breaks a traditional rhythm to suit his own flow:

> The erudite moon is up, less fair than she
> who hath tied silk cords about
> > a heart in agony,
> She at such ease
> > so all my work is vain.

And some of the poems are amusing:

> In fleecy coats with five white tassels,
> affable snakes, the great duke's vassals glide
> from his hall
> to tuck their court rations inside.

Too often, however, when the tone becomes serious and Pound the Confucian philosopher takes over, the sound and rhythm become thick and dull:

> Praise to King Wen for his horse-breeding,
> that he sought the people's tranquility
> and saw it brought into focus.
> > WEN! Avatar, how!

And there are not a few among Pound's admirers who when they read in the *Classic Anthology* the poem beginning:

> Pick a fern, pick a fern, ferns are high,
> 'Home,' I'll say home, the year's gone by,
> no house, no roof, these huns of the hoof. . . .

remember with a sense of loss the young man who forty years earlier had worked out the same poem from Fenollosa's notes, creating something more interesting which gave promise of a poetry certainly not realized in the later translations. The earlier version, 'Song of the Bowmen of Shu', was the opening poem of *Cathay*:

Here we are, picking the first fern-shoots
And saying: When shall we get back to our country?
Here we are because we have the Ken-nin for our foemen,
We have no comfort because of these Mongols.
We grub the soft fern-shoots,
When anyone says 'Return,' the others are full of sorrow.
Sorrowful minds, sorrow is strong, we are hungry and thirsty.

Publication of the English text of the *Classic Anthology* by Harvard – in England it was issued by Faber in 1955 – was to have been followed by a volume containing a transcription of each syllable of the Chinese originals, together with the Chinese text and Pound's English. As Pound gave the work to Harvard University Press on condition that they brought out the second volume also, he was extremely angry when it failed to appear. He had a right no doubt to be annoyed, and there was truth in his statement that there could be no 'real understanding of a good Chinese poem without knowledge both of the ideogram reaching the eye, and the metrical and melodic form reaching the ear or aural imagination'. But it was possibly unreasonable of him to believe, as he did, that the original text was an essential part of any book of Chinese translations – especially when he himself could not always read the originals without crib and a dictionary.

As time went on Pound was granted new privileges: he was allowed to receive his visitors on the lawns in summer, was permitted 'evening privileges', which meant that he could sit out until 8 p.m., and was allowed to play tennis. His writing-paper at this stage carried the motto: 'J'Ayme Donc Je Suis.' In addition to such regular visitors as Dorothy Pound and David Horton, and the political wing of his following, there was a steady stream of friends, writers and professors from the United States and abroad, who came bearing gifts and seeking conversation. Marianne Moore, whom at this time he helped with her translation of La Fontaine, visited him twice; Conrad Aiken came, Robert Lowell, Thornton Wilder (who spoke of his visit and *The Pisan Cantos* with great pleasure when I saw him in 1967), and also Zukofsky, whose son Paul, a violin prodigy aged ten, delighted Pound with his playing of Bach, Mozart, Corelli and the Janequin motet 'Les Oiseaux' – this last as reproduced in canto 75 in a violin arrangement by Gerhart

Münch. When Williams called, Pound lectured him on economics and Roosevelt's criminality; Eliot continued to visit him regularly and was subjected to criticism on account of Faber's publishing programme and his choice of religion. On 9 August 1955 Pound wrote to Hemingway: 'Possum more relaxed this year, last year rather edgy/he had got over annoyance at adjective applied to his religion in private correspondence.' The adjective was 'lousy'. Eliot never lost sight of the ultimate goal, which was to secure Pound's release from the hospital; in the meantime he did what he could to keep his friend's work before the public eye.

On 29 October 1953 Caresse Crosby wrote to Eliot from London, enclosing a copy of Pound's recent translation of *The Women of Trachis*. In passing it to John Hayward for his opinion on 9 November, Eliot wrote that Christopher Sykes was anxious to have it for the BBC; when Caresse Crosby had asked him about this, he had replied that from Pound's point of view he thought it would be 'excellent advertisement' to have the translation put on the air. The play was first performed on the BBC's Third programme on 25 April 1954, with one of Pound's active supporters, Denis Goacher, playing the part of Hyllos, son of Herakles and Daianeira. It was produced by Sykes and a follower of Pound's during the 1930s, D. G. Bridson, who had been included in the poet's *Active Anthology*. As poetry *The Women of Trachis* is mostly inferior, but it contains some experiments with word-sounds and this passage of word-blending:

> Daysair is left alone,
>   so sorry a bird,
> For whom, afore, so many suitors tried.
> And shall I ask what thing is heart's desire,
> Or how love fall to sleep with tearless eye,
> So worn by fear away, of dangerous road,
> A manless bride to mourn in vacant room,
> Expecting ever the worse,
>   of dooms to come?

The Women of Trachis was first published in book form by Neville Spearman of London in November 1956, with an American edition by Laughlin the following year.

In addition to the play, Bridson produced other Pound programmes for the BBC; his 'Ezra Pound, A Critical Study' was broadcast in August 1954 and later he made several other programmes for both wireless and television. Broadcasts of Pound's work over the BBC during the 1950s included pages from canto 88 (based on Benton's *Thirty Years' View*) and Marius Goring reading *Homage to Sextus Propertius*. Broadcasts in other parts of the world at this time included 'A Tribute to Ezra Pound', by the Yale Broadcasting Company on 5 December 1955 for the poet's seventieth birthday, and a tribute by Louis Dudek in Canada. One of the writers and producers of the Yale programme, Frederic D. Grab, was another of Pound's visitors, highly thought of by the poet.

Despite the shadow cast over his career a few years earlier by his wartime propaganda, he was probably more widely appreciated by the mid-1950s than at any other time. Newspapers and magazines in England, the United States, Italy, Spain, Portugal, Germany, Mexico, Brazil and many other parts of the world carried reviews and articles. In September 1953 the English Institute meeting at Columbia University, New York, devoted one of its conferences to 'The Cantos of Ezra Pound', and in the autumn of the following year the magazine *Perspectives* (published by Hamish Hamilton of London for Intercultural Publications Inc. of New York) announced that it had received nearly two thousand replies to a questionnaire: 'On the question as to which American authors our readers would like to see represented, the vote was not expected save in one case. The poet Ezra Pound received as many requests as several of the more popular novelists. In fact he was the only poet to attain a place in their favoured company.' And on 28 October 1954 *The New York Times* in a story from Stockholm announced that Hemingway had been awarded the Nobel Prize, adding that others who had been considered included 'Ezra Pound, American poet, whom the [Swedish] academy regards as one of the world's distinctive lyricists.' In December Hemingway said the prize might well have gone to Pound rather than himself; in a reference to Pound's detention he remarked: 'this would be a good year to release poets.'

Nowhere was there more interest in Pound's fame as a poet and his detention in St Elizabeths than in Italy, due largely to the efforts of Olga Rudge and her daughter, both of whom visited him in the hospital – Miss Rudge in 1952, Mary de Rachewiltz in 1953. The latter went for two months in the spring but her father insisted that she stay for three; on her return to Italy she and her husband took a renewed interest in Pound's work and began organizing on his behalf. Their home was Brunnenburg, a castle perched on a jutting point of land, in the village of Tirolo, overlooking Merano, in the Italian Tirol; but they lived for part of the time in a flat in the Via Monserrato in Rome. Gradually Brunnenburg became something of a centre of Poundian activities and for Pound a haven to which one day he would retire.

Part of the activities consisted of distributing cuttings and offset or mimeographed copies of articles about Pound, such as Camillo Pellizzi's 'Ezra Pound, A Difficult Man' published in *Il Tempo* of 20 March 1953 and letters from Dorothy Pound, Shakespear & Parkyn and three

Italian friends of Pound, including the anti-Fascist journalist Carlo Scarfoglio, which appeared in the *Mercure de France* in April 1949.

In October an International Congress of Poetry, held in Venice, sent an official invitation to Pound, through the U.S. embassy in Rome; his daughter attended the congress and read a message he had sent for the occasion. As this new wave of interest took form, articles began to appear frequently in the Italian press. *La Fiera Letteraria* devoted a large part of its issue of 25 October to Pound, with translations of his poetry, articles on his work, and reproduction of a drawing of him by Gaudier; on 19 November the poet Eugenio Montale contributed a sympathetic article entitled 'Uncle Ez' to the *Corriere d'informazione*, belonging to the influential *Corriere della Sera*, and on the evening of 30 March 1954 Duarte de Montalegre (who was really J. V. de Pina Martins, Portuguese poet and professor of Portuguese at Rome University), broadcast an account of some of his work and an appeal for his release over the Vatican radio. The broadcast was repeated at half-past ten that same night over the Italian radio and was followed by the publication of articles and letters – the latter including a long one from Carlo Scarfoglio headed 'The Ezra Pound Case' and another by John Drummond, an English friend of the poet since the 1930s, who lived in Rome. Both were published in the *Paese Sera* of 16 June.

This campaign continued in one form or another throughout 1954 into 1955, with Pound following the moves from St Elizabeths and helping to distribute copies of some of the material. At Rapallo *Il Mare* ran a number of articles between October and December 1954, one of which, in the issue of 31 October, was built around a letter from Eliot dated London, 27 October. After describing Pound as the greatest living master of English poetry Eliot said that he still remembered vividly a visit he had made to Pound and Rapallo some twenty-five years earlier. He was so strongly attached to his memories of the occasion that he would like, he said, to be able to make another visit and again to find Pound there when he did.

There were also appeals to the Italian government to make representations to Washington and appeals to the American ambassador in Rome, Clare Boothe Luce. One of the appeals to Mrs Luce was the work of his daughter, assisted by her husband and the Italian publisher, Vanni Scheiwiller; all of the signatories were anti-Fascists and included such well-known writers as Montale, Giovanni Papini and Salvatore Quasimodo. Mrs Luce took the matter up with the State Department and twice on trips home discussed it with government officials, including, on one occasion, the Attorney General. As she explained later, much of the indignation in Italy was based upon the false idea that although innocent of treason Pound had been sentenced and sent to prison and that the American government was being harsh in refusing him a pardon. She pointed out that the Italian government, no doubt because it knew the legal facts through its embassy in Washington, made no official representations on the subject. It is not without interest that on 6 February 1956 the magazine *Life*, owned by Mrs Luce's husband, Henry Luce, published an editorial drawing attention to the strange legal position in which Pound was caught and suggesting that the matter was due for attention: 'Pound's room at St Elizabeths has been called "a closet which contains a national skeleton". There may be good arguments for keeping him there, but there are none for pretending he doesn't exist. The crimes of World War II have aged to the point of requital, parole or forgiveness. For this reason, if no other, the arguments for quashing the indictment against Ezra Pound should be publicly considered.'

It was at this stage that Vanni Scheiwiller, son of Pound's earlier Italian publisher, Giovanni Scheiwiller, became an important pillar of Pound's world, publishing some fifteen of his books, large and small, in four years, including the first edition of *Section: Rock-Drill* (cantos 85–95). This came out in September 1955, the first book of cantos since the Pisan section. The name derived from a review by Wyndham Lewis of *The Letters of Ezra Pound* in the *New Statesman* of 7 April 1951; it was headed 'The Rock Drill' and at one point read: 'His rock-drill action is impressive: he blasts away tirelessly. . . .' Pound was very pleased with this idea and the praise heaped on him by his old friend who had lost some of his ferocity and at times was even benevolent.

The eleven *Rock-Drill* cantos do not form a whole or connect in any significant way with other sections. Consisting mainly of jottings from his notebooks they display lines and passages nicely fashioned, and moments of beauty, but have no centre of reference. Like the *Thrones* section, published four years later, *Rock-Drill* contains much more about magic and the retrogressive and pathological remnants of paganism than do earlier cantos.

Among the other Scheiwiller publications at this time was *La Martinelli*, a booklet of reproductions of paintings by the American artist, Sheri Martinelli, a strange, rather scatterbrained young woman who visited Pound regularly in St Elizabeths. Published in February 1956 it contained an introduction by Pound and among the plates a portrait of him. In the introduction he described her as possessing, like himself, a quality he called 'unstillness' and said that she was 'the first to show a capacity to manifest in paint, or in la ceramica what is most to be prized in my writing'. Miss Martinelli is said to appear in *Rock-Drill* and to have inspired canto 90, which is perhaps the most lyrical of the later cantos.

Scheiwiller also brought out in a single volume in February 1954, under the title *Lavoro ed Usura* ('Work and Usury'), Pound's three wartime pamphlets on economics. On the reverse of the title-leaf Pound published in English, with Italian translation, his recently-composed definition of usury: 'a charge for the use of purchasing-power, levied without regard to production, sometimes without regard even to the possibilities of production.' Early in 1953 Pound wrote to McNair Wilson that the definition was the result of a visit from a 'well meaning' professor who wanting to explain usury to his class had showed Pound '3 pages of muddle' on the subject. This may have been Hugh Kenner who in 1967 told me that it was he who elicited from Pound his definition of usury.

It is perhaps a measure of Pound's fame and the fascination he held for so many people both young and old that dozens of correspondents in the United States, Canada, England, Australia, South America, Germany and Italy, contributed to *The Pound Newsletter* published between 1954 and 1956 by the Department of English at the University of California, Berkeley; it was edited by John Edwards and William Vasse who afterwards used the material gathered through the *Newsletter* for their *Annotated Index to the Cantos of Ezra Pound* (1959), an indispensable book for anyone hoping to understand many of the references in cantos 1 to 84. Those who came, from all over the United States and abroad, to visit Pound at the hospital, were mainly interested in him as a great literary figure holding court under strange conditions. Dressed in 'tan shorts too big for him, tennis shoes and a loose plaid shirt' or perhaps in 'a loose sweatshirt, an old GI overcoat, baggy trousers, heavy white socks, bedroom slippers, long underwear showing at his ankles', he was generally very polite and ceremonious with visitors, including Jews, although after they were gone, he might, in letters to friends, express suspicion of a visitor's motives or accuse some writer or professor of intellectual cowardice or laziness. It is my impression, judging from his own letters and conversations with people who visited him, that he greatly enjoyed this period of his life, despite the drawbacks. We get something of the atmosphere in an account of a visit written by David Rattray and published in *The Nation* of 16 November 1957:

Before we had a chance to talk about anything, Pound jumped up again: 'You'll have tea, won't you?'

I said that I would, and immediately he was everywhere at once, in a frenzy of activity, loading himself with jars of various sizes, tin boxes of sugar and tea, spoons and a saucer. I stood up in embarrassment, not knowing what I ought to do, but Mrs Pound beckoned me from her corner: 'Let's sit here and talk while he makes the tea.' She was sitting behind a ramshackle old upright piano, so as not to see the people in the hall or be seen by them. Miss Martinelli was making sketches for a portrait of her.

Suddenly Pound was standing there, holding out a peanut-butter jar full of hot tea. When they got settled again, Pound, lying back in the canvas lawn-chair he always used, glared up at Rattray and said, 'Well, what specific questions have you? Or did you just come to talk? I'd just as soon talk.' Pound talked – about Byzantium, medieval Greek, the troubadours, usury – and then suddenly sprang from his chair and strode across the hall to his room, beckoning Rattray to follow. The room was strewn with papers, books, bits of envelopes, pencils, string, cardboard files, trunks, old paint tins and jars containing teabags or food. On the walls were paintings, some by Sheri Martinelli, and there was a dressing-table with a large mirror. Pound gave his guest a copy of Del Mar's *Roman and Moslem Moneys* and then dived under the table looking for food-tins, which he found and pried open. They contained doughnuts and bread which he put into a paper-bag and gave to Miss Martinelli; he then poked around under the bed for a box containing boiled eggs and salami which he gave to Rattray to give to John Châtel, one of his disciples in the alcove outside. It would appear from this and other accounts that Pound not only schooled his disciples but helped to feed some of them as well.

No sooner did a disciple or group of followers fall away, or a magazine or journal he was trying to capture, prove unwilling, than he was busy gathering new followers, forming new groups, helping to establish or capture other publications. Among the magazines in the United States with which he attempted to co-operate was *Shenandoah*, published at the Washington and Lee University, Lexington, Virginia. Between 1952, when they published a translation of his 1922 *Mercure de France* article on Joyce, and 1956, he was party to several attempts to make the magazine over into a Poundian vehicle; but although a good deal of Poundian material appeared in its pages the actual take-over attempts always misfired and Pound was not disposed to play much of a part himself after his offer of canto 88 was rejected in 1955.

In England two of his followers, Denis Goacher and Peter Whigham, made attempts to make use of Sir Oswald Mosley's magazine *The European*, but without much success. Goacher was a poet and BBC actor, and his friend Whigham a poet and school-teacher; both made the pilgrimage to St Elizabeths. One day on the lawn, during Whigham's visit, Pound was delighted to discover that Whigham's wife, Jean, was a niece by marriage of Bride Scratton, with whom both Pound and Dorothy were still in touch. Mrs Scratton was, Pound told them, one of the handful of people in England worth worrying about and insisted they see her. She lived in Cambridge where she was an authorized guide to the city's historical and architectural monuments and well known for her work on behalf of cats and other animals. Among her books and papers, which include first editions of some of his early work, typescripts of cantos 28, 29 and 30, and cuttings about him, were some of the Square Dollar books, sent by Pound to keep her abreast of the latest direction in his activities. She died in the early 1960s at the age of eighty-two.

Goacher and Whigham were active on behalf of a society formed in England to work for Pound's release and in this connection Whigham wrote a graceful account of Pound's life and work which was privately printed as a small pamphlet and distributed in high places. In 1955 Goacher wrote a foreword about Pound's imprisonment for the Neville Spearman edition of *The Women of Trachis* and he and Whigham together also contributed an 'Editorial Declaration', which was an attempt to interpret and reap the benefit of Pound's teachings in the light of their own work and interests. It included the announcement of a series of books 'now difficult or impossible to obtain', of which the following were said to be in preparation: a selection of Blackstone's *Commentaries on the Laws of England*; Arthur Golding's translation of Ovid's *The Metamorphoses*; a new translation of Richard of St Victor's *Benjamin Minor*; *Selected Speeches* of the early American statesman, Randolph of Roanoke; and Gavin Douglas's translation of *The Aeneid* – all of them books pronounced important by Pound. Although Whigham edited the Randolph speeches and S. V. Yankowski, a Polish classical scholar living in Australia, translated the Richard of St Victor, the series did not materialize, and gradually during the late 1950s the effort initiated by Goacher and Whigham drifted apart.

One of the most industrious and voluble pockets of Poundian activity was in Melbourne where between 1954 and 1957 the poet William Fleming and I were instrumental in having some of Pound's work published and in propagating his ideas. Canto 90 was first published in the Summer 1955 issue of the Australian magazine *Meanjin*, edited by C. B. Christesen, together with articles and other material collected by me for the occasion; and when Professor G. Giovannini of the Catholic University in Washington reported that an article on Pound which he had been commissioned to write for the Catholic journal *America*, had been turned down, it was published on 26 August 1955 in a Melbourne Social Credit paper *The New Times* – much to Pound's delight – and a large number of copies shipped to Washington for distribution. *The New Times* soon became Pound's main means of alerting the world to the presence and dangers of economic injustice and political degradation, and between late 1955 and early 1957 it published eighty or more unsigned or pseudonymous items sent from St Elizabeths. Although the editor was aware that Pound was embellishing his columns, he probably did not know to what extent, for Pound sent the items to me – ranging from snippets to one of more than a thousand words – and I distributed them over the 'Magazine Section' of the paper, with the result that Pound was a dozen different people – he was John Vignon of Boston who wrote about English Common Law, John Foster who wrote from New York, he was a Paris correspondent, a Mexico City correspondent and a London correspondent, and he contributed numerous items under such initials as M.L., D.E.J. and J.T. and some were published unsigned.

With pieces supplied by Pound and still others inspired by his ideas, it is not surprising that the 'Magazine Section' of *The New Times* often resembled his wartime articles and broadcasts, both in manner and content; copies of each issue were sent to Washington and then distributed by Pound to followers in other parts of the world. His friend Henry Swabey was at this time editing in England a Social Credit paper called *Voice*, in which the diligent researcher may discover many Pound items including several signed A. Watson.

At a slightly higher level than *The New Times* was another Melbourne publication, called *The Edge* at first, and then simply *Edge*. This came into being in October 1956 when another magazine failed to start and I was left holding a group of translations by Pound from the French of Rimbaud and Tailhade. The first issue opened with these five translations, one of which was of Rimbaud's 'Au Cabaret-Vert':

Very nice when the gal with the big bubs
And lively eyes,

Not one to be scared of a kiss and more,
Brought the butter and bread with a grin
And the luke-warm ham on a coloured plate,

Pink ham, white fat and a sprig
Of garlic, and a great chope of foamy beer
Gilt by the sun in that atmosphere.

Another was of Rimbaud's 'Les Chercheuses de poux':

They set the kid by a wide-open window where
A tangle of flowers bathes in the blue air
And run fine, alluring, terrible
Fingers through his thick dew-matted hair.

Of Tailhade, he translated 'Rus':

> What lures the antient truss-maker from his shoppe whose
>   luxury
> Sucked in the passers-by,
> Is his garden at Auteuil where zinnias void of all odour or
>   stink
> Look like varnished zinc.

The translations were brought out by Scheiwiller in a bilingual edition in 1957 and later included in an enlarged edition of *The Translations of Ezra Pound* published by New Directions in 1963.

Altogether Pound contributed more than thirty items, mainly prose, to the eight issues of *Edge*, including an advertisement for a New Directions edition of Williams's *In the American Grain*; this appeared on the back cover of *Edge* no. 7 (August 1957). The second issue (October 1956) was devoted entirely to an English translation by Henry Swabey of Thaddeus Zielinski's *La Sibylle* ('Three Essays on Ancient Religion and Christianity') which Pound considered an important work, and no. 4 (March 1957) contained an English translation of a 'Notebook of Thoughts' said to have been written by Mussolini during his captivity in Ponza and La Maddalena in 1943 before being rescued by the Germans and taken to northern Italy. When he sent it for publication Pound did not say whose translation it was; if he himself did not have a hand in it he certainly tidied or revised it. He acted as *Edge*'s contributing editor, advertising manager and circulation representative, and in 1957 composed, and had mimeographed, a publicity sheet which he distributed with his letters.

To describe and give illustrative extracts from the enormous correspondence Pound conducted from St Elizabeths would require a separate volume. It was much like his correspondence of the 1930s but more puzzling because the phrasing was often more condensed, as if composed under greater pressure; it was also more fragmentary. Among the range of subjects treated was the design of lunatic asylums. In letters to Hemingway in 1955 he expressed the need for a reform of asylum architecture, with more opportunities for sun and fresh air, and suggested that this might be something for Hemingway to write an article about. Later Pound composed a short note on the subject which was published in *The New Times*; he asked me to send the published note to one of the British medical journals, which I did, but as far as I know it was never reprinted.

XXII Return to Italy
1958/1969

Working behind the scenes MacLeish and Eliot had been trying to find a way for Pound to be released from St Elizabeths without the government exercising its right to press the treason charges. One of the biggest obstacles was that Pound was incapable of understanding his true position, and blind to the simplest realities, he had even written to the Secretary of State, Christian Herter. This made it very difficult, Eliot wrote to MacLeish, to persuade people that Pound was 'neither sane nor insane' and could safely be released without having to stand trial. MacLeish sent Pound a careful and friendly letter in which he tried to explain to him his position and the need for caution; he also drafted a letter to the Attorney-General which he sent to Eliot, Hemingway and Robert Frost for their approval. The final draft, typed on the writing-paper of the American Academy of Arts and Letters, and signed by Eliot, Hemingway and Frost, was dated 14 January 1957:

It is our understanding, based on inquiries directed to the medical personnel at St Elizabeths Hospital, that Pound is now unfit for trial and, in the opinion of the doctors treating him, will continue to be unfit for trial. This opinion, we believe, has already been communicated to the Department of Justice. Under these circumstances the perpetuation of the charges against him seems to us unfortunate and, indeed, indefensible . . . we cannot but regret the failure of the Department thus far to take steps to *nol pros* the indictment and remit the case to the medical authorities for disposition on medical grounds.

The Secretary-General of the United Nations, Dag Hammarskjöld, was interested in the case, as were other intellectuals, and it seems that the government was prepared to reconsider it. In an editorial on 1 April 1957 *The New Republic* said:

we would like to see the government give this old man and this eminent poet his freedom – if not as an act of justice, then as an act of largesse. There is every reason to believe that the U.S. Attorney General would be willing to quash the Pound indictment if his case were brought to trial, if only because

445

of the length of time Pound has already spent locked up. This cannot be done, however, until those empowered to act on Pound's behalf agree – which they have not yet done – to his undergoing the ordeal for another sanity hearing.

It was during this period that John Kasper became a national figure, with the *New York Herald Tribune* of 30 January 1957 publishing a front-page story headed: 'Segregationist Kasper is Ezra Pound Disciple.' Among those who were working for Pound's release was Harry Meacham, a poet and business-man from Virginia with connections in the world of poetry societies and writers' clubs. When he went to Pound and asked him to renounce Kasper, Pound's only comment, he said, was: 'Well, at least he's a man of action and don't sit around looking at his navel.' In July when MacLeish and Frost visited the Department of Justice they were told that nothing could be done for Pound while the 'Kasper mess' was boiling. With the South in turmoil the department not unreasonably feared that if Pound were released he might become involved personally in the trouble.

During the second half of 1957 Senator R. L. Neuberger and Representative Usher L. Burdick became interested in the case, with the result that early in 1958 H. A. Sieber of the Library of Congress produced a long report on 'The Medical, Legal, Literary and Political Status of Ezra (Loomis) Pound'. The actual men inside the government who did most to secure Pound's release were Dr Gabriel Hauge (President Eisenhower's Advisor on Economics) who received details of the case from Laughlin, and the president's right hand man, Sherman Adams. It was Adams who obtained from the president permission to go ahead. On 1 April 1958 the Attorney General, William P. Rogers, let it be known to the press that the Department of Justice was considering dropping the charges. Some years later Rogers told Harry Meacham that he had gathered from Frost that Pound had agreed to leave the country and this was a factor in his decision.

A well-known Washington lawyer, Thurman Arnold, of Arnold, Fortas & Porter, agreed to take the case, and on 14 April asked that the 1945 indictment be dismissed; his motion was accompanied by a statement about the difficulty the government would have, after fifteen years, in producing witnesses to the alleged acts of treason, and also an affidavit from Overholser in which he said that the poet was suffering from 'a paranoid state' and was incurably insane; there was also a 'strong probability that the commission of the crimes charged was the result of insanity'. Other documents presented by Arnold included an appeal by Robert Frost and statements by numerous other well-known writers. In a statement to the newspapers Abe Fortas, one of the members of Arnold, Fortas & Porter, said the firm had agreed to act following a request from Frost; they believed it was in 'the public interest' that they should, and there would be no fee.

In the District Court on 18 April Pound sat at the back of the courtroom, his wife at the counsel table with Arnold; also present was Omar Pound who at that time was a teacher at the Roxbury Latin School in Boston. Judge Laws announced that in view of the evidence about Pound's mental condition and the willingness of the government to see the matter at an end, he hereby dismissed the indictment. And so, twelve years, eleven months and two weeks after being taken into custody near Rapallo, Pound was free of the charge of treason. Although he was now allowed to leave the hospital to call on friends and to lunch out, he continued to live there for several more weeks, having his teeth seen to and gradually moving out his books, papers and other belongings. He was officially discharged from the hospital on 7 May into the custody of his wife.

Ten years earlier Pound had hoped that his struggle would soon be recognized for what it was and that he would 'float out' of St Elizabeths on an anti-Roosevelt tide. Even though this tide had missed him he was still unrepentant and believed that he had a part to play in politics, economics and education. It was as a man of affairs that on 29 April he called on Usher Burdick at his Washington home, to thank him for his part in obtaining his release; while there he spoke to the press as one who was feared by politicians and others for his defence of the American constitution.

Pound remained in the United States for a further two months because of passport difficulties; for part of the time he stayed with Professor Craig La Driere in Washington. One evening towards the end of May La Driere and Professor Giovannini heard him groaning and pacing irritably about as he read a copy of the proceedings of the National Institute of Arts and Letters, of which he was a member. The document was so offensive to him that he refused to belong to such an organization and despite attempts by his two friends to reason with him he sat down there and then and typed his resignation, which he took out and posted immediately.

Asked by a reporter about Frost's efforts on his behalf Pound is said to have replied: 'He ain't been in much of a hurry.' One day at lunch in a Chinese restaurant in Washington Harry Meacham reminded Pound of these words and then read aloud an editorial which said that after forty years Frost had repaid Pound for his help in London at the time of the publication of Frost's first book, *A Boy's Will*, in 1913. Suddenly a more likeable Pound came to the surface: referring to

Frost's second book, published in 1914, he smiled and said: 'Frost's debt was paid when he published *North of Boston*.'

With Meacham he visited Richmond, Virginia. They were having lunch with a group at the Rotunda Club when the head-waiter, an elderly negro, noticed that Pound was not wearing a coat. To Meacham he whispered: 'Mr Meacham, dat gentman have to wear a coat.' As Pound had not brought one, Meacham whispered back: 'Washington, you tell the manager to record in the annals of the staid old Rotunda that the only gentleman ever to eat in the dining-room without a coat was Ezra Pound.' Washington thought about this for a few moments and then asked: 'Who he?' Only later after he had read a story about Pound in the *Richmond News-Leader* was he reconciled to this breach of regulations.

One of the Mapel sisters was still alive and made a special visit from outside Washington to say goodbye to Pound before he left. Very old, but still with her wits about her, she sat in her hotel bed and for hours entertained Pound and his wife with her talk.

Since 1956 Pound had been corresponding with Carl W. Gatter who with his mother Mrs Elsie Gatter occupied the old Pound home at 166 Fernbrook Avenue, Wyncote. Gatter was interested in Pound's early life there and it greatly pleased the poet to answer questions and to send his correspondent in search of remembered details. After his release he arranged to visit Wyncote and to stay overnight with the Gatters. On 27 June, on his way to New York and the ship that would take him back to Italy, Pound arrived at Fernbrook Avenue in a car driven by T. D. Horton; others in the group were Mrs Pound, a student from Texas, Marcella Spann, and Mrs Horton.

Bounding up the path Pound remarked to the Gatters that they had 'dolled the place up a bit'. Although it was already dark he explored the house and searched the garden for Homer's trees. During dinner he told them that it was almost exactly half a century since he had last eaten a meal there; the Wyncote water tasted like champagne, he said, after the chemicalized Washington water. Lying on a couch afterwards he answered Carl Gatter's questions about the old days and recalled 'the patent' – a cast iron device that channelled heat from the fireplace to the back parlour and bedroom. Unfortunately it had set the house on fire and had had to be removed.

Late that night when the others had gone to bed Pound left the house and walked the streets of Wyncote alone. At Calvary Presbyterian church he stopped and wondered about a tree which he and another boy had planted behind the building, but it was too dark and too late to enter and see if it was still there.

Next day he walked barefoot in the garden and talked about his early life. Recalling the moneyed families who had moved to the area in his time, he mentioned that the Wideners had been butchers. The name was still to be seen, he said, over a meat stall at the Reading Terminal market, even after Mr Widener had built a mansion of one hundred and ten rooms – now the Faith Theological Seminary. During the day he was visited by some of his old friends; others he rang. Among the visitors was Priscilla Heacock, a lively old Quaker lady whose family had run the Chelten Hills school. When she asked whether she might call him by his old nickname '*Ra*' he replied: 'Well, I've been called worse things.'

After lunch on the twenty-eighth, Pound and his party left Wyncote for Hopewell, New Jersey, where they were the guests of Alan C. Collins, president of the literary agency, Curtis Brown, Ltd. Also present was Mrs Collins's father, Eugene C. Pomeroy, vice-president of the Defenders of the American Constitution. On Saturday night Pound talked; on Sunday he played tennis and swam in the pool next to the court. From Hopewell they went to Rutherford where Pound and his wife stayed with Williams; from there they went to New York where they boarded the *Cristoforo Colombo*. They were seen off by Omar Pound and a few friends – the Hortons, Norman Holmes Pearson, Robert MacGregor of New Directions, and Michael Reck, a student of Greek and oriental languages whose visit to Fenollosa's grave overlooking Lake Biwa in Japan in 1954 is celebrated at the end of canto 89. When the ship sailed on 30 June Pound and his wife were accompanied by Marcella Spann, a young woman who had first visited St Elizabeths in 1956 and was now helping Pound to compile an anthology of poetry.

The crossing was 'wonderfully smooth', Mrs Pound wrote later, and they 'were able to enjoy the grand cooking on board'. When Pound met reporters during a stop at Naples on 9 July he criticized the United States and the ignorance of senators and congressmen; he distributed copies of his one-page *Introductory Text-Book* and was photographed giving the Fascist salute. Next morning the story appeared in America: 'Pound, in Italy, Gives Fascist Salute; Calls United States an "Insane Asylum".' At Genoa he was greeted by a large crowd and according to one account began talking to reporters as he descended the gangplank; after passing through customs he began talking again to reporters, but an Italian friend interrupted, led the Pounds to a car, and took them to a private home. From Genoa, Pound, his wife and Miss Spann went to Verona where they spent the night of 11 July and the following day were met by Pound's daughter, who took them to the village of Tirolo by taxi. On the path which descends from Tirolo to Brunnenburg Castle he met, for the first time, his grandchildren – Walter, aged eleven, and Patrizia, aged eight; Walter was so excited after years of waiting that he burst into tears as his grandfather approached. Pound hugged the children and also his son-in-law, Boris de Rachewiltz. Through the wooden gate and archway, through the large wooden portal into the stone courtyard; Pound was given a spacious room in the tall square tower, with a view of hillside orchards and vines and of the Alps rising immediately to ten thousand feet. In the dining-room were the portraits of Hannah How and Mary Wadsworth Parker which had hung in the house in Fernbrook Avenue. Around the walls of a downstairs flat were his Gaudier drawings; the flat opens onto a private garden, and there, under the trees, stood his bust by Gaudier.

Home at last, surrounded by many of his books and papers, he was full of energy and despite his seventy-two years ready for work and to entertain his friends. At a party to celebrate his daughter's birthday and his arrival he did not stand on ceremony and opened the dancing well ahead of time, remarking that 'The rhythm of a Tirolean band gets you going.' Reporters were persistent and within a few days he agreed to meet them; he answered a few questions, talked about Merano and his work and handed out copies of *Introductory Text Book*, an Italian translation of which appeared in an account of the interview in the *Adige* of 16 July. About the castle he had a finger in everything that was going on. He helped his daughter with her translation of cantos 98 and 99 into Italian, refusing to accept her efforts and urging her to do better; he talked archaeology with his son-in-law, making notes in his notebooks for insertion in the later cantos; he took an interest in the cooking and set his granddaughter the task of writing out the menu before each meal, which she did, putting 'Brunnenburg' and the date at the top and decorating the list with drawings of cats and flowers; he also had a fit of gardening which consisted mainly of trimming everything in sight with a large pair of shears, and although he liked the local red wine he preferred white and was instrumental in having five hundred white vines planted that autumn in a section of the castle vineyard. At night he read aloud to the family – from his cantos and his translations of the *Classic Anthology*, *The Women of Trachis* and the Confucian *Analects*; he also read poems from the anthology he was preparing with Miss Spann, and for the children the Uncle Remus Tales.

Rising steeply on one side of Brunnenburg is a seven-thousand foot mountain called 'Mut'. Pound decided that he would like to build at the summit a marble temple with three columns; he was driven to a nearby quarry and the project was found to be within reach, but nothing more was done about it.

In July he received from Hemingway a cheque for a thousand dollars. Thanking him on 16 July he said that fortunately he did not need to cash it but would have it 'duly framed for posterity'. He later had it sunk in plexiglass for use as a paperweight. On 22 July he wrote asking Hemingway and his wife 'to drop in fer a week or two' at Brunnenburg, 'preferably before or after the cold weather'. Pound very badly wanted to see old friends and a large empty room at the castle was repaired and made ready as a reception-room in case Hemingway or others should come.

From drafts made in St Elizabeths Pound prepared cantos 96 to 109 for the press and began going through some of his pre-war papers and letters. There was so much to be done, he told correspondents, he could find work for four secretaries. Through Dorothy Pound he sent a message to the Gatters saying how pleased his mother would have been to see how well they were taking care of 'the old home'. In September the *Illustrazione Italiana* published canto 98 accompanied by his daughter's translation and an introductory note by Pound dated Brunnenburg, 22 July, in which he attacked 'Endowments' and the teaching of history in American universities, advertised the Square Dollar series, and made a few brief comments about 'the structure' of his cantos and the Confucian element running from canto 13, through 51–61, to canto 98.

He was made a life-member of the Merano racing club and attended meetings during the autumn; his big joy, during an outing, was to eat large quantities of ice-cream. For his seventy-third birthday the Merano tourist authorities arranged, with the help of his daughter and Vanni Scheiwiller, an exhibition of first editions, typescripts, photographs, paintings and other material. At the opening in Merano on 30 October he said, 'every man has the right to have his ideas examined one at a time and not all confused one with the other'. If he could get people to see this, then his life would not have been in vain.

In 1953 Pound had begun to nourish the idea that what Italy needed was the type of maple tree which in the United States and Canada yields maple syrup and he had sent seedlings to his daughter as an experiment. Although it did not succeed, he began to think about the idea again in 1958; he got in touch with a local newspaper, the *Alto Adige*, and explained it all to a reporter in great detail, adding that he would be glad to assist with the importation of new seedlings, if the idea were acceptable and an area were found in Italy in which the maple might flourish. The story appeared in the *Alto Adige* of 16 November. On 6 December he was visited by Sebastian Frobenius, grandson of Leo Frobenius. Pound called a press conference, explained who the young man was and how he was on his way to study in Japan. A story, with photograph, was published in the *Alto Adige* the following day.

As in Rapallo thirty years earlier Pound celebrated Burns' Night: a haggis was imported and some black label Johnny Walker whisky sent from Rome. With great gusto he read aloud from a tiny volume of Burns in which Sarah Angevine, Homer's mother, had written in violet ink, now faded: 'This little book was given to me by my father when I was eight years old, in the year 1844. This is the only one he ever gave me beside my school books.'

In America, meanwhile, canto 99 had appeared in the Summer issue of the *Virginia Quarterly Review* and in December canto 100 came out in a Pound issue of *The Yale Literary Magazine*. There was in England at this time a small group of followers who were high in Pound's favour, among them William Cookson, a young man just out of public school, who in the autumn of 1958 visited Brunnenburg with his mother, who was also interested in Pound's work. In January 1959 Cookson started a four-page Poundian leaflet called *Agenda* which owing to Pound's intervention later shed some of the outward signs of discipleship and eventually became an interesting eighty-page literary magazine.

At the beginning of 1959 there was still some faint hope that Mosley's *The European* might yet be guided into saner and more Poundian ways, and so Pound sent several short poems which he had recently unearthed from his files of the 1930s. These were published in the January *European* together with an extract from the *Institutes* of the famous seventeenth-century jurist Sir Edward Coke. The extract stated that a man who knowingly did not report treason to the authorities was guilty of a serious crime. Pound often cited this text in defence of his own conduct during the war, claiming or implying that he was only doing his duty in drawing attention to Roosevelt's intrigues and misdemeanours. He had discovered Coke only a year or two before and believed there was something seriously wrong with a system in which it was possible for a man like himself to remain in ignorance of such an important figure for most of his life. But once he had discovered him Pound made up for lost time and constantly recommended the *Institutes* and Catherine Drinker Bowen's life of Coke, *The Lion and the Throne*. He also copied extracts into his notebooks and put them into some of the later cantos. In canto 107 he called Coke 'the clearest mind ever in England'.

In February 1959 *The European* published canto 101, but this proved to be the magazine's final issue, extinguishing Pound's hopes for an outlet in that direction. Another English magazine, *Listen*, published by the Marvell Press at Hessle, East Yorkshire, was in favour at this time and in the spring brought out canto 102 and several other Pound items the following year. In September 1960 the Marvell Press published an enlarged edition of *Gaudier-Brzeska A Memoir* (but lacking the original preface); it was issued by Laughlin in 1961.

In January 1959 Pound was offered a reading engagement for the following summer by the mayor of Munich. This seems to have been to his taste, for on 7 January he wrote enthusiastically to Hemingway: 'Last news from the Bavarian front is that the mayor of Munich offers me 5 days swank with TWO companions.' He added that to Hemingway they offered, in addition to the fee that both of them would be paid, three days in the city plus his air fare from Cuba and back. Pound was ever anxious to take up again with Hemingway and for them to be able to meet again as if it were Paris in the 1920s, but somehow it could never be arranged. He was also very conscious of the honours that had passed him by and in the years after his release never lost hope of winning the Nobel Prize.

Although it was only six months since he had arrived at Brunnen-burg, by January 1959 he was already becoming restless; also there were difficulties involved in living at the castle and certain tensions which he felt unable to resolve, and so, with his wife and Miss Spann, he left and went to Rapallo, staying at the hotel Grande Italia e Lido on the seafront. He was becoming weary and readily agreed when Harry Meacham proposed to have copies made and posted of any letters or other material which Pound thought should be distributed among a few reliable and intelligent correspondents. As Meacham was an executive of Dun and Bradstreet in Richmond he was able to have the material reproduced by the office photo-copying machine.

It was at this time that Pound took his wife and Miss Spann on a tour of Italian towns and cities, including Pisa. Economics was never far from his mind, even now, and when he read or glanced at Erle Stanley Gardner's *The Case of the Perjured Parrot*, in a Penguin edition, he marked in red and blue the following passage on page 106: 'You might be interested in his economic philosophy, Mr Mason. . . He believed a dollar represented a token of work performed, that men were given these tokens to hold until they needed the product of work performed by some other man, that anyone who tried to get a token without giving his best work in return was an economic counterfeiter.' He was also interested in a reference to economic depression: 'In other words, the token itself came to mean more than what it could be exchanged for.' On the cover Pound wrote 'Keep' and also the relevant page number.

During the summer Pound took a flat for the three of them in a modern block in the heart of Rapallo not far from the water; there he continued to look through his old papers, made entries in his cantos notebooks and occasionally wrote a few paragraphs on economics and politics.

At times in his conversation he was extremely bitter against the

453

United States; but weary and bewildered by the press of events, facts and circumstances he was unable to plan or pursue any clear course in Italy. Above all he was nagged by the fact that not only had he been adjudged 'incompetent' but was in the custody of his wife who as 'committee for Ezra Pound' was officially in charge of all his money and property. No matter how gently or justly she carried out this side of her task he felt trapped and utterly dependent and by the end of September 1959 was worrying, he told Hemingway, about 'complications re/committee' and slow answers from the United States about 'incomprehensible' questions of taxation. To add to his feeling of hopelessness he discovered that he had got himself entangled over the lease of his flat. 'Not quick enough on the uptake', he wrote to Hemingway on 1 October, and added: 'Old man him tired.'

Soon after this he gave up the flat, Marcella Spann returned to America, and he and Dorothy returned to Brunnenburg. As I had moved from London and was living with my wife and children in one of the flats at the castle, I went to Rapallo to help his son-in-law with the packing and rode back to Tirolo in the motor-lorry containing furniture and many books and papers.

Pound had told me the previous May to begin examining the economic material already stored at the castle. When the publisher Henry Regnery of Chicago got in touch with him about his work Pound referred him to me. 'Ezra Pound has suggested', Regnery wrote on 4 June, 'that I write to you about some archives which, he says, are now at your disposal.' Out of this arose the idea of a book of previously uncollected writings on economics, politics and education including some published in Italy during the war. Throughout the autumn and early winter of 1959 I selected and typed the articles, referring my selection to Pound whenever it seemed that he should be consulted. As the idea was to include the main core of his economic thought I deleted sentences, paragraphs and even whole sections, to avoid too much repetition and fanaticism. Pound agreed there should be cuts, but left the actual cutting to me. Whenever corrections or changes in the text seemed called for, I took the matter to him, with the result that here and there he altered, or allowed me to alter, his original text. Thus in the long essay on Mencius, originally published in *The Criterion* in 1938, he changed his description of an ideogram and introduced a remark about the danger facing a self-educated Sinologist who attempts to read the ideograms as pictures. In an extract from a *New Age* article of 1922 was a reference to leisure. To this he attached a footnote saying: 'Leisure is time plus money, or at any rate time without monetary worry.'

While this work was in progress Pound received a long telegram from Eliot in response to a letter in which he had expressed doubts about the quality of his own work. Eliot told him not to worry, that he was one of the immortals and that part at least of his work was sure to survive. Pound was extremely bucked up by this and began reading again some of Eliot's books, including *After Strange Gods*. Years earlier he had thought it a poor book and had said so in *The New English Weekly*, but now he detected aspects which he had missed. One day while examining an article on the 'Immediate Need of Confucius', which I had chosen for the Regnery collection, he inserted, after a sentence about the Church, this footnote: 'Mr Eliot's "Primer of Heresy" (*After Strange Gods*) was not examined with sufficient care, nor did the present author chew on it sufficiently, especially in regard to the distinction between A Church, an orthodoxy, and a collection of intelligent observations by individual theologians, however brilliant. Eliot's use of Confucius in *The Rock* (section 5), is worth noting.'

On 7 December 1959 Scheiwiller and Laughlin brought out simultaneously a new book of cantos, *Thrones* (nos. 96 to 109); the Faber edition followed in March 1960. The economic collection, entitled *Impact*, was published by Regnery on 13 June. As soon as *Impact* was finished I prepared a selection of one hundred and forty-five unpublished letters by Pound, as well as other documents, which was accepted by Regnery for publication under the title *One Man's Aim*, but Mrs Pound decided to withdraw it.

Pound was restless and agitated over the Christmas of 1959 and early in the New Year left Tirolo to stay with an old friend, Ugo Dadone, at 80 Via Angelo Poliziano in Rome. He met and dined with Daniel Cory and his wife, gladly underwent a long interview with Donald Hall for *The Paris Review* (published in the Summer/Fall issue, 1962), and wrote to Carl Gatter that he was 'developing nostalgia for early scenes'. Although nothing came of a move to have *The Women of Trachis* staged at the Edinburgh Festival that year, it was performed with great success in Berlin. When it was staged at Darmstadt he attended with his daughter and his German translator Eva Hesse as the city's guest of honour and afterwards appeared on stage with the cast to acknowledge the applause. He no longer tried to keep up with his correspondence; when he did write it was mostly to friends such as Laughlin or Meacham. Back at Brunnenburg in the summer of 1960 he ate little and eventually had to be taken to Martinsbrunn, an all-purpose private clinic on the outskirts of Merano. No longer a commanding figure he had become suddenly old.

His work was still appearing occasionally. A translation of an ancient Egyptian poem which he had done several years earlier was published in Germany, with a German version by Eva Hesse, in January 1960, and in October that year in the *National Review* in New York and *X Quarterly* in London. It was called 'Conversations in Courtship' and had been translated from a literal rendering of the Egyptian original into Italian by his son-in-law. Accompanied by a group of poems which I had made from the same Italian source, 'Conversations in Courtship' was published by New Directions in November 1962 in a small book entitled *Love Poems of Ancient Egypt*.

In 1961 he returned to Rome; he went into a clinic there in May, and in June was brought back to Martinsbrunn. Apart from difficulty in concentrating he had a urinary infection which kept him in bed for some months. Towards the end of 1961 Olga Rudge took him to Rapallo where later he underwent a prostate operation. From this time onwards he lived with Miss Rudge at Sant' Ambrogio and in her house in Venice; he seldom spoke to outsiders, which visitors found disconcerting, especially as he cultivated the habit of staring his victim in the eye. His opera *Le Testament* was broadcast by the BBC in June 1962, in a version edited by the composer Murray Schafer, and was repeated the following August. Fragments of cantos, all written before 1960, were published in various magazines in 1962 and 1963. In a piece published in *The Paris Review* (Summer/Fall 1962) he said that his 'errors and wrecks' lay about him; and it was possibly of himself that he spoke in the following:

> A blown husk that is finished
> > but the light sings eternal
> a pale flare over marshes
> Where the salt hay whispers to tide's change

In canto 110, privately printed by Guy Davenport and Laurence Scott in Cambridge, Massachusetts, in 1965, he wrote:

> Falling spiders and scorpions,
> > Give light against falling poison,
> a wind of darkness hurls against forest,
> > > the candle flickers,
> > > > is faint

The old hand still held its cunning, creating here and there in these fragments lines and passages of unearthly beauty.

In 1962 when *Poetry* celebrated its fiftieth anniversary Pound received the Harriet Monroe Award of five hundred dollars and in September the following year an award of five thousand dollars from the Academy of American Poets. In 1964 New Directions published

Confucius to Cummings, the anthology he had made with the help of Marcella Spann. Although he had moments of doubt in which he spoke of ruining everything he touched, he was physically fit and able to travel and in January 1964 went to Vevey in Switzerland. When Eliot died on 4 January 1965 Pound flew to London and attended the memorial service in Westminster Abbey on 4 February. From London he and Miss Rudge flew to Dublin to see Yeats's widow. That summer he attended Gian Carlo Menotti's 'Festival of Two Worlds' at Spoleto where his opera *Le Testament* was given as a ballet. He also read, at a public reading there, poems by Marianne Moore, Robert Lowell and others, but none by himself; instead of mounting the stage he read sitting in Menotti's box, with a microphone beside him. It was sometimes difficult to distinguish all his words but when he had finished the audience stood and turned to the box to applaud. At Rapallo he swam with another octogenarian, an Italian friend, on a sheltered beach below Sant' Ambrogio, watched over by an attendant. During his trip to London earlier in the year Pound had met Peter du Sautoy, one of the directors of Faber and Faber and mention was made in passing of the possibility of publishing a selection from the cantos. Out of the blue a copy of the 1964 collected edition of the cantos arrived at the Faber office some months later with the selection marked out clearly in Pound's hand; it was published in 1967.

Pound turned eighty on 30 October 1965 and articles and tributes were published in many newspapers, periodicals and magazines in England, the United States, Germany, France and Italy, and he was also the subject of wireless and television programmes; he himself celebrated with a trip to Greece.

One night in June 1966, over coffee and brandy at Miss Rudge's house in Venice, he talked in a low voice about his early life and answered questions put him by an American professor about his acquaintance with John Butler Yeats, the poet's father, in New York in 1910–11; when Daniel Cory, who was also present, mentioned Sara Teasdale and asked whether Pound had read her work, he looked hard and replied: 'I remember the name, but not the poetry.' At Spoleto in July he read excerpts from *Mauberley* and the cantos, including some of the later fragments; his voice was weak and tremulous at first but became stronger, the syllables clearly enunciated, as he went along. At the house in Venice early in October Cory brought up the subject of the cantos and the conflicting opinions they had aroused. Pound intervened firmly, describing the work as 'a botch'. And when Cory persisted, 'You mean it didn't come off?' the poet replied: 'Of course it didn't. That's what I mean when I say I botched it.' He then went on to describe a shop window full of various objects: 'I picked out this and that thing that interested me, and then jumbled them into a bag. But that's not the way', he said, 'to make' – and here he paused – 'a *work of art*.'

In London half a century earlier Pound had given the corrected page-proofs of *Canzoni* and other papers to Brigit Patmore. This material found its way into a private collection and eventually to the University of Texas. It included the 114-line poem 'Redondillas, or Something of that Sort' which he had deleted entirely while correcting the *Canzoni* proofs in Paris in May 1911. He had forgotten about it when the text was sent to him in 1966; he did not think it was very good but said yes to a request from the magazine *Poetry Australia* in Sydney to be allowed to publish it for the first time. It appeared in the April 1967 issue and in 1968 was published as a book by New Directions in a signed edition limited to one hundred and ten copies.

In June 1967 he went to Paris for the publication of French translations of *ABC of Reading*, *How to Read* and *The Spirit of Romance*; at a meeting with French critics he maintained, according to the *Quinzaine littéraire* of 15–30 June, an 'obstinate silence', answering questions with a far-away look. He was sometimes worried about money, although he had no need to be, and was subject to periods of deep depression; but he was still able to travel and to read in public and cut a fine figure, with his white hair and white beard, before the television cameras of Italy and other countries. At Sant' Ambrogio he walked the hill-paths, in a landscape of cypress and olives, with the rocks and the sea far below. With Miss Rudge and sometimes with a caller he would visit the little church at Sant' Ambrogio and have coffee or a meal under the trees at the local restaurant. In Venice also he liked to walk – never tiring of the canals, the bridges, the network of footpaths and passageways, the succession of architectural fanfares, and the harmony of old stone and lapping sea. Mostly he and Miss Rudge ate at a restaurant called the Cici, just around the corner from her house in the San Gregorio section. When they had occasion to visit the San Marco area or the Fenice Theatre they walked along past Santa Maria della Salute to the customs house and there took a gondola ferry across the Grand Canal. He was particularly fond of opera and one night after a performance at the Fenice of Verdi's *Gerusalemme* Vanni Scheiwiller took him backstage to meet the conductor Gianandrea Gavazzeni.

On 4 June 1969 Pound and Miss Rudge flew to New York on a fortnight's visit to the United States. It was his first trip there since his departure aboard the *Cristoforo Colombo* eleven years earlier.

Although he had received a number of invitations in recent years, including one in 1968 from the Provost of Yale, and several times had been on the verge of going, these intentions were never carried through.

The visit, when it did occur, came as a surprise to his publisher James Laughlin who acted as his host.

On 5 June Pound attended the annual meeting of the Academy of American Poets in the boardroom of the New York Public Library. He sat in a large chair at the front, without speaking, but rose to shake hands whenever approached by an admirer. Next day, accompanied by their grandson Walter de Rachewiltz, a student at Rutgers University, Pound and Miss Rudge drove to Laughlin's home at Norfolk in Connecticut. Pound took a few short walks in the country and one day sat and watched children swimming in a nearby lake. Laughlin's small son Henry was fascinated by Walter's use of the Italian word *nonno* for grandfather. When Henry asked Pound whether he too could call him *nonno*, the poet quickly replied 'Honoured.' On Sunday 8 June the party drove to Hamilton College, Clinton, New York, for Laughlin to receive an honorary degree of Doctor of Letters. It was Pound's first visit to his old college since receiving his own honorary doctorate in 1939. He had lunch at the house of a Professor of English, Austin Briggs; according to Mrs Briggs he said 'almost nothing' during the meal.

Believing that the annual academic procession would be too arduous for Pound, the authorities arranged for him to take the platform after the others had assembled. Wearing his academic robes he was conducted from a side entrance by a college official bearing the stave and was given a standing ovation by the students when introduced by the president, John Chandler. He sat beside Laughlin on the platform, and although he did not at any stage speak, he shook hands with people afterwards. The following day, 9 June, Pound and Miss Rudge were driven to New York where Laughlin turned over to them his flat in Bank Street, Greenwich Village. Each day Miss Rudge worked out a programme that would not tire him. They visited the New York Public Library to see the draft of Eliot's *The Waste Land* bearing numerous cuts and suggestions in Pound's hand. There they met Eliot's widow, Mrs Valerie Eliot, who was preparing the draft for publication. Another day they went to a Hans Arp exhibition and one evening had dinner with Mrs Hemingway at the Voisin Restaurant. They dined also at the flat of the Robert Lowells and called on Marianne Moore who was confined to a wheelchair. Laughlin gave a number of small dinner parties in their honour at the Dorgene Restaurant, opposite the White Horse Tavern, in the Village. A guest at one of these was television producer Lewis Freedman; another was attended by the critic George Quasha and his wife; and still another by Frederick Morgan, editor-in-chief of *The Hudson Review*. Pound barely spoke, but he followed the conversations. He did a good deal of walking about

Greenwich Village and on one of his outings called and met the staff at the New Directions publishing office at 333 Sixth Avenue. One day Walter de Rachewiltz drove his grandparents to Philadelphia to see Priscilla Heacock and her sister – friends from Pound's Wyncote days who were also related to Miss Rudge.

Pound and Miss Rudge also had in mind a trip to his birthplace, Hailey, in Idaho, but wisely gave up the idea when they discovered how long and wearing a journey it would be. Numerous reporters sought interviews during their stay, but none was granted. Laughlin explained that Pound was not talking; and that, in any case, he had said all that he wanted to say in his books, which the reporters and public were at liberty to read. Pound and Miss Rudge flew home to Italy, via Paris, on 18 June.

With Yeats, Joyce, Lewis and Eliot dead he was the last survivor among the leading men of the formative years of the 'modern movement' in English literature – the movement in which he himself had played an important part, not only as innovator and renewer of language, but as impresario and publicity-agent, fund-raiser and office-boy. Later he lost touch with much that was going on in English Letters, so that by 1959 he knew little or nothing of such writers as Dylan Thomas, Hart Crane and Evelyn Waugh; but his influence was everywhere present in the way those who came after him were able to look with fresh eyes at the problems and responsibilities involved in the preservation of the language. And although after 1920 he was generally poor in his judgments of contemporary literature, and clung with unnecessary obstinacy to some lopsided ideas about earlier periods, he never lost touch with the language itself. In the 1930s when he was driving himself with egotistical fervour towards the brink of madness he was yet able to compose the usury cantos (nos. 45 and 51), admirably controlled and impersonal despite their force, and canto 49, imposing in its stillness; and at the Pisan camp he was sometimes able to blend, with the economy of the master, richly revived memories and vespertine colouring without losing an essential element of natural speech.

In the man himself, no matter how difficult and wrong-headed he sometimes may have been, there was much to admire, not least a generosity of spirit which caused him to yearn and work for beauty and justice and to dream of a realm in which perfect beauty might be fused with perfect justice.

But the world will know him mainly as that rare thing, a poet. And when the broadcasts and the manias, the economics and the sense of justice, are but footnotes in some learned history, men will remember him because he was one of the few to whom is granted the gift of giving words to that which is beyond words. If they recall the man it will be because of this, and the images that will come to mind will be most likely those associated with the essential other-worldliness that is somewhere present in all poetry. They will see a man of sixty in a prison-camp dreaming of a celestial city 'now in the mind indestructible' or a penniless young man, with no future, sitting on the steps of the customs house in Venice in 1908 gazing at the palaces and towers, the changing light and colour, and in his notebook writing poems to 'Venice of dreams'.

Index